INFRASTRUCTURE

More Praise for *Infrastructure*

"Read *Infrastructure* and you will never see the world quite the same again."
—TIM WU, Professor of Law, Columbia Law School (Concurring Opinions)

"The student of infrastructure policy will benefit from Frischmann's excellent treatment of public goods and social goods; spillovers and externalities; proprietary versus commons systems management; common carriage policies and open access regulation; congestion pricing strategies; and the debate over price discrimination for infrastructural resources. *Infrastructure* deserves a spot on your shelf whether you are just beginning your investigation of these issues or if you have covered them your entire life."
—ADAM THIERER, Senior Research Fellow, The Mercatus Center at George Mason University (Concurring Opinions)

"Brett Frischmann's excellent new book has crafted an elaborate theory of infrastructure that creates an intellectual foundation for addressing some of the most critical policy issues of our time: transportation, communication, environmental protection and beyond."
—LAURA DENARDIS, Associate Professor, School of Communication at American University (Concurring Opinions)

"Frischmann's book is an important contribution across a wide range of fields. It is a terrific achievement and I think its influence will continue to grow as we grapple with the implications of its analysis."
—MICHAEL BURSTEIN, Cardozo School of Law, PatentlyO.com

"It's unlikely that we are ever going to get a book as rigorous and comprehensive in its treatment of infrastructure as a commons than Professor Brett Frischmann's recently published *Infrastructure: The Social Value of Shared Resources* (Oxford University Press). This book is a landmark in the study of the social value of infrastructure, a theme that is generally overlooked or marginalized."
—DAVID BOLLIER, Bollier.org

"The book provides a new and productive way of analyzing all forms of infrastructure, especially those that are sources of major social value. Frischmann helps us recognize the importance of understanding how different types of policies balance provision and use. With its many fresh ideas, *Infrastructure* itself is likely to generate social value through additional research and the creation of innovative policies."
—EDELLA SCHLAGER, *Science* (July 13, 2012)

"A well-motivated, fundamental call for action. I hope that subsequent work will integrate the ideas developed in this book for the purpose of cost-benefit analysis and policy decisions on governance and market structure... Professor Frischmann has put the spotlight on the demand side. It is my hope and wish that his book will lead to more comprehensive debates and policy decisions."
—PAUL W.J. DE BIJL, Department of Competition and Regulation, CPB Netherlands Bureau for Economic Policy Analysis, *Journal of Information Policy* (2012)

Infrastructure

THE SOCIAL VALUE OF SHARED RESOURCES

Brett M. Frischmann

OXFORD
UNIVERSITY PRESS

OXFORD
UNIVERSITY PRESS

Oxford University Press is a department of the University of Oxford.
It furthers the University's objective of excellence in research, scholarship,
and education by publishing worldwide.

Oxford New York
Auckland Cape Town Dar es Salaam Hong Kong Karachi
Kuala Lumpur Madrid Melbourne Mexico City Nairobi
New Delhi Shanghai Taipei Toronto

With offices in
Argentina Austria Brazil Chile Czech Republic France Greece
Guatemala Hungary Italy Japan Poland Portugal Singapore
South Korea Switzerland Thailand Turkey Ukraine Vietnam

Oxford is a registered trade mark of Oxford University Press in the UK and certain other countries.

Published in the United States of America by
Oxford University Press
198 Madison Avenue, New York, NY 10016

First printing in paperback, 2013
ISBN 978-0-19-997550-1 (paperback : alk. paper)

Library of Congress Cataloging-in-Publication Data

Frischmann, Brett M.
 Infrastructure : the social value of shared resources / Brett M. Frischmann.
   p. cm.
 Includes bibliographical references and index.
 ISBN 978-0-19-989565-6 (hbk. : alk. paper)
 1. Infrastructure (Economics)—Social aspects. I. Title.
 HC79.C3F75 2012
 363—dc23

                                                      2011040968

Printed in the United States of America on acid-free paper

Note to Readers
This publication is designed to provide accurate and authoritative information in regard to the subject matter covered.
It is based upon sources believed to be accurate and reliable and is intended to be current as of the time it was written.
It is sold with the understanding that the publisher is not engaged in rendering legal, accounting, or other professional
services. If legal advice or other expert assistance is required, the services of a competent professional person should be
sought. Also, to confirm that the information has not been affected or changed by recent developments, traditional legal
research techniques should be used, including checking primary sources where appropriate.

*(Based on the Declaration of Principles jointly adopted by a Committee of the
American Bar Association and a Committee of Publishers and Associations.)*

To my wife, Kelly, and my three boys, Matthew, Jake, and Ben

Contents

Introduction   ix

PART ONE | FOUNDATIONS
1. Defining Infrastructure and Commons Management   3
2. Overview of Infrastructure Economics   10
3. Microeconomic Building Blocks   24

PART TWO | A DEMAND-SIDE THEORY OF INFRASTRUCTURE
AND COMMONS MANAGEMENT
4. Infrastructural Resources   61
5. Managing Infrastructure as Commons   91

PART THREE | COMPLICATIONS
6. Commons Management and Infrastructure Pricing   117
7. Managing Congestion   136
8. Supply-Side Incentives   159

PART FOUR | TRADITIONAL INFRASTRUCTURE
9. Transportation Infrastructure: Roads   189
10. Communications Infrastructure: Telecommunications   211

PART FIVE | NONTRADITIONAL INFRASTRUCTURE
11. Environmental Infrastructure   227
12. Intellectual Infrastructure   253

PART SIX | MODERN DEBATES

13. The Internet and the Network Neutrality Debate 317

14. Application to Other Modern Debates 358

CONCLUSION 365

ACKNOWLEDGMENTS 371

BIBLIOGRAPHY 375

INDEX 403

Introduction

This book devotes much-needed attention to understanding how society benefits from infrastructure resources and how management decisions affect a wide variety of interests. This book links *infrastructure*, a particular set of resources defined in terms of the manner in which they create value, with *commons*, a resource management principle by which a resource is shared within a community.

Too often, we take for granted the shared infrastructures that shape our lives, our relationships with each other, the opportunities we enjoy, and the environment we share. Think for a moment about the basic supporting infrastructures that you rely on daily. Some obvious examples are roads, the Internet, water systems, and the electric power grid, to name just a few. In fact, there are many less obvious examples, such as our shared language, legal institutions, ideas, and even the atmosphere. We depend heavily on shared infrastructures, yet it is difficult to appreciate just how much. It is difficult to fully appreciate how these resources contribute to our lives, because infrastructures are complex and the benefits provided are typically indirect. We don't pay much attention to infrastructure resources, because they are conveniently obscure, part of the background. We assume their continuous availability and pay attention to them only when catastrophe strikes, for example when a bridge fails or rolling blackouts deprive us of the electricity we need. And even then, the public attention given is reactive, isolated, and short-lived.

When a bridge collapses, for example, the immediate public outcry may be sufficient to support efforts to rebuild the particular bridge, but that is about as far as it goes. As the headline value of the disaster fades, the world moves on. According to the American Society of Civil Engineers (ASCE), "more than 26%, or one in four, of the nation's bridges

TABLE I.I   ASCE Report Card for America's Infrastructure (2009)

Infrastructure Type	2009 Grade
Aviation	D
Bridges	C
Dams	D
Drinking Water	D–
Energy	D+
Hazardous Waste	D
Inland Waterways	D–
Levees	D–
Public Parks and Recreation	C–
Rail	C–
Roads	D–
Schools	D
Solid Waste	C+
Transit	D
Wastewater	D–
America's Infrastructure GPA	**D**
Estimated Five-Year Investment Need	**$2.2 trillion**

are either structurally deficient or functionally obsolete."[1] In 2008, over 70,000 bridges in the United States were categorized as structurally deficient, and in addition, over 89,000 bridges were categorized as functionally obsolete.[2] And the problem is by no means limited to bridges. To take a rather simple illustration, the ASCE Report Card for America's Infrastructure (see table I.1) is abysmal, concluding with a "grade point average" of D and an estimated five-year investment need of $2.2 trillion.

While there are reasons one might quibble with the ASCE grading system or even particular grades, the basic point is that we have a major infrastructure problem in the United States. Our complacent, reactive, piecemeal approach to infrastructure is incredibly shortsighted and must change. A more proactive, systematic, long-term approach to infrastructure is desperately needed, as experts have long recognized.[3] For such change

---

[1] ASCE (2009).

[2] DEPARTMENT OF TRANSPORTATION 38 (2008) (Table 2-1-9 contains the relevant statistics on bridges).

[3] This need has long been recognized among expert communities. That is, engineers, economists, and other experts who focus on infrastructure have long argued for a proactive, systematic, long-term approach to infrastructure. What has not been recognized or at least explored methodically are the demand-side issues examined in this book.

to even begin to occur, however, citizens must learn to appreciate the social value of shared infrastructure.[4] We simply cannot assume continuous availability. As the ASCE Report Card indicates, both governments and markets struggle to adequately supply the public with the infrastructures that it needs. The reasons are many, and this book will not discuss them all. Infrastructure resources often require substantial investment to supply, maintain, and manage. The investment must come from somewhere, and the public must pay one way or another (taxes, user fees, etc.). As economists like to put it, there is no such thing as a free lunch. Raising sufficient capital to invest can be difficult. There are a host of "supply-side" obstacles to efficient infrastructure provisioning. Economic analysis of infrastructure tends to focus on these issues. But one critical reason, which is generally overlooked and which this book will confront at length, is that infrastructure users, as voters and consumers, may not adequately signal social demand for infrastructures. There are a host of "demand-side" issues to confront. At bottom, demand-side problems arise because we do not fully appreciate the social value that infrastructures provide.

Infrastructure resources entail long-term commitments with deep consequences for the public. Infrastructures are a prerequisite for economic and social development. Infrastructures shape complex systems of human activity, including economic, cultural, and political systems. That is, infrastructures affect the behavior of individuals, firms, households, and other organizations by providing and shaping the available opportunities of these actors to participate in these systems and to interact with each other. Transportation and communications infrastructures, for example, enable economic and cultural engagement between communities, expanding the scope of markets and communities by enabling people, goods, and ideas to travel more easily. Legal infrastructure, including laws and court systems, for example, enable an incredible variety of economic and social interactions within and across communities. Property and contract laws are a basic foundation for markets of all sorts. The First Amendment shapes the speech environment—the political, economic, cultural, and other conversations people have.

Infrastructure resources are at the center of many contentious public policy debates, ranging from what to do about our crumbling roads and bridges, to whether and how to protect our natural environment, to patent law reform, to electromagnetic spectrum allocation, to providing universal health care, to energy policy, to network neutrality regulation and the future of the Internet. The list could go on and on. Although the policy arenas may seem unrelated, all of them are, to some extent, the same. Each of these policy debates (and many others) involves a battle to control infrastructure resources, set

---

[4] Just as environmental movement helped society to see what it took for granted, this book aims to bring infrastructure to the foreground, so we can better see infrastructure where it exists and to sense its potential where it could come to exist.

the terms and conditions under which the public gets access, and determine how the infrastructure and various infrastructure-dependent systems will evolve over time.[5]

The battle is joined in each of these areas, with some groups arguing strongly for recourse to private property solutions[6] and other groups arguing strongly that such an approach would be fatal.[7] These groups draw on a broader intellectual debate about the merits of private control over (or, conversely, open access to) various types of resources. The intellectual debate takes place in a number of fields, including law, economics, and political science. On the private control side, there is robust economic theory in support of private ordering via markets with minimal government involvement. By contrast, on the open-access side, there is a frequent call for protecting the "commons," but the theoretical support for this prescriptive call is underdeveloped from an economics perspective. In fact, many who oppose privatization, deregulation, and commercialization view the entire discipline of economics with sincere suspicion and doubt.

This book advances strong economic arguments for managing and sustaining infrastructure resources as commons. For better or worse, economics has become the methodology of choice for many scholars and policy makers in these areas. The book offers a rigorous economic challenge to the prevailing wisdom about managing infrastructure. Within economics, infrastructure resources typically have been evaluated using public goods and club goods frameworks; under either framework the analysis typically has focused on the problem of ensuring adequate supply. This book explores a set of questions that, once asked, seem obvious: What drives the demand side of the equation, and how should demand-side drivers affect public policy? Demand for infrastructure resources involves a range of important considerations that bear on the optimal design of a regime for infrastructure management.

A demand-side approach facilitates a better understanding of how infrastructure resources generate value for society and how decisions regarding the allocation of access to such resources affect social welfare. The key insights from this analysis are that infrastructure resources are basic inputs into a wide variety of productive activities and infrastructure users who choose to engage in such activities often produce public and social goods that generate spillovers that benefit society as a whole. Managing such resources as commons may be socially desirable from an economic perspective because doing so facilitates these downstream productive activities. For example, managing the Internet infrastructure in this manner facilitates active citizen involvement in the production and

---

[5] The debates involve other issues as well. My point is that infrastructure issues are often at the core.

[6] E.g., "privatize public roads and bridges so that firms motivated by profit incentives will reduce costs and manage the resources efficiently" or "pay providers of ecosystem services for the benefits their land conveys to all of us" or "let the network owners control what traffic flows across their cables."

[7] E.g., "privatization benefits only a few, such as current politicians, the owners, and current users with the means to pay increased tolls" or "commodification will not solve environmental problems" or "network neutrality is essential to the future of the Internet."

sharing of public and social goods. Over the past decade, this has led to increased opportunities for a wide range of citizens to engage in entrepreneurship, political discourse, social network formation, and community building, among many other socially valuable activities.

To put the basic lesson more plainly: We should share infrastructure resources in an open, nondiscriminatory manner when it is feasible to do so. This is attractive public policy—not only for distributional or fairness reasons, but also for efficiency reasons. Society is better off sharing infrastructure openly. This book explains why. And it also explains that although many people question the feasibility of sharing, worrying that sharing will destroy incentives to invest or will lead to overuse, such concerns are greatly overstated and often can be addressed in a manner that preserves nondiscriminatory sharing.

The infrastructure commons ideas developed in this book have broad implications for scholarship and public policy across many fields, ranging from traditional infrastructure like roads to environmental economics to intellectual property to Internet policy. The book identifies resource valuation and attendant management problems that recur across many different fields and many different resource types, and it develops a functional economic approach to understanding and analyzing these problems. Accordingly, the theory is developed at a higher level of abstraction than would be appropriate if it focused exclusively on a single field or resource. This means that the theory needs refinement as it is applied in context. The book offers no universal prescriptions, because trade-offs will be different in different areas. Still, it is helpful and illuminating to take a step back and look across traditional disciplinary lines before examining the trade-offs. The first three parts of this book develop a general theoretical framework for examining the social value of shared infrastructure. The framework is not tailored to a particular type of infrastructure. Instead, it is based on a functional economic analysis of the characteristics of infrastructure resources. The final three parts of the book apply the framework to many different types of infrastructure, exploring nuanced trade-offs that arise in particular contexts as well as common issues that cut across different contexts. Despite their obvious differences, road systems, telephone networks, ecosystems, and ideas have much more in common than is conventionally appreciated.

Detailed Summary of Chapters

Part I lays the foundation for the economic arguments developed throughout the rest of the book. Chapters 1, 2, and 3 are building blocks. The concepts "infrastructure" and "commons" are used differently and often loosely across a wide range of disciplines, including engineering, economics, political science, and law. Moreover, the two concepts are rarely used together. Accordingly, chapter 1 sets forth a general description of the concepts, drawing on some of the key functional features of *infrastructure as resources* and *commons as a mode of resource management*. This discussion highlights some of the gaps in our understanding of how infrastructure generates social value and the role that commons management plays in facilitating value generation by infrastructure users. Chapter 2 gives an overview of infrastructure economics. Surprisingly, there is no particular subfield within economics devoted to infrastructure. The overview explains the basic supply-side orientation of public welfare economics and regulatory economics and highlights this book's point of departure—its focus on the demand side. Chapter 3 provides a detailed discussion of microeconomic concepts that serve as building blocks for the demand-side theory developed in Part II. The concepts are very important to understanding the value of infrastructure and evaluating and improving resource management. (Readers well versed in microeconomics may wish to skip this chapter. However, the chapter highlights some overlooked demand-side issues that arise in the analysis of public goods, social goods, and externalities.)

Part II develops a demand-side theory of infrastructure and commons management. It is the heart of the book. It delineates a set of infrastructure resources based on functional economic criteria and examines whether managing these resources as commons is an attractive resource management strategy.

Chapter 4 focuses on infrastructure resources. It aims to identify and evaluate infrastructure resources functionally from a systems perspective. First, it identifies and examines three economic criteria common to traditional infrastructure, such as transportation systems and telecommunications networks, and nontraditional infrastructure, such as the atmosphere and basic research. Specifically, infrastructural resources satisfy the following criteria:

(1) The resource may be consumed nonrivalrously for some appreciable range of demand.

(2) Social demand for the resource is driven primarily by downstream productive activity that requires the resource as an input.

(3) The resource may be used as an input into a wide range of goods and services, which may include private goods, public goods, and social goods.

These criteria delineate a set of resources that are functionally *infrastructural*. Bear in mind that the economic concepts woven together in these criteria are carefully explained in chapter 3. Second, chapter 4 develops a typology of different infrastructure (commercial, public, social, and mixed infrastructure) based on the distribution of productive activities the infrastructure facilitates. Third, it discusses how both the resource set delineated by the three criteria and the subsets delineated by the typology are dependent on demand, and how resources may evolve into or out of the set or subsets. The chapter explains how different types of demand-side market failures arise when spillovers from public or social goods are prevalent.

Chapter 5 connects the demand-side analysis of how infrastructure resources generate value for society with the management of such resources as commons. The case for commons management must be evaluated carefully and contextually. Chapter 5 first considers commons management as a private strategy. There are a variety of reasons why private firms choose to manage their infrastructure as commons. I discuss five primary reasons: (a) consumers generally dislike and react negatively to discrimination; (b) commons management may economize on information and transaction costs and avoid unnecessary complexity; (c) commons management may facilitate joint production or cooperation with competitors; (d) commons management may support and encourage value-creating activities by users; and (e) commons management may maximize the option value of infrastructure when there is high uncertainty regarding sources of future market value.

Chapter 5 next considers commons management as a public strategy. There are a variety of situations in which commons management is not an attractive private strategy but nonetheless is an attractive public strategy; markets sometimes fail to adopt commons management even when doing so would improve social welfare. The chapter explains the conventional forms of and justifications for such regulation. Next, it utilizes the typology developed in chapter 4 and articulates additional, powerful reasons to manage public, social, and mixed infrastructure in a nondiscriminatory manner. Specifically, commons management can be an efficient means of indirectly supporting public participation in a variety of socially valuable activities, namely activities that involve the production, use, and distribution of public and social goods. As such, commons management can be understood as serving two public functions: First, it diffuses pressure within both market and political systems to "pick winners and losers" and leaves it to users to decide what to do with the opportunities (capabilities) provided by infrastructure. Second, it functions like an option—a social option. When there is high uncertainty about which users or uses will generate social value in the future, as is typically the case for public, social, or mixed infrastructure, managing the infrastructure as a commons sustains the generic nature of the infrastructure, precludes optimization for a narrower range of activities, and avoids social opportunity costs associated with path dependency. Together, these public functions suggest a third public function: Commons management structures the relationships between infrastructure and infrastructure-dependent systems in a manner that creates a spillover-rich environment, where spillovers flow from the many productive activities of users. These activities yield new and unanticipated innovations, knowledge, social capital, and other public and social goods that lead to economic growth and development as well as social welfare improvements not fully reflected in traditional economic measures.

Though theory reveals a weight on the scale in favor of commons management that seems to be ignored in most contexts, the theory does not necessarily tip the balance; there are other relevant considerations, some more important than others, depending on the context. Part III focuses on three sets of complications that must be considered when evaluating the case for managing infrastructure as commons. The first set involve the impacts that commons management might have on pricing practices, and concerns that nondiscrimination rules must be accompanied by price regulation or government subsidies. The second set concerns congestion management and complications that arise when infrastructure is partially (non)rival and thus congestible, and the relationships between commons management and congestion management. Finally, the third set concerns the impact of nondiscrimination rules on supply-side incentives. As the chapters reveal, arguments based on these complications should be evaluated carefully. In many cases, the complications are manageable and do not undermine the case for commons management.

Part IV discusses examples of traditional infrastructure—specifically, transportation infrastructure (roads) in chapter 9 and telecommunications infrastructure (telephone networks) in chapter 10. These chapters illustrate how the demand-side theory applies to these traditional infrastructure resources and how commons management has been implemented. Both road and telecommunications infrastructures provide generic public capabilities, mobility and communication, that allow users to engage in an incredibly wide variety of productive activities. These activities generate private, public, and social goods and consequently substantial spillovers to the benefit of society. In the United States, the vast majority of road infrastructure is publicly owned, and the vast majority of telephone infrastructure is privately owned. The supply-side stories for these infrastructures are thus quite different. Yet both are sustained as commons, accessible to the public on nondiscriminatory terms. These chapters discuss a range of complications. Road infrastructure is complicated by congestion, negative externalities associated with environmental pollution, and public financing of maintenance and improvements. Telephone infrastructure is complicated by regulatory costs and the difficulties of transitioning from regulated monopoly to competition. While these chapters do not exhaustively cover these rich and complex fields, they begin to provide a more nuanced picture of how these fundamental infrastructure resources generate value for society, the critical role of commons management, and the various institutional means for sustaining commons when faced with an array of conflicting issues.

Part V shifts attention from traditional infrastructure to nontraditional infrastructure—specifically, environmental and intellectual infrastructure. It may seem odd to be grouping roads and telephone networks with lakes and ideas under the infrastructure umbrella. One reason for doing so is to highlight the demand-side similarities and the important, if varied, role of commons management. When feasible, society benefits tremendously by leveraging nonrivalry to support nondiscriminatory access to such resources because doing so enables the public to participate productively in a wide range of socially valuable activities. As with traditional infrastructure, many environmental and intellectual infrastructure resources are public, social, and mixed infrastructures that contribute immensely to our economic and social development. The case for commons management depends, however, on managing a host of competing considerations. Intellectual infrastructures face supply-side issues similar to those issues faced by traditional infrastructure. Attracting private investment can be difficult because of the cost structure of supply, high costs of exclusion, and misappropriation risks. Environmental infrastructures do not face the same supply-side issues, but environmental infrastructure face complex congestion and degradation problems. In short, pure open access to intellectual or environmental infrastructure typically is not feasible absent additional institutional support, whether in the form of public subsidies for basic research or in the form of command and control regulation of industrial polluters. Viewing foundational environmental and intellectual resources through the infrastructure lens yields interesting insights regarding commons management institutions. In particular, both environmental and intellectual property legal systems construct semi-commons arrangements that create and regulate interdependent private rights and public commons. Each does so in very different ways, however.

Part VI applies the infrastructure theory to modern challenges. Chapter 13 applies infrastructure theory to the particularly contentious "network neutrality" debate. At the heart of this debate is whether the Internet infrastructure will continue to be managed as a commons. Ultimately, the outcome of this debate may very well determine whether the Internet continues to operate as a mixed infrastructure that supports widespread user production of commercial, public, and social goods, or whether it evolves into a commercial infrastructure optimized for the production and delivery of commercial outputs. The chapter criticizes the current framing of the debate as well as the recent rule enacted by the Federal Communications Commission. It then proposes and defends a nondiscrimination rule that reflects the core commons management principle discussed throughout this book. Chapter 14 briefly discusses some additional modern challenges.

Foundations

THIS BOOK DRAWS heavily on different economic fields and involves a number of moving parts. Accordingly, Part I frames the issues in more detail, provides an overview of different economic approaches to infrastructure that incompletely address these issues, and examines the basic microeconomic building blocks used throughout the rest of the book.

1

DEFINING INFRASTRUCTURE AND COMMONS MANAGEMENT

INFRASTRUCTURE AND COMMONS are not typically thought to be related to one another. Both concepts have rich histories and varied meaning, and both involve complex phenomena that are the subject of study in various disciplines, including engineering, economics, political science, and law. There is no separate field of infrastructure study or commons study, and there are no settled universal theories or even definitions of infrastructure or commons. This chapter develops the foundation for bringing the concepts together. After a brief introduction to the modern conception of infrastructure and its traditional roots in large-scale, human-made physical resource systems, the chapter discusses a few observations about traditional infrastructure resources, including the important observation that traditional infrastructures are generally "managed as commons." This sets the stage for a more detailed discussion of "commons management" as a resource management strategy and for the economic analysis that takes place in subsequent chapters.

A. Infrastructure Resources

"Infrastructure" generally conjures up the notion of a large-scale physical resource made by humans for public consumption. Standard definitions of infrastructure refer to the "underlying framework of a system" or the "underlying foundation" of a system.[1] Familiar examples of "traditional infrastructure" include (1) *transportation systems*, such as highway systems, railway systems, airline systems, and ports; (2) *communication systems*, such as telephone networks and postal services; (3) *governance systems*, such as court systems; and (4) *basic public services and facilities*, such as schools, sewers, and water systems. The list could be expanded considerably, but the point is simply to bring to mind the range of traditional infrastructure resources on which we rely daily.

This book views infrastructure capaciously, emphasizing the functional role of infrastructure. As chapter 4 explains, infrastructure resources are *shared means to many ends*. I deliberately extend the scope of analysis beyond traditional infrastructure categories. Thus, while chapters 9 and 10 examine transportation and communications infrastructures, chapters 11 and 12 examine environmental and intellectual infrastructures. Much like traditional infrastructure resources, these "nontraditional" infrastructure resources enable, frame, and support a wide range of activities in our lives.

Three generalizations about traditional infrastructure help set the stage. First, the government has played and continues to play a significant and widely accepted role in ensuring the provision of many traditional infrastructures. The role of government varies according to the context, community, and infrastructure resource in question. In many contexts, private parties and markets play an increasingly important role in providing many types of traditional infrastructure due to, among other things, a wave of privatization as well as cooperative ventures between industry and government.[2] Nonetheless, the government's role as provider, subsidizer, coordinator, and/or regulator of traditional infrastructure provision remains intact in most communities in the United States and throughout the world. The reason, which relates to the next two generalizations and to the analysis to come in later chapters, is that "free" markets often fail to meet society's demand for infrastructure.

Second, traditional infrastructures generally are managed in an openly accessible manner whereby all members of a community who wish to use the resources may do so

---

[1] BLACK'S LAW DICTIONARY, "Infrastructure" 784 (1999); WEBSTER'S THIRD NEW INTERNATIONAL DICTIONARY OF THE ENGLISH LANGUAGE UNABRIDGED, "Infrastructure" 1161 (1993); MORRIS & MORRIS 309 (1988) (providing a historical account of how the term's meaning has evolved). The US National Research Council (NRC) identified a host of "public works infrastructure" along with a more comprehensive notion of infrastructure that included "the operating procedures, management practices, and development policies that interact together with societal demand and the physical world to facilitate" the provision of a range of services, including "the transport of people and goods, provision of water for drinking and a variety of other uses, safe disposal of society's waste products, provision of energy where it is needed, and transmission of information within and between communities." NATIONAL RESEARCH COUNCIL 4 n.1 (1987). The NRC recognized three conceptual needs that are central to the project undertaken in this book: first, the need to look beyond physical facilities; second, the need to evaluate infrastructure from a systems perspective; and third, the need to acknowledge and more fully consider the complex dynamics of societal demand.

[2] LEVY 16–17 (1996).

on equal and nondiscriminatory terms.[3] For many infrastructure resources, the relevant "community" is the public at large. "Roads and highways, canals, railroads, the mail, telegraph, and telephone, some owned by public entities, most owned by private corporations, have always been . . . required to interconnect and serve the public on a nondiscriminatory basis."[4] This does not mean that access is free. We pay tolls to access highways, we buy stamps to send letters, and we pay telephone companies to route our calls across their lines. Users must pay for access to some (though not all) of these resources. Nor does it mean that access to the resource is absolutely unregulated. Transportation of hazardous substances by highway or mail, for example, is heavily regulated. In short, the resource is accessible to all within a community regardless of the identity of the end-user or end-use—that is, without regard to who you are or what you are planning to do. Except for special cases, such as the narrowly defined priority given to a police officer driving with her siren and lights on, access to and use of most infrastructure resources are not prioritized based on such criteria. As discussed below, managing traditional infrastructure in this fashion often makes economic sense.

Third, traditional infrastructures generate significant spillovers (positive externalities)[5] that result in large social gains. As W. Edward Steinmueller observed:

> Both traditional and modern uses of the term infrastructure are related to "synergies," what economists call positive externalities, that are incompletely appropriated by the suppliers of goods and services within an economic system. The traditional idea of infrastructure was derived from the observation that the private gains from the construction and extension of transportation and communication networks, while very large, were also accompanied by additional large social gains.[6]

The economics of traditional infrastructure is quite complex, as reflected perhaps in the fact that economists sometimes refer to infrastructure "opaquely" as "social overhead capital."[7] There are ongoing, hotly contested debates in economics about the costs and benefits of infrastructure—for example, about the degree to which particular infrastructure investments contribute to social welfare or economic growth, and about how to prioritize infrastructure investments in developing countries. Regardless, most economists recognize that infrastructure resources are important to society precisely because infrastructure resources give rise to large social gains. As chapter 3 explains, the nature of some of the gains as spillovers may explain why we take infrastructure for granted: The

---

[3] Lessig 19–25 (2001b); Rose 752 (1986); Benkler 22–23, 47–48 (2001a). See generally Rose 723–49 (1986) (discussing the history of public access rights to various infrastructure resources).

[4] Cooper 14–15 (2005).

[5] On externalities, see chapter 3.

[6] Steinmueller 117 (1996).

[7] Button 148 (1996).

externalities are sufficiently difficult to observe or measure quantitatively, much less capture in economic transactions, and the benefits may be diffuse and sufficiently small in magnitude to escape the attention of individual beneficiaries.

One of the central objectives of this book is to explore the relationships among these three generalizations. Might the accepted role for government associated with infrastructure market failure be related to society's need for nondiscriminatory community access or to the generation of substantial spillovers or to both? The societal need for nondiscriminatory community access to infrastructure and the generation of substantial spillovers each appears to independently constitute grounds for identifying a potential market failure and for supporting some role for government. But the confluence of the two factors suggests that something more complex may be involved. Might society's need for nondiscriminatory community access to infrastructure be related to the generation of substantial spillovers?[8]

Carol Rose was the first to draw an explicit connection between commons and positive externalities.[9] She explained that a "comedy of the commons" arises where open access to a resource leads to scale returns—greater social value with greater use of the resource. With respect to road systems, for example, she considered commerce to be an

interactive practice whose exponential returns to increasing participation run on without limit. . . . Through ever-expanding commerce, the nation becomes ever-wealthier, and hence trade and commerce routes must be held open to the public, even if contrary to private interest. Instead of worrying that too many people will engage in commerce, we worry that too few will undertake the effort.[10]

---

[8] Similarly, NOAM (1994), in Part III.3, observes:

"Infrastructure" is a term of considerable vagueness. It can best be described as those services that are a basic input to most other economic activities, and which provide substantial positive externalities to the economy as a whole. Transportation, energy, communications, education, and protection are prime examples. Network industries, in particular, are considered infrastructure services. The positive externalities to members of the network increase positively with added membership, for example by the greater reach of the telephone.

Infrastructure services can greatly contribute to the economic growth of individuals, regions and the nation. In consequence, in most countries they are provided by government. When historically they were provided in the past by private firms, English common law courts often imposed some quasi-public obligations, one of which one was common carriage. It mandated the provision of service to willing customers, bringing common carriage close to a service obligation to all once it was offered to some.

[9] Rose 723, 775–81 (1986). Demsetz came close. He suggested that "[c]ommunal property results in great externalities. The full costs of the activities of an owner of a communal property right are not borne directly by him, nor can they be called to his attention easily by the willingness of others to pay him an appropriate sum." Demsetz 355 (1967). Demsetz focused exclusively on negative externalities (external costs) and failed to appreciate that communal property can result in great positive externalities (external benefits) and that such a result can be socially desirable.

[10] Rose 769–70 (1986); see also Cain (1998) ("[A]s long as Lake Michigan remained a 'fixed fact,' every railroad or town that was built and every farm that was settled north and west of the city would only increase the trade

Critically, (1) managing road systems in an open, nondiscriminatory manner is the key to sustaining and increasing *participation* in commerce, and (2) commerce is itself a *productive activity* that generates significant positive externalities. Commerce generates private value that is easily observed and captured by participants in economic transactions, as buyers and sellers exchange goods and services, but it also generates social value that is not easily observed and captured by participants—value associated with socialization, cultural exchange, and other such processes. Commerce is an excellent example of a *productive use* of roads that generates positive externalities and social surplus. There are many others, such as visiting other communities to see friends, relatives, or engage in recreation, or visiting state parks.[11] These activities generate private value that is easily observed and captured by participants as well as social value that is not easily observed and captured by participants. Rose's critical insight is that certain resources ought to be managed as commons because doing so increases participation in socially valuable activities that yield scale returns. This book intensively explores the relationship between nondiscriminatory access to infrastructure and the generation of substantial spillovers. Before delving deeper, I explain "commons management."

B. Commons Management

The term "commons" generally conjures up the notion of a shared community resource, such as a public park or a common pasture. The term gained some notoriety with the publication of Garrett Hardin's essay "The Tragedy of the Commons" in *Science* (1968). The term has more recently been used in a variety of different settings, ranging from environmental resources to spectrum policy. This book adopts a functional approach to understanding commons. As with infrastructure, the idea is to identify and examine the functional role of commons in complex systems. From this perspective, commons can be understood as a type of resource management strategy.

For purposes of this book, commons management refers to the situation in which a resource is accessible to all members of a community on nondiscriminatory terms, meaning terms that do not depend on the users' identity or intended use.[12] I use "commons management" to capture a *nondiscriminatory sharing* strategy, which can be implemented through

---

and prosperity of Chicago" (quoting 1 A. T. Andreas, History of Chicago from the Earliest Time to the Present 40 (1884)).

[11] See chapter 9. Cf. Branscomb & Keller (1996) ("Over the past half century, the U.S. highway system has advanced regional and national economic development by enhancing access to markets for goods, services, and people. It has also provided direct quality-of-life benefits, by providing easier access to both work and leisure.").

[12] Lessig 19–20 (2001b); Ostrom 1–7 (1990); Burger et al. 1–6 (2001); Bollier 2–3 (2001). I recognize that many commons arrangements discriminate against nonmembers, and even among members in some contexts where the contributions of members may vary or congestion issues arise. See chapter 7.

a variety of public and private institutions, including open access, common property, and other resource management or governance regimes. Grouping "open access" and "commons" under the "commons management" umbrella will be troublesome to some property scholars: Open access typically implies no ownership or property rights. No entity possesses the right to exclude others from the resource; all who want access can get access, typically for free.[13] Commons typically involves some form of communal ownership (community property rights, public property rights, joint ownership rights), such that members of the relevant community obtain access "under rules that may range from 'anything goes' to quite crisply articulated formal rules that are effectively enforced" and nonmembers can be excluded.[14] There are at least three dimensions of distinction between open access and commons as traditionally understood: first, ownership (none vs. communal/group); second, the definition of community (public at large vs. a more narrowly defined and circumscribed group with some boundary between members and nonmembers); and third, the degree of exclusion (none vs. exclusion of nonmembers). These distinctions are important, especially for understanding different institutions and how social arrangements operate at different scales. But our focus will be on infrastructure resources, for which the relevant community generally is the public at large. These "public commons" generally do not restrict membership and are available to users on nondiscriminatory terms; yet they are not always free, as is the case for pure open-access resources.

Accordingly, we put aside the distinctions between institutional regimes and focus on an important feature that they share: nondiscrimination, which means the underlying resource is accessible to members of a community on terms that do not depend on the users' identity or intended use.[15] We abstract from the institutional *form* (property rights, regulations, norms) to focus on a particular institutional *function* (nondiscriminatory sharing). Tying form and function together obscures the fact that a commons management strategy is implemented by a variety of institutional forms, which are often mixed (property and regulation, private and communal property).[16]

---

[13] Hess & Ostrom 121–22 (2003).

[14] Benkler 6–7 (2003a).

[15] See also Benkler (2011) (emphasizing the symmetric freedom to operate and the absence of asymmetrical power to exclude or decide how users operate).

[16] See chapters 5–13. There are many ways in which a resource can come to be managed in a nondiscriminatory manner. A resource may be open for common use naturally because its characteristics prevent it from being owned or controlled by anyone. Rose 89, 93 (2003) (discussing the traditional Roman categories of nonexclusive property, one of which, res communes, was incapable of exclusive appropriation due to its inherent character). For example, for most of the earth's history, the oceans and the atmosphere were natural commons. Exercising dominion over such resources was beyond the ability of human beings or simply unnecessary because there was no indication of scarcity. That has changed. A resource may be open for common use as the result of social construction. Laws or rules may prohibit ownership or ensure open access, or an open-access regime may arise through norms and customs among owners and users. For example, the Internet infrastructure has been governed by norms creating a nondiscrimination regime where end-users can access and use the infrastructure to route data packets without fear of discrimination or exclusion by infrastructure owners.

The general values of the commons management strategy are that it maintains openness, does not discriminate among users or uses of the resource, and eliminates the need to obtain approval or a license to use the resource.[17] Managing infrastructure resources as commons eliminates the need to rely on either market actors or the government to "pick winners" among users or uses. This catalyzes innovation through the creation of and experimentation with new uses. More generally, it facilitates the generation of positive externalities by permitting downstream production of public and social goods that might be stifled under a more restrictive access regime. Finally, it sustains the social option value of the infrastructure by precluding premature optimization of the resource for commercial gain. Chapter 5 examines these values.

Sustaining commons poses serious challenges, however. Environmental and information resources highlight the best-known and most-studied commons dilemmas. Environmental resources suffer from the "tragedy of the commons,"[18] a consumption or capacity problem, familiar to many infrastructure resources. Open access to some environmental resources may lead to congestion, depletion, and possibly ruin as users only take into account the private benefits and costs from their use and fail to account for negative externalities (costs to third parties) attributable to their consumption. If each user consumes rationally from a self-interested perspective but inefficiently from a social perspective, the resource may be overused to the point of ruin. Information resources suffer from a "free-rider dilemma," a production problem, also familiar to many infrastructure resources. Open access to some information resources may diminish incentives to invest in the creation and development of the resources because free-riding users consume the resources without paying an adequate contribution to investors, who in turn are unable to recoup their investments. These challenges are not insurmountable and should not stand in the way of managing infrastructure as commons.[19] Social institutions reflect a strong commitment to sustaining common access to certain infrastructure resources. This book shows the wisdom of that commitment.

See chapter 13. The open source and creative commons movements are two prominent examples. LESSIG 164–65, 255–56 (2001b); Reichman & Uhlir 430–32 (2003); see also David & Foray 87, 91 (1996) (The "activity of diffusing economically relevant knowledge is not itself a natural one." "Rather, it is socially constructed through the creation of appropriate institutions and conventions, such as open science and intellectual property...").

[17] LESSIG (2004b); LANDES & POSNER 15–16 (2004) (acknowledging such benefits with respect to the public domain).

[18] Hardin 1244–45 (1968).

[19] It is interesting how two frequently told stories of uncontrolled consumption—the tragedy of the commons and the free-rider story—came to dominate the policy discourse in the environmental and intellectual property areas and how both stories seem to lead to the conclusion that granting private property rights, typically with the power to grant access on discriminatory terms, is the best way to manage these resources. OSTROM 3 (1990) (connecting the tragedy of the commons with the prisoners' dilemma); Ghosh 1332 (2004); Lemley (2005). Both stories can be translated in game-theoretic terms into a prisoners' dilemma, another good story, although one that does not necessarily point to private property as a solution to the cooperation dilemma. See, e.g., Eastman (1997).

2

OVERVIEW OF INFRASTRUCTURE ECONOMICS

IN VARIOUS FIELDS of economics, there is widespread recognition that infrastructure is special. Macroeconomics recognizes that infrastructure is important for economic development and a key ingredient for economic growth.[1] Microeconomics recognizes that infrastructure resources often generate substantial social gains and that markets for infrastructure often fail and call for government intervention in one form or another. Development economics, which applies both micro- and macroeconomics to the process of development, recognizes similar ideas. Yet there are some gaping holes in our understanding of how infrastructure resources generate substantial social gains and contribute to development and economic growth. In particular, the importance of open infrastructure and user-generated spillovers at the microeconomic level and their relationships to technological innovation and growth at the macroeconomic level deserve attention.[2] A brief description of these fields helps to frame the discussion that follows.

---

[1] Ghosh & Meager (2004) ("Whether it is the Internet or freeways, infrastructure improves the functioning of an economy. Road building and improvements in telecommunications infrastructure have both been found to have a significant impact on productivity and growth for a wide selection of OECD countries. At the same time, in both policy quarters and academic circles, lack of proper infrastructure is often blamed for the poor performance of the less developed countries (see Easterly and Rebelo (1993); World Bank Development Report (1994)). This traditional wisdom— of a positive relationship between infrastructure and productivity/growth—has found support in the empirical macroeconomic literature (see for example Aschauer (1989), Fernald (1999), Roller and Waverman (2001)).").

[2] For example, innovation-driven economic growth may be fueled by certain types of infrastructural resources. I leave exploration of this issue for future work.

Microeconomics studies the behavior of individuals, firms, households, and other organizations, most often with respect to the allocation of resources (of all sorts, including money, time, labor, and both physical and intangible capital). While often associated with the study of market behavior, or the behavior of various participants in market systems, microeconomics studies the behavior of participants in nonmarket systems as well. Thus, microeconomics may be characterized as studying resource allocation within economic systems, or, more simply, *in-system behavior.*

Macroeconomics studies the performance of the economy on the whole. It is most often associated with the study of national income, growth, inflation, investment, international trade, monetary policy, and unemployment. Although some macroeconomic models are built from microeconomic foundations,[3] macroeconomics does not study in-system behavior of individuals, firms, households, and other organizations; rather, it focuses on the aggregate. Macroeconomics may be characterized as studying the behavior of economic systems, or, more simply, *system behavior.*[4]

Infrastructure resources are intermediate capital resources[5] that serve as critical foundations for productive behavior within economic and social systems. Infrastructure resources effectively structure in-system behavior at the micro-level by providing and shaping the available opportunities of many actors. In some cases, infrastructure resources make possible what would otherwise be impossible, and in other cases, infrastructure resources reduce the costs and/or increase the scope of participation for actions that are otherwise possible. The difference between these two sets of cases may very well depend on the existence of other infrastructure resources. So, for example, some form of transportation infrastructure may be a necessary precursor to the regular movement of people and/or goods from Region A to Region B and thus to economic and cultural engagement between the regions. Once such an infrastructure is in place, additional forms of transportation infrastructure may be more or less effective in lowering costs or increasing opportunities to participate in various activities enabled by the initial transportation infrastructure. Road and rail systems have a long history that illustrates these points. Both systems also depend on the advancement and availability of complementary technologies, institutions, and social practices.

Often, infrastructure resources structure in-system behavior in a manner that leads to *spillovers.* That is, infrastructure resources facilitate productive behaviors by users that

---

[3] There are rich, ongoing debates among macroeconomists about whether, and if so how, macroeconomics should be built from microeconomic foundations. See COLANDER (1996).

[4] Difficulties arise in the space where microeconomics meets macroeconomics. This is not surprising given similar experiences in other fields, such as physics, where scale matters and the dynamicism of systems quickly complicates both theory and empirical analysis. Nonetheless, economists have struggled for years to reconcile microeconomic and macroeconomic models. This is seen vividly in the literature on economic growth, for example. Infrastructure plays an important role in the intermediate space, mediating micro and macro.

[5] On capital resources, see chapter 3.

affect third parties (whether other users or non-users of the infrastructure). The third-party effects often are accidental, incidental, and not especially relevant to the infrastructure provider or user. To put it another way, the *social returns* on infrastructure investment and use may exceed the *private returns* because society realizes benefits above and beyond those realized by providers and users. Spillovers may be difficult to observe and account for fully in a microeconomic framework focused on in-system behavior, but the spillovers might be accounted for in a macroeconomic framework focused on system behavior.

This book focuses on the microeconomic analysis and leaves an examination of how infrastructure resources mediate micro and macro for future work. The remainder of this chapter provides an overview of the traditional microeconomic analysis of infrastructure.[6] There are two primary microeconomic perspectives on infrastructure: one that is grounded in *public welfare economics* and emphasizes the public goods attributes of infrastructure, and another that is grounded in *regulatory economics* and emphasizes the potential natural monopoly attributes of infrastructure industries. Both perspectives identify potential market failures that may justify some form of government intervention.[7] Neither tradition focuses on infrastructure exclusively. Yet the traditions converge in the infrastructure context.

A. Converging on the Supply-Side and Decreasing-Cost Phenomena

Public welfare economics classifies infrastructure as an impure public good, toll good, or club good, all of which share the public goods characteristic that the resource is consumed nonrivalrously over some range of demand.[8] Essentially, this means that consumption of the good by one person does not reduce the consumption opportunities of any other person. A pure public good is nonrivalrously consumed for all demand; it has infinite capacity and can be shared without running into capacity constraints. Traditional infrastructures are *impure* public goods, because capacity constraints mean that there is a limit to nonrivalrous consumption. Traditional infrastructure resources are durable goods with finite, renewable, and sharable capacity. The resources are sharable yet congestible.

Infrastructures are supplied jointly and thus are potentially available for access and use by many consumers. Public welfare economists have long recognized that jointness in supply (or *indivisibility*) often involves a peculiar cost structure: high fixed costs coupled

---

[6] An appendix provides a brief overview of macroeconomic perspectives on infrastructure.

[7] In the past few decades, concerns over government failures have served as a counterbalance and suggested that identifying a market failure alone does not warrant government intervention because the solution may be worse than the problem. There has been and continues to be much wrangling over these issues. This book will not focus on public choice analysis.

[8] Chapter 3 provides a more detailed discussion of these classifications.

with comparably low variable costs and, consequently, decreasing average costs. Most traditional infrastructures exhibit this cost structure. They involve high fixed costs that are "lumpy," meaning that the costs are sunk in discrete lumps. Constructing a bridge or a highway, for example, requires a lot of money to be committed up front. Once the bridge is built, those costs are sunk, and the ongoing variable costs of providing services to users are comparatively quite low. As the number of users increases, the total costs can be spread more widely, such that average costs decrease with output. This is referred to as short-term decreasing costs. Another form of decreasing costs, referred to as long-term decreasing costs, occurs when an enlargement of infrastructure (capacity expansion) causes a commensurate reduction of the unit costs of operation at capacity. These decreasing-cost phenomena are "widespread and important," especially with respect to infrastructure.[9]

The regulatory economics tradition focuses less on the characteristics of the resource and more on the characteristics of the relevant market, although these characteristics are related. Regulatory economists recognize that a market for infrastructure may be a natural monopoly. As W. Kip Vicusi, John Vernon, and Joseph Harrington explain:

> A market is a *natural monopoly* if, at the socially optimal output, industry cost is minimized by having only one firm produce. For the single-product case, if the average cost curve is declining for all outputs, then the cost of producing any industry output is minimized by having one firm produce it. In that case, the market is a natural monopoly regardless of market demand. Such natural monopolies are likely to exist when there is a large fixed-cost for components. For example, most public utilities, like local distribution of electricity and local telephone, are natural monopolies. In those cases, fixed costs (in particular, the cost of connecting homes and businesses to the distribution system) are large relative to marginal costs. Hence, the average cost declines for a wide range of outputs. For the relevant region of market demand, these markets constitute natural monopolies.[10]

A considerable regulatory economics literature explores the classification of natural monopoly markets, the attendant justifications for regulation, and the potential for deregulation and competition in various infrastructure industries. Natural monopoly status is not permanent, because it depends on both the cost structure, which may adjust due to various factors including technological advances, and demand, which may similarly

---

[9] KAHN 124–25 (1998).

[10] Vicusi et al. (2005). Vicusi, Vernon, and Harrington explain that "[i]n the real world a single-commodity producer is rare" and that "the definition of natural monopoly in the multiple-output case is that the cost function must be subadditive. Subadditivity of the cost function simply means that the production of all combinations of outputs is accomplished at least cost by a single firm" (333–35). Subadditivity "generally depends upon *both* economies of scale and economies of scope" (335).

change over time due to, for example, growth in infrastructure-dependent economic and social systems. Local telephone service may have been a natural monopoly in the days of wireline telephony, where each subscriber connected to the system through a dedicated copper wire, but technological advances, such as the emergence of wireless telephony, have changed the cost structure of the market, making it efficient to have multiple suppliers competing to provide telephone service. Natural monopoly classification also may change where an infrastructure market is modular and some portion of a vertical industry structure can be competitively supplied. For example, electric power generation, transmission, and distribution was long considered a natural monopoly, but that view "has given way to a general consensus that the generation segment of power supply . . . would be more efficient and economical if left to the forces of an open market."[11]

In the context of infrastructure, the core themes of the public welfare and regulatory economics traditions overlap considerably because of their convergence on decreasing cost phenomena, which invariably involve indivisibilities reflected in sunk costs as well as sharable capacity. Both traditions focus (myopically) on a complex trade-off between static and dynamic efficiency in the infrastructure market itself.[12] At any point in time, it is efficient from a static perspective to price access to infrastructure at the marginal cost of providing the service to a particular consumer. This is a basic prescription of microeconomics. From this perspective, decreasing-cost phenomena may seem quite attractive: Short of congestion, the more users, the merrier. Society benefits from having output or use increase at a price set equal to marginal cost until the full capacity of the infrastructure is utilized. But this cost structure poses complex problems associated with obtaining socially optimal supply in infrastructure markets. The reason is that it is not easy to set prices efficiently *and* in a manner that allows infrastructure providers to recoup their total costs.

As is generally true for both natural monopolies and public goods, average costs decrease as output expands and marginal costs are below average costs. For infrastructure, the difference between marginal and average costs may be substantial. This means that equating price with marginal cost will preclude providers from recovering their total costs. Consequently, from a dynamic perspective, providers will not have sufficient incentives to invest in producing the infrastructure at a socially optimal level.

Accordingly, society should expect underprovision of these types of goods. To solve this problem, there are a few standard solutions: (1) government provision of the infrastructure; (2) government subsidization to cover the lost portion of high fixed costs; (3) some form of nonprofit, nongovernmental, community-based provision; or (4) market

---

[11] McNerney 1 (1996).

[12] I say myopically focused on the infrastructure market itself because, as argued extensively in subsequent chapters, both perspectives tend to assume away (or minimize the importance of) externalities and assume that infrastructure consumers' willingness to pay for access and use of the infrastructure accurately reflects social demand for their access and use.

provision under conditions that allow providers to charge more than marginal costs. Each of these solutions has advantages and disadvantages and raises a host of complicated issues that are beyond the scope of this brief review. We discuss some of them in later chapters. But it is worth dwelling a bit longer on the fourth solution.

B. Market Provisioning and Pricing Infrastructure

In suggesting that society should expect underprovision, we've assumed that private providers would equate price with marginal cost, but this assumption is doubtful in many situations. Why would private infrastructure providers charge marginal costs rather than average costs or some other price well above marginal costs? There are two common restraints: *competition* and *regulation*. Competition generally drives price to (long-run) marginal cost, because attempts to charge more are disciplined through lost sales to competitors who are willing to charge less. There are a variety of limits on this dynamic, but it remains a foundational benchmark in economics. In regulated industries, regulators also aim to keep prices as close to marginal cost as possible. As Alfred Kahn explained, deviations may be justified to enable cost recovery, but marginal cost remains the economic benchmark.

There is a rich and complex literature on marginal cost pricing and deviations from it in all types of markets, ranging from perfectly competitive to fully regulated. The literature defies a simple overview. If an infrastructure market is not competitive and providers have at least some degree of market power, or if a market is regulated and regulators aim to ensure an acceptable rate of return for infrastructure providers, it may be feasible to employ a variety of pricing schemes that alleviate concerns about underprovision.

For example, providers may charge a price based on average costs rather than marginal cost. Doing so would allow providers to cover their costs and alleviate concerns about undersupply in the particular infrastructure market. This might appear to be an efficient solution. However, charging average costs may be inefficient for two reasons. First, from a static perspective, any price above marginal costs will lead to deadweight losses, where some consumers are "priced out" because they would be willing to pay for access at marginal cost but not at average cost. Second, from a dynamic perspective, average cost pricing can cause distortions in consumer behavior and resource allocation in other markets. Though imperfect, average cost pricing has the advantages of covering total costs and generally seeming fair in its distribution of cost among consumers.

Instead of average cost pricing, providers may implement more sophisticated pricing plans. For example, one approach is to implement two- or multipart pricing schemes that charge consumers (a) an initial access fee to cover a portion of fixed costs, (b) a variable fee to cover marginal (incremental) costs, and perhaps (c) additional fees for additional services. These pricing schemes are deployed in many different markets. The advantages can be effective cost recovery with a reasonable correspondence between price and the actual costs attributable to a given user. Disadvantages can include, inter alia, deadweight losses (e.g., for those who are unable to afford the access fee), high implementation costs, and the risk that pricing exceeds what is justified to recover costs and is obfuscated in a manner that makes detection and evaluation by regulators, potential entrants, or customers difficult.

Another approach is differential pricing, which involves charging different classes of consumers different prices for (more or less) the same good or service.[13] Differential pricing can be cost-based or value-based, or some combination. Cost-based differential pricing is common in regulated industries. It can be seen where infrastructure providers employ certain forms of congestion pricing—for example, where the price adjusts dynamically based on available system capacity or differentiates between on- and off-peak customers.[14]

In the rate-setting context, for example, the objective of regulators employing cost-based differential pricing is to set rates to cover total average costs in a manner that minimizes the distortions associated with prices above marginal costs. Frank Ramsey developed an ingenious though difficult-to-implement pricing scheme that aimed to fulfill this objective. Operating under a profit constraint, prices would be set in an inverse relationship to consumers' elasticity of demand (i.e., their relative responsiveness to changes in price).[15] This would spread the average costs among consumers in a manner that would lead to the least distortion. It can be difficult to implement because of information and transaction costs associated with segmenting customer groups based on demand elasticity and also because of customer backlash based on perceptions that it is unduly discriminatory, even though the provider does not realize excess profits. It is widely practiced in regulated industries throughout the world.

Value-based differential pricing (price discrimination)[16] occurs where prices vary not based on cost but instead on consumers' ability and willingness to pay—a measure of value—and the elasticity of their demand. Perfect price discrimination, or first-degree price discrimination, means that each unit of output is sold to the person that values it most and at that person's maximum willingness to pay. Thus, price varies both by person and by unit of output, being perfectly calibrated to each individual's preferences. Producers would love to be able to implement perfect price discrimination, because it

---

[13] Depending on the pricing scheme, providers may make slight alterations in the quality of the good or service to enable the differentiation. See, e.g., SHAPIRO & VARIAN (1998).

[14] See chapter 7.

[15] RAMSEY 47, 58 (1927); Fink 363, 365 (2009) (Ramsey pricing structures "minimize the consumption distortion of above-marginal cost pricing."); Cowan 252 (2006) ("Ramsey prices . . . maximize aggregate consumer surplus subject to a constraint on the level of profits.").

[16] Economists refer to price discrimination as the situation where "two or more similar goods are being sold at prices that bear different ratios to their marginal costs." Gifford & Kudrle 1239–40 (2010) (citing STIGLER 209 (1966)).

would maximize their gains by converting consumer surplus to producer surplus and would also, at the same time, maximize social welfare. In theory, if this scheme is perfectly implemented, everyone gets what they want: Consumers get exactly what they want at a price they are willing to pay; producers (and their shareholders) get maximal returns, which cover total costs and provide appropriate incentives to boot; and there are no deadweight losses.[17] Unfortunately, perfect price discrimination operates more as a lofty ambition than a realistic efficiency benchmark.[18] Perfect price discrimination is not feasible in the real world. It requires an inordinate amount of fine-grained information about consumers. As Daniel Gifford and Robert Kudrle note, "First-degree discrimination can only be roughly approximated and only occurs in specialized circumstances."[19]

Imperfect price discrimination, which includes second- and third-degree price discrimination, involves attempts to approximate perfect price discrimination and is quite common in infrastructure industries. Second-degree price discrimination occurs when price per unit varies based on the amount purchased—for example, when bulk purchasers receive a discount. "[T]he most familiar variant is the two-part tariff where there is an entrance fee into the market followed by a single price for all units purchased."[20] It is very common in infrastructure industries, for example, where the price of electricity or phone service varies nonlinearly with the amount purchased. Third-degree price discrimination occurs when price per unit varies based on separable consumer groups—for example, when students or seniors receive a discount. Essentially, amount purchased and group identity serve as proxies for the more difficult-to-obtain demand information necessary for first-degree discrimination.

Economists recognize that the welfare implications of imperfect price discrimination are ambiguous and vary considerably by context.[21] As subsequent chapters demonstrate, the welfare implications of imperfect price discrimination vary considerably according to the type of infrastructure. It is worth noting that existing economic analyses of price discrimination tend to focus on complete markets (that is, markets without externalities) and do not account for spillovers in downstream infrastructure-dependent systems. As we will see in chapter 6, this omission can have a significant impact on the analysis of the welfare implications of imperfect price discrimination in infrastructure markets.

---

[17] Truly *perfect* price discrimination would involve no deadweight losses because no one would be priced out. Marginal consumers would only have to pay what they would be willing to pay, constrained only by the marginal costs. Thus, if the marginal costs are zero, those who would only consume the good for free would be able to do so under perfect price discrimination. Of course, no one would be forced to consume the good.

[18] Chapter 6 considers this issue in more detail.

[19] Gifford & Kudrle 1241 (2010).

[20] *Id.*

[21] TIROLE 139, 149 (1988) (concluding that the welfare effects of imperfect price discrimination—technically, second- and third-degree price discrimination—are "ambiguous" and may be "socially suboptimal," depending on the context); Armstrong & Vickers 581–83 (2001) (comparing different scenarios of price discrimination).

C. A Myopic Focus on Supply-Side Issues

Microeconomic analyses of infrastructure—whether in the public welfare or regulatory economics traditions—converge on cost recovery, pricing, provisioning, and associated regulatory issues. These are very complex and important issues that attend decreasing-cost industries. Analysts recognize that public good or natural monopoly characteristics often justify government intervention in one form or another and proceed to analyze regulatory options. It is generally accepted that the market will fail in one way or another to efficiently provide society with infrastructure and that there is thus some role for government intervention. In some cases, the government supplants the market by supplying infrastructure directly or by contracting with providers on behalf of its citizens.[22] In other cases, the government attempts to correct the market failure through institutions, such as intellectual property and tax incentives, and continues to rely on private actors to assess demand for a resource and supply it to the public. In some cases, the government regulates private infrastructure providers to constrain monopoly power.

Critically, microeconomic studies of infrastructure are almost exclusively oriented on the supply side of the infrastructure market. The fundamental economic issue is cost recovery and preserving incentives to supply. Other issues are largely subsidiary. This is a significant and pervasive problem. First, consumers are largely passive in the analysis. They exist in these studies as ordinary purchasers of ordinary goods and services; access to and use of infrastructure is, for these consumers, no different than an apple, a haircut, or any other typical consumer good or service. Second, the fact that the demand for infrastructure is derived demand is not important because the markets from which infrastructure demand is derived are assumed to be complete. In other words, externalities (third-party effects) associated with consumer access to and use of infrastructure are largely assumed away.[23] This is a significant problem because it leaves too much out of focus and introduces analytic biases. Insufficient attention is paid to value creation, spillovers, innovation, growth, or the potential demand-side market failures of the sort discussed extensively in subsequent chapters. Yet assuming these issues away is what makes the microeconomic analysis more tractable; it is the cement that holds much of the regulatory economics analysis together. If this approach were substantially challenged, much would require adjustment, as Alfred Kahn recognized in the qualifications chapter of his seminal work on regulatory economics.[24]

The complex relationships between infrastructure resources and other economic and social systems remain largely unexamined from a microeconomic perspective, with some notable exceptions in the recently emergent fields of network economics and

---

[22] Viscusi et al., ch. 14 (2005); LEVY 16–17 (1996); Frischmann 386–87 (2000).

[23] Congestion and network effects are two exceptions. See chapter 7.

[24] KAHN ch. 7 (1998).

development economics. This book aims to begin such an examination by focusing extensively on demand-side issues and asking how and to what extent infrastructure resources generate value for society. Conventional economic analysis of many infrastructure resources fails to fully account for how society uses these resources to create social benefits, and as a result, the conventional analysis fails to fully account for the social demand for the resources. Economists—as well as regulators and politicians—recognize that there is a tremendous demand for public infrastructure and that infrastructure plays a critical role in economic development, but exactly why there is demand, how it manifests, how it should be measured, and how it contributes to human well-being are not well understood. Chapters 4 and 5, in particular, will develop a demand-side approach to infrastructure, picking up where microeconomic studies leave off. Chapter 3 provides a detailed discussion of the microeconomic building blocks woven together in chapters 4 and 5.

Appendix: Macroeconomics Perspective on Infrastructure

Macroeconomists that pay attention to infrastructure focus primarily on understanding and measuring the effects of infrastructure investments on productivity, economic growth, and development. There is a burgeoning literature analyzing the macroeconomic effects of infrastructure. A recent literature survey by World Bank economist Antonio Estache (2006: 7) noted:

> Since the late 1980s, over 150 published papers in English, French, or Spanish—and at least as many unpublished ones—have analyzed the macroeconomic effects of infrastructure. This is probably still the most widely covered theme in the economic literature on infrastructure, as well as the best known outside the infrastructure community. This literature boom has mainly been the result of conceptual and technical developments associated with new growth theory and associated discussions of regional policies.

It is widely accepted that infrastructure has positive impacts on productivity and economic performance and that, as noted in chapter 1, infrastructure resources give rise to large social gains. Quantitative assessments of the impacts of infrastructure tend to estimate social rates of return for infrastructure investments, relying on macroeconomic growth regressions. Estache observes that "[i]n recent years these methods have suggested economic returns on investment projects averaging 30–40 percent for telecommunications, more than 40 percent for electricity generation, and more than 200 percent for roads[,] although, when the outliers are excluded, the average is about 80 percent for roads." Arghya Ghosh and Kieron Meagher capture the conventional wisdom rather well:

> Whether it is the Internet or freeways, infrastructure improves the functioning of an economy. Road building and improvements in telecommunications

infrastructure have both been found to have a significant impact on productivity and growth for a wide selection of OECD countries. At the same time, in both policy quarters and academic circles, lack of proper infrastructure is often blamed for the poor performance of the less developed countries (see Easterly and Rebelo, 1993; World Bank Development Report 1994). This traditional wisdom—of a positive relationship between infrastructure and productivity/growth—has found support in the empirical macroeconomic literature (see for example Aschauer (1989), Fernald (1999), Roller and Waverman (2001)).

Still, both the *magnitude* of economic impacts and the *causal connection*[25] between infrastructure investments and productivity/growth have been and remain the subject of considerable debate among economists. According to a 2006 report of the OECD,[26] "[a] review of the more recent literature suggests that public infrastructure has a positive productive effect on the economy, but that the size of the effect is not as large as that estimated by earlier studies [such as those by Aschauer (1989)]. Based on samples of several OECD countries and broken down according to economic sectors, the findings indicate that the efficiency impacts of infrastructure tend to be positive—but relatively modest—in almost all sectors." Thus, the conventional wisdom of a positive relationship between infrastructure and productivity/growth is intact, but it is somewhat tempered and subject to qualifications and continued debate among macroeconomists.[27] Let me highlight a few issues relevant to themes discussed later in the book.

Acknowledging that infrastructure investments generally can yield substantial social benefits neither ensures that such benefits will occur in any particular case nor indicates how to prioritize or choose among different infrastructure investments.[28] Contextual details matter considerably. Priorities will vary based on the relevant community, development of the economy, existing infrastructure, available technology, and various societal needs, among other factors. Consider, for a moment, how decisions about infrastructure investment priorities vary across different societies—developed vs. developing countries, urban vs. rural communities, or even ancient vs. modern civilizations. Determining the optimal rate and direction of infrastructure investment is a complicated, community- and context-specific inquiry.

---

[25] E.g., does infrastructure cause productivity/growth or does productivity/growth cause infrastructure investment?

[26] OECD 15 (2006).

[27] The recent literature also suggests that infrastructure investments tend to yield benefits over the long term and that underinvestment in infrastructure witnessed in various regions may be due to difficulties in estimating these long-term impacts. *Id.* at 18. Compounding valuation problems, long-term investments may be discounted severely due to shortsightedness.

[28] Scarcity in funds for infrastructure investment requires prioritization and thus comparative evaluation of different infrastructure investments.

David Aschauer and others emphasize that the impact that infrastructure investments have on productivity/growth depends considerably on how well infrastructure is financed, managed, and used. As Aschauer put it, "[H]ow much you have is important," but so is "how you use it" and "how you pay for it."[29] Aschauer, building on the work of Charles Hulten, emphasizes that in addition to the amount of infrastructure capital, the effectiveness with which infrastructure resources are managed, maintained, and used affects economic growth. In some cases, investing in the maintenance, improvement, and more efficient use of existing infrastructure can yield substantially greater returns than investment in new infrastructure. Charles Hulten emphasized this point in the context of low- and middle-income countries, showing that ineffective use of infrastructure can significantly penalize developing countries. He refers to "[d]ata presented in the 1994 World Development Report (WDR) suggest[ing] that $12 billion in timely road maintenance in Africa over the preceding decade would have avoided the need for $45 billion in reconstruction and rehabilitation."[30] Manasi Deshpande and Douglas W. Elmendorf make a similar point with respect to the United States, arguing for better use of existing roads, highways, aviation infrastructure, and spectrum.[31]

Ghosh and Meagher explore the political economy of infrastructure investment. They observe that "the macroeconomic literature leaves us with a clear indication of the importance of infrastructure, but no deep understanding of the economic role of infrastructure and the processes determining the level of infrastructure." They suggest that variance in infrastructure development can be understood in part to be a function of who the winners and losers from such investments may be in a particular context. Consider, for example, why it is that maintenance of existing infrastructure or measures that improve infrastructure effectiveness (e.g., congestion pricing) take second seat to investments in new infrastructure. One simple reason is politics: The political system tends to reward politicians for delivering new infrastructure.

Their consideration of the political economy of infrastructure leads Ghosh and Meagher to connect infrastructure policy with competition policy (antitrust law). This move connects their approach to another school of macroeconomics, *institutionalism*, which focuses on the social institutions, including but not limited to legal regimes, that are critical to economic growth.[32] This highlights the basic fact that infrastructure resources are one of many factors that structure the economic environment and affect productivity and growth. Institutions, technology, politics, and various other factors, including nonstructural factors such as initial per capita income and savings rates, need to be taken into account when assessing macroeconomic performance.

---

[29] Aschauer (2000).

[30] Hulten (1996).

[31] Deshpande & Elmendorf (2008).

[32] BAUMOL ET AL. (2007); Baumol (1990); NORTH (1990).

One relevant area of macroeconomics that is not directly focused on infrastructure concerns endogenous growth theory. This field of study focuses on ideas (technological innovation) as a factor driving economic growth and considers technical change an endogenous process by which the economy creates new technologies. This modern approach to growth theory—sometime referred to as new growth theory—began with Robert Solow's famous 1957 paper, in which he added up the total labor and capital contributions to the US economy and estimated a national scale production function of the form

$$Y = AF(L,K).$$

He found that a substantial portion of US economic growth could not be accounted for using the labor and capital inputs and was instead attributed to the coefficient A, which became known as the *Solow residual*, or, more recently, as "total factor productivity," or in some circles simply as "technology." A tremendous amount of macroeconomic research has focused on figuring out how to account for the residual. What factors besides labor and capital inputs drive economic growth? The most common answer is technological innovation. The literature has grown tremendously over the last fifty years and offers many potential intersections with the ideas in this book. For the most part, those intersections will have to wait for future work. Let me highlight briefly two ways in which this literature is relevant to the arguments made in this book.

First, technology- or innovation-driven economic growth may be fueled by certain types of infrastructural resources. Infrastructure tends to be included in such growth models as a form of public capital and thus as a portion of K. Among other things, these models generally assume that capital involves decreasing returns, while technologies/innovation/ideas involve increasing returns due to the nonrival nature of the resource. But this division may not be appropriate for all infrastructural capital, because some infrastructural capital may be managed in a manner that sustains and leverages nonrivalry to achieve increasing returns. In a sense, certain infrastructure may contribute to the Solow residual by enabling user innovation and user-generated spillovers, though how this is achieved may depend on the type of infrastructure and how it is managed.[33]

Second, while this literature does not devote much attention to infrastructure, there is a particular line of work focused on general-purpose technologies (GPTs) that is complementary. GPTs are understood to be specific technologies that are of special significance

---

[33] The new growth models that have come to the forefront in macroeconomic theory rely heavily on increasing returns to scale from investments in ideas because ideas are nonrival, are sharable, and generate knowledge and other related externalities. See, e.g., Romer (1986); Romer (1996). This book may lead to potentially important contribution to that line of macroeconomic analysis because the book looks quite carefully at a broader set of resources that have similar economic features—nonrivalry and increasing returns to scale (and often scope) because of the externalities. Unfortunately, I cannot fully pursue this discussion in this book.

to the economy, and some but not all GPTs fall in to the category of infrastructure. In their book published in 2005, Richard Lipsey, Kenneth Carlaw, and Clifford Bekar present the following definition of a GPT: "a single generic technology . . . that initially has much scope for improvement and eventually comes to be widely used, to have many uses, and to have many spillover effects." Moreover, the authors emphasize that GPTs have considerable potential to transform economic, cultural, and other social systems. They present a list of proposed GPTs, which is revealing in that some are typically considered infrastructure, while others are not. As we will see in chapter 4, this definition shares some features with the demand-side criteria for infrastructural resources. GPTs and infrastructure (as defined in chapter 4) are essentially overlapping sets, and resources that fall within the shared area may be of particular interest.

Macroeconomic studies that are focused on productivity/growth do not account very well for other relevant economic measures of social welfare, such as quality of life or living standards. There have been significant developments in the macroeconomics literature, and particularly in the development economics field, that put such standards front and center.

This book will not focus on macroeconomics. The discussion in this brief overview is meant to give the reader some background and suggest that there are some connections with the microeconomic study on infrastructure that deserve further exploration.

3

MICROECONOMIC BUILDING BLOCKS

INFRASTRUCTURES ARE COMPLEX economic resources. This chapter provides a detailed discussion of microeconomic concepts that serve as building blocks for the demand-side analysis developed in Part II and applied in Parts III and IV. The concepts are very important to understanding the value of infrastructure and evaluating and improving resource management. Specifically, this chapter discusses the following microeconomic concepts:

- Public and Private Goods: (Non)rivalry and (Non)excludability
- Consumption Goods and Capital Goods
- Externalities: Incomplete and Missing Markets
- Social Goods: Nonmarket Goods, Merit Goods, Social Capital, and Irreducibly Social Goods

After discussing these concepts, I conclude the chapter with a brief discussion of speech. While not a building block, the speech example usefully illustrates how some of the microeconomic concepts relate to one another.

A. Public and Private Goods: (Non)rivalry and (Non)excludability

Economists classify resources based on two characteristics: rivalrousness of consumption and excludability.[1] Table 3.1 presents the standard classifications.

---

[1] CORNES & SANDLER 9 (1996).

TABLE 3.1   Classification Based on Rivalrousness of Consumption and Excludability

		(Non)excludability	
		Nonexcludable	Excludable
(Non)rivalrousness of Consumption	Nonrival	"Pure" public goods	Toll goods
	Rival	Common pool resources	"Pure" private goods

According to this classification scheme, whether a resource is deemed a public good or a private good depends only on the two characteristics and not on whether the resource is publicly or privately owned, provisioned, or financed. Despite frequent confusion on this point, resource classification does not in itself say anything about the role of government or markets.

Economists recognize that this classification scheme oversimplifies the true nature of resources. Both (non)rivalrousness of consumption and (non)excludability are matters of degree, therefore resources do not always fit neatly within the discrete boxes shown in the table. Moreover, these two characteristics often comprise only a piece of the economic puzzle, a point brought into relief below and in subsequent chapters. But it is a useful starting point.

I. (NON)EXCLUDABILITY

It is easy to see how (non)excludability varies by degree. (Non)excludability refers to the costs of exclusion—specifically, how costly it will be for one person to prevent another from consuming the resource.[2] Consider, for example, ideas and apples. It is very difficult to prevent someone from consuming an idea. If I have an idea, I can exclude others by keeping it secret. This involves some internal cost. I must take precautions to keep the idea secret and forgo opportunities to utilize the idea. I will face significantly higher costs if the idea is not kept secret and others share the idea. Ideas are notoriously slippery; it is difficult to maintain exclusive possession of them. By contrast, it is relatively cheap to maintain exclusive possession of an apple and thereby prevent another person from consuming it.

(Non)excludability is not a fixed or inherent characteristic of a resource; it is variable in the sense that the costs of exclusion depend on both context and technology. Social context can reduce the costs of exclusion where accepted norms and institutions condition access on permission.[3] Think for a moment about how parents endure the struggle of

---

[2] *Id.* at 4, 8–10.

[3] ELLICKSON (1991); McAdams (1997).

teaching children to ask for permission before taking another child's toy. Coupled with other related lessons (e.g., respect for others), parents collectively construct a powerful social institution that reduces the costs of exclusion. Technology, too, can greatly reduce the costs of exclusion. The inventions of barbed wire and encryption technology dramatically reduced the costs of exclusion for land and encrypted content, respectively.[4]

(Non)excludability is relevant to a supply-side analysis of whether markets work efficiently. Low cost exclusion is one key to a well-functioning market. If one can cheaply exclude others from consuming a resource, one can demand payment as a condition for access. If one cannot cheaply exclude others from consuming a resource, then the market may fail to satisfy consumer demand for the resource because suppliers will not be able to recoup their costs from consumers. Simply put, a producer of a good must exclude you from consuming the good it has produced if it wishes to charge you for it, and a producer needs to be able to charge you for access if it wishes to recover its costs. If the costs of exclusion are high, then producers must either absorb these additional costs and charge higher fees, or run the risk that consumers will "free ride" by consuming the good without paying. Either route may lead to market failure. Thus, *if* market provision of a resource is desirable but the cost of exclusion is too high, *then* government intervention to fix the market may be appropriate.[5] There are various institutional fixes to this form of market failure—property rights, for example, are a well-established means for reducing the costs of exclusion. For a variety of reasons, it may be that market provision is not desirable and that alternative provisioning mechanisms (e.g., government or community provision) fare better.

2. (NON)RIVALROUS CONSUMPTION

(Non)rivalry, or (non)rivalrousness of consumption, is a function of resource capacity and the degree to which one person's consumption of a resource affects the potential of the resource to meet the demands of others. It reflects the marginal cost of allowing an additional person to consume a good.

At the extremes, we can think of purely rivalrous goods, such as apples, and purely nonrivalrous goods, such as ideas. One person's consumption of an apple necessarily affects the availability of the apple for anyone else; apples are depleted when consumed. If A eats an apple, B cannot eat that same apple.[6] In a sense, the marginal costs of allowing B to eat *that* apple are infinite because A's consumption would render it impossible.

---

[4] Bollier 27–30, 57 (2001).

[5] It is a mistake to presume, as many do, that the market mechanism is always the superior mechanism for satisfying social demand for a resource. See CORNES & SANDLER 66 (1996); Benkler 406 (2006a); Cohen 1809–14 (2000); Justman & Teubal 51–52 (1996); Nelson 542–48 (1987a).

[6] We can imagine interesting exceptions to this general statement, for example, if we consider viewing the apple or taking a photograph of the apple. The exceptions highlight ambiguity in the term "consumption" and also

In addition to being consumed rivalrously, private goods are generally rivalrously possessed, meaning that A's possession of an apple precludes B from possessing that apple absent an exchange.

Putting aside transaction costs and distributional issues, most economists accept the following three principles: (a) social welfare is maximized when a rivalrous good is consumed by the person who values it the most, (b) the market mechanism is generally the most efficient means for rationing such goods, and (c) the market mechanism is generally the most efficient means for allocating resources needed to produce such goods.[7] To facilitate markets, producers of rivalrous goods are given exclusive control over the goods they produce through basic property rights, and those producers are then able to transfer their goods to consumers willing to pay the market price.

Consider a simple hypothetical: Assume we have one apple. Who should eat it? If we are aiming to maximize our joint welfare, presumably we should give it to the person who values it most, since only one person can consume it. How do we know who values it most? Should we rely on mere assertions? Perhaps we should auction it to see who is willing to pay the most for it. That would provide a reliable indicator of our valuations (although it would also depend on the putative consumer's ability to pay). Should we then bother to get another apple for the person who didn't get the one we possess? It depends on the costs of doing so (supply) and how badly the person wants an apple (demand). In essence, the hypothetical illustrates the three principles in action: Since the apple is rivalrous, we *must* allocate it exclusively to one person, and the optimal allocation would be to give the apple to the person that values it most; the market mechanism allocates goods based on price, which "serves efficiently both the function of rationing the existing inventory and rationing resources into replenishment of the inventory."[8] That is, what we are willing to pay for the apple provides reliable information on which to base our initial allocation decision (i.e., who gets the apple) as well as our future allocation decision (i.e., whether to invest resources in getting another apple).

At the opposite extreme, the story is quite different. Ideas, like other nonrival goods, have infinite capacity. One person's consumption of an idea does not affect the availability of the idea for anyone else; an idea is not depleted in quantity or quality when consumed, regardless of the number of persons consuming it. An idea only needs to be created once to satisfy consumer demand, whereas an apple must be produced for each consumer. Essentially, this means that the marginal costs of allowing an additional person to possess and use an idea are zero. Ideas are naturally sharable, which means that ideas

---

the fact that simple examples often rest on simplifying assumptions—in this case, that "the most prevalent uses of an apple involve rivalrous consumption." Frischmann & Lemley 257 n.53 (2007).

[7] Demsetz 295–96 (1970).

[8] *Id.*

always can be shared, possessed, and used simultaneously and repeatedly by many people.

Assume we have an idea—say, the nonrivalrous consumption concept about which I am writing. Who should "eat" it? As with the apple, we could aim to allocate it exclusively to the person who values it most and could rely on the market mechanism to generate information about who that might be. To facilitate the market, we might allocate exclusive rights to control the idea to the producer (see chapter 12). But we do not need to allocate the idea in this fashion. Instead, we can choose to allocate the idea on a nonexclusive basis. This is important because it reflects an additional degree of freedom in resource management that simply does not exist for rivalrous resources.

Nonrivalrousness thus calls into doubt the three principles noted above and suggests that "efficient allocation of rights to possess and use an idea does not require exclusivity and a market-driven search for the user that values the idea most."[9] As a result, most economists accept that it is efficient to maximize access to, and consequently consumption of, an *existing* nonrival good, because generally there is only an upside; additional private benefits come at no additional cost. Two caveats are worth noting: First, I have been careful to focus solely on sharing in terms of allowing access. I excluded distribution or transmission costs, which may vary considerably by resource type. Second, maximizing access does not mean free provision, nor does it mean force-feeding. Presumably, consumers bear any distribution or transmission costs, and consumers for whom the marginal benefits of consumption are less than the marginal costs of distribution may decline to access the good.

The static, *ex post* perspective on existing resources is obviously incomplete. One must adopt a dynamic perspective and consider how nonrival goods are produced and made available to society. From a dynamic perspective, nonrival, nonexcludable goods present a well-known supply-side problem: The inability to cheaply identify and exclude nonpaying users (sometimes called "free riders"), coupled with high fixed costs of initial production and low marginal costs of reproduction, presents risks for investors, which *may* lead to undersupply by markets.[10]

Taken together, the static and dynamic efficiency perspectives yield a complicated economic puzzle in terms of maximizing social welfare. As a policy matter, it *may* be necessary to strike a balance between maximizing access to reap static efficiency gains and restricting access to reap dynamic efficiency gains. As the next section and subsequent chapters discuss, there often are dynamic efficiency gains associated with maximizing access, since a wider range of productive users of the resources may generate increasing returns. Ultimately, whether and how to strike a balance between maximizing and

---

[9] Frischmann & Lemley n.56 (2007).

[10] On how the cost structure of supply and high exclusion costs may affect incentives to invest, see chapters 8 and 12.

restricting access depends on the resource, the costs and benefits of different allocations, the transaction and institutional costs, and available alternatives.

Nonrivalry often seems inextricably linked to nonexcludability and the associated risk of free riding. In a sense, nonrivalry opens the door to free riding, and in some cases it makes free riding likely—if not inevitable—because nonrival goods can be consumed by many persons simultaneously and jointly. Producers of nonrival goods seeking to maximize their returns face the risk that nonpaying consumers may obtain access to the goods (e.g., from competitors that need not bear the fixed cost of production and thus may sell the good at marginal cost), but this risk is really a function of excludability, not nonrivalry. Consider excludable goods, such as a telecommunications network, that exhibit similar cost structures (high fixed costs coupled with low marginal costs, and thus decreasing average costs). Such goods do not encounter the free-riding problem. Moreover, not all nonrival goods are produced by entities seeking to maximize profits or even to recoup their costs of production (consider, for example, national security), nor are all such goods even produced (consider, for example, sunshine).

Nonetheless, possible free riding drives analysts to focus on supply-side considerations and, more specifically, to correct market-oriented supply problems by designing property-based institutions to lessen the costs of exclusion and minimize free riding.[11] Yet markets may fail for many other reasons, and exclusion may aggravate other problems. Even if an owner can exclude users from a nonrival resource, and therefore meter use by charging a fee, dynamic inefficiencies still may abound—for example, if users are priced out of the market or if externalities are present (discussed below). Simply put, property rights and other institutions that lessen the costs of exclusion and facilitate market-driven provision of nonrival goods are no panacea. As Richard Cornes and Todd Sandler observed:

> Exclusion . . . can strengthen the motives for production of a public good and make possible the operation of a market. Given the efficiency problems associated with pure public goods, it is interesting to consider whether or not the possibility of exclusion is sufficient to restore the presumption that market provision is efficient. . . .
>
> . . . A number of writers have investigated the implications of price excludability under various assumptions regarding market structure and the amount of information about demand possessed by the supplier. There are no clear conclusions, except that Pareto efficiency is not guaranteed by the possibility of exclusion. Excludability alone cannot reinstate the presumptive efficiency of decentralized market provision, and most writers . . . have argued for a presumption of underprovision even when exclusion is possible.[12]

---

[11] I discuss free riding extensively in chapter 8; see also chapter 12.
[12] CORNES & SANDLER 56–57 (1996).

Critically, focusing on free riding and market-driven supply obscures the economic meaning and importance of nonrivalry. Nonrivalry enables sharing and opens the door to much more than free riding, as subsequent chapters demonstrate. Developing a more sophisticated understanding of what nonrivalry facilitates is crucial to providing a more robust economic argument for commons management.[13] Macroeconomists, building from the work of Paul Romer, have recognized that nonrivalry plays an important role in generating increasing returns and fueling economic growth. However, the microeconomic foundations of such insights remain underdeveloped.

We have discussed extremes, describing purely nonrival goods such as ideas and purely rival goods such as apples. The conceptual takeaway is that nonrival resources provide an additional *degree of freedom* with respect to resource management: Efficient allocation of a nonrival resource does not require exclusivity and a market-driven search for the user that values the resource most; where rivalry forces us to allocate possession and use on an exclusive basis, nonrivalry enables a wider range of choices, including allocating possession and use on a nonexclusive basis. Sharing is feasible, potentially on a wide scale; nonrivalry can be leveraged.

3. PARTIALLY (NON)RIVAL GOODS

There are a host of resources between the extremes, generally referred to as impure public goods.[14] An important subset of these in-between resources includes *partially (non)rival goods*.[15] Partially (non)rival goods are durable goods that have finite, *potentially* renewable, and *potentially* sharable capacity. Whether these resources are consumed nonrivalrously or rivalrously often depends on other conditions, such as how the resources are managed, the number of users, and the available capacity. I refer to these resources as partially (non)rival goods because they can be managed in a way that avoids rivalrous consumption (see table 3.2).

---

[13] David & Foray 87–88 (1996) (providing a strong economic argument for open access and knowledge distribution that focuses on "optimal utilization of a nonrival good" and the dominance of positive externalities derived from learning and productive use of knowledge); Benkler 404–5, 438–39 (2006a); Boyle 44–46 (2003).

[14] CORNES & SANDLER 9 (1996).

[15] The possibility of avoiding resource depletion and congestion while still allowing multiple users (uses) is what makes the resource partially (non)rivalrous. This terminology is a bit unusual in the sense that most economists would not characterize precongestion consumption as nonrivalrous. Instead, they would view consumption as depletion of the fixed capacity available and thus as rivalrous. As I see it, temporary depletion of renewable capacity that does not cause any congestion is not strictly rivalrous. Cornes and Sandler similarly refer to impure public goods and club goods as partially rival. CORNES & SANDLER (1996); Benkler (1998a) (discussing sharable resources with finite but perfectly renewable capacity); Benkler 21 (1998b) (same). Benkler suggests that I should use "congestible" rather than partially (non)rivalrous. Benkler (2011).

TABLE 3.2 Classification of Goods Based on Degree of Rivalrousness

(Non)rivalrousness of Consumption	Capacity	Type of Good
Nonrival	• Infinite • Sharable • Not congestible	Public good (idea)
Partially (non)rival	• Finite • Potentially renewable • Potentially sharable • Congestible • Depreciable	Impure public good (lake, road, the Internet)[a]
Rival	• Finite • Nonrenewable • Not sharable	Private good (apple)

[a] According to conventional classification (table 3.1), lakes are common pool resources (nonexcludable but rivalrously consumed), and roads are toll goods (excludable but nonrivalrously consumed). Yet the conventional classifications oversimplify: (1) modern regulatory institutions demonstrate that exclusion is feasible for lakes (see chapter 11), and (2) roads are congestible and can be rivalrously consumed (see chapter 9).

Consider a resource with finite, sharable capacity, such as a lake or computer network. Up to a point, the marginal costs of allowing an additional user to access and use the resource are zero; beyond that point, the marginal costs become positive and increase with each additional user.[16] Many partially (non)rival resources are *sometimes* nonrivalrously consumed and *sometimes* rivalrously consumed, depending on the number of users and available capacity at a particular time. Highways, in real space and cyberspace, offer excellent illustrations. During off-peak hours (imagine traffic at 2 a.m.), consumption of these resources is often nonrivalrous. At these times, users do not impose costs on other users, and the marginal cost of allowing an additional person to use the resource is zero. At some point (e.g., rush hour), nonrivalrous consumption turns rivalrous and congestion problems arise.[17] Congestion on the highway or on the Internet is a function of variable demand imposed on a system with finite capacity. As chapter 7 explains, managing congestion and various risks to sustainability of an infrastructure raises difficult management and governance issues.

---

[16] CORNES & SANDLER 272–77 (1996) (describing congestible resources); Bell & Parchomovsky 13 (2003) (observing that parks are impure public goods that "admit of nonrivalrous uses only to a certain point").

[17] "It should never be forgotten that the highway problem is essentially one of peak load. There is little traffic congestion, even in Manhattan, at three in the morning." Buchanan (1952).

There is a close connection between partially (non)rival resources and "club goods." Cornes and Sandler define club goods as a subclass of impure public goods that are partially rival, excludable goods.[18] Cornes and Sandler assume that exclusion is practiced for club goods and analyze decisions as to club membership, the provision quantity of a shared resource, and congestion management. Most, if not all, club goods are partially (non)rival in the sense that they can be managed in a fashion that eliminates congestion, often by keeping membership size small.[19] Cornes and Sandler emphasize, "Congestion is not something that must be completely eliminated; rather an optimal level of congestion must be found."[20] As chapter 7 examines, figuring out the optimal level of congestion is a critical question for infrastructure, yet in contrast with most club goods, keeping membership size small is not generally the preferred solution for infrastructure. Rather, infrastructures are open to the public to facilitate productive behavior by users that may lead to increasing returns for society.

For the purposes of this book, I focus on "partially (non)rival resources" (and do not often refer to impure public goods or club goods) for two reasons: (1) to emphasize that the degree of (non)rivalry of consumption is variable and often manageable; and (2) to emphasize that the means for managing congestion also vary. Chapter 7 considers these issues in detail. The key point, for now, is that commons management and congestion management often go hand in hand as joint means for leveraging nonrivalry.

4. TAKEAWAYS

Nonrivalry and partial nonrivalry are a defining characteristic of infrastructure and a key to analyzing infrastructure from a functional perspective. So let me reiterate some takeaways from this section:

- Nonrivalrous consumption describes the situation "when a unit of [a] good can be consumed by one individual without detracting, in the slightest, from the consumption opportunities still available to others from that same unit."[21] Nonrival resources have infinite capacity; they are naturally sharable and not congestible. As a result, nonrival resources may yield increasing returns to scale.[22]

---

[18] CORNES & SANDLER 349–50 (1996).

[19] *Id.* at 348–69.

[20] *Id.* at 524–25.

[21] *Id.* at 8.

[22] This is a core part of the new growth theory in macroeconomics. Romer 1002–37 (1986); JONES (1998). This theory focuses on ideas as a special economic resource because of nonrivalry. A host of other infrastructural resources exhibit nonrivalry, at least for an appreciable range of demand.

- (Non)rivalrousness of consumption is a resource characteristic that measures the degree to which one user's consumption of a resource directly affects another user's present consumption possibilities (and not how production costs are distributed among consumers). Resources do not necessarily have a single degree of (non)rivalrousness; many resources are partially (non)rival, which means that the degree and rate of rivalry may vary across time, among users, or across contexts. Partially (non)rival resources have finite capacity; they are potentially renewable, potentially sharable, and congestible. Complicated trade-offs arise in managing the boundary between rivalrous and nonrivalrous consumption.

- Nonrivalry calls into doubt the three principles applicable to rival goods, because efficient allocation of a nonrival resource does not require exclusivity and a market-driven search for the user that values the resource most. Where rivalry forces us to allocate possession and use on an exclusive basis, nonrivalry enables a wider range of choices, including allocating possession and use on a nonexclusive basis. Sharing is feasible, potentially on a wide scale. Exclusivity remains a potentially attractive tool for managing misappropriation risks and congestion in some contexts,[23] but it is not required and is not the only tool for dealing with such issues. Lowering the costs of exclusion through property rights or other institutions may alleviate certain types of market failures associated with misappropriation and congestion, but it also may aggravate other types of market failures associated with reduced sharing and productive use of a sharable resource.

B. Consumption Goods and Capital Goods

When analyzing nonrival and partially (non)rival resources, we must distinguish between consumption goods and capital goods. Consumption goods, like apples, are consumed directly to generate private benefits. They satisfy consumer demand and can be seen as *ends* (end-products or outputs) in themselves. In contrast, capital goods, such as a tractor or a harvesting process,[24] are used as inputs to produce other goods. They satisfy demand

---

[23] Exclusion is often a key ingredient to cooperation and coordination in nonmarket settings. Madison, Frischmann, & Strandburg (2010).

[24] The harvesting process can be described as technological or intellectual capital and distinguished from physical, capital goods. As a technological idea, the process is purely nonrivalous, while the tractor is partially (non) rivalrous. Of course, one person's use of the tractor rivals anyone else's opportunity to use that tractor at the same time—simultaneous use is not possible—but the tractor capacity is renewable and can be shared among users. The key point is that where one user's use does not actually affect another's desired use, there is no rivalry. Coordinating shared use of a tractor (or fleet of tractors or other related capital equipment) among a community of users might be costly and not worth the effort. I am not making a broad claim about managing all capital goods. Subsequent chapters delineate a special subset of capital resources—infrastructural capital—and examine

derived from demand for the outputs and are *means* rather than ends.[25] Economists refer to capital goods as "factors of production" that are not used up, exhausted, or otherwise transformed and incorporated into the final output on consumption, unlike raw materials (e.g., coal) or intermediate goods (e.g., a screw). In a sense, the definition of capital goods, or at least the way in which economists differentiate capital goods from raw materials and intermediate goods, suggests the breakdown presented in table 3.3.

Rival inputs, such as coal and screws, are subject to the same analysis as rival consumption goods, such as apples. Consumption of the good (or a unit of the good, in the case of raw materials such as coal) depletes the consumption opportunities of others and thus means that additional supply is needed to meet the demands of others. Accordingly, rivalrously consumed goods, whether private consumption goods, raw materials, or intermediate goods, are subject to the three economic principles identified above: (1) social welfare is maximized when a rivalrous good is consumed by the person who values it the most, (2) the market mechanism is generally the most efficient means for rationing such goods, and (3) the market mechanism is generally the most efficient means for allocating the resources needed to produce such goods.

TABLE 3.3 Consumption Goods, Intermediate Goods, and Capital

Nonrivalrousness of Consumption	Demand	
	Consumption	Derived
Nonrival or partially (non)rival	Public consumption good	Public capital good
Rival	Private consumption good	Private intermediate good (or raw material)

I. RIVAL CONSUMPTION GOOD (APPLE HYPO)

Suppose we have an apple and must decide how best to allocate our good between **A**, **B**, **C**, and **D**. Assume getting another apple would cost $.75. **A** would like to eat the apple

---

various resource management issues that arise with respect to that subset. The distinctions between different forms of capital resources, including intellectual, social, physical, and natural capital, are not important for this particular discussion. But it should be noted that there are distinct literatures focused on different types of capital resources. See, for example, Bourdieu (1986) (differentiating cultural, economic, and social capital). I discuss social capital in more detail below.

[25] I use input-output terminology to describe resource use in production processes. There are other ways to describe these relationships. One alternative refers to generic or basic inputs as platforms. Another refers to the relationships in terms of layers. As I am spanning a number of disciplines, there is bound to be some confusion with respect to terminology, which I can only hope to minimize.

and is willing to pay $.65; **B** would like to use the apple to make a pie and is willing to pay $.50; **C** would like for us to give the apple to a poor hungry child, **D**, down the street and is willing to pay us $.20 if we do so. Presumably, we should give the apple to **A**, who is, after all, willing to pay the most and appears to place the highest value on the apple.

Suppose **D**, though lacking in funds to pay, would be incredibly happy if she could eat the apple and satiate her hunger. The combined utilities of **C** and **D** might alter the analysis; should we give the apple to **D**? The hypo is complicated by the fact that **C** realizes value if **D** consumes the apple. But what exactly explains why or how **C** realizes $.20 in value? Perhaps altruism. Perhaps recognition that supporting a community of healthy, well-fed children will ultimately benefit **C** in some fashion that may be hard to predict or articulate. The hypo is also complicated by the fact that **D** is unable to pay.

The point of the hypo is only to show that there may be social value or surplus involved in the allocation of rival goods; it does not suggest, however, that the exception swallows the rule. To the contrary, the three principles still hold, for two important reasons: First, given the rivalrous nature of the goods in question, the goods must be allocated on an exclusive basis. Second, it is incredibly difficult to obtain information about valuations that depend on interdependencies of the sort described in the hypo. Imagine, if you will, how we would ever figure out in the real world how much value **D** would realize on consuming the apple. One important reason why the market mechanism is generally the most efficient means for rationing rival goods is that it relies on willingness to pay to provide reliable information about valuation. It is an imperfect mechanism, as we will see later, but in many contexts it is the best available.

2. RIVAL CAPITAL GOOD (STEEL SCRAP HYPO)

Suppose we need to figure out how to best use some steel scrap. **A** will pay the market rate of $300/ton to use the scrap in manufacturing stainless steel for kitchen appliances. **B** would like to use the steel scrap in building high-speed railway systems across major US corridors. **B** offers to pay $250/ton. Would we be better off allocating the steel scrap to the production of kitchen appliances or high-speed railways? The former involves using the steel as an input into the production of private goods, and the latter involves using the steel as an input into the production of an impure public good, which itself acts as an input into various productive activities (see chapter 4). As in the previous hypo, this hypo is intended to show that there may be social value or surplus involved in the allocation of rival goods. While it is tempting to lean toward allocating the steel scrap to **B** because of the potential social value, the temptation should be avoided, at least when considering how to allocate the steel itself. There are a few reasons, but the most important are the same as in the prior hypo: The steel is rivalrous and must be allocated exclusively, and the market mechanism is generally the most efficient means for doing so because it generates and depends on more reliable information about valuation; all the reliable information in the hypo suggests that **A** values the steel scrap more than **B** ($300 > $250).[26] Moreover, as the third principle suggests, the market mechanism is generally the most efficient means for attracting investment into the production of the rival resources being consumed— that is, it effectively signals to other steel producers the demand for steel scrap. Finally, I emphasize one additional point: To the extent that the output in question is socially valuable (above and beyond the value reflected in output markets), the standard solution is to directly subsidize or otherwise support output producers—in this case, high-speed transit systems; this would enable these producers to bid effectively for the inputs they need. If **B** receives stimulus funds from the federal government, for example, perhaps **B** will revise his bid. Then B's private demand for steel scrap may better reflect societal demand— demand derived from demand for high-speed transit systems.

3. NONRIVALROUS CONSUMPTION GOODS AND NONRIVALROUS CAPITAL GOODS

Nonrivalrous consumption goods are subject to the economic considerations set forth in the previous section. The three principles noted above do not hold because of nonrivalry. As discussed, there is a trade-off between static and dynamic efficiencies.

Nonrival capital may be used by multiple users as an input to produce other goods (outputs). This door opened by nonrivalry is worth exploring more carefully. Generally, demand for nonrival inputs depends on the full range of outputs. In essence, the wider the range of outputs, the greater the potential for increasing returns to sharing.

Suppose that instead of steel scrap, the resource to be allocated is a method for processing steel scrap, and both A and B value the method, say at $300 and $250, respectively. In this case we would not need to choose between kitchen appliances or railway because both A and B could use the resource. We could allocate the resource exclusively to A, exclusively to B, or nonexclusively to A and B. The possibility of allowing both A and B to use the method is a significant change in the hypo. It is an *additional degree of freedom* that doesn't exist with respect to rival resources, and it presents opportunities for leveraging the resource capacity to obtain increasing social returns. The three economic principles applicable to rival goods do not apply, and the trade-off between static and dynamic efficiencies is more complicated.

As the next two sections and subsequent chapters examine in more detail, demand-side problems arise where nonrival capital can be used to produce many different types of outputs, including public goods and social goods. Sharing the resource to facilitate these productive activities may generate beneficial effects *external* to the market mechanism. In some cases, the social benefits derived from widespread access to a nonrival input used to

---

[26] Note that, in our hypo, there is no reliable indicator of societal demand for steel scrap derived from demand for railways, other than the market price of $300/ton.

produce such goods may be quite large but underrepresented in markets.[27] A demand-side analysis is critical to valuing nonrival inputs, both in terms of measurement (i.e., the actual value of the resource) and in terms of understanding *how* the resource creates social value. These are related tasks, but one begins to grasp the true social value of infrastructure resources only when one looks to the downstream uses and applications. At a minimum, policy decisions aimed at balancing static and dynamic efficiency gains ought to explicitly take these issues into account. The next two sections examine in considerable detail how these effects external to the market mechanism arise and how they impact economic analysis.

C. Externalities: Incomplete and Missing Markets

Infrastructure resources generate different types of *externalities*, including third-party effects associated with incomplete or missing markets. As subsequent chapters discuss in detail, infrastructure resources often facilitate productive behaviors by users that affect third parties, including other users and non-users of the infrastructure. The third-party effects often are accidental, incidental, and not especially relevant to the infrastructure provider or user; nonetheless, they may be quite important from a societal perspective. This section summarizes the economics of externalities.

The term "externality" has been a contested concept in economics for many years.[28] Ronald Coase defined the concept broadly as "the effect of one person's decision on someone who is not a party to that decision."[29] Acknowledging that "externality is an ambiguous concept,"[30] Harold Demsetz suggested that "every cost and benefit associated with social interdependencies is a potential externality." In his view, actual externalities exist only where benefits or costs are not taken into account by parties, because "the cost of transacting in the rights between the parties (internalization) [] exceed[s] the gains from internalization." Kenneth Arrow defined externality as the absence of a functioning market; that is, an externality is functionally equivalent to an incomplete or missing market.[31] In a similar vein as Demsetz, Arrow made clear the importance of understanding that the existence or nonexistence of externalities is a function of the relevant institutional setting, incentive structure, information, and other constraints on the decision-making and exchange possibilities of relevant actors.

For purposes of the book, we adopt the following definition: Positive (negative) externalities are benefits (costs) realized by one person as a result of another person's activity

---

[27] LESSIG 87 (2001b); Rose 744 (1986); Benkler 369 (2006a).

[28] PAPANDREOU 13–68 (1994).

[29] COASE 24 (1988).

[30] Demsetz 348 (1967).

[31] Arrow 59, 67 (1970); CORNES & SANDLER 40–43 (1996).

without payment (compensation). We generate and realize externalities each and every day by virtue of our experiences in an interdependent society. Consider how many of your daily actions have small but nonetheless real effects on others around you. Many effects are small in magnitude and seem trivial—say, the effects of one person's loud cackling laugh on others trying to read at a coffeehouse. But such effects may become more significant if persistent or widespread—if the cackler persists for an extended period of time, perhaps every morning . . . or consider a person chatting loudly on her cell phone every morning on the public transit bus . . . or a person that maintains a beautiful flower garden to the benefit of those who pass by on the way to the bus . . . and so on. But many externalities are not small in magnitude. For example, the social importance of spillovers from innovation is well recognized.[32]

Externalities, whether positive or negative, are understood to be an important type of "market failure"—again, at times defined as the absence of a market. The perceived problem is that externalities generally are not fully factored into a person's decision about whether and how to engage in an activity and consequently may have a distorting effect on market coordination and allocation of resources.[33] Distortions may manifest on both the supply side—in terms of reduced incentives to invest in what would otherwise be optimal supply—and the demand side—in terms of lost signals about what consumers want and where investments should be directed. The "lost signals" description follows from the notion of externalities as missing markets or unpriced exchanges. Too few (many) resources may be allocated to activities that generate positive (negative) externalities because those persons deciding whether and how to allocate resources fail to account for the full range of benefits (costs). If only the unaccounted-for benefits (costs) were taken into account, or *internalized*, the actors might behave differently—for example, by reallocating their resources in a more efficient manner.[34]

To avoid distortions associated with externalities, the standard economic solution is to internalize externalities by pricing the exchanges or enabling missing markets to operate. How is internalization accomplished? For some time, most economists accepted A. C. Pigou's view that the government ought to "intervene" via the tax or regulatory system and force externality-producing agents to fully account for their actions.[35] Those who engage in activities that produce negative (positive) externalities, such as pollution (education), should be taxed (subsidized) at a level that takes into account external effects and aligns private and social costs (benefits).[36] However, Coase[37] challenged the Pigovian

[32] Frischmann & Lemley (2007) (collecting sources).

[33] CORNES & SANDLER 39–43 (1996); MEADE 15 (1973); Arrow 72–76 (1970).

[34] Still, even if internalized, the actors might not behave differently. See Frischmann 665–68 (2007b); Frischmann (2009b); Frischmann & Lemley (2007); Buchanan & Stubblebine 373–74 (1962). See also chapters 8 and 12.

[35] PIGOU (1920).

[36] CORNES & SANDLER 72–78 (1996); Buchanan & Stubblebine 381–82 (1962).

[37] Coase (1960).

tradition and, among other things, added *well-defined property rights* to the menu of options for dealing with externalities.[38] A rich legal and economic literature has developed around these issues.

In a series of articles, I have challenged the view that externalities are necessarily a problem to be solved. In certain contexts, society may be better off if it lets some externalities go without aiming to internalize them and, further, if it encourages participation in activities that generate externalities, again, without aiming to internalize them completely. Intellectual property systems are a good example; both patent and copyright systems are designed to enable some internalization of what would otherwise be external benefits and to promote some productive activities that generate externalities.[39]

Let me highlight two points of contention that are at the heart of the debate: I have argued, first, that externalities do not necessarily cause economic distortions and, second, that even when they do, the distortions may be welfare enhancing.

The first point is pretty straightforward, though often taken for granted. Claims—or, worse, assumptions—that internalizing externalities would necessarily lead to changes in behavior and/or resource allocation are overblown and lack theoretical or empirical support. Many externalities are simply "irrelevant"[40] in the sense that whether or not they are internalized by actors, the actors would not change their actions. To internalize or not to internalize in such cases is really a question of transferring wealth. While distributional considerations might warrant policies that aim to limit or promote such transfers, efficiency considerations do not.[41] This point places a significant limit on the supply-side rationale for internalization (i.e., the perceived benefits of internalization) and arguments about free riding and speculative diminution of incentives to invest.[42] It also connects with the empirical observations made by *many* scholars that in *many* different contexts, capturing value realized by others—through monetary returns or otherwise—is not necessary to support incentives to innovate because people prefer to innovate for their own reasons.[43]

---

[38] One important point to keep in mind is that internalization is not costless; this is one simple reason why externalities are ubiquitous—imagine how costly it would be to account fully for all the external effects from your own actions! Demsetz has emphasized this point in his work on how property rights systems evolve to meet demand for internalization of externalities. Demsetz (1967).

[39] See chapter 12.

[40] Buchanan & Stubblebine (1962). Some economists with whom I have discussed this point emphasized that the point only holds if externalities are defined capaciously to include all third-party effects. They argue such a broad definition sweeps in too much. It would be better, in their view, to limit the definition of externalities to those effects for which internalization is relevant. Then, analysis of externalities can more easily focus on the direct benefits and costs of externalities. I find this approach myopic and tautological.

[41] An exception might be strategic creation (withholding) of negative (positive) externalities. KELLY (2010).

[42] Lemley (2005).

[43] VON HIPPEL (2005); BENKLER (2006b); Tushnet (2009).

The second point is that even when internalization affects behavior and externalities are relevant, it may be best to leave them alone or even encourage their unmetered flow. It does not necessarily improve matters to internalize the externalities. First, the administrative, transaction, and/or institutional costs of internalization may be too high—it can be quite costly to set up the apparatus for a well-functioning market. Second, the reallocation of benefits or costs accomplished by internalization may affect the behavior of other actors besides the internalizing actor. In contexts involving incentive-relevant externalities, evaluating the benefits and costs of internalization must include not only impacts on internalizing actors but also impacts on third parties.

Letting spillovers flow, or even encouraging them to flow, may be worthwhile for society, particularly when beneficiaries are productive in ways that themselves generate social benefits. The reason is that transforming the beneficiaries into purchasers that must pay to act productively may shift their behavior, reducing the intensity of their productive activity or causing them to act differently altogether, and consequently may lead to fewer of the desired social benefits. This result is to be expected when purchasers cannot capture the full value of their own activities—that is, where their activities generate spillovers. Under these circumstances, the purchasers' private demand will fall short of social demand.

This demand-side problem may lead to market failure, but it may not. It may lead to underparticipation in the socially desired spillover-producing activity and undersupply of the spillovers. It may lead to optimization of the input being licensed for a narrower range of uses than would be socially desirable. It may have no impact other than to transfer wealth from licensee to licensor. The point is simply that we cannot *assume* the market mechanism will best aggregate demand information and allocate resources efficiently, and thus we need a better appreciation of demand in such contexts. Much of this book is devoted to this issue in the specific context of infrastructural resources.

Where externalities are incentive-relevant, the case for internalization depends, in part, on the degree to which all other markets are complete. Unless spillovers are internalized throughout society—which is impossible—the case for internalization in any particular context must account for cascading effects in other dependent markets and many incomplete and missing markets, including nonmarket systems. Such accounting is quite difficult and requires considerably more attention to context. It also requires acknowledgment of and engagement with the complexities often ignored or simplified in reductionist models.[44]

Externalities complicate and often confound various economic models and theories. This observation might be accepted only grudgingly by some economists, but it follows directly from the fact that many economic models and theories simply assume away externalities. Consider, for example, that much of the regulatory economics tradition

---

[44] Cf. Lunney (2008).

rests on an assumption of no externalities.[45] (One move that I lump together with assuming them away is the "acknowledge and then ignore completely" move often made in discussions of regulatory economics.)[46] Those models, theories, or economists that do not assume them away often work with a subset of externalities that are easily identified and for which the "missing market" may be constructed or captured via some championed institutional fix. This is seen vividly in the utilitarian economic theories of intellectual property. Where externalities are difficult to identify or capture, these exact difficulties may preclude further consideration: If we cannot easily identify, much less measure, externalities, how should we go about integrating them into our models and analyses? How do we know which external effects count or how to choose or weigh them? And so on. Talking about externalities may seem akin to academic handwaving.

Nonetheless, spillovers matter and should not be dismissed so easily. By definition, they represent value. Spillovers are ubiquitous and a necessary consequence of an increasingly interdependent society. That they are difficult to identify or capture only means we ought to pay much closer attention to their creation.[47] We should ask:

- How are they created?
- Which activities generate spillovers?
- What conditions support these activities?
- What types of externalities are created?
- How are the externalities distributed to or realized by third parties?
- Do third parties *realize* costs and benefits *cognitively* with awareness and appreciation (and perhaps a willingness to pay if a market were to form) or are the costs and benefits realized more passively, taken for granted, or perhaps appreciated only vaguely or in hindsight?[48]

---

[45] Kahn wrote the seminal treatise on the economics of regulation, and it remains a foundational text. He explicitly qualifies his analysis with the assumption that there are no externalities and notes that if that assumption is relaxed, much of the analysis may change. KAHN ch. 7 (1998). Essentially, the case for regulation (or more generally, government intervention in some form or another) is much stronger. This does not mean that the case is made—it depends on the degree to which government intervention can improve matters.

[46] For example, GOMEZ (2003) (initial chapter explains four justifications for government intervention, one of which is externalities, but then focuses completely on comparative analysis of institutions with natural monopoly/competition concerns being the basic "problem" to be addressed).

[47] "Social production of goods and services, both public and private, is ubiquitous, though unnoticed. It sometimes substitutes for, and sometimes complements, market and state production everywhere. It is, to be fanciful, the dark matter of our economic production universe." BENKLER ch. 4 (2006b).

[48] This inquiry is related but not identical to the behavioral economics considerations of bounded rationality, decision-making heuristics, and the like. In a sense, the inquiry is focused on identifying third-party effects that are unknown and, to some degree, unknowable to the individual third parties and yet still identifiable when analyzed from a broader social perspective, perhaps by focusing on categories of conduct and activities that generate such effects and/or on nonrival resources that can be leveraged to generate such effects. Designing institutions based on such an inquiry raises (a) a classic paternalism-elitism critique and (b) Demsetz's concern

- Can we differentiate among types of externality-producing activities and types of externalities in a manner that is relevant to decision making despite problems with quantification and measurement?

Paying attention to these questions presents fundamental challenges to an economic approach. Analytically, the challenge in employing economics derives at least in part from the difficulties in taking proper account of benefits and costs realized in noneconomic systems that are caused by or at least related to actions in economic systems. To illustrate, we might ask: *Are the cultural or political benefits I realize only passively as a result of the actions of others cognizable within economics?* For example: When others vote on issues that affect me, or participate in activities that build social capital in my neighborhood, or volunteer to maintain parks or mentor neighborhood kids or serve on school committees, or investigate political corruption, . . .[49] are the benefits I realize economically relevant, even if I do not participate or otherwise support those activities? I have always thought the answer is so obviously "Yes" that the question is not even worth asking. Yet Anne Barron, in a thoughtful critique of some of my earlier work, suggests that Mark Lemley and I necessarily venture beyond economics in our attempt to incorporate such values into an economic theory of intellectual property.[50] In her view (and others), these sorts of benefits and costs are strictly noneconomic. Barron's argument seems to rest to some degree on a conception of economics rooted in a narrow version of cost-benefit analysis. Among other things, this narrow conception disregards or makes simplifying assumptions about information, effects, and values that are difficult to observe, quantify, value, and/or monetize. As the next section discusses, this is not a position shared by all, or even most, economists.

If identifying and giving weight to such values *necessarily* takes one outside economics, then so be it—that is a boundary that must be crossed. But I do not think it does, or necessarily has to do so. In my view, it is a boundary worthy of attention and interrogation that we should acknowledge and explore, as I do in this book. Failure to do so truncates the economic analysis and isolates economics from other disciplinary approaches. The next section considers one approach to accommodating various social values, an approach focused on different types of social goods. Notably, social goods play a prominent role in the demand-side analysis of infrastructure that follows.

---

about the comparative competence of market, government, and other institutions. While I appreciate both types of criticism and acknowledge the need to keep them in mind, I do not believe either undermines the inquiry or effort to design institutions based on it.

[49] The list could go on and on, capturing the myriad ways in which social interdependence ties our actions and welfare together such that spillovers are realized but mostly passively, without awareness, formal transactions, or markets.

[50] Barron 9, 18 (2008).

D. Social Goods: Nonmarket Goods, Merit Goods, Social Capital, and Irreducibly Social Goods

Economists of many stripes within many different fields recognize the existence and importance of social values not reflected in existing preferences or markets. At the same time, many recognize that preferences are not fixed, inherent, or "exogenous," as conventional economic models assume. Rather, preferences are constructed and shaped during our lifetimes as we interact with our environment, social institutions, and each other.[51] But economists struggle to incorporate social values into their theories, models, and empirical studies. In this section, I introduce a few conceptions of social goods and then explain how social goods generate different sorts of externalities.

I. SOCIAL GOODS

One approach to incorporating social values in economic analysis is to delineate a category of *social goods*. The objective is to define the good, isolate its characteristics, and distinguish it from other categories of goods. In this section, I discuss four types of goods—nonmarket goods, merit goods, social capital, and irreducibly social goods—that do not fit neatly within the economic classification schema discussed earlier. Each involves social value not well reflected in markets and highlights characteristics that distinguish social goods.[52] Broadly speaking, social goods generate value through their impact on social interdependencies/systems. That such value is difficult to observe, measure, or appropriate does not make it insignificant, noneconomic, or incapable of recognition in economic analysis.[53]

Nonmarket goods are goods that are neither provided nor demanded through the market mechanism; we do not purchase such goods. We may recognize their value, but we do not simply rely on the market as a provisioning mechanism. Instead, we rely on

---

[51] NORTH 46–47 (2005); NORTH (1990). As North emphasizes, we learn from our experiences, and our preferences may change as a result. "[The] axiom that people influence each other in their beliefs, values, tastes, and virtually every other cognitive or affective process they engage in . . . is certainly well-founded in the literature on social psychology and sociology, and I would argue is at least as robust as the utility maximizing assumption about rational behavior." KRACKHARDT 5 (1994).

[52] Economists sometime use the label social goods to describe public goods (see, e.g., MUSGRAVE & MUSGRAVE (1984)), but I describe a distinct category.

[53] Many regard social goods to be noneconomic and thus beyond the purview of economics. Others suggest that investing in or otherwise supporting social goods reflects a sacrifice of efficiency for the sake of fairness or some other noneconomic value. My contention is that these framings are misleading. Public investments in social goods often promote efficiency and increase social welfare. That the social value generated by such investments is difficult to observe, measure, or appropriate does not make the value any less real.

other provisioning mechanisms, including government, community, family, and individuals,[54] if in fact these goods are "provided" at all.[55]

The concept of nonmarket goods is most familiar in environmental and ecological economics. Natural resources, ecosystems, and various environmental services critical to human life are not "provided" by markets. We inherit such resources, use them during our lives, and pass them on to future generations. We tend to take for granted the resources we inherit and the environment within which we live; our own preferences and values fail to account for the complex interdependencies between ourselves, our environment, and others. Our environment persistently contributes to our well-being, but most often it does so only indirectly. We rarely pay directly for its benefits, and when we value the environment in terms of individual preferences—measured by willingness to pay or revealed through our actions—it should not be surprising that we persistently undervalue it, in terms of its contributions to our well-being. The field of environmental and ecological economics has struggled with these issues for decades.[56] One approach to these issues is to employ so-called "nonmarket valuation" techniques to get a better estimate of the social value attributable to environmental resources where no functioning markets exist.

An incredible number of social goods we collectively value are nonmarket goods. Consider, for example, the preservation of certain resources, perhaps historic or environmental, for future generations. It may be that society as a whole considers such an objective worthwhile, but for various reasons the market mechanism simply will not accurately measure or respond to societal demand for preservation of this sort. Or consider abstract governing principles, such as the "rule of law," or even more concrete governing institutions, such as a criminal justice system. These resources are classic nonmarket goods. We do not buy or sell the "rule of law" or the criminal justice system. Demand for such institutions manifests not in markets through the operation of the price mechanism but, rather, through other sociopolitical systems.[57] Markets for such goods are doomed to fail.

Some of the nonmarket goods we collectively value may be reflected in our individual preferences, and those preferences may be meaningfully communicated to nonmarket "suppliers" through political and social mechanisms other than the price mechanism.

---

[54] On comparative institutional analysis of markets, politics, courts, and bureaucracies, see KOMESAR (2001); KOMESAR (1994).

[55] In contrast, private goods and public goods (pure and impure) are supplied by the market mechanism with varying degrees of effectiveness. For private goods, the market mechanism generally works well from both the supply and demand sides, assuming markets are competitive. For public goods, the market mechanism may work well in some cases, but in other cases, it may fail from the supply or demand side, even if markets are competitive.

[56] For a debate about this issue, see the *Journal of Economic Perspectives* 8, no. 4 (Autumn 1994), pp. 1–64.

[57] ALSTON, EGGERTSSON, & NORTH (1996).

Governance institutions are a good example. Some may be reflected in our preferences but remain unsupplied or latent because there is no effective mechanism for expressing or satisfying those preferences. For example, some people may have had a strong desire (a) to make their creative works—music, poetry, short stories, home videos, whatever—freely accessible and usable to others throughout the world, or (b) to collaboratively create with hundreds or thousands of others throughout the world, but until recently, the means for doing so were not technologically available.[58] Some nonmarket goods we collectively value may even be emergent phenomena, not reflected in or responsive directly to our preferences; such goods may emerge over time through the evolution of complex cultural and social systems. Shared cultural meanings and language are examples. The nonmarket goods category is remarkably broad.

Merit goods are goods that society deems so valuable that everyone should have them. Merit goods may be provided by markets, but according to Musgrave's definition, merit goods will be underconsumed and underprovided in a market economy driven by consumer sovereignty.[59] Thus, if some people cannot afford to or would otherwise not choose to consume the goods, government may be warranted in forcing or encouraging consumption, for the betterment of society. Often, the case for classifying a resource as a merit good turns on the existence of external effects. Thus, education and health care are frequently cited as merit goods. Although both are provided by markets, the positive external effects from education and health care provide a basis for government support to ensure widespread consumption. Another basis for classifying a good as a merit good is when consumers have interdependent utility functions, that is, when consumption of the merit good directly affects the utility of another. Another basis for classifying a good as a merit good is when individual preferences diverge from individual welfare—for example, when ignorance, shortsightedness or myopia distort preferences, leading to underconsumption.[60]

What is interesting about the merit goods concept is that it turns, by definition, on a persistent demand-side problem: systematic undervaluation of the merit good in market settings. At the same time, the concept depends on political or collective recognition and

---

[58] BENKLER (2006b).

[59] Musgrave (2009). Musgrave discusses the concept of "community preferences" for merit goods, where "individuals, as members of the community, accept certain community values or preferences, even though their personal preferences might differ." *Id.* He notes, as examples, "maintenance of historical sites" and "respect for the arts" as well as "restrictions on drug use or of prostitution as offences to human dignity (quite apart from potentially costly externalities)." *Id.* He explains that the emergence of such "common values" or "community preferences" may reflect "the outcome of a historical process of interaction among individuals." *Id.* See also MUSGRAVE & MUSGRAVE (1984) ("by virtue of sustained association and mutual sympathy, people come to develop common concerns") and *id.* at 78 ("common concerns and values do exist in a coherent society and its historical tradition"). This social explanation reveals a close connection to social capital and irreducibly social goods, discussed below.

[60] *Id.*; BURKHEAD & MINER 126–27 (2007).

appreciation of the social value. Not surprisingly, this leads to controversy over *who* decides what constitutes a merit good and what level of government support is warranted, particularly when the good is provided to some degree by the market. Nonmarket and merit goods focus on the ineffectiveness of markets as provisioning mechanisms and thus overlap somewhat. The two types of social goods discussed below, social capital and irreducibly social goods, focus on the social nature of value creation.

Social capital is a concept developed outside economics but increasingly used in economics and other social sciences to capture a wide range of social goods.[61] Social capital is a special type of capital good whose value-generation has a social dimension. L. J. Hanifan described social capital as

> that in life which tends to make these tangible substances count for most in the daily lives of people: namely good will, fellowship, sympathy, and social intercourse among the individuals and families who make up a social unit. . . . The individual is helpless socially, if left to himself. . . . If he comes into contact with his neighbor, and they with other neighbors, there will be accumulation of social capital, which may immediately satisfy his social needs and which may bear a social potentiality sufficient to the substantial improvement of living conditions in the whole community. The community as a whole will benefit by the cooperation of all its parts, while the individual will find in his associations the advantages of the help, the sympathy, and the fellowship of his neighbors.[62]

James Coleman suggests a more functional definition:

> Like other forms of capital, social capital is productive, making possible the achievement of certain ends that would not be attainable in its absence. Like physical capital and human capital, social capital is not completely fungible, but is fungible with respect to specific activities. A given form of social capital that is valuable in facilitating certain actions may be useless or even harmful for others. Unlike other forms of capital, social capital inheres in the structure of relations between persons and among persons. It is lodged neither in individuals nor in physical implements of production.[63]

---

[61] For an overview, see FIELD 13–47 (2008). According to the Social Science Citation index, references to social capital grew tremendously in the 1990s. *Id.* at 5 (table 1.1; figure 1.1). Robert Putnam's book *Bowling Alone* captured public attention with its observation that social capital in the United States is declining and connected to lower levels of civic engagement and of trust in public institutions. PUTNAM (2000).

[62] Hanifan 130 (1916).

[63] Coleman 94 (1988).

The core idea is that "social networks have value. Just as a screwdriver (physical capital) or a college education (human capital) can increase productivity (both individual and collective), so do social contacts affect the productivity of individuals and groups."[64] As John Field put it, "The theory of social capital is, at heart, most straightforward. Its central thesis can be summed up in two words: relationships matter."[65]

Social capital may be viewed solely in terms of the networks or more broadly in terms of various associations, institutions, social norms, and many other intangible resources that constitute and shape social interactions; some social scientists suggest that social capital is the trust embedded within such resources.[66] Sociologist Pierre Bourdieu defines social capital as "the aggregate of the actual or potential resources which are linked to possession of a durable network of more or less institutionalised relationships of mutual acquaintance and recognition."[67] Robert Putnam suggests that social capital "refers to features of social organization, such as trust, norms and networks, that can improve the efficiency of society by facilitating coordinated actions."[68]

Social capital provides a useful way to think about value creation where social structure, networks, and relationships play an integral role in shaping opportunities and interactions.[69] Social capital is often infrastructural. As a form of capital,[70] demand is derived from different types of activities—often from a wide range of them. Still, the prevalent definitions of social capital do not say enough about how demand is derived, or from what types of activities demand is derived, other than to define demand for coordination vis-à-vis some relationship.[71]

The category of *irreducibly social goods* is rather narrow. Charles Taylor delineates this category in his critique of welfare economics, particularly its commitment to methodological individualism and the atomistic notion that society and other collectives/groups can be reduced to collections of individuals. Taylor suggests that these social goods are

---

[64] Putnam (2000).

[65] Field 1 (2008).

[66] Putnam 167 (1993).

[67] Bourdieu 249 (1986).

[68] Putnam 167 (1993).

[69] Some have raised concerns about the social capital concept. Haynes (2009).

[70] Social capital is a capital good in the sense described above; it is a factor of production not used up, exhausted, or otherwise transformed and incorporated into the final output upon consumption. Yet some very prominent economists, including Kenneth Arrow and Robert Solow, have suggested that social capital is not a form of capital. See Arrow (1999); Solow (2000).

[71] Suppose we assume that demand is derived from social activities—activities that depend on the existence of social networks, relationships, interdependencies, or, put in a slightly different way, activities that constitute participation in social systems. Then, at least for some social systems, we might expect that social demand differs from private demand and that spillover effects might be prevalent because individual actors affect others both when they access and use social capital to participate and when they contribute to the resource itself. Cf. Portes (1998) (discussing the "deliberate construction of sociability for the purpose of creating this resource").

not decomposable; the goods are not only valuable to the extent that they deliver benefits to individuals but are valuable above and beyond, or in a different way than, the value realized by individuals. The key characteristic appears to be that their value is necessarily social and not decomposable. The value is functionally dependent on the existence and nature of interdependent social relations and is not adequately reflected in aggregations of individual utilities.[72] Taylor highlights how irreducibly social goods are enabling, how they "make conceivable" participation in socially/culturally valuable/valued activities/ways of life, and this seems to capture what was missing from definitions of social capital—namely, a sense of what sources demand derives from. Many infrastructure resources are enabling in this fashion.

The theories behind nonmarket goods, merit goods, social capital, and irreducibly social goods are still in development. Much work remains to be done in identifying and examining social values not well reflected in preferences or markets. Not surprisingly, the analysis and application of theories about these types of social goods remain outside mainstream economics and related public policy fields, except for some very limited cases, such as the study of nonmarket goods in environmental economics and the World Bank program focused on social capital. Nonetheless, the concepts highlight a number of characteristics relevant to our analysis of infrastructure.

2. THE RELATIONSHIP BETWEEN SOCIAL GOODS AND EXTERNALITIES

Social goods generate value through their impact on social systems and interdependencies—that is, because of the social nature of the goods themselves. Their value is inherently social because it depends on the existence and nature of interdependent social relations. The value of social goods may manifest as *system-effects*—that is, effects seen at a macro-level analysis of the system (or network) rather than at the micro-level analysis of individual actors within the system and perhaps measurable in terms of system performance, scope, robustness, or growth. The value may manifest as individual effects distributed across a social group, for example, when the good satisfies preferences shared by group members. Or there may be some combination of these effects.

Social goods differ from classic private or public goods in two related ways: first, in terms of how they generate value; and second, in terms of the types of externalities associated with the good.

The value of both private and public goods is realized upon consumption or use. Upon obtaining access to a good, a person may consume or use it to accrue benefits (value,

---

[72] Although TAYLOR (1995) emphasized the noninstrumental value of irreducibly social goods, such as a culture or a language, I believe Russell Hardin was correct in his analysis of the issue when he suggested that even irreducibly social goods are contingently good rather than inherently good. See HARDIN 67–68 (1997). James Coleman made the same point with respect to social capital, and Alejandro Portes emphasizes that social capital can have harmful consequences as well. Coleman (1988); Portes (1998).

utility, happiness, etc.). Due to their rivalrous character, private goods generate value for a particular consumer. Public goods may be consumed by many. The production of public goods has the potential to generate positive externalities. Whether the benefits are external to production depends on the conditions of access and the degree to which the producer internalizes the value realized by others. For example, consider a flower garden. A person who plants flowers in his front yard creates the potential for positive externalities that may be realized by those who walk by and appreciate their beauty. The view of the flowers is nonrivalrous; consumption by one person does not deplete the view or beauty available for others to consume. Consumption depends on access, however, and the realization of potential externalities depends on whether the homeowner builds a fence that effectively obstructs the public's view. If the homeowner builds an effective fence, then he has restricted access, and the potential for positive externalities remains untapped. If the homeowner does not build such a fence, then people who pass by obtain access to the view, consume it, and realize external benefits.[73]

By contrast, the value of social goods is realized in a more osmotic fashion and not necessarily or fully through direct consumption or use of the "good" itself. Social goods change environmental conditions and social interdependencies in ways that affect social welfare. Take, for example, active participation in democratic dialogue or education. While participants may realize direct benefits as a result of their activity, nonparticipants and nonconsumers also benefit—*not* because they also may gain access to the good (dialogue or education), but instead because of the manner in which dialogue or education improves societal conditions and has systemic effects. The institutional and social environment improves. These effects are not contingent on access and use conditions in the same way as for private and public goods and are not related to the characteristics of public goods (nonrivalry, nonexcludability). Instead, these effects depend on the nature of the relationships and interdependencies among members of a social group or community and how the good in question relates to those relationships and interdependencies.

In sum, the production of public goods has the potential to generate positive externalities for nonpaying consumers and users, and the production of social/nonmarket goods generates diffuse externalities. As the next section and subsequent chapters examine, some public goods are inputs into the production of social goods, potentially leading to externalities at different levels: first, the input user/output producer may realize some effects; and second, those affected by the social good output may realize other effects.

---

[73] I like to refer to such persons as incidental beneficiaries, although some would use derogatory, loaded labels such as "free riders," "thieves," or even "pirates." At least in the context of an open view of a flower garden, however, we do not expect people to stop and compensate the homeowner.

E. Speech: An Example That Illustrates the Building Block Concepts

In this section, I use speech as an example to illustrate how many of the economic concepts discussed in this chapter relate to each other. It also highlights my preliminary attempt to explore, in the context of speech, some of the questions noted in section C concerning different types of externalities. Finally, I note that speech is integral to our discussion of certain infrastructure resources later in the book.

Speech—a term that includes various forms of communication—is an activity that regularly generates externalities: costs or benefits realized by parties other than the speaker or listener that are not fully accounted for in the decision to speak or transactions related to the speech. Quite frequently, people do not account for the costs or benefits to third parties when deciding whether to speak, what to say, where to speak, and so on. Some external effects are positive; others are negative. The nature of the effects depends on many factors, including, but not limited to, the content of the speech, the parties, and the context. More broadly, speech often impacts the very systems that give rise to and shape social interdependence. Speech affects social interdependence—our relationships with each other—in many different ways.

We begin with the notion that speech involves the communication of ideas[74] and that it involves the sharing of a public good. It is quite difficult to maintain exclusive possession of an idea (putting secrecy aside), and the marginal costs of allowing another person to consume an idea are zero. Ideas are naturally sharable. If I communicate an idea to you, we both "possess" the idea, and you may in turn share it with others. I may not fully account for such sharing and the benefits and costs that third parties may obtain from consuming or possessing the idea. In short, one important category of externalities regularly generated by speech involves the sharing of public goods (that can be shared, and shared, and shared again).[75]

For example, consider a joke. (If my use of "joke" throws you off, please substitute "anecdote," "story," or another form of expression. The points made below are not limited to jokes, and I am making no claims about the benefits and costs from joke telling.) Suppose I tell my original joke to John and Jenn at the water cooler. They both laugh when they hear the punch line. The next day, John and Jenn each tell the joke to their spouses, who laugh and the following day tell the joke to their colleagues at work, who laugh and retell it again. Assume, for simplicity, that everyone in the distribution chain forgets the joke after retelling it (it was funny but easily forgettable), and assume that no one "learns" anything from the joke or uses the joke in any other way than retelling it.

---

[74] For now, put aside the distinction between speech as an activity (communicating an idea), and speech as a thing (the set of expressed ideas); we revisit the distinction in chapter 12.

[75] Speech produces public goods as well. Many communications involve the sharing of already produced public goods, but many communications involve the spontaneous creation and sharing of public goods. For ease of discussion, I leave this complication aside for now.

This assumption is meant only to isolate the fact that the joke generates purely consumptive value and is not productive of any other good. In other words, assume the joke has an immediate consumptive value (laughing at the punch line) and is sharable (can be possessed and retold by many). The external effects from my speech (joke telling) might include the third-party benefits realized with each retelling. Note that the public good (the joke) need not change or be used in any particular manner; the public good generates value (or harm) when people receive the "message." People who retell the joke also may derive value from being able to communicate the speech, and this also may give rise to external effects.

The set of external effects derived from sharing public goods is quite important and pervasive. While the magnitude of the effects may be small in many cases, the communicative practice of retelling is so widespread and fundamental to our social lives that the aggregate welfare effects may be incalculably high.

But the set of speech externalities discussed so far may be the least interesting. The speech externalities that appear to matter most are those associated with productive uses of speech. In addition to being a public good that can be shared, speech is often an intermediate or capital good, an essential input into other activities—the range of activities is as wide as the range of ideas and frequently includes the production of public and social goods. The sharable nature of speech allows it to be *consumed* and retold over and over again, and often it also allows it to be *used* productively over and over again.

The line between *idea consumption* and *idea use* is difficult to draw. It is not a bright or fixed line. We might say that *idea consumption* is an end, whereas *idea use* is instrumental, a means to another end. While this division doesn't always work well, it does capture the basic distinction. Consider *idea consumption* to be associated with value derived from mere appreciation or possession of an idea, as illustrated in the joke example above by the joy expressed in the listener's laughter. We might also define *consumptive ideas* as those ideas that generate value primarily when consumed—where possession directly yields value (that is, by appreciation).

Idea use, then, may be associated with value derived from something other than mere appreciation or possession of an idea, something that involves other activities and/or other people. Some ideas may be deliberately "put to use" in the sense that the possessor sets out to derive value through some external actions—for example, opening a business, developing a product, building a reputation, or developing a new idea.

Idea use also may be less deliberate and less well-planned, for example, when one's ideas affect another's (a) beliefs, knowledge, and understanding (for simplicity, "beliefs")[76] and

---

[76] Despite numerous complications, for purposes of illustration, I will conflate beliefs with knowledge and understanding. Ideas and information are distinguishable from beliefs, knowledge, and understanding because beliefs, knowledge, and understanding all depend on the human capacity to comprehend ideas and information. So, for example, sufficient language and education may be necessary complements for information and ideas to produce beliefs, knowledge, and understanding. Speech is an activity that communicates ideas/information and

(b) preferences. Shaping the beliefs or preferences of others through one's speech is at the heart of what it means to communicate; we engage in such communications throughout our lives and play both roles—speaker and listener—in a reciprocating, discursive process. We generally do so deliberately. Still, it seems plausible to argue that the most subtle and powerful way in which speech generates externalities is through the accidental, playful, or ad hoc sharing and use (and resharing and reuse) of productive ideas that shape beliefs and preferences. Speakers account for some of the effects their speech will have on others; such effects are often intended. *But not always, and often not fully.* For example, when speech recipients do not simply consume, as in our joke example, but rather *learn* something, it can be incredibly difficult to predict, observe, or map out potential effects, particularly where speech-enabled learning impacts behavior in other social systems.

Speech often has dynamic and systemic implications that are unanticipated and underappreciated by speakers and their audience. The effects may be small in magnitude and may not be immediately salient to the speaker or audience. This is probably the case for the vast majority of speech. Nonetheless, we should expect the aggregate impact across many participants in many conversations to be substantial, for two reasons.

First, and perhaps most obvious, small external effects add up. Just as the small external benefits from a joke told and retold and retold and so on can become substantial if the joke spreads widely across a community, the small external effects from the shaping of beliefs or preferences can become substantial. Note that I am not claiming that the external effects are necessarily positive or that the shaping leads to Truth. My claim is simply that small external effects add up as speech, information, and ideas propagate.

Second, sometimes the effects are not so small in magnitude; sometimes the unanticipated and underappreciated effects of ideas communicated turn out to be quite large in magnitude. Yet, for a variety of well-understood reasons, it is not easy to "pick winners," to foresee or even recognize early on those "killer ideas" that yield substantial social value, occasionally through systemic change.[77]

Consider the speech of a nonprofessional blogger pertaining to some political issue (for example, the Iraq war, civil rights, or property tax reform). The speech may have external effects beyond those who write, read, or comment on the blog itself because the speech—the ideas and information communicated—may impact awareness and opinion within the community affected by the political issue being discussed, and ultimately the speech may affect political processes. The likelihood that any particular speaker will have a noticeable impact may be small, but that is beside the point. Society benefits when its members participate because of the aggregate effects, and there is a persistent risk of

---

builds human capacity to comprehend through the development/practice of language and educational skills. Mill seemed to recognize this when he suggested that engaging ideas, even those that were false, improved one's understanding and confidence in the truth. MILL 45 (1869); Balkin 35–36 (2004).

[77] KUHN (1962).

underparticipation in the process and of underproduction of the speech. Speech affects community systems and community members, even community members who do not participate in the conversation.

The external effects from speech are not limited to political systems. Speech externalities are often due to complex interdependencies between communication-information systems and other complementary human systems that depend on speech inputs—we can attach many different overlapping labels to describe these systems, including cultural, economic, educational, political, social, and so on.[78] Many of these systems may be characterized as nonmarket systems.

This discussion of speech aimed to suggest that speech regularly generates externalities and to explore some, though not all, of the different ways in which this happens. At its core, speech involves the creation and sharing of nonrivalrous goods. But we should not stop our analysis there. The picture is complicated by the fact that ideas communicated are often a form of intellectual and social capital and, as such, are often used productively to generate third-party effects in complementary social systems.

Appendix: The Shortcomings of Pursuing Optimality

Public goods play an important role in this book; as the next chapter explains, infrastructure resources are a special type of public good that often facilitates production of many more public goods. This section discusses a technical economic issue at the heart of public goods theory—specifically, Paul Samuelson's optimality condition—and suggests that pursuing optimality may be a mistake with respect to infrastructure.

In his seminal work on public goods, Samuelson suggested that since public goods simultaneously enter into the "indifference curves" or "consumption functions" of many people,[79] optimal production would have to account for the aggregate value for the consuming population; investment in production of a public good should expand so long as the aggregate marginal benefits to consumers exceeds the marginal cost.[80] Samuelson suggested that accurately measuring demand and achieving optimality are difficult because consumers may act strategically and understate their actual preferences in the hope that others will bear a greater proportion of the costs. To make matters worse, regardless of strategic behavior of this sort, accurately measuring the marginal benefits to each

---

[78] Ed Baker has explored various types of externalities associated with media content. See Baker 350–51 (1997).

[79] Samuelson 387 (1954). The reason why this occurs for public goods is related to nonrivalry, infinite capacity, and the sharable nature of the resource.

[80] The optimality condition is framed in terms of marginal rates of transformation and substitutions as follows: Public goods production should expand until the marginal rate of transformation equals the sum of the marginal rates of substitution. *Id.*

consumer is an incredibly difficult enterprise in the real world, akin to the informational demands that make perfect price discrimination impossible.[81]

Samuelson recognized that competitive markets would struggle with measuring demand for public goods, and while he thought the government would solve the demand-revelation problem in some contexts through voting and political processes rather than market processes, he recognized that all of these processes are imperfect and that optimal production would be elusive.[82] In this book, I go one step further and suggest that optimal production, like perfect price discrimination, may be a distracting red herring because we are inevitably in a complex second-best world where attempts to perfect one market can be expected to cause unpredictable and often harmful distortions in many other markets and nonmarkets.[83]

The fact that demand-measurement problems exist for each public good does not mean that markets will undersupply *all* public goods. To the contrary, markets work rather well in supplying various public goods because demand manifests sufficiently to support investment (e.g., when average costs are recoverable),[84] and expanding investment or production yields diminishing if any additional returns.[85] This may seem to contradict the Samuelson condition, but it does not.

Keep in mind that the Samuelson condition sets forth optimality conditions for evaluating whether public or private investment in public goods production is justified, and effectively that evaluation is situated at the margin between investment in further public goods production and alternative investment opportunities (e.g., in private goods production). Imagine that a stream of potential investments being evaluated and the issue is whether or not to expand investment in public goods production. (Expanding investment might mean either investing more in an existing public good to improve its quality or investing in a new public good. In both cases, though, the point is the same.) Thus, for each potential public good investment, one must compare the aggregate benefits to the production cost, which includes the cost of capital and opportunity costs associated with alternative investment opportunities (i.e., rate of substitution). While this may be a useful way to think about social investments at the margins, keep in mind that a substantial amount of investment in public goods production occurs well before such marginal evaluation becomes relevant; in other words, if the stream of potential investments described above is conceptualized as a market for investments, then a substantial amount of

---

[81] See chapter 6.

[82] Samuelson (1958: 334); Samuelson (1954). Also, note that effectiveness of political systems to accurately measure demand is suspect for a variety of reasons. In reality, measuring demand for public and social goods is an incredibly complex task.

[83] See Lunney (2008); Lipsey & Lancaster (1956).

[84] See chapter 8.

[85] While it is analytically useful to assume continuous production functions, such as assumption does not make sense for many public goods.

investment in public goods production is *inframarginal*. As discussed below, it may be better to eschew marginal evaluation and optimality conditions because of the complexity of the systems involved and the variety of possible equilibriums.

In the basic model discussed thus far, the basis for measuring benefits to be aggregated is consumer preferences or willingness to pay for the public good in question. The basic model effectively assumes a single market, the public goods market. Since Samuelson's seminal work, economists have extended the model and noted that the Samuelson condition applies when the public good is an intermediate good used as an input to produce private goods. A substantial economics literature has developed. But insufficient attention has been given to the impact of externalities on demand measurement.[86] Unfortunately, externalities from public goods production tend to be assumed away or marginalized. Analysts often focus on a limited subset of externalities from public goods production, typically benefits realized by free-riding competitors or consumers of the particular public good. But, as this and subsequent chapters discuss at length, public goods production can lead to significant external effects of different types, and this fact dramatically complicates the demand measurement problem. Even if we assume that consumers do not actively conceal their true preferences in a deliberate effort to free ride, demand measurement problems persist, and *optimal* production may remain practically impossible. "The absence of any reliable way to determine the aggregate marginal value that consumers place on a public good makes it all but impossible to determine the optimal level of production for any public good."[87] The demand-side analysis gets much more complicated when the public good is used productively (rather than merely consumed) and such productive use generates externalities. Even if consumers cooperate and accurately reveal their preferences for particular public goods, those preferences do not account for various third-party effects. Unless externalities are internalized throughout the entire system (incomplete markets are completed, missing markets are made functional, etc.), which is impossible, we must acknowledge and grapple with systematic demand-side problems of both types—distortions associated with measuring actual consumer preferences and distortions associated with externalities.

I am unaware of work that addresses demand-measurement problems attributable to externalities in various output markets, either where there are streams of public good inputs into public good outputs that further serve as inputs into outputs and so on, or where there are public good inputs into private, public, and social good outputs. In this book, I focus mainly on the latter, although I discuss both complications in the context of intellectual resources and the cultural environment (chapter 12).

---

[86] I recognize that the literature on network effects considers this issue, but only to a limited degree because of the specific type of effect involved. On network effects, see chapter 4.

[87] Yoo 670 (2007).

In concluding this section, I emphasize that the demand-measurement problems posed by measuring actual consumer preferences and significant external effects call into question the utility of focusing on optimality conditions. Samuelson seems to have anticipated this point; consider the following two statements he made in an essay reflecting on his public goods theory:

> Having called attention to the nature of the [first demand-measurement] difficulty, I do not wish to be too pessimistic. After all, the world's work does somehow get done. And to say that market mechanisms are non-optimal, and that there are difficulties with most political decision processes, does not imply that we can never find new mechanisms of a better sort.[88]
>
> . . .
>
> [It] should be possible for the theorist to go beyond the polar cases of (1) pure private goods and (2) pure public goods to (3) some kind of a mixed model which takes account of all external, indirect, joint-consumption effects. I shall not write down such a mathematical model. But if I did do so, would we not find—as Pigou and Sidgwick so long ago warned us is true of all external economies and diseconomies—that *the social optimum could not be achieved without somebody's taking into account all direct and indirect utilities and costs in all social decisions?*[89]

Samuelson recognized the importance of external effects and the severe limits they posed on efforts to perfect market and government systems and achieve optimal production of public goods.

Again, speech is a useful example. We do not aim to optimally produce speech. It makes little sense to rely on government or markets to optimally produce speech. It is simply too difficult to even begin measuring demand, and not just because some consumers will misrepresent their preferences in the hope of free riding. Governments and markets produce plenty of "inframarginal speech," as we all do every day. The societal objective in this area is precisely the opposite of optimal production of speech; it is to provide an open, supportive environment for speech and speech-related activities.

As the following chapters examine, the prevalence and variety of external effects suggest that we live in a very complex second-best world.[90] Pursuing optimality may be a fool's errand. Accordingly, I set aside optimality conditions and instead focus on how to improve market and government systems for the bulk of investments that are not at the "edge" in terms of being the last few projects that would satisfy the Samuelson conditions. We simply know too little about the territory leading up to the edge; to make the

---

[88] Samuelson 334 (1958).

[89] *Id.* at 335 (emphasis added).

[90] Lipsey & Lancaster (1956).

analysis tractable, we have to assume away too much. Subsequent chapters elaborate on these demand-measurement problems, the corresponding difficulty/impossibility of achieving optimal government or market selection among public good investments, and how sustaining infrastructure commons supports a wide range of public and social goods producers.

A Demand-Side Theory of Infrastructure and Commons Management

PART II DEVELOPS a theoretic approach to understanding and analyzing societal demand for infrastructure resources.[1] The conceptual model developed is generic and meant to highlight the common functional characteristics of infrastructural resources that are relevant to societal demand. Like the conventional supply-side view of infrastructure, however, the demand-side model is incomplete, in at least two ways. First, it puts aside many of the supply-side issues. Second, due to its generic nature, it initially abstracts away from many of the contextual details that become relevant when one focuses acutely on a particular infrastructure resource. These considerations are important and will be revisited in subsequent parts.

---

[1] A note on societal demand: Demand is defined within economics in terms of an individual's willingness and ability to pay for something. Payments need not be monetary and can be understood in terms of an exchange of resources, whether money, time, labor, raw materials, or something else. (Money is useful as a common denominator.) A preferred exchange is essentially a resource reallocation that would, in one's estimation, make a person better off (satisfy her preferences, increase her utility, make her happier, etc.). When an exchange is voluntarily consummated, presumably both parties are better off. When discussing demand,

Part II is organized along the conceptual distinction identified in chapter 1: Chapter 4 focuses on infrastructure as a type of resource (a resource set), and chapter 5 focuses on commons management as a type of resource management strategy. Basically, if a resource satisfies the criteria set forth in chapter 4 and qualifies as "infrastructure," then the arguments for and against commons management set forth in chapter 5 should be examined. Thus, while this is a useful organization structure, one should not assume the simple equation "If infrastructure, then commons."

I refer broadly to humans' desire to realize value (utility, happiness, preference satisfaction, or some other measure of well-being), recognizing that such desire may be contingent on, among other things, one's knowledge of opportunities and consequences. When discussing societal demand, I refer to society's aggregated desires. In this book, I do not engage in the age-old, ongoing, and notoriously contentious debates over which values count (utility, happiness, preference satisfaction, capabilities, or some other measure of well-being); how to measure or account for different, at times incommensurable, values; or how to aggregate (move from private individuals to society). My approach is functional and can accommodate various approaches to these tough questions. With respect to infrastructure resources, one must better understand how value is created and realized by human beings, and thus where demand for infrastructure comes from. Only with such an understanding can one analyze and compare provisioning mechanisms (supply systems such as markets, government, community, family), and institutions aimed at improving these mechanisms (laws, norms, subsidies, taxes). This is because a critical aspect of comparative analysis concerns the relative effectiveness of these mechanisms to generate, communicate, process, and respond to demand signals.

4

INFRASTRUCTURAL RESOURCES

THIS CHAPTER EXAMINES societal demand for infrastructure resources. It aims to identify and evaluate infrastructural resources functionally from a systems perspective and to better understand how individuals who obtain access to infrastructure resources both realize and create social value.

The chapter identifies and examines three economic criteria common to traditional infrastructure, such as transportation systems and telecommunications networks, and nontraditional infrastructure, such as the atmosphere and basic research. It develops a typology of different infrastructure (commercial, public, social, and mixed infrastructure) based on the types of systems dependent on the infrastructural resource and the distribution of productive activities it facilitates. It also discusses how both the resource set delineated by the three criteria and the subsets delineated by the typology are dependent on demand, and how resources may evolve into or out of the set or subsets. Throughout, the chapter explains how different types of demand-side market failures arise when spillovers from public or social goods are prevalent.

A. Delineating Infrastructural Resources

Infrastructural resources satisfy the following criteria:

(1) The resource may be consumed nonrivalrously for some appreciable range of demand.

(2) Social demand for the resource is driven primarily by downstream productive activities that require the resource as an input.

(3) The resource may be used as an input into a wide range of goods and services, which may include private goods, public goods, and social goods.

These criteria delineate a set of resources that are functionally *infrastructural*, and this set of resources will be the focus of analysis hereinafter. It is worth noting that relative to common perceptions of what counts as infrastructure, the defined set may be both under-inclusive and overinclusive. Some resources one might consider infrastructure are excluded from this set; for example, while some might think of an oil reserve as infrastructure, it is not within the set, because it is rivalrously consumed. Some resources one might not consider infrastructure are included in the set; for example, lakes, ideas, and laws can be infrastructural. Keep in mind, however, that the set's definition is functional, not semantic. Together, the criteria comprise a tool for analyzing resources and evaluating management strategies.

The first criterion captures the consumption attribute of nonrival and partially (non)rival goods, as detailed in the previous chapter. Infrastructural resources are either *pure or impure public goods*, shown in the shaded sections of table 4.1.

Nonrivalry over some appreciable range of demand opens the door to widespread, shared access and productive use of the resource. For purely nonrival resources of infinite capacity, the marginal cost of allowing an additional person to access the resource is zero over all demand. Thus, for infrastructural ideas, such as the scientific idea of gravity or the political idea of representative democracy, it is costless to share and allow others to possess and use the idea. For partially nonrival resources that have finite but potentially renewable and potentially sharable capacity, the marginal cost of allowing an additional person to access and use the resource is zero over some range of demand but not necessarily over all demand. The resource is congestible, though not necessarily congested, and it

TABLE 4.1 Infrastructures' Degree of Rivalrousness

(Non)rivalrousness of Consumption	Capacity	Type of Good
Nonrival	• Infinite • Sharable • Not congestible	Public good (idea)
Partially (non)rival	• Finite • Potentially renewable • Potentially sharable • Congestible • Depreciable	Impure public good (lake, road, the Internet)
Rival	• Finite • Nonrenewable • Not sharable	Private good (apple)

may be physically depreciable, which means there may be some resource exhaustion or depletion at a rate that does not immediately transform the infrastructure but still may reduce its capacity and require maintenance or replenishment over time.[2] For infrastructural lakes and roads, sharing is feasible but not necessarily costless; it depends on the contextual details, such as how the resource is managed, the number of users, and available capacity. Chapters 7, 9, and 11 explore these complications.

In short, the first criterion describes the sharable nature of the resource. Sharing is technologically feasible. This is the additional degree of freedom discussed in the previous chapter. Infrastructural resources can be accessed and used concurrently by multiple users for multiple uses. This presents an important but often overlooked and unappreciated opportunity. Nonrivalry can be leveraged for a variety of purposes. The second and third criteria focus on the manner in which infrastructure resources create social value, in a sense on how nonrivalry can be leveraged. These criteria move beyond the public goods characterization of infrastructure and raise additional demand-side implications.

The second criterion emphasizes that infrastructure resources are *capital goods* that create social value when utilized productively. In contrast with raw materials (e.g., coal) or intermediate goods (e.g., a screw), also inputs for which demand is derived, infrastructure resources are not used up, exhausted, or otherwise transformed and incorporated into the final output when used (see table 4.2).

Societal demand for infrastructure is derived demand. Infrastructure resources are inputs that satisfy demand derived from demand for the outputs. Essentially, they are *means* rather than ends. Whether we are talking about transportation systems, the electricity grid, ideas, environmental ecosystems, or Internet infrastructure, the bulk

TABLE 4.2 Demand for Infrastructures

(Non)rivalrousness of Consumption	Demand	
	Consumption	Derived
Nonrival or partially (non)rival	Public consumption good	Public capital good
Rival	Private consumption good	Private intermediate good or raw material

---

[2] Marc Poirier has argued that the infrastructure theory does not apply to environmental resources very well because congestion and depletion of natural environmental resources is inevitable. In essence, he questions whether there is any meaningful range of demand within which resource consumption is nonrivalrous. See Poirier (2008).

of the social benefits generated by these resources derives from their downstream uses. They create value downstream by serving a wide variety of end-users who rely on access to them. As a result, it makes more sense to talk about infrastructure use (users) than infrastructure consumption (consumers).

While some infrastructure resources may be consumed directly to produce immediate benefits, most of the value derived from the resources results from productive use rather than consumption. A road system, for example, is not socially beneficial simply because we can drive on it. I may realize direct consumptive benefits when I go cruising with the windows down and my favorite music playing, but the bulk of social benefits attributable to a road system derives from the various activities it facilitates, including, for example, commerce, labor, communications, and recreation.[3]

Infrastructure valuation, management, and policy must pay closer attention to and be guided by the activities, systems, and *ends* enabled by infrastructure. As the National Research Council points out, "Infrastructure is a means to other ends, and the effectiveness, efficiency, and reliability of its contribution to these other ends must ultimately be the measure of infrastructure performance."[4] Despite general recognition that social demand for infrastructure is driven by downstream activities and systems, theoretical modeling of this relationship and empirical measurement of value creation downstream remain underdeveloped.

The third criterion emphasizes that infrastructures are generic (general-purpose) inputs and that the range of outputs may span private, public, and social goods. The criterion emphasizes both the variance of potential downstream outputs and the nature of those outputs.[5] Note that here I use input-output terminology, but at other times I refer to (a) the productive activities, processes, or uses by which users generate the outputs, and/or (b) the downstream systems (markets and nonmarkets) that arise between and among infrastructure users and consumers of the outputs produced (see figure 4.1).

Infrastructure resources enable many systems (markets and nonmarkets) to function and satisfy demand derived from many different types of users. Infrastructure resources

---

[3] Rose 768–70 (1986); Benkler 22–23 (2001a).

[4] Comm. on Measuring & Improving Infrastructure Performance, Nat'l Research Council, Measuring and Improving Infrastructure Performance 5 (1995); CORNES & SANDLER 483–505 (1996) (on difficulties in assessing social demand for the infrastructure resource in traditional infrastructure industries).

[5] Justman & Teubal 21–23 (1996) (defining technological infrastructure as "a set of collectively supplied, specific, industry-relevant capabilities, intended for several applications in two or more firms or user organizations"); Tassey 59, 59–60 (1995) (similarly defining technological infrastructure as generic and jointly used inputs); see also Justman & Teubal 24 n.5 (1996) (describing genericness as having broad relevance from a demand perspective for multiple users/uses).

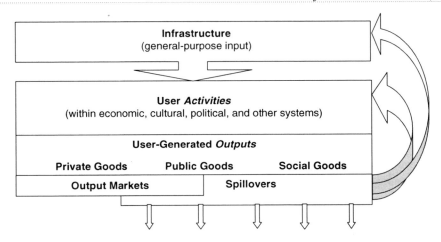

FIGURE 4.1

are not special-purpose resources, optimized for a particular user or use to satisfy the demand derived from a particular downstream market. Instead, they provide basic, multipurpose functionality.

An electricity grid, for example, delivers power to the public, supporting an incredibly wide range of uses, users, markets, and technologies. It is not specially designed or optimized for any particular use, user, market, technology, or appliance; it provides nondiscriminatory service for a toaster and a computer, for Staples and a pizzeria, and so on. The same could be said of the national highway system, the Internet, and Lake Michigan. These resources provide basic functionalities and thereby support and structure complex systems of user activities, but do not determine them.

Users determine what to do with the capabilities that infrastructure provide. Genericness implies a range of capabilities, options, opportunities, choices, freedoms. Subject to standardized compatibility requirements, users decide what to plug in, run, use, work with, play with. Users decide which roads to travel, where to go, what to do, who to visit. Users choose their activities; they can choose to experiment, to innovate, to roam freely. Users decide whether and what to build. Users decide how to use their time and other complementary resources. Infrastructure (providers) enable, support, and shape such opportunities.

To understand societal demand and how value is created and realized, it is necessary to pay closer attention to the nature of the user activities and the outputs users produce. Ultimately, the value of an infrastructure resource is realized by producers and consumers of these outputs. It is thus the demand for these outputs that determines demand for the infrastructure. This is why the third criterion also emphasizes the nature of the downstream outputs and, more specifically, the potential production of public and social goods. When infrastructure supports these productive activities, there are good reasons to question how well markets will work in assessing demand and supplying infrastructure resources; a gap between private demand and social demand arises because the social value created by allowing users to access and use the resource to produce public and social goods is underrepresented in the prices people are willing to pay for infrastructure. The social value may be substantial but extremely difficult to measure.

The reason for the gap is relatively straightforward: Infrastructure users' willingness to pay reflects private demand—the value that they expect to realize—and does not take into account value that others might realize as a result of their use. That is, it does not account for external effects associated with the production of public and social goods. This means that infrastructure users who produce public and social goods are not necessarily optimal purchasers of access and use rights, because they do not themselves capture the full social value of their use.

Difficulties in measuring and appropriating value generated in output markets translates into a problem for infrastructure suppliers and, consequently, the public. This "demand-manifestation" problem may affect infrastructure allocation, design, investment, and management, as well as other supply-side decisions. At least in market contexts, infrastructure suppliers base such decisions in large part on the prospect of foreseeable returns in downstream markets. Demand signals manifested in those markets, aggregated and, in a sense, communicated upstream by dynamic operation of the price mechanism, provide critical raw information for making assessments about prospective returns. To society's detriment, demand-manifestation problems can lead to the undersupply of infrastructure essential to various producers of public and social goods, and this undersupply can lead to an optimization of infrastructure design or prioritization of access and use of the infrastructure for a narrower range of uses than would be socially optimal. I discuss these issues in the next two sections.

* * *

Since introducing these criteria in earlier papers, I have found that people often focus on one or two and forget that all three work together to delineate a set of infrastructural resources. Before proceeding, I explain how they relate to each other. The first criterion isolates those resources that are potentially sharable at low (or at least manageable) marginal cost, and the latter criteria further narrow the set to those resources for which the marginal benefit of allowing additional users to access and use the resource may be substantial but difficult to measure. The latter criteria focus on resources that are more likely to give rise to an assortment of demand-side market failures associated with externalities, high transaction and information costs, and path dependency. The demand-side focus is intended to draw attention to the functional means-ends relationship between infrastructure resources and society's capabilities to generate social value in infrastructure-dependent systems.

B. Commercial, Public, and Social Infrastructure

This section develops a typology of different infrastructure based on the types and distribution of productive activities infrastructure facilitates. Building from the three criteria discussed above, it delineates three types of infrastructure, as illustrated in table 4.3: commercial, public, and social infrastructure. These categories are neither exhaustive nor mutually exclusive. Real-world infrastructure resources often fit within more than one of these categories at the same time. For example, the Internet is a combination of all three types of infrastructure. I refer to such infrastructure resources as "mixed" and to infrastructure resources that fall within only one category as "pure." At the outset, let me acknowledge that pure infrastructure may be rare. Nonetheless, this schema provides a means for understanding the social value generated by these infrastructure resources and identifying different types of market failures.

1. COMMERCIAL INFRASTRUCTURE

Commercial infrastructure resources support production of a wide variety of private goods. Consider the examples listed in table 4.3. Basic manufacturing processes, such as die casting, milling, and the assembly-line process, are nonrival inputs into the production of a wide variety of private manufactured goods.[6] Similarly, basic agricultural

TABLE 4.3   Typology of Infrastructure Resources

Type	Products	Examples
Commercial infrastructure	Wide variance of private goods	1. Basic manufacturing processes 2. Basic agricultural processes and food-processing techniques 3. Road systems 4. The Internet
Public infrastructure	Wide variance of public goods	1. Basic research 2. Ideas 3. Language 4. The Internet
Social infrastructure	Wide variance of social goods	1. Lakes 2. The Internet 3. Road systems 4. Law

---

[6] I am referring to the process, not the mill or assembly line.

processes and food-processing techniques are nonrival inputs into the production of a wide variety of private agricultural goods and foodstuffs. These processes are essentially infrastructural ideas that generate substantial value across a range of discrete, well-functioning markets. Demand for access to and use of these processes derives from these downstream markets, where producers actively seek to satisfy consumer demand for the various private goods. At times, such processes create new opportunities to develop final products; often the processes reduce costs and improve efficiencies, ultimately to the benefit of consumers.

Many transportation infrastructure resources are used productively by a wide variety of suppliers as a delivery mechanism for manufactured goods, agricultural goods, foodstuffs, and many other commercial products. Similarly, many other infrastructure resources, such as the electricity grid, telephone networks, and the Internet, are inputs into these commercial activities (provisioning private goods), contributing value by way of new opportunities, cost reductions, scale efficiencies, and so on, ultimately to the benefit of consumers.

For pure commercial infrastructure, competitive output markets should work well and effectively create demand information for the input,[7] and market actors (input suppliers) will process this information and satisfy demand efficiently. Simply put, for commercial infrastructure, output producers should adequately appropriate the benefits of the outputs via sales to consumers and accurately manifest demand for the required inputs in upstream markets. Because the outputs are private goods, there are no incomplete or missing markets and no production externalities associated with public or social goods. Therefore, with respect to demand for commercial infrastructure, the key is maintaining competition in the output markets, where producers are competing to produce and supply private goods to consumers. Competition is the linchpin in this context because the public's consumptive demands can be best assessed and satisfied by competitive markets.

2. PUBLIC AND SOCIAL INFRASTRUCTURE

Public and social infrastructure resources are used to produce a wide variety of public and social goods, respectively. Consider, for example, abstract ideas and scientific principles. These resources are intellectual infrastructure: nonrival inputs into a wide variety of

---

[7] Commercial infrastructure may face a similar demand-side market failure as public and social infrastructure. Consumer surplus is the portion of the value created by outputs that is not captured by output producers. If (1) access is prioritized (e.g., due to capacity constraints) and (2) perfect price discrimination is not effective in the input market, infrastructure suppliers may bias access priority or optimize infrastructure design in favor of output markets that generate the highest levels of appropriable returns, perhaps at the expense of output markets that generate a larger aggregate surplus (consumer surplus plus producer surplus). I thank Mark Lemley for raising this issue. I leave further consideration for future work.

public good outputs, including various applications and implementations, more refined or applied ideas and principles, research, and so on. Language is an excellent example of mixed infrastructure with strong public and social components, for language serves as the foundation for the production and exchange of knowledge and the development and operation of social systems and interdependencies. Many traditional infrastructures, including transportation and communications infrastructures, contribute to the production of a wide range of public and social goods because of the ways in which they connect communities and social systems.

For much of the analysis that follows, I group public and social infrastructure together because the demand-side problems and arguments for commons management generally take the same form. For both public and social infrastructure, the ability of competitive output markets to generate and process information effectively regarding demand for the required input is less clear than in the case of commercial infrastructure.

Infrastructure users that produce public goods and social goods suffer valuation problems because they generally do not fully observe, much less measure or appropriate, the potential benefits of the outputs they produce and consequently do not accurately represent actual social demand for the infrastructure resource in market settings. Instead, for public and social infrastructure, demand generated by competitive output markets will tend to reflect the individual benefits realized by particular users and not take into account positive externalities. Infrastructure users will pay for access to infrastructure only to the extent that they benefit rather than to the extent that society benefits from the outputs produced. Difficulties in measuring and appropriating value generated in output markets translate into valuation/measurement problems for infrastructure suppliers. Competitive output markets may fail to accurately manifest demand for public and social infrastructure because of the presence of demand-side externalities associated with the production, distribution, and use of public and social goods. To the extent that private demand manifested by infrastructure users falls short of social demand, there is a risk that users will be undersupplied with the infrastructure needed to produce the dependent public and social goods society desires.

Although the demand-side problems are similar in form for public and social infrastructure, there are some important differences that warrant distinguishing between the two types. As described in chapter 3, public goods are a particular type of good, having the characteristics of nonrivalry and nonexcludability, which present specific economic challenges. But markets can provide public goods with varying degrees of effectiveness. The externalities associated directly with the public goods nature of a resource are production externalities that can be traced to the capacity for sharing the resource. Sharing the good may generate external effects not observed, appropriated, or otherwise taken into account (internalized) by the producer. Production of a public good *may* generate external effects; whether in fact such effects are generated depends on the conditions of access and consumption/use.

In the infrastructure context, downstream markets for public goods are not necessarily doomed to fail. In some cases, depending on the public goods themselves, market provision may work rather well and demand for infrastructural inputs needed to produce such public goods similarly may work well. Thus, for example, *if* public goods producers are sufficiently supported in their productive activities via employment, subsidies, or other means, we might not expect underproduction or demand manifestation problems by these user groups. Consider, for example, the case of industry researchers and some academic researchers; employment, government funding, and other forms of institutional and community assistance provide support for their productive activities. Presumably, the researchers appreciate what infrastructural inputs they need and are capable of effectively manifesting demand via the price mechanism, like any other infrastructure user.

This example highlights an important point that I discuss in more detail later: The classic economic solution to the public goods problem downstream is to provide a subsidy directly to the public goods producer. When difficulties arise in choosing among a wide variety of possible public goods producers, however, there may be room for alternative or complementary solutions at the infrastructure level, including commons management and directing subsidies to infrastructure provision, which may indirectly subsidize a variety of public goods producers.

Social goods are different from public goods in terms of how they generate value and the demand-manifestation problems associated with different types of external effects. Each of the four types of social goods discussed in chapter 3 raises correspondingly different complications for the market mechanism. Nonmarket goods, for example, involve persistently missing markets, and merit goods generally involve either persistently missing or persistently incomplete markets. Social capital and irreducibly social goods raise similar complications, particularly where such goods shape environmental conditions and affect social interdependencies in ways that improve social welfare.

Social goods involve diffuse externalities that are not realized by producers or consumers of the good. Beneficiaries are not potential purchasers or licensees waiting in the wings for transaction costs to decrease; nor are they free-riders in any meaningful sense. These types of externalities constitute *persistently* missing or incomplete markets because constructing or perfecting markets is not feasible; internalization is futile. As Harold Demsetz might say, the costs of internalizing the externalities persistently outweigh the benefits of internalization.

Thus, if these effects are to exist, they will exist as externalities. This does *not* mean that the effects are either insignificant or inevitable. The value of the effects might be quite significant, as chapter 3 explained. Keep in mind that the statement *Costs of internalization > Benefits of internalization* says nothing at all about the magnitude or distribution of the external effects. While this is a simple, perhaps obvious, point, people often assume otherwise. Social goods may generate incredibly large external benefits that are impossible—infinitely costly—to internalize. The impossibly high costs may be attributable to the nature of the effects, their diffusivity, and their dependence on social relationships, systems, and interdependencies. Equally important, such externalities are not inevitable. Social goods often require substantial investment, coordination, development, and commitment—consider any of the examples from the previous chapter (e.g., rule of law, system of copyright law, education, community trust). Social goods often depend on infrastructure and communities of infrastructure users.

Social goods involve inescapable demand-manifestation problems. Demand for social goods manifests incompletely, if at all, in markets, and as a result, market demand for infrastructural inputs needed to produce such goods suffers dramatically. Demand-manifestation problems for social goods lead to similar problems upstream, at the infra-structure level, where demand is derived. To the extent that we, as a society, wish to support social goods, we need to consider more carefully what types of infrastructure are essential for their production.

Classic economic solutions to social goods problems include direct government inter-vention, typically government provision of the social good, and provision by other non-market provisioning mechanisms, such as community or family provisioning. As discussed below, there may be room for alternative or complementary solutions at the infrastruc-ture level, including commons management and directing subsidies to infrastructure pro-vision, which may indirectly support a variety of social goods producers.

Social infrastructures tend to be mixed and support production of private and/or public goods as well as social goods. It may be sufficient, analytically, to identify mixed infrastructures that have a strong social component—that support production of some social goods[8]—because doing so (a) calls into doubt a reliance on partial equilibrium analysis and (b) suggests a potential trade-off among social values, some of which may be reflected well within markets but some of which may not.

It is worth emphasizing (again) that such a trade-off does not necessarily take us outside a utilitarian or economic framework; we might abandon utilitarianism or economics for other reasons, but committing oneself to support various social goods not well reflected in markets does not necessitate such a departure. It may reveal starkly the limitations of certain modes of economic decision making, such as constrained versions of cost-benefit analysis, and may force explicit consideration of complex trade-offs involving values that are incommensurable, in part because observing, tracing, and measuring diffuse external effects are too difficult. I stress this point because it is too easy to quarantine social goods by falsely framing these sorts of trade-offs as, for example, efficiency/welfare-maximization versus fairness/(re)distribution. Social does not mean noneconomic or nonutilitarian; in many cases, it will be social welfare– or utility-maximizing to support social goods.

* * *

Infrastructure market failures can be two-sided and dynamic when spillovers from public or social goods are prevalent. On the supply side, private owners are not necessar-ily optimal suppliers of infrastructure, because they have an incentive to investigate and

---

[8] The typology recognizes the social infrastructure category primarily to maintain the distinction between public and social goods and the types of demand-side issues that arise.

support only those uses that generate observable and appropriable private returns, which may or may not be the uses with the greatest social value. On the demand side, users are not necessarily optimal purchasers of access, because if they are productive users they do not themselves capture the full social value of their use. Society may want, need, or depend on infrastructure use to a substantial degree more than private demand would suggest. This raises two sets of related social/market failure concerns. First, as the next section examines further, there are concerns about undersupply and underuse of infrastructure and undersupply of infrastructure-dependent public and social goods. Second, as the following section examines, there are concerns about dynamic shifts in the nature of infrastructure resources—that a resource will evolve from infrastructure to noninfrastructure or from public, social, or mixed infrastructure to commercial infrastructure. Infrastructure development may be skewed in socially undesirable directions.

C. How Demand-Manifestation Problems Lead to Supply Problems

For commercial infrastructure, the conventional economic analysis of public goods and regulatory economics applies rather well. The focus is on the supply side of the infrastructure market, and the fundamental economic issue is cost recovery and preserving incentives to supply. Consumers are largely passive in the analysis, and the fact that infrastructure demand is derived from downstream markets is not important, because the downstream markets are complete. The supply-side issues are complicated; the dueling between *ex ante* and *ex post* efficiencies gives rise to a familiar but complex trade-off. Marginal cost pricing may appear attractive from a static efficiency perspective, but it is not sustainable from a dynamic efficiency perspective and will lead to underprovision without some form of subsidy to cover the fixed cost of production.[9] In the absence of such support, commercial suppliers must spread the fixed cost of producing the infrastructure across their consumer base.

The manner in which commercial infrastructure access is priced will depend on market factors—for example, whether the infrastructure market is competitive and/or whether some form of price discrimination is feasible. But, in general, market allocation of commercial infrastructure should work rather well, provided that markets are competitive. Downstream producers of private goods accurately manifest demand for infrastructure because consumers realize the value of those goods and are willing to pay for such benefits (i.e., there are no relevant externalities). Accordingly, from the demand side, there is less reason to believe that government intervention into markets for commercial infrastructure is necessary, absent anticompetitive behavior. The special case of natural monopolies, in which it is efficient for a single producer to supply commercial infrastructure to a particular market, triggers similar considerations over the risk of anticompetitive

---

[9] See chapters 6 and 8.

behavior (e.g., leveraging into output markets), pricing issues for the input, and reduced output.

Consider a basic manufacturing process, such as die casting, milling, and the assembly-line process, that can be used to reduce manufacturing costs in a wide variety of markets for finished goods.[10] If the process is publicly known and not patented—that is, it is in the public domain—we would expect the process to be widely used for free. If the process is patented,[11] we would expect the process to be widely used at prices that reflect market conditions, such as the availability of competing processes, the magnitude of the cost reduction in different industries, transaction costs (including the costs of identifying license opportunities and negotiating licenses), and the feasibility of price discrimination, among other things. In some cases, a patent owner seeking to maximize revenues may choose to license a basic process on nonexclusive, uniform terms to reduce transaction costs and encourage widespread adoption.[12] In other cases, a patent owner may utilize exclusive licenses for particular fields of use or markets in an effort to maximize licensing revenues. In still other cases, a patent owner may develop more sophisticated licensing schemes. It is unlikely that a patent owner would not take advantage of the basic nature of the invention by seeking to license it in multiple markets,[13] but the manner in which a patent owner does so varies considerably based on the context.

It is too difficult to generalize about the efficiencies of such licensing practices, but it should be noted that licensing schemes that deviate from a commons (nonexclusive, uniform terms) often involve supply-side efficiencies without demand-side inefficiencies because the schemes appropriate rents differentially without further reducing or biasing use of the process among downstream markets. The conventional economic concerns about pricing above marginal cost, deadweight losses, and imperfections in price discrimination schemes remain, but the infrastructural nature of the patented invention does not necessarily aggravate those concerns relative to a noninfrastructural invention. This brief analysis suggests that patents on commercial infrastructure are not especially troublesome from a policy standpoint and that imposed sharing obligations should be unnecessary. It may be that pure commercial infrastructure inventions normally are hard to find, because candidate inventions will almost always be mixed infrastructure that also supports production of public goods such as more research, knowledge, and improvement technologies. (See chapter 12.)

---

[10] Basic agricultural processes and food-processing techniques are nonrival inputs into the production of a wide variety of private agricultural goods and foodstuffs.

[11] If the process is not patented but protected as a trade secret, it still might be licensed for use in multiple markets, though the licensor should take the risk of losing trade secrecy protection into account and would likely curtail licensing efforts. Patenting might be preferable for basic processes because doing so may enable broader licensing opportunities.

[12] Mimura (2010).

[13] Given the basic nature of the process, it is unlikely that the patent owner will be able to fully exploit the invention independently without licensing use by others.

For public or social infrastructure, the conventional economic analysis of public goods and regulatory economics tells only half the story and obscures dynamic problems that originate on the demand side but affect supply-side decisions about the management, design, and development of infrastructure. When these demand-side concerns are taken into account, the case for government intervention becomes much stronger. Again, despite significant differences between public and social infrastructure, the basic problem for both types concerns demand manifestation: The market mechanism will not fully take into account or provide the services for the broader set of social benefits attributable to public or social goods.

The first set of market failure concerns—undersupply and underuse of infrastructure and undersupply of infrastructure-dependent public and social goods—can be understood by way of a simple comparison of demand curves for commercial and public/social infrastructure. Recall that demand for infrastructure is derived from the output markets. For commercial infrastructure, the demand curve reflects users' willingness to pay and thus can be interpreted as a ranking of individual uses according to private and social value from left to right. For public/social infrastructure, the demand curve again reflects users' willingness to pay and ranks individual uses according to private value from left to right, but this ranking does not necessarily or likely rank individual uses according to social value. The social demand curve is a demand curve shifted up (or down) from the private demand curve to reflect the aggregate spillovers that comprise the difference between social and private value. (See figure 4.2.)

Each point (x, y) on the private demand curve represents a user's (x's) willingness to pay (y) for infrastructure, and each point $(x, y + s)$ on the social demand curve represents society's willingness to pay $(y + s)$ for x to use the infrastructure, where s is the aggregate spillover effect caused by x's use of the infrastructure.

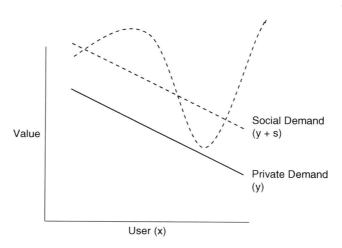

FIGURE 4.2 Demand for Infrastructure.

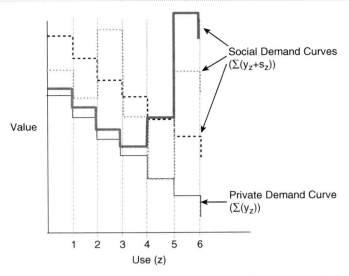

FIGURE 4.3 Four Demand Curves. The private demand curve ranks uses 1 through 6 according to the market value of each use, reflected in users' aggregated willingness to pay. The social demand curves show the social value of each use, reflected in the sum of users' aggregated willingness to pay and spillovers from their use.

There is a temptation to draw a social demand curve with the same shape as the private demand curve; doing so would assume that each user generates an identical spillover, at least in magnitude. This assumption is inappropriate, however. It may be the case that willingness to pay and the magnitude of the externality are correlated in some contexts, but there is no reason a priori to assume such a correlation, and making such an assumption can often be misleading. The shape of the social demand curve may diverge substantially from that of the private demand curve, because there is no necessary or obvious relationship between the private and social value of different users' use of the infrastructure. It is impossible to generalize about how y relates to s.

From the demand curves, we can construct rankings of uses (or, more broadly, infrastructure-dependent activities). For each infrastructure type, (1) imagine a private demand curve ranking uses (z) based on users' aggregated willingness to pay (Σy_z), and (2) imagine a corresponding social demand curve based on social value generated by the uses ($\Sigma(y_z+s_z)$). The individual uses have been grouped by type, and the value derived from the uses is aggregated. This allows us to consider ranking of infrastructure uses based on market value and corresponding social value.[14] (See figure 4.3.)

---

[14] We can go one step further and construct a three-dimensional diagram with the individual users ranked according to their willingness to pay within each use type. The size of the population of potential users would be as important as the ranking within uses. We expect to see considerable variance in the numbers of potential users as well as the private and social valuations.

For commercial infrastructure, we should expect significant overlap if not identical ordering for the two rankings. For public and social infrastructure, the rankings likely are quite different because there may be many potential uses (users) with low market value (willingness to pay) that (who) would generate great social value.

Consider two ways in which divergence in the ranking might occur. First, social surplus, the amount by which the social value exceeds the private value, might be driven by the magnitude or size of the external effect generated by a particular infrastructure use (or user). There may be some infrastructure-enabled activity, use, or application that generates substantial spillovers by virtue of the nature of the public or social goods produced. Akin to the "killer application" phenomena in computer programming, it may be very difficult, if not impossible, to predict what activities, uses, or applications will turn out to be so valuable. Killer apps, such as e-mail or the World Wide Web, tend to emerge unheralded from a soup of innovations.[15] In this context, the set of potential infrastructure users whose willingness to pay for infrastructure may fall well short of the social value of their activities are the applications developers. Applications developers—or, more broadly, innovators, entrepreneurs, and others who experiment with infrastructure capacity to develop uses—do not capture the full social value of the public and social goods they develop, even when they are successful. Most are not successful. Risks considered ex ante (when investments are made but prior to success) only aggravate the demand-side problem. To be clear, the point is not limited to innovation and the search for new killer apps. The large magnitude effect may be due to the communication of a politically salient idea, a scientific breakthrough, or a new opportunity for socialization between isolated communities.

Second, social surplus might derive from a large number of outputs that generate positive externalities on a much smaller scale. In this case, it is not the magnitude of the effect from each good that drives the analysis; instead, it is the number of users participating in production of this type of good and the number of goods produced. As I discussed in the speech context, small-scale externalities may add up to a significant social surplus. Here, the demand-side problem is less focused on whether especially valuable public or social goods will be produced and is more focused on the extent of participation.

I have described two extremes: At one end, a particularly valuable public or social good output generates a large social surplus, and at the other, a large number of public or social good outputs generate small social surpluses. The "killer app" phenomenon end of the spectrum appears to be reasonably well understood (if not fully appreciated), but the other end is not; the small-scale but widespread production of public and social goods by

---

[15] Innovation scholars focus on different types of innovation—disruptive, radical, incremental, user-driven, etc. CARRIER 129–30 (2009). My demand-side point is not limited, however, to innovation. It applies to a broad range of social and cultural activities that yield public and social goods; infrastructures provide basic capabilities, and users decide whether, when, and how to exercise them.

end-users that obtain access to the infrastructure appears to be underappreciated and undervalued by most analysts. There is a middle ground as well. I highlight the extremes to illustrate different ways that value is created.

The social costs of restricting access to public or social infrastructure can be significant yet evade observation or consideration within conventional economic analysis. In essence, the deadweight losses ordinarily associated with pricing above marginal cost must be extended to include lost spillovers. We might frame the issue as one of high transaction costs and imperfect information, but that does not quite capture the problem. Even if the market participants (i.e., infrastructure suppliers and buyers) have perfect information and face low or even zero transaction costs, input buyers would still not accurately represent social demand, because it is the external benefits generated by the relevant outputs that escape observation and appropriation.

The external effects from public and social goods are, as Arrow suggested, missing markets. What stands in the way of completing or constructing the markets and internalizing the externalities? Why is it that beneficiaries cannot be made to pay, to reveal their preferences, or to participate in a market? Perhaps one might posit that it is just another layer of high transaction costs and imperfect information, but that conflates too much. As chapter 3 discussed, there are a host of obstacles, ranging from the difficulty in identifying missing markets to difficulties in tracing effects across economic and noneconomic systems; even when feasible, internalization may reduce aggregate welfare because of distortions affecting other incomplete or missing markets. Thus, there may be substantial social costs in trying to internalize externalities above and beyond the direct costs of setting up the apparatus for a well-functioning market.

An alternative to completing or constructing markets to facilitate transactions and make beneficiaries pay is to subsidize producers of public and social goods. Economists have long recognized that there is a case for subsidizing public goods producers, because the market undersupplies such goods.[16] Recall the discussion about how government-subsidized producers of public goods, such as academic researchers, may effectively manifest demand for the infrastructure they need. To the extent that such producers are identified and adequately supported, concerns over underproduction may be alleviated. (See figure 4.4.)

But the effectiveness of directly subsidizing such producers will vary considerably based on, among other things, the capacity for subsidy mechanisms to identify and direct funds to worthy recipients. There are significant, well-understood limitations on the capacity, resources, and effectiveness of government in this regard. Government must assess demand and figure out which public and social goods are worth supporting. Certain types of public goods and social goods may be well funded, particularly those

---

[16] CORNES & SANDLER 153–58 (1996).

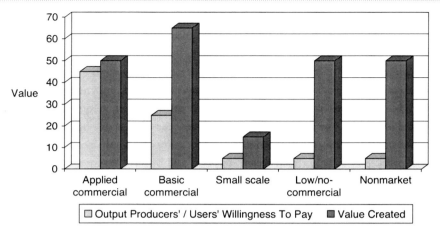

FIGURE 4.4   Basic Research as Infrastructure

Note: Uses are ranked (1, 2, 3, 4, 5) based on users' willingness to pay. Applied commercial research (Use 1) yields appropriable returns and likely some positive externalities. This type of research tends to be more predictable, less risky, and generally has a short-term focus. Basic commercial research (Use 2) has the potential to yield both appropriable returns and a larger degree of positive externalities. This type of research tends to be less predictable, more risky, and generally has a longer-term focus than applied research. By "small scale" (Use 3), I mean the small-scale production of research results that are not necessarily applied or commercial. Individual researchers, educators, or other members of the public may learn from and extend basic research results in directions not focused on by commercially driven entities. "Low/no-commercial" uses (Use 4) refers more generally to basic and applied research that springs from basic research but is not directed at ends with high commercial value (e.g., vaccine research relevant to developing country populations—see the appendix to chapter 12). Finally, "nonmarket" uses (Use 5) refers broadly to pure science and other nonmarket production processes. With respect to the latter two categories of uses, there may not be prospective users that are willing to pay for access to basic research results in the absence of government or nonprofit funding. Yet such research has the potential to yield substantial positive externalities and social surplus. The assigned values are arbitrary and intended only for illustration.

that are visible and historically recognized, have politically powerful proponents, and promise to deliver returns in the short to medium term, *but many are not*. It should not come as a surprise that governments face many of the same problems as markets.

In some cases, it may be better to focus on infrastructure as an indirect means of supporting public and social goods producers. The most extreme form of government intervention would be to supplant the market altogether and rely on government to supply society with public, social, or mixed infrastructure. Less extreme options include subsidies and, as the next chapter examines, regulation that requires private infrastructure providers to manage their infrastructure in an open and nondiscriminatory manner.

Private infrastructure providers will tend to treat public, social, and mixed infrastructure as if it were commercial infrastructure. That is, infrastructure providers will allocate access based on private demand and will not take into account social demand. Pricing schemes will vary, as described above. One key concern, then, is that the social costs associated with deadweight losses are greater and more difficult to measure. A second key concern is the risk of misdirected prioritization, optimization, or design of infrastructure as the infrastructure evolves. This concern is discussed in the next section.

D. Understanding the Dynamic Nature of Infrastructure

This section considers the dynamic nature of infrastructure in two steps: First, it explains that both the resource set delineated by the three criteria and the subsets delineated by the typology are dependent on demand. This means that resources may evolve into or out of the set or subsets. Second, it explains how systemic (market), organizational (firm), and cognitive (individual) biases lead to the second key concern noted above—that is, the risk of misdirected prioritization, optimization, or design of infrastructure. Note that by "bias" I mean a propensity or inclination in decision making. I do not mean to imply irrationality or mistake, at least from the perspective of the decision maker. A propensity to take one path—for example, the path that maximizes profits—may be perfectly rational for the decision maker yet fail to maximize social welfare and thus constitute a mistake from the perspective of society.

1. EVOLVING INTO AND OUT OF INFRASTRUCTURAL STATUS

Over time, resources may become and cease to be infrastructural. In addition, infrastructures may shift types, among commercial, public, social, and mixed. Both the resource set delineated by the three criteria and the subsets delineated by the typology are contextual and dependent on demand and often design. Resources may evolve into or out of the set or subsets (see figures 4.5a and 4.5b). This subsection explores some of the dimensions along which such change occurs.

The genericness of a resource, the nature of the outputs it can be used to produce, and thus its status as infrastructure are not fixed. Rather, these attributes are a function of demand and design, and may vary over time. If downstream demand dries up and leaves only a narrow set of viable uses, or if strong downstream demand pushes owners to optimize for a particular use, an infrastructural resource may cease to be infrastructure.

For example, railroads in South Dakota and Wyoming were built to accommodate a wide range of uses, such as farm-to-market and production-center-to-hinterland transportation. Demand for these activities has fallen to almost nil. But several railroads in this region are very successful because they carry coal from the Powder River Basin to power plants farther east. While these railroads are still connected to the national rail system and may constitute an element of that infrastructure, they are no longer infrastructure for the region when viewed in isolation. Note that this is almost entirely a change on the demand side. On the supply side, almost nothing happened other than removing some sidings that are no longer needed and strengthening bridges and rails for heavy coal trains.

This example also highlights an important feature of many infrastructural resources: A track of road or railway may be special purpose and noninfrastructural in isolation but at the same time constitute a segment of an infrastructural networked system, such as a road or rail system. A similar feature can be seen in the environmental context with respect to a fishery or a particular species—both can be seen as special-purpose resources (with narrow range and variety) when viewed in isolation, and yet the resource may be an integral part of a larger whole (ecosystem) that is infrastructural. This feature complicates analysis, but does so in a revealing fashion, because it forces consideration of how resources generate value at different scales, both in isolation and in conjunction with other resources as part of a larger system.

Change also may occur from the opposite direction: a resource designed and used for a particular special purpose may evolve into infrastructure. This may occur when a special-purpose road or railway begins to serve a wider variety of users within the communities connected or becomes part of a larger network. For example, the communities connected by the road or railway may grow and diversify their interactions; or they may demand increased connectivity with each other and other communities, such that isolated, special-purpose segments are integrated into a larger, general-purpose system.

This sort of evolution often occurs along with or as a result of scientific and technological progress, which may reveal new and often completely unforeseen uses, and may generate a wide range of different sources of demand. In fact, scientific ideas and technologies themselves may evolve in this manner. Although technological advancement had long been conceptualized as a linear process where basic (generic) research evolves

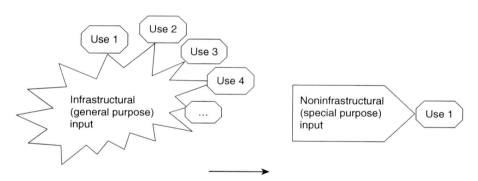

FIGURE 4.5A Evolution from Infrastructure to Noninfrastructure

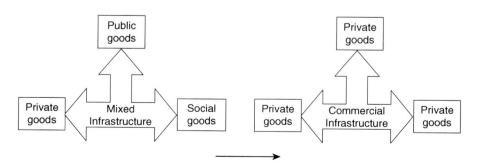

FIGURE 4.5B Evolution from Mixed Infrastructure to Commercial Infrastructure

toward more applied (special-purpose) research and applications, this conceptualization has been rejected and replaced with a more dynamic complex systems understanding, which recognizes that evolution may proceed nonlinearly and in many different directions. The literature on general-purpose technologies, for example, recognizes that many basic technologies begin as special purpose, in the sense that they are developed to provide functionality to accomplish a particular objective, and over time the range of uses increases as entrepreneurs and others adopt and adapt the technology.

Peter Lee has written about how various intellectual resources may evolve into infrastructure.[17] Lee directly links the evolution of a resource into "infrastructure status" to shifts in societal demand. He suggests that "resources can become infrastructure based on widespread social use and reliance":

> [T]rademarked terms can enter the vernacular as generic words such as "aspirin" or "thermos." Particularized expressions can become stock literary elements, such as the Swiss bank account that has become a standard plot device in international espionage stories. Inventions can quickly become standard platforms for technological development, such as the technique for gene splicing, a fundamental innovation around which a significant portion of the biotechnology industry has coalesced. Through widespread adoption and reliance, applications can evolve into infrastructure.

Infrastructure is often as contingent on supply-side decisions—for example, regarding design for and allocation to particular uses/markets—as it is on demand. The railroad example above shows how changes in demand may lead to changes in the range of actual uses with minimal changes in design. It is also possible for changes in capacity to affect infrastructure status. For example, partially (non)rival infrastructure—that is, infrastructure with fixed, congestible capacity—may become persistently congested, to the point that nonrivalrous consumption is not possible at any time and the marginal user necessarily crowds out or imposes costs on another potential user. In addition, capacity expansion may enable nonrivalrous sharing of a previously rivalrous generic capital resource.

Demand also may interact dynamically with supply and lead to shifts in design, management, and allocation priorities for infrastructure. Consider telecommunications and cable networks. Both networks were initially designed to deliver particular services—transmission of voice communications and transmission of television, respectively. Demand for these services shaped the design, management, and allocation priorities for the underlying infrastructure. Both networks have shifted and continue to shift design, management, and allocation priorities considerably to accommodate demand for transmission of data over the Internet.

---

[17] Lee 43 (2008).

Consider also how the Internet evolved. It began as computer networking infrastructure built to meet the demands of government and academia. The early backbone networks, such as ARPANET and NSFNET, primarily focused on three sets of objectives: (1) to establish a secure, reliable communications and control system for national defense purposes, (2) to facilitate cooperative research among government agencies and among academic institutions via better communication of data and more efficient use of expensive equipment (from supercomputers to scanning electron microscopes), and (3) to advance the computing and networking technologies themselves. During the 1990s, the Internet evolved rapidly into the mixed infrastructure we know today, which supports an incredibly wide range of unanticipated uses and satisfies demands from all sectors of society. The rapid explosion in range and variety of uses followed an important shift in the management of the infrastructure, including lifting a ban on using the publicly owned backbone network for commercial purposes and privatization of the infrastructure. The supply-side shifts in ownership and management were in part driven by pent-up demand of commercial entities that wanted to deliver commercial traffic over the backbone.[18]

Infrastructures evolve over time, at different rates and in different manners, depending on the infrastructure in question. Changes may occur, for example, by exogenous changes in the environment, changes in demand, emergence of unforeseen uses, new knowledge about the relative values of different uses, and supply-side changes in design, management, or priority. These drivers may interact and influence each other dynamically in incredibly complex ways. In some cases, we may manage or nudge the process, and in others, there may be little that we can do. Given the social and economic importance of infrastructure, however, various actors—public and private—are bound to try.

2. THE RISK OF MISDIRECTED PRIORITIZATION, OPTIMIZATION, OR DESIGN

This subsection considers the possibility of dynamic failures in infrastructure markets. The concern is with how private infrastructure providers manage the evolution of infrastructure. There are two predictable biases in the decision making associated with managing infrastructure evolution in market settings: (a) appropriable value bias and (b) anti-uncertainty bias.[19]

---

[18] Frischmann par. 18 (2001). Another important driver was that the government recognized the need to leverage public funds with private funds and shift the financing and management of Internet infrastructure to industry. *Id.*

[19] I will not unpack these two biases into more specific decision-making biases that behavioral and organizational psychologists, economists, and social scientists study—for example, status quo bias, endowment effect, and so on. My aim is not to generate a testable theory to explain (a) when and how such biases arise, (b) how various biases interact and counteract each other in practice, or (c) how firms and other organizations use various institutions to manage biases. Rather, my aim is to describe in general terms systematic decision-making propensities

First, to the extent that infrastructure resources can be optimized (or prioritized by design) for particular applications, which often is the case, there is a risk that infrastructure suppliers will favor applications that generate more readily appropriable benefits at the expense of applications that generate positive externalities, even if society would be better off if the latter set of applications were prioritized, or at least treated with equal priority. This bias toward infrastructure uses that generate appropriable value is a direct, predictable, and quite natural consequence of the ordinary operation of the market system. To be clear, this is a feature (not a bug) of the market system; we expect and encourage firms, entrepreneurs, and other market participants to behave in this fashion. Private firms generally aim to maximize expected value to the firm (rather than society).[20] In setting prices and output levels, firms aim to maximize their profits. In deciding how to allocate investments in infrastructure creation, design, maintenance, and improvement, infrastructure providers aim to maximize their returns on those investments. In choosing which investments to make, how to design or modify infrastructure, what research and development projects to pursue, and, most broadly, what exactly to supply to consumers, firms rely on existing and projected demand to forecast profit potential or expected value to the firm. Value to the firm means appropriable value—value that can be captured in market exchanges. It does not include spillovers—value realized by third parties that is not captured. Effectively (if not formally), firms rank downstream uses or applications according to private demand and make supply-side decisions about managing infrastructure and its evolution accordingly. When feasible, firms manage infrastructure evolution, for example, through prioritization of investments, design choices, and access to various user communities, and they will do so to maximize expected value to the firm. It should not be surprising or controversial that profit potential often will be a significant driver of evolution within infrastructure markets. Whether or not this basic fact should lead one to conclude that there is a societal problem worthy of attention is another matter, the evaluation of which depends considerably on the infrastructure resource in question and the context. It is important, however, to recognize the bias and understand how it constitutes a dynamic cousin of the market failure/societal concern noted in the previous section.

Second, to the extent that infrastructure resources can be optimized (or prioritized by design) for particular applications, there is a risk that infrastructure suppliers will favor applications that currently exist or are anticipated to exist with a reasonable degree of certainty over more uncertain or even unknown applications. Infrastructure providers operate in a dynamic and uncertain environment. For many infrastructure resources,

---

that are for the most part uncontroversial. We expect to see, and in fact do see, the two biases mentioned in the text at work and often count on them to lead to efficient outcomes.

[20] Organizational theorists have developed more nuanced theories of the firm that account for differing incentives for managers and owners, for example, but the basic point remains, especially when one moves from individuals and firms to the market system more generally.

there may be considerable uncertainty as to how the infrastructure may evolve. Prospective uncertainty can exist along various dimensions that affect investment and management decisions.[21] It may be difficult to predict what will be technologically feasible (and, more broadly, the course and impact of technological change), what unforeseen uses may emerge, what people will want, how much people will be willing to pay, what other options for users will be available, and what complementary goods and services may arise in the future. Such uncertainty complicates decision making and increases information and transaction costs, especially costs associated with identifying and dealing with future contingencies. Prospective uncertainty in various dimensions may steer managers toward the known or reasonably foreseeable subset of uses (markets), biasing design, investment, development, or licensing efforts. As a result, firms may find themselves prematurely locked in to development paths, technologies, or business models.[22] Uncertainty may even deter market actors from entering markets altogether.

Firms, especially big dominant firms or incumbents, are prone to gravitate toward what they already know and do well. (Firms, like individuals, are creatures of habit.) Innovation scholars have studied various examples. AT&T offers a good illustration of this point. AT&T controlled the telephone network for most of the twentieth century, and for most of that time AT&T managed and optimized its network for the business it knew and performed reasonably well: communications by telephone. Though innovation and experimentation were technically feasible, the network was not open to new uses or experimentation by users. AT&T exercised its control over the network and devices attached to the network in a manner that constrained users and maintained the business it knew and could control. Through a series of regulatory decisions, the Federal Communications Commission essentially divested AT&T of some of that control and enabled users to innovate and experiment with devices, so long as there was no harm to the network. As Tim Wu, Jonathan Zittrain, and others have observed, this small space for users yielded advances such as the answering machine, the fax machine, the cordless phone, and the dial-up modem, all of which created new markets and generated substantial benefits for AT&T as well as society at large.[23]

That markets, firms, and individuals may have a bias for the known or reasonably foreseeable is not surprising or controversial. This does not necessarily give rise to a societal problem or market failure. Optimization might be socially desirable; the social value of an infrastructure optimized for the set of known and/or reasonably foreseeable applications at some point in time may exceed the social value of an infrastructure that is not

---

[21] Frischmann 362, 366–67, 374–75 & n.104 (2000); Scotchmer 31–32 (1991) (uncertainty makes ex ante contracting between input suppliers and output producers difficult); Flores 47 (2003) ("[D]emand for the environment has dynamic characteristics that imply value for potential use, though not current use, and that trends for future users need to be explicitly recognized in order to adequately preserve natural areas.").

[22] CHRISTENSEN 131 (1997); CARRIER (2009).

[23] ZITTRAIN 23–24 (2008).

optimized in that fashion. Moreover, even if it is not, markets may correct the problem. For example, if firms prematurely optimize their infrastructure, other firms may not follow that path and consumers may switch providers, allowing market forces to discipline the first set of firms. This self-correction argument only gets you so far, however. First, it is easily overstated, and one can rely on it too heavily. One must keep in mind the premises on which it depends, such as (a) the existence of competitors providing an alternative, and (b) relatively low switching costs for consumers. Second, the self-correction argument does not alleviate concerns about underproduced public and social goods because of demand-manifestation problems—competitors and consumers do not account for the lost spillovers.

It is generally quite difficult, if not impossible, to do the sort of counterfactual analysis that would evaluate the full range of benefits and costs associated with decisions to optimize. Nonetheless, the bias is important to recognize. Optimization entails opportunity costs of the sort often associated with path dependency.[24] There is a risk that infrastructure providers make strategic choices and sink costs into the development and/or design of infrastructure that constrain the opportunities of users to determine what they do with the infrastructure. Technological design is one way to optimize or choose a path, but prioritization of user activities coupled with discriminatory pricing is another way. Of particular concern in the infrastructure context, optimization for the known and/or reasonably foreseeable may preclude—or at least significantly raise the costs for—future innovation and experimentation among applications exhibiting prospective uncertainty along one of the various dimensions noted above.

Some people view uncertainty as a negative, something that should be, and inevitably will be, reduced over time. According to this view, progress will reduce uncertainty. But in a sense this view misunderstands uncertainty. It sees uncertainty as high information costs, a lack of knowledge, or risk, all of which need to be reduced or eliminated. But uncertainty can also be understood as flexibility, freedom, opportunities, options, path *in*dependency. With respect to infrastructure resources, sustaining the infrastructure to support unknown or not reasonably foreseeable uses, activities, and (non)markets—in short, sustaining uncertainty—leaves options on the table and room for development and innovation; it avoids lock-in and the constraints of path dependency. In fact, recent work in real options theory has shown that in highly uncertain environments, where the value of potential applications is uncertain, it may be efficient to maintain a flexible, decentralized management structure, one that is not optimized or prioritized for a particular application or narrow range of applications.[25] The next chapter explains how

---

[24] Path dependency is a process in which something becomes fixed into a seemingly unshakeable trajectory of development; the costs of deviating from or changing the trajectory may be substantial for a variety of reasons.

[25] Gaynor (2003).

common management can be understood as a commitment to sustaining infrastructure flexibility in the face of uncertainty.

Appendix 1: Lessig's Figure

Larry Lessig used the diagram in figure 4.6 to summarize the series of distinctions I draw with the three criteria and typology. Here is his description of the figure:

> Each diamond marks a distinction. Resources are either rival or [nonrival (NR)]. If they are NR, they are either consumption or intermediate. If they are intermediate, they are either specific, or generic. If they are generic, they support either commercial goods exclusively, or public or social goods as well. The column on the left [includes] those categories for which the market is presumptively an adequate mechanism. . . . The row at the bottom [includes] those goods where even well

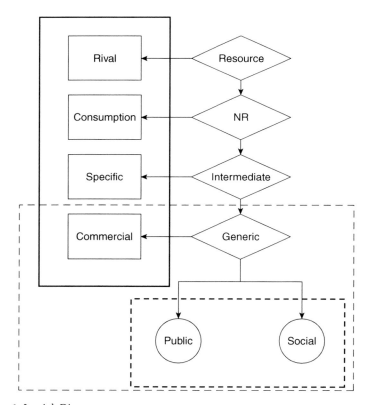

FIGURE 4.6   Lessig's Diagram.

functioning markets would fail adequately to value resource. And the box at the bottom includes all goods properly considered "infrastructure."[26]

Appendix 2: Distinguishing the Demand-Side Analysis of Infrastructure from Network Effects

Most, if not all, traditional infrastructure resources are networks.[27] In recent years economists have devoted substantial effort to unravel the peculiar economic features of networks, commonly referred to as "network effects."[28] Network economists realize that many non-network industries exhibit network effects and have extended their analysis accordingly.[29] Nicholas Economides, a pioneering network economist, provides the following explanation of networks: "Networks are composed of complementary nodes and links. The crucial defining feature of networks is the complementarity between the various nodes and links. A service delivered over a network requires the use of two or more network components. Thus, network components are complementary to each other."[30]

Network effects often, though not always, result in positive externalities (generally referred to as network externalities).[31] Network effects exist when the utility to a user of a good or service increases with the number of other people using it, either for consumption or production (specifically, to produce functionally compatible goods).[32] Economists differentiate between direct and indirect network effects, which arise on so-called actual and virtual networks, respectively. Direct network effects arise because the number of connections an end-user (consumer) can make increases with the size of the network. Standard examples of goods that exhibit direct network effects include telephones and fax machines. As Mark Lemley and David McGowan have explained:

> [O]wning the only telephone or fax machine in the world would be of little benefit because it could not be used to communicate with anyone. The value of the

---

[26] Lessig (2005).

[27] Amitai Aviram observes that "[o]ften, though not always, realization of network effects requires interconnection between the users. The institution that facilitates interconnection between users of a good or service exhibiting network effects, thus enabling the realization of the network benefits, is called a network." Aviram 1182 (2003). Traditional infrastructure resources often act as such a network.

[28] See Economides 673–74 (1996a); Economides 213 (1996b).

[29] Economides 673 (1996a).

[30] Economides 4 (2003); Economides 3 (2008).

[31] Katz & Shapiro 96–100 (1994); see also Katz & Shapiro 436 (1985); Economides 5 (2003); Economides 3 (2008).

[32] See *id.* at 3 ("A market exhibits network effects (or network externalities) when the value to a buyer of an extra unit is higher when more units are sold, everything else being equal."); Lemley & McGowan 488–94 (1998).

telephone or fax machine one has already purchased increases with each additional purchaser, so long as all machines operate on the same standards and the network infrastructure is capable of processing all member communications reliably.[33]

Basically, the idea is "The more the merrier."[34]

Indirect network effects arise under similar conditions, except that it is not the number of connected end-users that generates value; rather, it is the increased availability of compatible, interoperable, and thus complementary goods.[35] "Computer software is the paradigm example."[36] Indirect network effects in the software industry may arise from horizontal compatibility, such as the compatibility between word-processing software (e.g., WordPerfect and Microsoft Word),[37] and from vertical interoperability, as in the case of operating systems and application programs (e.g., Microsoft Windows and word-processing software).[38] Lemley and McGowan explained it as follows:

> [S]oftware may be subject to "increasing returns" based on positive feedback from the market in the form of complementary goods. Software developers will write more applications programs for an operating system with two-thirds of the market than for a system with one-third because the operating system with the larger share will provide the biggest market for applications programs. The availability of a broader array of application programs will reinforce the popularity of an operating system, which in turn will make investment in application programs compatible with that system more desirable than investment in application programs compatible with less popular systems. Similarly, firms that adopt relatively popular software will likely incur lower costs to train employees and will find it easier to hire productive temporary help than will firms with unpopular software. Importantly, the strength of network effects will vary depending on the type of software in question.

---

[33] *Id.* at 488–89.

[34] Rose 768 (1986). Congestion may act as a significant constraint. See Aviram 1201 n.71 (2003). As Aviram notes:

> Congestion is a major limit on efficient scales in rivalrous networks, i.e., networks in which, besides the positive network externality, there is a negative externality imposed by an additional member of the network on the other members. Rivalrous networks include, inter alia, cellular phones, broadband Internet and peer-to-peer information networks. Nonrivalrous networks, such as languages, PC or video cassette standards, etc., do not suffer from congestion; it is no more difficult for me to express myself in English merely because many millions of additional people also express themselves in English.

> *Id.*; see Lemley & McGowan 497 (1998). See also chapter 7.

[35] Economides 5 (2003).

[36] Lemley & McGowan 491 (1998).

[37] *Id.*

[38] See Weiser 564–68 (2003).

Network effects will be materially greater for operating systems software than for applications programs, for example.[39]

Nicholas Economides has noted that the "key reason for the appearance of network externalities is the complementarity between network components."[40] The essential difference between direct and indirect effects is whether "customers are identified with components," in which case the effect is direct.[41]

Although both types of network effects are prevalent for infrastructure resources and may generate significant positive externalities, network externalities are not the only type of demand-side externalities generated by infrastructure. The other positive externalities generated by infrastructure resources may be attributable to the production of public and social goods by end-users who obtain access to the infrastructure resource and use it as an input.

There is a critical difference between network effects and "infrastructure effects"[42] and the resulting types of externalities. Network effects tend to increase consumers' willingness to pay for access to the resource.[43] By definition, network effects arise when users' utilities increase with the number of other users.[44] Economists assume that consumers appreciate the value created by network effects and thus are willing to pay more for access to the larger network, which may lead to the internalization of some network externalities.[45] Thus, although the generally applicable law of demand holds that "the willingness to pay for the last unit of a good decreases with the number of units sold,"[46] the opposite may hold true for goods that exhibit network effects. The presence of network effects may cause the demand curve to shift upward as the quantity of units accessed (sold) increases, leading to an upward-sloping portion of the demand curve.[47]

Infrastructure effects do not necessarily increase users' willingness to pay for access to the infrastructure resource. As discussed earlier, a user's willingness to pay for access to the infrastructure resource is limited to benefits that can be obtained by the user, which depends on the nature of the outputs produced, the extent to which such outputs

---

[39] Lemley & McGowan 491–92 (1998) (footnotes omitted). Lemley and McGowan also discuss other examples of virtual networks. *Id.* at 491–94.

[40] Economides 6 (2003); Economides 5 (2008).

[41] *Id.*

[42] I hesitate to use this term, because it is very difficult to isolate a narrow definition. For now, I use "infrastructure effects" to refer to situations where managing infrastructure as a commons generates positive externalities through the production of public and social goods.

[43] Economides 6 (2003).

[44] See *id.* at 7.

[45] See *id.* at 11.

[46] *Id.* at 6.

[47] *Id.*; Economides 682 (1996a).

generate positive externalities, and the manner in which those externalities are distributed. Infrastructure effects resemble indirect network effects in the sense that a larger number or a wide variance of applications may lead to an increase in consumers' valuation of the infrastructure or network.[48] However, the externalities generated by public and social infrastructure are even more indirect; they are diffuse, derived from public and social goods, and not simply a function of increased availability of desired end-users or end-uses. Further, the externalities generated by public and social infrastructure often positively affect the utility of nonusers, that is, members of society who are not using the infrastructure itself also benefit. In a sense, the positive externalities generated by the outputs are closely connected to the nature of the outputs and only loosely connected to the complementary relationship between the infrastructure and the output. This is important because the prospect of infrastructure suppliers' internalizing complementary externalities is much less likely,[49] making the possibility of a demand-side market failure much more likely.

---

[48] Aviram 1197 (2003).

[49] On the theory of "internalizing complementary externalities," see Farrell & Weiser 89, 100–126 (2003). See also Lichtman 617 (2000).

5

MANAGING INFRASTRUCTURE AS COMMONS

IN CHAPTER 1, I observed that markets often fail to meet societal demand for infrastructure, infrastructures often generate substantial spillovers that result in large social gains, and infrastructures are often managed as commons. I suggested that these three generalizations might be related to each other. In chapter 4, I addressed the first two observations: Specifically, I explained how infrastructure market failures can be complicated by demand-side considerations and how different types of infrastructure generate different types of spillovers by supporting and enabling production of various public and social goods. In this chapter, I consider how managing infrastructure as commons directly relates to the first two observations.

Before proceeding, it helps to restate what I mean by commons as a resource management strategy. Recall the discussion of commons as resource management in chapter 1. Commons refers to a shared resource and often brings to mind the related concept of open access, or, more generally, openness. Commons typically are distinguished from open access because commons are open only to community members and often subject to a particular governance regime, while open-access resources are open to the public without ownership or attendant governance regimes. I do not draw a firm line between commons and open access. Instead, I focus on commons from a functional and relational perspective. "Commons regimes [can be] defined both by the *degree of openness and control* that they exhibit with respect to contributors, users, and resources, and by the *assignment of control, or custody of the power to administer access [and use]*." According to this perspective, "openness is a functional variable that describes the degree to which possession and use of a resource is controlled, and it is a relational variable that describes the structure of relationships among [owners and] potential resource users."[1]

For the purposes of this book, commons management is a functional concept that describes the situation in which a resource is shared among members of a community on nondiscriminatory terms. In general, *nondiscriminatory terms are terms that do not depend on the users' identity or intended use.* Members of the community have equal opportunities to use the resource as they see fit, under conditions that are more or less uniform. Users decide what to do, with whom to interact, or how to use the shared resource; their choices are not predetermined or prioritized by the terms or conditions set by infrastructure providers. This does not mean that use of the resource is free or comes without any terms and conditions.

Typically, at least in market contexts, users must cover the costs of providing and sustaining the resource, and in many cases, managing congestion can be difficult. Cost recovery and managing congestion often require complex pricing and other terms and conditions. But such complications can be accommodated within a commons management regime and need not disrupt the basic nondiscrimination rule, which holds that pricing and other terms and conditions do not depend on the users' identity or intended use. For example, as discussed in detail below, terms that vary by time or amount of resource use are often effective ways to deal with cost recovery and to manage congestion without deviating from the nondiscrimination rule.

Still, having emphasized nondiscrimination as one basic feature of a commons, I must also reiterate that exceptions arise in many contexts—for reasons of emergency (recall the police officer's priority when sirens are blaring) or securing the commons itself. In some cases, sustaining a resource as a commons requires narrowly tailored exceptions to address specific, identifiable uses that degrade, deplete, or otherwise harm the resource itself or risk harm to the community of users. (Chapter 7 discusses the importance of such use restrictions.) That such exceptions exist in some contexts for certain types of infrastructure resources does not undermine the basic nondiscrimination rule, as long as the exceptions do not swallow the rule.

For the purposes of this book, I view resource management as a form of governance. The decision about whether and how to manage a given resource as a commons might be made privately or publicly, depending on the context. Commons may be voluntarily adopted by private or public owners of infrastructure; commons may be imposed on private owners by government; and commons may arise collectively as the result of a give-and-take among owner and users—in a sense, a community decision with private and public aspects.

This chapter does not address implementation questions or the specific means by which commons management is achieved. Questions of ownership, community definition, institutional design, regulation, boundaries, exclusion of nonmembers, exceptions from the nondiscrimination rule, and pricing are not specifically addressed. Instead, to frame the discussion, we assume (a) private ownership and provisioning of infrastructure,

---

[1] Madison, Frischmann, & Strandburg 685 (2010).

and thus market pricing, and (b) the public at large as the relevant community of potential users. Commons management does not imply market or government provision. Government-owned infrastructures often are managed as commons, as are privately owned infrastructures. This chapter analyzes commons management in terms of private and public strategy for different infrastructure resources.

Due to their nonrival or partially nonrival nature, infrastructure resources can be managed as commons. Whether in fact they should be, and if so, how, remain incredibly difficult questions that must be answered contextually. This chapter begins to explore the economic arguments for managing infrastructure as commons. Subsequent chapters build from this analysis and apply it to particular contexts.

From an economic perspective (and others), it makes sense to manage certain infrastructure resources as commons. Doing so permits a wide range of downstream producers of private, public, and social goods to flourish. As Benkler noted, "[t]he high variability in value of using both transportation and communications facilities from person to person and time to time have made a commons-based approach to providing the core facilities immensely valuable."[2] The point is not that all infrastructure resources (traditional or nontraditional) are or should be managed as commons.

Rather, for certain classes of resources, the economic arguments for managing the resources as commons vary in strength and substance. Moreover, as we will see, the degree of openness itself may vary to accommodate competing interests. But for public, social, and mixed infrastructure, openness is a reasonable baseline objective, and deviations from it require justification.

Commons management may be an attractive private or public management strategy for infrastructure resources. For both private and public managers of infrastructure as well as public regulators, the case for commons management must be evaluated carefully and contextually. Sections A and B set forth the economic arguments for managing different types of infrastructure as commons. Keep in mind that discrimination is not inherently bad, unjust, or inefficient; to the contrary, it is often good, just, and efficient. In essence, we must evaluate the comparative advantages of discrimination and nondiscrimination. Both sections assume the simplest case of a nonrivalrous infrastructure.

Section A considers commons management as a private strategy. There are a variety of reasons why private firms choose to manage their infrastructure as commons. I discuss five primary reasons: (1) consumers generally dislike and react negatively to discrimination; (2) commons management may economize on information and transaction costs and avoid unnecessary complexity; (3) commons management may facilitate joint production or cooperation with competitors; (4) commons management may support and encourage value-creating activities by users; and (5) commons management may maximize the option value of infrastructure when there is high uncertainty regarding sources of future market value.

---

[2] Benkler 47–48 (2001a).

In debates concerning nondiscrimination rules, opponents at times argue that firms, or more generally markets, will choose commons management when it is efficient to do so, and that government should not intervene to impose commons management. As section A demonstrates, there is some truth to the argument that firms will choose commons management in various contexts. But it is a serious mistake to assume that firms will do so efficiently in all contexts and that there is no role for government intervention. There are a variety of situations in which commons management is not an attractive private strategy but nonetheless is an attractive public strategy; that is, markets sometimes fail to adopt commons management when doing so would improve social welfare.

Section B considers commons management as a public strategy. First, it explains the conventional forms of and justifications for government regulation requiring private infrastructure providers to manage infrastructure in a nondiscriminatory manner. Specifically, it considers open-access regulation, essential facilities doctrine, and common-carrier-style nondiscrimination rules. Next, it utilizes the typology developed in chapter 4 and articulates additional, powerful reasons to manage public, social, and mixed infrastructure in a nondiscriminatory manner. Specifically, I argue that commons management can be an efficient means of indirectly supporting public participation in a variety of socially valuable activities, namely activities that involve the production, use, and distribution of public and social goods. As such, commons management can be understood as serving two public functions: First, it diffuses pressure within both market and political systems to "pick winners and losers" among infrastructure users/uses and leaves it to users to decide what to do with the opportunities (capabilities) provided by infrastructure. Second, it functions like an option—a social option. When there is high uncertainty about which users or uses will generate social value in the future, as is typically the case for public, social, or mixed infrastructure, managing the infrastructure as a commons sustains the generic nature of the infrastructure, precludes optimization for a narrower range of activities, and avoids social opportunity costs associated with path dependency. Together, these public functions suggest a third function: Commons management structures the relationships between infrastructure and infrastructure-dependent systems in a manner that creates a spillover-rich environment, where spillovers flow from the many productive activities of users. These activities yield new and unanticipated innovations, knowledge, social capital, and other public and social goods that lead to economic growth and development as well as social welfare improvements not fully reflected in traditional economic measures.

Before proceeding, I note that moving from resource to resource management is not as simple as it may seem, since infrastructure and management institutions affect each other dynamically. Openness may be a characteristic of the resource; open infrastructure is functionally a different "thing" than closed infrastructure.[3] Openness describes the terms and conditions of access and use, and such terms and conditions effectively determine the

---

[3] Madison (2005).

manner in which users relate to the resource; open (closed) infrastructure enables (restricts) user opportunities and degrees of freedom, whether by pricing or technological design. Moreover, management institutions may shape and be shaped by infrastructure resources—whether those institutions are private or public.

A. Commons Management as Private Strategy: The Business Case

We begin with commons management as a private strategy. There are many reasons why private owners of infrastructure voluntarily choose to manage infrastructure in an open, nondiscriminatory fashion. It often makes good business sense to do so. Private firms generally aim to maximize their private returns, and while price discrimination may be an attractive private strategy for increasing revenues in certain contexts, it is hardly the optimal private strategy across the board. Rather, in a variety of contexts, a commons management strategy may better serve the firm's objective.[4] In this section, I describe five primary reasons why firms choose to adopt a commons management strategy for privately owned infrastructure. (There are additional reasons that I will not discuss. For example, firms may adopt a commons management strategy to avoid regulation or the attention of regulators.)

First, consumers generally dislike discrimination, especially where similarly situated consumers are charged or otherwise treated differently. For example, a survey by the Annenberg Public Policy Center of the University of Pennsylvania suggested that many consumers have a strong distaste for price discrimination and inaccurately believe that various forms are unlawful.[5] Although discrimination is practiced by firms and tolerated by consumers in many markets—whether discounts for seniors or high-volume purchasers, higher prices for business class than coach, or different rates for commuter and weekend travelers—firms nevertheless may be reluctant to implement discriminatory pricing or other conditions, at least in a manner transparent to consumers, because of a fear that customers will react negatively. One famous example involved Amazon.com: "In September 2000, Amazon.com got headlines when customers found that the same DVDs were being offered to different buyers at discounts of 30, 35 or 40 percent. Amazon insisted the discounts were part of a random 'price test,' but critics suggested they were based on customer profiling. After weeks of bad press, the firm offered to refund the difference to buyers who had paid the higher prices. The company vowed it wouldn't happen again."[6]

---

[4] We will not discuss internal management of infrastructural resources. Firms, and other organizations, sometimes manage infrastructural resources as commons within the organization such that members may share the resource openly and nonmembers are excluded or allowed access on special terms. See Madison, Frischmann, & Strandburg (2010).

[5] Turow, Feldman, & Meltzer (2005).

[6] Turow (2005).

As Andrew Odlyzko remarks, "price discrimination is an ancient technique that is widespread in the economy, although it is often disguised to avoid negative public reactions."[7] In some market contexts, aversion to price discrimination may reflect a consumer preference regarding the conditions upon which a good or service is provided to them. Put another way, consumer desire for nondiscriminatory infrastructure reasonably can be thought of as a product attribute that providers must take into account.

Second, an open, uniform platform may be easier and cheaper to manage than a closed, discriminatory one. The expected costs of implementing a strategy involving price discrimination or use prioritization may exceed the perceived benefits. This trade-off is discussed extensively in the economic literature on price discrimination.[8] The information costs associated with identifying different consumer groups may preclude implementation of an effective price discrimination scheme; preventing arbitrage by consumers may be quite costly; and it may be difficult to differentiate among suppliers of complementary goods. Many of these costs are contingent on the current state of technology, so the attractiveness of price discrimination (commons management) may change over time. Odlyzko suggested that significant advancements in information gathering, aggregation, and storage and processing technologies have increased and will continue to increase incentives to price discriminate.[9] Nonetheless, in many contexts, commons management may economize on information and transaction costs and avoid unnecessary complexity.

Third, firms may adopt a commons management strategy to facilitate joint production or cooperate with competitors more generally. While cooperation among competitors may seem counterintuitive and contrary to the notion of competition, infrastructure industries often require limited cooperation among competitors with respect to interconnection and standardization. The interconnection of networked infrastructure to create a more robust meta-network, for example, may lead private owners to share resources on a nondiscriminatory basis among the community of interconnecting infrastructure providers. There are competing concerns that push in the opposite direction. The point here is only to acknowledge that the strategy makes good business sense in some contexts. Another example along these lines is joint research ventures or patent pools, where firms may adopt a commons management strategy to facilitate joint production because independent research efforts are inhibited by complexity, expense, strategic concerns, transaction costs, or other impediments. In such cases, commons management allows firms to overcome collective action problems, sometimes mere coordination problems and sometimes more difficult prisoner's dilemma problems.

Fourth, private infrastructure owners may adopt a commons management strategy to support or, put more strongly, encourage value-creating activities by users. Although there

---

[7] Odlyzko 189 (2004b).

[8] Hemphill (2008).

[9] Odlyzko (2004a and 2004b) (making this point and providing various examples).

are many examples of firms failing to appreciate the benefits of such activities, there are also many counterexamples, particularly in high-technology industries.[10] Open infrastructure can be an important foundation for "modular industry structures," which may facilitate innovation by, and at the same time competition among, suppliers of complementary goods and also may improve the prospects of developing beneficial network effects.[11] As Joseph Farrell and Philip Weiser explain, open standards and interfaces facilitated innovation within and entry into the computer and Internet industries. Private firms often will "internalize complementary efficiencies" and in some cases will choose a commons management strategy to encourage experimentation and innovation among complementary applications. Farrell and Weiser explain how the logic of "internalizing complementary efficiencies" suggests that firms will adopt a commons management strategy—"open access" or "modularity" in their article—when it is efficient to do so and will decline to adopt the strategy when that is the efficient choice. For example, firms generally will take into account the benefits consumers realize from applications developed by others. In many cases, demand for infrastructure is driven by demand for infrastructure-dependent applications; recognizing this, infrastructure providers have a strong incentive to take the potential complementary efficiencies into account. A strong version of the argument is that infrastructure provider monopolists are good stewards for the system on the whole—infrastructure and dependent applications—because the monopolist gains the most from efficient applications markets.[12] Providers have a strong incentive to maximize the use value of their own platforms, and this often (though not always) boils down to encouraging as many applications as possible and as widespread adoption by users as possible—the more, the merrier. This can lead to both direct and indirect network effects, where consumers' willingness to pay for the platform/infrastructure increases with the number of other users, including application providers and other consumers. Since network effects operate on users' willingness to pay, much of the value can be internalized by providers.

The strategy may be employed both to encourage widespread adoption by users and to encourage user innovation and experimentation with new applications and uses of the platform. Private infrastructure providers may choose to adopt a commons management strategy when they recognize that users may be best positioned to create value, some portion of which, at least, is appropriable by the infrastructure provider. Put a slightly different way, the strategy may be attractive when firms *know or have reason to believe* that users will be the primary sources of future value. As the previous chapter discussed, this mindset may run counter to the culture of some firms, particularly that of dominant incumbents, and in a sense it may be foreclosed by path dependencies and the costs of getting established managers (and other employees) to adjust their dispositions.

---

[10] Barnett (2011).

[11] Farrell & Weiser (2003).

[12] Farrell and Weiser explore a number of exceptions to the ICE logic. *Id.* at 104.

Finally, another important reason why private infrastructure owners may adopt a commons management strategy is to maintain flexibility in the face of genuine uncertainty. In contrast with the scenario just described, where infrastructure providers recognize that users are the likely source of future value, in this scenario providers are uncertain about the future sources of the value. Infrastructure providers operate in a dynamic and uncertain environment, and for many infrastructure resources, there may be considerable uncertainty as to how the infrastructure may evolve, what will be technologically feasible, what unforeseen uses may emerge, what people will want, how much people will be willing to pay, what complementary goods and services may arise in the future, and so on. Simply put, firms may be unable to accurately predict the likely sources of future market value. Mark Gaynor explains how a decentralized management structure—akin to commons management—can be an efficient private strategy for infrastructure providers in an uncertain environment.[13] Building on the work of Carliss Baldwin and Kim Clark on the value of modularity in computer systems and his prior work with Scott Bradner on the value of modular standards, Gaynor develops and applies a real options framework to the management decisions of private infrastructure providers and demonstrates how a firm's choice of management structure depends—*or at least, should depend*—on the degree of market uncertainty, which Gaynor defines in terms of future market value. In settings characterized by high market uncertainty, commons management may be an attractive private strategy because it takes advantage of the increased value of experimentation by users, the increased range of potential value-creating services, market selection of the best services that eventually emerge, and learning over time about user preferences and possible paths for continued development. In essence, managing infrastructure as a commons maintains flexibility and avoids premature optimization or lock-in to a particular development path or narrow range of paths. Commons management thus may maximize the *option value* of infrastructure.

Though commons management may be an attractive private strategy in some contexts, there are many reasons why private owners of infrastructure choose not to manage infrastructure in an open, nondiscriminatory fashion. For example, price discrimination may be feasible; in a particular market, consumers may not object to the practice; or even if they do, consumers may be unwilling or unable to switch providers. This scenario could provide a good opportunity for the firm to increase profits. Or a closed, centralized management structure may lead to a variety of efficiencies commonly associated with vertical integration, such as those generally associated with technological interdependence or complementarities in process or manufacturing operations, or with governance controls and procedures that can be leveraged efficiently for upstream and downstream operations.[14] Even in uncertain environments, there are a variety of reasons why firms may

---

[13] GAYNOR (2003).
[14] Williamson (1971).

decide not to adopt this strategy. As Gaynor explains, a centralized management structure may offer significant business and technical advantages that must be weighed in firms' decisions about management strategy.[15]

In addition, a variety of biases may cloud the judgment of firm managers. For example, managers may be shortsighted, focusing on prospective returns in a relatively short time frame and unduly discounting potential gains in the medium to long term.[16] Firms may be afflicted by an institutional form of the endowment effect—that is, firms may be strongly biased in their estimation of the future value of services to favor existing or expected services that they currently offer, sponsor or otherwise control and to disfavor those that they do not. Similarly, firms may not recognize that they are operating in a highly uncertain market environment because they are reasonably certain about the potential market value of known or expected services and simply discount the potential value of uncertain prospects.[17]

In sum, there are a variety of reasons why private owners of infrastructure may choose to manage infrastructure as commons or not. We might presume that firms will choose efficiently whether or not to adopt a commons management strategy, taking into account the considerations noted above and any other relevant factors, and in general, we might presume firms are better situated to make such decisions than public officials because, among other things, firms are better informed about consumers, relevant technologies, potential market opportunities, and implementation costs. These presumptions may be defensible in scenarios where the disciplining effect of markets will correct errors: That is, where mistakes lead to market opportunities for other firms, competition may correct inefficient choices. The next section considers situations where this presumption holds and situations where it does not.

B. Commons Management as Public Strategy: The Case for Government Intervention

Commons management may be an attractive public strategy even if it is not attractive as a private strategy. For both public managers of infrastructure and public regulators, the case for commons management must be evaluated carefully and contextually. We focus

---

[15] GAYNOR (2003).

[16] Managers must respond to the short-term expectations of shareholders, and thus in some cases, it may be shareholders, rather than the managers, who are shortsighted. On shortsightedness, see Frischmann (2005d); Frischmann & McKenna (2011).

[17] There is an important difference between risk and uncertainty. Risk implies probabilities are available to guide decisions while uncertainty implies a lack of adequate information to estimate probabilities. See KNIGHT (1921). I refer to uncertainty rather than risk. Of course, there will be situations where firms can estimate probabilities for some of the future prospects, and this capacity itself may influence decisions, for example, where firms are averse to uncertainty. Epstein (1999) (defining uncertainty aversion).

on public regulators and the case for government intervention in infrastructure markets to impose a commons management strategy via some form of nondiscrimination rule. At this stage, our focus is not extensively on the form or means of implementing the rule, although we will briefly discuss a few conventional examples. Instead, we will consider why commons management might be an attractive public strategy.

We begin with a brief discussion of the conventional means and justifications for imposing nondiscrimination rules on private owners of infrastructure. As we will see, these conventional means and justifications are undertheorized and do not fully capture the range of situations in which commons management is an attractive public strategy. Yet they do indicate public recognition of the importance of nondiscrimination rules for certain types of infrastructure.

Next, we turn to the demand-side arguments raised in this book. This allows us to examine both situations in which the conventional means apply and situations in which they do not but perhaps should apply. To facilitate analysis, we return to the infrastructure typology developed in chapter 4 to distinguish between commercial, public, and social infrastructure based on the nature of outputs and the potential for positive externalities.

I. CONVENTIONAL MEANS AND JUSTIFICATIONS FOR NONDISCRIMINATION RULES IN INFRASTRUCTURE INDUSTRIES

Government intervention in infrastructure markets to impose commons management can take a number of forms. Categorizing broadly, we can identify four primary types of intervention:

1. public regulation of private infrastructure providers mandating nondiscriminatory access for *competitors*;
2. public regulation of private infrastructure providers mandating nondiscriminatory access for *consumers*;
3. dedication of privately produced infrastructure to the public domain; and
4. public provision of infrastructure on a nondiscriminatory basis.

Given our assumption of private provisioning, we leave public provision of infrastructure on a nondiscriminatory basis for discussion in later chapters. Public refusal to recognize or protect private property rights in infrastructural resources and concomitant dedication of the resources to public ownership, communal ownership, or nonownership is an important means for sustaining certain types of infrastructure commons. This type of intervention is not often considered in discussions of infrastructure policy because it typically applies to nontraditional infrastructure, such as intellectual infrastructure (e.g., ideas) and environmental infrastructure (e.g., oceans). Accordingly, we also leave it for discussion in later chapters. Note, however, that the justifications explored in this section apply to nontraditional infrastructure.

Government intervention in traditional infrastructure markets to impose commons management is generally constrained to the first two types of interventions, one focused on nondiscriminatory access for *competitors* and one focused on nondiscriminatory service to *consumers*. At times, these different types of intervention are conflated or confused. It is worth distinguishing them because they generally involve different institutions, rationales, and economic consequences.

In the first type, government may require an infrastructure owner to provide nondiscriminatory access to a (potential) *competitor*. Typically, this means that competitors gain access to the infrastructure resource on terms and conditions no less favorable than those granted to the owner's current internal or external users. The central purpose for mandating such access is to facilitate competition and entry and to prevent foreclosure. The intervention is limited to situations in which the infrastructure market is not competitive.

There are two primary means for imposing this type of nondiscriminatory access. First, open-access regulation may require an infrastructure owner to allow competitors access on nondiscriminatory terms through policies such as unbundling, wholesaling, and functional separation, among others.[18] Open-access regulation typically involves a complex regulatory regime administered by a sector- or industry-specific agency, and often such regulation is part of broader efforts to privatize public facilities and/or deregulate regulated monopolies. For example, open-access regulation has been and remains an integral, though sometimes controversial, part of the electric, gas, railway, airline, and communications industries, among others, throughout the world. (See chapter 8.C.3.)

Second, nondiscriminatory access may be imposed when the infrastructure is deemed to be an "essential facility" within the meaning of antitrust law.[19] Under the essential facilities doctrine, courts may impose obligations of equal and nondiscriminatory access to an infrastructural resource where

1. a monopolist controls access to an essential facility;
2. the facility cannot be reasonably duplicated by a competitor;
3. the monopolist denies access to a competitor, and
4. it was feasible to grant access.[20]

---

[18] Berkman Center (2009).

[19] Related to this, antitrust law also may lead to similar obligations being imposed as a merger condition in consent decrees. See, e.g., Silicon Graphics, Inc., 120 F.T.C. 928 (1995); Decision and Order at II.A, Intel Corp., FTC Docket No. 9288 (Aug. 3, 1999); United States v. AT&T Co., 552 F. Supp. 131, 142–43, 195–200 (D.D.C. 1982); Final Judgment at III, United States v. Microsoft Corp., No. 98-1232 (CKK) (D.D.C. Nov. 12, 2002); see also Wigod (2002) (analyzing open access provisions of consent decree authorizing merger between AOL and Time-Warner).

[20] MCI Commc'ns Corp. v. Am. Tel. and Tel. Co., 708 F.2d 1081, 1132–33 (7th Cir.), cert. denied, 464 U.S. 891. For further discussion, see Frischmann & Waller (2008).

The essential facilities doctrine applies only to a specific competitor that has been denied access to the infrastructural facility, and whether the doctrine should apply is determined in a judicial setting through the application of antitrust law. In contrast, open-access regulation applies to all potential competitors and is implemented in a regulatory setting. These institutional differences affect the scope and timing of the intervention as well as the evidence and criteria on which decisions to intervene are made.

Regardless of the means used, the conventional justification for this type of intervention is to support viable competition in the infrastructure-access market and other market(s) dependent on the infrastructure, and thus to preclude foreclosure of potential competition. Competition may not be viable otherwise because of barriers to entry—for example, potential competitors may be unable to enter the market if the costs of duplicating the infrastructure are substantial. Such costs often are substantial for both the potential entrant and the community being served.[21] Restricting access to the infrastructure also may harm competition by encouraging firms to exit the market or by raising the operating costs of rival competitors.[22] The conventional justification, rooted in antitrust and regulatory economics, is premised on the idea that competition is socially desirable yet unattainable under certain conditions, and nondiscriminatory access may be an efficient means of facilitating competition.

Yet the antitrust and regulatory economics traditions largely disfavor this type of intervention—through either means. The reasons are many and complex. Here are some of the traditional concerns leading to such disfavor:

- Monopoly is not necessarily bad.
- Government intervention may stifle incentives.
- The complex business (and often technological) interface between infrastructure owners and competitors requires careful attention, presents opportunities for strategic behavior, and may require considerable oversight by regulators.
- Regulatory agencies are likely to be cumbersome, inefficient, wasteful, and possibly captured by the regulated entities.
- Courts are not likely to make good economic decisions with respect to determining whether the essential facilities doctrine applies and to administering the remedy.
- Nondiscrimination rules inevitably must be accompanied by price regulation (to avoid monopoly pricing).

I discuss many of these issues in chapters 6 and 8.

---

[21] Rey & Tirole 1 (2007).
[22] Id. at 8; Krattenmaker & Salop (1986).

In the second type of intervention, government may require an infrastructure owner to provide nondiscriminatory access to all *customers*. In such cases, the owner may be deemed to be a "common carrier." Common carrier obligations arose in common law for a range of businesses that opened their doors to the public, ranging from innkeepers to freight carriers. It was applied broadly to early communications and transportation industries—for example, telegraph and railroads. It became a core concept in the regulatory regimes developed to govern public utilities and modern network infrastructure, though in some of these contexts the nondiscrimination rule is not called common carriage.[23] Historically, common-carrier-style obligations for infrastructure were said to arise in markets "affected with the public interest."[24]

This type of intervention typically requires an infrastructure provider to provide nondiscriminatory service to all customers at reasonable rates. A duty to provide such service is not absolute, however. Providers could refuse service when facing unreasonably high risks or capacity constraints. Price discrimination based on identity generally was disallowed, yet common carrier regulation sometimes permitted certain types of discrimination among customers. Permissible discrimination, which varied under different common carrier regimes, involved categorical differentiation among classes of customers, often based on cost (e.g., charging different rates for transporting goods based on weight or standard of care), but also sometimes based on value (e.g., charging different rates for transporting equal weights of coal and diamonds), or on some mix of cost- and value-based criteria.[25]

The conventional justifications for common-carrier-type regulation include both economic and noneconomic concerns. Like the first type of intervention, the second type has at times been justified to deal with antitrust and regulatory economic concerns about monopolistic supply and economic consequences for consumers in dependent markets.[26]

But it also can be justified to deal with a host of other public interest concerns. Barbara Cherry, Thomas Nachbar, and other scholars have suggested that common carrier and similar access-promoting doctrines historically depended on various public interests justifications that do not depend on concerns about competition. For example, Cherry emphasized how common carriage fundamentally addressed "economic coercion arising from inequality of bargaining power between provider and customer of an essential service."[27] Bargaining-power inequality is not contingent on a lack of competition in the relevant market; for example, it arises regularly in contexts where consumers cannot effectively switch providers because of information asymmetries, transaction costs, lock-in/switching

---

[23] Though often confused, commons carriers are not the same as public utilities. Cherry (2003); Noam (1994).

[24] EPSTEIN 279–318 (1998) (history of common carrier regulation); Hamilton 1100–01 (1930).

[25] Hemphill (2008) (collecting cites on price discrimination and common carriage).

[26] EPSTEIN 156, 279–318 (1998).

[27] Cherry 268 (2003). In subsequent work, Cherry has gone further and incorporated speech and other related public interests. Cherry (2006).

costs, or other impediments. Nachbar emphasizes that common-carrier-style obligations have been imposed on owners of facilities that are part of a network even if the facilities in question are not essential or do not give rise to market power.[28] Nachbar suggests that nondiscrimination may be an attractive public strategy for reducing transaction costs associated with standardization of terms and rates in network markets.[29] The public interest concerns often have an economic ring to them but depart somewhat, though not radically, from the conventional antitrust and regulatory economic traditions. In a sense, the arguments attempt to put some meat on the bones of the key concepts of "essentiality" and "affected by the public interest."

Still, one might reasonably ask: *essential to what?* To what, if anything besides competition, is nondiscriminatory infrastructure access essential? Nachbar suggests that one answer is network standardization and perhaps the further consequence of development and growth contingent on standardized network terms and conditions. Cherry suggests fair, equal, and reasonable access unbiased by economic coercion;[30] she also suggests that speech values may justify nondiscrimination.[31] These public interests, Nachbar and Cherry suggest, are not fully accounted for in the conventional antitrust and regulatory economic traditions. Though both interests seem worthwhile, it remains unclear why and how important they are.

Following the conventional economic approach to studying infrastructure, Nachbar and Cherry focus on the infrastructure market (providers and consumers), and as a result they do not appreciate fully the significance of both "network standardization" and "equal, unbiased access" to user participation in infrastructure-dependent markets *and nonmarkets*, and, more specifically, to the generation of spillovers in infrastructure-dependent systems.[32] Nondiscriminatory access to infrastructure may be *essential* to public participation in a range of socially valuable activities, including economic, cultural, political, and other social systems, and it is in this sense that we can say some infrastructures are "affected by the public interest."

The infrastructure criteria and typology developed in chapter 4 suggest that the conventional justifications may be incomplete and may have been applied to a subset of a

---

[28] Nachbar 102 (2008). He emphasizes that being part of or connected physically to a transportation network is quite common.

[29] *Id.* at 108. This may be an important reason for nondiscrimination in some contexts, but it is not clear from Nachbar's analysis why private actors will not voluntarily and efficiently choose to adopt a common management strategy. Thus, it is not clear why or when the government intervention is needed to impose nondiscrimination for the purpose of standardization and reducing transaction costs. See Farrell & Weiser (2003).

[30] Cherry (2003).

[31] Cherry (2006).

[32] Some of the public interest concerns raised by Cherry and Nachbar map onto the theoretical framework developed in this book; as noted, Cherry emphasizes speech values. Some of the public interests can be described in terms of infrastructure-dependent public or social goods produced by users. But the mapping is imperfect and incomplete.

broader phenomenon. First, there is a wider range of resources that are "affected by the public interest" and are candidates for similar institutional treatment. The infrastructure model provides a useful means for identifying such resources and examining some of the arguments for commons management. Second, the institutional response—whether via essential facilities doctrine, common carrier regulation, or some related public intervention—need not be justified purely on the argument that it is necessary to facilitate competition. When uses of an infrastructure resource include the production of public goods and social goods, the case for commons management may be substantially stronger because of the positive social welfare effects attributable to the production, dissemination, and use of such goods.

The next two subsections evaluate the case for government intervention to impose nondiscrimination in the context of different types of infrastructure. The first subsection discusses commercial infrastructure and ties the analysis back to the conventional means and justifications discussed above. The next subsection extends the analysis and discusses public, social, and mixed infrastructure.

2. PUBLIC STRATEGY: COMMERCIAL INFRASTRUCTURE

For commercial infrastructure, the arguments for government intervention into infrastructure markets to impose a nondiscrimination rule are quite limited. The nonrival nature of the resource presents an opportunity for commons management and the familiar trade-offs. Recall from chapter 4 that demand manifestation problems are not significant. Accordingly, the conventional analysis applies rather well.

In some contexts, antitrust and regulatory economics principles provide a sufficient basis for government-imposed commons, and associated legal regimes provide mechanisms for doing so, but those contexts are relatively rare. The case for government intervention is constrained to situations in which the infrastructure market is not competitive, and even in such situations, the case is rather limited.

If the commercial infrastructure market is competitive, two assumptions are appropriate: first, that competition will effectively discipline providers for poor strategic decisions; and second, that any observed discrimination or prioritization may be associated with product differentiation, cost-based differences among consumers, attempts to realize efficiencies through vertical arrangements, or other factors that do not raise public concern. Generally, there is no particular problem to solve, and, in the event that any problems do arise—for example, a firm inefficiently prioritizes one set of applications or users over another—the market system should adjust and correct any such problems over time. There are certain exceptions to this line of reasoning—for instance, network effects and switching costs may make it more difficult for consumers to switch providers—but in general it holds up rather well.

If the commercial infrastructure market is not competitive, however, intervention may be warranted based on the conventional antitrust and regulatory economics principles discussed above. We must acknowledge at the outset that monopoly is not unlawful or necessarily a bad thing. In fact, as economists are prone to emphasize, the prospect of obtaining a monopoly may serve as a significant inducement for firms to compete, innovate, and invest heavily in infrastructure. Consequently, the possessor of a lawfully obtained monopoly generally has the freedom to charge a monopoly price, engage in price discrimination, and refuse to deal with competitors. This point is very important to keep in mind because it serves as a critical baseline for most economists. Nonetheless, exceptions to this general freedom arise as a result of two important and well-recognized economic concerns: (a) deadweight losses from pricing above marginal cost and (b) foreclosure of potential competitors.[33]

In the regulated industries context, an important justification for intervention concerns minimizing deadweight losses. Pricing above marginal cost may be inevitable, absent subsidies to cover the fixed costs, because commercial infrastructure involve decreasing-cost phenomena and indivisibilities. As Duffy observes, "reputable economics encompasses the . . . view—'that, generally, prices which deviate in a systematic manner from marginal costs will be required for an optimal allocation of resources, even in the absence of externalities.'"[34] There are a variety of different pricing schemes that providers and rate setters might employ to facilitate cost recovery and minimize deadweight losses. If the market is monopolized, the monopolist presumably would choose between the uniform monopoly price and a price discrimination scheme that allowed it to extract a greater proportion of the surplus. Such a choice would be guided by the considerations set forth in the previous section. In this context, a nondiscrimination rule (imposed by government) standing alone may not help consumers, and in fact it might hurt. Imagine imposing a nondiscrimination rule on a monopolist: What price would the provider set for access to the infrastructure? Presumably, the monopoly price. Absent competition (or at least the threat of entry), there is no downward pressure on price to push price to average cost. When compared to the monopoly price, price discrimination may look attractive because it may increase output and lessen deadweight losses. Average cost pricing is a nondiscriminatory pricing regime that would lessen deadweight losses compared to this alternative, but no monopolist would voluntarily choose average cost pricing over the monopoly price. Thus, government intervention to impose a nondiscrimination rule may be insufficient; price regulation might be required. I discuss these issues further in the next chapter. Still, mandating nondiscriminatory access may improve matters in some cases, even if the monopolist charges the monopoly price. For example, in the access to competitor scenario, the essential facilities doctrine or open-access regulation may facilitate competition by a more efficient competitor who has been denied access to the

---

[33] There are other concerns, but for the sake of brevity, we focus on these.

[34] Duffy 38 (2004) (quoting Baumol and Bradford 265 (1970)).

essential infrastructure facility. Such access does not inevitably enhance or decrease welfare and must be evaluated carefully in a particular context.[35]

In the antitrust context, an important justification for intervention concerns foreclosure of potential competitors, or, more generally, manipulation of the competitive process, where a firm unlawfully attempts to monopolize a market (and not earn it lawfully) or a monopolist acts in an anticompetitive manner to maintain its monopoly. In general, antitrust does not impose nondiscrimination rules for infrastructure,[36] with a narrow (and increasingly disfavored) exception: the essential facilities doctrine, discussed above.[37] While the essential facilities doctrine does not alleviate concerns about deadweight losses attributable to monopoly pricing, it serves to protect the public against foreclosure of potential competitors, as was seen vividly in the *MCI v. AT&T* case.[38]

To summarize, the case for imposing commons on privately owned commercial infrastructure is limited to well-understood rationales reflected in antitrust and regulatory economic traditions. The basic overarching concerns for commercial infrastructure are supply, cost recovery, and sustaining incentives to invest in the first place. Demand-side concerns are not particularly important. For some infrastructure, the regulatory economics classification as natural monopoly leads to an emphasis on minimizing deadweight losses. Within this setting, nondiscrimination rules may work with price regulation and lead to average cost pricing as the baseline from which deviations must be justified, for example, by showing that deadweight losses are reduced. This focus is a very different orientation than antitrust law, which focuses on the competitive process, assumes that monopolies may be lawful and even desirable, and does not involve price regulation. Antitrust law imposes commons management in very rare circumstances.

---

[35] Frischmann & Waller (2008).

[36] The Robinson-Patman Act prohibits price discrimination with respect to "different purchasers of commodities of like grade and quality, . . . where the effect of such discrimination may be substantially to lessen competition or tend to create a monopoly in any line of commerce, or to injure, destroy, or prevent competition with any person who either grants or knowingly receives the benefit of such discrimination, or with customers of either of them." 15 U.S.C. § 13(a). The Act allows for price differentials based on cost. *Id.* The Act does not apply to infrastructure industries.

[37] Nondiscrimination obligations are occasionally included in merger approvals and consent decrees. In addition, antitrust law has recognized a duty to deal in situations that extend beyond the essential facilities doctrine, for example, where a monopolist's refusal to deal raises rivals' costs and has no efficiency or procompetitive justification. Aspen Skiing Co. v. Aspen Highlands Skiing Corp., 472 U.S. 585 (1985); Associated Press v. United States, 326 U.S. 1 (1945); see generally Frischmann & Waller (2008).

[38] MCI Commc'ns Corp. v. Am. Tel. and Tel. Co., 708 F.2d 1081, 1132–33 (7th Cir.); see Frischmann & Waller (2008).

3. PUBLIC STRATEGY: PUBLIC, SOCIAL, AND MIXED INFRASTRUCTURE

For public and social infrastructure, the arguments for government intervention into infrastructure markets to impose nondiscrimination rules are not limited to the rationales reflected in antitrust and regulatory economics, though such arguments still may apply. Rather, the arguments extend further to encompass information, transaction cost, and externality problems that inhibit efficient operation of both markets and targeted government subsidies where downstream production of public and social goods is concerned. As chapter 4 described, public, social, and mixed infrastructure present demand manifestation problems and associated market failure concerns. Specifically, there are two overarching sets of related concerns: First, there are concerns about undersupply and underuse of infrastructure and undersupply of infrastructure-dependent public and social goods. Second, there are concerns about dynamic shifts in the nature of infrastructure resources, concerns that infrastructure development might be skewed in socially undesirable directions—for example, if private infrastructure owners prematurely optimize infrastructure for uses that they expect will maximize their private returns and in doing so choose a path that forecloses production of various public or social goods that would yield greater net social returns.

Competition among infrastructure providers does *not* eliminate these concerns, because the problems originate on the demand side and dynamically affect the supply side. Market demand for infrastructure access and use fails to reflect social demand because of spillovers from the production of public and social goods. Accordingly, there is no ready mechanism for the market to adjust or correct for incomplete or missing markets. This means first that government interventions aimed at promoting competition are no panacea, and second, and more importantly, that relying on such interventions alone is likely to distort infrastructure use and development over time. In the end, competition policy is orthogonal to the market failures associated with spillovers from public and social goods, and thus it is false hope to place too much reliance on competition policy where such failures arise. Competition policy and environmental policy are orthogonal, for the same basic reason. No economist would argue that competition alone will lead to an efficient amount of pollution, because pollution involves negative externalities not accounted for by market actors.

With respect to the undersupply of public and social goods, the conventional solutions involve interventions that directly target public and social goods production. Government may produce or subsidize production of such goods, or structure institutions that enable markets to function where they would otherwise be incomplete or missing—for example, through the creation of intellectual property rights. These solutions directly target producers of public goods. In many cases, these solutions are reasonably effective, though it is very difficult to know confidently how effective. Nonetheless, even if we assume they are reasonably effective in some contexts, we must recognize how these interventions are *systematically ineffective* for many different types of public and social goods.

Consider, for example, the problem of intellectual public goods, discussed briefly in chapter 3 and extensively in chapter 12. The direct interventions targeted at this problem are intellectual property and government subsidization. The intellectual property regimes of patent and copyright primarily aim to solve the problem by enabling markets to function more efficiently. Intellectual property regimes provide owners with a legal right to exclude others from using qualifying inventions and creative works, facilitate a range of different transactions with respect to such public goods, and thereby improve incentives to invest resources in production, development, and commercialization of inventions and creative works. Both regimes are very difficult to evaluate, and my objective here is not to engage the ongoing debates about intellectual property reform. Rather, I make a simple, uncontroversial but important observation: Both intellectual property regimes encourage certain types of intellectual goods to be produced and discourage or fail to affect many other types. The same is true of government funding of research and related subsidization.

These direct targeted interventions are imperfect and incomplete, and the reasons why are worth noting. To the extent that the intellectual property systems aim to solve the underproduction problem, they do so in deliberate and unavoidable reliance on the market mechanism, which exhibits a predictable bias for intellectual goods that generate the most appropriable value in consumer markets.[39] As a result, various socially desirable intellectual goods—basic research, drugs for diseases in small markets, well-reasoned political dialogue, and "fair and balanced" news reporting, to name just a few—remain underproduced even with intellectual property regimes in place.

For such goods, government provision or subsidy may seem more appropriate. There are many ways in which governments subsidize intellectual public goods production, including research grants, procurement programs, contracted research, and tax incentives.[40] Such mechanisms exhibit a range of biases that result from political and other decision-making processes that influence resource allocation. To subsidize production of public goods (or social goods), the government needs to pick winners by assessing social demand for such goods based on the social value they create.[41] Resources are limited, and decisions about what and who to fund and how much money to allocate to different projects entail prioritization and ranking just like markets, albeit according to different decision-making processes, criteria, and values. Indeed, there are winners and losers, and

---

[39] See chapter 3. In addition to copyright and patent, trademark can also have this distorting effect. Hemphill & Suk 1177–78 (2009).

[40] Governments allocate a tremendous amount of money to support research. Basic research funding is allocated by government agencies and institutions like the National Science Foundation, the Department of Energy, and the National Institutes of Health. Decisions about what and who to fund and how much money should be allocated to different projects entail prioritization and ranking just like markets, albeit according to different decision-making processes, criteria, and values.

[41] Frischmann 386–91 (2000) (discussing government assessment of demand for public goods).

good reasons to question the efficiency of these mechanisms for various types of public and social goods. Most would agree, for example, that government provision or support is not the best way to get well-reasoned political dialogue or high-quality news reporting.

It is particularly difficult for government to directly support private production of social goods. Government certainly provides a variety of social goods directly (e.g., governance, law). But it may be quite difficult if not impossible for the government to create private property rights in many nonmarket goods, merit goods, social capital, or irreducibly social goods, given the systematic inefficiencies in market provisioning, unacceptable deadweight losses, intractable definitional and boundary-setting issues, and the social nature of the goods. Direct subsidization may be appropriate in some cases—say, for merit goods like education or health care—but there is often considerable controversy about the role and degree of government intervention in such areas. For many social goods, government subsidy mechanisms run into the same set of problems as public goods (i.e., problems associated with prioritization and selection among different types of social goods), and those problems may be exacerbated because social goods are often produced, developed, and adapted by communities rather than an identifiable "producer" to whom a subsidy could be directed. Finally, government intervention into some social and cultural systems may destroy, distort, or disrupt the social processes, trust, community bonds, and so on that enable social capital and irreducibly social goods to emerge.

In many cases, indirect interventions are a more efficient and politically attractive means for supporting the production of public and social goods. Specifically, government intervention at the infrastructure level may be a more efficient and politically acceptable means for supporting the production of various infrastructure-dependent public and social goods. Public, social, and mixed infrastructures constitute a special type of merit good. Infrastructure users' private demand for access to and use of the infrastructure—their preferences—are systematically distorted because of persistent information and appropriability problems associated with the production of public and social goods. Many criticisms of Musgrave's theory of merit goods focus on the disadvantages of relying on government or elites to "correct" individual preferences and override consumer sovereignty, but these criticisms seem much less persuasive in the infrastructure context.

The appropriate form of intervention depends on the type of infrastructure. The most direct intervention would be to publicly provide infrastructure or publicly subsidize infrastructure provision. Let us put this option aside for now and, consistent with our assumption of private ownership and provisioning of infrastructure, consider the case of imposing commons management. Specifically, government may require an infrastructure owner to provide nondiscriminatory access to all users and thereby preclude owners from differentially allocating and prioritizing infrastructure access and use.

Managing infrastructure as a commons may be a more effective means for supporting the production of public and social goods than targeted subsidies.[42] Commons management is not a direct subsidy to infrastructure users who produce public or social goods, but it effectively creates cross-subsidies and eliminates the need to rely on *either* the market or the government to "pick winners"—that is, to prioritize or rank infrastructure-dependent users worthy of access and support. As discussed above, the market picks winners according to the appropriable value generated by outputs and, consequently, output producers' willingness to pay for access to the infrastructure, and the government picks winners by assessing social demand for such goods based on their estimated social value. The inefficiencies, information problems, and transaction costs associated with picking winners under either system may justify managing public and social infrastructure resources as commons. Cross-subsidies arise between those uses/users/goods that would be winners and those that would be losers. Cross-subsidization is admittedly a rather blunt tool, and economists generally prefer the precision of both price discrimination and direct subsidies. Nonetheless, where such precision is either not feasible or introduces its own set of distortions, cross-subsidization can be an attractive public strategy.

It is worth noting that the cross-subsidization can be quite complex, and it may be hard to predict how the cross-subsidies flow among different user types. In part,[43] this is because it is often impossible to predict which infrastructure use/user is producing spillovers, much less to predict more detailed information about the magnitude of any spillovers or the correspondence between private and social demand. As chapter 4 discussed, the social demand curve need not have the same shape as the private demand curve. In fact, the shapes of the curves can be wildly different. Where the shape of the social demand curve is unknown and unknowable, it is impossible to say how the cross-subsidies flow.

Such imprecision may be troubling. Without a doubt, it would be wonderful if we had the information needed to fully evaluate and know the social demand curve, but we do not and practically cannot. This does not mean that we should ignore or discount the effects. That spillovers from infrastructure-dependent public and social goods are not easily quantified or appropriated does not make their value insignificant, inevitable, or noneconomic. One way or another, infrastructure management decisions shape the opportunities for users to produce such goods, and it is critical to consider the consequences of such decisions.[44]

---

[42] This is an argument I developed in a series of articles. Frischmann (2005a); Frischmann & Lemey (2007); Frischmann & van Schewick (2007). Other scholars have picked up on the idea. Lee & Wu (2009); Hemphill (2008).

[43] It is very difficult, if not impossible, to engage in the counterfactual analysis, which would require identifying winners and losers under both market and government subsidy systems.

[44] In future work, I plan to explore alternative empirical methods for measuring the consequences, even if valuation in conventional economic terms remains out of reach.

Managing public, social, and mixed infrastructures as commons has important dynamic implications apart from cross-subsidies. Commons management maintains flexibility and the generic nature of the infrastructure resource and thus addresses the persistent and systematic uncertainty about where social value will come from, the social opportunity costs of failing to support a wide range of public and social goods, and how well markets and government will pick winners. Absent government intervention, there are strong incentives in many cases for private infrastructure providers to prioritize access and use of the infrastructure—whether through technological design or price or quality discrimination. In essence, a nondiscrimination rule precludes differentially allocating and prioritizing infrastructure access and use on the basis of expected private returns and also indirectly limits infrastructure evolution or optimization on that basis.

Public commitment to an infrastructure commons can be understood in terms of options theory, similar to the discussion above regarding the private strategy. Recall that where market uncertainty is high, managing infrastructure as a commons may be an attractive private strategy because it maintains flexibility, avoids premature optimization or lock-in to a particular development path or narrow range of paths, and thereby maximizes the option value of the infrastructure. Commons management supports experimentation by users; increases the range of potential value-creating activities; defers market selection of the best services; leaves room for unforeseen innovations, markets, and value-creating activities to emerge; and facilitates learning over time.

With respect to public, social, and mixed infrastructure, commons management serves the same critical functions. A similar argument in favor of commons management applies, except that the nature of the uncertainty is different. The relevant uncertainty is not limited to market value and instead must include social value. Even if there is little uncertainty about what infrastructure uses will generate market value in the future, there still may be considerable uncertainty about what infrastructure uses will generate social value in the future. Again, there is no obvious or necessary correlation between market and social value of different infrastructure uses.

Low market uncertainty suggests a very weak case for commons management as a private strategy, because price discrimination or use prioritization, if feasible, would be quite attractive as a profit-maximization strategy. However, the strongest case for commons management as a public strategy is *precisely* when there is low market uncertainty and high uncertainty about what infrastructure uses will generate social value in the future. In this scenario, private owners have strong incentives to pursue a strategy of discrimination or prioritization because of the prospective private returns, but the public would be better off with a commons management strategy because of the prospective social returns. It is this wedge between private and social returns that may warrant government intervention.

In the event that there is low uncertainty about future social value—for example, when it is known or reasonably foreseeable which infrastructure uses will generate social value—we might expect that the government could effectively support those uses directly. But in an uncertain environment, commons management may be an attractive public strategy for maximizing the option value of the infrastructure.

Note that for commercial infrastructure, there is low uncertainty about future social value and variable (low, medium, or high) uncertainty about future market value. The reason why there is low uncertainty about future social value is that the infrastructure is not used to produce public and social goods. Accordingly, with respect to commercial infrastructure, the case for commons management largely turns on the degree of market uncertainty, which is presumably something that private firms are better at evaluating than public officials.

For public, social, and mixed infrastructure, however, there is variable uncertainty about both future market and future social value. Thus, with respect to public, social, and mixed infrastructure, the case for commons management largely turns on the degree of social value uncertainty. There is no reason to defer to private firms in this context. First, there is no reason to believe that firms are better informed or better able to allocate resources, or that firms are likely to resist the pressure to discriminate, prioritize, or optimize the infrastructure. Second, there is no reason to think that the market will correct misallocations. Still, to the extent that there is also high market uncertainty (and firms recognize this), government intervention may be unnecessary because private firms may choose to adopt a commons management strategy for the reasons discussed in the previous section (so long as market uncertainty remains high and firms continue to recognize it).

Let me reiterate the basic lesson: When an infrastructure resource serves as a foundation for the production of a wide variety of public and/or social goods, managing access to and use of that resource in a manner that does not discriminate in price, quality, or priority among users or uses may be an efficient and politically attractive public strategy. Nondiscrimination rules effectively function as a social option, maintaining generic infrastructure, precluding premature optimization, and reducing pressure on both market and government allocation systems to pick winners. Given systematic failures of both markets and governments in supporting production of public and social goods, supporting infrastructure commons can be an attractive public option.

I should note that the argument being made is theoretical, abstract, and general. Application to specific infrastructure resources requires attention to the contextual details. The infrastructure definition and typology are doing work in delineating a set, and then particular subsets, of resources that behave functionally as special types of infrastructural capital. This is important to keep in mind because it constrains the reach of the arguments. For the vast majority of resources and markets, the arguments do not apply directly. The arguments apply to infrastructure, and, as discussed, the arguments diverge from the conventional economic analysis only with respect to public, social, or mixed infrastructure. We assumed nonrivalrous infrastructure and thus assumed away congestion and depreciation; these issues are considered in chapter 7. We also assumed private owner-ship and provisioning without considering how government intervention to impose com-mons management may affect incentives to supply; this issue is considered in chapter 8. Before considering congestion or incentives, however, we examine, in chapter 6, how commons management affects pricing.

3

Complications

PART III ADDRESSES complications that must be considered when evaluating whether to manage infrastructure as commons. As Part II discussed, the social value of infrastructure may greatly exceed the private value manifest in markets, so commons management may be justified as a means for sustaining opportunities for users to generate public and social goods that contribute to the wedge between social and private market value. In a sense, the demand-side analysis reveals a weight on the scale in favor of commons management, but the weight does not necessarily tip the balance. There are other relevant considerations, some more important than others, depending on the context.

Part III focuses on three sets of complications. The first set involves the impacts that commons management might have on pricing practices, and concerns that nondiscrimination rules must be accompanied by price regulation or government subsidies. The second set concerns congestion management and complications that arise when infrastructure is partially (non)rival and congestible, and the relationships between commons management and congestion management. Finally, the third set concerns the impact of nondiscrimination rules on supply-side incentives. As the chapters reveal, arguments based on these complications should be evaluated carefully. Although opponents of commons management often portray these complications as sources of substantial conflict, such claims are hyperbolic; in many contexts, the complications are manageable and do not undermine the case for commons management.

6

COMMONS MANAGEMENT AND INFRASTRUCTURE PRICING

THIS CHAPTER ADDRESSES three complicated issues concerning commons management and infrastructure pricing. First, it examines how commons management interacts with different forms of price discrimination. Second, it considers the relationship between commons management and price regulation. Although nondiscrimination rules and price regulation may complement each other, particularly in the context of regulated monopolies, one does not necessitate the other. Finally, it focuses on infrastructure pricing and subsidies aimed at reducing prices to marginal cost.

Infrastructure pricing practices vary considerably across different contexts, depending on the infrastructure and the community, among other things. For example, electricity, road, and telecommunications infrastructures involve very different pricing practices within and across countries. Moreover, pricing practices have changed considerably in many industries over the past few decades. The deregulation movement, in particular, has swept the world and brought significant reform in many industries. Some general observations are possible. Infrastructure resources often involve decreasing average costs, and this significantly complicates pricing and cost recovery when compared with non-infrastructure industries. Generally speaking, infrastructure pricing follows a pattern that depends on the degree to which and manner in which the infrastructure market is regulated or competitive.

At the extremes, theory suggests similar pricing principles and outcomes. The reason is that both regulation and competition should impose a profit constraint on infrastructure providers. Classic rate-of-return regulation, for example, imposes such a constraint by regulating the rate of return on capital. Other forms of price regulation, such as price cap regulation, constrain profits and aim to maintain cost-based pricing.

Competition imposes a different profit constraint because industries that generate above-normal profits attract entry and price-cutting. There are different models of competition in infrastructure industries that suggest different outcomes (e.g., Bertrand competition between duopolists drives price to marginal cost, while Cournot competition drives price to average cost), but generally, competition imposes a profit constraint and restrains pricing practices, typically driving price to average cost.[1] We expect short-run deviations and strategic behavior, of course. The basic point is premised on the idea that firms will not enter the market if they cannot reasonably expect to recover their total costs; at the same time, it assumes that attempts to price above average cost will be disciplined in a competitive setting. There is a substantial economics literature on these issues.[2]

Most infrastructure markets are not and probably never will be fully regulated or perfectly competitive. Rather, most infrastructure markets fall into the "gray area," with some exceptional sectors. Infrastructure markets involve a "mix of inevitably imperfect regulation and inevitably imperfect competition."[3]

A. Commons Management and Price Discrimination

This section examines how the following nondiscrimination rule interacts with different forms of price discrimination:

> Infrastructure owners must provide access on terms and conditions that do not discriminate on the basis of the identity of the user or use.

This rule precludes many forms of value-based price discrimination. It does not preclude various forms of cost-based differential pricing, including variable load pricing (discussed below) and congestion- or usage-based pricing (discussed in chapter 7). The reason is that cost-based differential pricing does not discriminate on the basis of the identity of users or their specific activities (uses); instead, it discriminates based on the quantity of infrastructure use (or capacity utilized) and the marginal cost of such use,

---

[1] TIROLE (1988).

[2] For more details, see LANDSBURG 169–218 (2008); ARNOLD 492–504 (2008). Not all models lead to average cost pricing in equilibrium. BAUMOL & BLINDER 235–62 (2009).

[3] KAHN xxxvii (1998) (The "central institutional issue of public utility regulation remains . . . finding the best possible mix of inevitably imperfect regulation and inevitably imperfect competition.").

taking into account contextual details such as timing and available system capacity but not identity characteristics. To implement most forms of cost-based differential pricing, an infrastructure owner does not need to know *who is doing what*. The focus is on *when* and *how much*. In sharp contrast, price discrimination relies directly on identity characteristics that aim to best approximate individual users' subjective valuation of infrastructure use; *who* and *what* are *essential to the discrimination scheme*.

The suggested rule is both broader and narrower than the traditional common-carrier-style nondiscrimination rule for consumers. It is broader in that it does not allow for value-based discrimination, whereas common carrier rules sometimes permitted limited forms of value-based price discrimination. It is narrower in that it does not require price to be reasonable or fair. We could adjust the rule to be more or less like traditional common carriage, but such changes would not be tied to the arguments made in the previous chapter. So we will not make such adjustments as a general matter but may invoke them in certain contexts. For example, tolerating some forms of value-based discrimination might make sense where doing so demonstrably increases output and improves incentives to invest in the infrastructure. Moreover, imposing a requirement that prices be reasonable or that a provider serve all customers might make sense in cases where certain underserved populations are left behind without such a requirement.

Value-based discrimination is at the core of the rule because it is estimated appropriable value that drives private allocation, prioritization, and optimization decisions and potentially leads the infrastructure to evolve in a manner that forecloses production of various public and social goods. Disabling value-based discrimination is not costless. To the contrary, price discrimination may constitute an attractive private strategy that enables owners to increase private returns. Moreover, conventional economic analysis of price discrimination suggests that in some cases, price discrimination can improve aggregate social welfare (relative to uniform pricing) by increasing output and, by virtue of the increased private returns, improving incentives to invest in the infrastructure. Yet, like many conventional analyses of infrastructure markets, conventional economic analysis of price discrimination adopts a partial-equilibrium-style analysis, assumes away incomplete or missing markets associated with dependent public and social goods, reduces dynamic considerations about infrastructure evolution resulting from discrimination, and thus paints an incomplete picture.[4] I do not intend to challenge the substantial economics literature on price discrimination here, however. Instead, I make a few general observations.

Perfect price discrimination would eliminate many allocation concerns. Recall from chapter 2 that perfect price discrimination means that each unit of output is sold to the person that values it most and at that person's maximum willingness to pay. Thus, price would vary both by person and by unit of output, being perfectly calibrated to each

---

[4] On price discrimination through a partial equilibrium lens, see Lunney (2008).

individual's preferences. The producer would capture the entire consumer surplus. By definition, all users that desired access to the infrastructure would be given access at their respective willingness to pay, and thus deadweight losses would be eliminated. In other words, no one would be priced out: Marginal consumers would have to pay only what they would be willing to pay, constrained only by the marginal costs. Thus, if the marginal costs are zero (as in the case for nonrival infrastructure), those who would only be willing to consume the good for free would be able to do so under perfect price discrimination. Accordingly, the fact that private willingness to pay for infrastructure access does not account for spillovers from the resulting production of public and social goods is not a cause for great concern.

Despite the superficial appeal of perfect price discrimination, there are (at least) three reasons to be wary of it. First, perfect price discrimination is *not* feasible in the real world. It simply requires an inordinate amount of fine-grained information about consumers.[5] The unattainable but theoretically appealing ideal of perfect price discrimination operates more as a distracting red herring than a useful analytical baseline. Second, the path to perfect price discrimination may be fraught with peril for society. Pricing practices in many industries evolve over time.[6] When unchecked by competition or regulation, producers often drive toward price discrimination. To progress on this path, producers often depend on adapting law, technology, and other institutions to their needs. For example, to facilitate price discrimination, producers may lobby for changes in the law (for example, special legal protection for digital rights management technologies or relaxing antitrust scrutiny of patent licensing), invest in technologies (for example, deep packet inspection), or alter conventional relationships with consumers (for example, by collecting massive amounts of personally identifiable information). These steps may involve considerable social costs and unintended consequences, such as a dramatic diminution in privacy to satisfy the immense information requirements for price discrimination.[7]

Finally, perfect price discrimination would eliminate cross-subsidies that arise when infrastructure is managed as a commons. This may have dynamic effects on production of public and social goods in situations where the consumer surplus that is converted to producer surplus would otherwise be necessary to support certain productive activities by infrastructure users. This latter point is completely missing in the literature because infrastructure-dependent markets are generally assumed to be complete.

Given the unattainable nature of perfect price discrimination, the appropriate trade-off to consider is between common management and various forms of imperfect

---

[5] I suspect the further one goes down the path toward perfect price discrimination, the greater the distortions one introduces into the environment and subjects being studied.

[6] Odlyzko (2004a and 2004b).

[7] In future work I hope to explore the relationship between price discrimination and privacy. For some interesting efforts along these lines, see Odlyzko (2004b); Edwards 593–94 (2006); Fudenberg & Villas-Boas 422 (2006).

price discrimination. Imperfect price discrimination is quite common in various infrastructure industries. Second-degree price discrimination occurs when price per unit varies based on the amount purchased—for example, when bulk purchasers receive a discount. Third-degree price discrimination occurs when price per unit varies based on consumer groups—for example, when students or seniors receive a discount. Essentially, amount purchased and group identity serve as proxies for the difficult-to-obtain demand information necessary for first-degree discrimination. To implement either pricing scheme, providers must be able (1) to identify different users, segment them, and prevent arbitrage (i.e., prevent a consumer in the low-price group from reselling to a consumer in the higher-priced group, and prevent bulk purchasers from acting as resellers), or (2) to set up mechanisms that allow users to self-select into the appropriate segment (e.g., first class versus coach). These requirements entail costs, and in many cases, the feasibility and efficiency of price discrimination schemes fail because of these costs.

Economists recognize that the welfare implications of imperfect price discrimination are ambiguous and vary considerably by context.[8] In some contexts, imperfect price discrimination may increase social welfare, and in other contexts, it may decrease social welfare.[9] The trade-offs between commons management and imperfect price discrimination are best examined in particular contexts. A few general points about the nature of the trade-offs are in order.

First, a complete picture of the welfare implications of price discrimination requires further consideration of the infrastructure in question and its relationship with dependent markets and nonmarkets, both incomplete and missing. Thus, for public, social, and mixed infrastructure, the deadweight losses should not be limited to forgone consumer surplus but must also include forgone spillovers that are otherwise unaccounted for. To the traditional welfare analysis, one must add the social benefits associated with user-generated public and social goods. Those benefits may be difficult to observe and quantify, and the social demand curve based on such benefits would not necessarily take the same shape as the private demand curve, but these complications do not justify ignoring the benefits altogether. Recall from chapter 4 how the social demand curve need not take the same shape as the private demand curve. This means that the prioritization of infrastructure use that accompanies price discrimination (i.e., ranking of uses based on users' willingness to pay) can introduce distortions in the production of public and social goods.

---

[8] TIROLE 139, 149 (1988); CARLTON & PERLOFF 448–50 (1990); Armstrong & Vickers 581–83 (2001).

[9] There is an extensive literature. ROBINSON (1933); Schmalensee 242–47 (1981); Varian (1985); Varian (1996); Katz (1987); DeGraba (1990); Yoshida 240–46 (2000); Stole (2007). Given both the lack of attention to spillovers in studies concerning price discrimination and the infeasibility of perfect price discrimination, I am not willing to rely too much on the existing empirical work, which focuses on price discrimination is very particular market settings.

Second, commons management does not preclude all forms of price discrimination. Commons management precludes discriminating on the basis of the identity of the infrastructure user or use. Second-degree price discrimination, for example, may or may not run afoul of the nondiscrimination rule, depending on how the scheme operates. Third-degree price discrimination tends to categorize consumers based on their identity and thus generally conflicts with commons management. Typically, second-degree price discrimination presents all infrastructure users with the same price schedule and price variations are based on the quantity of use; users decide what to choose from the menu. This does not conflict with the commons management rule. The price schedule may differentiate among customer classes in a fashion that depends on user identity in a very coarse and attenuated sense—for example, residential, business, and industrial classes. These categories are typically based on differences in the quantity of infrastructure capacity demanded, the costs of providing service, and group elasticity of demand, meaning that those charged a higher per unit cost are less likely to alter their consumption. (*Who is doing what* is not really important to the categories or the pricing scheme; the focus is on how much capacity and at what cost.) Second-degree price discrimination of this sort is very common in infrastructure industries—for example, where the price of electricity or phone service varies nonlinearly with the amount purchased or consumed. Generally, residential consumers of electricity and phone service consume less but pay more on a per unit basis than business consumers, in part because servicing the residential consumers costs more in terms of maintaining infrastructure capacity for that group.

In the context of regulated industries, regulators have developed many sophisticated pricing mechanisms that often involve differential pricing. These pricing systems often are complemented by various forms of nondiscrimination rules (e.g., open access, interconnection, common carriage) and by additional constraints (e.g., entry and exit). The differential pricing schemes are cost-based,[10] generally do not depend on the identity of the infrastructure user or use, and do not conflict with commons management. For example, two prominent forms of differential pricing employed in traditional infrastructure industries are Ramsey pricing and variable load pricing. Both pricing systems are fundamentally designed to facilitate cost recovery in ways that are more efficient than average cost pricing, *but neither is focused on profit maximization.* Ramsey pricing (described in chapter 2) "sets prices such that the percentage deviation of price from marginal cost is inversely proportional to the price elasticity of demand."[11] While prices vary based on demand elasticity, Ramsey pricing operates under a profit constraint, which

---

[10] Most economists define price discrimination by explicitly excluding cost-based price differentials and would not describe regulatory pricing as price discrimination. Meurer (2001); TIROLE 133–34 (1988).

[11] Berry 111 (1992) (Ramsey pricing is "the second-best Pareto-optimal solution for a multi-product regulated monopoly where prices set equal to marginal costs fail to cover average costs."). Ramsey focused on the problem of optimal taxation, but economists recognize it to be the equivalent to the second-best pricing problem. Spulber 239 n.1 (1986).

minimizes distortions from prices exceeding marginal cost.[12] Variable load pricing involves varying price based on the timing of use and contemporaneous load on the resource. Such adjustments also may incorporate Ramsey pricing principles and adjust price according to differences in demand elasticity (again to minimize distortions associated with pricing above marginal cost, *not* to increase profits). One simple example of variable load pricing is peak-load pricing, which involves adjusting price during peak (high-load) and off-peak (low-load) periods. Under this pricing system, peak users bear both the marginal operating costs and the marginal capacity costs, and off-peak users bear only the marginal operating costs.

These differential pricing systems do not discriminate on the basis of the *identity* of the user or use. This should not be surprising. The systems do not involve value-based price discrimination and do not aim to increase profits by converting consumer surplus to producer surplus. These pricing systems categorically differentiate among users, but not based primarily on the users' identity or activity. The characteristics that define user categories include the quantity or volume of infrastructure capacity used, the marginal costs of providing service, and demand elasticity. Demand elasticity implicates user identity, but it is typically evaluated on a broad group basis as a means of allocating cost without affecting consumption patterns. Still, this potentially gives rise to a conflict with the rule in some contexts and may require clarification in some settings.

Disabling value-based price discrimination is not necessarily costless. It might involve a trade-off. The economics literature recognizes two principal advantages of value-based price discrimination: (1) increased output and reduced deadweight losses when compared with uniform pricing, and (2) increased profits for infrastructure providers that may improve incentives to invest in the supply, maintenance, and improvement of infrastructure.[13] Of course, neither of these potential advantages is guaranteed.[14]

---

[12] Ramsey 47, 58 (1927); Fink 363, 365 (2009) (Ramsey pricing structures "minimize the consumption distortion of above-marginal cost pricing."); Cowan 252 (2006) ("Ramsey prices . . . maximize aggregate consumer surplus subject to a constraint on the level of profits. There is no particular reason to think that uniform prices are efficient [for multiproduct monopolies] and indeed, when marginal costs and price elasticities differ across markets, price discrimination, *constrained by regulation*, will generally raise aggregate welfare.") (emphasis added).

[13] We can add a third: In some particular contexts, price discrimination may lead to increased spillovers. Price discrimination might increase welfare by (a) increasing output in a manner that leads to more spillover-generating users or (b) maintaining or even reducing output but reallocating capacity to users that generate greater net welfare because of spillovers. Both scenarios are theoretically plausible. The first scenario might involve increasing output to low willingness to pay users who happen to be the types of users that generate spillovers. The second would depend on the price discrimination scheme and how it reallocated capacity. Other complications include differentiating between the discrimination among user activities and discrimination among users within activities, which will differ with the price discrimination scheme employed. I thank Scott Hemphill for raising this point.

[14] Moreover, even if a particular price discrimination scheme provides these advantages, the scheme is not necessarily welfare enhancing. Economists recognize that increasing output is a necessary condition for price

First, whether or not value-based price discrimination increases output and reduces deadweight losses when compared with uniform pricing depends on the infrastructure in question, the price discrimination scheme employed, and other contextual factors. Second-degree price discrimination tends to generate these advantages, yet this form of price discrimination does not necessarily conflict with commons management. Third-degree price discrimination tends to conflict with commons management, and the welfare implications of third-degree price discrimination are generally more ambiguous.[15]

Second, whether or not increased profits from value-based price discrimination improve incentives to invest and the supply of infrastructure also depends on the infrastructure in question, the price discrimination scheme employed, and other contextual factors. For some traditional infrastructure involving (a) investments with very high fixed costs and (b) long-term, irreversible commitments by investors and by the affected community, imperfect value-based price discrimination might be necessary to cover total costs. We should expect to observe such pricing practices within partially regulated industries where price regulation has been removed (deregulated) and imperfectly competitive markets where price taking, consumer switching, and (potential) competition are insufficient constraints on pricing practices. It is often asserted that price discrimination serves as an efficient means for cost recovery and privately financing infrastructure.

Thus, commons management rules may threaten to foreclose a preferred method for recovering costs in some infrastructure industries. But the threat must not be overstated. There is no doubt that precluding infrastructure owners from engaging in discrimination, prioritization, or optimization of the infrastructure that they own often affects incentives to invest, but as always, the question is to what degree and in comparison with what alternatives. Put simply, *the additional private returns from price discrimination may be the difference between attractive and unattractive investments in some settings, but certainly not always and not nearly as often as claimed.* Here are three of the reasons for skepticism of such claims:

- In many, if not most, contexts, average cost pricing is a reasonable means of recovering costs and ought to be the relevant supply-side benchmark. Cost-based differential pricing, such as variable load pricing, may improve the efficiency with which average costs are recovered, but it does not entail increasing the ratio of producer-to-consumer surplus to improve incentives to invest. If an infrastructure project cannot be justified based on recovering average costs, it is

---

discrimination to increase welfare, but it is not a sufficient condition. *See, e.g.,* Varian (1985). As Cowan 420 (2007) explains: "The problem with the output test is that it does not always produce conclusive results. When output is known to increase, this does not imply that welfare rises because an output increase is necessary for welfare to rise, but not sufficient." Cowan examines how the welfare implications of price discrimination depend on demand and the curvature of the demand function. *Id.*

[15] Schmalensee (1981); Armstrong & Vickers 581–83 (2001); TIROLE 139, 149 (1988).

difficult to explain why the project should be undertaken, unless one accounts for spillovers.[16]

- In many contexts, infrastructure owners may be unregulated monopolists capable of securing monopoly rents (via a uniform price), and this is usually a sufficient inducement for investment in infrastructure.[17]

- In both of these contexts, the additional gains in terms of supply-side incentives derived from imperfect value-based price discrimination may be minimal, and thus the impact of a nondiscrimination rule on incentives may be minimal. This point should not be understood to mean that infrastructure providers' gains are minimal. The gains may be substantial but not relevant to the incentive to invest in the undertaking. There is a mistaken tendency to believe that any gain in profits corresponds to an equal or proportional gain in investment incentives, but this belief oversimplifies the decision-making process and underlying economics and ignores the relevance of alternative opportunities for investment.[18] The conversion of consumer surplus to producer surplus may be a mere wealth transfer with no meaningful impact on producers' investment incentives, or it may be otherwise, but there is no theoretical or empirical basis for assuming that producer gains from discrimination are incentive-relevant. Moreover, the promise of substantial gains above and beyond total cost may lead to wasteful rent dissipation.

Unfortunately, the claim that commons management will dramatically reduce incentives to invest in infrastructure is frequently made and left unchallenged in policy debates. It is all too easy to assume the worst-case scenario in terms of the alleged impacts of nondiscrimination rules on cost recovery and incentives. Commons management does not conflict with most forms of cost-based price discrimination, and it does not interfere with incentives as dramatically as is often alleged. Moreover, to the extent that supply-side incentives are an obstacle, there may be alternative means for dealing with the issues. Chapter 8 examines these issues in more detail.

B. Commons Management and Price Regulation

Price regulation is practiced in many infrastructure industries, and thus we briefly examine how nondiscrimination relates to price regulation. There are two points to make clear: First, commons management does not conflict with price regulation or the types of cost-based differential pricing practiced in regulated industries. Second, although

---

[16] See chapter 8 for more details. There are some practical difficulties with implementing average cost pricing.

[17] See chapter 8.

[18] For an explanation, see Frischmann & Lemley (2007).

nondiscrimination rules and price regulation may complement each other, one does not necessitate the other.

When infrastructure markets are noncompetitive, nondiscrimination rules may be accompanied by price regulation, at least in many traditional infrastructure industries. There is a substantial economics literature on the advantages and disadvantages of price regulation, the upshot of which is that price regulation typically involves a considerable regulatory apparatus, is very costly to administer, provides significant opportunities for regulatory capture and gaming, and is generally disfavored. Deregulation efforts worldwide have focused considerable attention on transitioning from rate-of-return–style price regulation to incentive-based price regulation to unregulated market pricing.

Modern price regulation is fundamentally guided by cost-based pricing principles. The regulatory objective is to approximate prices that would emerge in a competitive market, taking into account the special characteristics of infrastructure. This means that average cost pricing is the baseline, along with a profit constraint. Regulators who employ classic rate-of-return regulation, for example, impose such a constraint by regulating the rate of return on capital. Rate-of-return regulation depends heavily on detailed and constant information about costs and requires substantial interaction between regulators and regulated entities. Not surprisingly, this can lead to gaming, cost inflation, and regulatory capture.

A widely employed alternative to rate-of-return regulation is price-cap regulation, which sets a cap on prices that includes an adjustment factor.[19] Price caps are typically cost-based and effectively constrain profits, but price caps include pricing flexibility to create incentives for providers to reduce costs. As a result, price caps also involve flexibility with respect to rate of return and introduce potential risk for firms (e.g., if costs increase) and potential gains (e.g., if costs decrease). Cost savings achieved by a producer may lead to positive profits, but those are constrained by the adjustment factor and the frequency with which rates are reviewed. Compared with rate-of-return regulation, price-cap regulation improves incentives of regulated entities to be more efficient—for example, by improving productivity or innovating to reduce costs and capture the savings.[20] The overarching objective is minimizing cost while enabling cost recovery.

The primary industries subject to price regulation are natural monopoly industries, typically traditional infrastructure such as electricity and gas transmission, fixed telecommunications, and railways.[21] In such contexts, price regulation is justified in large part by concerns about the economic consequences of monopoly, such as deadweight losses

---

[19] Gönenç et al. 30–31 (2001); Cowan 249–52 (2006).

[20] In practice, price cap regulation may mimic rate of return regulation, particularly if the time period between regulatory reviews is short. Gönenç et al. 30–31 (2001); Cowan 251 (2006).

[21] Gönenç et al. 33 (2001); Cowan 248 (2006).

associated with monopoly pricing. Not surprisingly, public utility regulation and similar regulatory regimes often involve both price regulation and nondiscrimination rules.

Open access and interconnection regulations[22] often go hand in hand with a form of price regulation called access pricing. Access pricing begins with cost-based principles, such as "long-run average incremental costs" incurred by the incumbent provider. The basic idea is to enable entry or facilitate interconnection while supporting the incumbent's ability to recover its costs. As with rate-of-return regulation, difficulties in estimating and attributing costs have led to a variety of more sophisticated approaches, including the use of Ramsey pricing to distribute costs while minimizing distortions from setting prices above marginal costs. A considerable literature in economics addresses these issues.

The bottom line for our purposes is that, while heavily criticized, price regulation remains integral in many traditional infrastructure industries. The approaches regulators take to price regulation vary considerably and are being adjusted through reform efforts. Still, the basic pricing principle underneath all of the complex methodology and difficult accounting is cost recovery. Commons management does not conflict in any meaningful way with that principle or price regulation as it is practiced in most regulatory settings.

When infrastructure markets are noncompetitive and unregulated, imposing a nondiscrimination rule may lead infrastructure owners to charge consumers the monopoly price. The other obvious alternatives are average or marginal cost, but there is no reason for profit-maximizing infrastructure owners to choose those other options unless some other constraint operates.[23] In this setting, there is nothing inherently wrong with charging the monopoly price. Society would be better off in the short run if prices were lower and deadweight losses reduced, but from a long-run perspective, society may be willing to tolerate monopoly prices and may even be better off for doing so. The prospect of monopoly rents may induce innovation and ex ante investments, and monopoly prices also may attract entrants and investments in disruptive innovations.[24] One should not assume that imposing a nondiscrimination rule in noncompetitive and unregulated

---

[22] Open access and interconnection regulations are quite different. Open-access regulations generally involve efforts to stimulate entry by ensuring entrants nondiscriminatory access to an incumbent's facilities. Interconnection generally involves coordination among different providers of infrastructural services, often (a) through a standardized interface, (b) in a networked environment, (c) involving the exchange of traffic, and/or (d) in different markets or geographic regions. Werbach 1275–79 (2007).

[23] "[T]here is often much more involved in context that will constrain the monopolist's ability actually to charge the monopoly price—for example, existing regulation, contractual (RAND-like) commitments, or even the EU's explicit concern with fair and reasonable pricing." Frischmann & Waller 29, n.84 (2008).

[24] Verizon Communs., Inc. v. Law Offices of Curtis V. Trinko, LLP, 540 U.S. 398, 407–08 (2004) ("The opportunity to charge monopoly prices—at least for a short period—is what attracts 'business acumen' in the first place; it induces risk taking that produces innovation and economic growth.").

infrastructure markets must be accompanied by price regulation.[25] In some settings, the two regulations operate effectively together, and in other settings, price regulation is not needed. It depends on a variety of factors and trade-offs associated with price regulation in general and the particular infrastructure market.

Some claim that implementing a nondiscrimination rule necessarily requires price regulation, either by a regulatory agency or by the courts.[26] Such claims are hyperbolic and misleading. It is true that where nondiscrimination rules apply, there is a restriction on pricing practices (or the supposed "freedom" to price), and someone must evaluate claims of discrimination and conduct an inquiry into pricing practices. But this is not price regulation as conventionally understood.[27] In fact, determining whether an infrastructure provider has discriminated on the basis of identity characteristics is the type of inquiry courts undertake regularly in a variety of settings, including "civil rights, employment discrimination, common carrier duties, licensing decisions, school segregation, prison conditions, access to health care, and numerous other areas of the law."[28] Such an inquiry does not necessitate reliance on the elaborate regulatory regimes.[29] In some industries—for example, in classic public utility markets—regulatory agencies may be better equipped than courts to apply the nondiscrimination rule. This raises an important question of comparative institutional competence.[30] But the bottom line, for our purposes, is that nondiscrimination does not require price regulation, nor should it be equated with price regulation. In some contexts, price regulation may be a potentially

---

[25] The nondiscrimination rule may constrain the distortionary impact of the monopoly to the infrastructure market (rather than dependent markets) and to the form of price (rather than priority/quality), and as a result, it may "force a sort of transparency that provides better signals regarding the need for price regulation or even government provision/subsidization of infrastructure expansion." Frischmann & Waller 29, n.84 (2008). The threat of regulation or government entry alone may serve as a pricing constraint.

[26] This concern is frequently raised in the network neutrality debate. See, e.g., Hahn & Wallsten 1 (2006) ("'[N]et neutrality' is actually a friendly-sounding name for price regulation. We fear that such regulation could substantially reduce investment incentives, distort innovation, and ultimately harm consumers. The government must weigh policy choices carefully: are the benefits of price regulation likely to exceed its costs? We believe that the history of price regulation clearly teaches us that the answer is likely to be no (see, for example, Paul Joskow and Roger Noll's overview of regulation)."). Adam Thierer similarly suggests that the "real Net Neutrality debate" is about choosing between "price flexibility versus price regulation." Thierer (2005). He also seems to suggest that nondiscrimination rules require price regulation to be effective: "[I]n practice, common carriage law is toothless without price regulation." *Id.*

[27] I acknowledge that there is necessarily a restriction on pricing flexibility, but conflating such a restriction with price regulation and then appealing to the lessons learned from the history of price regulation is a misleading rhetorical move. Moreover, it is worth noting that there are competing views within economics on the "lessons to be learned" from the history of price regulation. See, e.g., Cowan 257 (2006) (noting that price cap regulation has been "successful in encouraging operating efficiency in regulated utilities" and "in general investment incentives in the UK and USA have not been dented").

[28] Frischmann & Waller 41–42 (2008)

[29] Frischmann and Waller (2008).

[30] KOMESAR (2001); KOMESAR (1994).

attractive complement to a nondiscrimination rule because it may push prices toward average cost pricing rather than monopoly pricing, but that involves a policy choice above and beyond the decision to impose a nondiscrimination rule.

C. Subsidies, Marginal Cost Pricing, and the Marginal Cost Controversy

This section examines infrastructure pricing and subsidies. It focuses on the Marginal Cost Controversy, a famous debate in economics between Harold Hotelling and Ronald Coase over the wisdom of Hotelling's suggestion that government should subsidize the fixed costs of certain public utilities to keep price at marginal cost.[31] The discussion dovetails with the previous two sections. It builds from the critical observation that in some contexts, commons management alone may be insufficient to achieve the social value of open infrastructure. The reason is simple: Commons management alone says nothing about the *magnitude* of prices.[32] For many infrastructure resources, prices may be well above marginal costs. When pricing above marginal cost generates substantial deadweight losses, especially when extended to include lost spillovers, subsidies may be an attractive complement to consider.

In the early to mid-twentieth century, economists debated whether marginal cost pricing should be the goal. The magnitude of prices was at the heart of the debate. Although the debate involved many major economists, it can be summarized briefly and reasonably in terms of the debate between two famous economists, Harold Hotelling and Ronald Coase.[33]

In 1938, Hotelling argued in favor of marginal cost pricing. Specifically, he argued that "the optimum of the general welfare corresponds to the sale of everything at marginal cost" and that general government revenues should "be applied to cover the fixed costs of electric power plants, waterworks, railroad, and other industries in which the fixed costs are large, so as to reduce to the level of marginal cost the prices charged for the services and products of these industries."[34]

---

[31] The debate involved many economists. Ruggles (1949) (reviewing debate).

[32] A monopolist infrastructure owner constrained only by a nondiscrimination rule presumably would charge the monopoly price. In a competitive market, infrastructure owners constrained only by a nondiscrimination rule presumably would set prices approximating average costs. As discussed in the previous section, in some industries, price regulation may push monopoly pricing toward average cost pricing. Given the cost structure of supply, there is no reason to think that private infrastructure owners would set the price at marginal cost, whether or not the owners are required to conform to a nondiscrimination rule. See chapter 8 for more details.

[33] Duffy (2004); Hotelling (1938); Coase (1946); Ruggles (1949); Baumol & Bradford (1970); LERNER (1944); Meade (1944); Coase (1947).

[34] Duffy 37 (2004) (quoting Hotelling 242 (1938)).

Hotelling's argument can be simplified as follows: The economic baseline for efficiency is marginal cost pricing because that would equate marginal benefits to marginal costs, the result expected for perfectly competitive markets. But public utilities involve very high fixed costs that would not be recovered under marginal cost pricing, and therefore we would need to resort to average cost pricing. But any deviation from marginal cost pricing will have deadweight losses. Thus, Hotelling offered government subsidization of the fixed cost component as a solution that would enable marginal cost pricing throughout the economy.

In his 1946 article *The Marginal Cost Controversy*, Coase responded critically to Hotelling, suggesting that Hotelling proposal "would bring about a maldistribution of the factors of production, a maldistribution of income and probably a loss similar to that which the scheme was designed to avoid." Coase articulated the following five arguments:[35]

1. Marginal cost pricing eliminates or at least truncates demand signals, significantly reducing the available information necessary for investment decisions about how much infrastructure to build, where to build it, when to add capacity, and so on. (This critique concerns an intramarket distortion originating on the demand side of the infrastructure market.)

2. Relying on the government to subsidize the fixed cost component in decreasing-cost industries raises significant concerns about institutional competence. How will the government know *when* and *who* and *how much* to subsidize? How will the government determine *what* costs constitute the fixed costs? Coase was skeptical of rote confidence in government institutions, and both in his reply to Hotelling and in much of his other writing, Coase challenged economists to evaluate critically any claims that relied on the expertise, competence, and benevolence/public-mindedness of government officials.

3. Relying on the government to subsidize the fixed costs also raises serious concerns about distortions caused by government taxation. Hotelling discussed a number of different means for raising revenue and argued that income taxation would be superior, but Coase challenged this view. The revenue needed to carry out Hotelling's proposal would be substantial, and Coase maintained that the impact of increasing income or other taxes to raise such revenue could not be ignored. (This critique concerns a more general economy-wide distortion originating from taxation.)

4. Relying on government taxation and spending also raises concerns about interpersonal comparisons and redistribution of wealth from the general population to public utility consumers. Hotelling acknowledged that the scheme

---

[35] Other economists raised many of the same arguments. Ruggles (1949).

would have distributional effects. Indeed, various economists criticized marginal cost pricing because of difficulties with interpersonal comparisons. For example, Pegrum noted that the consumers who benefit under the scheme were not necessarily identical to the taxpayers who paid for the fixed costs.[36] (This critique overlaps with the previous one but also raises distinct distributional concerns.)

5. Coase pointed to alternative institutional arrangements that relied on private rather than government pricing. Specifically, Coase noted that multipart pricing or Ramsey pricing would allow for average cost recovery while minimizing the distortions from pricing above marginal cost. This alternative would retain market-based demand signals and generate better information to guide investments.[37]

In a more recent article, Duffy summarized the outcome of the debate:

> Modern regulatory policy generally accepts that a declining average cost industry—that is, a so-called "natural monopoly"—will not have its fixed costs subsidized from general government revenues and that therefore the industry must be allowed to price above marginal cost so that it can cover its fixed costs. The rejection of the Hotelling thesis is so complete that reputable economics encompasses the very opposite of Hotelling's view—"that, generally, prices which deviate in a systematic manner from marginal costs will be required for an optimal allocation of resources, even in the absence of externalities." Indeed, in the parlance of public utility regulation, the very phrase "marginal cost pricing" now refers not to Hotelling's proposed marginal cost pricing and subsidy scheme, but rather to a pricing system akin to the "multi-part" pricing system that Coase advocated as the more efficient alternative to Hotelling's proposal. In short, modern public utility theorists generally do not recommend using pervasive public subsidies to chase the Holy Grail of global marginal cost pricing.[38]

As Duffy makes clear, Hotelling's argument sparked considerable commentary and debate but ultimately was found unpersuasive. The arguments marshaled by Coase not only succeeded in this particular debate but more generally serve as part of the foundation for modern economics, particularly institutional, regulatory, and public choice economics as well as law and economics.

---

[36] Pegrum 60–63 (1944).

[37] Coase advocated cost-based differential pricing rather than value-based price discrimination. He criticized Nordin for misreading his work to conclude that Coase favored value-based price discrimination. Coase (1947).

[38] Duffy (2004) (quoting Baumol & Bradford 265 (1970)).

Coase's arguments apply well to commercial infrastructure. For commercial infrastructure, the price mechanism works rather well in directing investments and indicating demand. The first and second arguments listed above emphasize the demand-side problems associated with relying on government to choose which commercial infrastructures to subsidize. Government intervention not only would distort demand signals within an existing infrastructure market but also, and perhaps more importantly, would disrupt private decision making, planning, and investment in yet-to-be-discovered and discovered-but-yet-to-be-built infrastructure markets.[39] From a static efficiency perspective focused on a given public utility, Hotelling's argument may seem quite strong, but the strength of the argument wanes when generalized, approached from a dynamic efficiency perspective, and applied to a range of potential infrastructure projects. Moreover, to the extent that deadweight losses from pricing above marginal cost are the economic problem to solve, private firms, and public regulators in some contexts, have reasonably attractive alternatives to employ. Finally, it is also worth noting that the third and fourth arguments are relevant and suggest the need for some additional justification for imposing costs on the general public beyond reducing the deadweight losses for a set of potential infrastructure users.

The five arguments described above remain relevant and important, but despite the strength of Coase's arguments with respect to commercial infrastructure, they may be less persuasive for public, social, and mixed infrastructure. In the remainder of this section, I do not go as far as Hotelling did in his argument for marginal cost pricing throughout the economy. My goal is much more modest.

I suggest only that government subsidies that aim to push prices toward marginal cost may be economically defensible for public, social, and mixed infrastructure, particularly when such infrastructure is subject to a commons management rule and the infrastructure market is not competitive. The basic reason is that government subsidy may dramatically lessen deadweight losses and indirectly subsidize a wide variety of public and social goods.

Coase's arguments work well for commercial infrastructure because that economic setting best reflects the assumptions underlying Coase's analysis. The Hotelling-Coase debate takes place (largely) in terms of partial-equilibrium-style analysis. Both participants acknowledged the need to consider the impacts of taxation on the economy, recognizing that other sectors of the economy might be affected by decisions made in the sector under consideration. But neither considered how the pricing of infrastructure would impact the more immediate infrastructure-dependent markets. Those markets

---

[39] Mandel (2008).

were assumed to be complete and fully functional, with externalities assumed away. This is appropriate for commercial infrastructure resources, which serve as inputs for a wide variety of private goods and services.

If we relax the assumption of complete markets, refrain from focusing myopically on commercial infrastructure, and instead consider public or social infrastructure, the case for marginal cost pricing coupled with government subsidization of fixed costs takes on a different form than it does in the argument articulated by Hotelling. If the infrastructure market in question is competitive and subject to a commons management rule, we might presume average cost pricing pricing, perhaps modified by some cost-based differential pricing scheme if feasible. If the infrastructure market in question is not competitive and is subject to a commons management rule, we might presume pricing above average cost, perhaps monopoly pricing.[40] In either scenario, the case for government subsidization of fixed costs to drive prices to marginal costs may be attractive for (at least) two reasons: (1) Hotelling's concern with deadweight losses associated with pricing above marginal cost may become even more pressing, and (2) Coase's argument about demand signals being distorted may cut in the opposite direction—in favor of Hotelling.

Recall the earlier discussion about how social demand may deviate from private demand for public and social infrastructure because of various types of externalities generated by infrastructure users. To the extent that infrastructure users are priced out of the infrastructure market, which may be quite substantial for monopoly pricing, the relevant social losses include not only the forgone consumers but also the forgone spillovers, thus affecting the magnitude of the deadweight losses in a more complicated fashion than ordinarily assumed. In either scenario, exclusive reliance on demand signals generated by the market would involve reliance on already truncated demand signals (private demand in lieu of social demand), which could lead to a misallocation of infrastructure (via pricing or prioritization) among downstream markets.[41] Marginal cost pricing would not improve demand signals by bringing additional information to the table; however, it would eliminate the false sense of security associated with market pricing and would push toward different, potentially more coarse, mechanisms for assessing infrastructure

---

[40] We could complicate the analysis with alternative market structures and pricing models, but doing so would add little.

[41] Inderset and Shaffer suggest that price discrimination in intermediate good markets can improve welfare where the discriminating intermediate good supplier effectively selects or prioritizes "more efficient" or more productive downstream purchasers (or dependent markets). This argument makes sense where the downstream markets are complete and private demand provides the best information about how to allocate the input—for example, in the commercial infrastructure context—but the argument may cut in the opposite direction where private demand systematically distorts—for example, in the context of public or social infrastructure. Inderst & Shaffer (2009).

demand—for example, on a group, community, or societal basis.[42] Moreover, government subsidization of infrastructure coupled with commons management may alleviate pressure on government to identify and direct subsidies to various producers of public and social goods. In other words, pursuing Hotelling's strategy with respect to public and social infrastructure may focus government on more "upstream," basic investments that enable and support social systems, rather than more applied (or final) public and social goods and services. Government may be more competent in identifying and managing such investments, although that proposition is certainly subject to debate.

Furthermore, with respect to justification, the spillover effects from public and social infrastructure often involve benefits that flow to non-users. This suggests that while Hotelling's marginal cost pricing proposal imposes costs on the general public by taxation, it also may confer general welfare benefits as well, thus weakening Coase's fourth argument noted above. In fact, Hotelling seemed to believe the fourth objection (interpersonal comparison and redistribution from the general public to infrastructure users) was insufficient, for two reasons: First, general welfare would increase under marginal cost pricing, and second, there might be spillovers from the public investment that benefited those non-users who had to bear some of the fixed costs. His argument coincides with the idea of indirectly subsidizing public and social goods through public investments in infrastructure. Unfortunately, Hotelling did not make this argument forcefully or very clearly.

To illustrate his marginal cost pricing proposal, Hotelling used the example of the costs and benefits of introducing cheap electricity to a region. Although cheap electrification might have the effect of raising the region's economy so much that the benefits received by individual residents could far exceed the costs of development, it might not be possible to cover the total costs via lump-sum taxes on local inhabitants. Thus, he argued that, given the large-scale positive externalities the electrification would generate, it would be better to sell the electricity at its marginal cost and make up the difference from revenues derived from other parts of the country. Hotelling defended this recommendation by pointing out that the project's positive benefits would not be confined to that region alone and that when many such projects are viewed as a whole, their widespread effects would benefit the entire country.[43]

This section revisited the Marginal Cost Controversy and opened a line of inquiry. Many readers of my prior work on this topic have suggested that commons management

---

[42] Hotelling 247–48 (1938) (deciding whether demand was sufficient to justify the costs of building a bridge "would be a matter of estimation of vehicular and pedestrian traffic originating and terminating in particular zones, with a comparison of distances by alternative routes in each case, and an evaluation of the savings in each class of movement").

[43] Ruggles 108–09 (1949).

alone is an insufficient intervention to achieve the social value of open infrastructure because if such a rule is imposed, prices will skyrocket to the monopoly price in many infrastructure industries. Of course, it depends on whether there are any constraints on pricing—for instance, competition or regulation. Nonetheless, in many cases, the magnitude of price may be as important as, if not more important than, the uniformity of price, in which case revisiting the Marginal Cost Controversy may be necessary.

7

MANAGING CONGESTION

CHAPTERS 5 AND 6 assumed pure nonrivalry and infinite capacity for shared use. This assumption allowed us to focus on what nonrivalry enables and how commons management may be an attractive private or public strategy to leverage nonrivalry and encourage productive activities and spillovers. I put aside two complications addressed in this and the following chapter. This chapter considers partially (non)rival infrastructure and congestion. Chapter 8 considers supply-side incentives and problems that may arise with sustaining investments in infrastructure subject to commons management.

Recall from chapter 3: (Non)rivalrousness is a characteristic that measures the degree to which one user's consumption of a resource directly affects another user's present consumption possibilities. It describes a continuum. Pure nonrivalrous consumption describes the situation "when a unit of [a] good can be consumed by one individual without detracting, in the slightest, from the consumption opportunities still available to others from that same unit."[1] Pure rivalrous consumption describes the situation when consumption of a unit of a good by one individual necessarily detracts from the consumption opportunities still available to others from that same unit. Resources do not necessarily have a single degree of (non)rivalrousness. In fact, many resources are partially (non)rival, meaning the degree and rate of rivalry may vary across time, among users and uses, or across contexts. In contrast with pure nonrivalrous resources, partially

---

[1] CORNES & SANDLER 8 (1996).

(non)rival resources generally have finite capacity and are potentially renewable, sharable, and congestible. Complicated trade-offs arise in managing the boundary between rivalrous and nonrivalrous consumption. This chapter considers these trade-offs.

For partially (non)rival infrastructure, leveraging nonrivalry may depend on managing congestion (potential rivalry). Commons management often remains an attractive and viable option, but we need to consider and compare different institutional solutions to congestion problems. In some settings, a commons management rule might need to be adapted to better manage the boundary between rivalrous and nonrivalous consumption.

A. Partially (Non)rival Infrastructure and the Congestion Problem

There are various types of purely nonrival infrastructure, such as intellectual infrastructure like basic research, languages, and infrastructural ideas, as well as social infrastructure like rules of law and community norms. But the assumption of pure nonrivalry does not hold for many infrastructure resources, including most traditional infrastructure.

Indeed, many infrastructure resources have finite capacity and are partially (non)rivalrous. Partially (non)rival goods are durable goods that have finite, *potentially* renewable, and *potentially* sharable capacity. The marginal cost of allowing an additional person to access and use the resource may be zero over some range of demand but not over all demand. As a result, the resource is congestible, though not necessarily congested. Further, it may be physically depreciable, which means there may be some resource exhaustion or depletion at a rate that does not immediately transform the infrastructure or impose costs on other users but still may reduce its capacity and require maintenance or replenishment over time.[2] For infrastructural lakes and highways, the Internet, and other partially (non)rival infrastructure, nondiscriminatory sharing is technically feasible and may be socially desirable, depending on careful consideration of potential congestion and the need to manage the boundary between nonrivalrous and rivalrous consumption.

For many partially (non)rival infrastructure resources, the boundary between nonrivalrous and rivalrous consumption is crossed regularly over time, sometimes according to predictable time patterns. At any particular time, the marginal cost of allowing an additional person to access and use the resource may depend on the number of users and available capacity. Highways, in real space and cyberspace, offer excellent illustrations. During off-peak hours (imagine traffic at 2 a.m.), consumption of these resources is

---

[2] Most partially (non)rival infrastructure resources depreciate with use; they are subject to ordinary "wear and tear" and need to be maintained over time to remain useful. Such depreciation ordinarily does not rise to the level of congestion, such that a user's consumption directly impacts another user's consumption opportunity within a relevant timeframe, but it does raise a cost allocation issue and potentially raises a risk to the sustainability of the infrastructure over the long run.

often nonrivalrous. At these times, users do not impose costs on other users and the marginal cost of allowing an additional person to use the resource is zero. But nonrivalrous consumption turns rivalrous at rush hour, when congestion problems arise.

Congestion on the highway or on the Internet is a function of variable demand on a system with finite renewable capacity. As a general matter, congestion dissipates over time and the capacity of the resource is renewed. Thus, it is not permanently depleted unless the system is overwhelmed and crashes. Some infrastructure resources, such as the power distribution system, are more vulnerable to "instability, cascading failures, or collapse."[3] The devastating economic and social consequences of blackouts from such failures attest to the important governance, design, and investment issues these resources present. But even short of catastrophic failures, persistent congestion or traffic jams can give rise to substantial costs. Congestion leads not only to direct costs associated with inefficient use of the congested infrastructure and the immediate costs for frustrated users but also to substantial indirect economic and social costs associated with impacts on productive activities in dependent systems. Prior chapters emphasized the positive externalities from infrastructure use, but negative externalities also arise, for example, when congestion arises and retards productive activities.

The basic congestion problem involves a situation in which demand exceeds available supply. In other words, capacity is scarce. In some situations, congestion may be tolerable and may not be worth addressing, and in other situations, congestion needs to be addressed. Congestion problems often depend on contextual details about the nature of the resource, the community of potential users, the range and nature of potential resource uses, and interdependencies among uses.

One way to conceptualize the congestion problem is in terms of the *tragedy of the commons* story.[4] Assume a partially (non)rival resource, such as a meadow or a highway, is shared freely without restriction. That is, assume the resource is presumptively open to all comers and there is no mechanism for coordinating the actions of resource users, such as owners of sheep or automobiles. Consumption may remain nonrivalrous if, for example, the population is small and the resource capacity is large. Yet in many situations, the straightforward prediction is that the resource is likely to be overconsumed because individual users rationally decide to use the resource at a rate and in a manner that maximizes private gains but disregards the effects that such use has on other users or more generally on the sustainability of the resource. Herders maximize the size of their own flocks and graze the shared meadow to a degree that maximizes their individual returns,

---

[3] Wilson 1302 (2002) (discussing technological transmission constraints and vulnerability to "instability, cascading failures, or collapse at great cost").

[4] Hardin (1968). The "tragedy of the commons" model is useful, but reality often is much more complicated than the model suggests. Ostrom (2007). When a series of specific assumptions hold and fully describe the resource setting, the model predictions map well to reality and experimental results. But this is an exceptional result, rather than the norm. *Id.*

and drivers plan their trips in terms of timing, routes, frequency, and so on with only their self-interest in mind. If each individual acts in such a fashion, then the aggregate consumption may exceed the threshold for nonrivalrous consumption. This may lead to congestion, in the form of crowding, increased waiting time in queues, slower service, pollution, noise, reduced quality of service due to increased interruptions of service, and so on.[5] It may lead to rapid depreciation and depletion of the shared resource. For many resources, such as a meadow, unconstrained consumption is not sustainable and can lead to ruin. Hardin labeled this "the tragedy of the commons" because of these socially harmful consequences. At its core, the tragedy of the commons illustrates a standard externality problem that manifests in a failure of collective action.[6] Avoiding tragedy requires collective action in one form or another to manage use of the shared resource. Broadly speaking, two classic economic solutions aimed at internalizing the externality are government regulation and allocating private property rights. A third important solution involves community management, which may entail reliance on social norms or the formation of a club.[7] One common feature among the institutions is the introduction of constraints on consumption.

Congestion *may* involve an externality, where individual users do not account for the congestion costs imposed on other users as a result of their consumption decisions. Congestion externalities arise when the marginal social cost exceeds the marginal private cost and the reason for the cost divergence is related to competing uses of scarce resource capacity. Congestion externalities are necessarily related to costs associated with rivalrous uses of resource capacity. Like network effects, congestion effects arise among users and do not implicate non-users. Thus, external harms realized by non-users are not congestion externalities, nor are costs arising from interpersonal preferences, such as a preference for other users to have certain personal attributes.

It is a mistake to assume that observed congestion necessarily involves an externality, much less an externality that ought to be internalized. First, internalization does not mean elimination of congestion. Observed congestion may remain even when congestion costs have been internalized. In many cases, consumers prefer a congested infrastructure to an uncongested one, perhaps preferring to pay less in money (e.g., tolls, taxes) and more in reduced quality (e.g., waiting time, service interruptions). Consumers choose different levels of congestion for a variety of services, including more or less crowded

---

[5] Cornes and Sandler list a variety of different forms of congestion, including, among others, "greater accident rates on highways, higher bacteria counts in swimming pools, . . . and increased noise levels at public performances." CORNES & SANDLER 348 (1996). They equate congestion with crowding and also explain that congestion can be analyzed in terms of externalities or as a public bad.

[6] EASTMAN 749–51 (1997); OLSON 2 (1965); OSTROM 99–100 (1998).

[7] See various works of Elinor Ostrom. See also Madison, Frischmann, & Strandburg (2010).

restaurants, shopping centers, and Internet service providers.[8] Individuals may not directly account for the direct costs imposed on others as a result of each particular consumption decision, but congestion effects may be shared in a reciprocal manner, and market pricing may indirectly account for the costs of congestion—particularly in cases where infrastructure owners are able to employ congestion pricing, which is discussed below. As Richard Cornes and Todd Sandler point out, "Congestion is not something that must be completely eliminated; rather an optimal level of congestion must be found."[9] Second, for the reasons discussed in chapter 3, internalization may not be worth it; the social costs of internalization may exceed the benefits.

It is helpful to compare congestion with network effects. Both congestion and network effects arise as a result of consumption decisions. Network effects arise when a user's utility function responds positively to an increase in the number of other users. The telephone system is a classic example of a system exhibiting network effects: An increase in the number of users connected to the system increases the value realized by individual users via an increase in the potential number of people users may communicate with using the system. Congestion effects, on the other hand, arise from the manner in which a user's utility function responds negatively to an increase in the number of other users. In a sense, both types of effects are related to the number of consumption opportunities available to demanding users. For network effects, the number of opportunities increases with the number of users; for congestion effects, the number of opportunities decreases with the number of users because of rivalrousness and possibly even depletion. Whether these effects constitute externalities depends on whether the relevant benefits or costs are priced or otherwise reflected in market transactions. Network effects tend to increase consumers' willingness to pay for access to the resource; economists assume that consumers generally appreciate the value created by network effects and thus are willing to pay more for access to the larger network. Over time, this may lead to the internalization of some network externalities as network providers adjust prices. Congestion effects may be internalized in a similar fashion as the market evolves. Consumers' willingness to pay may adjust to congestion, and over time market prices may reflect the direct costs of congestion, particularly when markets are competitive.

There is an important difference between congestion and network effects, however, and that is the immediate impact of congestion on capacity. Network effects are pure demand-side effects and are not consumptive, while congestion directly affects available supply. While congestion may lead to demand-side adjustments in consumers' willingness

---

[8] In infrastructure industries, there is not always a viable option to choose between congested and uncongested, and we must be careful to avoid ascribing preferences to consumers where none have been revealed. In the road congestion literature, some argue that congestion is a tremendous economic and social problem in desperate need of solution; others argue that the problem is slight, if it is truly a problem at all, because people do not want to pay in taxes or tolls what it would take to fix the problem.

[9] CORNES & SANDLER 524–25 (1996).

to pay and thus could lead to the internalization of some congestion externalities, dynamic supply issues still remain important, as seen below. Efficient use of the resource at a given time as well as sustaining the resource over time may require more targeted interventions to manage congestion.

B. Conventional Approaches to Managing Congestion

There are many different approaches to managing congestion, each of which has its advantages and disadvantages and fits different contexts better than others. Decades of economic and engineering research has focused on congestion problems and potential solutions, and to date, there is no panacea. Congestion seems to be a persistent, inevitable part of modern society.

The basic economic model of congestion assumes homogenous uses.[10] The shared meadow is used for grazing sheep (not for grazing other animals or for other activities); the shared highway is used to complete trips (in more or less identical vehicles). When considering homogenous use, economists utilize a congestion cost function that relates the marginal social cost of infrastructure use (e.g., feeding sheep, completing a trip) to utilization rates (traffic) and resource capacity (e.g., acreage, number of lanes). Economists refer to such congestion as "anonymous crowding" because the determinants of crowding are utilization and facility size, and attributes of individual users play no part in the equation.[11] Resource management options focus on the three interdependent dimensions of the problem—resource capacity, membership size, and external costs. For example, internalization of external costs through taxes, user fees, or private property rights may be unnecessary and overly costly when the user population is small or excess capacity is large, but the situation may change as the population grows.[12]

The following chart frames the discussion that follows by identifying a contributing cause of the congestion problem to be targeted and the associated approach to managing congestion.

Target Variable / Cause of Congestion	Solution
Resource capacity / insufficient capacity	Expand capacity, maintain excess capacity
Number of users / too many users	Limit community membership, user population
External cost / distorted price	Institute congestion-/usage-sensitive pricing

---

[10] Heterogeneity arises with respect to uses and users in different ways. Below, I focus on heterogeneous uses, rather than users. The population of infrastructure users also will be mixed with respect to tastes, endowments, and other attributes. I do not discuss these complications.

[11] CORNES & SANDLER 355 (1996).

[12] Hardin (1968).

The conventional solutions to congestion are also "anonymous," in the sense that the solutions focus on the determinants of crowding and not the attributes of individual users. These solutions do not conflict with the commons management rule discussed in chapter 5 because they do not discriminate among users on the basis of the identity of either user or use.

Congestion can arise in many different ways on complex infrastructure systems, such as interconnected networked infrastructure. There may be particular links or nodes in a network, or interconnection points between networks, that create bottlenecks. There may be access or "on-ramp" congestion. This section proceeds with a rather abstract notion of congestion for the purpose of explaining the primary approaches to managing congestion, recognizing that in practice multiple sources and types of congestion on a given infrastructure may require different combinations of solutions targeted to the sources. For example, congestion on the Internet is composed of congestion at different links and servers, on different networks, and may not be reducible to a single "problem." Managing Internet congestion might require a combination of different approaches that target different bottlenecks and sources of congestion.

1. RESOURCE CAPACITY: EXPANDING CAPACITY AND MAINTAINING EXCESS CAPACITY

Congestion arises because capacity is finite and, at peak times, demand exceeds supply. "Congestion is essentially a peak load problem,"[13] where "peak" and "off-peak" depend on capacity and utilization rates. The most obvious way to avoid congestion is to over-supply infrastructure capacity. Maintaining infrastructure capacity in excess of anticipated peak demand significantly reduces the likelihood that demand will exceed supply, at least in the short run. In essence, the goal would be to avoid peaking (congestion) by maintaining a sufficient capacity cushion. In fact, it is standard industry practice in many infrastructure industries to maintain a significant capacity cushion.

The "tragedy of the commons" story implies that the user population necessarily will overtake the carrying capacity of the shared resource, but this need not be the case. Whether it will be depends on the size of the existing user population, the rate of population growth, existing resource capacity, resource renewal rates, utilization rates and patterns, pricing, and the cost of expanding resource capacity, among other things. Assuming that congestion exists or is likely, capacity expansion may be an attractive solution, if it is feasible. But it is by no means a panacea.

Four related difficulties arise when one considers investment in capacity as a solution to a congestion problem: cost, cost recovery, waste, and dynamic inefficiencies. First, the cost of capacity expansion may be prohibitive for many infrastructure resources.

---

[13] Buchanan 98 (1952).

For some, the cost is infinite; expansion is impossible—for example, one cannot expand the capacity of many environmental infrastructures. For others, it is simply too expensive relative to the benefits of reducing congestion—for example, adding capacity to existing highway infrastructure in certain urban settings is technically feasible but cost infeasible. The high costs of capacity expansion are often a function of physical constraints, technological limitations, and path dependency. In some situations, these influences may diminish and the costs of capacity expansion may recede.

Second, even if investing in capacity is a feasible option, financing can be a major obstacle. As noted, users may be unwilling to pay for the extra capacity needed to avoid congestion, whether payment is collected as taxes, tolls, or user fees. Even if some consumers are willing to do so, the risk of free riders may deter private investment, particularly if exclusion costs are high. Public funding may be necessary—and is common in many infrastructure industries for this reason—but public funding raises a host of complicated and contentious issues, many of which surfaced in the Marginal Cost Controversy discussion in chapter 6. The deterioration of many infrastructure resources across the United States evidences the difficulty in raising public funds for infrastructure maintenance, improvements, and capacity expansion.[14]

Third, even if the first two difficulties are overcome, maintaining excess capacity may be wasteful. Buchanan makes the point quite clearly in the context of highway congestion:

> In attempting to decide how many resources should be devoted to highways and streets, society must choose between providing a structure which is too large in off-peak periods and one which is too small in peak periods. It seems certain that if enough resources were to be devoted to highway construction to reduce congestion to acceptable proportions in peak traffic periods, overinvestment in highways would be present. A highway system of compromise size would appear preferable. This would mean that some highway resources would be wasted in off-peak period.[15]

The costs associated with waste during off-peak periods need to be compared with the benefits of avoiding congestion during peak periods. In some contexts, it may make sense to maintain a sufficient capacity cushion to avoid congestion during peak periods, despite waste during off-peak periods, and in other contexts, it may make sense to tolerate certain levels of congestion during peak periods.

---

[14] The 2009 Report Card for American Infrastructure, for example, gave the nation's infrastructural resources a cumulative "D" grade, lamenting that "years of delayed maintenance and lack of modernization have left Americans with an outdated and failing infrastructure that cannot meet our needs." American Society of Civil Engineers iii (2009). The Report Card estimated that an investment of $2.2 trillion would be needed over a five-year period in order to bring the nation's infrastructure up to a good condition. *Id.* at 6.

[15] Buchanan 97 (1952).

Beyond the question of waste (underutilization or idle supply), inefficiencies may result from distorted incentives among users. Investing in capacity expansion to stay ahead of demand and stave off congestion may be a futile exercise over the medium or long term because expanded capacity may spur additional users and uses to emerge. For example, new highway construction may lower transportation costs and spur invest-ments in new residential or industrial development.[16] Without some intervention to internalize the congestion costs, investments in capacity may operate as an indirect sub-sidy to these new activities. This may lead to an inefficient allocation of resources; absent some reason to justify the subsidies, the investments in new residential or industrial development might have been better utilized elsewhere in the economy. Finally, even when investments in capacity are cost-justified, are reasonably well financed, and do not inefficiently distort incentives, there remains the possibility that alternative means for managing congestion would have been more efficient. Maintaining a capacity cushion is a simple but rather blunt approach to managing congestion, and it is often most effec-tive when coupled with one or more of the other approaches discussed below.[17]

2. NUMBER OF USERS: LIMITING COMMUNITY MEMBERSHIP OR USER POPULATION

A second approach to managing congestion problems targets the user community. Hardin emphasized the impact of population growth on the management of shared resources. The aggregate consumption by a community of users depends on the number of users as well as the intensity of their use. Membership size is critical to evaluating resource management options.

One prevalent means for managing congestion of shared facilities is to restrict community membership. Private clubs created to facilitate sharing of some congestible facility—such as a swimming pool, golf course, or ski resort—regularly restrict member-ship to manage congestion.[18] There is a rich economic literature on club theory and the role of membership size in controlling congestion. Clubs can be member-owned,

---

[16] This may increase demand and lead to another round of congestion. Strahilevitz 1247 n.76 (2000); Nash (2008).

[17] One approach to handling congestion in the power industry is the process of "peak shaving," wherein large electricity consumers employ "peaking power plants," often backup generators, to produce some of their elec-tricity during peak consumption hours. This is done in order to avoid the higher prices charged for peak elec-tricity, or qualify for electric company discounts. See THUMANN & MEHTA 266 (2008) ("Peak shaving is the practice of selectively dropping electric loads or generating on-site electricity during periods of peak electric demand . . . most commonly used to reduce annual electricity costs."); see also California Energy Commission, Distributed Energy Resource Guide: Peak Shaving, available at http://www.energy.ca.gov/distgen/back ground/peak_shaving.html (last visited Feb. 1, 2011) (diagrammatically describing peak shaving in practice).

[18] I leave aside "discriminatory clubs" in which club membership may be determined based on identity character-istics. CORNES & SANDLER 385–87 (1996). In such clubs, congestion or crowding is associated with character-istics of the members, such as "beauty, congeniality, intelligence, . . . race, rudeness."

firm-owned, or government-provided; formal or informal; large or small. Generally, club membership is voluntary.[19] For our purposes, the key club function is managing membership size (exclude nonmembers) to avoid congestion or keep congestion at tolerable levels.

Rationing is a related approach to managing congestion that focuses on controlling the number of users. The government may ration a publicly owned resource to a limited user community by granting exclusive licenses to select actors. For example, the FCC issues broadcast licenses to avoid interference. Park facilities, such as soccer fields, basketball courts, and baseball diamonds, are often rationed with permits during peak periods (e.g., summer recreation leagues), and left open to the public for use on a first-come-first-served basis during off-peak periods.

Rationing also may occur dynamically in response to congestion or perceived threats of congestion. For example, a resource may be open to users on a first-come-first-served basis until demand rises to level that poses a risk of congestion, at which point potential users may be queued (or prices may rise; see below). This does not eliminate congestion; potential users bear the costs while waiting for an opportunity to use the resource.[20] "[O]ne appeal of rationing is that is relatively easy to implement. Indeed, it is common today to see file servers, Web servers, and other network services that reject additional users when the load is too high."[21] Such rationing depends on effective mechanisms for measuring load and implementing exclusion and queuing—ranging from bouncers at a bar to sophisticated technological systems such as load management programs used by utilities. The Internet, for example, relies on standardized technical protocols to manage congestion. Informal or uncoordinated rationing also arises through social customs, such as rules regarding pickup basketball at outdoor basketball courts or queuing at lookout points for scenic views.

Club membership and rationing can be effective in avoiding or at least managing congestion. The feasibility and effectiveness of these solutions depend on transaction costs (administration, billing) and the cost of excluding nonmembers. Like investments in capacity, restricting membership size can be blunt when implemented alone. A fixed membership size may lead to inefficiencies and waste quite similar to capacity cushioning— for example, it can be underrestrictive during peak periods and overrestrictive during off-peak periods. Managing membership size and use dynamically to overcome this

---

[19] CORNES & SANDLER (1996). This is true for private clubs. Economists have used club theory to analyze publicly provided club goods and examine intersections with the theory of public goods. One can consider jurisdictions as clubs that provide and manage a range of shared resources, including many infrastructure resources. To the extent that citizens can opt out of the club by moving to another jurisdiction, membership appears to be voluntary. Tiebout (1956).

[20] CORNES & SANDLER 387 (1996). The opportunity cost of their time in the queue can determine membership size. *Id.*

[21] MacKie-Mason & Varian (1995).

problem can be information-intensive, raise implementation costs, and require more adaptable exclusion mechanisms. Thus, controlling total club membership size may be combined with dynamic rationing to more efficiently allocate the shared resources. Technology may play a critical role in monitoring utilization rates, managing queues, and enforcing rules. While dynamic rationing can be nondiscriminatory, as is the case when access is provided on a first-come-first-served basis, it can also be discriminatory—for example, when priority is given to certain users or uses. Clubs often invest in capacity, employ a variety of pricing mechanisms to internalize congestion costs, and utilize use restrictions.

3. COST INTERNALIZATION: INSTITUTING CONGESTION PRICING

A third approach to managing congestion is pricing. Economists strongly prefer pricing mechanisms that fully account for costs, including the costs of congestion. Utilization rates depend on price (whether taxes, tolls, or market prices), and congestion problems often arise because pricing does not reflect congestion costs. As the "tragedy of the commons" story highlights, congestion often arises because individual users do not account for the congestion costs imposed on other users as a result of their consumption decisions. This may be due to the fact that the resource is open to all users on a first-come-first-served basis without any restriction or toll (i.e., price is set at zero), or it may be due to tolls that are insensitive to congestion costs (e.g., a fixed membership fee).

In theory, each resource user should pay a price that reflects both the direct and external costs of his or her use—the marginal social cost—and that price should be sensitive to utilization rates, available capacity, and potential congestion. Economists have long argued that congestion pricing will lead to efficient use of the shared resource. As Barbara van Schewick and I noted in an article that evaluated arguments about congestion pricing in the Internet context, "there are a variety of pricing mechanisms employed by facility owners to internalize congestion costs, and the relative attractiveness of different mechanisms depends upon contextual factors and transaction costs."[22]

A common and straightforward example of congestion pricing utilizes the two-part tariff scheme discussed in chapter 2. Such a scheme can include a membership (subscription) fee—typically, a lump-sum fee—that aims to recover fixed costs and a variable fee—typically, a per-use fee—that aims to recover marginal costs, which in theory would reflect fully the user's marginal contribution to congestion costs. Ideally, the variable component would vary over time with utilization rates and the load on the resource. During off-peak periods, the variable fee drops to zero. As utilization rates increase and congestion looms, the fee adjusts to account for users' marginal contribution to

---

[22] Frischmann & van Schewick (2007).

congestion. There is a rich literature on different approaches to this pricing problem, and, as noted, congestion need not be eliminated.

Congestion pricing is not costless. Its utility depends on significant information and transaction cost considerations. Much like rationing, implementation requires effective metering of individual *and* aggregate usage of system capacity to determine each user's marginal contribution to congestion costs. Metering can be quite difficult and costly, depending on available monitoring and information technologies as well as the complexity of the infrastructure resource being used. Metering the use of a pasture may be substantially less difficult than metering use of networked infrastructure, such as interconnected transportation or communications systems. Congestion pricing also can involve complex billing practices, which raise transaction costs and can raise concerns among consumers. In some contexts, consumers prefer to experience some congestion over a complex, dynamic pricing schedule.

In lieu of congestion-sensitive pricing, many providers utilize flat-rate pricing, where the variable fee does not adjust dynamically based on congestion. Instead, users pay a fixed per-use fee, which may be based in part on average congestion costs. This approach differentiates heavy and light users and thus can help to internalize congestion costs, albeit imperfectly. Imperfections arise because such flat-rate pricing is insensitive to actual congestion and thus, depending on the fee, usage patterns, capacity, and other factors, may over- or undercharge users. For example, during off-peak periods, the per-use fee may exceed actual marginal costs and inefficiently tax users; during peak periods, the per-use fee may fall below the actual marginal cost and fail to internalize congestion costs fully. Nonetheless, this type of congestion pricing can be attractive in situations where transaction costs associated with metering and usage-sensitive pricing are high or where consumers prefer less complex pricing schedules.

There are intermediate approaches. One prominent example is time-of-day pricing, which adjusts the variable fee according to the time of day based on utilization patterns. Thus, heavy users in peak time periods pay more than heavy users in off-peak time periods. There are many other examples, such as weekday and weekend calling plans. In essence, this is an imperfect form of usage-sensitive congestion pricing. Yet it may be quite attractive in various contexts because it targets the congestion problem and internalizes congestion externalities to a greater degree than flat-rate pricing but without introducing overly complex pricing and metering.

As with perfect price discrimination, perfect congestion pricing may be impossible because of the information demands such pricing imposes. Perfection is itself an ambiguous and elusive concept in this context because complete internalization is not necessarily "perfect." Consumers sometimes prefer some degree of congestion. The interaction between consumer preferences for congestion and for less complex pricing schemes complicates the idea of perfect congestion pricing. Moreover, the fact that such preferences may be shaped by consumers' experience with particular infrastructure suggests that path dependencies also complicate the concept of perfection.

Putting perfection aside, there are significant economic advantages to congestion pricing of one form or another, including (a) more efficient use of existing capacity; (b) more accurate signals about demand, which inform both investments in capacity expansion and management of membership size; and (c) generation of funds to pay for capacity. More efficient use of capacity is a potential advantage because congestion externalities may distort resource allocation. When congestion costs are not reflected in the price paid by users, overuse is expected. Users maximize their private welfare and do not account for the costs imposed on others. Incorporating those costs raises the price of using the resource and may reduce use. This may prevent overuse and reduce congestion.[23] Further, assuming there are no other relevant externalities—for example, positive spillovers—congestion pricing better allocates capacity during peak periods because the reduction in use is accomplished by the pricing mechanism, which means that the rationing process is driven by consumer demand rather than more arbitrary criteria, such as first-come-first-served. Congestion pricing also generates better information about consumer demand. It provides signals about what people are willing to pay; demand elasticity and whether people are willing to change their consumption patterns; consumer preferences for (tolerating) congestion; and demand for additional capacity. Finally, congestion pricing generates funds to pay for capacity expansion as well as congestion management. This can be a significant advantage over pure rationing approaches. Related to the three advantages just discussed, congestion pricing also may affect the timing of investments in capacity expansion. For example, (premature) investments may be delayed as the use of existing capacity is spread more evenly by consumer adjustments in the timing of their activities. Conversely, by providing more accurate signals about consumer preferences as well as funds, congestion pricing can hasten investments in capacity.

Yet, as economists have shown, congestion pricing can lead to perverse incentives. For example, providers may see congestion pricing as a means of boosting revenues. Thus, one should not assume that providers will use congestion charges to expand capacity; sometimes providers may prefer moderately congested systems because that may increase revenues. Even when providers do commit to using congestion charges to expand capacity, customers may act strategically in their decision making. For example, some users may consume more in what would otherwise be off-peak periods to create congestion, trigger congestion pricing, and, as a result, force off-peak users to contribute toward capacity expansion.[24]

---

[23] As noted above, congestion may persist. For example, if demand is inelastic, a change in price might not affect consumption very much and the utilization rate and level of congestion may remain unchanged.

[24] Bauer & Faratin (2005).

Not surprisingly, in many cases congestion pricing is used in conjunction with capacity expansion and club membership practices. As with the other approaches to managing congestion, pricing is no panacea.

C. Infrastructure Congestion, Heterogeneity, and Cross-Crowding

In reality, most uses of partially (non)rival infrastructure are *heterogeneous* rather than *homogenous*.[25] Infrastructure resources are general-purpose rather than special-purpose resources. A lake may be used exclusively for swimming, or it may be used for swimming, fishing, wastewater treatment, and a variety of other purposes that involve different costs and generate different benefits. Similarly, although a highway could be used exclusively for transportation of people in automobiles on predetermined routes, most highways are general-purpose infrastructure used for transportation of people and goods in many different types of vehicles by whatever route users choose. Different activities may place different demands on the resource, potentially leading to complicated trade-offs among uses.

Heterogeneity impacts analysis of costs and benefits and is relevant to diagnosing congestion problems and comparing solutions.[26] In particular, we consider how heterogeneity introduces (a) variance in capacity consumption rates and (b) cross-crowding or interuse congestion. These issues complicate analysis of congestion management options.

Situations involving heterogeneous uses of infrastructure give rise to a fourth approach to managing congestion: the implementation of use restrictions. In contrast with the three conventional approaches to managing congestion discussed above, use restrictions involve discrimination based on the identity of the use and conflict with commons management.

Target Variable / Cause of Congestion	Solution
Resource capacity / insufficient capacity	Expand capacity, maintain excess capacity
Number of users / too many users	Limit community membership, user population
External cost / distorted price	Institute congestion-/usage-sensitive pricing
Heterogeneous uses / cross-crowding	*Establish use restrictions*

---

[25] CORNES & SANDLER ch. 12 (1996) (heterogeneous clubs, mixed clubs, and multiproduct clubs).

[26] Club theorists have analyzed multiproduct clubs and noted the importance of economies of scope, which arise "whenever the costs of providing the services of a sharable input to two or more product lines are subadditive (i.e., less than the total costs of providing these services for each product line separately)." In essence, economies of scope involve cost advantages from joint production as infrastructure supply costs—common costs—can be shared by multiple products. When relevant, economies of scope can push clubs (a) to increase membership size so as to accommodate a greater number of club goods (i.e., outputs dependent on use of the shared facilities) and (b) to increase provisioning of infrastructure capacity correspondingly.

I. VARIANCE IN CAPACITY CONSUMPTION

Heterogeneity introduces variance in the capacity consumption of different uses. E-mail and video conferencing consume bandwidth at different rates. Grazing sheep on a meadow imposes a different burden than grazing goats or buffalo, much less flying a kite. Driving an SUV on the highway imposes a different burden than driving a Honda Civic or a Mack truck, much less a motorcycle or a bicycle. Some uses may be particularly intense, whereas others are not. Some uses may be particularly sporadic or bursty in their utilization rates, while others may be more uniform. Such variations among uses of the shared resource can complicate congestion management, including provisioning of capacity, membership size, and pricing.

Capacity cushioning and membership limits remain useful approaches to managing congestion when heterogeneous uses lead to such variations. Some complications do arise, however. For example, capacity cushioning may need to account for the effect of variable utilization on predicted utilization patterns and anticipation of peak volumes. Membership size may need to account for the expected activities of users—for example, the greater the number of intense users, the lower the total membership size must be. These complications often are manageable.

Multiple uses and variable utilization rates among uses also complicate congestion pricing. Congestion pricing in this scenario aims to account for different marginal contributions to congestion costs associated with different types of uses. This additional accounting can dramatically increase transaction costs. As a result, the transaction costs of use-specific, usage-sensitive pricing may exceed the marginal benefits of increased complexity. Less fine-grained approaches may be more efficient, whether employed through flat-rate per-use pricing or intermediate options.

To see how heterogeneity can increase the complexity and transaction costs of congestion pricing, consider the following example: our shared pasture that is well suited for grazing livestock. If only sheep graze the pasture, a flat per-use fee can be based on the marginal costs of each additional sheep, assuming that differences between individual sheep are negligible. If sheep, donkeys, buffalo, and other livestock graze the pasture, the per-use fee cannot be uniformly based on sheep; instead, it must account for the different marginal costs for the different animals. Further, monitoring and enforcement mechanisms must account for the different animals to make sure that the pricing scheme is not gamed. As variety increases, so may the transaction costs of metering, monitoring, and enforcement.

Yet such complications do not always arise. In some situations where heterogeneity introduces variance in the capacity consumption of different uses, congestion pricing applied per unit of capacity consumed may be feasible and efficient, provided that per-unit consumption can be metered cost-effectively. For example, while e-mail and video conferencing consume bandwidth at different rates, the variable component of congestion pricing can be applied on a per-bit basis without regard for the application.

Thus, time-of-day congestion pricing applied on a per-bit basis need not identify transmitted bits of data as e-mail or video conferencing bits. The fact that different uses consume capacity at different rates is not relevant in this scenario.

2. CROSS-CROWDING: CONGESTION AMONG USES

Heterogeneity also introduces potential interdependencies among uses, referred to as *interaction effects*. Some interaction effects can be positive, as when uses are complementary. Some can be negative. Interaction effects may generate (or constitute) *interuse congestion*, referred to as *cross-crowding*. Various infrastructure uses may interact with each other in a manner that goes beyond competition for scarce capacity. Rivalrousness in consumption may arise because a certain use raises the marginal costs for another use, reducing consumption opportunities for that use, even if the capacity of the underlying resource is not scarce. For example, imagine that sheep and buffalo tend to fight with each other; herding both types of animals on a common pasture would then give rise to interaction effects and rivalry, even if the capacity of the pasture is more than enough to support both flocks.

Certain uses may be nonrivalrous with some uses and rivalrous with other uses, sometimes at different rates of use. For example, various recreational uses of an environmental resource, such as a lake, may be nonrival with respect to each other and at the same time rival with respect to industrial uses. Certain pollutants may render swimming and fishing unsafe or unhealthy—the uses of the resource are incompatible, at least at certain intensity levels. In some contexts, even swimming and fishing may be rivalrous with each other (try swimming in the same area as a group of people fishing). Industrial uses need not crowd out recreational uses, however; for example, industrial uses may be regulated with the health and safety of other users in mind.

Interaction effects may depend on the scale of use (population of users), timing, spatial proximity, and other contextual factors. Some uses may be congestive only for short durations—for example, when swimming in a particular location precludes fishing. Other uses may affect the resource renewal rate and have a longer-term impact on other uses, as when industrial waste pollutes a lake. For example, *E. coli* bacteria may render a swimming area unsafe for a few hours or days, while dumping significant amounts of a highly toxic pollutant into a lake may have much longer-term effects.

More sophisticated economic models of congestion introduce heterogeneity among users and uses and interaction effects (e.g., interuse congestion that occurs between buses and cars, hikers and loggers).[27] A full exploration of different congestion problems

---

[27] ARNOTT (2001) suggests that the margins of choice explored in the economics literature on urban traffic congestion are too constrained and ought to be expanded to include a variety of individual micro-decisions that impact congestion, for example, "decisions such as how rapidly to accelerate or decelerate, which determines my

is best left for particular contexts where specific interaction effects can be discussed. Subsequent chapters explore such problems in the context of highways, environmental infrastructure, and the Internet.

Cross-crowding complicates the conventional approaches to managing congestion. A sizable capacity cushion does not necessarily eliminate cross-crowding; nor does restricting total membership size of the user community; nor does congestion pricing. Interaction effects arise because of interdependencies among uses that are unrelated to scarce capacity. As a result, where interaction effects are significant, some manner of coordination may be necessary. In particular, managing cross-crowding may entail managing the membership size of subsets of users or the intensity of their usage based on the identity of their use.

3. USE RESTRICTIONS

Heterogeneity does not imply unlimited variation. It introduces another choice variable—the scope of uses. In addition to resource capacity, membership size, and pricing, the scope of allowable uses is a variable to consider. As chapter 4 discussed, the genericness of infrastructure implies a wide variety of uses, but the range of uses may be constrained and may change over time. Design and management decisions about the range of possible uses are influenced by many considerations (technical, economic, and social), and many use restrictions reflect initial design, construction, and management decisions. For example, building a road system that connects certain communities but not others, or even one that supports certain routes but not others, enables a range of uses and disables a range of other uses. (Similar decisions about the scope of uses of a facility are made for many noninfrastructural facilities—for example, when a swimming pool is open for swimming but not washing laundry.) In many situations, initial design, allocation, and use decisions shape expectations about how a resource can and should be used and guide investments by owners and users; as path dependencies set in, a particular scope of uses may be perceived as "natural" or fixed. While such processes affect the scope of uses and thus non-uses (use restrictions), let us put aside such macro-level decisions, for now, and instead focus on use restrictions as a deliberate approach to managing interuse congestion.

Use restrictions run the gamut from outright bans on particular uses to rationing capacity based on use-type to differential use-based pricing, which taxes certain uses at a

---

speed and the distance between my car and the car in front . . . whether to accept an opportunity to overtake, whether to honk my horn, whether to enter an intersection after the light has turned yellow (or in Boston red) or when it is blocked, and whether to shift to an apparently faster lane." He suggests that while many of the behavioral choices might be trivial, the cumulative effect can be quite significant. He goes on to suggest a number of additional margins of choice reflected in policy and technology (automobile characteristics) that contribute to urban traffic congestion.

different rate than others. The basic idea is to regulate a particular use because of the interuse congestion attributable to it. For example, as chapter 11 examines, environmental regulations often (aim to) restrict particular industrial uses of environmental infrastructure to levels that minimize cross-crowding and consequently sustain a range of recreational and other uses.

Where two uses are interdependent in a fashion that gives rise to interuse congestion, both uses *cause* the congestion. Cross-crowding is not attributable uniquely to one use or the other; the interuse congestion would not arise unless both uses were present. Thus, interaction effects between industrial pollution and swimming in a lake are attributable to both uses, and not, as is often assumed, to the industrial use alone.[28] Eliminating interaction effects between these uses can be accomplished by eliminating either of the two uses, or perhaps by restricting the intensity, timing, or some other characteristic of one use or the other. Deciding how to coordinate uses, and which use(s) to restrict, are difficult questions that must be evaluated in context. Subsequent chapters discuss these issues.

Another way to view use restrictions is as a form of deprioritization, or, conversely, as a prioritization of other uses. Suppose community members must coordinate use of their shared pasture. Choosing to prohibit buffalo herding because of the potential cross-crowding with other livestock reflects a choice to prioritize the other livestock over buffalo. One can imagine a community making the opposite decision, perhaps restricting access to the pasture to buffalo alone. The interaction effects might be what drive the need to choose, but presumably the choice itself is based on a more holistic evaluation of the social costs and benefits. Perhaps this presumes too much. Political, cultural, and historical factors probably play a much larger role in many of these types of decisions than an evaluation of the social costs and benefits, and probably for good reason, given how difficult it can be to tally the various costs and benefits. Alternatively, one might say that incorporating these factors into a holistic decision-making process actually constitutes an effective form of cost-benefit analysis. The relevant point is that cross-crowding creates demand for use restrictions of one form or another, and this can lead to (de)prioritization or discrimination of the sort discussed in previous chapters. This complicates the case for commons management by adding an additional variable to the mix.

Use restrictions may be an attractive approach to managing congestion, even in the absence of interaction effects. In lieu of the three approaches discussed above, an infrastructure owner might choose to single out a particular use that characteristically consumes a lot of capacity and contributes heavily to congestion and either prohibit that use or tax it more heavily than other uses. For example, recall how grazing different animals on our shared pasture might complicate congestion pricing because the per-use

---

[28] Coase (1960).

fee could not be based on sheep and would need to account for differences among animals' contributions to congestion. Suppose that most of the animals are more or less equivalent to sheep in this respect, with the exception of buffalo. Rather than differentiating among animals, which not only requires figuring out different prices but also requires more expensive monitoring and enforcement mechanisms, it might be more efficient to ban buffalo and use a uniform price for the remaining allowed animals. The basic idea is that the transaction costs of metering all users and employing some form of rationing or congestion pricing may render those options less attractive when compared to the alternative of restricting the intensely consumptive use. The comparative analysis here depends on empirical information about transaction costs.

Another example involves congestion on broadband networks. Yoo claims that use restrictions employed by broadband providers might be justified on this basis. For example, a broadband provider, such as Comcast, might block certain uses of its Internet access service, such as peer-to-peer applications, because users of such applications have overloaded Comcast's system and drained a disproportionate share of its resources.[29] Yoo claims that this type of network management decision can be justified because the transaction costs of metering traffic and employing some form of congestion pricing, such as usage-sensitive congestion pricing, are prohibitive.[30] In his view, the identity of the application (for example, the common file-sharing program known as Bit Torrent) serves as an efficient proxy for usage, and rather than metering usage, broadband providers should be free to restrict use of the application directly. Van Schewick and I strongly disputed both the empirical claim about transaction costs and the argument that use restrictions of this sort are justified as a matter of public policy. Nonetheless, in terms of *private* congestion management strategy, Yoo's theoretical argument is plausible. It may make sense from the perspective of a rational broadband provider to employ use restrictions in this manner. For the reasons set forth in chapter 5, justifying use restrictions as a private strategy should be distinguished from justifying them as public strategy, at least where public, social, or mixed infrastructures are concerned. The network neutrality debate in general, and the FCC decision in 2009 finding Comcast's restriction of Bit Torrent unreasonable in particular, are not focused on whether use restrictions are rational private strategies for broadband providers; rather, the focus is on whether permitting or regulating use restrictions is rational public policy, given the broader range of social values involved.

As previously mentioned, use restrictions involve discrimination based on the identity of the use, which raises a conflict with commons management. Thus, for partially (non)

---

[29] In re Formal Compl. of Free Press & Public Knowledge Against Comcast Corp. for Secretly Degrading Peer-to-Peer Applications, 23 F.C.C.R. 13,028 (2008); see also Comcast Corp. v. FCC, 600 F. 3d 642 (DC Cir. 2010) (vacating the order on jurisdictional grounds).

[30] Yoo (2008); Frischmann & Van Schewick (2007) (challenging his claims).

rival infrastructure, the case for commons management must account for the possibility that use restrictions are necessary for managing congestion. As the next section examines, where cross-crowding requires coordination through use restrictions, a commons management regime may admit narrow exceptions and retain much of its force.

D. Managing Infrastructure Congestion

The move from nonrivalrous to partially (non)rivalrous infrastructure brings congestion management to the table and invites reconsideration of the analysis in chapter 5. To be clear, the potential social benefits of leveraging nonrivalry to encourage productive activities and spillovers remains undiminished, but reaching that potential requires managing the boundary between nonrivalrous and rivalrous consumption. This management requires consideration of the sources of congestion and means for managing congestion, perhaps to avoid it altogether and sustain nonrivalrous consumption but more often to keep congestion at minimal levels and durations. Congestion may be inevitable in many contexts. The key is preventing congestion from retarding or disabling the many productive activities that infrastructures enable.

It is very difficult to generalize about the relative advantages and disadvantages of different approaches to managing infrastructure congestion. Comparative analysis is best done in specific contexts with more detailed information about the resources, communities, and institutional and social settings. The approaches can be roughly broken down to the four types discussed: capacity expansion; rationing, or limitations on membership size; congestion pricing; and use restrictions. In practice, there are many models of each of these types, and infrastructure managers employ complex combinations of approaches.

Yet there are some general limits on viable approaches to managing infrastructure congestion. First, not all infrastructure resources can be expanded. It may be impossible to expand the capacity of certain environmental infrastructure; the costs of expanding capacity of an urban road system may be prohibitive. In such scenarios, the focus is on how to best manage existing capacity. In some cases, expanding capacity may be feasible in terms of cost but may involve financing problems. Congestion pricing may help with financing, but government involvement may be required for capacity expansion to be an option. Second, for many infrastructure resources, the relevant user community is the public at large. This means that, for social and economic reasons, restricting membership size to manage congestion may be less palatable for such infrastructure than in the case of congestible resources that are not infrastructural. Infrastructure resources often are essential to participation in various economic, cultural, political, and other social activities. In such scenarios, the focus may be on ensuring the availability of sufficient capacity for public consumption; if feasible, congestion pricing may be attractive for the reasons discussed in the previous section. Third, the scale and complexity of many infrastructures significantly complicate the approaches to managing congestion that depend on metering, rationing, and pricing. (We might conflate this into "excessive transaction costs.") Thus, for many interconnected networked infrastructures, congestion pricing may be impossible to implement on a system-wide basis because doing so would require cooperation, commitment, and shared intelligence among various networks and other providers of subsystems (or infrastructure components) to a degree that is infeasible from a cost perspective, a strategic behavior perspective, and a governance perspective. The technology necessary to implement system-wide congestion pricing may be too expensive. In such scenarios, the focus may be on piecemeal solutions that aim at managing congestion at persistent bottlenecks; capacity expansion and congestion pricing may be attractive for certain components (e.g., access networks), but not others. In some contexts, such as the Internet, congestion management technologies provide feedback about congestion at different locations and facilitate dynamic rationing and routing of traffic. These technologies facilitate complex coordination among different interconnected networks that subscribe to standardized protocols.[31]

The case for commons management set forth in chapter 5 may be complicated for partially (non)rival infrastructure, but perhaps not as significantly as one might suspect. Most approaches to managing congestion comply with the commons management rule. Capacity expansion, management of membership size, and congestion pricing generally do not discriminate based on the identity of the user or use. Only use restrictions generally conflict with commons management.

In some cases, congestion pricing and management of membership size (rationing) may raise concerns about how reductions in use attributable to these approaches might affect the production of spillovers. In other words, reducing congestion externalities may also reduce positive externalities, particularly where the congestion management technique is imperfect. This suggests that, in some cases, there may be reasons to prefer capacity expansion or to refrain from managing congestion where the external costs from congestion are less than the positive external benefits from the congestive use. This complication is best dealt with in specific contexts.

The primary complication is posed by use restrictions, essentially a form of use (de) prioritization. In the context of cross-crowding, use restrictions may be the only feasible approach to reducing or eliminating congestion. This does not mean that use restrictions are necessary. Tolerating cross-crowding may be an option, depending on the nature of the effects and the magnitude of the costs involved. Again, this is the same basic point I made earlier with respect to congestion in general. It need not be eliminated. In some cases, tolerating congestion may be the best option. In some cases, it is not. Cross-crowding may involve incompatible uses such that use A completely precludes use B,

---

[31] As discussed in chapter 13, TCP accomplishes such coordination on an anonymous basis and thereby maintains the infrastructure commons.

perhaps for technological or health and safety reasons. Such cross-crowding may require coordination by some form of use restriction. Where incompatibilities like this arise, use restriction is inevitable: It will result from either a deliberate decision (restrict use A or let use A preclude use B) or indecision (effectively, let use A preclude use B).[32]

In situations where use restrictions are required, commons management still may be preserved to a significant degree. In fact, in some cases, use restrictions may be predicated on the idea that prohibiting or regulating the intensity of certain uses preserves the non-discriminatory access regime for a wide range of other uses. In essence, narrowly tailored and well-specified use restrictions may constitute limited exceptions to the general non-discrimination rule. Such exceptions are quite common for infrastructure. A few examples: Common carriers typically are obligated to provide nondiscriminatory service and a high degree of care to protect customers from harm; the latter obligation provides a narrow exception to the former in that common carriers are obligated to discriminate against users/uses that pose a risk to others. While highways are generally managed as commons, various regulations, such as restrictions on the transportation of hazardous materials, aim to reduce cross-crowding.[33]

As chapter 11 illustrates, environmental infrastructures give rise to this scenario. Environmental infrastructures are partially (non)rival and cannot be expanded. Accordingly, environmental management and regulation focus on managing existing capacity and sustaining the resources. Regulation of various industrial uses generally aims to minimize cross-crowding and sustain the commons for a wide range of recreational and other uses. The key point, for our current purposes, is that targeted regulation of a subset of industrial uses that risk precluding a wide range of other socially valuable uses is a classic example of use restrictions that do not completely dismantle the commons management regime; to the contrary, such use restrictions protect and sustain the commons.

It is also worth noting that use restrictions might be employed to regulate uses that generate public bads and yield negative externalities (as opposed to public goods yielding positive externalities). Government regulation of the use of highways to transport hazardous materials or prohibition of the use of interstate communications networks to communicate fraudulent information can be viewed as a discriminatory use restriction aimed at reducing activities that generate harmful external effects that have little to do with congestion. Absent some regulatory obligation, private infrastructure owners have little incentive to employ use restrictions in this fashion, because the costs are external.

---

[32] To make this less abstract, we can substitute (1) industrial pollution (buffalo grazing) for use A, and (2) swimming (sheep grazing) for use B.

[33] Absent regulation, transporters of hazardous materials may externalize considerable costs in the form of risks of severe harm to other drivers, and such risks may crowd out other users. Note that it is the interdependency among use types that causes crowding—comparable to how industrial pollution crowds out swimmers.

In a sense, this is the flipside of the argument developed in previous chapters concerning the production of public and social goods.

The case for managing partially (non)rival infrastructure as commons follows the same basic structure and arguments as set forth in chapter 5. For commercial infrastructure, the arguments are quite limited and are reasonably articulated in traditional doctrines like the essential facilities doctrine and common carriage. For public, social, and mixed infrastructure, the arguments for commons management do not change substantively either. Leveraging nonrivalry may require managing congestion, but it is important to keep in mind that there are many nondiscriminatory means for managing congestion problems. In many situations, commons management and congestion management are perfectly compatible.

8

SUPPLY-SIDE INCENTIVES

THIS CHAPTER CONSIDERS the relationship between nondiscrimination rules and supply-side incentives to invest in infrastructure. We encountered the issue throughout chapter 6. This chapter frames and evaluates the oft-made claim that government-imposed commons management will significantly impair incentives to invest in infrastructure. The impact of rules requiring nondiscriminatory sharing of infrastructural resources on the supply-side incentives to provide, maintain, and improve those resources is complex, context-specific, and not amenable to generalized, a priori conclusions. Yet policy debates are muddled with assertions about purported effects on incentives; such assertions typically are hyperbole.

To be fair, these assertions are sometimes made in situations in which nondiscrimination rules are accompanied by price regulation, which triggers a host of reasonable concerns that bear more directly on investment incentives. But as chapter 6 explained, there is no necessary correlation between nondiscrimination rules and price regulation. The two may be complementary institutions employed in certain regulated industries, but one does not require the other. Unfortunately, analysis and debate about nondiscrimination rules is stunted by unwarranted generalizations based on faulty assumptions.

There is a limit to how much can be said in this chapter about any general relationship between commons management and supply-side incentives, because there are considerable differences in the relationship for different types of infrastructure and different types of commons management institutions. Consider how different the supply-side analysis of different infrastructure resources can be. Traditional infrastructure tends to involve significant irreversible investments, decreasing average costs, and a host of related supply-side considerations that may be more or less relevant for nontraditional infrastructure, such as intellectual infrastructure or environmental infrastructure. Even among traditional infrastructure, the supply-side issues vary considerably. The same is true of various institutions that implement nondiscrimination rules. The essential facilities doctrine and common carriage, for example, may interact with supply-side incentives quite differently. I leave a more detailed analysis of these relationships for subsequent chapters. Here I confront the general claim that government-imposed commons management will significantly impair incentives to invest in building and sustaining infrastructure.

First, the chapter briefly discusses typical assumptions underlying this claim. Unfortunately, tragedy is often assumed rather than demonstrated. I address a few of the powerful rhetorical devices/analytical heuristics that influence modern debates about nondiscrimination rules. Next, the chapter considers a series of issues that require context-specific attention in order to evaluate the relationship between commons management and incentives to invest. The chapter ends with two examples of situations where a conflict between commons management and supply-side incentives arises.

A. Rhetoric Underlying Typical "Commons Destroys Incentives" Claims

Claims that nondiscrimination rules reduce incentives to invest are often mere rhetoric. Opponents of government imposed nondiscrimination rules make incentive arguments that rely heavily on (1) a fear of free riding (or a sense of entitlement to be free from free riding), (2) concerns about dynamic efficiency in the infrastructure market, and (3) a general aversion to government regulation. I address each in turn.

I. FREE RIDING

We encountered the idea that commons management invites free riding in chapter 7 when we discussed the "tragedy of the commons" story. Recall, first, how unconstrained consumption led to tragedy because each user has incentives to maximize private returns without accounting for external effects and, second, how this can lead to congestion and depletion of the resource. With respect to public goods, the inability to exclude can lead to unconstrained consumption, often referred to as "free riding" because the user consumes the good without paying the producer.[1] Though congestion and depletion are

---

[1] The expression "free riding" is normative and rhetorical in and of itself. In many cases of alleged free riding, the user in fact has paid for access and use of the resource but is deemed a free rider for using the resource in a manner that displeases the producer or exceeds the scope of what the producer intended to authorize.

not an issue for public goods, free riding can have dynamic effects on incentives to produce. The difficult question is determining when free riding produces such effects.

Simply put, free riding can only be evaluated in particular contexts. It makes no sense to appeal abstractly to the idea that commons management invites free riding and therefore diminishes incentives to invest. *Both premises are flawed.* Let us take them in reverse order.

First, free riding does not necessarily diminish incentives to invest.[2] We discussed similar points in chapters 3 and 6. There is a mistaken tendency to believe that any gain or loss in profits corresponds to an equal or proportional gain or loss in investment incentives, but this belief greatly oversimplifies the decision-making process and underlying economics and ignores the relevance of alternative opportunities for investment. The conversion of surplus realized by a free rider into producer surplus may be a wealth transfer with no meaningful impact on producers' investment incentives or it may be otherwise, but there is no theoretical or empirical basis for assuming that such producer gains are systematically incentive-relevant.[3]

To the contrary, free riding is pervasive in society and a feature, rather than a bug, of our economic, cultural, and social systems. There are innumerable examples of free riding in society, and there is little reason to think that such behavior is inefficiently suppressing investment incentives systematically throughout society. Rather, idea diffusion and competition, among other important social processes, depend significantly on free—unauthorized, unlicensed, unapproved, and often unpaid—riding. These processes distribute surplus among interdependent markets (complete, incomplete, and missing) and thereby sustain the capabilities of others (free riders) to participate in productive activities. In many cases, the surplus is value/opportunities realized from shared capital resources. Arguably, deviation from the norm of free riding requires strong justification because restricting free riding in one market can lead to distortions that ripple through other interdependent markets.

Only in particular *exceptional* settings does society employ legal regimes, such as intellectual property, to limit free riding and thereby sustain incentives to invest in certain types of productive activities.[4] It is critical to keep in mind, however, that even in these

---

[2] It may increase investment incentives in certain areas. Frischmann & Lemley (2007).

[3] The tendency to assume that surplus conversion is systematically incentive-relevant may be a function of marginalism in neoclassical economics. Many investments are profitable and thus motivated by sufficient incentives to invest, based on returns from inframarginal consumers rather than marginal consumers.

[4] I should note that some might confuse my claim that free riding is normal with a claim against property rights in general, the right to exclude others from one's property in particular, or the freedom to refuse to deal with others. These claims are distinct and are not mine. While property rights often provide the means for restricting free riding and may even be justified to serve this exact purpose, property rights systems do not extend to all resources and activities that support free riding (ideas, risk taking, etc.). Though some would like to recognize property rights in all of the fruits of one's labor or investment, society does not and need not recognize such rights.

settings, the legal regimes limit *but do not eliminate* free riding. In fact, the legal regimes often sustain free riding by protecting certain user freedoms.[5] (Chapter 12 examines this point in the context of intellectual property regimes.)

More importantly, commons management does not invite *free* riding. Commons management does not imply free, except in the sense of freedom from discrimination. In some cases, resources managed as commons are free—for example, ideas in the public domain. But, as with the relationship between commons management and price regulation, there is no necessary correlation between commons management and any particular price level (much less a price of zero). An infrastructure owner subject to a nondiscrimination rule would be free to charge the monopoly price, absent some other constraint such as competition or price regulation.

Another version of the free-riding argument focuses on the irreversible nature of many infrastructure investments. Once investments are made, the costs are sunk and the resources cannot be recommitted elsewhere if and when it turns out that markets do not meet expectations (e.g., demand fails to materialize or demand shocks cause the market to shrink). This means that when facing uncertainty, the option of delaying investment can be quite valuable, and, conversely, that making investments in the face of uncertainty involves taking a risk. (Recall our discussion of option theory in chapter 5.) In the situation of irreversible infrastructure investments, commons management may facilitate free riding on risk taking. Being the first mover entails taking risks that subsequent entrants may be able to avoid by taking advantage of a commons management regime.[6] Commons management appears to give latecomers the option to wait and see whether the initial venture is successful or not. If it is, they may enter; if it is not, they may avoid the market altogether. Put another way, competitors may share in the benefits of successful ventures while avoiding the costs of failures. Thus, commons management may reduce the incentives of first movers (to make irreversible investments, undertake risks, and be the first mover) and at the same time distort incentives of other potential entrants (e.g., encouraging them to wait and see rather than invest independently). In some contexts, these effects on supply-side incentives can be quite significant.

But, as a generic argument divorced from the details of a specific context, this is simply another version of the standard free-riding argument. The points made above apply to this argument as well: First, commons management does not determine the price level, and therefore, in the absence of price regulation, market pricing should account for the risk. If price regulation accompanies nondiscriminatory access, then the option

---

[5] See chapters 3, 11, and 12.
[6] There may be substantial first-mover benefits. BARON & SHANE 268–69 (2008) (discussing various benefits).

value might be taken into account by regulators.[7] But there is no reason to think *discrimination* is generally necessary to safeguard risk taking, even if such risk taking involves irreversible investments. Second, free riding on the risk taking of others is a feature rather than a bug of our economic and social systems. Again, there are special circumstances in which society limits such free riding by providing exclusionary rights or exclusive franchises. Absent such special circumstances (or a more detailed analysis of a specific context), there is no reason to credit this or the more generic free-riding argument when evaluating the case for commons management.

2. DYNAMIC VERSUS STATIC EFFICIENCY

Related to free-riding arguments are arguments that set up a presumed trade-off between static efficiency and dynamic efficiency.[8] Where such a pure trade-off exists and the expected values on each side of the trade-off are at least roughly equivalent, Glen Robinson and Dennis Weisman are correct that "dynamic efficiency always trumps static efficiency."[9] But such pure trade-offs are quite rare and should not be mistaken for the general case when evaluating the case for commons management.

Robinson and Weisman support the maxim with the following quote from Alfred Kahn: "[W]herever mandatory sharing, for the sake of jump-starting the entry of competitors, would interfere with the more creative and dynamic investment in facilities-based competitive entry and innovation by incumbents and challengers alike, it is the latter that must take primacy."[10] To put this statement in context, one must appreciate that Kahn, Robinson, and Weisman are discussing a particular (de)regulatory regime that required an infrastructure owner to share certain facilities with competitors. This regime primarily aimed to facilitate a transition from a regulated monopoly to competition (a topic discussed below), and thus one might presume that these rules are justified on the basis of static efficiency at the expense of dynamic efficiency. On one hand, granting competitors nondiscriminatory access to an incumbent monopolist's facilities may introduce competition and thereby bring prices down to a competitive level for the benefit of current consumers; on the other hand, this type of sharing among

---

[7] Hausman (1997); Hausman, Pakes, & Rosston (1999).

[8] Static efficiency concerns the efficiency of an existing system, evaluated in terms of optimal resource use within a stable set of initial conditions. Economists evaluate static efficiency in terms of both allocative efficiency and productive efficiency. ANDERTON 100–01 (2000). Dynamic efficiency concerns the efficiency of a system capable of change, evaluated in terms of optimal resource use where some resources may be used to generate new knowledge and change the conditions. Dynamic efficiency depends on innovation and is associated with technological advancement and economic growth. *Id.* at 100–02.

[9] Robinson & Weisman (2008).

[10] KAHN 22 (2001).

competitors may reduce incentives to invest in both the existing facilities and in new facilities.

But to be clear, in this context, price regulation accompanied the nondiscriminatory sharing regime and raised legitimate concerns about the relationships between rate setting for the shared facilities and incentives to invest. My point here is not to engage those particular concerns or the broader debate about that particular (de)regulatory regime. Instead, I aim to show that Kahn properly framed the trade-off with care, in a context-specific manner, and to explain that this frame does not apply to all nondiscriminatory sharing regimes. In short, the maxim is not generalizable.

Kahn states a version of the economic principle proposed by Robinson and Weisman: Dynamic efficiency should trump static efficiency. Two related points are worth noting, however. First, Kahn does not assume that mandatory sharing interferes with "more creative and dynamic investment[s]." Second, Kahn does not suggest that mandatory sharing always should be seen as a choice between static efficiency gains and dynamic efficiency gains. Instead, he is careful to suggest that *wherever* mandatory sharing (a) would interfere with dynamic investments and (b) is done only for the sake of introducing competition, then we ought to choose dynamic efficiency over static efficiency. These two conditions may fit the (de)regulatory context considered by Kahn, Robinson, and Weisman, but it would be a mistake to assume that the two conditions are satisfied generally when evaluating the case for managing infrastructure as commons.

Both chapter 6 and the previous subsection, outlined the basic reasons why the first condition is not uniformly met. Nondiscrimination rules do not necessarily interfere with dynamic investments by infrastructure owners or potential entrants. The freedom and ability to discriminate is not essential to many infrastructure investments. Average cost pricing and monopoly pricing, for example, are two nondiscriminatory pricing regimes that provide sufficient cost recovery and support investment incentives for many types of infrastructure investments, although certainly not all socially desirable infrastructure investments (see the next section). In some cases where discrimination is not essential, it still may be an efficient means for reducing deadweight losses, but that is a different matter.[11]

Chapter 5 explains why the case for commons management is not limited to static efficiency benefits associated with introducing competition for the sake of current consumers. The case for commons management may be driven by a variety of dynamic efficiency considerations. In some contexts, commons management indirectly subsidizes a wide range of dynamic investments in innovation and entrepreneurship by users. In such contexts, the "dynamic efficiency always trumps static efficiency" principle is

---

[11] Recall that both average cost and monopoly pricing lead to deadweight losses that would be eliminated under a regime of perfect price discrimination. But also recall that perfect price discrimination is a false hope and that imperfect price discrimination has more ambiguous results.

useless because it does not tell us how to trade-off among different sources of dynamic efficiencies. Notably, dynamic efficiency benefits are quite difficult to measure, evaluate, and trade off against one another.[12] Moreover, in a system of interdependent markets, there is no reason to systematically prioritize dynamic efficiencies in one market over another.

The point is to explain the problems with generic claims about commons management (nondiscrimination rules) and trade-offs between static and dynamic efficiencies and to question the relevance of the maxim that dynamic efficiencies trump static efficiencies. Generalizations about these complex relationships and trade-offs too often operate as analytical heuristics, establishing priors and cutting off needed theoretical and empirical analysis.

3. AVERSION TO GOVERNMENT REGULATION

Beneath particular claims about how nondiscrimination rules reduce incentives to invest often rests a more basic claim that any government interference with private resource management decisions will reduce incentives to invest in those resources. This type of claim would not be worth paying attention to if it were not so prevalent in policy debates. It is remarkable how deeply unsubstantiated assertions of this sort permeate public discourse. At bottom, this type of claim seems to reflect an aversion to government regulation and may be related to a range of cultural beliefs about the idealized relationship between government and private enterprise.[13]

Government regulation involves various costs, and there are many ways in which government failures can be substantial.[14] I do not deny these facts. But these basic facts do not support the broad claim that any government interference with private resource management decisions will reduce incentives to invest in those resources, much less the more specific claim about nondiscrimination rules reducing incentives to invest.

Broad claims of this sort conveniently ignore the fact that markets depend on a variety of government institutions to function; the claims fail to differentiate one type of government regulation from another; the claims rest on ideological and perhaps cultural beliefs rather than proven theory or empirical fact. Ultimately, there is no reason to credit these claims with predictive or prescriptive value when evaluating whether government-imposed commons management will impact incentives to invest in infrastructure.

---

[12] Canoy et al. 161 (2004).

[13] On how cultural values shape public risk perceptions and related policy beliefs, see Kahan & Braman (2006).

[14] There is an extensive literature in economics and political science. On regulatory inefficiency and capture, see, for example, Dal Bo (2006); PELTZMAN (1998); Laffont & Tirole (1991); Peltzman (1976); Stigler (1971).

B. Economic Characteristics of Infrastructure and Infrastructure Markets That Affect Supply-Side Incentives to Invest

This section explores economic characteristics that affect infrastructure supply and incentives to invest. I consider two related topics: First, characteristics of *infrastructure resources* that determine the *cost structure for supply*; and second, characteristics of the *infrastructure market* that determine whether the market is classified as a *natural monopoly*. After a brief discussion of each topic, I note implications for the relationship between commons management and incentives to invest.

1. ECONOMIC CHARACTERISTICS OF THE RESOURCE THAT INFLUENCE THE COST STRUCTURE FOR INFRASTRUCTURE SUPPLY

The economic characteristics of *infrastructure resources* shape the supply-side analysis. Recall the discussion in chapter 2 about the microeconomic perspectives on infrastructure. Infrastructure resources are durable and sharable. Supplying infrastructure typically involves high fixed costs coupled with comparably much lower variable costs and, consequently, decreasing average costs. Infrastructure resources exhibit economies of scale associated with indivisibilities. This is true of infrastructure resources that are pure public goods (nonrival) and those that are impure public goods (partially (non)rival). Most traditional infrastructures have high fixed costs that are "lumpy," meaning that the costs are sunk in discrete lumps. Lumpy fixed costs can vary in magnitude over time. For example, fixed costs can encompass significant upfront investments followed by maintenance and repair as well as periodic upgrades to expand capacity or improve technology; these fixed costs do not vary with each unit of production or each infrastructure user and thus must be shared. Often such fixed cost investments are irreversible, meaning that once they are made it may be impossible to repurpose the infrastructure. As a result of these characteristics, infrastructure supply tends to involve a complex trade-off between static and dynamic efficiencies.

At any point in time, it is efficient from a static perspective to price access to infrastructure at the marginal cost of providing the service to a particular consumer. Society benefits from having output or use increase at a price set equal to marginal cost until the full capacity of the infrastructure is utilized.[15] But marginal cost pricing will cause providers to be unable to cover their total costs, and consequently, from a dynamic perspective, providers will not have sufficient incentives to invest in producing the infrastructure at a

---

[15] Technically, the price charged to the marginal consumer should be set at marginal cost. Inframarginal consumers need not be charged marginal cost, at least if we follow the conventional approach of assuming such consumers are mere consumers and not productive users that generate spillovers. If we reject that assumption, the case for constraining the price charged inframarginal consumers to marginal cost needs to be revisited.

socially desirable level. Simply put, incentives to invest depend on expectations of positive returns, which means recovery of total costs, including a reasonable return on capital. If market provisioning of infrastructure is going to work efficiently, we expect pricing above marginal costs. This raises two important supply-side considerations:

First, pricing infrastructure above marginal costs means that there may be substantial deadweight welfare losses, as some potential users for whom the marginal benefits of using the infrastructure would exceed the marginal costs would be priced out. Although conventionally viewed as mere static efficiency losses, this can lead to both static and dynamic efficiency losses. In many contexts, the deadweight losses that accompany market provisioning can be a sufficient problem to justify government intervention in one form or another. As chapter 6 discussed, Hotelling proposed government subsidization of the fixed cost component of infrastructure investment in order to eliminate these deadweight losses. In many contexts, such as the natural monopoly context described below, government regulation or provisioning is justified because the deadweight losses that otherwise would accompany market provisioning are not tolerable. Each of these solutions to the deadweight loss problem introduces its own set of costs/problems to be considered and compared.

In some cases, price discrimination may mitigate concerns over deadweight losses, but not always, and not without introducing other costs/problems that must be considered. Recall that at a minimum, price discrimination must increase output to be beneficial.[16] A comparative analysis of deadweight loss mitigation strategies—government regulation, government provisioning, market provisioning with price discrimination—is required in those situations where price discrimination may be beneficial. One important consideration when evaluating the case for commons management is the potential impact on these deadweight loss mitigation strategies. Chapter 6 discussed the potential conflict between commons management and different forms of price discrimination. Note that even if there is a conflict (e.g., commons management would preclude a price discrimination strategy that would effectively reduce deadweight losses), such a conflict does not necessarily have a meaningful impact on supply-side incentives to invest in infrastructure.

An effective price discrimination scheme might reduce deadweight losses and increase producer returns, but it still may have only a negligible impact on supply-side incentives. In such a situation, the difficult empirical question—not answerable in the abstract based on theory—is whether the additional producer returns from discrimination have a relevant impact on the profitability of the investment and its attractiveness relative to alternative investment opportunities.

One might wonder whether there is some inconsistency here, because I have hypothesized an effective price discrimination scheme, yet I claimed that it need not improve incentives. The point is to distinguish between deadweight loss mitigation and incentives

---

[16] See chapter 6.

to supply. Generally, reducing deadweight losses is not directly relevant to producer incentives. Producers choose their pricing strategy to increase profits, and deadweight losses are a consequence of such choices. Producers certainly prefer to utilize price discrimination when doing so increases their profits, and reducing deadweight losses can be a consequence of such choices, but it is incidental to the providers' decision making. In some cases, there may be an indirect relationship between reducing deadweight losses via price discrimination and producer incentives. Specifically, where substantial deadweight losses are anticipated, the prospect of burdensome government regulation may discourage investment. Reducing deadweight losses via price discrimination may be an effective way to serve a broader population and limit the need for regulation.

Finally, in some special cases, price discrimination may be necessary to both reduce deadweight losses and maintain sufficient incentives to invest, and in those cases, the case for nondiscrimination rules may be particularly difficult. The key is to identify when price discrimination is necessary for infrastructure investment to be profitable. I explore this issue in the next section.

Second, the fact that market provisioning depends on pricing above marginal costs raises the question of whether providers will be able to sustain prices above marginal costs. If prices cannot be sustained at a level that at least approximates average cost pricing and enables a reasonable rate of return, adjusted to account for the risks involved, then market provisioning will fail to meet societal demand. Recall that there are two general constraints that might "push" price to marginal costs—competition and regulation. But these constraints are not always as forceful as one might think in decreasing average cost industries. In both competitive and regulated markets, prices generally exceed marginal cost.[17] One important reason is that decision makers who would effectively "put the pressure on"—(potential) competitors and regulators—recognize the prevailing cost structure and the need to recover total costs.

In the conventional model of a perfectly competitive market, price is pushed to marginal cost because rivals compete for any excess profits. If abnormal profits are made in a particular market, new entrants will be attracted to the market, and price-cutting to compete for customers will drive prices to marginal costs. While it is difficult to generalize about infrastructure markets, it is safe to say that infrastructure markets do not tend to follow the simple model just described. Since infrastructure markets typically involve significant up-front commitments and fixed costs that may be irreversible, entrants must evaluate whether they will be able to recoup those costs.

Absent government subsidies, we expect average cost pricing rather than marginal cost pricing to be the relevant (lower-bound) baseline for these actors.[18] Even in regulatory

---

[17] Duffy (2005); BAUMOL & BLINDER 276 (2009).

[18] BAUMOL & BLINDER 276 (2009).

contexts that purport to employ marginal cost pricing, the pricing methodology often incorporates a fee or transfer to account for some contribution to fixed costs.[19] Whether the relevant constraint is competition or regulation depends on the market conditions, which in turn depend on the cost structure of supply and demand. As the next section explains, some infrastructure resources are amenable to competitive supply, in which case competition should drive market prices toward average cost pricing; other infrastructure resources are not amenable to competitive supply, in which case market provision will tend toward monopoly, and, consequently, monopoly pricing absent regulation or average cost pricing with regulation.

What does the cost structure of infrastructure supply suggest about the relationship between commons management and incentives to invest?

- The cost structure of supply affects incentives to invest. Sufficient incentives to invest depend on an expectation of recovering total costs, including a competitive return on capital investment. The cost structure suggests that incentives to invest will be insufficient and undersupply will result, unless pricing above marginal cost and (at least) approximating average cost is sustainable. This means that a trade-off between static and dynamic efficiencies arises and deadweight losses are an important concern.
- The cost structure does not, however, suggest that discrimination is essential to incentives to invest. Price discrimination is not necessary for infrastructure investment to be profitable, at least not generally. Average cost pricing and monopoly pricing are two nondiscriminatory pricing regimes that often are sufficient for recovering total costs. Moreover, while firms and regulators sometimes employ pricing schemes that involve nonlinear pricing to reduce deadweight losses while covering total costs, these schemes do not necessarily conflict with commons management (see chapter 6).
- Nondiscriminatory pricing regimes that involve substantial deadweight losses may impact incentives to invest indirectly. Specifically, deadweight losses may create demand for government intervention, and the potential for such intervention may introduce risk for investors. This possibility should not be ignored or overstated. It is difficult to assess in the abstract. The likelihood of government intervention is greatest for infrastructure markets classified as natural monopolies, as discussed below. The likelihood is slight or nonexistent in competitive markets with average cost pricing.

---

[19] Brown & Sibley 67–68 (1986).

2. ECONOMIC CHARACTERISTICS OF THE MARKET: NATURAL MONOPOLY

In many infrastructure contexts, the economic characteristics of the *infrastructure market* raise additional concerns. Regulatory economists have long recognized that a market for infrastructure (with the cost structure described in the previous section) may be a natural monopoly. As W. Kip Viscusi, John Vernon, and Joseph Harrington explain:

> A market is a natural monopoly if, at the socially optimal output, industry cost is minimized by having only one firm produce. For the single-product case, if the average cost curve is declining for all outputs, then the cost of producing any industry output is minimized by having one firm produce it. In that case, the market is a natural monopoly regardless of market demand. Natural monopolies are likely to exist when there is a large fixed-cost component cost. For example, most public utilities, like local distribution of electricity and local telephone, are natural monopolies. In those cases, fixed costs (in particular, the cost of connecting homes and businesses to the distribution system) are large relative to marginal costs. Hence, average cost is declining for a wide range of outputs. For the relevant region of market demand, these markets are natural monopolies.[20]

Note that the cost structure of supply and market demand are both relevant. Shubha Ghosh explains:

> The natural monopoly situation arises when average total cost declines as a firm produces more output relative to demand in the marketplace. In such a situation, the relationship between [the] market price for the good, the marginal cost of production, and the average total cost are not in the necessary alignment for the long-run equilibrium required for competition. When average total cost is declining, several elements work against the forces of competition. First, a single firm can expand production while average total costs are falling and meet more of the market demand. As average costs fall, the single firm can afford to lower the price it charges and take demand away from other firms. Second, if firms try to compete in this way by expanding output and lowering price, the market price will be forced down until it becomes unprofitable for firms to continue in the marketplace. This downward pressure on price arises from the increased supply of product in the marketplace and the tendency of competition to force price down to marginal cost. These forces together result in what has been labeled destructive competition. Because of the

---

[20] VICUSI, VERNON, & HARRINGTON 309 (2005). Vicusi, Vernon, and Harrington explain that "[i]n the real world a single-commodity producer is rare" and that "the definition of natural monopoly in the multiple-output case is that the cost function must be subadditive. Subadditivity of the cost function simply means that the production of all combinations of outputs is accomplished at least cost by a single firm." *Id.* at 333–35.

destructive tendencies of competition, the argument goes, only one firm can profitably survive in the marketplace.[21]

Yet a significant change in the cost of supply might change the situation. For example, when a new production technology dramatically reduces fixed costs, competitive entry may be feasible and competitive supply may be sustainable. Or a significant expansion or contraction in demand also might change the classification of a market. For some very small markets, it makes sense only to have one provider sink the fixed costs, and for some very large markets, it makes sense to have multiple providers sink fixed costs.[22] Industries with very large minimum efficient scale, such as electricity, water, and sewer systems, are prone to natural monopoly where the minimum efficient scale is larger than the size of the market. The smaller the market or the larger the minimum efficient scale, the more likely a natural monopoly industry.[23] If market demand expands substantially, a natural monopoly situation may shift toward a competitive market situation.

Natural monopoly classification has some important economic implications. I note three: First, natural monopoly implies that society is better off if a single provider supplies the entire market, because this minimizes the cost of production, avoids wasteful duplication of large fixed costs, and, in some cases, limits disruption in local communities. For a natural monopoly, economies of scale exist at all reasonable scales, which means that it is more efficient for a single provider to expand production than for new firms to enter the market. Productive efficiency is achieved, but traditional concerns about allocative efficiency arise because of monopoly pricing and associated deadweight losses.

Second, natural monopoly implies that the market will tend toward monopoly. The first-mover may capture the market because of economies of scale and resulting barriers to entry; new entrants may be reluctant to challenge an incumbent that has already committed significant capital, has established a sizable customer base, and enjoys lower average costs. Even if multiple firms enter at the same time and compete, they are likely to compete for the market, and a single winner is likely to emerge. This is important because it suggests that monopoly in such a market might be more durable and impervious to competition than in markets not subject to decreasing average costs.

The previous two implications suggest a third: Natural monopoly implies the need (or least, a plausible case) for government regulation, or, in the alternative, government provisioning. Government regulation of natural monopoly markets typically involves restrictions on firms' ability to make decisions about price, quantity, entry, and exit. It also may address quality, investment, and other variables. The key regulatory objective is controlling deadweight welfare losses that otherwise would accompany private provisioning.

---

[21] Ghosh 1153 (2008).

[22] GAL 28 (2003) ("[S]mall market size . . . increases the prevalence of natural monopolies.").

[23] TAYLOR & WEERAPANA 288 (2009).

Government regulators must obtain information about the regulated variables, and in many cases, the best source of such information is the regulated entity. This leads to a rather basic problem of asymmetric information and moral hazard. Simply put, the regulated entity has better information than the regulator and has an incentive to play games. As Ghosh explains:

> Since the regulator depends upon the information supplied by the regulated body to set rates, the regulated body has the incentive to inflate the cost data in order to have the benefit of rates set as high as possible. This inflation may occur through fraud, but auditing and oversight can detect such abuses. More pernicious is the inflation that occurs from the lack of incentive to curtail cost. Economists Averch and Johnson first reported on the incentive of the regulated entity to gold plate its facilities by not producing the good or service in as efficient a manner as possible.[24]

Concerns over gold plating and cost inflation led to significant regulatory reforms in the late twentieth century. In some contexts, regulatory reforms aim to improve the regulatory system, for example, by shifting to modes of regulation that incorporate better incentives for firms to reduce costs. In other contexts, regulatory reforms aim to shift away from regulation altogether, for example, by removing certain regulatory restrictions, such as restrictions on entry.

In general, natural monopoly implies the need for price regulation to avoid monopoly pricing and push pricing toward the average cost baseline. Yet price regulation requires a significant administrative apparatus to determine costs and set rates, and there are a number of strong criticisms of the enterprise. The prospect of error in the assessment of cost and regulation of price may deter investment. Accordingly, alternative deadweight loss mitigation strategies, including price discrimination, should be considered.

Where price discrimination effectively increases output, it is possible that an unregulated monopolist practicing price discrimination could reduce deadweight losses to the same extent as, or an even greater extent than, price regulation, and improve incentives to invest relative to price regulation. We cannot assume this is the general case, however. Price discrimination and price regulation both entail costs, and both are imperfect. It is not enough to identify price discrimination that increases output; rather, output must increase to the same degree as it would under the comparable price regulation regime. The costs of implementing imperfect price discrimination in a manner that reduces deadweight losses to a level equivalent to those realized under imperfect price regulation may be substantial. Since those would be private costs (in contrast with imperfect price

---

[24] Ghosh 1163 (2008) (citing Averch & Johnson (1962)).

regulation), the infrastructure owner might not choose that level, absent regulatory or competitive pressure.

There is a tremendous amount of regulatory economics research on the classification of an industry as a natural monopoly, the attendant justifications for regulation, the benefits and costs of different regulatory modalities, and the potential for deregulation and competition in various infrastructure industries. The point is to emphasize the importance of natural monopoly as

> a construct used to identify certain market conditions that support only one supplier in order to promote efficiency. This construct is used to recognize that in some situations, the norm of competition may not lead to the most socially desirable result from the perspective of efficiency. In the case of natural monopoly, market competition may even be destructive to social goals.[25]

What does natural monopoly classification suggest about the relationship between commons management and incentives to invest?

- Natural monopoly status may affect incentives to invest in a variety of complex manners. The prospect of monopoly is a significant inducement for investment, and the potential durability of natural monopoly may be especially attractive to investors.[26] It is the potential monopoly profit that attracts investment more readily than alternative opportunities, and the prospect of government regulation may dampen that inducement. But it should not be assumed, on the basis of natural monopoly status, that monopoly profits are necessary to attract investment or that any additional investment attracted by the prospect of monopoly profits is an efficient allocation of resources. Average cost recovery is an appropriate baseline for evaluating whether incentives to invest are sufficient, and there is no reason to assume that monopoly pricing is needed. In some cases, it might be—for example, when externalities are relevant—but the case needs to be made.
- Natural monopoly status implies regulation, and that may impact incentives to invest. Firms may be reluctant to make substantial, irreversible fixed cost investments absent some commitment by the government that total costs will be recovered. In various contexts (for example, franchise agreements), public officials and

---

[25] *Id.* at 1152.

[26] The first mover may have a higher probability of earning monopoly profit but may also face a higher risk of failure. HILL & JONES 227 (2008) (describing risks and disadvantages balanced against the first-mover advantage, including high pioneering costs and fixed costs, mistakes due to early market uncertainty, risk of catering to the initial customer base instead of the mass market, and investing in older or obsolete technology).

private infrastructure suppliers effectively reach an agreement recognizing such a commitment and establishing regulatory terms.[27] Price regulation aims to cover total costs, including a reasonable return on capital taking risk into account. But the prospect of error in the assessment of cost and regulation of price may deter investment. Similarly, firms may be concerned that technological changes may support competitive entry in the future and jeopardize those irreversible investments.[28] These types of supply-side concerns have shaped regulatory regimes, including rate-setting practices, entry restrictions, universal service obligations, and exclusive franchising. (A complete survey of such regulation is beyond the scope of this discussion.)

- Natural monopoly status does not suggest, however, that commons management impairs incentives to invest, for reasons that parallel the discussion in the last section. Average cost recovery remains the relevant economic baseline for sufficient incentives to invest. Average cost pricing and monopoly pricing are two nondiscriminatory pricing schemes that generally maintain sufficient incentives; we discuss an exception in the next section. Regulators employ a variety of sophisticated pricing methodologies that deviate from these two regimes to mitigate deadweight losses, typically in a manner compatible with commons management.

- In some cases, commons management may preclude price discrimination that would reduce deadweight losses more effectively—that is, at lower cost and with less error—than alternatives, such as price regulation. This is a cost to be considered (in such cases), but it does not imply a corresponding impairment on incentives to invest. Deadweight losses and investment incentives are different economic concerns that may or may not correlate in different contexts.

3. CONCLUSIONS

The bottom line is that there is no reason to conclude that commons management negatively impacts incentives to invest in infrastructure in general. There is no doubt that the cost structure generally leads to pricing above marginal cost and consequently deadweight welfare losses, that a range of deadweight loss mitigation strategies may be desirable, and that commons management may conflict with one such strategy (price discrimination), but these features do not suggest that commons management generally will have a negative impact on incentives. Furthermore, there is no doubt that many infrastructure markets may be classified as natural monopolies and that the deadweight

---

[27] DOERN & GATTINGER 47 (2003); SIDAK & SPULBER 28 (1998); ROSSI 2–3 (2005); GOMEZ (2003).

[28] Yet entrants may be reluctant to enter the market and compete with an incumbent with a significant customer base. The incentives for different actors are quite complex and vary considerably from one context to another.

losses that would accompany monopoly pricing might justify government regulation (particularly where the monopoly is durable infrastructure), but these market conditions do not support the argument that commons management will have a negative impact on incentives.

C. Special Contexts Where Commons Management May Conflict with Supply-Side Incentives

This section first discusses the idea that average cost pricing generally maintains sufficient incentives to invest, and then turns to two special contexts where commons management may conflict with supply-side incentives. First, it considers the special case where price discrimination is necessary for sufficient incentives to invest; specifically, the case where the social value of infrastructure exceeds the total cost of provision, which in turn exceeds the market value appropriable under nondiscriminatory pricing schemes (e.g., average cost and monopoly pricing). In this scenario, market provisioning may depend on either price discrimination or government subsidies; otherwise, public provisioning may be necessary. Second, I consider the context of deregulatory transitions from regulated monopoly to competitive supply, a context in which particular nondiscrimination rules raise important incentive conflicts.

1. SUFFICIENT INCENTIVES TO INVEST AND THE AVERAGE COST BENCHMARK

Nondiscrimination rules do not necessarily or generally conflict with incentives to invest, or, conversely, discrimination is not necessary for sustaining sufficient incentives to invest. Various nondiscriminatory pricing regimes—for example, average cost pricing, monopoly pricing, nonlinear pricing (e.g., two-part tariff), peak load pricing, and congestion pricing—maintain sufficient incentives to invest in various contexts. This subsection unpacks the claim that average cost pricing generally maintains sufficient incentives to invest.

Average cost pricing, or, more accurately, average total cost pricing,[29] is a reasonable economic benchmark for thinking about the sufficiency of incentives to invest. I am not claiming that average cost pricing is *efficient*. My focus is on the supply side, particularly the relationship between pricing and the sufficiency of incentives to invest. When feasible (when the demand curve intersects the average total cost curve), average cost pricing

---

[29] When I refer to average cost pricing, I mean pricing based on average total cost, setting prices where the average total cost curve intersects with demand. In industries with long-run constant costs or long-run increasing costs, the competitive equilibrium price will be the point where short-run marginal costs and average total costs are equal. But in industries with long-run decreasing costs, the same equilibrium does not emerge, because marginal cost pricing would not cover average total cost.

covers total costs, including a reasonable return on capital. It does not over- or undercompensate investors and does not over- or underattract investment relative to alternative investment opportunities available in the market. In fact, average cost recovery reflects equilibrium in the market for investment. As John Duffy explains:

> If a certain class of investments in a capital good can, ex ante, be identified as returning more than average fixed costs (including a reasonable return on capital), then that class of investments is earning greater returns than other investments. Capital markets are very good at equalizing such supra-market levels of returns. Indeed, it is generally assumed that capital will flow from sectors of the economy that are underperforming (compared to the market average) to ones that are performing better.[30]

From a sufficiency of incentives to invest perspective, average cost recovery is an appropriate baseline, even though it may lead to inefficient outcomes from a broader welfare perspective because of the deadweight losses associated with pricing above marginal cost.

Certain types of investment may require "supra-market" returns, for example, to encourage substantial risk taking or account for external effects, but the economic case for such returns must be made in context and cannot simply rest on the cost structure of supply or natural monopoly concerns. Nonetheless, even when such a case is made, monopoly pricing is a nondiscriminatory pricing regime that may be sufficient. Or government subsidies might be appropriate. An even more exceptional case is where both average cost pricing and monopoly pricing provide insufficient incentives to invest and price discrimination is necessary for maintaining sufficient incentives, absent government subsidy. I explore that exceptional case below, but first a few caveats regarding my claim that average cost pricing is an appropriate economic benchmark for sufficient incentives.

Average cost pricing is imperfect. We are inevitably in a second-best world of competing imperfect alternatives with trade-offs to be evaluated. First, an average cost pricing scheme involves deadweight losses. Deviation from average cost pricing may be efficient because it reduces deadweight losses. (Chapter 6 discussed cost-based differential pricing regimes that deviate from average cost pricing in a manner that minimizes deadweight losses while still operating under a profit constraint.) But this does not mean that deviation is necessary to support investment or to improve investment incentives. Reducing deadweight losses and improving investment incentives are different economic objectives that may or may not correlate in different contexts.

Second, there are various practical difficulties with implementing average cost pricing. Since average cost decreases with the number of infrastructure users, average cost pricing

---

[30] Duffy 1079 (2005).

is not necessarily uniform for all users for the lifetime of the infrastructure. In practice, prices vary across time periods, production scales, and markets. As an economist might put it, both the average total cost curve and the demand curve change over time, and thus so does the efficient scale of production.

There are many complicated issues about how to distribute the fixed costs of infrastructure among different cohorts of users—across generations and among different products and services. Although it is convenient to assume that an infrastructure owner sells a single product, the infrastructural input, and to apply average cost pricing principles to that input, many infrastructure providers supply a range of products and services—trips of different length, freight of different size and weight, calls to different locations over varied distances. First, the marginal costs of providing different services may vary; second, it may be quite difficult to apportion common or joint costs based on the causal responsibility of each unit supplied. This means that average cost pricing must admit some variance or differentiation based on cost principles. There is an extensive economic literature on this topic. Let me highlight a few obstacles.

One significant obstacle to implementing average cost pricing is *information*—it is hard to know the actual costs of providing infrastructure and how those costs should be allocated among different users, different products or services, or different generations. This difficulty may be less of a concern in an unregulated market when average cost pricing is implemented privately and can be adjusted dynamically. In this context, private firms presumably have the best information about their costs. But, as noted, it is a significant concern in regulated markets when regulators obtain this information from regulated firms. On one hand, investors may be concerned about regulatory error in assessing costs and regulating prices, which may lead to undercompensation and deter investment. On the other hand, consumers, and the public more generally, may be concerned about asymmetric information and moral hazard, which may lead to overcompensation. This implementation problem is one that afflicts price regulation in particular.

A second, related obstacle to implementing average cost pricing is *time/timing*—it can be very difficult to (a) select the appropriate time frame over which to average costs, (b) allocate time-dependent costs, and (c) decide when to make irreversible investments.

- It can be difficult to determine the time period over which costs should be averaged (or fixed costs should be spread). Many infrastructure investments involve substantial up-front fixed costs that must be recovered over a relatively long time period. To support sufficient incentives to invest, it may be necessary to recover large fixed costs over a longer time period so that the fixed costs can be spread over a larger user group. For example, spreading fixed costs over a one-year period rather than a twenty-year period can dramatically affect pricing. Rates based on a one-year time horizon for fixed cost recovery would be substantially higher than rates based on a twenty-year horizon. The former may be too steep for most consumers, and the resulting market returns may be insufficient to cover total costs, making the investment unprofitable. Spreading the fixed costs over a larger group of consumers over a longer period of time increases the size of the consumer base and may make the investment economically viable. A countervailing concern is the time horizon for private investors and the discount rate applied to future returns on investment. If the time frame over which fixed costs must be spread for an infrastructure investment to be viable exceeds the time horizon for private capital investment, then average cost pricing may not yield sufficient incentives to invest. Put another way, private capital markets may be too short-term focused to support long-term infrastructure investments. This is one reason why government finances or supplies infrastructure in many contexts.

- Many of the costs that must be recovered through average cost pricing vary over time. The cost of capital needed for infrastructure includes depreciation, interest, profits, and certain taxes, and "[e]xcept for the portion of depreciation that varies with the extent to which the facilities are used . . ., these costs are a function of time—so much per dollar of investment per year—instead of a function of the rate of output from given facilities." Average cost pricing can recover these costs from consumers in different ways—for example, spread equally over time periods, spread equally over sales units, or through prices that fluctuate with the business cycle.[31]

- It can be difficult to know *when* to invest. Where investment is large, capital-intensive, and irreversible, investors must have a reasonable degree of confidence about the market demand for the infrastructure and its prospects for growth. Where there is uncertainty about future demand, how the market and related technologies will evolve, and the possibility of government intervention, investment can be risky—note that risk can arise from one or more different factors and can be cumulative. There may be gains to waiting, to delaying investment until more is known about how things will shape up. It can be quite difficult to determine what the risk-adjusted rate of return ought to be. This is related to the point made above regarding time horizons. Some infrastructure investments may be presently too risky for private capital markets, in which case additional inducement may be needed to support incentives to invest. Otherwise, government provisioning is an option.

There are volumes of economic literature on these topics. The point is that while average cost is an appropriate economic baseline for the sufficiency of incentives to invest in infrastructure, there are practical complications. The long-term, irreversible, capital-intensive, and risky nature of infrastructure investments may lead to supply-side problems. The expected returns from such investments may be insufficient to attract

---

[31] KAHN 105 (1998).

private capital and may require "supra-market" returns to attract private investment and encourage earlier deployment than might otherwise occur. But the case for such returns must be made in context rather than assumed. "Supra-market" returns may result from government subsidies or from sustained pricing over average cost—for example, monopoly pricing. The prospect of a monopoly in an infrastructure industry can be a significant inducement for investment.

2. SUFFICIENT INCENTIVES TO INVEST AND DISCRIMINATION

This section considers *when discrimination is necessary to support sufficient incentives to invest.* In many contexts, market provisioning of infrastructure is feasible without discrimination. Neither the cost structure of supply nor natural monopoly suggests that discrimination is necessary to support investment incentives, although in some cases discrimination may be an attractive option for mitigating deadweight losses.

Still, in some special cases, the additional returns appropriable by price discrimination can make an unprofitable investment profitable. As Kahn explains, in the "extreme case, price discrimination might make it economical for a private firm to construct [infrastructure] that would not otherwise be feasible because . . . at no single price . . . would revenues be large enough to cover total costs."[32] In this case, the average total cost curve never intersects the demand curve. Average cost and monopoly pricing are both incapable of providing sufficient revenues to cover total costs. Yet the investment could yield social welfare gains *if* the area under the demand curve exceeds total costs. In this situation, price discrimination would yield sufficient revenues to cover total costs and thus make the investment economical. So would a government subsidy that lowered the average total cost curve such that it intersected the demand curve. (See figure 8.1.)

The fact that the average total cost curve exceeds the demand curve seems to suggest that society should be less concerned with making this investment. In a sense, the investment appears quite costly relative to the gains, and it depends on price discrimination to be worthwhile. The net social welfare gains from making this type of investment, rather than others, may not be substantial.

There may some social value to waiting before accepting price discrimination or awarding subsidies. The option value may exceed the benefits from price discrimination or subsidies: As noted, these curves are dynamic; they shift over time. Perhaps the demand curve will shift upward and intersect the average total cost curve, or perhaps the average total cost curve will shift downward with some new technological development. Both demand-side economies of scale (network effects) and supply-side economies of scale may take time to kick in.

---

[32] *Id.* at 132, n.17.

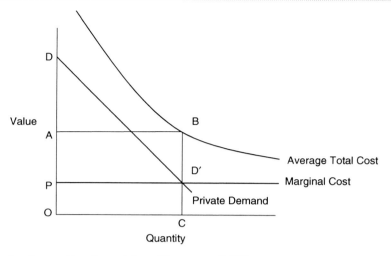

FIGURE 8.1 Average Cost Curve. Adapted from KAHN (1998).

Note: There is no single price on the demand curve that would cover total costs. However, if the area under the demand curve (ODD'C) is greater than the total cost (OABC), then the investment would be justified, and price discrimination could yield sufficient revenues.

If the question posed is whether or not to subsidize this type of investment (via government subsidies or toleration of price discrimination), the case appears rather weak, assuming that the private demand curve accurately reflects societal demand for the infrastructure, because the social gains do not appear substantial. Perhaps more importantly, the market would be capable of processing and responding to the relevant information about costs and benefits, and this presumably would provide incentives for entrepreneurial activity along the dimensions just noted (developing demand, production technologies). A price-discriminating infrastructure monopolist, on the other hand, presumably would savor the status quo and would be much less likely to invest in cost-reducing technology that would enable average cost pricing and potential entry.

Suppose, however, that the private demand curve fails to accurately and completely reflect societal demand for the infrastructure. As previous chapters discussed extensively, public, social, and mixed infrastructures facilitate production of public and social goods and thereby generate spillovers. Societal demand for such infrastructure may exceed private demand by a substantial margin. Suppose the private demand curve falls short of the average cost curve, but the social demand curve, which reflects both the value realized by the users and spillovers from their use, does not. Without price discrimination or government subsidies, market provisioning will not work in this context because revenues will not cover total costs, for the same reasons as the case without spillovers. The difficult question, however, is whether to solve the supply-side problem with price discrimination, government subsidies, or even government provisioning.

Interestingly, the demand-side perspective developed in this book supports arguments in favor of commons management in general but against commons management in the special case discussed in this section. Yet the supply-side argument to abandon commons management in favor of price discrimination is not overwhelming.

For commercial infrastructure, the case for both commons management and price discrimination is weak. There is less to be gained or lost, so it is probably best to let the market sort it out. For public, social, or mixed infrastructure, it would initially appear that the demand-side case for commons management and the supply-side case for price discrimination are both strong and thus a stalemate arises. But this initial impression must give way to a more contextual evaluation of the price discrimination scheme. (*Perfect* price discrimination would alleviate concerns on the demand and supply sides, but it is a red herring.) The supply-side case for price discrimination relies on an appeal to spillovers or social gains not reflected in market demand, but there is a risk that imperfect price discrimination will distort the productive activities of users and reduce the very social gains relied on to justify discrimination. Alternative institutional solutions, including government provisioning or government subsidies that aim to bring the costs down, are probably better candidates for addressing the supply-side problem and sustaining spillover-producing activities.

This section indicates a situation where commons management does conflict with incentives to invest and suggests the need for comparative analysis of alternative solutions to supply-side problems. In considering whether price discrimination is the best option, however, one must take into account the impact of imperfect price discrimination on both user activities and the generation of spillovers. In many cases where this situation arises, public subsidies or provisioning may be a preferable alternative to price discrimination.

Note that one should not assume that this situation is the general case for infrastructure. The claim that price discrimination is necessary for incentives to invest or that commons management conflicts with incentives to invest holds only for a special class of cases where (1) the average total cost curve fails to intersect the private demand curve, and (2) price discrimination yields benefits in excess of total costs (i.e., the area under the demand curve exceeds total costs).

Even when these two conditions are met, the argument for price discrimination (against commons management) is not necessarily strong. The strength of the argument depends on number of additional considerations:

- a comparative analysis of alternative institutional solutions that might solve the incentive problem in a more efficient (less costly) manner than price discrimination;[33]

---

[33] For example, government subsidy can reduce the average total costs and make the investment profitable without relying on price discrimination. Government subsidies also can be directed at research and development in technologies that may reduce the costs of infrastructure supply and facilitate competitive entry.

- the magnitude of the net social welfare gains;
- the option value of waiting and allowing demand to rise, supply costs to fall, economies of scale to kick in; and
- the social costs of imperfect price discrimination, including the impacts on the productive activities of users and the generation of spillovers.

I end this section with a caveat. I emphasize that the situation where price discrimination is necessary for incentives to invest is not the general case and suggest it is exceptional. But that might not be quite accurate, for two reasons: First, to my knowledge, no empirical evidence defines what is ordinary and what is exceptional in this context. Second, I may have framed the question in too static a fashion. Perhaps some/many infrastructure resources fall into this box (price discrimination is necessary for incentives to invest) at some point in time but as time passes they move out of the box as technology, demand, economies of scale, and so on develop. Regardless, the point is more or less the same—the two conditions need to be met for the claim to be valid, and the argument in favor of price discrimination faces additional hurdles.

3. TRANSITION FROM REGULATED MONOPOLY TO COMPETITIVE MARKETS

The structure, nature, form, and extent of economic regulation in various infrastructure industries dramatically changed over the past half-century (as in the half-century before it). Much of the recent change around the world has involved transitioning from fully regulated monopoly, and, in many cases, public ownership, to partially regulated, partially competitive markets—toward the goal of a complete transition to unregulated, competitive markets.

The objective in most contexts is to facilitate competitive supply whenever feasible. Whether the best policy path to competition involves full deregulation (eliminating controls on price, quantity, entry, and exit) or partial deregulation (e.g., eliminating most controls but leaving in place price regulation for the incumbent) depends on the context and is a highly contentious topic. There is an extensive economic literature.[34]

In most contexts, the transition from regulated monopoly to competition relies on mandatory sharing of the incumbent monopolist's facilities. This typically involves an open-access-style nondiscrimination rule that aims to facilitate entry into markets historically dominated by the monopolist. A persistent anxiety is whether mandatory sharing of incumbent facilities will undermine incentives to invest. First, there is a concern that incumbents will have less incentive to maintain or expand facilities or to invest in innovations

---

[34] The shift from fully regulated monopoly to competition is incredibly complex and involves a host of transaction costs and strategic issues that are hard to escape. A complete survey is beyond the scope of this chapter.

that would improve the quality or reduce the cost of their facilities. Second, there is a concern that entrants will simply elect to free ride on the incumbents' investment and will not invest independently in facilities. Third, given the difficulty in determining exactly what should be shared and on what terms, there is a more general concern that administrative costs, transaction costs, and uncertainty increase the cost of doing business and reduce incentives to invest. These incentive conflicts are real and need to be evaluated in context. The conflicts arise in large part because of the nature of the transition, the existing regulatory structure, and the continued presence of an incumbent.

To aid our analysis of incentive conflicts, consider two scenarios where the transition from regulated monopoly to competitive supply potentially leads to a conflict between commons management and incentives to invest: (1) partial transitions where natural monopoly segments remain and must be integrated with emergent competition in complementary segments, and (2) full transitions where natural monopoly erodes in all industry segments but incumbent monopolist(s) must share particular resources on a nondiscriminatory basis to facilitate the transition.

Although my description suggests that there is a bright line between these two scenarios, in reality it may be quite difficult to draw such a line. The first scenario may be a sustainable industry structure for a long period of time, or it may be an intermediate point on the path to the second scenario. For a transition to competition in an infrastructure industry, the key preliminary issue to resolve is what industry segments are natural monopolies and what industry segments can be competitive. If all segments fall into the latter category, then the second scenario applies, although the transition might be accomplished in multiple steps. I distinguish the two scenarios because each gives rise to somewhat different transitional objectives and, as a result, regulatory rules and incentive conflicts.

The electric power industry illustrates the first scenario. Electric power generation, transmission, and distribution was long considered a natural monopoly, but that view "has given way to a general consensus that the generation segment of power supply . . . would be more efficient and economical if left to the forces of an open market."[35] Generators can compete to supply power, but only if transmission and distribution are accessible on a nondiscriminatory basis. Generators need such access to reach customers. It is cost-prohibitive for generators to build independent facilities, and the risk of discriminatory practices by facility owners would deter new generators from entering the market. The transitional objective is not to introduce competition into the transmission and distribution infrastructure; those sectors remain regulated natural monopolies in most cases. Rather, the objective is to introduce and sustain competition in the generation market, which can significantly reduce the price of electricity for consumers.

---

[35] MᴄNᴇʀɴᴇʏ 1 (1996).

Nondiscrimination rules thus operate at the interface between the relevant markets (or industry segments). Price regulation typically applies to the natural monopoly segments of the industry and raises a host of complicated, well-known regulatory issues. But it important to make clear that incentive conflicts are primarily due to (and a major concern of) price regulation and are internal to the regulated monopoly segments of the industry. Nondiscrimination rules are not the source of conflict with incentives to invest in those segments.

The US telecommunication industry illustrates the second scenario. It has undergone an impressive transformation over the past fifty years, involving (attempted) transitions from monopoly to competition in long-distance and local services, as well as other related markets (e.g., customer premises equipment). The transformation involved a complicated mix of economic, political, technological, and regulatory forces, and it occurred in stages.[36] In various markets, the transition is far from complete. Nonetheless, the 1996 Telecommunications Act reflects a strong view that the objective is to introduce competition throughout the system, and quickly.[37] Arguably, two transitional objectives are in conflict: First, given the paradigm shift away from natural monopoly, the desired outcome is facilities-based competition—multiple competitors utilizing their own independent, though interconnected, networks to compete for customers. Yet a second objective seemed to be accelerated progress toward competition, which need not be facilities-based. As Robinson and Weisman state, Congress "wanted immediate results." In contrast with the electric power industry scenario, this transition involves nondiscrimination rules that are not limited to the interface between complementary markets. Instead, since the overarching policy objective is *opening* the market to competition, the rules apply to competitors within the same market—the incumbent and its competitors—and the goal is to facilitate competition with the incumbent. As a result, the rules are more controversial and the incentive conflicts more pronounced.

Perhaps most contentious is the requirement that incumbent local exchange carriers (ILECs) provide "to any requesting telecommunications carrier for the provision of a telecommunications service, nondiscriminatory access to network elements on an unbundled basis at any technically feasible point on rates, terms, and conditions that are just, reasonable, and nondiscriminatory. . . . An incumbent local exchange carrier shall provide such unbundled network elements in a manner that allows requesting carriers to combine such elements in order to provide such telecommunications service."[38] The basic idea is to "require the ILECs to offer pieces of their networks as unbundled building

---

[36] For a detailed history, see Robinson (1991).
[37] Robinson & Weisman 510 (2008).
[38] Section 251(c)(3).

blocks, which the CLECs can lease, repackage, and use to compete against the ILECs in telecommunications markets across the country."[39]

Critics argued that unbundling would radically undermine incentives to invest for all involved: Incumbents would be less inclined to maintain or improve their networks or invest in innovation, and entrants would be less inclined to invest in building their own facilities. (Both possibilities depend on the pricing.) In *AT&T v. Iowa Utilities Board*, Justice Stephen Breyer expressed concern about the incentive costs of overly broad sharing:

> Even the simplest kind of compelled sharing, say, requiring a railroad to share bridges, tunnels, or track, means that someone must oversee the terms and conditions of that sharing. Moreover, a sharing requirement may diminish the original owner's incentive to keep up or to improve the property by depriving the owner of the fruits of value-creating investment, research, or labor. And as one moves beyond the sharing of readily separable and administrable physical facilities, say, to the sharing of research facilities, firm management, or technical capacities, these problems can become more severe. One would not ordinarily believe it practical, for example, to require a railroad to share its locomotives, fuel, or workforce. Nor can one guarantee that firms will undertake the investment necessary to produce complex technological innovations knowing that any competitive advantage deriving from those innovations will be dissipated by the sharing requirement. The more complex the facilities, the more central their relation to the firm's managerial responsibilities, the more extensive the sharing demanded, the more likely these costs will become serious. . . . And the more serious they become, the more likely they will offset any economic or competitive gain that a sharing requirement might otherwise provide. The greater the administrative burden, for example, the more the need for complex proceedings, the very existence of which means delay, which in turn can impede the entry into long-distance markets that the Act foresees.[40]

---

[39] Covad Communication v. FCC, DC Cir. 2006, at p. 4. The court explained:

The basics of unbundling are relatively simple. Suppose a CLEC (such as Covad) wants to serve customers in Washington, D.C. One way of doing so is for Covad to purchase its own switches, trunks, and loops, which it can then use to offer service to its new customers. However, given that the local ILEC (e.g., Verizon) has already deployed switches, trunks, and loops to serve the market, it might be economically impossible for Covad to duplicate competitively Verizon's infrastructure. Through regulatory unbundling, however, Covad might be able to lease Verizon's switches, trunks, and loops as UNEs. Covad could then use combinations of UNEs to cobble together a network and compete against Verizon in Washington.

[40] 525 U.S. 366, 428–29 (1999).

Breyer worried that unbundling would go too far, forcing incumbents to share "virtually every aspect of its business." In a sense, too broad an unbundling regime risked limiting the intended full transition to a partial transition in which the incumbent monopolist remained the only actual network in town and meaningful competition in that market was only a fiction created by regulation—in other words, a bunch of alleged competitors that merely operated as resellers whose costs were fully determined by regulators.

The second scenario highlights a complicated question of whether an incumbent's facilities that can be shared should be shared, even if the facilities are not subject to natural monopoly conditions. In the presence of natural monopoly, competition in complementary markets depends on access to the monopolist facilities, and nondiscriminatory sharing is essential. Absent natural monopoly conditions, sharing may not be essential to competition, but still might be needed to accomplish other important transitional objectives, such as reducing competitive advantages that linger from the incumbent's monopoly position, facilitating a more rapid transition from monopoly to competition, inducing entry that involves different combinations of existing and new facilities, or reducing wasteful duplication. Yet the incentive effects of such sharing can be significant. A new entrant that can lease facilities from the incumbent on a forward-looking, incremental cost basis may be much less likely to build duplicative independent facilities. As I have repeatedly emphasized in this and previous chapters, *pricing* plays an important role in shaping incentives in these contexts, but disabling price discrimination generally does not. The scope of nondiscriminatory sharing obligations among competitors within a market is highly contested, in part because of differing opinions about what the primary objectives of a transition from regulated monopoly to competition are and how those objectives should be prioritized. Consider a few of the possible objectives:

- Minimize (reduce) natural monopoly or the competitive advantages that linger from monopoly position in market.
- Maximize (increase) competition in any form.
- Maximize (increase) facilities-based competition in particular.
- Maximize (increase) the rate of transition to competition.
- Encourage or induce entry.
- Remove (artificial) barriers to entry.
- Minimize (reduce) regulation.
- Minimize (reduce) wasteful duplication of facilities.

Policy choices need to be made, and trade-offs are inevitable. Subsequent chapters revisit some of these issues.

4

Traditional Infrastructure

BUILDING FROM CHAPTERS 4 and 5, Part IV illustrates how the demand-side analysis applies to traditional infrastructure resources and how commons management is implemented. Specifically, chapter 9 examines transportation infrastructure (roads), and chapter 10 examines telecommunications infrastructure (telephone networks). Both road and telecommunications infrastructures are the foundation for markets "affected with the public interest." These infrastructures provide generic public capabilities, mobility and communication, that allow users to engage in an incredibly wide variety of productive activities that generate private, public, and social goods and, consequently, substantial spillovers to the benefit of society. These infrastructures are mixed infrastructure and are not optimized or prioritized for any particular use, user, or market. The vast majority of road infrastructure is publicly owned, and the vast majority of telephone infrastructure is privately owned. The supply-side stories for these infrastructures are quite different. Yet both types of infrastructures are sustained as commons, accessible to the public on nondiscriminatory terms. Building from chapters 6, 7, and 8, these chapters also discuss a range of complications. Road infrastructure highlights complications, such as congestion, negative externalities associated with environmental pollution, and public financing of maintenance and improvements. Telephone infrastructure highlights other complications, such as regulatory costs and the difficulties of transitioning from regulated monopoly to competition. These chapters show how these fundamental infrastructure resources generate value for society, the critical role of commons management, and the various institutional means for sustaining commons when faced with various complications.

9

TRANSPORTATION INFRASTRUCTURE

Roads

TRANSPORTATION INFRASTRUCTURES have been critical to the prosperity and growth of human civilization and are integral to modern society. From ancient long-distance walking tracks for people and animals to modern aviation, transportation infrastructure evolved with society and its needs and with technological progress. Today, many different modes of transport interconnect to form an incredibly complex, global meta-network. Local, regional, national, and international transport occurs on land, over water, and in the air. Many trips are intermodal, meaning that users depend on more than one mode of transport to complete their trip.

Transportation infrastructures facilitate the movement of people and goods. This basic functionality fuels the development of commercial and noncommercial relationships; cultural, economic, educational, and social exchange; markets and other nonmarket social systems; and interdependence within and across communities. In the United States, the human capability supported by basic transportation infrastructure—*personal mobility*—is valued in practical, instrumental terms and as a foundational component of personal liberty.

This chapter illustrates many of the economic concepts discussed in previous chapters. First, road infrastructure exhibits the classic supply-side economic characteristics, which are commonly discussed in transportation, public welfare, and regulatory economics. The cost structure of supply and strong natural monopoly tendencies indicate that markets will fail to provide road infrastructure efficiently and that provision by either the government or a regulated monopolist will be necessary. In the United States, government provision dominates as the solution to this problem. Second, road infrastructure exhibit the demand-side economic characteristics explored in chapters 4 and 5. Road infrastructure is mixed infrastructure that generate massive spillovers for society by enabling users to engage in an incredibly wide variety of productive activities that yield private, public, and social goods. The case for commons management is quite strong. Not surprisingly (given government provisioning), road infrastructure is managed openly as commons. Government provisioning alleviates supply-side objections to commons management, but two major concerns remain: congestion and the generation of substantial negative externalities from environmental pollution. This chapter shows how to address these significant concerns in nondiscriminatory ways that sustain the road infrastructure commons. With respect to congestion, a combination of approaches, including capacity expansion, congestion pricing, and rationing, may be required to manage congestion. In addition, use restrictions are necessary to manage interaction effects among uses of certain types of roads. With respect to environmental externalities, the current approaches regulate fuels and vehicles and target particular pollutants in an effort to internalize external costs, minimize pollution, and incentivize innovation in more environmentally sound and energy-efficient technologies. These approaches have been quite effective with respect to many types of air pollutants. It may be that such approaches are insufficient to reduce greenhouse gas emissions and combat climate change and that more drastic interventions may be required if reductions are to come from the transportation sector.

A. Overview of Roads

Roads are ubiquitous in modern societies. "Between 1900 and 2000, the length of paved roads in the United States increased from 240 km to 6,400,000 km with virtually 100% of the U.S. population having almost immediate access to paved roadways."[1] In the United States, there are over 4 million miles of public roads and thousands of miles of private roads.[2] Most mileage is rural, but a majority of road usage occurs in urban areas.[3]

---

[1] Levinson 175–88 (2005); PEAT (2002).

[2] In many other countries, and even in the United States' past, private roads play a more significant role. Beito 23 (1993). Private roads and highways are common in Asia and Europe. BARSBY (1997). Build-own-operate-transfer (BOOT) models, and variants thereof, are common financing model for large highway infrastructure projects in the developing world, where the infrastructure provider privately owns the roadways for a specified duration, recouping construction costs and earning income from the collected tolls. INTERNATIONAL FINANCE PROJECT 91 (1999).

[3] DOT (2008). For all functional classifications of roads, passenger vehicles contribute the greatest number of VMT. *Id.*

The national road system is a complex, extensive network. Transportation experts classify roads functionally:[4]

> Roads serve two important functions: access and mobility. The better any individual segment is serving one of these functions, the worse it is at serving the other. Thus, routes on the Interstate Highway System allow a driver to travel long distances in a relatively short time, but do not allow the driver to enter each farm field or business along the way. Contrarily, a subdivision street allows a driver access to any address along its length, but does not allow the driver to travel at a high rate of speed and is frequently interrupted by intersections, often containing traffic control devices.

The functional hierarchy is similar to that of other networked infrastructure, such as telecommunications. When viewed from a systems perspective, the complex network of roads from arterials to local roads constitutes a general-purpose infrastructure. But when individual segments are evaluated independently, arterials and collectors appear infrastructural, while local roads seem less so; arterials and collectors focus on mobility and the generic opportunities mobility provides, whereas local roads serve the more specific functional purpose of providing access to particular properties. The same analysis applies to a host of complementary resources, such as bridges and tunnels, which are integral components of road infrastructure. For example, a bridge may appear less infrastructural when viewed in isolation, because it facilitates access to two specific locations—each side of the bridge—and in that sense is special-purpose. But the resource-specific analysis will vary based on the locations being connected by the bridge; a bridge that connects two arterials is different than a bridge that connects a local road to a private property. More generally, as with many individual road segments, a system-based analysis recognizes that these complementary resources are integral parts of the interconnected road infrastructure. For the sake of brevity, I focus on roads and refer generically to road infrastructure, keeping in mind that road infrastructure includes these complementary resources.

B. Economic Characteristics of Road Infrastructure

The supply-side characteristics of road infrastructure are familiar: Road infrastructure requires significant capital investments in the construction and maintenance of physical

---

[4] "Arterials provide the highest level of mobility, at the highest speed, for long and uninterrupted travel. Arterials typically have higher design standards than other roads. They often include multiple lanes and have some degree of access control. . . . Collectors provide a lower degree of mobility than arterials. They are designed for travel at lower speeds and for shorter distances. Generally, collectors are two-lane roads that collect travel from local roads and distribute it to the arterial system." DOT (2008).

assets that are "extremely long-lived and expensive to replace." As Kenneth Button observed, "we still use ports and roads constructed in Roman times."[5] Maintaining the condition and performance of road infrastructure requires periodic capital investments because large volumes of traffic, particularly heavy trucks, along with weather and environmental factors, deteriorate the physical assets. The large capital investments tend to be sunk costs; once these infrastructure resources are built, there are rarely alternative uses to which they can be put. The fixed costs are substantial, but the marginal cost of infrastructure use is generally quite small, absent congestion and putting aside negative externalities associated with pollution (discussed below). Off-peak marginal costs can approach zero. (Recall our hypothetical from chapter 3 of a driver using the highway at 2 a.m.) Road infrastructure involves significant economies of scale.[6] Economists recognize that for road infrastructure, supply-side economies of scale kick in due to the cost structure of supply, and demand-side economies of scale kick in due to network effects. Due to the physical nature and scale of roads, location-specific advantages, the substantial fixed costs involved, and the disruptive nature of road construction and maintenance for communities and the environment, road infrastructure exhibits strong natural monopoly tendencies.[7]

Road infrastructure raises the conventional supply-side concerns discussed in the previous chapter. The cost structure of supply and natural monopoly tendencies imply market failure and either government provisioning or provisioning by regulated monopoly. In the United States, most road infrastructure is publicly owned and openly accessible. Public providers struggle with managing congestion and with financing maintenance and improvements.

From the demand side, road infrastructure raises many of the issues discussed in previous chapters. Road infrastructure is mixed infrastructure—partially (non)rival input into a wide variety of productive activities that yield private, public, and social goods.

The sharable but congestible nature of road infrastructure raises many of the issues discussed in chapter 7. The institutional approaches to managing the boundary between nonrivalry and rivalry—to leverage nonrivalry and manage congestion—vary across contexts. We consider this issue in detail below. Congestion is a significant public concern for road infrastructure because the consequential costs of delays and the environmental pollution from congested traffic can be substantial.

---

[5] BUTTON 13 (2010).

[6] WALKER (1942).

[7] BROWN 97 (2010). If one focuses on (a) individual road segments or (b) origin-destination pairs, competition might look feasible and attractive, but this is too narrow a focus; one needs to consider the road system more broadly.

Road infrastructure is generally described as a form of public capital. Users of road infrastructure demand access and use of the infrastructure to satisfy their demand to engage in activities at the "ends." As Button observed:

> Possibly the most important characteristic of transport is that it is not really demanded in its own right. . . . People wish, in general, to travel so that some benefit can be obtained at the final destination. The trip itself is to be as short as possible. Of course, there are "joy riders" and "tourists" but they tend to be in the minority. Similarly, users of freight transport perceive transport as a cost in their overall production function and seek to minimize it wherever possible. The derived nature of the demand for transport is often forgotten in everyday debate but it underlies all economics of transport.[8]

At a foundational level, people understand that mobility is a rather basic and important capability. While movement or travel for its own sake is occasionally romanticized, for the most part, people move because of—and recognize that the value of movement derives from—the opportunities movement creates. The range of economic, social, recreational, educational, employment, and other opportunities is extensive.[9]

By facilitating a wide range of productive activities, road infrastructure generates many positive externalities. In modern society, access to transportation infrastructure is essential to meaningfully exercising the capability to move about freely and, consequently, to participating in a host of socially valuable activities, many of which involve economies of scale and scope.[10] Foremost, at least in the minds of economists, may be commerce. As chapter 1 noted, Rose explained that commerce is an "interactive practice whose exponential returns to increasing participation run on without limit. . . . Through ever-expanding commerce, the nation becomes ever-wealthier, and hence trade and commerce routes must be held open to the public, even if contrary to private interest. Instead of worrying that too many people will engage in commerce, we worry that too few will undertake the effort."[11]

Managing road systems in an openly accessible manner is the key to sustaining and increasing participation in commerce, and commerce itself is a productive activity that generates significant positive externalities. Commerce generates private value that is easily observed and captured by participants in economic transactions, as buyers and sellers

---

[8] BUTTON 13 (2010).

[9] See *id.*

[10] One might disagree with my claim that transportation infrastructure is *essential* to participation, because many activities might occur on a smaller local scale. But without access to transportation infrastructure, economic, social, and other relationships might be severely restricted and prevent exploitation of economies of scale in various social, political, and cultural activities.

[11] Rose 769–70 (1986).

exchange goods and services, but it also generates social value that is not easily observed and captured by participants, value associated with socialization, cultural exchange, and other such processes. Road infrastructure expands the scale and scope of commercial opportunities, including the range of products available, the sources of raw materials, and the possibilities of specialization and "exploitation of other major economies of scale."[12] This is what makes road infrastructure critical to economic development and growth.[13]

While commerce is an excellent example of a productive use of roads that generates positive externalities and social surplus, there are many others, such as traveling to other communities to see friends and relatives or enjoy recreational activities, or visiting state parks. These activities generate private value that is easily observed and captured by participants as well as social value that is not as easily observed and captured.

More generally, transportation infrastructure expands opportunities for social intercourse and exchange of ideas, cross-cultural opportunities such as the exchange and examination of art and historical items, and even the range of "life-style options open to people."[14] Transportation infrastructure brings people and communities together, and still allows them to live apart—for example, enabling people to separate work from home. The development of cultural, economic, political, and social relationships within and across geographically separate communities builds social capital and value not reflected or captured fully in market transactions or macroeconomic metrics such as GDP.[15] The list could go on extensively.[16] Road infrastructure is undoubtedly mixed infrastructure.

C. Commons Management

In the United States, most road systems are owned and provided by government,[17] and, not surprisingly, most road systems are managed as commons. It is worth emphasizing at

---

[12] BUTTON 17 (1993).

[13] Road infrastructure enables the creation and expansion of all types of markets—for finished goods, raw materials, labor, services, and so on. Simarmata 30 (1998). Developed road infrastructure is an essential factor facilitating and accelerating economic growth, which in turn enables the addition of more roads. Ortiz-Moctezuma et al. 259 (2010).

[14] BUTTON 48–49 (2010) (quoting THOMSON (1974)).

[15] As Kenneth Button notes: "Without transport, social relationships and contacts are normally very restricted. Transport permits social intercourse, and with it may come a greater understanding of the problems and attitudes of various geographically distant groups." BUTTON 49 (2010). Button goes on to describe the profound effects of transport-enabled social interactions in the developed and developing world.

[16] Perhaps it can be said that we, as a society, value mobility as a basic capability because it is a freedom we value individually *and* because of its spillover potential. Transportation infrastructures make the capability a reality. In future work, I plan to examine the relationships between infrastructure, capabilities, and spillovers. Cf. Sen (1993); SEN (2009).

[17] Public ownership and provisioning has not always been the norm in the United States. In the nineteenth century, private roads comprised a significant portion of the road system, including private turnpikes between

the outset that public ownership and provisioning makes commons management much easier to implement and much less objectionable economically and politically when compared to imposing commons management on privately owned and provisioned infrastructure. While the decision to rely on public provisioning raises its own set of concerns, the point is that solving the supply-side dilemma through public provisioning eliminates many of the arguments against commons management: private providers' supply-side incentives are not relevant; the case for price discrimination disappears; the costs of government regulation imposing commons management and policing implementation also disappear. While some might argue that public roads should be privatized or that future construction of road infrastructure should rely more on private provisioning than on public provisioning, few would argue that government-owned road infrastructure should not be managed as a commons. Again, commons management does not mean free. Many, including me (below), argue that certain forms of nondiscriminatory road pricing schemes should be employed to manage congestion and finance construction, maintenance, and improvements. There are considerable debates about the details of any road pricing scheme, and there are many different approaches to implementation. But few advocate price discrimination as a general solution.

Most road infrastructure is accessible to the public on nondiscriminatory terms. Roads are not optimized for a particular user or market, although they could be.[18] Priority is not

---

towns and cities as well as short turnpikes and plank roads that connected communities to canals and railways. Klein & Fielding (1992). Klein and Majewski suggest that turnpike investments were community investments that "promised little in the way of direct dividends and profits, but [] offered potentially large indirect benefits." Klein & Majewski (2008). *Id.* As Henry Clay told Congress:

> I think it very possible that the capitalist who should invest his money in these objects [turnpikes] might not be reimbursed three percent annually upon it; and yet society in various forms, might actually reap fifteen or twenty per cent. The benefit resulting from a turnpike road made by private association is divided between the capitalist, who receives his toll, the land through which it passes and which is augmented in its value, and the commodities whose value is enhanced by the diminished expense of transportation.

Annals of Congress 1377 (1817–18). Toll roads often involved discriminatory concessions, such as toll exemptions. Common carriage did not apply to private toll roads, although some state charters imposed comparable obligations, and common-law obligations sometimes applied under a "common callings" theory or "public utility" theory. REGIONAL STUDIES ASSOCIATION 186 (1989). Common callings encompassed "what we would today call infrastructure services in transportation and communications, together with associated facilities such as inns." NOAM 213 (2001). Under the "public utility" theory, a public utility was "obliged to serve all those who desire its services and are able to pay for them." DODD 161 (1954). This notion gave rise to the public utility approach to regulation, wherein a private enterprise was granted an exclusive franchise to provide monopoly service in exchange for, among other thing, nondiscriminatory rates and serving all customers. STERLING ET AL. 22–23 (2008).

[18] Road infrastructure generally is generic, mixed infrastructure, not optimized for any particular use or downstream market. Use of road infrastructure for the movement of people and freight are interdependent. Trucks and cars share roads. So do other users, such as bicyclists and pedestrians. Optimization is feasible, and in some

given to "high-value" users, except in very rare circumstances such as an emergency vehicle with its sirens blaring. *Priority is not for sale.*[19] Instead, roads provide a basic capability to all users on an equal basis,[20] allowing them to move about and connect with others; users decide how and when to exercise that capability. Commons management effectively sustains road infrastructure as mixed infrastructure and fuels the comedy of the commons.

Since roads are funded typically through indirect taxes rather than direct usage-based fees, users may perceive roads to be "free." Users pay for vehicles and fuel, and they pay taxes and fees, but these payments are not directly tied to infrastructure use. There are exceptions, of course: Many arterial highways are partially funded by tolls. The tolls tend to be usage-based and tend to vary based on both distance traveled and vehicle type to account for differences in wear and tear. Although use of such roads is not free, the fees are nondiscriminatory and essentially cost-based.

The combination of commons management and perceived "free" access leads to three complications raised in chapter 7. Specifically, three different forms of the tragedy of the commons arise: First, roads are partially nonrival and subject to congestion. Second, interaction effects arise because some uses are interdependent in dimensions other than capacity consumption. For example, trucks, automobiles, bicycles, in-line skaters, and pedestrians affect each other in complicated ways while sharing roads; the most obvious are safety risks. Such effects often constitute externalities because users do not fully account for the risks posed to other users by their own activities. As a result, safety risks often require use prioritization or other arrangements. Third, certain uses not only consume road capacity but also consume other shared resources subject to the tragedy of the commons, such as the atmosphere. Specifically, fuel consumption leads to pollution and significant negative externalities. The tragedy arises because both resources—road and environmental infrastructures—are managed as commons. I address each of these complications below and explain how commons are (can be) sustained.

I. ROAD CONGESTION

While most roads are not congested most of the time, road congestion is a persistent feature of many road systems and a source of significant social costs. Congestion occurs

---

cases it may be desirable. Consider optimization for freight. Road infrastructure optimized (prioritized) for freight transport might reduce accidents, congestion, and environmental pollution and, in some contexts, might be attractive if alternative modes of public transport are available. Alternatively, consider optimization for automobiles, bicycles, or even pedestrians, perhaps on safety grounds or to encourage bike riding or walking for health and environmental reasons. When some roads cease to be useful as general-purpose infrastructure, conversion to special-purpose modes may be worthwhile. But that is not the norm.

[19] For those aching to disagree and raise the example of paid-for priority on some highways, keep in mind that such arrangements are very much the exception and not the rule. See below.

[20] Benkler (2011) refers to this as a "symmetric freedom to operate."

when one user's use of the shared resource (e.g., road, bridge, or tunnel) causes another user delay in using the resource. Congestion often arises because demand exceeds supply, when the number of users (vehicles) exceeds available resource capacity. Such "bottle-neck delays are the single largest cause of delays [on highways] nationwide."[21] In this con-text, congestion is a function of variable demand imposed on a resource system with finite renewable capacity and thus implicates the boundary between nonrivalrous and rivalrous consumption. This boundary is crossed regularly over time, often in predictable patterns that allow for the delineation of peak and off-peak periods.

Congestion also arises because external factors can influence traffic. Prominent exter-nal causes include traffic incidents, bad weather, work zones, and poor signal timing.[22] These factors may reduce the available resource capacity—for example, when a four-lane highway is reduced to two lanes to accommodate a work zone—or these factors may influence the behavior of drivers—for example, the familiar experience of delays caused by rubbernecking, where drivers slow to observe an accident. These factors may be more variable, less predictable, and consequently more difficult to manage than bottlenecks.

The costs of congestion are substantial. They include the costs associated with delay, less reliable travel times, use of additional fuel, drivers' frustration, and a host of other economic and social costs. In 2009, the Congressional Budget Office (CBO) reviewed the best available estimates:

> According to one widely cited study, highway congestion caused 4.2 billion hours of delay and the use of 2.9 billion gallons of additional fuel in 2005, at a cost of $78 billion to highway users. Other similar studies have found that highway users faced significant delays and costs because of congestion at major urban intersections, on major transportation corridors between cities, and at locations with large amounts of truck traffic. Moreover, the costs of highway congestion extend beyond the high-way users themselves. One recent study estimated that highway congestion cost businesses in one major metropolitan area up to $1 billion per year in increased production and distribution costs, over and above the costs borne by highway users themselves. Congestion is estimated to represent half of all the "external costs" that an automobile user imposes on other members of society. (Other external costs include costs imposed by pollution generally, greenhouse gases, and accidents.)[23]

It is widely understood that traffic congestion is a significant problem that requires attention. As the CBO notes, "Highway congestion has been increasing and is expected

---

[21] Congressional Budget Office (CBO) 1 (2009), Figure 1-1.

[22] *Id.*

[23] *Id.* See Komanoff 129 (1994) (traffic congestion drains US economy of approximately $168 billion 1990 dollars).

to be even more prevalent in the coming years. According to estimates by the Department of Transportation Federal Highway Administration, 11 percent of the major highways in the United States experienced peak-period congestion in 2002, but by 2035, that figure is expected to rise to 40 percent." The problem is especially acute for urban infrastructure.[24]

As chapter 7 explained, there are four conventional approaches to managing congestion: (1) capacity expansion, (2) limitations on the user population, (3) congestion pricing, and (4) use restrictions. Of these, capacity expansion and congestion pricing are the primary options for mitigating congestion on the national road infrastructure. Capacity expansion is the dominant approach to managing road congestion in the United States. Congestion pricing is exceptional, although it has attracted significant attention in the past decade. Limiting the user population is not a politically feasible or economically attractive option.[25] Since most roads are publicly owned, the public at large remains the relevant user population. As discussed below, rationing road capacity during congested periods is a useful option in certain contexts—for example, allocating three out of four lanes to a particular direction (inbound/outbound) during peak periods. As the next section explains, use restrictions are important for managing interaction effects; for example, many major roads restrict access to designated vehicular traffic and do not allow pedestrians or bicyclists. Use restrictions are less viable as a solution to highway congestion.

Maintaining capacity in excess of anticipated peak demand, that is, maintaining a capacity cushion, is one way to avoid bottleneck congestion. This can be quite difficult with respect to road infrastructure. Supplying roads, bridges, and tunnels is lumpy and can be intensely disruptive to the local population and environment. For most road infrastructure, it is not easy to add capacity in a modular fashion; moreover, even where feasible, expanding one road or road segment can induce demand and have impacts on other segments, making it difficult to fully anticipate the impact of modular expansion on the road system.

Investing in new road infrastructure capacity runs into the difficulties discussed in chapter 7. It can be incredibly expensive and difficult to finance. Public provisioning overcomes these obstacles but not without considerable controversy, tremendous politicization, special-interest influence, and waste. As one commentator notes, "New road

---

[24] "Some 70 percent of all urban interstates are congested during rush hours." Poole 166 (1996); SMALL ET AL. 80–81 (1989) (providing additional data on increasing levels of metropolitan road congestion). The 2010 Urban Mobility Report analyzed congestion in 439 US urban areas, suggesting that congestion has increased significantly since the metrics were first tracked in 1982. Texas Transportation Institute (2010). The report tabs the total 2009 cost of congestion at $115 billion, burning 3.9 billion gallons in wasted fuel, and causing the average commuter thirty-four hours of peak delay.

[25] Programs to limit the user population, such as quota systems, have gained traction in other countries, such as China. Zhao (2011); Yujie (2011).

construction has been described as the quintessential form of political pork."[26] Tolls and increased gas taxes notwithstanding, it is generally very difficult to cover the costs of new infrastructure capacity directly from users. Moreover, adding capacity can create classic inefficiencies: Maintaining sufficient capacity to avoid congestion during peak periods entails waste during off-peak periods, and adding capacity can induce demand and distort incentives among users, for example by diminishing incentives to choose alternative routes, modes of transportation, or travel times. Despite such difficulties, capacity expansion remains the dominant approach in the United States.[27]

In lieu of expanding capacity, government has two options for reducing congestion: rationing and congestion pricing. As examples of rationing, "the government might have lanes that reverse direction depending on the extent of traffic flow during different times of day," or "the government might dedicate particular lanes to 'express use' (i.e., limited ability to enter into, and leave from, those lanes to the rest of the expressway and other roads)."[28] These efforts partition traffic and allocate road capacity based on anticipated traffic patterns.[29] They can increase the efficiency with which existing capacity is used, but they are imperfect and have limited scope. Rationing alone does not improve drivers' incentives, because external costs are not internalized, and existing capacity remains a constraint; thus, rationing may be an insufficient fix if congestion persists or demand increases. Moreover, rationing may impose costs on other users; for example, converting a lane from inbound to outbound traffic for the afternoon rush hour may cause congestion for inbound traffic.

High Occupancy Vehicle ("HOV") lanes are a form of rationing that encourages users to internalize congestion costs, to a degree. Congestion arises not only from users' choice of route and travel time, but also because many users choose to travel alone or in vehicles that are not fully occupied. Demand for trips can be met with less infrastructure congestion if travelers share rides in carpools, vanpools, or buses.[30] Whether or not to share a ride is a relevant choice parameter. HOV lanes ration capacity by restricting access to vehicles carrying more than one passenger (the minimum number of required passengers

---

[26] Nash 702 (2008).

[27] Nash suggests the best explanation of the preference for capacity expansion is rooted in public choice theory. *Id.*

[28] *Id.*

[29] For example, transportation authorities in Chile in 2001 put in place a system that varied the direction of traffic on six major axes in the city, with results showing a 43 percent savings on travel times on reversible-flow roads during the morning peak hours. BULL 62–63 (2004).

[30] HOV lanes are only one of multiple ways to encourage ride sharing. Offering preferred parking and reduced parking costs for carpools, as well as instituting carpool rider–matching services and commute rewards programs (prize drawings), encourages ride sharing and may qualify for federal or state benefits. SORENSEN ET AL. 311 (2008); US Environmental Protection Agency (US EPA) (2001). Dynamic ride sharing, wherein riders and drivers are matched in real time through GPS-equipped cell phones, is touted as the wave of transportation's future. *Id.*; Barringer (2011).

varies). Dedicating HOV lanes provides the impetus to consider ride-sharing options. Not surprisingly, as a result of this restriction "HOV lanes are less congested than their open-access counterparts."[31] However, due to the imposed restriction HOV lanes "often operate at volumes well below the traffic carrying capacity of such facilities, even during peak hours."[32]

In some cases, HOV lanes have been converted to HOT lanes that restrict access like HOV lanes but also permit vehicles that fall under the occupancy threshold to purchase access by paying a toll. This is one (rare) example of paid priority on the highway.

Economists generally prefer congestion pricing of roads as a commons management strategy, for good reasons.[33] As chapter 7 explained, congestion pricing aims to internalize the external congestion costs and better match price with the marginal social cost of road use. In theory, congestion pricing leads to (a) more efficient use of existing capacity, (b) more accurate signals about demand, which inform both investments in capacity expansion and rationing, and (c) generation of funds to pay for maintenance and capacity expansion. More efficient use of existing capacity may involve shifts in the timing of trips, increased carpooling, increased use of buses, or decreased use of the road system and corresponding increased use of public transit. The extent of any such changes depends on how prices are set and collected.

An extensive economic and engineering literature devoted to the issue identifies and examines a host of objections and complications that challenge both economic models of congestion and prescriptions based on those models.[34] Often, the issues debated range well beyond congestion management; for example, congestion may serve as the indicator that roads need to be priced, but discussion of how roads should be priced incorporates broader concerns such as recovering fixed costs and whether roads should be privatized. Though important, the objections and complications do not appear to undercut the economic case for some form of congestion pricing. As Lindsey concludes:

> [E]conomists do agree that highway congestion should be solved by pricing. Beyond that primary insight, however, there is much disagreement. Economists disagree over how to set tolls, how to cover common costs, what to do with any excess revenues, whether and how "losers" from tolling previously free roads should be compensated, and whether to privatize highways. These disagreements fill a lot of pages, while the main point of agreement is largely taken for granted.[35]

---

[31] Strahilevitz 1238 (2000).

[32] Federal Highway Administration (FHWA) 14–10 (2008).

[33] Lindsey (2006).

[34] I recommend a fascinating article reviewing the economic literature on road pricing. *Id.*

[35] *Id.*

The primary insight noted by Lindsey is important and should not be lost in disagreements about tangential issues, implementation details, or theoretical notions of perfect congestion pricing. "Perfect" congestion pricing of roads probably is neither feasible nor worth the effort, given the substantial information and transaction costs involved. Prices must reflect each user's marginal contribution to congestion costs, which requires dynamic metering of individual and aggregate usage of system capacity. Furthermore, as noted previously, the very notion of perfection is dubious in this context.

Despite various disagreements among economists, imperfect congestion-sensitive pricing (in one form or another) offers substantial gains in each of the three dimensions noted above when compared to congestion-insensitive pricing.[36] Relatively simple, crude congestion-pricing schemes may suffice. For example, time-of-day (peak = rush hours, non-peak = non–rush hours) and/or time-of-week (peak = weekday, non-peak = weekend) pricing may provide substantial efficiency gains. Such schemes are much more likely to be politically palatable than complex pricing schemes.[37] Simple, transparent, understandable, and predictable congestion pricing may be politically feasible and over time may help the public to get accustomed to congestion pricing.[38] Moreover, as a number of economists have suggested, improvements on crude pricing schemes can be made periodically. For example, "periodic adjustment of tolls is now official policy for Singapore's electronic road-pricing system where tolls are adjusted every three months to maintain average vehicle speeds within a prescribed range."[39] Similarly, a published pricing schedule may set maximum prices that vary based on time of day and time of week, and actual prices may be dynamically adjusted based on actual congestion levels; published schedules also may be adjusted on an annual or semiannual basis according to historic averages.

For example, the I-15 highway in San Diego employs a dynamic pricing scheme, wherein drivers are provided with stickers or electronic transponders and dynamically adjusting prices are displayed on electronic boards before drivers enter on-ramps. In contrast, State Route 91 in Orange County, California, features four variably priced express lanes in the

---

[36] Frischmann & Van Schewick (2007) for analysis of trade-offs.

[37] Economists disagree about the relative attractiveness of simple, crude congestion pricing compared to more elegant congestion-pricing schemes, such as variable fees that are responsive to actual congestion. Lindsey 329–32 (2006) (discussing and quoting various commentators). Others studies and surveys have pointed to various factors that affect public resistance to congestion pricing, and possible means for overcoming this resistance. Harrington et al. 98–27 (1998); Jaensirisak et al. (2005); Lindsey & Verhoef (2000). Implementing congestion pricing on newly built highways, or new lanes on existing highways, may be the easiest way to acclimatize the public to congestion pricing. Harrington et al. (1998); CBO, Statement of Douglas Holtz-Eakin, Congestion Pricing on Highways, May 6, 2003, available at http://www.cbo.gov/doc.cfm?index=4197&type=0 ("Where congestion pricing has been successfully implemented in the United States, it has been applied to new highways or new lanes of existing highways.").

[38] Plowden 94 (2005) ("Since there is little to be gained from a more elaborate [congestion pricing] system, a simple one could and should be introduced very soon."); May et al. 89 (2004).

[39] Lindsey 328 (2006).

median, with the toll schedule revised and adjusted every three months based on observed traffic during the three-month period.[40]

There are a number of different approaches to implementation. Two types of congestion pricing practiced for road infrastructure are "cordon charges, which apply to all highways, bridges, or tunnels serving a congested area, such as the center of a city, and corridor charges, which apply to part or all of one congested highway, bridge, or tunnel."[41] Cordon charges often are congestion-sensitive, typically based on time of day. Singapore, London, and Stockholm have successfully implemented cordon pricing.[42] Corridor charges involve charging a fee to use a designated resource, whether a highway, bridge, or tunnel, or even a particular lane; the fee is congestion-sensitive, typically based on time of day. The CBO discusses an illustrative example of corridor charges:

> The bridges and tunnels of the Port Authority of New York and New Jersey (PANYNJ) provide an example of how variably priced facilities can reduce congestion. In March 2001, PANYNJ implemented a congestion-pricing system on its six bridges and tunnels, which carry about 350,000 vehicles in each direction each day. Tolls are collected only in the eastbound direction into New York City, with no tolls in the other direction. Under that system, users who paid cash were charged $6.00 at all hours, while users of the E-ZPass electronic toll collection system paid $5.00 at peak hours and $4.00 at off-peak hours. As a result of the program, traffic in the peak morning period declined by 7 percent compared with that in the previous year, traffic in the peak evening period declined by 4 percent, and overall traffic remained the same. Among trucking carriers, 6 percent shifted their operations to off-peak hours as a result of the change in tolls.[43]

Although there have been some successful implementations[44] and a series of pilot projects are under way, congestion pricing of road infrastructure remains rare and is still in its infancy.[45]

Political opposition to congestion-pricing plans remains powerful in various communities. For example, a comprehensive congestion-pricing plan for New York City stalled

---

[40] Congressional Budget Office (CBO) (2009); FHWA 6 (2006).

[41] CBO 5 (2009). Cordon charges and corridor charges can be broken down further.

[42] See Leape (2006). For the fee schedule utilized by Stockholm during its pilot project, see http://www.ops.fhwa.dot.gov/publications/congestionpricing/images/stockholm.jpg.

[43] CBO 8 (2009).

[44] State Route 91 in Orange County, California, is a prominent example of a successful congestion-pricing project. Express lanes occupy a ten-mile stretch of the freeway median between Orange and Riverside Counties, and the lanes are subject to congestion pricing that varies both by time of day and day of week. For a toll schedule, see http://www.octa.net/images/tollcard070110.jpg.

[45] For a list of pilot projects under way in the United States, see CBO 6, table 2-1 (2009).

in 2008 because of a number of serious objections, including concerns about the distributional impacts of the plan, the planned use of revenues generated by the charges, and the privacy of tolling data.[46]

There are a host of distributional issues considered in the literature. After reviewing the literature and data from a series of projects, the FHWA concluded:

> Any change in the way charges are made for road use will benefit some individuals more than others. Those who have higher incomes will tend to use congestion-priced facilities more often, which leads to a perception that wealthy people are favored; however, income-related equity concerns may not be entirely warranted. Although data from priced lanes that are operated in the United States show that high-income motorists do use the lanes more often, the lanes are used by all income groups, serving drivers' needs when they absolutely have to get to their destinations on time (e.g., getting to a daycare center before late fees kick in). Moreover, approval ratings are equally high for all income groups, in the 60–80 percent range, because all income groups value the "insurance" of a reliable trip time when they absolutely need it.
>
> Low-income travelers who take transit more frequently will benefit from transit-service improvements that generally accompany congestion pricing.... Low-income transit riders can benefit significantly from toll-financed transit improvements, which are generally included in any pricing package. In cases in which effects on low-income drivers are perceived to be particularly severe, such drivers could be provided with toll exemptions, rebates, or other forms of monetary compensation, such as tax rebates or income supplements. Pricing schemes may include protections for low-income individuals, such as toll credits.[47]

On balance, given both the magnitude of congestion costs for many road infrastructures and the improved technologies for metering and electronic toll collection, the economic case for congestion pricing is strong in many contexts. This is not to say that the gains necessarily exceed the costs. One must consider administrative costs associated with setting and collecting fees, impacts on drivers' trip planning (e.g., whether drivers

---

[46] In 2007 New York mayor Michael Bloomberg unveiled a plan that would charge drivers an $8 fee to enter the congested areas south of Manhattan's 60th Street, with the generated funds and federal grants going toward mass transit improvements, along with tax credits to low-income residents. Confessore (2008). This was a scaled-back version of the original plan, which would have charged the $8 fee for entry south of 86th Street, and $4 for movement within the zone. *Id.* However, in the face of significant opposition from residents of New York's outer boroughs and suburbs, who felt that the system disproportionately burdened them while subsidizing already-wealthy Manhattanites, the proposal was declared dead in 2008. *Id.*

[47] FHWA (2008).

will shift from priced to unpriced roads/destinations), and political feasibility, among other things.[48]

* * *

A combination of the conventional approaches to managing congestion is probably best.[49] Expanding capacity alone is a rather shortsighted approach. Adding capacity may be the dominant approach to managing congestion in the United States, but it falls well short of expectations and needs. On most accounts, the state of the national road infrastructure is abysmal, and significant investment is needed to maintain and update existing infrastructure and to expand capacity in many congested areas. Where feasible, capacity expansion can be combined with congestion pricing, and in some cases rationing, to improve the efficiency with which the infrastructure capacity is used.[50] Notably, these approaches to congestion management are compatible with commons management and generally help to sustain road infrastructure as commons.

2. INTERACTION EFFECTS (INTERUSE RIVALRY)

Road use is heterogeneous in ways that give rise to interaction effects. As chapter 7 discussed, interaction effects arise because some uses are interdependent in dimensions other than infrastructure capacity consumption. For example, trucks, automobiles, bicycles, inline skaters, and pedestrians not only consume road capacity at different rates but also affect each other in complicated ways while sharing roads; the most obvious effects are safety risks. Such effects often constitute externalities because users do not fully account

---

[48] As revealed by the many disagreements among transportation economists and engineers, congestion pricing raises various complex issues that I have not discussed; for example, I have not addressed the differential impact that congestion pricing can have on freight and passenger traffic, nor have I discussed how prices should be set.

[49] For the sake of brevity, I have focused on bottleneck congestion and relevant congestion management options, and I have not focused on options for dealing with the other major causes of congestions, such as traffic incidents, work zones, weather, and so on. Improved operations management and information and communications technologies can help mitigate congestion in these circumstances.

[50] Transportation experts are exploring and communities are testing a host of additional mechanisms for improving road users' transportation decisions. Many are complementary. Congestion pricing helps users in this regard by putting a price on their contribution to congestion. Other techniques leverage significant advances in information and communications technologies. Section 1201 of the SAFETEA-LU (Pub. L. 109-59, 119 Stat. 1144) requires the "Secretary of Transportation to establish a Real-time System Management Information Program to provide, in all States, the capability to monitor, in real-time, the traffic and travel conditions of the major highways of the United States and to share that information to improve the security of the surface transportation system, to address congestion problems, to support improved response to weather events and surface transportation incidents, and to facilitate national and regional highway traveler information." Traveler information systems utilize a range of new technologies to monitor road infrastructure operations and communicate to travelers information regarding traffic, alternative routes, weather conditions, accidents, special events, and so on. Online travel planning tools can integrate such information and assist travelers in making informed decisions; online tools can also assist travelers in comparing alternative travel options, such as public transit, as well as in coordinating carpools.

for the risks posed to other users by their own activities. As a result, safety risks often require discrimination based on use (i.e., use-specific regulation) or use prioritization.

Use restrictions are necessary on some roads. Although I have claimed that roads are managed as commons, this claim requires refinement. Many roads restrict certain uses altogether. One cannot ride a bicycle on the interstate, for example. Identity-based discrimination does not exist in these circumstances, and the right to ride a bike on the interstate is not for sale (paid priority is not available for even the richest bicyclist). Major arterials[51] are managed as commons with respect to certain classes of vehicles but categorically exclude other classes of vehicles and users in general. The reason for such exclusion is safety. The safety risks associated with mixed traffic on the high-speed, high-traffic arterials are unacceptable. The risks are not a function of capacity consumption or demand exceeding supply. Rather, the risks arise because of the interdependent relationship between the different types of traffic during their contemporaneous use of the infrastructure and the resulting interaction effects.[52] (The interaction effects are effects among users and do not impact non-users. The next section considers environmental externalities, which involve effects that impact non-users.) The risks may be asymmetric, in the sense that trucks pose a substantial risk of harm to bicyclists and pedestrians but not vice versa; however, as Ronald Coase argued, mixed uses jointly create these types of risks;[53] the resource management issue is whether to allow mixed use or not. For many road infrastructure resources, interaction effects in the form of safety risks make some use restrictions necessary. Traffic is mixed on some roads where lower speed limits and other rules of the road lessen the risks. Many roads are partitioned (a form of rationing) to accommodate different types of traffic and mitigate interaction effects; for example, many roads include lanes designated for automobiles, bicycle lanes, running lanes, and sidewalks.

Another example of interaction effects involves transport of particular goods, such as hazardous materials, which pose a risk to other users (and, in some cases, non-users). Transporting such materials on shared road infrastructure may magnify the risks associated with the materials because of the speed and proximity of traffic. To mitigate the risks, the transport of hazardous materials is heavily regulated. This constitutes a form of use-based discrimination. Access to and use of the shared road infrastructure for transporting hazardous materials is restricted; government imposes significant costs/regulatory burdens on those who wish to use the roads to transport hazardous materials. The targeted use restriction is justified as necessary to manage the risks and sustain the commons for others users/uses.

---

[51] I refer to arterials only to illustrate the point. The point applies to some bridges, tunnels, and other roads as well.

[52] Recall the discussion in chapter 7 about buffalo fighting with the other grazing animals.

[53] Coase (1960).

3. ENVIRONMENTAL POLLUTION

Road transport generates significant negative environmental externalities.[54] For example, emissions from automotive vehicles contribute substantially to air and water pollution and climate change;[55] noise from traffic has been shown to have adverse health impacts;[56] road infrastructure also contributes to runoff that pollutes water resources;[57] finally, building and maintaining road infrastructure has a dramatic impact on landscapes and ecosystems.[58]

In contrast with congestion and interaction effects among users, these negative effects impact non-users. The environmental externalities associated with road infrastructure are social costs that require attention and, at least at first blush, appear to conflict with commons management. If one conceives of the environmental externalities as a product of the tragedy of the commons, intervention to eliminate, or at least internalize, the externality would appear to require elimination of the commons.[59] But it does not. The regulatory means for addressing environmental externalities do not eliminate the commons; rather, regulation tends to sustain road infrastructure as a commons.[60] Environmental regulation targets particular social "bads" (pollutants), but for the most part, environmental regulation either focuses on the means used to access and use the road infrastructure (vehicles and fuels) or applies directly to all users in a nondiscriminatory manner (e.g., carbon taxes). Environmental regulation of mobile sources does not involve identity or use-based discrimination, except in the attenuated sense that vehicle types or fuel types are differentiated. Such differentiation is cost-based and focused on the relationship between the category (vehicle type, fuel type) and the environmental harms being targeted. To illustrate, consider air pollution from road transport.

Air pollution from road transport includes the emission of greenhouse gases, such as carbon dioxide, that contribute to climate change. Combustion-based engine technologies burn fossil fuels, such as gasoline and diesel, and produce emissions. The transportation

---

[54] OECD 198 (2010).

[55] Id.

[56] Id.

[57] Id.

[58] OECD 198 (2010).

[59] There are a few commons at issue: the road infrastructure and various environmental resources. For further discussion of environmental resources, see chapter 11.

[60] Perhaps it is more accurate to say that the atmospheric commons is eliminated because a particular class of use/user—road infrastructure users—is not given access to the atmospheric commons on the same terms as other classes of uses/users. While road infrastructure commons may be sustained by environmental regulation, the atmospheric commons is not. In chapter 11, I argue that the atmosphere can be understood to be an environmental infrastructure managed as a semi-commons. The semi-commons label captures the idea that (a) access to and use of the resource is managed/regulated/constrained for a narrow set of heavily regulated uses that threaten the sustainability of the resource while (b) the resource is managed as a commons—access and use is open and nondiscriminatory—for a broad set of unregulated uses that do not threaten the sustainability of the resource.

sector is the largest contributor to greenhouse gas emissions in the United States. Globally, energy consumption from road transport has grown steadily over the past few decades and is projected to continue growing at a comparable rate and to double between 2000 and 2040.[61]

There is substantial debate about how best to reduce greenhouse gas emissions from transport.[62] A number of feasible policy interventions appear to have promise. Fuel taxes and fuel economy standards are useful policy instruments for getting consumers to better internalize the costs of transport-based carbon emissions and for enhancing incentives to innovate in technologies that reduce emissions as well as in the development of alternative fuels.[63] Government coordination and funding of research and development in these areas also can be beneficial. For example, the National Vehicle and Fuel Emissions Laboratory of the US Environmental Protection Agency (EPA) conducts Clean Automotive Technology research aimed at developing cost-effective, energy-efficient technology for vehicles.[64] In addition, since fuel consumption increases under congested conditions, congestion management also is an effective way to reduce emissions. Providing alternative modes of transport, such as public transit, that are more efficient and consume less fossil fuel can be an attractive approach.[65] For example, intercity buses, vanpools, and rail transport are more energy-efficient forms of passenger transportation on a per-passenger-mile basis than automobiles and light trucks.[66] With respect to freight transport, trucking is less efficient and more energy-intensive than rail transport on a per-ton-mile basis.[67] Finally, "land use and economic development policies . . . that encourage efficiency in the location of economic activities [can affect trip generation and trip lengths]. . . . Ensuring that origins and destinations are more closely spaced could reduce travel demand [and thus transportation energy consumption] while maintaining accessibility to economic and social opportunities."[68] None of these policy instruments is a silver

---

[61] OECD 200 (2010). Much of the growth is projected to occur in developing countries. For example, "in China, . . . road energy consumption is expected to grow by a factor of five between 2000 and 2030." *Id.* at 201. Without a technological breakthrough or significant policy intervention, carbon dioxide emissions from transport are projected to follow a similar growth trend. *Id.* at 203–04.

[62] OECD 231–32 (2010).

[63] TUCKER 369 (2008); Hamelink 975 (1998).

[64] For details, see http://www.epa.gov/nvfel/.

[65] According to the American Public Transportation Authority, public transportation produces 95 percent less carbon monoxide and nearly 50 percent less carbon dioxide and nitrogen oxide per passenger mile than a private vehicle. American Public Transportation Authority, "Public Transportation: Benefits for the 21st Century" (2007), available at http://www.apta.com/resources/reportsandpublications/Documents/twenty_first_century.pdf.

[66] National Surface Transportation Policy and Revenue Study Commission (NSTPRSC) 3–20 (2007) (exhibit 3-13 displays energy intensity for different modes of passenger transport).

[67] *Id.* at 3–21 (exhibit 3-14 displays energy intensity for different modes of freight transport).

[68] *Id.* at 3–20.

bullet, however. Transportation "is inherently dependent on energy" and is currently, and for the foreseeable future will remain, heavily dependent on petroleum-based fuels.[69]

Road transport also generates a host of other air pollutants. Among the most important are particulate matter, nitrogen and sulfur oxides, ozone, and volatile organic compounds.[70] The harms caused by these pollutants include a range of health impacts, damage to buildings and other materials, crop losses, and damage to forests and other ecosystems.[71] The federal Clean Air Act mandates that the EPA regulate mobile sources of air pollutants by uniform emissions standards, with an exception to federal preemption granted to California. The EPA has set emissions standards for mobile sources and gradually tightened them over the past few decades.[72] This has driven significant technological innovation: "Emissions-control technology for mobile sources has developed in a series of interactive steps with the promulgation of emissions standards for new vehicles and engines and for fuel regulation."[73] It also drove dramatic emissions reductions. According to the US Bureau of Transportation Statistics, emission of these air pollutants from highway vehicles has steadily decreased over the past few decades.[74] For example, as the National Research Council of the National Academies summarized with respect to light-duty vehicles: "light-duty-vehicle emissions control evolved to today's complex regulation of fuel properties, exhaust emissions, and evaporative emissions, which require the use of sophisticated engine and emissions control technologies. These strategies enabled per-mile-exhaust emissions of new, properly operating light-duty vehicles to decrease by 95–99% in 2004 compared with emissions of 1967 model-year vehicles."[75]

The social costs of environmental pollution and other environmental impacts from road infrastructure must be taken into account and may suggest that there are decreasing returns at certain levels of infrastructure use in certain contexts. Whether the environmental costs of road transport tip the scales and render alternative modes of transport

---

[69] *Id.* at 3–18 ("In 2005, petroleum-based fuels represented 97 percent of the total energy consumed by the American transportation network.").

[70] Colvile et al. 188–90 (2002).

[71] Each of these impacts may involve multiple pollutants. *Id.* In contrast with the climate change impacts from greenhouse gas emissions, the "impacts from air pollutant emissions depend on location. Air pollutants that are emitted in densely populated areas cause considerably more harm than pollutants emitted in remote areas." OECD 200 (2010).

[72] For a review of the EPA's Office of Transportation and Air Quality (OTAQ) efforts to regulate emissions from mobile sources, see US Environmental Protection Agency, Transportation and Air Quality, http://www.epa. gov/oms/(visited January 30, 2011).

[73] NATIONAL ACADEMIES PRESS (NAP) 114 (2006); Driesen 257 (2010). The EPA's emission standards have generally been of "a 'technology-forcing' character, with the introduction of performance standards that cannot be met with existing technology and as such have not been demonstrated in practice." OECD 65–66 (2008).

[74] Bureau of Transportation Statistics ch. 4, tables 4-40 through 4-47 (2010).

[75] NAP 1 (2006).

more attractive from a social welfare perspective is an important issue, one that I do not attempt to resolve here.

Appendix: Public Investment Shortfalls

Public provision of road infrastructure makes commons management much easier because it alleviates concerns about the impact of commons management on supply-side incentives for private investment in building and maintaining infrastructure. However, supply-side issues arise as governments struggle to raise sufficient funds to maintain, upgrade, and expand roads, bridges, and other critical components of road infrastructure. To be clear, this is not a consequence of commons management. Nor does it undermine the case for commons management; as noted, no one (seriously) argues that public roads and bridges should be allocated according to a value-based pricing scheme or otherwise prioritized in a manner that conflicts with commons management. Even where privatization of publicly owned resources or a shift toward private provisioning is proposed or undertaken, commons management remains integral, via regulation, contractual provisions, or some other institution.

As discussed in the chapter, the absence of *any* pricing—that is, free, open access— leads to congestion and environmental externalities. Thus, a shift from free access to a nondiscriminatory pricing regime may be necessary to internalize negative externalities and sustain the commons; moreover, such a shift would yield the significant added benefit of generating revenues to support supply and maintenance and lessen the pressure on other sources of public funding.

Public ownership and provisioning presents its own set of supply-side issues. A full-fledged analysis is beyond the scope of this book. There are many complex and highly contested reasons for public underinvestment in road infrastructure. I briefly note a few relevant factors: Multiple levels of government share financing responsibility;[76] multiple

---

[76] All three levels of government share responsibility for financing highway construction and maintenance. In 2006, "$166.0 billion was generated by all levels of government . . . for the purpose of highway invest-ment"—$34.8 billion from federal government revenues; $83.7 billion from state governments; and $47.6 billion from local governments. DOT, 2006 Highway Statistics, table HF-10, available at http://www.fhwa.dot.gov/policy/ohim/hs06/index.htm. The majority of the federal government's contribution consists of grants to state and local governments. Actual highway spending in 2006 was about $161.1 billion. Here is a breakdown of how the money was spent:

> $78.7 billion (48.8 percent) of this total was spent on capital projects. Another $40.4 billion was tar-geted toward maintenance (25.1 percent), while $14.5 billion (9.0 percent) was used for highway patrol and safety activities and $13.2 billion (8.2 percent) was spent on administrative costs; $14.2 billion (8.8 percent) was used for interest and bond retirement. . . . Of the $78.7 billion of capital spending in 2006, $40.4 billion was spent for rehabilitating the existing system; $16.2 billion was used to construct new roads and bridges; $13.8 billion was used for widening existing facilities; and $8.2 billion supported system enhancements such as safety, operational, and environmental enhancements.

needs press for significant capital investment; the processes for allocating scarce public funds are highly political; and, finally, the lack of political will to raise fuel taxes, vehicle fees, and tolls—which account for most of the public funds for road infrastructure—has led to funding shortfalls.

The nation's investment needs for road infrastructure far outstrip the funds available. Consider the incredible number of bridges and roads in need of repair. In its 2009 Infrastructure Report Card, the American Society of Civil Engineers (ASCE) gave the nation's roads a D-minus. ASCE noted: "One-third of America's major roads are in poor or mediocre condition and 45% of major urban highways are congested. Current spending of $70.3 billion per year for highway capital improvements is well below the estimated $186 billion needed annually to substantially improve conditions."[77] ASCE also graded the nation's bridges, awarding them a D. ASCE explained:

> More than 26%, or one in four, of the nation's bridges are either structurally deficient or functionally obsolete. While some progress has been made in recent years to reduce the number of deficient and obsolete bridges in rural areas, the number in urban areas is rising. A $17 billion annual investment is needed to substantially improve current bridge conditions. Currently, only $10.5 billion is spent annually on the construction and maintenance of bridges.[78]

According to the DOT, in 2008 over 70,000 bridges in the United States were categorized as structurally deficient, and in addition, over 89,000 bridges were categorized as functionally obsolete.[79] Repair of bridges and roads is essential to maintaining the existing road infrastructure, but it is hardly sufficient to meet growing demand for both passenger and freight traffic.[80]

Most observers recognize that government revenues, at all levels, dedicated to road infrastructure fall well short of investment needs. The National Surface Transportation Policy and Revenue Study Commission suggested that "[p]erhaps the principal reason why revenues have fallen short of meeting investment requirements . . . has been the lack of a demonstrated will at all levels of government to raise taxes and fees to the levels required to maintain transportation condition and performance."[81]

DOT ES-10 (2008). This high-level breakdown provides only a rough sense of how funds are allocated. The incredible variety of projects and investment needs defies a short summary.

[77] American Society of Civil Engineers (2009).

[78] Id.

[79] DOT 38 (2008) (table 2-1-9 contains the relevant statistics on bridges).

[80] NSTPRSC ch. 4 (2007).

[81] Id. at 5–14.

10

COMMUNICATIONS INFRASTRUCTURE

Telecommunications

COMMUNICATIONS INFRASTRUCTURES, like transportation infrastructures, have been an important factor in the prosperity and growth of human civilization and are integral to modern society. In fact, for most of human history, transportation infrastructures served as communications infrastructures in the sense that most communication of information over a distance occurred through messengers who literally transported the message from one location to another. It was not until Claude Chappe's invention and deployment, in the early 1790s, of a system of towers to relay visual messages across hundreds of miles of French countryside that the first modern communications network was born.[1] Technology has been a persistent driving force in the evolution of communications infrastructures. Transmitting intangible messages from sender to receiver by telegraph, telephone, radio, or satellite depends on a series of fundamental technological innovations. Today, there are many different modes of communication that compete with each other at various scales. Local, regional, national, and international communications occur through various communications infrastructures, including the Internet.

In this chapter, I focus narrowly on telecommunications infrastructure and keep the discussion brief. Telecommunications infrastructure is mixed infrastructure with a long history of public commitment to commons management. As chapter 6 discussed, the

---

[1] NUECHTERLEIN & WEISER 1 (2005) (describing the towers as having six arms and being spaced twenty miles apart, forming a network that spanned the breadth of France).

industry transformed dramatically over the past century and continues to be quite dynamic. This chapter provides an overview of the basic economic issues and the industry transformation and highlights the consistent role of commons management.

A. Overview of Telecommunications Infrastructure

In the United States, the national telecommunications system consists of various interconnected networks with a functional hierarchy similar to the national road system. Simply put, local exchange networks provide basic local telephone service to customers within a particular region. Interexchange networks provide long-distance telephone service, connecting local exchange networks at each end of a given long-distance telephone call. Interexchange networks pay local exchange networks for the use of their networks and access to their customers. The "local loop" or "last mile" is the portion of the local exchange network that connects individual customers to the main local switch, at which point the connection is handed off to an interexchange carrier for long-distance interconnection to a local exchange carrier in another region.

For most of the telecommunications industry history, these networks consisted of wires and switches; the networks transported communications between users, who had standard equipment (i.e., telephones) in their homes or offices. The switches evolved from manually operated switchboards to sophisticated computers that route traffic. Numerous other technological advances have altered the industry. Customer premises equipment, for example, includes not only telephones but also fax machines, answering machines, computer modems, and so on. The emergence of wireless telecommunications dramatically altered and continues to shape the telecommunications industry.[2]

The architecture of wireless telephony is similar to traditional telecommunications, but the infrastructure is made more complex by the unique and congestible nature of spectrum.[3] To operate a network on a particular range of frequencies, a carrier must purchase an exclusive license from the Federal Communications Commission (FCC), which can cost billions of dollars for spectrum suitable for cellular telephone service.[4] In wireless telecommunications, the "last mile" or local loop is not wired, but a wireless transmission between the closest cell tower and the end-user's device. Generally, to enter the market, a wireless carrier must become a licensee with the FCC, build cell towers in a particular region or lease service from existing towers owned by others, and purchase "backhaul"

---

[2] Besides the following paragraph, this chapter focuses on wireline telecommunications infrastructure and does not wade into debates about wireless spectrum or the Internet. Chapter 13 discusses the Internet. Spectrum would be an excellent candidate for future work.

[3] Spectrum allocation raises a host of complex and incredibly important issues. See FCC ch. 5 (2010); BENJAMIN, LICHTMAN, SHELANSKI, & WEISER chs. 1–4 (2006).

[4] For an overview of the FCC licensing regime, see FCC ch. 4 (2010).

service. Backhaul is a large-scale wireline infrastructure that functions similar to interexchange networks discussed above, and even arterial highways in the transportation infrastructure. It permits interconnection between the carrier's network and other networks (including other wireless carriers or the Internet).[5]

In contrast with road infrastructure, the US telecommunications infrastructure is mostly built, managed, and owned by private firms. For most of the twentieth century, telecommunications markets were considered natural monopolies and regulated as such, with state public utility commissions regulating local and intrastate services and the Federal Communications Commission regulating interstate services. As the end of the twentieth century approached, the paradigm shifted. The natural monopoly characterization gave way to the possibility of competitive provisioning in various sectors; public recognition of the high costs of regulation along with the risk of "regulatory capture" spurred a strong deregulation movement;[6] and technological advances pushed the industry beyond classic telephony toward more sophisticated, varied, and data-intensive services.

B. Economic Characteristics of Telecommunications Infrastructure

The supply-side characteristics of telecommunications infrastructure are familiar. The natural monopoly designation made sense for a while. Three primary reasons stand out. First, the standard argument that a single provider is most cost effective fit the industry rather well. The cost structure of supply involved very high fixed cost investments in building the initial network of wires and switches. Once that network was built, the marginal costs of adding a customer were nearly zero. Particularly with respect to the local loop, most agreed that it was efficient to have a single provider build and operate the infrastructure. Moreover, the variable nature of demand for telephone service further supported the natural monopoly designation. Individual users' demand for telephone service varies quite a lot each day, although users typically prefer to have service available on demand. The existence of multiple providers would lead to considerable idle capacity because each provider would have to build sufficient capacity for redundant on-demand service. A single provider could more efficiently invest in total capacity and reduce waste.[7]

---

[5] Some vertically integrated wireless carriers own and operate their own backhaul services.

[6] "[T]he term 'regulatory capture' [] receives both a broad and narrow interpretation. According to the broad interpretation, regulatory capture is the process by which special interests affect state intervention in any of its forms. . . . According to the narrow interpretation, regulatory capture is specifically the process through which regulated monopolies end up manipulating the state agencies that are supposed to control them." Dal Bo (2006). For an extensive review, see *id.* See generally Stigler (1971); Peltzman (1976).

[7] See, e.g., BENJAMIN, LICHTMAN, & SHELANSKI 719 (2001). For the sake of brevity, I leave aside additional economic arguments about natural monopoly in the telecommunications industry (e.g., economies of scope and density).

Second, the telecommunications industry displays "network effects," meaning that the value of the network to each user increases (decreases) with the addition (subtraction) of other users. All else equal, a single large network is more valuable than two or more competing but smaller networks because the single network maximizes the total number of users with whom each user can connect. This demand-side effect is distinct from the supply-side effect of sharing the fixed costs of the network over a larger base. Both effects push toward monopoly as the market evolves. An unregulated network-effects industry has a tendency to slide into monopoly where the largest network would dominate and competitors wither away.[8] As this occurs, there is wasteful duplication of facilities, needless clogging of public spaces with cables and devices, and higher prices. Along the way, network effects may spur some competitors to invest in their networks and reach as many customers as possible.[9] But "eventually there will be only a single company."[10]

Third, if society is committed to a policy of universal access, a single provider may be the most cost-effective way to execute that policy. Theodore Vail successfully made this argument on behalf of the Bell System, capturing the idea in the slogan "One Policy, One System, Universal Service."[11] The concept of universal service has been repeatedly advanced by incumbent telecommunications providers to stave off attempts to introduce competition.[12] In a competitive market, market participants will avoid unprofitable services or sets of consumers and thus obstruct the achievement of universal service. A single, integrated provider, however, could accomplish a few things through various cross-subsidies that a bunch of providers competing with each other could not. The single provider could take a loss on one service or with one set of customers and make up for the loss by increasing prices on another service or for a different set of customers. For example, business services would subsidize the cost of residential services; urban would subsidize rural; long distance would subsidize local. Pricing local telephone service at its true cost would render universal service impossible, due to its high cost structure. To reduce its price, some other related service must be priced above cost to effectively subsidize local telephony. The identity of the higher-priced service changed over time—from interstate private lines to interstate long distance to intrastate long distance and even to cellular service—but the argument remained the same: Introducing competition in the

---

[8] NUECHTERLEIN & WEISER 4 (2005).

[9] Id. at 4.

[10] "You can start with a competitive free-for-all . . . but eventually there will be only a single company, because until a company serves the whole market it will have an incentive to keep expanding in order to lower its average costs. In the interim there may be wasteful duplication of facilities, . . . higher prices to . . . subscribers . . . [and] higher costs to other users of the public ways . . ." Omega Satellite Prods. v. City of Indianapolis, 694 F. 2d 119, 126 (7th Cir. 1982).

[11] BENJAMIN ET AL. 608 (2001); BENJAMIN ET AL. 696 (2006).

[12] Blumenfeld & Kunin 108 (1998). Blumenfeld and Kunin reexamine the universal service argument against competition, questioning the presumptions underlying the argument "in light of the technology and society of the 1990s."

higher-priced service would drive down prices and hamper the universal availability of local telephony.[13]

The regulatory bodies at the state and federal levels built such cross-subsidies into the rates. Regulators adopted two basic pricing principles: value-of-service pricing and system-wide price averaging. Value-of-service pricing takes into account elasticity of demand and enables differential pricing for different types of services—for example, creating a different price structure for business and residential subscribers.[14] System-wide price averaging mandates similar rates for similar services, regardless of varying actual costs—for example, charging the same price for basic telephone service irrespective of the higher costs associated with wiring and servicing subscribers located farther away from the local exchange. Regulatory agencies also set rate-of-return and rate-base regulations, reflecting administrative judgment of the amount of profit that the public utility may appropriately generate.[15] The regulatory agencies protected the integrity of the rate structure by restricting entry. Competition among providers would eliminate the opportunity for such cross-subsidies, for example, if a competitor decided to enter the market where prices are raised (known as cream-skimming).

The notion of communications networks as "a natural monopoly that had to be publicly owned and accountable to some notion of the public interest" has "undergone a dramatic transformation."[16] A useful way to quickly see how is to examine how the three primary reasons just discussed have changed.[17] First, the standard argument that a single provider is most cost effective no longer fits for certain segments of the industry. The emergence of new technologies dramatically lowered the fixed cost investments required to enter certain markets, and as a result, competition is feasible. For example, competition in the long-distance market emerged as a result of new microwave transmission technology. (Similarly, wireless telephone technology has provided an inroad to promote competition in the local loop, the market segment with perhaps the strongest natural monopoly tendencies.)[18] The microwave transmission technology sidestepped two major sources of fixed costs for entrants: "first, digging the trenches and, second, obtaining the

---

[13] *Id.* at 108.

[14] Notably, such pricing schemes differentiate among customer classes in a fashion that depends on user identity in a very coarse sense. The business and residential categories are based on differences in the quantity of infrastructure capacity demanded, the costs of providing service, and group elasticity of demand. See chapter 6.

[15] WILSON 60 (2000).

[16] WILKIN 29 (2001). For a detailed history and discussion of the forces behind the transformation, see Robinson (1991). See also ROBINSON 434–795 (2008) (describing the legal aspects of the regulatory changes in the telecommunications industry, including the effects of the 1996 Telecommunications Act, and the advent of mobile wireless telecommunications and the Internet).

[17] A host of books provide more detailed accounts. See, e.g., BENJAMIN ET AL. (2006); NUECHTERLEIN & WEISER (2005); KELLOGG, THORNE, & HUBER (1992); WU (2011).

[18] Complications presented by the need for backhaul and the small number of backhaul providers may push in the other direction, however.

rights of way needed to lay the transmission cable essential for providing telephone service. . . . [This] helped to reduce the entry barriers . . . by greatly reducing the need to lay cable. A firm could transmit information by microwave, incurring only the more modest costs of constructing transmission and relay towers at sufficient intervals."[19] Not surprisingly, introducing competition in the long-distance market was a drawn-out, messy affair. It eventually led to the breakup of Bell and a complete transformation of the industry.[20]

Second, while it remains true that telecommunications infrastructure exhibits network effects, the accepted implications of this observation are no longer that monopoly is desirable or inevitable. Due to the presence of network effects, a large network may have an incentive to refuse to interconnect with competitors for strategic reasons. But interconnection, either voluntary or government-imposed, may be a solution that is well short of tolerating a regulated monopoly. The basic idea is that interconnection creates a meta-network (network of networks) that enables network effects to improve social welfare without the corresponding risk of network-effects-induced tipping toward monopoly. Interconnection allows multiple networks to function as one, permitting society to benefit from the network effects without suffering the harms of an unregulated monopoly. Interconnection is not easy or costless to implement, but the costs are likely a reasonable price to pay for competition among networks.

Third, while universal service remains a policy objective in the United States, it is no longer accepted that weaving elaborate cross-subsidies into the rate structure of a regulated monopoly is the most effective means of accomplishing the objective. There are more direct and cost-effective means that may cause less distortion in other sectors. For example, many believe that to the extent that market provisioning fails to meet the demand of certain populations, perhaps because the market is too small or the costs of service are too high, the government can provide subsidies to the underserved population or even directly provide services. In other words, resort to cross-subsidies should be reserved for situations where direct subsidies are not feasible. This view is fully consistent with the arguments made in chapter 5 regarding commons management and the social utility of cross-subsidies, because universal service subsidies can be directed toward easily identified user groups. How best to achieve universal service objectives depends on a comparative analysis of different means.

Even though the supply-side characteristics have shifted over time and natural monopoly classification no longer applies in various sectors, the cost structure of supplying telecommunications infrastructure continues to present the difficulties that were discussed extensively in previous chapters. Shifting from a regulated natural monopoly paradigm to a competitive market provisioning paradigm leaves cost recovery, investment incentives, pricing, and deadweight loss issues on the table.

---

[19] BENJAMIN ET AL. 719 (2001).

[20] There is an extensive literature. See, e.g., BENJAMIN ET AL. (2006); NUECHTERLEIN & WEISER (2005); KELLOGG, THORNE, & HUBER (1992); WU (2011).

The demand-side characteristics of telecommunications infrastructure are familiar. Telecommunications networks comprise mixed infrastructure: partially (non)rival inputs into a wide variety of user activities. Telecommunications networks are consumed nonrivalrously over an appreciable range of demand; they are sharable and congestible. Usage-based and congestion pricing are prevalent means for managing congestion. Telecommunication infrastructures exhibit network effects, making interconnection of networks and expanding the scope of opportunities to connect quite important.[21] Telecommunications infrastructure supports the basic capability of communication, and communication leads to the creation and sharing of a vast range of public and social goods (recall the discussion of speech in chapter 3). Moreover, much like transportation infrastructures, telecommunication infrastructures facilitate a significant number of social and economic interactions between people and communities that are distant, expanding the scale and scope of markets and nonmarket systems. Telecommunications facilitate all sorts of personal, social, and business interactions as people talk, exchange ideas, make plans, and socialize; develop business and personal relationships; participate in political discourse; and so on.[22]

C. Commons Management

The telecommunications industry has a long and deeply ingrained tradition of commons management. In some cases, infrastructure providers voluntarily adopted commons management as a private strategy—for example, when opting to interconnect with a competing network on nondiscriminatory terms. But for the most part, commons management has been imposed on infrastructure providers through various forms of government intervention. Nondiscriminatory access can be provided to potential competitors or to consumers. Granting nondiscriminatory access to current and potential competitors, on terms similar to those granted current users, is done for the purpose of facilitating market entry and competition and preventing foreclosure. Granting nondiscriminatory access to consumers attempts to achieve reasonable pricing and prevent fine-grained price discrimination, among other things.

This section briefly discusses three important ways in which commons management has been achieved: common carrier requirements, antitrust laws (notably the essential facilities doctrine, consent decrees, and merger conditions), and open-access regulatory regimes.

---

[21] See, e.g., NUECHTERLEIN & WEISER 4–10 (2005); WILSON 58–59 (2000).

[22] I keep this discussion brief because the material here overlaps considerably with that in other chapters. See chapter 3 (speech); 13 (Internet). See also chapter 9 (roads).

I. COMMON CARRIAGE

The imposition of commons management principles through *common carriage* requirements has a long history.[23] Historically, common-carrier-style obligations for infrastructure were said to arise in markets "affected with the public interest."[24] Throughout its legal
development, common carriage implied a duty to serve all comers through equal access
and nondiscrimination.[25] In the case of communications networks, common carriage
derived its meaning both from the law of bailment, which sought to assign liability strictly
to common carriers, and from the law of franchise and monopoly, under which state-
authorized communications providers were required not to discriminate.[26] For example,
various state statutes imposed nondiscrimination rules on telegraph companies.[27] The
common carriage label gradually attached to communications companies when lumped
together with railroad and transportation companies in federal statutes.[28] Title II of the
Communications Act of 1934 more systematically outlined common carriage obligations,
including interconnection requirements for carriers[29] and the requirement to furnish
service on reasonable request, charge just and reasonable rates, and provide service
without "unjust or unreasonable discrimination in charges, practices, classifications,
regulations, facilities, or services."[30] Although by no means perfect or without cost or
controversy,[31]

> the common carrier system has served telecommunications participants well: it has
> permitted society to entrust its vital highways of information to for-profit compa-
> nies, without the specter of unreasonable discrimination and censorship by govern-
> ment or private monopolies; it was an important element in establishing a free flow
> of information, neutral as to its content; it reduced the administrative cost and the
> burden of liability of a carrier, since it needed not, at least in theory, inquire as to a
> user's background and intended use; and it protected the telephone industry from

---

[23] There is an extensive literature. Noam (1994); Brenner (1998); EPSTEIN 279–318 (1998); Jones (1980).

[24] Hamilton 1100–01 (1930).

[25] Crawford 878 (2009).

[26] Jones 9–10 (1980).

[27] Crawford 879 (2009).

[28] *Id.*

[29] On interconnection requirements, see, e.g., Speta (2002), Werbach (2007).

[30] 47 U.S.C. 202. Crawford 880; Weinberg 217 (1999).

[31] Many criticisms of common carriage focus on the price regulation that accompanied the basic nondiscrimination rules. For example, rate averaging and cross-subsidies that aimed to further the goal of universal service
have been highly criticized.

various pressure groups who would prevent it from offering service to their targets of protest or competition.[32]

2. ANTITRUST

Antitrust law has played a very important role in the telecommunications industry. The *essential facilities* doctrine, for example, can be invoked to ensure commons-style nondiscriminatory access in cases where a competitor has been denied use of an incumbent's facilities. The doctrine "requires a firm with monopoly power in one market to deal equitably with competing firms operating in adjacent markets that depend on it for essential inputs."[33] Various private antitrust lawsuits were brought against incumbent telecom giants, and many of these suits invoked this doctrine and related doctrines. In 1974, for example, MCI sued AT&T, alleging that it had failed to provide essential facilities by attempting to block MCI's access to Bell System's local facilities.[34] Southern Pacific Communications (today known as Sprint) filed suit in 1978, alleging denial of access to essential facilities; a similar charge was also leveled by Mid-Texas Communications Systems, a company that was attempting to provide local phone service and claimed to have been denied interconnection with AT&T's long-distance network.[35] Between 1968 and 1974, no less than thirty-five private antitrust suits were brought against AT&T, often based on similar allegations.[36]

The government brought three major antitrust suits against AT&T's telecommunications monopoly. The first one, in which the government sought to stifle AT&T's aggressive acquisitions charge, ended in 1913 with a negotiated settlement known as the Kingsbury Commitment; AT&T agreed to cease its predatory practices, divest itself of Western Electric, and not attempt to acquire a controlling interest in independent phone companies located in the same market as a Bell subsidiary. The Kingsbury Commitment formalized and entrenched AT&T's formidable monopoly, while assuring interconnection between the various local and long-distance monopolists.[37] The prevailing view at the time was that the telecommunications industry as a whole was a natural monopoly.[38] This was reflected in the Kingsbury Commitment itself[39] and in the legislative history of

---

[32] Noam (1994) (analysis of the inevitable demise of commons carriage and rise of "contract-carrier based network system").

[33] KELLOGG, THORNE, & HUBER 139 (1992). See chapter 5.

[34] *Id*. at 159.

[35] WILSON 138 (2000).

[36] BROCK 295 (1981).

[37] NUECHTERLEIN & WEISER 13 (2005).

[38] Sen. Rep. No. 75, 67th Cong., 1st Sess. 1 (1921).

[39] NUECHTERLEIN & WEISER 13 (2005).

the Communications Act of 1934. During House debate, Alabama Democrat George Huddleston said, "Any man of observation is bound to recognize that there are certain natural monopolies. . . . [T]here are monopolies which ought to exist in the interest of economy and good service in the public welfare and . . . the telephone business is one of these."[40] The very real consequence of local telephone exchange competition—the need to have multiple phones in a home or office to access the various networks—led the House Committee to declare that "[t]here is nothing to be gained by local competition in the telephone business."[41]

The second antitrust suit was brought by the government in 1949 and had its roots in an FCC study undertaken in the aftermath of the 1934 Communications Act that examined whether further legislation was required.[42] Although only minor changes to the 1934 Act were implemented, the report inspired the 1949 suit, which resulted in a settlement (consent decree) in 1956. This settlement espoused a more liberal approach to the sharing of patents with AT&T's competitors, granting all present and future comers nondiscriminatory and nonexclusive access to Bell System patents.[43] Additionally, under its terms, AT&T would provide manufacturing know-how for a reasonable fee and limit Western Electric's manufacturing to just telephone equipment.[44] Finally, AT&T agreed to limit its activities to the "business of common carriage."[45]

The third and final government antitrust suit, launched in 1974,[46] once again ended in a settlement. It had sweeping implications that radically changed the telecommunications landscape in the United States: AT&T agreed to divest itself of its local operating companies and disassemble its vertically integrated businesses.[47] The mammoth Bell System, colloquially known as "Ma Bell," was broken up into seven independent Regional Bell Operating Companies, known as the "Baby Bells." In exchange, AT&T was freed from the constraints of the 1956 settlement and allowed to enter the computer business.[48]

That the Bell/AT&T monopoly persisted for so long after competition might in theory have been introduced is a testament to the company's entrenchment within the economy and regulatory policy of the United States. By 1984, AT&T was the world's largest private employer, with 1 million employees, and ranked first in categories such as assets owned

---

[40] 61 Cong. Rec. 1988 (1921) (remarks of Rep. Huddleston).

[41] H.R. Rep. No. 190, 67th Cong., 1st Sess. 1 (1921).

[42] BROCK 179 (1981).

[43] KELLOGG, THORNE, & HUBER 203 (1992).

[44] Id.

[45] WILSON 109 (2000).

[46] United States v. American Tel. & Tel. Co. (modified final judgment), 552 F.Supp. 131 (D.D.C. 1982), aff'd sub. nom., Maryland v. United States, 460 U.S. 1001 (1983).

[47] The Modification of Final Judgment was the final 1982 consent decree that modified the original 1956 settlement and set out the terms of the divestiture.

[48] A Brief History: The Bell System, AT&T, http://www.corp.att.com/history/history3.html, accessed October 13, 2011.

and net income.[49] Moreover, AT&T's successful invocation of the universal service argument to ensure its continued dominance was, in many ways, a validation of public choice theory, which holds that private economic actors will extract "rents" from policy makers by leveraging their political influence.[50] This union of interests between regulatory agency and corporate entity gave AT&T the ability to formalize its monopoly, while also providing tax-averse politicians with a way to subsidize local telephony.[51] The universal service argument could not hold up in the face of technological change, and in the early 1970s it began to unravel.[52]

3. POST-"MA BELL" OPEN ACCESS REGULATION

The first competitive inroads were made into segments where prices and call volumes were so high that competitors could utilize new technologies to build cost-effective rival networks, notably in the business-oriented long-distance services used to subsidize local telephony.[53] Access services, which allowed high-speed connections between local exchanges and long-distance networks, were next.[54] Finally, the Telecommunications Act of 1996 repudiated the natural monopoly premise altogether, introducing competition in all spheres of telephony, including local networks.[55] The 1996 Act loosened ownership restrictions and prohibited state and local government from erecting barriers to entry in the local telephone exchange markets, enticing new players and new technologies to enter the market.[56] Critically, Congress also required telecommunications carriers to interconnect with any requesting carrier,[57] thereby maintaining the communications meta-network and continuing the basic commons management traditions.

As chapter 6 described, Congress implemented an open-access policy through unbundling. "Open access policies seek to make it easier for new competitors to enter and compete in [] markets by requiring existing carriers to lease access to their networks to their competitors, mostly at regulated rates."[58] To this end, Congress "grant[ed] new entrants rights to lease capacity on the facilities owned by the incumbent telephone company,

---

[49] BOLTER, McCONNAUGHEY, & KELSEY 106 (1990).

[50] Farber & Frickley (1987).

[51] NUECHTERLEIN & WEISER 14 (2005).

[52] Kearney & Merrill 1384 (1998) (explaining reasons for this early transition, including the regulatory familiarity with public choice theory and the possibility that their regulations could help industry participants while hurting the public interest).

[53] NUECHTERLEIN & WEISER 15 (2005).

[54] *Id.*

[55] *Id.* at 15.

[56] Becker 3, 5 (1998).

[57] NUECHTERLEIN & WEISER 15–16 (2005).

[58] Berkman Center for Internet & Society 11 (2009).

enabling them to 'participate' in the incumbent's economies of scale by availing them-selves of the same low per-unit cost."[59] In the intervening years, there has been little con-sensus on the parameters of this open-access regime. Significant criticism of the regime has arisen,[60] and "[w]hile Congress adopted various open access provisions in the almost unanimously-approved Telecommunications Act of 1996, the FCC decided to abandon this mode of regulation for broadband in a series of decisions in 2001 and 2002. Open access has been largely treated as a closed issue in U.S. policy debates ever since."[61]

* * *

The telecommunications industry remains a work in progress, undergoing transforma-tions driven by technological innovation, shifting business practices, and an evolving regulatory environment. The paradigm shift described above occurred on the supply side; it involved increased potential for competition among providers (as well as technolo-gies). An important shift also occurred on the demand side, as the basic capability pro-vided to users by the communications infrastructure has expanded to include data communications. This shift dramatically increased the scope of possible user activities, introduced substantial market and social value uncertainty, increased the social option value of the infrastructure, and correspondingly strengthened the case for commons management as public strategy. I leave a discussion of this demand-side shift for chapter 13, which focuses on the Internet and the network neutrality debate.

Appendix: Private Investment Shortfalls

While public provisioning of infrastructure faces risk of underfunding and political obstacles,[62] private provisioning suffers from supply-side problems as well. One obvious example is underinvestment in areas expected to be unprofitable. Private industry will suffer the high fixed costs associated with building new infrastructure only if there is positive expectation of profit. Thus, for example, a local exchange carrier will build a net-work in a region only if the number of customers it expects to obtain is sufficient to bring

---

[59] Nuechterlein & Weiser 16 (2005).

[60] For further discussion, see chapter 6.

[61] Berkman Center for Internet & Society 11 (2009). In 2009, Harvard's Berkman Center for Internet & Society conducted a comprehensive study of international broadband policies and the economic impact of these poli-cies on the development of broadband Internet access in each country. *Id.* The study found that internationally, implementation of open-access policies has been extremely successful in stimulating competition and innova-tion. In the United States and Canada, broadband providers offered the lowest speeds for the highest prices, whereas countries with open-access requirements consistently demonstrated the highest speeds for the lowest prices. See *id.* at 11–13. The Berkman Center's findings indicated that open-access policies "played a core role" in the development of first-generation broadband services in countries with successful infrastructure models. *Id.* at 11.

[62] See discussion in chapter 9 (road infrastructure).

in more revenue than the cost of building and maintaining the network. As the universal service discussion suggested, this can present a problem in smaller markets, such as remote, rural municipalities, where consumers are spread far apart and require more investment to reach each additional potential customer.

Another example is a lack of competition in infrastructure markets where competition is feasible and desirable.[63] Competitive entry may be deterred by the threat of preexisting competitors, especially when there is a powerful incumbent. If an incumbent has already expended the fixed costs of building a network and dominates the market it serves, a new entrant must overcome a series of obstacles, such as cost disadvantages, the risk of predatory pricing, marketing difficulties, and switching costs. Moreover, potential entrants have to worry about political battles, as the incumbent is likely to wage war by lobbying government officials to raise costs or otherwise impede entry, often through regulation. There is a rich economic literature on these issues.

Suffice it to say that, as discussed in chapter 2, private investment shortfalls (undersupply) present a strong justification for government intervention in communication infrastructure markets. This intervention can take the form of subsidies, such as universal service, or direct government provision of infrastructure. Direct government provision of broadband Internet, for example, has been successful in several countries, including Sweden, South Korea, and Japan (who are also the world's leaders in fiber deployment).[64] While telephone services are nearly ubiquitous in the United States, supply-side problems are apparent in the failure of broadband Internet to reach many areas.[65] In the United States, many municipalities have attempted publicly funded broadband provision, utilizing different models with varying degrees of success and, notably, with considerable political opposition by incumbents.[66]

The case for government intervention is strengthened by the demand-side analysis. Universal service commitments are not solely normatively grounded in distributional concerns; the commitments also have positive efficiency implications. To a private

---

[63] Deregulation has been justified in part based on the beliefs that the natural monopoly paradigm no longer applied and deregulation would stimulate competition. However, as discussed previously, the transition from regulation to competition has been difficult.

[64] Berkman Center for Internet & Society 13 (2009). The United States' $7.2 billion investment allocated by the American Recovery and Reinvestment Act, "adjusted per capita, is commensurate with, and mostly higher than, investment made in other countries." *Id.*

[65] See, e.g., FCC (2010) at 20–21 (reporting that, nationally, 7 million housing units do not have access to broadband Internet access with speeds greater than 4mbps and that "[i]t is unlikely there will be a significant change in the number of unserved Americans based on planned [broadband Internet] upgrades over the next few years, although some small companies may upgrade their networks to support broadband in currently unserved areas.").

[66] Many states have passed laws prohibiting, restricting, or regulating municipal provision of broadband infrastructure. For a state-by-state list of related legislation, see Cyber Telecom, http://www.cybertelecom.org/broadband/muni.htm.

infrastructure provider, the value of infrastructure provision is profit, pure and simple. But the social value generated by telecommunications infrastructure, particularly broadband Internet because of its enhanced capabilities, far exceeds the value reflected by the private markets. Specifically, the communicative, cultural, social, and economic value that society gains by broadband Internet provision is not accounted for in private actors' investment decisions. The wedge between private and social returns in investing in such infrastructure is significant.[67] When supply-side problems arise, the case for government provisioning of such essential public infrastructure is quite strong.

---

[67] This is discussed further in chapter 13.

5

Nontraditional Infrastructure

IN THE NEXT TWO CHAPTERS, I shift attention from traditional infrastructure to nontraditional infrastructure, specifically, from transportation and communications infrastructure to environmental and intellectual infrastructure. It may seem odd to be grouping roads and telephone networks with lakes and ideas under the infrastructure umbrella. The primary reason for doing so is to highlight the demand-side similarities and the important, if varied, role of commons management. When feasible, society benefits tremendously by leveraging nonrivalry to support nondiscriminatory access to such resources, because doing so enables the public to participate productively in a wide range of socially valuable activities. As with traditional infrastructure, many environmental and intellectual infrastructure resources are public, social, and mixed infrastructures that contribute immensely to our economic and social development. In fact, there are interesting parallels between environmental and intellectual infrastructure resources: Both are inputs into complex dynamic processes—natural ecosystem processes and cumulative intellectual processes, as well as social and cultural processes—that have the potential to yield significant positive externalities that benefit society as a whole. Sustaining these fundamental resources in an open manner is critical to realizing this potential.

Feasible leveraging depends, however, on managing a host of competing considerations. Intellectual infrastructures face supply-side issues similar to those issues faced by traditional infrastructure. Attracting private investment can be difficult because of the cost structure of supply, high costs of exclusion, and misappropriation risks, among other factors discussed below. Environmental infrastructures do not face the same supply-side issues. Human beings do not supply environmental infrastructure in the same manner as traditional infrastructure or intellectual infrastructure. We inherit and manage environmental resources.[1] But, like traditional infrastructure, environmental infrastructures are partially (non)rivalrous and, as a result, face complex congestion and degradation problems. In short, pure open access to intellectual or environmental infrastructure typically is not feasible absent additional institutional support, whether in the form of public subsidies for basic research or in the form of command-and-control regulation of industrial polluters.

Viewing environmental and intellectual infrastructure through the infrastructure lens yields important insights regarding commons management institutions. In particular, both environmental and intellectual property legal systems construct semi-commons arrangements that create and regulate interdependent private rights and public commons. Each system does so in a very different way, as explored below. Though these areas of law are often conceptualized as necessary departures from commons because of the tragic effects that commons might have on incentives—whether leading to overconsumption of environmental resources or undersupply of intellectual resources—greater analytical clarity may be achieved by conceptualizing these legal regimes in a more nuanced fashion and appreciating that an overarching objective and consequence of these regimes is sustaining (rather than eliminating) commons for an appreciable range of use(r)s.

---

[1] Of course, each generation also inherits an incredible wealth of intellectual and cultural resources—our cultural environment—and as with the inherited natural environment, these inherited resources are the foundation for our current reality and future development and progress as a society.

11

ENVIRONMENTAL INFRASTRUCTURE

THE ENVIRONMENT CAN BE VIEWED as a natural infrastructure that supports life on Earth. Like "traditional" infrastructure, such as road systems and telephone networks, environmental infrastructure resources play an incredibly important role in society and generate substantial social value by serving as *shared means to many ends*. The natural environment serves as a critical form of capital, which economists refer to as natural capital. The environment functions instrumentally as an essential input into a wide range of human and natural goods and services, including "agricultural output, human health, recreation, and more amorphous goods such as quality of life,"[2] as well as "purification of air and water, detoxification and decomposition of wastes, regulation of climate, regeneration of soil fertility, and production and maintenance of biodiversity."[3] Richard Revesz and Robert Stavins observe that "[t]his effect is analogous to the manner in which real physical capital assets provide service flows used in manufacturing. As with real physical capital, a deterioration in the natural environment (as a productive asset) reduces the flow of services the environment is capable of providing."[4]

---

[2] Revesz & Stavins 499 (2007).

[3] Daily et al. 2 (1997); Freeman 3 (2003a) ("Examples include nutrient recycling, organic material decomposition, soil fertility generation and renewal, crop and natural vegetation pollination, and biological control of agricultural pests.").

[4] Revesz & Stavins (2007).

As with other resource systems discussed in this book, we can identify infrastructure at a very high level of abstraction (i.e., the environment) and at progressively lower levels of abstraction. Thus, we can say that the environment comprises many interdependent environmental infrastructures, such as rivers, lakes, forests, and the atmosphere, which act as essential inputs into a wide range of human and natural processes. These resources interact to sustain both complex natural systems (ecosystems) and complex human systems (cultural, economic, and social).

The complexity of relationships and the spatial and temporal range of the benefits that environmental infrastructures produce make valuation and management of resources extremely difficult. Accurate valuation and effective management requires appreciation of the full range of different activities, uses, and processes that generate value. It also requires consideration of a host of other complexities, including significant uncertainties, long-term implications such as effects on future generations, and risks of path dependency—for example, where marginal changes increase the likelihood of similar incremental changes that have cumulative, sometimes nonlinear effects.

Environmental resources are often associated with the tragedy of the commons, discussed in chapter 7. Recall how that story of unconstrained consumption and consequent ruin seemed to lead inexorably to two solutions—(1) private ownership of the resource so as to enable market transactions, internalization of externalities, and efficient management of the resource; or (2) government management/regulation of resource use to constrain consumption to efficient levels and avoid ruin. Both "solutions" allegedly solve the problem by eliminating the commons. Without engaging the volumes of literature on the story, with attendant predictions and prescriptions for environmental policy, I question the notion that commons are or should be eliminated. At least with respect to environmental resources that are infrastructural, society often is better off sustaining commons to the extent feasible, to leverage the sharable, nonrival nature of the resources. In fact, it is plausible that the strongest case for environmental protection or preservation depends on the social values attributable to the comedy of the commons rather than the social harms attributable to the tragedy of the commons. In some cases, the true tragedy would be eliminating the commons and the social value that flows from shared public use of environmental resources.

Consider, for a moment, the limits of the first solution—privatizing environmental infrastructure by granting ownership to a private party. To make matters manageable, assume a single owner of a resource with reasonably well-delineated boundaries: Imagine that you owned Lake Michigan.[5] Now imagine the difficulty in managing access to the lake, even assuming the costs of exclusion are low. In terms of appropriating maximum benefits (so as to maximize your own welfare, a key reason for granting you ownership), it should not be surprising that it would be much easier and more profitable to deal with

---

[5] The example is drawn from Frischmann (2005a).

a smaller number of large-scale commercial users than with a much larger number of small-scale commercial and noncommercial users.

Difficulties in appropriation may be a function of transaction costs that result from dealing with a wide variety of different types of users. Such costs may relate to information acquisition and exchange, negotiation and enforcement of commitments, demand-side coordination and collective action problems, and other related costs. Appropriation difficulties may result because the downstream users themselves generate positive externalities that they do not internalize. Consider a pristine view. While appreciation of the view of Lake Michigan yields direct consumptive benefits that people certainly appreciate and value,[6] it also acts as an input into cultural and social processes that yield, among other things, artwork, literature, memories, community identity, and culture.[7] Various types of recreational use may generate small-scale spillovers, as discussed below.

More importantly, difficulties in appropriation arise in situations where there are simply no human agents engaged in production downstream. For example, socially valuable outputs may be products of natural rather than human processes. Many environmental resources, including lakes, support a wide range of socially valuable ecosystem services. The social benefits of such services are diffuse, indirect, and difficult to observe, much less appropriate. Further, as discussed below, there is no representative agent to manifest demand for the natural capital in markets or political systems.

If all uses were compatible and nonrivalrous in consumption, society presumably would choose to make the lake accessible to all. But interuse congestion, incompatibilities, and rivalrous consumption complicate matters and are the reason for granting you ownership in the first place. So what would you, our rational property owner, do?

Though this lake example focuses on the problems faced by a hypothetical infrastructure owner seeking to maximize his or her own welfare, the underlying information, valuation, and planning problems are quite similar to those faced by a regulator or other manager of a public resource.[8] As discussed in detail below, it is often quite difficult, if not impossible, to identify, understand, and assess the value of various downstream uses of infrastructure resources and thus to make decisions about how the resources should be managed. This difficulty is a common theme that connects infrastructure analysis with the ecosystems literature (discussed below). Both approach questions of valuation and management with an eye on systems, processes, goods, and services that are often taken for granted in market and other decision-making frameworks.

---

[6] Given the market value of property adjoining the lake, it is clear that these property owners realize and to some extent appropriate substantial benefits from the view. Bell & Parchomovsky 20–23 (2003) (describing the "proximate property principle," which explains the high value of land located near commons).

[7] At a macro level, the "identities" of communities surrounding the lake, including the city of Chicago itself, are intimately tied to the lake.

[8] Brown & Peterson 221–22 (2003).

A closer look at the second solution—that is, how government regulates environmental infrastructure—suggests that commons are not eliminated altogether; government regulators or managers do not micromanage each and every use of environmental infrastructure. Rather, a *regulatory semi-commons* arises, where government (or some community organization)[9] (1) assigns and regulates private rights (access, use, exclusion, and/or exchange) for certain fields of use, such as resource extraction for industrial purposes; (2) defines commons in terms of community rights (access and use) for certain fields of use, such as recreational use; and (3) sustains the integrity of the resource for nonhuman users and future generations. The first action involves use-based discrimination and thus conflicts with a pure nondiscrimination rule—hence the semi-commons label. It is critical to recognize what is often ignored or taken for granted, however: that the first action supports the second and third; and that regulating certain fields of use to manage rivalrous consumption preserves the commons for a wide range of other use(r)s and, as a result, the social option value of the resource. To put it in a slightly different way, we must manage the environmental commons to sustain its ability to function as infrastructure. I elaborate on these issues below.

* * *

This chapter begins to explore how infrastructure arguments apply to environmental resources and contribute to the difficult tasks of valuing and managing these resources. It is organized into four sections. Section A briefly discusses some difficult valuation and management problems that plague economic analysis of environmental resources. Section B applies the infrastructure criteria and delineates environmental infrastructure. It shows how environmental infrastructures are mixed infrastructure and discusses the many different ways in which users generate massive social value, some of which is reflected in markets and much of which is not. Section C considers commons management and various complications. While the demand-side case for commons management is quite strong, there are strong countervailing concerns, including congestion, degradation, and depletion (conventional tragedy of the commons problems); interuse rivalrousness and incompatibilities (e.g., when pollution and swimming conflict); and negative externalities associated with the production of "public bads" that cause harm in interdependent systems (e.g., pollution that causes adverse health effects to people regardless of whether or not they use the resource). This section offers a few insights regarding how environmental regulation addresses these concerns while sustaining commons to the extent feasible. Section D considers how infrastructure analysis relates to the literatures on ecosystem services and multiple-use management.

My objectives are primarily conceptual: to illustrate how the demand-side infrastructure analysis applies to environmental resources, explore how it "fits" within existing environmental theory, and raise issues for future consideration in specific contexts. I do not

---

[9] OSTROM (1990).

claim to make major contributions to the existing environmental literature. Rather, the following may or may not constitute modest contributions:

- an economic framework for approaching difficult valuation and management issues and thinking about the social demand for environmental infrastructure;
- a connection with related areas of resource management (traditional infrastructure and intellectual infrastructure);
- a better understanding of competing tragedies and comedies of the commons and why the best argument for environmental protection may be an argument about sustaining commons; and
- a better understanding of the regulatory semi-commons concept and how environmental regulation sustains rather than supplants commons.

With a few exceptions, the discussion remains at a relatively high level of abstraction, for two reasons. First, a more detailed analysis of various environmental infrastructure resources would be a nice idea for another book, but it is beyond the scope of this one. Second, there is value in thinking about the environment abstractly as infrastructure, or perhaps "infra-infrastructure."[10] Doing so helps the process of drawing connections with other resource systems discussed in this book and with identifying principles that apply across different areas of environmental policy.

A. Valuing and Managing Environmental Resources

Valuing and managing environmental resources is extremely difficult. We tend to take for granted the environment within which we live; our own preferences and values can fail to recognize the complex interdependencies between ourselves, our environment, and others. Consequently, our decisions about how to manage our interactions with the environment are not likely to maximize social welfare.[11] It persistently contributes to our well-being, but most often it does so only indirectly.[12] We rarely pay directly for its benefits, so when it comes down to individual preferences or valuation—for example, preferences measured in terms of willingness to pay or revealed through our actions—it should not

---

[10] Daly (1992) refers broadly to the "biophysical infrastructure of the entire human niche" as "infra-infrastructure" and emphasizes how public investments in natural capital—for example, to "conserve [existing] natural capital and encourage its natural growth by reducing our level of current exploitation"—constitute infrastructure investments.

[11] Daily et al. 395 (2000) ("Often, the importance of ecosystem services is widely appreciated only upon their loss.").

[12] For a framework that links ecosystem services and human well-being along many important dimensions, see Millennium Ecosystem Assessment vi, fig. A (2005).

be surprising that we persistently undervalue the environment, in terms of its contributions to our own well-being (putting aside notions of intrinsic and existence values).

One reason we undervalue[13] the environment is that it is hard to understand; it is complex and involves many different sets of interdependent resource systems. Until recently (i.e., the past half-century), we haven't had to pay much attention or seek to better understand our interactions and interdependencies with the environment. But that has changed; we no longer have the luxury of abundance or ignorance. Environmental problems that have arisen with industrialization, population expansion, and increased use of the environment for recreational purposes have drawn public attention to the environment.

Ordinary individuals frequently fail to appreciate environmental resources. One reason is that many of them do not understand environmental science, as demonstrated by pervasive misunderstanding of various environmental risks, such as climate change.[14] This poses a significant problem for economic valuation based on individual preferences. It is hard to value what one does not understand.[15]

Another reason individuals fail to appreciate the environment is the confluence of its relative obscurity and our inescapable dependence on it. Like many infrastructure resources, it remains in the background, taken for granted, and insufficiently reflected in existing preferences.[16] It seems reasonable to argue that we, as individuals and as a society, haven't learned to appreciate the environment yet. Most people lack both the information and experience necessary to make accurate judgments concerning the value of the environment in terms of its actual contributions to our welfare. I emphasize experience to suggest that context and cultural factors affect our capacity to judge value, especially but not only where complexity and uncertainty make such judgments difficult.[17] Information may reduce uncertainty and bring complex phenomena within reach of human understanding, but knowledge and the related capacity to judge value require experience.[18]

---

[13] We probably overvalue some environmental resources as well.

[14] Environmental science has vastly improved in the past century, and to some degree, this has improved our appreciation of environmental systems. But science alone cannot solve environmental valuation and management problems.

[15] Salzman 134 (2006) (discussing ignorance of ecosystem services); Salzman, Thompson, & Daily 311 (2001) (discussing "[o]ur unthinking reliance on ecosystem services"); Heal et al. (2001) (ecosystems are under threat because they are unrecognized and, even when recognized, easily ignored or forgotten).

[16] Ruhl & Salzman make this point succinctly. Ruhl & Salzman 157 (2007). Some economists may see this statement as either incorrect or overly strong; they might argue that any inaccuracy in valuing resources is associated with the measurement tools rather than the preferences themselves.

[17] Daily et al. 396 (2000) (noting "serious pitfalls" in relying on "individual preferences to construct social values").

[18] Participation in recreational activities may provide the information, context, and experience needed to shape preferences and enable improved valuation of the environment. Learning to appreciate what one takes for granted is an exercise that shapes preferences, and it may be the case that society would make better decisions and be better off over the long run if such shaping took place. Morton 473–78, 481–82, 483 (1999) (comparable dynamics with respect to wilderness recreation).

Despite such problems, most economic approaches to valuing environmental resources and weighing different management options rely on aggregated individual preferences.[19] Economists use a range of sophisticated methods, such as stated preference methods and revealed preference methods, to approximate preferences.[20] Although used in many policy and resource management settings,[21] these methods are, *at best*, incomplete proxies for measuring the social value of environmental resources.[22] Even if economists could accurately measure everyone's current preferences, the resulting valuation would nonetheless be skewed in a manner that undervalued the environment's "true" contribution to human well-being.

Economists generally do not attempt to identify the absolute value of environmental resources, although some have tried to do so with macroeconomic approaches.[23] Besides, "it is trivial to ask what is the value of the atmosphere to humankind, or what is the value of rocks and soil infrastructure as support systems. Their value is infinite in total."[24]

Instead, economists value environmental resources "at the margin," meaning that they aim to estimate marginal values based on incremental changes in the amount or quality of the resource. Such valuation may be based on the expected incremental effects from proposed public policy options.[25] The marginal approach to valuation makes sense because valuation is used to evaluate discrete trade-offs that are inevitable in resource management or policy making. As James Salzman notes, "The tough decisions revolve

---

[19] Two principal types of valuation methods that do not rely on individual preferences are production function methods and replacement cost methods. On the methods, see NATIONAL RESEARCH COUNCIL 95–152 (2005); RUHL ET AL. 70–71 (2007).

[20] A PRIMER ON NONMARKET VALUATION. Stated preference methods, such as contingent valuation, rely on statements made by individuals in response to questions about various hypothetical scenarios. *Id.* at 21, chs. 4–7. Revealed preference methods rely on observations of how people act in actual scenarios. *Id.* at 21, chs. 8–11. Revesz & Stavins 12–20 (2007) (providing an accessible account of these and other methods).

[21] McCollum 483 (2003).

[22] Bishop 537, 539 (2003) ("true economic values are unobservable"); Revesz & Stavins 12 (2007) (These and other related methods attempt to "infer [individuals'] willingness to trade off other goods (or monetary amounts) for environmental services."); *id.* at 9 ("[T]he benefits of environmental policy are defined as the collection of individuals' willingness to pay (WTP) for the reduction or prevention of environmental damages or individuals' willingness to accept (WTA) compensation to tolerate such environmental damages."); Salzman & Ruhl 623 (2000) ("environmental law relies almost entirely on proxy measures").

[23] Costanza et al. (1997); Pearce (1998). In his reply to Pearce, Costanza et al. explained that their estimate of the value of Earth's ecosystems at a global scale employed macroeconomics and necessarily differed from more traditional microeconomic approaches. Costanza et al. (1997); Sutton & Costanza (2002) (looking at special patterns of conventional GDP and at the value of nonmarketed ecosystem services not currently included in GDP).

[24] Costanza et al. 255 (1997).

[25] Freeman 3 (2003a); Salzman (1997); Turner et al. 493–510 (2003); Driesen 17 (2010) (discussing cost-benefit analysis of environmental regulation).

not around whether protecting ecosystems is a good thing but, rather, how much we should protect and at what cost."[26] Similarly, Revesz and Stavins note:

> Protecting the environment usually involves active employment of capital, labor, and other scarce resources. Using these resources to protect the environment means they are not available to be used for other purposes. Hence, the economic concept of the value or benefit of environmental goods and services is couched in terms of society's willingness to make trade-offs between competing uses of limited resources, and in terms of aggregating over individuals' willingness to make these trade-offs.[27]

Despite inevitable trade-offs and reasonable appeals for marginal valuation, we should not pretend that such proxies accurately capture the social value humans derive from environmental resources. If individuals' willingness to pay is systematically biased against making trade-offs that would improve their own welfare and the welfare of future generations, we must resist approaches that rely on aggregating individuals' willingness to pay to guide valuation and management decisions, and we must develop better approaches.[28]

B. Delineating Environmental Infrastructure

Applying the infrastructure criteria to environmental resources delineates a class of environmental resources that create benefits for society primarily through the facilitation of a wide range of uses (user activities and natural processes), many of which generate positive externalities. Oceans, lakes, forests, and the atmosphere are a few examples of environmental infrastructure.

Recall that the first infrastructure criterion focuses attention on the "sharability" of the resource and degree of rivalry among users and uses. Environmental infrastructures are not purely nonrivalrous. For most environmental infrastructures, at some point(s), consumption of the resource by one user imposes costs on other users and diminishes the resource capacity to support other users.[29] At the same time, in contrast with some nonrenewable

---

[26] Salzman (1997).

[27] Revesz & Stavins 9 (2007).

[28] Nothing that I have said should be interpreted to suggest that the costs of regulation do not matter. The costs of regulation are one of the reasons there is a trade-off to be evaluated, and the costs obviously extend beyond the opportunity costs involved. My focus is on the benefits. The fields of environmental and ecological economics recognize that many of the benefits are difficult if not impossible to quantify. My observations in this regard are not original or surprising.

[29] *Id.* at 64–65 (describing risk of congestion); *id.* at 52 (describing a "threshold of irreversibility" and noting that "once thresholds are crossed, it can take enormous spans of time to rebuild natural capital through ecological processes").

natural resources (such as oil), environmental infrastructures are not purely rivalrous in consumption, such that consumption by one user necessarily diminishes the capacity of the resource to support other users.

Like road infrastructure, environmental infrastructures are partially (non)rival, meaning that the resources have finite, *potentially* renewable, and *potentially* sharable capacity.[30] As discussed, realizing these potentials requires effective management of the boundary between rivalrous and nonrivalrous consumption. Unfortunately, there is substantial evidence of unsustainable degradation of many environmental resources that amounts to a "persistent decrease in the capacity" of ecosystems to deliver services.[31]

For many environmental infrastructures, the degree and rate of rivalry varies across uses and across time. The possibility of avoiding or at least minimizing congestion and resource depletion while allowing multiple users (uses) is what makes the resource partially (non) rivalrous. The degree of rivalry can be thought of in terms of the degree of scarcity or even joint costs. Where an environmental resource is consumed nonrivalrously—for example, when someone appreciates a scenic view—there is no scarcity or cost involved; however, when it is consumed rivalrously—for example, when pollution precludes swimming (or vice versa)—scarcity arises and opportunity costs must be weighed.

Resource management involves managing trade-offs among potentially competing rival uses. To manage rivalry and begin to evaluate such trade-offs, managers need information about which parameters drive rivalry among specific uses—for example, which water quality characteristics, such as heat, salinity, and concentration of various chemicals, give rise to costs for joint use—and whether impacts on the resource or resource characteristics are reversible. Over the long term, regulators may have to choose between extending access to the maximum number of use types while monitoring use along relevant parameters or excluding some uses entirely and allowing the remaining user community unrestricted common use.

Beyond straightforward congestion and depletion problems, the cumulative impact of resource use can be nonlinear in both spatial and temporal scales. As the UN Millennium Ecosystem Assessment observed, "[T]here is *established but incomplete* evidence that changes being made in ecosystems are increasing the likelihood of nonlinear changes in ecosystems (including accelerating, abrupt, and potentially irreversible changes) that have important consequences for human well-being. Examples of such changes include disease emergence, abrupt alterations in water quality, the creation of 'dead zones' in coastal waters, the collapse of fisheries, and shifts in regional climate."[32]

---

[30] Millennium Ecosystem Assessment 1–2, 39–48 (2005).

[31] "Human use of all ecosystem services is growing rapidly. Approximately 60% (15 out of 24) of the ecosystem services evaluated in this assessment (including 70% of regulating and cultural services) are being degraded or used unsustainably." *Id.* at 39.

[32] *Id.* at 1. On "accounting for cumulative impacts across nonlinear scale domains" in spatial and temporal models, see RUHL ET AL. 53–56 (2007). For a discussion of how the nonlinearity of externalities may depend on different

Concerns about renewal rates, reversibility, nonlinearity, and sustainability, which are prevalent in environmental scholarship, highlight another important dimension along which the degree and rate of rivalry varies: *time*. We must consider valuation and management problems in a manner that takes into account the degree and rate of rivalry among users and uses across time (generations). Thus, in contrast with congestion on traditional infrastructure such as transportation and communications infrastructure, we cannot take comfort in the fact that congestion will usually dissipate in a relatively short time period, leaving the infrastructure intact and unchanged. Rather, sustaining environmental infrastructure depends on governance institutions that take a longer view and consider potential rivalry between current and future use(r)s.[33]

The partially (non)rival nature of environmental infrastructure is only part of the puzzle, in a sense, highlighting the relative costs of supplying infrastructure to different profiles of users. The second and third infrastructure criteria focus attention on the manner in which environmental infrastructure generates value for society, and, in particular, on the diversity and nature of uses/outputs (private, public, and social goods). The social value of environmental infrastructure derives from infrastructure-dependent human and natural systems that directly and indirectly contribute to human well-being in a wide variety of different ways. As with traditional infrastructure, the social value in sustaining environmental infrastructure may be incredibly high yet undervalued. The case for environmental protection or preservation depends in large part on the massive systemic value attributable to environmental resources and the systems they support.

Briefly consider some examples: Consider a lake (or a river, or an ocean, etc.). Like a road system, a lake is socially valuable primarily because it facilitates a wide variety of different uses (user activities) that produce social benefits, often in the form of positive externalities. Think about the wide variety of uses to which many lakes are put. They can be used for fishing, boating, swimming, and other recreational activities. Further, lakes can be used as subject matter for artwork, for commerce, for transportation of goods, for waste processing, as a sink for pollution, or as a drinking water source, to name just a few. These uses are in addition to both the incredibly valuable role lakes play in supporting complex ecosystems and the complex interactions between lakes and other environmental infrastructures.

Consider "wildland ecosystems," which Pete Morton described in infrastructural terms:

Wildland ecosystems represent natural capital capable of producing a wide range of goods and services for society. Some of these outputs, such as timber, are freely

---

forms of spatial and temporal differentiation among environmental degradations, see Nash 13–19 (2007). For a discussion of how nonlinearities may call for spreading a pollutant around or trying to isolate it in relatively few locations, see Nash & Revesz 577–80 (2001).

[33] I discuss intergenerational issues briefly below. Unfortunately, although intergenerational issues are incredibly important and interesting, a detailed examination of them is beyond the scope of this chapter.

exchanged in formal markets. Value is determined in these markets through exchange and quantified in terms of price. However, many other outputs, watershed protection, carbon storage, scenic beauty, trophy caliber wildlife, and native fish for example, contribute to our quality of life, but are without formal markets and therefore without prices. Although highly valued by society, the benefits of nonmarket goods and services are typically underestimated in production and consumption decisions—i.e., underproduced by private markets.[34]

In contrast with these examples, some partially nonrival environmental assets are special purpose (only support a narrow range of uses), and thus would not constitute infrastructure within the scope and meaning of the criteria. For example, a small river, a woodland, or even a single species might not individually constitute infrastructure. Some small lakes, including some human-made lakes, are not infrastructural for this reason. Even though the resource is sharable (partially nonrival), it may not support a wide range of different activities and thus should not be considered infrastructural. Much like an isolated road or bridge, however, these resources may be important components of a networked infrastructure (biodiversity; ecosystem). It should be clear that, on one hand, environmental infrastructures are a subset of environmental resources, yet on the other, environmental resources outside the infrastructure subset may combine with others to constitute infrastructure.

Typically, environmental infrastructures are mixed infrastructure that support the production of private, public, and social goods. Environmental infrastructure users generate a tremendous variety of private goods that are easy to identify, discuss, quantify, and appreciate. Many private goods produced by environmental infrastructure users are simply extracted or cultivated materials, such as food, timber, fiber, biochemicals, genetic resources, and freshwater. Many others are more finished commercial products that depend on the services of the environmental infrastructure to support a part of the production process, such as when an industrial user relies on a lake for processing waste or cooling turbines. Restaurants, resorts, and related tourism services may similarly depend on the environmental infrastructure to support their services to consumers. Finally, many direct consumptive uses of environmental infrastructure, including recreational uses such as swimming, can be squeezed into the private goods category.[35]

---

[34] Morton (1999).

[35] In some contexts, it might make sense to conflate consumptive uses of the infrastructure with private goods production. The same move could be made for other infrastructure resources. For example, in our discussion of road infrastructure in chapter 9, we could have made the same point with respect to people who drive for the sake of driving and who are thus purely consumptive and not productive users. But given that the overwhelming reason for using roads is to get from one place to another in order to engage in some activity at the destination, we did not make this point. With respect to environmental infrastructure, however, a considerable number of users and uses may fall into this category of consumptive use; recreational uses, for example, are primarily

Environmental infrastructure (users) generate a host of public goods.[36] In contrast with private goods, the public goods may not be as easy to identify, discuss, quantify, and appreciate. Some public goods, such as scenic views, are not necessarily produced by users and thus seem consumptive. The aesthetic benefits of a scenic view may be captured in a painting, photograph, story, or song. As noted, environmental infrastructures act as inputs into cultural and social processes that yield artwork, literature, memories, community identity, and culture, among other things. More importantly, many incredibly valuable public goods associated with environmental infrastructure—a host of ecosystem services, such as flood prevention, pest control, water purification, and climate control— are not produced by human beings. Nonetheless, some individuals often are in a position to disrupt the flow of such services to others. Alison Power describes the problem with respect to agriculture:

> One of the inherent difficulties of managing ecosystem services is that the individuals who control the supply of such services, such as farmers and other land managers, are not always the beneficiaries of these services. Many ecosystem services are public goods. While farmers do benefit from a variety of ecosystem services, their activities may strongly influence the delivery of services to other individuals who do not control the production of these services. Examples include the impact of farming practices on downstream water supply and purity and regional pest management.[37]

Environmental infrastructure users also generate a host of social goods. Though often taken for granted, social goods directly attributable to environmental infrastructure are a bit easier to identify and discuss, if still quite difficult to value. Recall our discussion in chapter 3 of four types of social goods—nonmarket goods, merit goods, social capital, and irreducibly social goods. These types of goods tend to generate social value through diffuse mechanisms and not necessarily through direct consumption. Most of the ecosystem services noted above (and discussed further below) are nonmarket goods. Typically, these services are not bought and sold in markets. There are various exceptions; for

---

consumptive. From the demand side, whether recreational swimmers or fishers are consumptive users or productive users may not matter much because the relevant observation is that the benefits of the activity are largely if not entirely captured by the participant and thus reflected in their willingness to pay for access and use of the resource. Note, however, that I challenge this view below and suggest that recreational activities, even if consumptive, also may generate small-scale spillovers.

[36] Resource use also can generate "public bads" and negative externalities that are not directly related to rivalrousness. For example, resource use may impact other resource systems in a manner that harms third parties, or it may affect the health of third parties. Interdependencies among environmental and other infrastructure resources also can be relevant. I discuss this issue in the next section.

[37] Power (2010). Power suggests, "The challenge is to use emerging information about ecological production functions and valuation to develop policies and incentives that are easily implemented and adaptable to changing ecological and market conditions."

example, while the vast majority of pollination services are not bought and sold in markets, there is a substantial market for such services in some contexts.[38] But most ecosystem services are nonmarket goods.

Consider how important certain environmental resources can be for certain communities. Environmental infrastructures play an integral role in community identity and culture. For example, the "identities" of communities surrounding Lake Michigan, including the city of Chicago itself, are intimately tied to a particular conception of the lake—that of a wonderful natural resource accessible for community use.[39] The same is true of countless communities across the country.[40] Shared community identity and culture are a form of social capital and may be irreducibly social goods; their value is inherently social because it depends on the existence and nature of interdependent social relations and it shapes those relations over time.

Environmental infrastructure resources also play a critical foundational yet underappreciated role in supporting many public and private investments in other infrastructure and capital resources. The value of (or generated by) those resources ultimately depends on environmental infrastructure. Consider, for example, how the value of various capital investments in a mining town depends on the existence of ore to mine; it is easy to see how depletion of the ore affects those investments.[41] Now extend the thought to a lumber town, wharf, or tourist destination, and note that a very similar relationship exists. Many communities depend on natural resource endowments to support their economy, identity, and culture. The deterioration of natural capital—woodlands, fish stocks, air and water quality—often leads to significant reduction in the value of physical and human capital built up around the natural capital.[42] Yet it is important to emphasize that, in

---

[38] Pickert (2009); Heimbuch (2010).

[39] Perched on edge of Lake Michigan, Chicago is defined by its proximity to the lake. Its tallest buildings, its most expensive neighborhoods, and a third of its population are located along the lakefront. The eighteen-mile-long Lakefront Trail offers runners, bicyclists, and tourists a magnificent view of the lake, while passing alongside the city's most prominent institutions, including Soldier Field, Navy Pier, and several museums and public beaches. A similar symbiotic relationship has developed between Lake Michigan and other cities on its shores, including Milwaukee and Green Bay.

[40] Florida's tropical coastline has earned it the title of the "Sunshine State," drawing droves of retirees with whom the state has come to be identified. Similarly, ski towns in Colorado, mining towns in Appalachia, beachfront towns in New Jersey and New York, and vineyard towns in California have all forged their community identity around the conception and economic exploitation of their immediate environmental resources.

[41] Note that the ore is not infrastructure because it is rivalrously consumed. See chapter 5 for further discussion.

[42] Consider, for example, the far-reaching effects of the BP oil spill that affected the Gulf of Mexico in 2010. In the aftermath, BP set up a $20 billion compensation fund for victims of the spill; the difficulty in assessing claims made to this fund highlights the complex interactions between human and physical capital and the natural capital. Restaurants, hotels, and business owners claimed significant negative economic effects from the oil spill. Economic losses went far beyond the reach of the spill—businesses in towns such as St. Pete Beach, Florida, far from the actual oil spill, were significantly impacted by the public perception that the oil had or would eventually reach those towns, even though it never did. Segal (2010). Indeed, lawyers estimated that more than 100,000 entities in Florida would make "proximity claims" based on indirect harm from the spill. *Id.* Moreover, the true

contrast with depletion of ore, deterioration of natural capital is not a foregone conclusion; sustainable practices are feasible.

In general, one advantage of the infrastructure lens is that it differentiates the infrastructural asset (resource) from the users that depend on it as well as the outputs those users produce. This perspective can be analytically useful in framing trade-offs. In the environmental context, it can be a little confusing. The remainder of this section explores a modified approach focused on categories of uses to show how the second and third infrastructure criteria apply and then explores the concept of a "nonhuman" user.

Freeman explains that environmental and resource "service flows" may be classified according to the "economic channel through which human well-being is affected" (market system or nonmarket system) and whether the flow affects humans directly, indirectly through impacts on other living organisms, or indirectly through impacts on inanimate systems.[43] Adapting his classification slightly, we differentiate between market, direct nonmarket, and indirect nonmarket uses. In examining infrastructure uses, we consider whether the infrastructure uses can be expected to yield positive or negative externalities due to the character of the activity, the nature of its output, or its joint products. Just as the degree and rate of rivalry varies across uses, so does the degree and rate of positive and negative externalities. It is worth noting that externalities arise in similar categories as for other infrastructure types, such as road infrastructure. Conventional congestion/network externalities may arise among more or less homogenous users—for example, where a fisher harvested too many fish from a lake without regard for the impact on other local fishers. Some externalities are due to interdependencies among different user groups, thus giving rise to interuse externalities or interaction effects—for example, when a polluter fails to account for the costs imposed on swimmers or fishers. Finally, other externalities are due to interdependencies between infrastructure users and nonusers—for example, when users degrade ecosystems and such degradation impacts human health. Finally, it is necessary to consider the degree to which streams of external benefits and costs associated with user activities are (un)known, (un)observable, or (un)foreseeable and whether the activities have feedback effects on the system.

I. MARKET USES

Environmental infrastructures support a variety of commercial activities. For example, users extract food, wood, fiber, biochemicals, genetic resources, freshwater, and other resources; release waste products for dilution and assimilation; and use environmental

---

long-term economic impact from the spill is far from quantifiable; researchers have uncovered huge underwater oil plumes that are breaking down at a rate far slower than anticipated, stoking fears of long-term damage to the economically important local ecosystem. Gillis & Collins (2010). Already, scientists expecting to see "subtle effects" from the oil on underwater coral life are instead finding an "ecosystem in collapse." Rudolf (2010).

[43] FREEMAN 12–13 (2003b).

infrastructure as transportation infrastructure. The goods and services derived from these activities are bought and sold in markets, and the benefits derived from them are largely captured in market transactions. In other words, the degree and rate of positive externalities may be insignificant. Many joint products or by-products of these activities can produce negative externalities due to rivalry with other uses of the environmental infrastructure (e.g., resource extraction may displace or lessen the attractiveness of various recreational opportunities), collateral effects on neighboring communities (e.g., pollution associated with resource extraction may have negative health effects on local communities), and depletion of the resource in an unsustainable manner that negatively impacts future users (e.g., resource extraction at a rate that exceeds renewal rate).

2. DIRECT NONMARKET USES

Environmental infrastructures also support a variety of noncommercial activities. The use of the environment as a source of raw materials and a sink for waste products is often noncommercial and not accounted for in market systems. For example, emission of carbon dioxide by a wide variety of household and individual activities uses the atmosphere freely and without restriction. In fact, many day-to-day human activities use environmental infrastructure without mediation by the market system. Some of these activities have the potential to generate externalities, both positive and negative.[44] Most everyday activities are consumptive, such that the bulk of the value from using the environmental infrastructure is captured by the particular user and does not generate benefits for others. Yet, as global warming demonstrates, many of these activities may generate small-scale negative externalities that aggregate into a significant cumulative effect.[45] Driving is an obvious example.

Many of the human uses that generate public and social goods discussed above should be categorized as direct nonmarket uses. Many such uses generate substantial positive externalities that are not easily observed or captured by the users.

It is worth discussing a category of noncommercial uses that have grown tremendously in popularity and developed cultural significance over the past century: recreational activities. Environmental infrastructures support a variety of recreational uses, including swimming, fishing, boating, camping, hiking, running, biking, and sightseeing, among others. The value derived by recreational users typically depends on various characteristics of the environmental resource, such as the air or water quality, that in turn depend on other uses. Recreational uses tend to be potentially rival with other uses, particularly commercial uses that introduce waste (pollution) or extract resources (e.g., timber, minerals, wildlife). Recreational uses tend to be weakly rivalrous with other recreational uses

---

[44] Lazarus 234–36 (2005).
[45] *Id.* at 236.

but strongly rivalrous with commercial uses. In some cases, recreational uses can also be strongly rivalrous with other noncommercial uses, such as spiritual uses.[46]

Access to the infrastructure for recreational use is generally nondiscriminatory, such that "access is typically open to all comers at a zero price or a nominal entrance fee that bears no relationship to the cost of providing access."[47] Economists see recreational uses as consumptive, such that willingness to pay is an accurate assessment of value derived from use.[48] Thus, although access generally is not allocated via the market system, some economists have argued that it should be.[49]

For purposes of this argument, recreational activities should be distinguished from many day-to-day activities that use the environment for a few reasons. First, demand for recreational activities is comparatively elastic. Second, recreational activities are often tied directly to a particular environmental infrastructure resource (e.g., lake or woodland). Third, recreational users are often engaged directly with their setting and are aware of the connection with the environment. Finally, recreational activities are more easily privatized and allocated through the market mechanism (and regulated) than many of the day-to-day activities. Thus, when it comes to resource management, recreational uses are more easily seen as "available" to trade off with other uses.

It might be worth exploring whether recreational uses of environmental infrastructure generate (small-scale) spillovers. It seems reasonable to view recreational uses as primarily consumptive but partially productive of the following: health, community, and environmental appreciation. Recreational activities such as swimming and hiking promote good health, and that has some positive spillovers; note that the availability of other forms of exercise that promote good health but do not depend on the same environmental infrastructure implies a limit to the magnitude of spillovers. For example, suppose my favorite bike trail is closed. My opportunity to bike does not drop to zero; rather, it drops only as much as the difference in value to my next-best alternative, my second-favorite trail. This might limit the size of the spillovers.

Recreational activities also promote community values and support social networks, and that may have some beneficial spillovers.[50] Perhaps most importantly, participating in recreational activities that depend on environmental infrastructure—that derive value from the specific connection to the environmental setting—may provide the experience,

---

[46] Bluemel (2005a); Bluemel (2005b).

[47] FREEMAN 417 (2003b).

[48] *Id.* at 418. Economists have developed other approaches, such as the travel cost model of valuing recreation. Even if entry fee is negligible, some people travel a long way at great expense to engage in recreational activities in certain environments, and the travel costs reflect valuation.

[49] FRIEDMAN (1962) (arguing there were no externalities associated with using national parks and owners should be able to capture the full economic value of uses through admissions fees) (cited in FREEMAN 249 (2003b)).

[50] Poirier 101–03 (2006) (drawing a connection between infrastructure, recreation, and these types of benefits in light of Carol Rose's work); Rose 713–14, 779–81 (1986).

context, and connection necessary to appreciate and value the environment; such learning may have significant external effects if it impacts individuals' behavior and influences culture and public policy.

3. INDIRECT NONMARKET USES

Environmental infrastructures support an incredible diversity of life (users) and a wide variety of natural processes (uses) that provide incalculable value to human beings. An especially important set of uses, which may be classified as indirect nonmarket uses, includes a wide variety of ecosystem services, such as flood prevention, pest control, water purification, and climate control, to name just a few.[51] These services provide tremendous value to humans, yet often indirectly and not through the agency of human users.

The ecosystem services literature has developed a number of quite refined typologies to differentiate among ecosystem services.[52] For example, J. B. Ruhl emphasized the importance of distinguishing between provisioning and regulating services:[53] *Provisioning services*, such as pollination, that support the human production of food and fiber commodities are used indirectly by humans, and thus the value of such services is embedded in the commodities' value.[54] *Regulating services*, such as storm surge mitigation, gas regulation, groundwater recharge, and thermal regulation, are used directly by human beings, meaning that there is no intermediate step or conversion to another form of good or service, and thus the value of such services is not embodied in marketable commodities.[55] Both categories of ecosystem services give rise to complex valuation problems. Ruhl observes that "[f]rom the perspective of formulating economic and regulatory policies for managing ecosystem services, this distinction between direct and indirect use will be of utmost importance, because it reflects the human perception of the service use values."[56]

---

[51] For more comprehensive lists, see RUHL ET AL. 23–30 (2007); Balvanera & Prabhu 3 (2004); Costanza et al. 254 table 1 (1997) (providing a list of "renewable ecosystem" services organized into seventeen groups); Daily et al. 2 (1997); Holmlund & Hammer (1999). Economists attempt to approximate the value of such services indirectly. A Primer on Nonmarket Valuation, U.S. EPA, Ecological Research Program Multi-Year Plan FY 2008–2014 app. A (Feb. 2008) (Draft Review); Brown & Peterson (2003).

[52] RUHL ET AL. 26–27 (2007).

[53] *See id.*; Millennium Ecosystem Assessment 1–2 (2005).

[54] Ruhl describes this category in terms of "structure-based benefits of indirectly used ecosystem services." RUHL ET AL. 29 (2007).

[55] Ruhl describes this category in terms of "dynamics-based benefits of directly used ecosystem services." *Id.* at 29.

[56] *Id.* Ruhl and his coauthors show how directly used service benefits present the "most difficult problems for envisioning ecosystem service law and policy." *Id.*

4. A NOTE ON NONHUMAN AND UNBORN USERS

The last category of uses is perhaps the most difficult to conceptualize. In earlier work, I suggested that one way to think about ecosystem services was to imagine a nonhuman user[57] of the environmental infrastructure that produced ecosystem services. Such a user would not have "preferences" measured in terms of willingness to pay (or some other measure), would not be able to participate in market or political systems, and would be difficult to account for in policy-making discussions.[58]

In a sense, the nonhuman user was already incorporated into the notion of an ecosystem, which is defined as the complex system of *living communities* (plant, animal, and microorganisms) and *nonliving environmental resources* that interact as a unit.[59] "Ecosystem" brings together environmental infrastructure and users within a system but expands the notion of users beyond humans to encompass all organisms. Therefore, in evaluating the economic value of certain ecosystem services, one might focus on the services provided by a particular living species, such as pollination by bees or pest control by wasps.[60] The ecosystems literature acknowledges and evaluates the contributions of non-human users and, in some contexts, even seems to recognize a resource–resource-user relationship.[61]

For purposes of valuation and examining management strategies, it may be helpful to maintain our focus on the infrastructure resource and continue to differentiate among different types of users and uses. I do not mean to suggest that the preferences of nonhuman users should be incorporated into valuation studies; that would be impossible. My point is that acknowledging both the demand/needs and contributions of nonhuman users complicates the analysis. It highlights the demand-manifestation problem with stark clarity. Thinking of the nonhuman user that produces ecosystem services as an entity that fails to manifest demand in either market or political systems is important because it highlights the complex interdependencies involved as well as a persistent and systematic source of undervaluation and thus distortion.

---

[57] The next few paragraphs explore the idea of nonhuman users. I find this a useful conceptual tool, but the arguments being made in this chapter are not contingent on your acceptance of this construct.

[58] Heal et al. 342 (2001).

[59] Millennium Ecosystem Assessment v (2005). On a more holistic theory of environmental ethics not centered on humans, see TAYLOR (1986).

[60] Losey & Vaughn (2006) (study of wild insects).

[61] Many organisms depend on habitats that are spatially or temporally segregated from locations where those organisms deliver ecosystem services. Kremen et al. (2007) ("Some ecosystem services, such as pollination, pest control and seed dispersal, are produced at a local scale by mobile organisms foraging within or between habitats [internal citations omitted]. We call these services mobile agent-based ecosystem services (MABES). Although these mobile organisms deliver services locally, their individual behaviour, population biology and community dynamics are often affected by the spatial distribution of resources at a larger, landscape scale."). Note that habitats are sometimes referred to as an example of ecosystem structure, which can be a type of environmental infrastructure. RUHL ET AL. 27 (2007).

In their lack of representation in market or political systems, nonhuman users are similar to the other relevant class of user: the unborn members of future generations.[62] Granted, future generations are not users that generate value for current users; instead, they are recipients of whatever we leave for them.[63] But the same could have been said in the past. Working out the details of an intergenerational theory is beyond the scope of this chapter, but three points need to be emphasized.

First, the ethical and moral obligations to transmit environmental infrastructure to future generations of users seem quite strong. At a minimum, the very existence of future generations depends on an environment that can sustain life;[64] further, the welfare of future generations, as well as the present generation, certainly depends on the quality of the inherited environment.[65] Moreover, no particular generation has a stronger moral claim than any other generation to the inherited environment. At a minimum, it seems reasonable to follow Edith Brown Weiss and require "each generation to pass the planet on in no worse condition than that in which it received it and to provide equitable access to its resources and benefits. Each generation is thus both a trustee for the planet with obligations to care for it and a beneficiary with rights to use it."[66]

Although intergenerational commitments may extend beyond environmental resources, the injustice of excessive degradation of the environment seems to be of a different kind than any injustice associated with underinvestment in other types of infrastructure. In part, this is because of the inherited nature of the environment; in part, this is because the different types of capital are not entirely substitutable.[67] Physical, intellectual, technological, and social capital, while very important, are not fully interchangeable substitutes for natural capital.[68] Technological progress offers significant hope for improving the efficiency with which each generation uses environmental resources,[69] but there are significant limits, reflected in the "plain and uncontestable" facts: "the biosphere is finite, nongrowing, closed (except for the constant input of solar energy), and constrained

---

[62] BARNES (2006).

[63] I am intrigued by Marc Poirier's suggested connection between infrastructure theory and intergenerational stewardship obligations. Poirier (2008). I briefly explored this issue and would like to explore it in the future. Frischmann (2005d). *See generally* BROWN WEISS (1989); Revesz 987–1016 (1999).

[64] Some might argue that the present generation owes no obligations to the future or that the future generations have no right to exist. I will not engage this philosophical debate here.

[65] Brown Weiss 335–36 (1995).

[66] Brown Weiss 200 (1990).

[67] I have not explored substitution across infrastructure types (or even within types). This may be an important issue to consider in future research.

[68] If forced to choose between (1) a world full of natural capital but empty of the other types of capital and (2) a world empty of natural capital but full of the other types of capital, each generation would presumably choose the former.

[69] For an examination of how to encourage environmentally beneficial technological innovation and of the social benefits of doing so, see DRIESEN (2003).

by the laws of thermodynamics."[70] It seems rather shallow to rely completely on technological progress to alleviate all burdens on the present generation with respect to the environmental conservation.

Second, despite some conceptual difficulties, valuing and managing environmental infrastructure can take into account these classes of users (nonhuman users and future generations). As noted, the ecosystems valuation literature incorporates nonhuman users. Manifesting the demand of future users within existing decision-making frameworks may require clever institutions, such as the public trustee. In a provocative book, Peter Barnes argues that we could create common property trusts to be managed by trustees with obligations to these sets of users.[71]

Third, infrastructure analysis relies on functional economic concepts that are useful in understanding relationships among people, resources, and institutions, but ultimately, economics does not provide definitive answers to these difficult social questions. What type of environment we live in and how we structure relationships within that environment involves complex trade-offs among values that transcend economics.[72] Nonetheless, economics helps frame the trade-offs and questions we need to ask ourselves. Sustaining environmental infrastructure for current and future generations of human and nonhuman users can be understood in terms of social welfare economics, although incorporation of the contributions of nonhumans and the welfare of future generations may be theoretically difficult and empirically impossible. There are other attractive approaches to articulating ethical and moral obligations and framing these trade-offs. For example, Marc Poirier discusses potential parallelism and intersections with various versions of intergenerational ethics, including two that have influenced my thinking—Brown Weiss's notion of fairness to future generations, and the capabilities approach developed by Amartya Sen and Martha Nussbaum.[73] I leave exploration of such approaches for another day.

C. Managing Environmental Infrastructure

Managing environmental infrastructure is extremely difficult. The infrastructure frame highlights three reasons, all of which also afflict infrastructure management in other areas: First, the sharable but congestible and depletable nature of environmental resources

---

[70] Daly (2005).

[71] BARNES (2006). On the public trust doctrine, see Poirier 189–92 (2008); Sax (1970).

[72] In an essay commenting on my previous article, Marc Poirier suggested that I "seem[ed] to skirt the issue of the possibility that there are deep disagreements of values, not simply questions of quantification, at stake." Poirier 193 (2008).

[73] *Id.* at 200–02.

means that the boundary between nonrivalrous and rivalrous consumption must be tended, and that is a complex and difficult task. Second, the multiplicity of users (human and nonhuman) and outputs (which in this context refers to beneficial flows of resources and services) and the interdependence among users and outputs dramatically complicates matters. Third, the significant number of outputs that constitute public and social goods means that much of the social value is not well reflected in market processes, may be quite difficult to observe and quantify directly, and may be quite difficult to value. Unfortunately, if value is unseen or vastly underestimated, it often will not be taken into account in management decisions, leading to bias or prioritization in favor of more easily observed and captured value. This is the same demand-side concern raised throughout this book.

Despite the powerful lessons taught by the tragedy of the commons story, there are lessons from the comedy of the commons story as well. While environmental infrastructure resources are congestible and depletable, that does not mean that the resources are necessarily doomed to tragedy and thus commons must be eliminated. Environmental infrastructures are partially (non)rival, which means they are congestible and exhaustible but also sharable. The second and third infrastructure criteria help to show how environmental infrastructure generate social value and how, similarly to other infrastructural resources, managing environmental infrastructure as a commons can support many different types of value-creating activities. Yet the partially (non)rival nature of environmental infrastructures, particularly the risk of degradation and even catastrophic loss through cumulative and nonlinear effects, suggests that pure commons management is not sustainable.

Resource management requires, among other things, consideration of the following functional economic variables that describe the relationship between infrastructure resource and the systems it supports:

Degrees and Rates of Rivalry among Uses
- Relevant resource characteristics
- Interdependence among uses
- Path dependence and reversibility

Nature of Outputs from Uses
- Private, public, and social goods
- Rate and degree of externalities
- Degree to which observable, known, and foreseeable

Nature of Infrastructure User / Output Producer
- Market actor
- Nonmarket human
- Nonmarket nonhuman

This is only the first step toward framing the resource management problem. Sustaining environmental infrastructure poses numerous challenges for policy makers, including, inter alia, reconciling competing values; determining an appropriate discount rate or how to trade-off current and future welfare effects; dealing with uncertainty; and a host of institutional design questions.[74]

Managing environmental infrastructure in a sustainable manner leaves trade-offs to manage. There is a very strong demand-side case for sustaining environmental infrastructure in a nondiscriminatory manner, that is, in a manner that does not discriminate in favor of the more easily observed and captured value and instead supports the full range of users and sustains the option value of the resource for current and future generations. However, there are strong countervailing pressures, including both the demand-pull toward present extraction of observable, appropriable value and the vulnerabilities of environmental infrastructure to congestion, degradation, and catastrophic loss.

In practice, the dominant approach in the environmental area appears to be a mixed strategy that regulates some uses and sustains a commons for many others. Environmental infrastructure resources are often sustained through complex institutional arrangements that form something akin to semi-commons property regimes,[75] although often through regulatory regimes rather than pure property regimes.[76] This approach to constructing semi-commons (1) assigns and regulates private rights (access, use, exclusion, and/or exchange) for certain fields of use, such as diversion for industrial purposes; (2) defines commons in terms of community rights (access and use) for certain fields of use, such as recreational use;[77] and (3) sustains the integrity of the resource for nonhuman users and future generations. It is worth noting that often we regulate fields of use which are strongly rivalrous with each other and many other activities—and thus are likely to give rise to congestion, surpass renewal rates, or risk depletion—and which also may be less spillover intensive (i.e., the users observe and capture much of the value associated with their use). By managing these uses, we sustain commons (a) for a wide variety of other uses that often are nonrivalrous (or only weakly rivalrous) and may be more spillover intensive as well as (b) for users that are not well represented in current market or political systems.

---

[74] A detailed discussion of these topics must be left for another day, or at least another book.

[75] Smith (2000).

[76] The public trust doctrine seems to follow this model. Poirier (2008) (explaining that the public trust doctrine may couple nondiscriminatory access with congestion management).

[77] Some recreational uses are regulated. In some cases, regulations focus on safety issues associated with the recreational activity itself. *See, e.g.*, Illinois Boat Registration and Safety Act, 625 ILL. COMP. STAT. 45 (2008) ("It is the policy of this State to promote safety for persons and property in and connected with the use, operation and equipment of vessels and to promote uniformity of laws relating thereto."). In some cases, regulations focus on how participation in the activity affects the environmental resource or other resource users. In national parks, for example, recreational uses are often limited to protect environmental resources through park general management plans. Bluemel (2005a and 2005b).

D. Multiple-Use Management and Ecosystem Services

The concept of environmental infrastructure seems to fit well within existing environmental scholarship. Specifically, it appears to complement bodies of work on (1) multiple-use management (MUM) strategies for public lands and forests, and (2) ecosystem valuation and management.[78]

MUM primarily focuses on valuing and managing natural resources that have multiple competing *human* uses.[79] Different sets of uses are characterized and valued under different scenarios; where uses are rival, the different scenarios consider shared but coordinated use versus dedicated use. In managing a forest unit, for example, one would compare the net benefits of joint production of timber and recreational amenities with the net benefits of dedicating the unit to a "dominant use" (timber production or recreation).[80] MUM does not directly incorporate ecosystems services as a set of "uses" within the multiple-use framework.[81] This is a potential shortcoming when one considers the complex interaction of nonhuman users and infrastructures and increasing concerns about long-term sustainability. In her critique of a MUM approach, Janet Neuman argues that "the Tillamook State Forest ecosystem is much greater than the sum of its parts. Until a true ecosystem approach is adopted, the forest managers, the interest groups, and the public will all fail to see the forest for the trees . . . or the fish . . . or the off-road-vehicle trails . . . or any other single interest."[82] MUM has evolved to incorporate some ecosystem planning and management principles.[83]

The ecosystems literature brings together resource management perspectives in economics, ecology, and other related fields and takes a more holistic view of systems of nonliving environmental resources and the living resources that support and are supported by the environment.[84] Economists attempt to value a wide range of ecosystem services, some of which involve direct human agency in the exploitation and use of the

---

[78] For an excellent exploration of these complex, interdisciplinary literatures, see NAGLE & RUHL (2006).

[79] BOWES & KRUTILLA (1989). A related body of environmental scholarship focuses on managing multiple-use common pool resources. It addresses the complexity attributable to multiplicity of use when devising management strategies, for example, the added institutional difficulties where multiple, heterogeneous user communities share a common pool resource. Steins & Edwards (1999).

[80] BOWES & KRUTILLA ch. 3 (1989).

[81] NAGLE & RUHL 489–90 (2006); Neuman 194 (2007); Ruhl & Salzman 168 (2007).

[82] Neuman 194 (2007).

[83] Federal Interagency Ecosystem Management Task Force, Memorandum of Understanding to foster the Ecosystem Approach between the Council on Envtl. Quality et al. (December 15, 1995), *available at* http://www.fhwa.dot.gov/legsregs/directives/policy/memoofun.htm; *see also* Multiple Use Sustained Yield Act of 1960, 16 U.S.C. § 528 (2006) (creating a multiple-use framework for the federal regulation of national forests); Lynch 433 (1996).

[84] NATIONAL RESEARCH COUNCIL 153 (2005) ("Valuing ecosystem services requires the integration of ecology and economics.").

resource and some of which involve nonhuman agency and indirect provision of services. As discussed, these services can be split into direct market, direct nonmarket, and indirect nonmarket uses. The first category involves value that is well reflected in markets; the latter two categories do not. As a result, valuing ecosystem services typically relies on nonmarket valuation methods (e.g., revealed preference methods, stated preference methods, and avoided and replacement cost methods). Ruhl observes, "Each technique has its own set of limitations, but each can also reveal the tremendous monetary values of ecosystem services that are currently 'hidden' from the marketplace. Given the level of knowledge about ecosystem services that members of society have at any time, the results of these techniques are first approximations of the values assigned by individuals to ecosystems services and the functions they perform."[85]

Built on an understanding that the methods are imperfect, that trade-offs are inevitable, and that "society has to choose how to allocate natural resources necessarily requires valuation of ecosystem services in some form or another,"[86] the literature reflects a concerted effort to grapple with the complex systems involved, to improve economic valuation methods, and gradually to improve decision-making processes and regulatory frameworks.[87] The idea that priorities are misdirected because of difficult-to-observe and difficult-to-measure benefits is a foundational theme in the ecological economics and ecosystems valuation literature. As John Losey and Mace Vaughn observe:

> Natural systems provide ecological services on which humans depend. Countless organisms are involved in these complex interactions that put food on our tables and remove our waste. Although human life could not persist without these services, it is difficult to assign them even an approximate economic value, which can lead to their conservation being assigned a lower priority for funding or action than other needs for which values (economic or otherwise) are more readily calculated. Estimating even a minimum value for a subset of the services that functioning ecosystems provide may help establish a higher priority for their conservation.[88]

A hotly debated question is whether economic valuation is likely to improve decision-making processes and regulatory frameworks or merely provide further support for insufficient regulation and unsustainable practices. Many agree with the sentiment expressed

---

[85] RUHL ET AL. 58 (2007).

[86] *Id.* at 31 (citing Costanza et al. (1997)).

[87] Difficulties of scale, jurisdiction, and fractured regulatory regimes present significant challenges for existing ecosystem management and governance regimes. One federal commission recently called for a more holistic form of governance, one that is "effective, participatory, and well coordinated among government agencies, the private sector, and the public." Eagle 153 (2006) (quoting US COMMISSION ON OCEAN POLICY, AN OCEAN BLUEPRINT FOR THE 21ST CENTURY: FINAL REPORT (2004)).

[88] Losey & Vaughn (2006).

by Losey and Vaughn: "Estimating even a minimum value for a subset of the services that functioning ecosystems provide may help establish a higher priority for their conservation." Surely it is better to identify and attempt to value ecosystem services; assigning some value is better than assigning no value. However, others have argued that such comfort is misplaced because it accepts and promulgates the analytical paradigm and provides a false sense of security that ecosystems are being sufficiently valued and protected.[89]

While sympathetic to both sides of this argument, I have reservations about overreliance on ecosystem valuation as a tool to guide regulatory policy. As part of a dynamic, adaptive, and interdisciplinary approach to learning about and improving our interactions with our environment, ecosystem valuation can be useful. But let me highlight two reservations. First, as discussed, I am suspicious of valuation based on existing preferences and thus of methods that at best approximate existing preferences. Relying on such methods, even if (unrealistically) assumed to be accurate approximations, runs the risk of merely confirming already biased perceptions or simple misperceptions of value. It assumes stable preferences and ignores the possibility that we need to learn how to appreciate the environment and judge value. It also ignores the possible advantages of developing our "undeveloped tastes" to make better use of natural resources.[90]

Second, I worry that ecosystem valuation studies frequently focus only on valuing ecosystem services, too often a single service or small subset of services, and too often those that are most amenable to valuation techniques:[91] for example, environmental products that either have a readily traceable market value, or whose market value is indirectly discernable through its contribution to the value of other products, how much people are willing to pay for it, or the results of surveys.

There are many complex interactions between ecosystems, between ecosystems and services, and between services themselves. The complex and dynamic interactions make valuation difficult and the risk of distortion by omission significant. The National Research Council stresses the importance of differentiating between valuing an entire ecosystem

---

[89] Kysar (2004) (discussing the deceptive lure of CBA's comprehensive rationality). This has led some scholars to argue forcefully that reliance on incomplete valuations may make matters worse. HEINZERLING & ACKERMAN (2005).

[90] "[G]ame ranching and fruit gathering in a natural tropical forest may, in terms of biomass, be more productive than cattle ranching. But undeveloped tastes for game meat and tropical fruit may make this use less profitable than the biologically less productive use of cattle ranching." While cutting down the forest to make room for the cattle ranch may maximize value measured on the basis of existing preferences, it is by no means clear that this is the best management decision; "a change in tastes can increase the biological productivity with which the land is used." Daly 5 (1992). The scenario gets more complicated when other ecosystem services are taken into account. It might be that cattle ranching is not only biologically less productive than game ranching and fruit gathering in terms of outputs for human consumption, but also might be more strongly rivalrous with various ecosystem services.

[91] Power (2010).

and valuing a single ecosystem service, noting that "single service valuation exercises may provide a false signal of the total economic value of the natural processes in an ecosystem."[92] Moreover, an overly narrow valuation may ignore important trade-offs among ecosystem services. Power notes, "In general, ecosystem services are not independent of one other and the relationships between them are likely to be highly nonlinear." She suggests:

> Tradeoffs among ecosystem services should be considered in terms of spatial scale, temporal scale and reversibility. Are the effects of the tradeoff felt locally, for example on-farm, or at a more distant location? How quickly does the tradeoff occur? Are the effects reversible and if so, how quickly can they be reversed? Management decisions often focus on the immediate provision of a commodity or service, at the expense of this same or another ecosystem service at a distant location or in the future. As either the temporal or spatial scale increases, tradeoffs become more uncertain and difficult to manage.
>
> Management is further complicated by biophysical and socioeconomic variation, since every hectare of a given habitat is not of equal value in generating a given ecosystem service. For natural ecosystems, habitat quality, size of unit and spatial configuration are likely to influence the services provided by the ecosystem. . . . Furthermore, the values of both market and non-market goods and services will vary according to various biophysical and socioeconomic factors.[93]

The more general ecosystem literature—the interdisciplinary literature that incorporates economic valuation but extends well beyond economics—reflects an incredible step forward in terms of its systemic approach to the study of complex social-ecological systems. In fact, the approach offers much that might be mapped over to other areas discussed in this book.

There are a number of potential affinities between MUM and ecosystems approaches and the infrastructure approach. All three approaches explore from a functional perspective how social value is generated in complex social-ecological systems, and how across many different systems we fail to appreciate or simply massively discount values that are difficult to observe, measure, and capture in markets. It is not that the existence of these values is doubted; it is that their magnitude, persistence, comparative weight, and distribution are underappreciated. Tremendous uncertainty about how complex social-ecological systems work exacerbates the problem. All three approaches aim to develop an improved appreciation of these values by seeking to identify, understand, and better account for the complex interactions and interdependencies in social-ecological systems.

---

[92] NATIONAL RESEARCH COUNCIL 156 (2005).
[93] Power (2010).

12

INTELLECTUAL INFRASTRUCTURE

THIS CHAPTER EXPLORES how infrastructure theory applies to cultural-intellectual resources and delineates a class of infrastructure—hereinafter, *intellectual infrastructure*. Intellectual infrastructure, such as basic research, ideas, general purpose technologies, and languages, creates benefits for society primarily by facilitating a wide range of downstream productive activities, including information production, innovation, and the development of products and services, as well as education, community building and interaction, democratic participation, socialization, and many other socially valuable activities. The foundational role of intellectual infrastructures in cumulative, dynamic, and complex systems merits attention. Courts and commentators frequently refer to intellectual infrastructure resources as "building blocks" to capture their role as basic inputs. But while the "building blocks" metaphor is evocative, it fails to fully reflect the complex relationships among participants in intellectual systems that derive value from intellectual infrastructures as producers, users, consumers, or incidental beneficiaries.

Applying infrastructure concepts to cultural-intellectual resources is more difficult in some respects than applying them to other resources. The difficulties stem in part from the fluid, continuous, and dynamic nature of cultural-intellectual systems. Distorting reductionism seems inevitable when we attempt to delineate clear boundaries around discrete cultural-intellectual resources or to separate resources (inputs, outputs, products, things) from activities (processes, practices, uses). Intellectual infrastructures, such as basic research, often seem to be both resources and activities. Difficulties also stem from the fact that infrastructure appear to exist on many different scales within cultural-intellectual systems. Nonetheless, the analysis yields important insights about societal demand for intellectual infrastructure and the case for commons management.

This chapter is organized into four sections. It begins in section A with the idea of the cultural environment as infrastructure. This discussion provides an important connection to the previous chapter and establishes a context for examining intellectual-cultural resource systems and governance institutions. It also explains some of the complex relationships between intellectual-cultural resources and people—for example, the mutual dynamic shaping that takes place as society lives within, interacts with, shapes, and is shaped by its interactions with the cultural environment. Section B describes the economic characteristics of intellectual resources. The economic analysis of intellectual resources is quite complex; while I discussed most of the general issues in previous chapters, this section extends the analysis in a few ways. First, it explains how (non) excludability and nonrivalry[1] give rise to distinct economic considerations concerning systematic risk of undersupply of some intellectual resources. Next, it considers an added layer of complexity associated with "information [being] both input and output of its own production process. . . . This characteristic is known to economists as the 'on the shoulders of giants' effect."[2] The added complexity centers on the dynamics of intellectual processes and systems and how intellectual progress occurs. An appreciation of the "on the shoulders of giants" effect is critical to understanding how productive use of intellectual resources generates spillovers. It also reconnects the economic analysis with the broader notion of the cultural environment.

---

[1] I use (non)excludability because this characteristic is context-dependent, is variable with the costs of exclusion, and can be addressed though various institutional interventions. I use nonrivalry (without the parentheses) because this characteristic in inherent or fixed for intellectual resources. While some dispute this point and argue that I am too much of a Platonist, I have never found this argument persuasive. The marginal cost of allowing another person to consume an intellectual resource is always zero because the resource has infinite capacity to be possessed, consumed, and used; the resource is not depleted. This does not mean that each possessor, consumer, or user will realize the same (or even any) value. An idea might bring me some positive value (benefit), someone else no value, and someone else negative value (harm). Regardless, the idea is nonrival and sharable. If I write a PhD thesis and capture all of the value from an idea that can be realized in the process of being awarded a PhD and I effectively preclude someone else from using the idea for her PhD, the preclusive effect is a function of the external environment, the PhD rules or market, or whatever one calls it, but this does not mean the idea is anything other than nonrival. A second comer could possess the idea, and even write a PhD thesis, but the person would not, according to the rules, be awarded a PhD. This may reduce the use value realized by a second user who wishes to make a particular use of the idea, but that has nothing to do with nonrivalry. The PhD queue may be congestible, but the idea is not. Similarly, a person might need a certain level of knowledge or language skills (absorptive capacity) to effectively use an idea, but that important prerequisite also has nothing to do with nonrivalry.

[2] Benkler 37 (2006a).

I argue that the complexity of dynamic cultural systems and the resulting economics should lead to a reframing of the economic objectives in this area. Specifically, I suggest that pursuing optimal production of public goods is a fool's errand because of the pervasiveness and diversity of externalities in the cultural environment. It is more appropriate to improve the efficiency of inframarginal investments,[3] for example, by reducing the costs of public goods production for as wide a variety of potential public goods producers as possible. This shift in perspective has implications for the subsequent discussion of intellectual infrastructure (section C) and intellectual property laws as semi-commons arrangements (section D).

Section C focuses on applying the infrastructure criteria to delineate intellectual infrastructure. Through a series of examples, this section describes some of the practical difficulties to doing so. The section then turns to ideas as an example of intellectual infrastructure. Focusing on the First Amendment, copyright law, and patent law, it examines legal recognition of both the infrastructural nature of ideas and the social value of commons management. It then considers the struggle in patent law to differentiate abstract ideas from patentable inventions, reflected most recently in the Supreme Court's decision in *Bilski v. Kappos* (2010), and suggests that patent law should follow more explicitly the analytical framework employed in copyright law. I argue that despite some confusion and controversy on how to draw lines and separate ideas from expression and invention, ideas are and should be "free as the air to common use."[4]

Section D considers intellectual property laws. It examines intellectual property laws as a semi-commons regime and compares it to the regulatory semi-commons discussed in the previous chapter. It shows first how intellectual property laws, like environmental regulation, are targeted exceptions/interventions to the default commons regime for the cultural environment. The laws enclose and regulate a select (albeit very broad) set of intellectual resources to overcome supply-side market failures. Given tremendous difficulties in establishing and maintaining boundaries around this set and the dynamic and complex nature of cultural-intellectual resource systems, the laws also sustain semi-commons arrangements for enclosed resources. This leads to a second point. Many intellectual infrastructure resources are excluded from the enclosed set—that is, the resources remain in the public domain and are not patentable or copyrightable, but many intellectual infrastructures are patentable or copyrightable. For these resources, intellectual property laws seem to recognize the social demand for commons management and mediate access to intellectual infrastructure accordingly. I argue that a more deliberate approach is needed and provide some preliminary suggestions.

---

[3] See chapter 3, appendix.
[4] International News Serv. v. Associated Press, 248 U.S. 215, 250 (1918) (Brandeis, J., dissenting).

A. The Cultural Environment as Infrastructure (Meta- or Infra-infrastructure)

We can identify infrastructure at a very high level of abstraction and broad scale—the cultural environment—and at progressively lower levels of abstraction, on smaller scales, and within different systems or fields. In parallel with such efforts, we can study different commons management institutions. Thus, we analyze both infrastructure and commons as nested phenomena operating at different levels that may interact with one another.[5] The scaling issue arises in other contexts—for example, recall how our discussion of road infrastructure varied in scale from a particular road or bridge to the national highway system.[6]

At a relatively abstract level, the basic similarities between the natural and cultural environments concern the functional and relational meanings of the common term "environment." An environment might be defined as a complex system of interconnected and/or interdependent resources (or even resource systems) that comprise the "surroundings," "setting," or "context" that we inherit, live within, use, interact with, change, and pass on to future generations. We inherit the natural physical environment; we live within, use, interact with, and change it; and we pass it on to future generations. Similarly, we inherit, live within, use, interact with, change, and pass on to future generations a cultural-intellectual environment, comprised of many overlapping sub-environments, if one would like to distinguish culture(s), science(s), and so on. The world we live in comprises multiple, complex, overlapping, and interdependent resource systems with which we interact and that constitute our environments—the natural environment is one type, and (socially) constructed environments, such as the cultural environment, are another.

Thus, we can envision a cultural environment that consists of the various cultural, intellectual and social resource systems that we inherit, use, experience, interact with, change, and pass on to future generations.[7] This is analogous to the move made in the previous chapter envisioning the environment as a meta–natural environment that consists of various overlapping and interdependent natural resource ecosystems.[8]

---

[5] Madison, Frischmann, & Strandburg 674 (2010) ("By 'nesting,' we mean that a particular commons phenomenon might be analyzed at many levels; these levels may interact strongly with one another. One of the issues that must be resolved in any particular inquiry is the appropriate level of complexity at which a particular commons should be studied. Ostrom analogizes this nested analysis to a set of maps at different levels of detail, such as one sees when using the zoom function in Google Maps. All of these maps are accurate, but the usefulness of a particular map depends on the question one seeks to answer. Moreover, some questions can be answered by focusing only at street level, while others may require zooming back and forth to different levels. Similarly, analyzing a commons institution may require more or less detailed knowledge of the larger cultural institutions within which it resides.") (citing OSTROM 58–62 (2005)).

[6] See chapters 7, 8, and 9 (identifying infrastructure at different scales and levels of abstraction).

[7] I explored this is greater detail in prior work; see Frischmann 1091–96 (2007a); Madison, Frischmann, & Strandburg 685 (2010). On cultural environmentalism, see Boyle 70–74 (2003); Boyle 108–16 (1997); BOYLE (1996); Opderbeck (2009).

[8] I owe a significant intellectual debt to Jamie Boyle for his work on cultural environmentalism. I discussed his work extensively in Frischmann (2007a).

The cultural environment provides us with resources and capabilities to act, participate, be productive, and "make and pursue life plans that can properly be called our own."[9] It also shapes our very beliefs and preferences regarding our lives (life plans) and relationships with each other and the world we share. Human beings are not born with fully formed preferences, knowledge, and beliefs about the world they enter;[10] rather, preferences, knowledge, and beliefs are learned and experienced and thus contingent to a degree on the cultural environment a person experiences.[11]

We have an incredibly complex and dynamic relationship with the cultural environment.[12] Science and culture, for example, are cumulative and immersive systems that develop with society, while simultaneously developing society. Put another way, the cultural environment provides for, shapes, and reflects us, and at the same time, we provide, shape, and reflect it. I stress this point because the cultural environment has a normative dimension that is sometime lost. As John Breen puts it, culture can be understood as a society's answer to a series of "fundamental questions" about what it values. He explains:

---

[9] Benkler 146 (2006a).

[10] DeMartino 77–79 (2000); Krackhardt 5 (1994); North 46–47 (2005). I have always loved how Julie Cohen made this point in an article about privacy:

> Autonomous individuals do not spring full-blown from the womb. We must learn to process information and to draw our own conclusions about the world around us. We must learn to choose, and must learn something before we can choose anything. Here, though, information theory suggests a paradox: "Autonomy" connotes an essential independence of critical faculty and an imperviousness to influence. But to the extent that information shapes behavior, autonomy is radically contingent upon environment and circumstance. The only tenable resolution—if "autonomy" is not to degenerate into the simple, stimulus-response behavior sought by direct marketers—is to underdetermine environment. Autonomy in a contingent world requires a zone of relative insulation from outside scrutiny and interference—a field of operation within which to engage in the conscious construction of self. The solution to the paradox of contingent autonomy, in other words, lies in a second paradox: To exist in fact as well as in theory, autonomy must be nurtured.
>
> A realm of autonomous, unmonitored choice, in turn, promotes a vital diversity of speech and behavior. The recognition that anonymity shelters constitutionally-protected decisions about speech, belief, and political and intellectual association—decisions that otherwise might be chilled by unpopularity or simple difference—is part of our constitutional tradition. But the benefits of informational autonomy (defined to include the condition in which no information is recorded about nonanonymous choices) extend to a much wider range of human activity and choice. We do not experiment only with beliefs and associations, but also with every other conceivable type of taste and behavior that expresses and defines self. The opportunity to experiment with preferences is a vital part of the process of learning, and learning to choose, that every individual must undergo.

Cohen (2001) (footnotes omitted). Cohen's argument strongly influenced my own thinking.

[11] Of course, not everyone experiences the same cultural environment. Individual cultural experience is inextricably linked to the extent of one's access to artistic and cultural resources; these resources are distributed spatially in ways that make any particular resource more relevant or less so to a given individual, based on accessibility and proximity. Cohen 1180 (2007).

[12] Breen 29–30 (2006) (quoting works of Pope John Paul II).

A culture ... constitutes the response that a given people have to these fundamental questions, a response that is constantly being revised and worked out over time. It is expressed not only through the customs and traditions of a people, but through their language, history, art, commerce and politics. Indeed, "[a]ll human activity takes place within a culture and interacts with culture." ... As such, every culture is, in essence, a normative and didactic enterprise. It indicates what is desirable and permissible within a given society. It instructs both the observer and the participant as to how they ought to act. ... That is, a culture is a societal answer to the question of value. Every culture renders a whole series of judgments as to what is truly important in life.

For this reason, I deliberately choose "cultural environment" rather than "information environment" or "intellectual environment."[13] "Cultural" captures the contextual, contingent, and social/relational aspects of the resources that constitute the meta-environment; the resources are resources vis-à-vis their *meaning* to and among people.[14] As Yochai Benkler suggests, "[Culture] is a frame of meaning from within which we must inevitably function and speak to each other, and whose terms, constraints, and affordances we always negotiate. There is no point outside of culture from which to do otherwise."[15] In a real sense, culture itself is an environmental concept.

One of the most important differences between the natural environment and cultural environment is the degree to which cultural resources are manufactured, both by humans and by law. Natural resources typically are given. Yet this difference is easily misunderstood or taken too far. Although the natural environment is given and not made by humans, it is continuously and unavoidably affected by humans and, in a sense, made and remade and unmade with irreversible consequences through those interactions. And although the cultural environment is made by humans, it is also inherited, subject to considerable path dependencies that can have irreversible consequences, and even contingent on human interactions with the physical environment.[16]

Viewed through the infrastructure lens, two points are clear: First, the cultural environment constitutes mixed infrastructure.[17] Human beings produce an incredible

---

[13] The other adjectives seem reductionist in the sense that they "cleanse" the discussion of normative values.

[14] Frischmann 1094 (2007a). Another reason is to connect this discussion with the "movement and ideas" associated with cultural environmentalism. See *id*. See Boyle (1997).

[15] Benkler 282 (2006a).

[16] Gordon (1993) (discussing path dependencies in the cultural environment).

[17] It is nonrival and sharable. As noted, it is comprised of nonrival resources. One might argue that some resources that are integral parts of cultural systems are partially nonrival—for example, libraries or even communications infrastructure. Such an argument does not undermine the point I am making and can be integrated into the discussion. I leave this additional layer of complication aside and focus on the intangible, intellectual, cultural, and social resources that are nonrivalrously consumed.

diversity of private, public, and social goods simply by living in and interacting with the cultural environment. It would be a mistake to assume that such productivity is inevitable or natural. In some respects, some may be; one way or another, human beings experience their lives, and "[e]xperience constitutes an important intellectual resource that simultaneously relates human beings to their inherited and evolving environment(s) and constitutes a resource that may shape the intellectual environment."[18] But the fact that the cultural environment shapes both our capabilities to be culturally or intellectually productive and our beliefs and preferences regarding the exercise of such capabilities is a reason to pay close attention to the dynamic relationships between users and the cultural environment. Whether people are active participants in intellectual, cultural, and social resource production, actively shaping the cultural environment, or passive consumers shaped by the cultural environment (or by those who are shaping it) depends on the cultural environment and how it is managed.[19] Different evolutionary paths are possible— for our environment and for us:

> [People] may become more aware, conscious of their (potential) roles as listeners, voters, and speakers, but also as consumers and producers, as political, cultural, and social beings, as members of communities. They may learn to be productive—or learn to want to be productive, if such desire is not simply latent. This very awareness that one can play different roles and that the environment is not fixed or fully determined by others is encouraging. It encourages participation and the development of facilitative social practices, and perhaps over time, the adoption of a participatory culture. . . .[20]

Second, the case for commons management is incredibly strong. Managing the cultural environment as a public commons maintains flexibility and maximizes the social option value of the infrastructure. At this scale and level of abstraction, commons management aims to limit both government and market shaping of the environment and our lives, plans, beliefs, and preferences. In other words, commons management is a strong default position for the cultural environment because users—autonomous individuals as well as social groups and communities—get to shape the environment and choose what to say and do and how to plan their lives, experiences, and interactions with each other

---

[18] Madison, Frischmann, & Strandburg 685 (2010). "Experience (or perception or observation) is not enclosed within IP regimes except when expressed and embodied in a particular qualifying form, such as a copyrightable work of authorship or a patentable invention." *Id.*

[19] Benkler 150–51 (2006a). I discuss this point further in my review of Benkler's book. Frischmann 1123–28 (2007a).

[20] See *id.* See also chapter 13 (considering how the Internet affects society and the cultural environment). Wendy Gordon makes this point well in the copyright context. Gordon (1993).

and the environment.[21] The cultural environment is spillover-rich because of the many different user activities that produce, distribute, use, and reuse public and social goods.

Support for commons as a default position at this macro level seems to be reflected in both the First Amendment, which restricts the exercise of government power to control the cultural environment,[22] and the related conception of a robust public domain, which limits private ownership, control, and exclusion over swaths of cultural, intellectual, and social resources.[23] Nonetheless, whether commons management truly *is* the default position is debatable.[24] Markets and government have played and will continue to play incredibly important roles in shaping the cultural environment. These social systems and institutions depend on and are essential to the cultural environment. As Benkler aptly describes (and critiques), the reality of our modern existence is that the industrial information economy and mass media system have had a tremendous influence on both the cultural environment and the American people.[25] Still, the case for commons management is incredibly strong; it should be the default position and government and market interventions and institutional structures should be understood as targeted exceptions. I return to this idea below in the context of intellectual property laws and my view that these legal systems should be understood as important, targeted exceptions.

The cultural environment as infrastructure has an intergenerational dimension. Each generation is blessed beyond measure with the intellectual and cultural resources it receives from past generations; each generation experiences and changes the cultural environment and passes it on to future generations. That we "stand on the shoulders of giants" is often noted to emphasize the cumulative nature of cultural or scientific progress.[26] But "the expression also reflects an understanding of intergenerational dependence: each generation is both dwarf and giant; the current generation stands on the shoulders of the past and also serves as the shoulders for the future."[27] Essentially, "shoulders" refers to the "fundamental blessings"[28] of resources preserved, created, and transmitted. While each generation faces supply-side problems (discussed below), it does so within the existing cultural environment, while also shaping the cultural environment for the future.

---

[21] Benkler (2006a) provides a richer account.

[22] Frischmann (2008b).

[23] On the public domain, see, for example, Litman (1990); Benkler (1999); LESSIG (2001b); Samuelson (2006).

[24] This is tricky because the question can be approached as a matter of normative commitment—that is, does society demonstrate a normative commitment to this baseline via legal or other forms of public commitment?— and the question can be approached empirically—to what degree are markets and/or government actually shaping the cultural environment?

[25] Benkler (2006a).

[26] Scotchmer 29 (1991).

[27] Frischmann & McKenna (2011); Gordon (1993).

[28] Lincoln, Lyceum Address (referring to "fundamental blessings").

B. Economic Characteristics of Intellectual Resources

The economic characteristics of intellectual resources are complex. We discussed most of the basic economic issues in chapter 3: intellectual resources are public goods, often a form of capital, and often the source of various types of externalities. An added layer of complexity not discussed in chapter 3 is the fact that intellectual resources are part of cultural, intellectual, and social progress, and thus a part of our complex and evolving cultural environment. In this section, I explain the supply-side problems that flow from the public goods nature of intellectual resources, and then I discuss the added layer of complexity.

I. SUPPLY-SIDE PROBLEMS

Intellectual resources face well-known supply-side problems, common to public goods, discussed in chapters 3 and 8. First, the inability to (cheaply) exclude competitors and nonpaying consumers (free riders) presents a risk to investors perceived ex ante (prior to production of the good), and this risk may lead to undersupply. This problem is a function of (non)excludability. Second, even if exclusion is feasible at low cost, nonrivalry suggests that markets still undersupply various intellectual resources.

a. (Non)excludability

Recall that (non)excludability is not a fixed or inherent characteristic of a resource; the costs of exclusion vary considerably with technology and context. In the absence of some institutional solution, there would be a significant underinvestment in *some types* of intellectual resources because of the risk that competitors would appropriate the value of the resources and undermine the ability of investors to recover their costs.

Whether private incentives are in fact inefficiently suppressed by this potential misappropriation risk depends on the type of investment, the intellectual resource in question, and the particular context. Many intellectual resources are not subject to this particular supply-side concern; we generate the resources without being disabled by concerns over misappropriation. For example, human experience generates substantial intellectual resources naturally. Paying attention to and recording one's experience entails fixed costs that we may choose to avoid. This highlights a distinction between creating the intellectual resource and identifying it as a resource, and converting the intellectual resource from a purely intangible creature of human intellect—referred to as tacit knowledge—to a recorded or fixed form that can more easily be preserved and shared. Underinvestment in these extra steps may constitute a supply-side problem that warrants attention.

In many situations, people make investments because the expected private benefits exceed the fixed costs, regardless of whether or not others free ride. Appropriating benefits through market exchange of the intellectual resource or some derivative product may not be *relevant* to the investor. For example, we engage in many intellectually productive activities because participation itself provides sufficient private benefits.[29] Participation can be fun, intellectually stimulating, educational, or service-oriented, among other things. Participation may not be effortless or free; it may require substantial investment. Regardless, the private value derived from participation may be sufficient, and external benefits conferred to others that use or consume the output (i.e., the intellectual resource) may be irrelevant to incentives to invest. Even if those benefits could be internalized, such internalization could potentially decrease incentives to invest and prove quite costly.[30]

In many situations, people create, invent, and innovate because the anticipated returns from their own use of the results are sufficient to justify the investment. There is a rich literature on user innovation that demonstrates quite clearly how many significant innovations result from users seeking to solve their own particular problems, needs, or curiosities.[31] The key point is that similar to folks who participate in intellectually productive activities because of the direct benefits of participation, people often engage in such activities because the results (outputs) may be beneficial for themselves, and they do so without disabling concern over free riding.

In some contexts, people produce intellectual resources and welcome free riding by others. Sharing intellectual resources can be a viable strategy for increasing returns generated through other means. Benkler describes a bunch of different examples, ranging from lawyers who write articles to attract clients to software developers who share software and make money by providing services to users.[32] Sharing may help attract attention, build a reputation, lead to reciprocal sharing, and so on.

Finally, even where free riding is a concern and appropriating benefits through market exchange of the intellectual resource or some derivative product is relevant to investment decisions, self-help mechanisms, such as lead-time advantages and barriers to entry, may provide sufficient protection against free riding by competitors to support the investment. In some instances and in certain industries, self-help mechanisms are preferred for gaining a competitive advantage. Surveys of R&D managers show that factors such as securing lead-time advantages, increasing learning, developing complementary products, and ensuring secrecy are more relevant to incentives to invest in R&D than any perceived

---

[29] Madison, Frischmann, & Strandburg (2010); FREY 35 (2008).

[30] As discussed in chapter 3, the transaction and institutional costs may be significant, and internalization may affect other dependent markets and activities. The shift to internalization may even affect the attractiveness of the activity itself; participation in the activity may be less attractive when commercialization of the outputs occurs. PINK 37 (2010); AMABILE 17 (1996); Benkler 298 (2006a).

[31] VON HIPPEL (2005).

[32] Benkler 42–46 (2006a).

ability to secure traditional intellectual property protection.[33] The extent of the benefits that inure from such self-help mechanisms vary by industry and depend on a multitude of external factors, including technology-enhanced access and copying opportunities. Such mechanisms are imperfect and do not suffice for many types of intellectual resources, but when relevant, they can be quite important and should be evaluated in comparison with each other and alternative institutions.

Intellectual property laws are a prominent but by no means exclusive means of addressing the supply-side problem where free riding is a concern and appropriating benefits through market exchange of the intellectual resource or some derivative product is relevant to investment decisions. Consider patent law.[34] In the absence of patent law, there would be a significant underinvestment in some types of inventions because of the risk that competitors would appropriate the value of the inventions. Granting inventors patents lessens the costs of exclusion, raises the costs of free riding, encourages licensing, and, as a result, makes a greater portion of the surplus generated by the invention appropriable by the inventor. The exclusivity provided by patent law does more than affect investment in invention, however. Patents affect the supply-side functioning of markets for inventions as well as markets for derivative products, including additional improvements, innovations, and commercial end-products. The reward, prospect, and commercialization theories of patent law take patent-enabled exclusivity as the relevant means for fixing a supply-side problem—the undersupply of private investment in the production of patentable subject matter or in the development and commercialization of patentable subject matter that would occur in the absence of patent-enabled exclusivity.[35] The theories differ largely in terms of where in the supply chain patent-enabled exclusivity is needed, and in terms of the degree of control/exclusivity needed. In reality, these needs vary by industry and context, giving each of the theories some support. As the next section explains, intellectual property laws also set boundaries around intellectual resources in a manner that reduces transaction costs and reduces information costs. This boundary-setting function creates legal "things" that can be more easily subject to market exchange.[36]

The supply-side benefits provided by patent law are not costless. The appropriation of a greater portion of the surplus presumes an increase in price. Absent exclusivity,

---

[33] Mansfield (1981); Mansfield 174 (1986); Levin et al. 795–97 (1987); Cohen, Nelson, & Walsh table 1 (2000); Barnett 1257–69 (2004).

[34] A similar story can be told with respect to copyright law, although in many contexts the emphasis shifts to supply-side problems further down the supply chain than authorship, i.e., facilitating the development, commercialization, and distribution of works of authorship.

[35] LANDES & POSNER (2003) (reward); Kitch (1977) (prospect); Kieff (2001) (commercialization); see also Ghosh 1353–57 (2004) (connecting prospect and commercialization theories with the theoretical work of Demsetz).

[36] Madison (2005).

competitive distribution and use of the invention would drive price to marginal cost (zero), in which case consumers would capture the full consumer surplus. When relevant, patents may enable pricing above marginal cost and, as result, introduce deadweight losses. Keep in mind, however, that the magnitude of the deadweight losses depends on both the strength of the legal rights conferred and the market conditions. (A patent might enable average cost recovery because the patent owner can exclude other competitors from free riding on sunk fixed costs and thus push competitors to sink their own fixed costs in developing a competitive substitute, but the patent need not, and typically does not, confer market power.) There are transaction and administrative costs to consider as well. But this simple explanation of patent law reveals the basic trade-off between static and dynamic efficiencies; we tolerate some deadweight losses along with transaction and administrative costs to mitigate the supply-side risk of underinvestment.

b. Nonrivalry

Addressing the excludability problem for intellectual resources through intellectual property or other means does not eliminate the nonrival nature of the resources or ensure efficient market provisioning.[37] Some scholars have suggested that private property rights convert the public good into a private good, but this is not correct.[38] As chapter 3 discussed, (non)excludability should not be confused or conflated with nonrivalry. It may be the case that exclusion can prevent sharing, but that in no way affects the capacity of the resource or the corresponding option to share among many users. Consider three important implications.

First, nonrivalry enables sharing and an extra degree of freedom in managing or allocating the intellectual resource. For purely consumptive ideas,[39] this prompts the classic trade-off between static and dynamic efficiencies—for an existing idea, open sharing

---

[37] Lunney 994 (2002) (quoting Samuelson 387 (1954)).

[38] Samuelson 335 (1958):

> You might think that the case where a program comes over the air and is available for any set owner to tune in on is a perfect example of my public good. And in a way it is. But you would be wrong to think that the essence of the phenomenon is inherent in the fact that the broadcaster is not able to refuse the service to whatever individuals he pleases. For in this case, by use of unscramblers, it is technically possible to limit the consumptions of a particular broadcast to any specified group of individuals. You might, therefore, be tempted to say: A descrambler enables us to convert a public good into a private good; and by permitting its use, we can sidestep the vexing problems of collective expenditure, instead relying on the free pricing mechanism. . . . Such an argument would be wrong. Being able to limit a public good's consumption does not make it a true-blue private good. For what, after all, are the true marginal costs of having one extra family tune in on the program? They are literally zero.

[39] Chapter 3.

generally maximizes social welfare[40] because the marginal cost of sharing with someone is zero, but such sharing may have consequences for dynamic efficiency if it lessens investment incentives. Exclusion does not eliminate this trade-off; it simply provides the entity with the capability to exclude with the opportunity to decide whether or not to do so. For ideas, nonrivalry prompts a more complicated trade-off among static efficiency and various types of dynamic efficiencies.[41] In sum, the private and public opportunity to leverage nonrivalry remains an important economic consideration, even when the costs of exclusion are minimal.

Second, demand-measurement problems still lead to undersupply by markets even when the costs of exclusion are minimal.[42] There are two notable demand-measurement problems, one focused on "optimality conditions" and difficulties in accurately measuring consumer preferences, and one focused on externalities. I discussed both extensively in previous chapters. With respect to the first, Paul Samuelson noted that a second type of free riding occurs when consumers strategically misrepresent their true preferences in the hope that other consumers will bear a greater proportion of the costs. This problem, however, is independent of exclusion. The same is true of demand-measurement problems associated with externalities. The bottom line is while exclusion facilitates market provisioning, markets still systematically undersupply *some* public goods because market demand fails to accurately reflect social demand. I revisit the demand-side issues in the next section.

Third, reducing exclusion costs fixes an important supply-side problem and brings the supply-side analysis of market provisioning of intellectual resources in line with the discussion in chapter 8. Specifically, while natural monopoly is less often a concern, the cost structure of supply can impact incentives to invest and impose deadweight losses during fixed cost recovery. Excludability does not eliminate this issue either. As chapter 8 explained, the relevant economic baseline for evaluating the sufficiency of market incentives to invest should be average cost recovery. Sufficient incentives to invest depend on

---

[40] Caveats: First, open sharing does not mean force-feeding. People who want the idea can get it, but no one is forced to consume it. Second, I am assuming that the idea is beneficial rather than harmful. Third, I am assuming away negative network effects, for example, where my consumption of the idea makes it less valuable to you.

[41] As chapter 8 discussed, the conventional characterization of access vs. incentives as static efficiency vs. dynamic efficiency is often a gross and distorting oversimplification.

[42] If exclusion is coupled with *perfect* price discrimination, the first demand manifestation problem goes away. On why I reject that red herring, see chapter 6. Lunney explains:

> The literature also establishes that we can achieve a Pareto efficient outcome in the production of the public good by enabling perfect price discrimination with respect to the public good. In this context, perfect price discrimination creates personalized markets for the public good, where each consumer's consumption of the public good becomes a distinct commodity with its own market and its own price. If it could be achieved, the resulting equilibrium, known as a Lindahl equilibrium, would essentially convert the public good into a private good and ensure a Pareto efficient outcome. Lunney 451–52 (2008).

an expectation of recovering total costs, including a competitive return on capital investment. The cost structure suggests that incentives to invest will be insufficient and undersupply will result, unless pricing above marginal cost and (at least) approximating average cost is sustainable. Without exclusion enabled by intellectual property or other means, it might be impossible for suppliers to recover their average costs because free-riding competitors would drive prices to marginal cost. Exclusion can enable sustainable average cost pricing and competition, in a sense facilitating markets. Enabling average cost pricing does not ensure actual cost recovery, however. As chapter 8 discussed, there are a number of practical obstacles to effectively implementing average cost pricing. Moreover, competition and innovation can jeopardize cost recovery, for example, when a new entrant figures out a way to compete with lower fixed costs. If exclusion is limited in scope to actual misappropriation (in essence, free riding on the fixed cost investment of the first entrant), then whether the first entrant is capable of recovering its costs will depend on the fixed cost investments that others must make to enter the market as well as lead-time advantages and other possible barriers to entry.[43] On the other hand, exclusion also can enable monopoly pricing and eliminate competition.

What exclusion enables depends on the strength and scope of exclusion and the market context. The legal right to exclude can be narrowly or broadly constructed along various dimensions. For example, it can be limited to actual copying of an entire intellectual work, broadened to block copying of parts of the work, broadened to block similar but not identical copying, or broadened beyond instances of copying to block independent creation, among other things. It can also vary in other dimensions such as duration, the strength of remedies, and so on. At the extreme, government could grant monopoly franchises with legal entry barriers. The point is that exclusion can vary in strength, scope, and market impact.

---

[43] People sometimes emphasize the magnitude of fixed costs. In many cases, this doesn't really matter so long as a second comer would have to sink the same amount. High fixed costs may actually be a decent barrier to entry, provided that misappropriation is precluded and average cost pricing is feasible. What seems to matter in such circumstances is the rate of fixed-cost-reducing innovation—whether a second comer can figure out a way to enter more cheaply. Of course, this is true in all sorts of markets. Certainly in some cases, incredibly high fixed costs may exceed capital constraints for any single firm, but that raises a different problem altogether.

A difficult supply-side question[44] to confront is whether patent or copyright law should do more than address *actual* free-riding risks.[45] If patent and copyright laws aim to facilitate competitive markets for intellectual resources and derivative products, a narrow focus on such risks would be appropriate. However, if the laws aim to induce investment in intellectual resources above and beyond what competitive markets would provide, a broader focus on conveying market power and the ability to appropriate supracompetitive returns might be appropriate. If the latter objective is chosen, however, then one

---

[44] I raise this question because it gets insufficient attention in intellectual property scholarship, and, as a result, some unfortunate assumptions/overstatements are made. I highlight two:

- First, a common overstatement in intellectual property discourse suggests that intellectual property laws *create* incentives to invest. Intellectual property laws do not create incentives exactly. Generally, incentives to invest exist independently of intellectual property laws. The motivations briefly described in the previous subsection constitute incentives to invest, and those motivations—whether driven by the value of participation, prospective use of the output, or prospective appropriation of value through market exchange—are not constructed or "created" by intellectual property laws. Rather, intellectual property laws address risks that may distort markets and deter some people from doing (investing in) what they would otherwise be inclined to do (invest in)—in a sense, intellectual property laws assist in the construction of a market. To the extent that the risks are irrelevant and do not distort markets, then the justification for intellectual property is greatly diminished from an economic perspective. (Some might argue that intellectual property rights are still necessary to reduce transaction costs and facilitate coordination, but this argument is significantly diminished where the risk of free riding is irrelevant because it is not clear what intellectual property offers above and beyond what traditional means for coordination already provide.) By addressing free-riding risk when it is relevant, intellectual property (re)aligns incentives to invest, but it seems odd to say that in doing so the law *creates* those incentives. One reasonably could say that intellectual property laws counteract the particular disincentive associated with misappropriation risks and, in that very limited sense, create incentives.
- Second, the conventional economic explanation of intellectual property sometimes slips into a story about temporary monopoly or market power that allows intellectual property owners to extract monopoly rents. This story would seem to support the argument that intellectual property rights create incentives because the prospect of extra-market returns would induce investment above and beyond what would otherwise exist in a competitive market. But recall our discussion in chapter 8 about the appropriate economic baseline for sufficient incentives to invest; the baseline is average cost recovery. To the extent that incentives to invest hinge on prospective appropriation of value through market exchange, the market creates those incentives rather than intellectual property law; providing exclusion by legal means lessens the otherwise disabling costs of exclusion associated with public goods provision and may reduce information and transaction costs associated with appropriation of value through market exchange, but absent additional justification, there is little reason to put a thumb on the scale and provide further inducement to invest via the prospect of extramarket returns. I am not suggesting that additional justifications do not exist; I discuss some in the following sections. But those justifications are complicated and cannot be based exclusively on the risk of free riding or mere evocation of public goods. Moreover, to the extent that society wishes to provide such additional inducement, a comparative institutional analysis would be required.
[45] I emphasize *actual* free riding *risks* to remind you that free riding does not always present a risk to investment because alternative means of exclusion may exist and alternative motivations may provide sufficient incentives irrespective of free riding. See chapters 3, 8; Lemley (2005); Frischmann & Lemley (2007); Liivak (2010); Le 32 (2004).

would have to both justify the need for extra inducement (Why put a thumb on the scale in favor of investments in intellectual resources rather than other types of investments? Is the increase in deadweight losses worth the gain?) and explain from a comparative institutional standpoint why intellectual property laws are the preferred institution for making this social investment—why intellectual property rights rather than government subsidies, a prize system, or other alternatives.[46] Patent and copyright law differ substantially in their institutional design—for example, patent provides a stronger right to exclude than copyright but for a much shorter duration—and it might be argued that patent law is more directly attuned to the latter objective. Note, however, that most intellectual property rights do not in fact convey market power that would allow a supplier to sustain prices above competitive levels, which we might expect to gravitate toward average cost pricing over the medium to long run. In some cases, market power does arise, but it is debatable whether such market power is attributable to the granting of the intellectual property right, the success of the innovation, or other context-specific factors.[47]

An important implication of the cost structure of supply is that market provisioning involves deadweight losses and the magnitude of those losses may be quite significant given the high ratio of fixed cost to marginal cost. There are a host of deadweight mitigation strategies, ranging from price discrimination to government prizes. Even the limited duration of intellectual property rights can be understood as deadweight mitigation strategy. I return to this issue in the context of intellectual infrastructure.

2. INTELLECTUAL RESOURCES AND ACTIVITIES, PRODUCTS AND PROCESSES

The previous section focused on the basic supply-side problem; this section focuses on the added complexity associated with "the other crucial quirkiness . . . that information is both input and output of its own production process." [48] As noted, this effect is interesting and complex because it reveals necessary dependence among generations, but there is more to it than that. It implicates the cumulative, dynamic, and evolutionary nature of progress in intellectual-cultural systems, or, more broadly, in the cultural environment. I examine a few distinct but related points that often are conflated or ignored in discussing this quirkiness.

Benkler focuses on how the "on the shoulders of giants" effect makes "property-like exclusive rights less appealing" because it increases the deadweight losses from pricing

---

[46] FISHER 200–04 (2004); Madison, Frischmann, & Strandburg 685 (2010). Note that alternatives might include support for infrastructures that enable nonmarket production.

[47] FTC ch. 3 (2003) (collecting evidence that "issues of fixed cost recovery, alternative appropriability mechanisms, and relationships between initial and follow-on innovation" vary by industry); Burk & Lemley 1577–1589 (2003) ("Recent evidence has demonstrated that this complex relationship [between patents and innovation] is . . . industry-specific at each stage of the patent process").

[48] BENKLER 37 (2006b).

above marginal cost of zero by making productive use of the nonrival resources more costly. He notes: "Today's users of information are not only today's readers and consumers. They are also today's producers and tomorrow's innovators."[49] Simply put, users are both consumers and producers. Obviously, I agree (given the discussion of this general problem in earlier chapters). The fact that many intellectual resources are a form of nonrival capital that supports production of even more nonrival capital suggests the possibility of increasing returns to investing in such resources and leveraging nonrivalry.[50]

Yet we take the "on the shoulders of giants" effect for granted.[51] For example, we often take for granted the intellectual or cultural backdrop within which and on which we (and others) build; this may be due to a romantic notion of authorship, an inflated sense of self, or any number of things.[52] Similarly, we often take for granted the various intellectual outputs that emerge from our experience and engagement with the cultural environment; we only have so much time and attention. Regardless, we use, make, and reuse intellectual resources continuously in our lives. This seemingly trivial observation has some interesting implications. First, we need intellectual inputs to be intellectually productive and to make intellectual progress in our lives. Second, the intellectual resources to which we have access will shape the intellectual outputs we are capable of producing as well as our beliefs and desires about what to produce; in a sense, they shape who we become (our beliefs, knowledge, preferences) as we engage with the environment. Third, each producer and producer's output is thus dependent or contingent on various inputs. "In order to write today's academic or news article, I need access to yesterday's articles and reports. In order to write today's novel, movie, or song, I need to use and rework existing cultural forms, such as story lines and twists."[53] In a sense, this is a more micro-way of

---

[49] *Id.*

[50] This is a key dimension to Romer's growth theory. Romer (1996); OCHOA 10–15 (1996). Although I refrain from discussing macroeconomics much in this book (to keep some limit on the scope!), there is an interesting connection between these features of intellectual resources and processes/activities and some of the new growth models. SCHMIDT 11 (2003); Romer (1996).

[51] To the extent that this effect is taken seriously in economic and legal scholarship, attention is devoted to the relationship between two stages, the first- and second-generation producers, the pioneer and improver. For example, Suzanne Scotchmer has focused on this effect. She emphasizes the importance of licensing intellectual property between first- and second-generation inventors, and adequately compensating and maintaining investment incentives to both stages of inventorship, given that many products are the result of numerous improvements on previous inventions. Scotchmer (1991); Green & Scotchmer (1995); Scotchmer (1996); Lemley (1997); Merges & Nelson (1994); Merges & Nelson (1990). See also TECHNOLOGICAL INFRASTRUCTURE POLICY: AN INTERNATIONAL PERSPECTIVE at 8 n. 2 ("Cumulative forms of knowledge are those in which today's advances lay the basis for tomorrow's, which in turn lay the basis for the next round. The integrative aspect of the production of knowledge means that new knowledge is selectively applied and integrated into existing systems to create new systems.").

[52] Many scholars have discussed this point. See, e.g., Litman (1990); BOYLE 122 (2010); Lessig 9–13 (2001b); VAIDHYANATHAN 117–48 (2001). See also Lemley (forthcoming 2012).

[53] BENKLER 37 (2006b).

making the point I made earlier with respect to the cultural environment. As Julie Cohen suggests, we are situated within the cultural environment, shaping it while being shaped by it.[54]

Continuous situated engagement implies a stream of input-output relationships (i.e., input → output/input → output/input . . .). In many contexts, it may not be worth the effort to pay attention to the continuous streams of relationships. Surely, we do not need to acknowledge and consider each incremental addition associated with sensory experience or thinking. Instead, we may conflate many input-output relationships into a *process* (activity or practice) and pay attention only to particular outputs that are worthy of attention.[55] Note that such a conflation begs for deeper interrogation. Why would we do this? How do we choose to distinguish between resources and processes? When do we decide to pay attention to the outputs? When are they, and how do they become, meaningful or worthy of attention?[56] When is something an input, an output, both, or an aspect of a process? And so on. This is not the place to address such questions, however. I make two observations and then push on:

- It is common to talk about intellectual resources as identifiable, discrete things with known properties and boundaries. The very notion of a "resource" or "public good" implies such features. But this is a significant oversimplification. Intellectual resources often have a dual nature—creation, invention, and innovation may be resources and activities. Consider basic research: Is it a thing—a result, an input, an output, both—or is it a process or activity that one engages in? It is both, right? Maybe this seems like a semantic point, but isolating one from the other (product from process) for purposes of the law, economic analysis, or just discussion loses something quite valuable.
- Can we "discretize" cumulative intellectual processes of creation, invention, and innovation in a manner that makes analytic sense? We try to do so regularly within copyright and patent law, but are we truly granting patents and copyrights over discrete outputs—over discrete "things"? When we are dealing with streams of input-output relationships that may or may not culminate in a consumer good, it can be difficult to isolate the "thing" we might identify as *the* invention or work of authorship, much less the intellectual contribution made by the person claiming patent or copyright.[57] We recognize and enforce (artificial)

---

[54] Cohen (2005) focuses on the situated user and the importance of the dynamic relationships between creators and context. Her situated user "engages cultural goods and artifacts found within the context of her culture through a variety of activities ranging from consumption to creative play." *Id.* at 370.

[55] Frischmann (2000).

[56] Benkler explores this in the context of communications. Benkler (2006a).

[57] I discuss this issue further below. On the difficulties and importance of delineating "things" in a variety of contexts, see Madison (2005).

boundaries for purposes of constructing property rights and facilitating exclusion, coordination, and market provisioning, but our focus on "things" (inputs, outputs, resources, goods, and so on) often obscures the continuity and complexity of the system.

Even if we reduce the number of input-output relationships we are willing to entertain, we must acknowledge that intellectual progress involves a stream of such relationships, and this requires acknowledgment of a potential stream of spillovers, or what we might refer to as *cascading spillovers*. This is the case even if we assume a simple string of single public good input-output relationships, where a single public good is produced at each stage. In reality, each stage of production may involve multiple input and outputs, each of which can be used productively to produce different outputs and potentially support different production paths by many people. Many intellectual and cultural activities yield social goods as well, in which cases the diffusion of a different set of externalities cascade as well.

The conventional model of intellectual production represents progress in a linear fashion, for example, from basic research to applied research and finally to commercial application; or, alternatively, from idea conception to invention to commercial development; or something similar. Linear models are intuitive and qualitatively appealing because many economic and social policy questions that follow seem to have straightforward answers.[58] For example, the government should support basic research as a form of public goods production; the basic research pool should supply inputs for applied research; private firms should step in at some point and bring the benefits of research results to the public through commercialization.[59] Yet the linear model is not an actual scientific model of innovation or intellectual progress. Rather, as Benoît Godin explains, a host of different actors—scientists seeking funding, economists advising government agencies—constructed the linear model of innovation to classify research activities, establish a connection between basic and applied research and eventually commercial activities, and advance political and other agendas.[60] Godin explains that the simple three-stage "basic research → applied research → development" model became standardized when official government statisticians appropriated the three-stage model as a means for classification of research to aid in statistical categorization, measurement, and quantitative analysis.[61] Yet the linear model has been roundly criticized and rejected.[62] As Nathan Rosenberg

---

[58] Although many trace the linear model to Bush (1954), Godin suggests that "[o]ne would be hard-pressed . . . to find anything but a rudiment of this model in Bush's manifesto." Godin 639 (2006).

[59] Frischmann (2000).

[60] Godin (2006).

[61] *Id.* See also OECD 12 (1962).

[62] Kline & Rosenberg (1986).

claimed in 1994, "Everyone knows that the linear model of innovation is dead."[63] Yet as Godin shows, the linear model remains intact in the discourse despite its many criticisms. He observes that alternative models have struggled to replace the linear model because they pose more difficult measurement issues, and "with their multiple feedback loops look more like modern artwork or 'a plate of spaghetti and meatballs' than a useful analytical framework."[64]

Intellectual production processes, and intellectual progress more generally, are often nonlinear, multidirectional, stochastic, full of feedback loops, and difficult to model.[65] There are various nonlinear innovation models that incorporate dynamic interactions between different types of research and even nonresearch activities as well as the background cultural environment within which such interactions take place.[66] For example, the "Chain-Linked Model," developed by S. J. Kline, incorporates feedback loops between research and the "existing corpus of knowledge" and emphasizes the importance of various different activities, procedures, and external influences that play a role in innovative progress; there are multiple paths, feedback loops, and various actors.[67] As Kline and Rosenberg point out, the linear model's omission of feedback loops, learning from "shortcoming and failures," and other features renders it incapable of dealing with radical and incremental innovation.[68]

The dynamic nature of progress often leads to unexpected spillover effects. For example, an idea developed in one sector may lead to beneficial progress in another unrelated (or marginally related) sector.

The practice of science is becoming increasingly interdisciplinary, and scientific progress in one discipline is often propelled by advances in other, often apparently unrelated, fields. For example, who would have thought that nuclear physics research (the study of the inner workings and properties of the atomic nucleus) and data gathering techniques developed for experiments on elementary particles (quarks and such) would lead to a device that has advanced the boundaries of biomedical research and health care? Yet both of these lines of inquiry led ultimately to Magnetic Resonance Imaging (MRI), a tool now used in laboratories and hospitals around

---

[63] ROSENBERG 139 (1994).

[64] Godin 639 (2006). Frankly, this seems like yet another example of looking for what can be measured more easily rather than what actually matters, or, to return to the old joke, looking for one's lost keys only under the lamppost.

[65] Dreyfuss (2010); Godin (2006); Knudsen 13, 24 (2003) (examining the policy implications of self-reinforcing processes and traps such as feedback loops in intellectual progress).

[66] Padmore & Gibson (1998); OECD (2000).

[67] Kline & Rosenberg (1986); Kline (1991a); Kline (1991b).

[68] Kline & Rosenberg (1986). To be clear, many scholars that study innovation systems recognize these complexities.

the world both to conduct basic biological research and also to diagnose illness. Such cross-over between fields is yet another example of the unexpected payoffs that can come from basic research.[69]

There are countless examples in science, technology, and innovation, but these phenomena are equally relevant in cultural systems too. James Boyle presents one such example of cross-genre evolution in the music field: the story of an amateur hip-hop song entitled "George Bush Doesn't Care about Black People," released in 2005, that sampled Kanye West's song "Gold Digger" from the same year and was named after Kanye's outburst criticizing former president George W. Bush for his response to Hurricane Katrina. West's song had, in turn, sampled the 1950s R&B/soul song "I Got a Woman" by Ray Charles, which, it turns out, was a rewording of the Christian hymn "Jesus Is All the World to Me," penned in 1904.[70] In a more direct way, music sampling reflects the cross-pollination of musical genres, albeit through conscious appropriation rather than organic development.[71] Literature is rife with examples of similar developments. Genres blend into each other and form new hybrids whose existence is sometimes fleeting, sometimes stable: Twentieth-century American musicals spawned cowboy musicals and gangster musicals like *Guys and Dolls*;[72] the cult classic *Blade Runner* drew thematic elements from pulp genres such as film noir and science fiction to create a subgenre of its own.[73] Cultural systems affect each other in complex and unpredictable ways; for example, geographically driven changes in the interactions of ethnic groups affect literary traditions, art, and architecture.[74]

The cultural environment and its constituent innovation, science, culture, knowledge, and other systems are dynamic evolutionary systems. Since how and what direction the systems, environment, and consequently society evolve are not predetermined or inevitable, institutions and social policies matter considerably; the cultural environment we construct and sustain reflects deep normative values.[75]

---

[69] Staff of House Comm. on Science (1998); see, e.g., Nelson 459 (1982) (discussing the spillover effects of government research motivated by national security interests into other applied areas).

[70] BOYLE 122–25 (2010).

[71] MCLEOD & DICOLA (2010) (music sampling).

[72] SCHATZ (1981) (describing the hybridization of film genres); Schatz 44 (1977); ALTMAN (1989).

[73] Doll & Faller (1986) (describing the literary and motion picture genre cross-pollination that led to the making of *Blade Runner*).

[74] Miller xvii (2007).

[75] I am tempted to digress into a discussion of how we have lost sight of values in our focus on perfecting the means to achieve optimality. What do I mean by this? Utilitarianism and utilitarian economics has become the dominant mode of analysis, for various reasons, and a host of normative values are either forced into commensurability boxes to be traded off against each other within the utilitarian economic framework or are simply ignored. Utilitarian economics may be the analytical framework best able to provide answers to policy questions, but that does not mean the answers are correct or the best indicator of what society actually wants.

The dynamic, nonlinear, and multidirectional nature of these processes/activities involves considerable uncertainty, and this can be daunting and possibly viewed as something we hope to control, diminish, or eliminate over time. Yet when coupled with the nonrival nature of intellectual resources, it suggests considerable *social opportunity*—the opportunity to leverage nonrivalry. The nonrival nature of the resources means that intellectual capital generated at different points in the "stream" may flow along many paths, potentially being used simultaneously by different people in different settings as an input into multiple intellectual-cultural processes. There are a variety of obstacles to the free flow and use of intellectual capital (e.g., limited absorptive capacity, education, or capabilities to productively use the resources),[76] and in particular contexts, there are good reasons to restrict the free flow and use of intellectual capital (e.g., to prevent misappropriation and protect supply-side incentives to invest). My point is that in light of nonrivalry and the "on the shoulders of giants" effect, the social opportunity deserves recognition and further attention.[77]

I conclude this section by revisiting the point I made in the appendix to chapter 3. The complex, dynamic, nonlinear, and multidirectional nature of intellectual progress and the prevalence and variety of external effects in the cultural environment suggest that focusing on optimality conditions may be a red herring (or worse). We are inevitably in what economists call a second-best world because of the incredible number of incomplete and missing markets in the cultural environment.[78] Rather than focus on achieving optimal government or market selection of public good investments, society is likely (much) better off focusing on indirect interventions that (a) support public capabilities to participate in intellectual-cultural activities and (b) aim to lower the costs of public goods production for a wide range of public goods while (c) maintaining flexibility in the opportunities available to potential participants. In my view, this would better leverage nonrivalry, facilitate progress along many paths, and sustain a spillover-rich cultural environment in which and with which members of society are capable of interacting productively. This shift in focus has important implications for the subsequent discussion of intellectual infrastructure (section C) and for an appreciation of intellectual property laws as semi-commons arrangements (section D).

But failing to question or deal deliberately with the underlying normative values effectively deals with them. In any event, this is simply too big a digression. See, e.g., Frischmann & McKenna (2011). For an excellent discussion of a range of normative values within the liberal tradition, see Benkler (2006a).

[76] Bontis 134–35 (2005) (discussing this issue and listing strategies such as improving tertiary education, implementing R&D policies, encouraging tourism, and hosting international conferences, as means to promote the accumulation of intellectual capital assets); Albert & Bradley 79 (1997) (describing barriers to the flow of intellectual capital).

[77] Benkler (2006a) explores this social opportunity in the context of commons-based peer production.

[78] Lipsey & Lancaster (1956).

Here I briefly note what this would mean for intellectual property laws: First, the laws should focus on misappropriation risks with an aim to facilitate average cost recovery and competition, rather than market power or monopoly; to the extent that certain areas warrant subsidies, then targeted subsidies seem more direct and less distorting than adjusting the legal system for all areas, and such subsidies can be directed at infrastructural investments in the targeted area—for example, basic research in biotech or even directly funding clinical trial system. This first point suggests that exclusion is important but should be limited in scope. Second, in addition to facilitating exclusion, intellectual property systems should aim to reduce information and transaction costs because such cost reductions would apply to a wide range of public goods investments. This can be done in a manner similar to traditional property law systems, by providing recordation, registration, dispute resolution, and so on. Also, given the multitude of intellectual property owners, private ordering solutions to collective management problems should be facilitated as well. Third, and related to the first point, it should be understood that the division of surplus often has efficiency consequences (rather than mere distributional or equity consequences) because consumers are often productive users, even if their productive use does not immediately generate a marketable good. This has consequences for a variety of economic issues in intellectual property law. Fundamentally, and in stark contrast with the conventional economic perspective, intellectual property systems should be understood as exceptional, targeted interventions that construct semi-commons and sustain a spillover-rich cultural environment.

C. Intellectual Infrastructure

1. APPLYING THE CRITERIA TO DELINEATE INTELLECTUAL INFRASTRUCTURE

Applying the infrastructure criteria to intellectual resources delineates a broad set of resources that create benefits for society primarily through the facilitation of downstream productive activities, many of which generate spillovers. The definition of infrastructure can be reduced as follows to fit intellectual infrastructure: *nonrival input into a wide variety of outputs*. This seems incredibly capacious. Like environmental infrastructure, intellectual infrastructure can be identified and analyzed at various levels of abstraction, ranging from the meta-environment itself to a discrete general-purpose input, such as a basic idea, to a specific expression that has broad communicative power and social meaning. The resource set is much more highly and diversely populated than traditional infrastructure. Each of the following categories, for example, contains innumerable examples:

- Basic research
- Infrastructural ideas

- General-purpose technologies[79]
- Languages

Rebecca Tushnet once told me that the infrastructure concept seemed to have a fractal nature when applied to intellectual resources because you could identify infrastructure at various scales and observe repeating patterns, similar characteristics, and so on. She suggested the concept seemed to apply too easily and to too many different resources, and as a result, it seemed to lose its usefulness. While I agree with her observations, I reach a different conclusion. It seems to me that the dynamic, cumulative and interactive features of cultural-intellectual resources and practices may mean that more cultural-intellectual resources potentially function as infrastructure. Keep in mind that the infrastructure criteria describe functional relationships and are only part of the broader resource management question. That the functional relationships repeat at different scales means that choosing the appropriate scale for evaluating resource management options and trade-offs is critical. Different types of rules may be appropriate at different scales; for example, a default open-access-style rule (ex ante, broadly applicable) may be appropriate for intellectual infrastructure at high levels of abstraction, while a less demanding rule, such as an essential-facilities-style rule (*ex post*, case-specific), may be appropriate for intellectual infrastructure at low levels of abstraction.

Still, many intellectual resources do not fall within the scope of the general definition of infrastructure. A few examples illustrate this point as well as a number of complications that arise in applying the criteria.

First, consider a common construction wire nail ("common nail").[80] While the tangible nail itself satisfies the latter two prongs of the definition (input into wide variety of outputs), it fails to satisfy the first prong because nails are rivalrously consumed and cannot be managed in a way that renders consumption nonrivalrous. Consumption of the tangible good depletes the consumption opportunities of others and means that additional supply is needed to meet the demands of others. A common nail must be made for

---

[79] General-purpose technologies are those drastic innovations that have "the potential for pervasive use in a wide range of sectors in ways that drastically change their modes of operation." Helpman 3 (1998). These technologies often, but not always, fit into our definition of infrastructure but involve some added complications. See the appendix to chapter 2. Basically, new general-purpose technologies appear to require the development of new intermediate goods, and perhaps new infrastructure or meta-infrastructure, before the technologies can be effectively implemented. Aghion & Howitt 121 (1998). Developing these intermediate goods requires time and a critical mass of demand, which may result in a possibly painful transition as resources are taken out of production and put into R&D activities aimed at developing these new goods. *Id.*

[80] I thank Scott Kieff for this example. A "wire nail" is made from wire of the same size as the shank of the nail, by a machine that cuts the wire in even length, heads it, and points it. They are said to be stronger for driving vand less prone to splitting the wood, and are thus earned their stripes with carpenters a century ago. KIDDER 324 (1899). Common wire nails are today ubiquitous, and although newer specialized nails compete for use, they "are still the most frequently used fasteners." Faherty 5.3 (1999).

each user.[81] But what about the *idea* of a common nail? Ideas are nonrival goods. The idea itself is not infrastructural, however, because it fails to satisfy the third criterion; it is special purpose rather than general purpose. The idea of a common nail is a nonrival input into the production of a *single* output—a tangible common nail, which is an input into a wide range of outputs. There is little reason to believe that demand-manifestation problems in the output markets will distort the input market.[82] Competitive markets for common nails work well in manifesting demand for production of such nails and in allocating them.

This example highlights three boundary issues that arise when applying the criteria to distinguish infrastructure and non-infrastructure. I note the issues here and then discuss each of them further in the examples that follow.

- First, it may be difficult to draw lines where there is a stream of cumulative inputs (idea of a nail → nail → range of outputs). Although this does not seem terribly significant in this particular example, it can be incredibly difficult where the stream is of the type described in the previous section, that is, streams of public goods.
- Second, it may be difficult to choose the appropriate level of abstraction. At a more abstract level, the idea of a nail—perhaps expressed as the idea of a pin-shaped fastener or the idea of a fastener that holds materials together by shear strength laterally and friction axially—may be infrastructure because the variety of outputs expands significantly with the abstraction. The common construction wire nail is but one of many different tangible embodiments of the more abstract idea.[83]
- Third, it may be difficult to choose the appropriate scope of uses. I implicitly narrowed the scope of relevant uses of the idea of a common nail when I declared it to be a nonrival input into the production of a tangible common nail. Specifically, I limited the scope of relevant uses to implementing the idea through the transformation of physical resources to produce a tangible embodiment. I maintained the same scope at a higher level of abstraction in the previous paragraph. At both levels of abstraction (idea of nail and idea of common construction wire nail), we

---

[81] Recall the discussion in chapter 3 of rivalrous consumption goods, raw materials, and intermediate goods. Three principles apply: (1) social welfare is maximized when a rivalrous good is consumed by the person who values it the most, and the market mechanism is generally the most efficient means for (2) rationing such goods and (3) allocating resources needed to produce such goods.

[82] Put another way, demand-measurement problems associated with externalities are not significant. Keep in mind that the demand-measurement problem identified by Samuelson—consumers misrepresent their actual preferences for the public good in an effort to free ride—might arise in the (public good) input market but does not arise in the (private good) output market.

[83] KIDDER 324–25 (1899) (describing various types of nails); Faherty 5.3–4 (1999) (describing nails).

could expand the scope of relevant uses to include uses of the ideas to communicate or to develop new ideas, in addition to using the idea to produce tangible embodiments.[84] In applying the criteria, the scope issue should be resolved by considering which uses are the primary drivers of social demand.[85] Thus, one basic reason for maintaining the narrow scope for the idea of a common nail is that social demand for this idea is driven primarily by production of tangible nails and not the other possible but less relevant uses. (This is very similar to the reason given in chapter 3 for describing apples as rivalrously consumed and largely ignoring the potential nonrivalrous use of a tangible apple as an input into the production of a painting.) Such a narrow scope may be questionable, however, at the higher level of abstraction. I revisit this particular example and issue below in the discussion of ideas.

As a second example, imagine that scientists discover a drug to cure a particular disease. While the discovered knowledge is a nonrival input and thus satisfies the first two prongs of the infrastructure definition, the range of outputs may be relatively narrow, for example, curing the particular disease and perhaps some closely related research on improving the cure (e.g., to hasten the recovery). In some cases, the range may broaden to the point that the discovery is infrastructural. Putting that possibility aside, however, I would not classify the discovery as infrastructure based only on the social value of the resource. It is not the magnitude of social value associated with the resource that makes it infrastructural, although infrastructure may generate substantial social value; rather, it is the functional nature of the resource and the manner in which it generates social value that matters. As this example highlights, one of the difficulties in applying the third criterion is figuring out how wide a variety of outputs qualifies something as infrastructure. How basic or generic must the input be? At what level of abstraction do we assess genericness? There are no easy answers to these questions. To some degree, these questions permeate patent and copyright law, as I discuss below. Although it important to acknowledge and be aware of this difficulty, we do not need easy answers. There is some fuzziness at the boundaries, which is probably inescapable given the complex resource systems involved.

Regardless of whether the discovery is classified as infrastructure, there still may be a strong case for government intervention in one form or another on social welfare or other

---

[84] Including these additional types of uses does not involve abstraction. The scope issue arises at each level of abstraction.

[85] Alternatively, the scope issue can be resolved by looking at the institutional framework. For example, even if we consider all possible uses of the idea of a common nail, different legal regimes focus on different types of uses— patent focuses on implementation by physical transformation or tangible embodiment and copyright law focuses on communication; neither focuses directly on idea production, although both indirectly affect idea production. I discuss this further below.

grounds. If privately owned and controlled, a host of government interventions ranging from open access, essential facilities (essential medicine), price regulation, or even government expropriation might be justified by significant public health concerns.[86] On the other hand, there may be a strong case for encouraging price discrimination, particularly where markets can be segmented geographically or along similar broad market-by-market categories. Price discrimination may enable cost recovery for drugs that require incredibly high fixed cost investments in research, development, and clinical trials while significantly reducing deadweight losses and improving access to critical medicines in markets where resources are limited.[87] *This is a very complex problem.* My basic point is that the range and variety of downstream uses is often quite narrow for a particular drug; as a result, maintaining flexibility or the social option to pursue different paths downstream is less pressing, and to the extent that market failure arises, targeted approaches are probably more attractive than commons management. All of this being said, however, there are good reasons to look further upstream from the drug itself to examine the basic research and drug discovery system, which probably constitutes mixed infrastructure and is subject to substantial risk of demand-side failures and associated misallocation of resources because of distorted prioritization.[88]

Third, consider the 80386 microprocessor chip developed by Intel Corporation, commonly referred to as the "386 chip."[89] Many people might regard the 386 chip as infrastructural because it constituted a significant advance for desktop computing and was a substantial platform for innovation in software. The chip could handle 4 million operations per second and up to four megabytes of memory. It was backward compatible, meaning it worked with Intel's previous line of processors for IBM PCs and could run software written for those processors. Applying the criteria follows a similar path as the previous examples but raises a few wrinkles. The actual chip, like a nail, satisfies the latter two prongs of the definition (input into wide variety of outputs) but fails to satisfy the first prong. Each chip is a tangible, rivalrously consumed good. While the chip is durable and is not depleted or transformed upon use, it is still rivalrous. When used in an IBM PC, for example, a 386 chip cannot be used in another IBM PC. The concept of sharing a 386 chip among multiple users makes sense if the computer itself is being shared, perhaps

---

[86] Various versions of open-access regimes and open-source research collaborations have been proposed as pharmaceutical R&D models to increase access to essential medicines. Srinivas 263 (2010). Several countries have external price regulations whereby these governments set the price or reimbursement rate for pharmaceuticals and vaccines based on the prices charged in other countries. McElligott 426 n. 49 (2009). Similarly, compulsory licensing schemes have been proposed that invoke the essential facilities doctrine for public health reasons. Liu (2008).

[87] FISHER & SYED (forthcoming).

[88] *Id.*

[89] Chris Yoo raised this example at a colloquium at Wharton, and the lively discussion that followed suggested that it was worth including here.

among a community of users, such as a family or among library patrons, or among users on a network. Put this way, the computing power of the chip is sharable. In this sense, the 386 chip (or the computer) is comparable to the harvesting equipment discussed in chapter 3 (or an automobile or other types of capital equipment), in that it can be shared over time among a community of users because of its durability. There are, however, significant limits on the capacity of the resource that correspondingly limit such sharing arrangements and the opportunity to leverage nonrivalry. I do not mean to diminish the importance of this potential for sharing, but the relevant community cannot be the public at large (unless perhaps a fleet of capital equipment is shared).[90] This example highlights an underspecified part of the first criterion, specifically, what constitutes an "appreciable range" of demand. I leave that open for now and again acknowledge that there are some fuzzy boundaries around the infrastructure set.

If the 386 chip itself is rivalrous in the sense that a chip must be made for each computer, what about the *ideas or design* behind the 386 chip? Similar to the previous examples, the "idea of the 386 chip" does not satisfy the third criterion because it is special purpose in that it is used primarily to generate the 386 chip itself. As with the previous example, however, there is some room to argue because the ideas are relevant to research. This highlights another difficulty, choosing the relevant idea and the appropriate level of abstraction for analysis. The specific chip design is more easily dismissed as not infrastructure because it is primarily used to produce actual chips, but more abstract descriptions of various ideas that surround, enable, and in a sense constitute the "idea of the 386 chip" are less easily categorized. Consider, for example, the idea of backward compatibility. While relevant to describing the 386 chip and perhaps even a defining feature of the chip, this idea is separable and infrastructural, at least when stated at this level of generality. The idea of backwards compatibility applies to an incredibly wide range of products and services.

These examples test the boundaries of the infrastructure criteria and demonstrate some fuzziness, which is unavoidable. Nonetheless, focusing on intellectual resources that satisfy all three criteria for infrastructure helps to distinguish different types of intellectual resources based on the manner in which they create social value. All intellectual goods are nonrival; some are primarily valuable as consumption goods, while others are primarily valuable as intermediate goods, as intellectual capital. We are concerned with intellectual capital that is generic in nature—that can be used by many (people, firms, etc.) as an input into a wide variety of productive activities—and once we have identified such resources, we are further interested in the nature of the productive activities and whether users produce private, public, or social goods. This set of resources deserves careful

---

[90] On such community sharing, see Benkler (2004); Levine (2009) (describing the increasing popularity of Zipcars, fleets of cars parked in garages in various cities in North America and Europe, that members can use via an online reservation system; almost 5 million people in New York City live within a ten-minute walk from a Zipcar). Sharing initiatives in more traditional ways may accomplish similar goals, as with computer clusters at public libraries or car rental agencies.

attention because the benefits of open access (costs of restricted access) may be substantially higher than for intellectual resources that are not infrastructure.

The next section considers ideas as an example of intellectual infrastructure. Then, the following section considers intellectual property systems more generally and how those systems mediate access to intellectual infrastructure.

2. IDEAS

> If nature has made any one thing less susceptible than all others of exclusive property, it is the action of the thinking power called an idea.
> —JEFFERSON (1813)

> The general rule of law is, that the noblest of human productions—knowledge, truths ascertained, conceptions, and ideas—become, after voluntary communication to others, free as the air to common use. Upon these incorporeal productions the attribute of property is continued after such communication only in certain classes of cases where public policy has seemed to demand it.
> —INS V. AP

Should ideas once disclosed to the public be "free as the air to common use," as Justice Brandeis famously propounded and as courts and commentators often suggest? If so, why? Why are these intellectual goods deemed the "noblest"? Why should they necessarily be placed in the commons? The exclusion of (abstract) ideas from patent and ideas from copyright is a foundational and yet somewhat confusing area of intellectual property law.

Despite the bedrock nature of the general rule that the fundamental intellectual building blocks cannot and should not be subject to the embarrassment of exclusive rights,[91] there has not been much attention devoted to understanding *why* this should be the case. There have been numerous pronouncements by courts declaring ideas to be outside the intellectual property system, and the copyright statute expressly excludes ideas and other intellectual building blocks. Often the rhetoric employed by courts has analogized ideas to fundamental forces or products of nature.[92] As Jefferson famously suggested:

> That ideas should freely spread from one to another over the globe, for the moral and mutual instruction of man, and improvement of his condition, seems to have been peculiarly and benevolently designed by nature, when she made them, like fire, expansible over all space, without lessening their density in any point, and like the air in which we breathe, move, and have our physical being, incapable of confinement or exclusive appropriation.[93]

---

[91] Jefferson (1813).

[92] O'Reilly v. Morse, 15 How. 62 (1854)

[93] Jefferson (1813).

Ideas are not forces or products of Nature. Ideas are intangible products of the human intellect. As such, why shouldn't they be subject to exclusive property? The short answer is that ideas are often, though not always, intellectual infrastructure. Jefferson recognized the special infrastructural characteristics of ideas; the quote above indicates that he not only took notice of the nonrivalrous nature of ideas, but also saw how ideas are productive inputs, "for the moral and mutual instruction of man, and improvement of his condition."[94] The noble stature of ideas seems to be rooted in appreciation of both the instrumental nature of ideas as means to human flourishing and societal progress, and the egalitarian potential of leveraging nonrivalry so that everyone can benefit and have the capacity to participate.[95]

This section is divided into two subsections. The first discusses infrastructural ideas, and the second examines legal recognition of the infrastructural nature of ideas and the social value of commons management, focusing on the First Amendment, copyright law, and patent law. I argue that despite some confusion and controversy on how to draw lines and separate ideas from expression and invention (which I suggest are outputs from particular uses of ideas), ideas are and should be "free as the air to common use."[96]

a. Ideas as Infrastructure

Ideas are a particularly good example of intellectual infrastructure, because they are non-rival inputs into a wide variety of productive uses.[97] Broadly categorized, the scope of uses includes (1) further idea production/research, (2) expression/communication/education, and (3) implementation/transformation of the physical or social world. Many others have explored this metaphysical terrain in a more sophisticated and detailed fashion.[98] My point here is to segregate uses of ideas roughly along functional lines. Frankly, the lines also coincide with legal categories, as we will see below.

Ideas implicate each of the three boundary issues discussed in the previous section: First, it is difficult to draw lines where there is a stream of cumulative inputs, as is often the case with ideas. Second, it is difficult to choose the appropriate level of abstraction. Third, it is difficult to choose the appropriate scope of uses. The line-drawing consideration

---

[94] *Id.* Jefferson was not the first to recognize the power of ideas. His views reflect a much broader historical tradition.

[95] We might say that ideas are "essential" and "affected with the public interest" in a similar way as traditional infrastructure. See chapter 5.

[96] International News Serv. v. Associated Press, 248 U.S. 215, 250 (1918) (Brandeis, J., dissenting).

[97] Frischmann & Lemley 281 (2007) ("intangible infrastructure, such as ideas, ... may be the cleanest example of the benefits of commons because the advantage of private ownership in solving the tragedy of the commons does not apply to information, which is inexhaustible. Ideas themselves are a good example of infrastructure, because they are not merely passively consumed but frequently are reused for productive purposes.") (footnote omitted).

[98] See, e.g., LOCKE (1975); HUME (1986).

arises directly and acutely in the context of intellectual property. For present purposes, I leave it aside and focus mostly on the latter two difficulties.

Ideas constitute intellectual infrastructure when we consider ideas on an abstract, philosophical level. Even at less abstract levels, ideas are infrastructural. So when are ideas not infrastructural? Some ideas are inputs into a rather limited range of uses or outputs. In the previous section, I discussed two examples of ideas that were not infrastructural—the idea of a common construction wire nail and the idea of the 386 chip. Both ideas are inputs into a rather narrow range of outputs—the common nail and the 386 chip. Recall that this discussion raised boundary issues because applying the infrastructure criteria depended on the level of abstraction. For example, I concluded that the relatively concrete (applied) idea of the 386 chip would not qualify as infrastructure, but the more abstract (basic) idea of backward compatibility would. Similarly, I suggested that the idea of a common nail is not infrastructural because the idea is an input into the production of a tangible nail and not much else. Again, the idea is rather concrete (applied) and tied to the specific tangible embodiment. To expand the range of outputs rather dramatically, we could drop the specifications of common construction wire nail. At a more abstract level, the idea of a nail—expressed as, the idea of a pin-shaped fastener or the idea of a fastener that holds materials together by shear strength laterally and friction axially—is infrastructural. The more abstract idea of a nail leaves considerable room for variety in implementation, for example, in terms of design, the material or process used to produce the nail, the dimensions, and so on.

Thus far, I have narrowed the *scope* of relevant uses of the idea by focusing on implementation of the idea through transformation of physical resources (i.e., producing tangible embodiments). The reason for doing so is that these uses are most prevalent from the demand side. I could have mentioned uses that involve further idea production, such as research and development. Also, I could have mentioned uses that involve communicating the idea, such as expression—the idea of a nail is certainly used expressively in instructions, plans, illustrations, or even metaphorically (e.g., the gymnast "nailed" the landing). Expanding the scope of relevant uses adds variety and thus might lead one to more easily classify the idea as infrastructural. In fact, this expansion would apply to the abstract idea as well as the more concrete ideas of a common nail and the 386 chip. Admittedly, I hesitate to include such additional uses in all cases, for the same reason that when discussing the rivalrousness of an apple in chapter 3, I narrowed the scope of relevant uses by excluding some possible nonrivalrous uses of an apple, such as using an apple as the subject matter of a painting or photograph. Possible does not mean relevant. The uses seem considerably less important from the demand side. The vast majority of social demand for (value attributable to) apples is derived from rivalrous consumption. Similarly, the vast majority of social demand for (value attributable to) the idea of a common nail is derived from the production of tangible nails.

Yet this conclusion depends substantially on what level of abstraction we are working at. The more abstract idea of a nail may yield significant social value both from (a) further idea production, research and development, or simply refinement of the abstract idea to make it more concrete and capable of implementation, and (b) expressive use that communicates the idea so people may internalize it as knowledge. This example demonstrates another way in which ideas are quite different from apples. It also shows why it makes sense to categorize ideas as intellectual infrastructure, at least as a default.

b. Commons Management via First Amendment, Copyright, and Patent Jurisprudence

The infrastructural nature of ideas and the social value of sustaining the public commons appear to be reasonably well established in various areas of the law, especially the First Amendment and intellectual property. The First Amendment is fundamentally about ideas. It protects the freedoms of speech and of the press from government interference.[99] As chapter 3 discussed, speech involves the communication of ideas. The same can be said of the press.[100] In the First Amendment context, ideas are recognized as a basic input for a host of socially valuable activities, including public debate, discourse, and education on commercial, political, and various other societal issues. Consider political speech, for example.

> Political speech, at the core of protected First Amendment speech, involves the communication of ideas used productively in political systems. The public good nature of ideas enables repeated sharing and productive use, which often has dynamic and systemic implications in political systems that speakers may not anticipate or appreciate fully. As Posner suggests, because political speech generates many different types of spillovers the category is especially susceptible to underproduction. Government regulation, which Posner helpfully analogizes to a tax, would only exacerbate the problem. As important as the problem of underproduction is the serious concern about error costs from misdirected regulation. Posner, Farber, and many others have noted that First Amendment protection is especially needed for political speech because otherwise political speakers (candidates, political parties, etc.) might introduce considerable bias into the system. The First Amendment constraint on government intervention sustains the flow of spillovers from the repeated sharing and productive use of ideas communicated through political speech.[101] In other words, the First Amendment recognizes the complex relationships

---

[99] "Congress shall make no law respecting an establishment of religion, or prohibiting the free exercise thereof; or abridging the freedom of speech, or of the press; or the right of the people peaceably to assemble, and to petition the Government for a redress of grievances." Though tempting, I leave aside discussion of religious freedom and freedom of association, both of which support the basic argument I am making.

[100] Baker (2007).

[101] This paragraph draws from Frischmann 323–24 (2008b). See also Posner 22–23 (1986); Farber 563 (1991); Farber 935 (2006).

between the activity of speech, the power of communicated ideas, and the consequences for political and other social systems. Nothing less than the fate of democracy itself is said to rest on our First Amendment freedoms and the various idea-dependent activities and social practices those freedoms support.

Freedom of speech is frequently associated with the metaphor of a "marketplace of ideas." Justice Holmes is credited with bringing the concept into the First Amendment jurisprudence when he stated that it may be logical for people who hold strong opinions about the truth or superiority of their ideas to try to fix those ideas "in law and sweep away all opposition," but "the ultimate good desired is better reached by free trade in ideas... that the best test of truth is the power of the thought to get itself accepted in the competition of the market, and that truth is the only ground upon which their wishes safely can be carried out."[102] As many have pointed out, sustaining an open and vibrant "marketplace of ideas" is *not* about sustaining an actual market with transactions mediated by the price mechanism; rather, the marketplace of ideas metaphor concerns an open exchange of ideas, unbiased competition among many different ideas, and a diverse and wide range of competitors (idea producers and users).[103] In essence, the "marketplace of ideas" metaphor reflects a strong commitment to a public commons.

The First Amendment not only constrains the government's ability to "pick winners" directly, for example through censorship or favoring particular viewpoints, but also constrains the government's ability to eliminate the public commons.[104] At a macro level, at least, the First Amendment limits the extent to which the government can privatize and propertize ideas. In *Eldred v. Ashcroft*, the Supreme Court described the exclusion of ideas from copyright protection as a "built-in First Amendment accommodation" that "strike[s] a definitional balance between the First Amendment and the Copyright Act by permitting free communication of facts while still protecting an author's expression." The Court explained that "[d]ue to this distinction, every idea, theory, and fact in a copyrighted work becomes instantly available for public exploitation at the moment of

---

[102] Abrams v. United States, 250 U.S. 616, 630 (1919) (Holmes dissenting). Holmes recognized that ideas are means to "the ultimate good desired."

[103] For further discussion, see Frischmann n.6 (2008b); Netanel 158–60 (2005).

[104] The First Amendment plays other important roles in structuring the cultural environment. See Balkin (2009); Balkin (2004). For example, the First Amendment may impose an obligation on government to ensure sufficient speech capabilities for its citizens. Such capabilities may depend on various shared public infrastructures (e.g., public spaces, communications technologies, laws). See *id.* (advancing the concept of "an infrastructure of free expression"); Ammori (forthcoming 2012) (arguing for the First Amendment requires government provision, or at least assurance of availability, of sufficient public "spaces"). I agree with much of what Balkin and Ammori have to say, but leave aside this topic for future research.

publication."[105] The First Amendment can be understood as a constitutional commitment to public commons in ideas.[106]

Similarly, based on a firm recognition that ideas are basic inputs for cultural, scientific, and technological progress, the copyright and patent laws exclude ideas from protection and allocate ideas to the public commons, generally referred to as the public domain.[107] In theory and formally, copyright law extends protection only to original expression of ideas,[108] and patent law extends protection only to new, useful, and nonobvious inventions,[109] which constitute implementations or embodiments of ideas. Put another way, the intellectual property system relies on different bodies of law to address different subsets of idea uses—patent law addresses uses related to physical implementation, and copyright law addresses uses related to expression. Patent law is concerned with whether the idea can be implemented; if so, then a patent may issue. Copyright law, on the other hand, attaches to particular expressions of the idea, for example an illustration or textual description. Patent law does not aim to regulate expression; to the extent that patent law deals with expression, it generally pushes expression of ideas toward the public commons (e.g., via public disclosure, written description) to ensure public dissemination of the expressed ideas. Similarly, copyright law does not aim to regulate idea implementation; to the extent that copyright law encounters issues pertaining to implementation, it generally pushes implementations or embodiments of ideas toward patent law or the public commons. Neither patent nor copyright directly addresses the use of ideas to generate more ideas. Ideas generated in cumulative stages of idea production, research and development, and so on remain outside the scope of patent and copyright. Copyright and patent laws grant exclusive rights only to certain qualifying outputs produced from the use of ideas, leaving ideas "free as the air to common use," at least after voluntary communication to others.[110]

In reality, the intellectual property regimes struggle mightily to separate unprotectable ideas from copyrightable expression and patentable invention. The struggle stems in part

---

[105] Eldred v. Ashcroft, 537 US 186, 219 (2003) (citing Feist, 499 U.S., at 349–350). See also Harper & Row, Publrs. v. Nation Enters., 471 U.S. 539, 556 (1985). Of course, it also may be understood to reflect other commitments. See previous note. There is a rich literature on the relationship between the First Amendment and copyright law. See, e.g., NETANEL (2008); Benkler (1999); Baker (1997); Lessig (2001a); Patterson (1987); Nimmer (1970). On how the First Amendment affects congressional power in patent, see Burk (2000); Sawkar 3048 (2008); Pollack (2002)

[106] Frischmann (2008b).

[107] 17 U.S.C. § 102(b) ("In no case does copyright protection for an original work of authorship extend to any idea, procedure, process, system, method of operation, concept, principle, or discovery . . ."); Diamond v. Chakrabarty, 447 U.S. 303, 309 (1980) ("The laws of nature, physical phenomena, and abstract ideas have been held not patentable.").

[108] 17 U.S.C. § 102 (a) & (b).

[109] 35 USC 101, 102, 103.

[110] INS. v. AP (Brandeis, J., dissenting).

from many of the complications noted in the previous section—for example, the dynamic and complex nature of intellectual systems, the continuity or fluidity of resource streams, and dual product-process nature of intellectual resources. Typically, ideas are not discrete things that can be easily identified, delineated, and isolated from other ideas or the context within which they are developed and their meaning derives and evolves. An idea can be stated or implemented; such actions effectively construct a discrete thing bounded by the specificity of action and the output (i.e., the statement or implementation), but the output/thing is not the idea.

Expression and invention describe both the action and the output. That is, "expression" ("invention") describes the act of stating (implementing) and the statement (implementation). While this duality of meaning may pose some complications, expression and invention are discrete things that can be identified, delineated, and isolated, at least when manifest in tangible form such as a written note or a working embodiment.

If copyright and patent protection only extended to such discrete things—that is, if copyright only protected the literal expression fixed in the tangible form of the note and patent only protected the actual working embodiment created by the inventor and disclosed in a patent application—then the struggle to separate unprotectable ideas from copyrightable expression and patentable invention would probably go away. But copyright protection and patent protection are not so limited in scope, nor should they be. In both areas, courts have explained why the scope of protection must be broader if the legal regimes are to effectively serve their purpose of promoting Progress in Science and the useful Arts:[111]

- "It is of course essential to any protection of literary property . . . that the right cannot be limited literally to the text, else a plagiarist would escape by immaterial variations. That has never been the law, but, as soon as literal appropriation ceases to be the test, the whole matter is necessarily at large, so that . . . the decisions cannot help much in a new case. . . ."[112] In essence, the court suggests that once the scope of protection exceeds the literal text, each case must be decided carefully on its own facts.
- "Courts have also recognized that to permit imitation of a patented invention which does not copy every literal detail would be to convert the protection of the patent grant into a hollow and useless thing. Such a limitation would leave room for—indeed, encourage—the unscrupulous copyist to make unimportant and insubstantial changes and substitutions in the patent which, though adding nothing, would be enough to take the copied matter outside the claim, and hence outside the reach of law. One who seeks to pirate an invention, like one who

---

[111] US CONST. art. I, § 8, cl. 8.
[112] Nichols v. Universal Pictures Corp., 45 F. 2d 119 (2d Cir. 1930).

seeks to pirate a copyrighted book or play, may be expected to introduce minor variations to conceal and shelter the piracy. Outright and forthright duplication is a dull and very rare type of infringement."[113]

The recognized need to expand scope to preclude "plagiarism by immaterial variation" and "copying by unimportant and insubstantial changes and substitutions" resonates with classic misappropriation. It reflects, in economic terms, the basic supply-side problems described earlier in the chapter: high exclusion costs and the associated risk that competitors will free ride on the fixed cost investment of the author or inventor. Note that the recognized need to expand the scope of protection to exclude this type of free riding does not resolve a series of fundamental questions: How *much* should scope be expanded? In what ways should scope be expanded? Recall how the scope of exclusion can vary in many different dimensions.

The struggle to separate unprotectable ideas from copyrightable expression and patentable invention thus stems from the difficulty in choosing the appropriate scope of protection and, consequently, in choosing the appropriate "level of abstraction" to effectuate that choice.[114] The *scope* of relevant uses is more or less chosen by the institutional structure, with patent focused on implementing uses, and copyright focused on expressive/communicative uses. I briefly explain how this abstraction issue arises in both copyright and patent law.

In copyright law, Learned Hand famously introduced a level of abstractions analysis:

Upon any work, and especially upon a play, a great number of patterns of increasing generality will fit equally well, as more and more of the incident is left out. The last may perhaps be no more than the most general statement of what the play is about, and at times might consist only of its title; but there is a point in this series of abstractions where they are no longer protected, since otherwise the playwright could prevent the use of his "ideas," to which, apart from their expression, his property is never extended. . . . Nobody has ever been able to fix that boundary, and nobody ever can.[115]

Despite his acknowledgment of the inherent struggle to draw a clear line between idea and expression, Hand proceeded to evaluate the similarities and differences between two

---

[113] Graver Tank & Mfg. Co. v. Linde Air Prods. Co., 339 U.S. 605, 607 (1950) ("The doctrine of equivalents evolved in response to this experience. . . . The theory on which it is founded is that, 'if two devices do the same work in substantially the same way, and accomplish substantially the same result, they are the same, even though they differ in name, form or shape.'") (quoting Union Paper-Bag Machine Co. v. Murphy, 97 U. S. 120, 125 (1877)).

[114] Chiang (2011).

[115] Nichols, 45 F. 2d at 122.

dramatic works (a play and a motion picture) at different levels of abstraction, focusing primarily on the "the characters and sequence of incident." The following is illustrative of the approach:

> If *Twelfth Night* were copyrighted, it is quite possible that a second comer might so closely imitate Sir Toby Belch or Malvolio as to infringe, but it would not be enough that for one of his characters he cast a riotous knight who kept wassail to the discomfort of the household, or a vain and foppish steward who became amorous of his mistress. These would be no more than Shakespeare's "ideas" in the play, as little capable of monopoly as Einstein's Doctrine of Relativity, or Darwin's theory of the Origin of Species. It follows that the less developed the characters, the less they can be copyrighted; that is the penalty an author must bear for marking them too indistinctly.
>
> In the two plays at bar we think both as to incident and character, the defendant took no more . . . than the law allowed. The stories are quite different. One is of a religious zealot who insists upon his child's marrying no one outside his faith; opposed by another who is in this respect just like him, and is his foil. Their difference in race is merely an obbligato to the main theme, religion. They sink their differences through grandparental pride and affection. In the other, zealotry is wholly absent; religion does not even appear. It is true that the parents are hostile to each other in part because they differ in race; but the marriage of their son to a Jew does not apparently offend the Irish family at all, and it exacerbates the existing animosity of the Jew, principally because he has become rich, when he learns it. . . . The only matter common to the two is a quarrel between a Jewish and an Irish father, the marriage of their children, the birth of grandchildren and a reconciliation.
>
> If the defendant took so much from the plaintiff, it may well have been because her amazing success seemed to prove that this was a subject of enduring popularity. . . . Though the plaintiff discovered the vein, she could not keep it to herself; so defined, the theme was too generalized an abstraction from what she wrote. It was only a part of her "ideas."[116]

In this framework, ideas are often assumed to be abstract, basic, or generalized inputs in the sense that ideas can be expressed in many different ways. This conforms to the basic rule that ideas are unprotected and expression is protected by copyright. Yet in applying the framework, courts evaluate whether ideas at various levels of abstraction are being expressed in a work and whether the scope of copyright protection extends to such expression. At intermediate levels of abstraction, ideas may be used communicatively (i.e., to generate expression), or may be used to produce more refined ideas at lower levels

---

[116] *Id.*

of expression (for example, an idea of a love story may be used to generate the more refined idea of a love story plot involving people from different religious backgrounds, which might in turn be used to generate an even more refined idea of a love story plot, etc.). In addition, for certain types of works, such as software, ideas at various levels of abstraction implement functional rather than expressive ends.[117] Courts have developed more sophisticated approaches to the levels-of-abstraction analysis. For example in *Computer Associates v. Altai*, the Court of Appeals for the Second Circuit developed an Abstraction-Filtration-Comparison approach with which a court filters out a range of unprotected elements at various levels of abstraction from the copyright owner's software program before comparing it with the defendant's program.[118]

Moreover, in some cases, courts recognize the existence of ideas that can only be expressed effectively in a limited number of ways, though the idea may be useful in many other ways and thus still infrastructural. For example, the idea underlying an algorithm may be expressed in a mathematical equation, and there may be a limited number of ways to effectively express the idea. Courts have developed a "merger doctrine" in such cases to limit protection.[119] In developing the doctrine, courts were concerned with copyright protection of the expression leading to de facto protection of the idea. The limitation imposed by this doctrine varies among different Courts of Appeals: In some jurisdictions no copyright protection is permitted, and in others protection is deemed "thin," meaning that the scope of protection is limited to literal or identical copying.[120]

The levels-of-abstraction framework has become a regular feature of copyright law, as a methodology employed in infringement analysis to separate unprotected ideas from protected

---

[117] Computer Associates International, Inc. v. Altai, Inc., 982 F. 2d 693, 712 (2d Cir. 1992); Lotus Development Corporation v. Borland International, Inc., 49 F. 3d 807, 815 (1st Cir. 1995). Judge Boudin's concurring opinion in Borland is particularly attuned to the additional social costs of limiting access to infrastructural elements of software programs and interfaces:

> Of course, the argument for protection is undiminished, perhaps even enhanced, by utility: if we want more of an intellectual product, a temporary monopoly for the creator provides incentives for others to create other, different items in this class. *But the "cost" side of the equation may be different where one places a very high value on public access to a useful innovation. . . . Thus, the argument for extending protection may be the same; but the stakes on the other side are much higher.*

Lotus Dev. Corp. v. Borland Int'l, Inc., 49 F. 3d 807, 819 (1st Cir. 1995) (Boudin, J., concurring) (emphasis added).

[118] Altai, 982 F. 2d 693, at 706.

[119] Toro Company v. R&R Products Co., 787 F. 2d 1208, 1212 (8th Cir. 1986) ("Under the copyright law doctrine of merger, a close cousin to the idea/expression dichotomy, copyright protection will be denied to even some expressions of ideas if the idea behind the expression is such that it can be expressed only in a very limited number of ways. The doctrine is designed to prevent an author from monopolizing an idea merely by copyrighting a few expressions of it."); Morrissey v. Procter & Gamble Co., 379 F. 2d 675, 678–79 (1st Cir. 1967) (denying copyright protection to the wording of rules for a sweepstakes contest, on account of the limited number of ways to express the rule).

[120] *Id.*; Apple Computer Corp. v. Microsoft Corp., 33 F. 3d 1435, 1439–42 (9th Cir. 1994) (thin protection); see also Nimmer on Copyright 13.03[B][3] (2010).

expression and more broadly as a conceptual tool for understanding the scope of the copyright system and its relationship with the First Amendment. The framework transforms the bright-line rule of "ideas out, expression in" into a context-specific standard to be applied on a case-by-case basis. There is no bright line rule telling courts (or anyone else) how to determine the "optimal scope" of copyright protection or how to choose the level of abstraction,[121] perhaps because such a rule cannot exist.[122] As a result, courts (and everyone else) must muddle ahead with an understanding of the struggle, the need to evaluate and determine scope in context, and healthy appreciation of the default rule (ideas out, expression in).

In patent law, courts also struggle with separating unprotectable ideas from patentable invention. The struggle is complicated by the fact that patent law is not very clear about the baseline rule of excluding ideas. In contrast with copyright, the patent statute does not refer to "ideas," much less expressly exclude them from protection. Instead, the patent statute focuses on "invention."[123]

Courts and commentators are all over the map on what constitutes an invention—is it an idea, or is it the implementation or tangible embodiment of an idea? Tun-Jen Chiang aptly describes the definitional confusion:

When forced to clarify what an "invention" really is, however, leading authorities take directly contradictory approaches. . . . Chief Judge Howard Markey of the Federal Circuit, one of the preeminent judges of patent law, has characterized an

---

[121] This has led to conflicting views on the merits of the approach. Compare, for example, Chiang [draft at 50] (2011) ("the abstractions test [] provide[s] an enormously useful framework, reminding judges of 'the difficulties that require courts to avoid either extreme of the continuum of generality.'") (quoting Nash v. CBS, Inc., 899 F. 2d 1537, 1540 (7th Cir. 1990)) with Cohen 732 (1987) (criticizing the doctrine for leading to "unpredictable, impressionistic" decisions) and Yen (2003) (criticizing idea-expression and fair use doctrines resort to abstraction and noting that "[i]t is dangerous to put free speech at the mercy of the idea/expression dichotomy and fair use because those doctrines do not have enough substance to adequately protect something so important."). Most recognize that the approach is imperfect because it is, among other things, inherently messy, unpredictable, and subjective. Nonetheless, it may be the best available means for evaluating and tailoring the scope of protection to the intellectual work.

[122] Cf. Fromer 745 (2009) ("Fixing the boundary between idea and expression can be difficult, not only because of the line drawing required to determine which abstractions of the expression are still protected enough to be more of an expression than an idea, but also because there is no sharp ex ante sense of what the copyright protects beyond the copyrighted work itself").

[123] The statute provides: "Whoever invents or discovers any new and useful process, machine, manufacture, or composition of matter, or any new and useful improvement thereof, may obtain a patent therefor, subject to the conditions and requirements of this title." 35 USC 101. The Supreme Court broadly construed "process, machine, manufacture, or composition of matter," noting that Congress chose expansive terms and even modified them with the "comprehensive 'any.'" Diamond v. Chakrabarty, 447 U.S. 303 (1980). In Chakrabarty, the Court concluded, "Congress intended statutory subject matter to 'include anything under the sun that is made by man.'" *Id.* (quoting S. Rep. No. 1979, 82d Cong., 2d Sess., 5 (1952); H. R. Rep. No. 1923, 82d Cong., 2d Sess., 6 (1952)). Immediately following this expansive construction of patentable subject matter, the Court noted, "This is not to suggest that 101 has no limits or that it embraces every discovery. The laws of nature, physical phenomena, and abstract ideas have been held not patentable." *Id.*

"invention" as the embodiment described by a specification. According to Chief Judge Markey, "Ideas are never patentable. Only embodiments of an idea, i.e. an invention, may be patented." Moreover, "idea" is a "mud word" that "appears nowhere in the statute, which speaks only of invention." This view of invention as embodiment is supported by some Supreme Court precedent as well as the statute that defines patentable inventions as tangible machines, products, and processes that can be made and used.[124]

On the other side, Judge Giles Rich of the Federal Circuit, another eminent judge who wrote much of the 1952 Patent Act, has opined that an "invention" is an abstract idea. According to Judge Rich, an invention is "an incorporeal, intangible abstraction in the nature of a product of the mind." An embodiment is "[p]opularly but inaccurately called 'invention.'" This view, too, has support in Supreme Court precedent, which states that "[t]he primary meaning of the word 'invention' in the Patent Act unquestionably refers to the inventor's conception rather than to a physical embodiment of that idea."[125]

On top of this confusion over what constitutes an invention, the Supreme Court has long held that "laws of nature, physical phenomena, and *abstract ideas*" are not patentable subject matter and that "[t]he concepts covered by these exceptions are 'part of the storehouse of knowledge of all men . . . free to all men and reserved exclusively to none.'"[126] Obviously, this rule mirrors the idea/expression dichotomy in copyright law.[127] However, it still leaves unclear what constitutes an abstract idea and what constitutes an invention.

Abstract ideas excluded
In *Bilski v. Kappos* (2010), the Supreme Court reiterated the rule that abstract ideas are not patentable.[128] The case involved a person trying to patent a method for hedging risk in energy markets. According to the Court, the key claims were 1 and 4; claim 1 described

---

[124] Chiang (2011) (citing Markey 333 (1983); Seymour v. Osborne, 78 U.S. 516, 552 (1870); 35 U.S.C. § 101); Rubber-Tip Pencil Company v. Howard, 87 U.S. (20 Wall.) 498, 507 (1874) ("An idea of itself is not patentable, but a new device by which it may be made practically useful is.").

[125] Chiang (2011) (citing Rich (1942)); Pfaff v. Wells Elecs., Inc., 525 U.S. 55, 60 (1998); Gill v. United States, 160 U.S. 426, 434 (1896) ("In every case the idea conceived is the invention.")).

[126] Bilski v. Kappos, 130 S.Ct. 3218, 561 U.S. _ (2010) (quoting Funk Brothers Seed Co. v. Kalo Inoculant Co., 333 U. S. 127, 130 (1948)). In many of the cases reiterating that basic rule, the Court has stated more broadly that ideas as such are not patentable. For example, in Benson, the Supreme Court stated, "It is conceded that one may not patent an idea." 409 U.S., at 71.

[127] LANDES & POSNER 305 (2003).

[128] The rule is rooted in both English and American law. See, e.g., Neilson v. Harford, Webster's Patent Cases 295, 371 (1841); Le Roy v. Tatham, 14 How. 156. 175 (1853); O'Reilly v. Morse, 15 How. 62 (1854); The Telephone Cases, 126 U. S. 1 (1888).

a series of steps instructing how to hedge risk, and claim 4 provided a formula that restated in mathematical terms the concept in claim 1. The Court "resolve[d] th[e] case narrowly on the basis of [its] decisions in *Benson*, *Flook*, and *Diehr*, which show that [Bilski's] claims are not patentable processes because they are attempts to patent abstract ideas. Indeed, all members of the Court agreed that the patent application at issue fell outside of §101 because it claims an abstract idea."[129] The Court discussed the three decisions and applied the underlying lessons as follows:

- In *Benson*, the Court considered whether a patent application for an algorithm to convert binary-coded decimal numerals into pure binary code was a "process" under §101.[130] The Court first explained that "'[a] principle, in the abstract, is a fundamental truth; an original cause; a motive; these cannot be patented, as no one can claim in either of them an exclusive right.'"[131] The Court then held the application at issue was not a "process," but an unpatentable abstract idea. "It is conceded that one may not patent an idea. But in practical effect that would be the result if the formula for converting . . . numerals to pure binary numerals were patented in this case."[132] A contrary holding "would wholly pre-empt the mathematical formula and in practical effect would be a patent on the algorithm itself."[133]

- In *Flook*, the Court considered the next logical step after *Benson*. The applicant there attempted to patent a procedure for monitoring the conditions during the catalytic conversion process in the petrochemical and oil-refining industries. The application's only innovation was reliance on a mathematical algorithm.[134] *Flook* held the invention was not a patentable "process." The Court conceded the invention at issue, unlike the algorithm in *Benson*, had been limited so that it could still be freely used outside the petrochemical and oil-refining industries.[135] Nevertheless, *Flook* rejected "[t]he notion that post-solution activity, no matter how conventional or obvious in itself, can transform an unpatentable principle into a patentable process."[136] The Court concluded that the process at issue there was "unpatentable under §101, not because it contain[ed] a mathematical algorithm as one component, but because once that algorithm [wa]s assumed to be within the prior art, the application, considered as a whole, contain[ed] no

---

[129] Bilski, 130 S.Ct. at 3230.

[130] 409 U.S., at 64–67.

[131] *Id.* at 67 (quoting Le Roy, 14 How., at 175).

[132] 409 U.S., at 71.

[133] *Id.* at 72.

[134] 437 U.S. at 585–586.

[135] 437 U.S. at 589–590.

[136] *Id.* at 590.

patentable invention."[137] As the Court later explained, *Flook* stands for the proposition that the prohibition against patenting abstract ideas "cannot be circumvented by attempting to limit the use of the formula to a particular technological environment" or adding "insignificant postsolution activity."[138]

- Finally, in *Diehr*, the Court established a limitation on the principles articulated in *Benson* and *Flook*. The application in *Diehr* claimed a previously unknown method for "molding raw, uncured synthetic rubber into cured precision products," using a mathematical formula to complete some of its several steps by way of a computer.[139] *Diehr* explained that while an abstract idea, law of nature, or mathematical formula could not be patented, "an application of a law of nature or mathematical formula to a known structure or process may well be deserving of patent protection."[140] *Diehr* emphasized the need to consider the invention as a whole, rather than "dissect[ing] the claims into old and new elements and then . . . ignor[ing] the presence of the old elements in the analysis."[141] Finally, the Court concluded that because the claim was not "an attempt to patent a mathematical formula, but rather [was] an industrial process for the molding of rubber products," it fell within §101's patentable subject matter.[142]

- In light of these precedents, it is clear that [Bilski's] application is not a patentable "process." Claims 1 and 4 in petitioners' application explain the basic concept of hedging, or protecting against risk: "Hedging is a fundamental economic practice long prevalent in our system of commerce and taught in any introductory finance class."[143] The concept of hedging, described in claim 1 and reduced to a mathematical formula in claim 4, is an unpatentable abstract idea, just like the algorithms at issue in *Benson* and *Flook*. Allowing petitioners to patent risk hedging would preempt use of this approach in all fields, and would effectively grant a monopoly over an abstract idea.

The Court's "analysis," in the excerpts quoted above, is not particularly helpful as guidance for differentiating abstract ideas from patentable inventions.[144] The Court does not indicate any reasons or characteristics that distinguish abstract ideas from nonabstract ideas. As Justice Stevens noted in his concurrence, "The Court, in sum, never provides a

---

[137] *Id.* at 594.

[138] Diehr, 450 U.S., at 191–92.

[139] 450 U.S. at 177.

[140] *Id.* at 187.

[141] *Id.* at 188.

[142] *Id.* at 192–93.

[143] 545 F. 3d at 1013 (Rader, J., dissenting).

[144] See Stevens concurrence; Schultz & Samuelson (2011).

satisfying account of what constitutes an unpatentable abstract idea."[145] Rather, the Court bases its conclusion fully on the consequences of classification for patent scope; that is, the concept of hedging and the mathematical formula are abstract ideas, says the Court, because of the preemptive effect of deciding otherwise.

A better way to understand the decision and the rule it was attempting to describe and apply is to view the analysis as identical to the copyright inquiry: Bilski's invention cannot be extended to the level of abstraction reflected in claims 1 and 4 because that would allow the scope of the patent to reach beyond the embodiment of the idea disclosed in the patent application and the family of related embodiments that reflect Bilski's inventive contribution. To make more sense of this alternative view, I turn to the question of what constitutes an invention.

Invention and patent scope

Chiang argues persuasively that invention has two different meanings in two separate but related contexts in patent law: First, invention refers to the embodiment, the "tangible and working apparatus or process" described in the patent specification.[146] Using an idea to create such a new and useful "process, machine, manufacture, or composition of matter" is what entitles a person to a patent. Second, invention refers to the claimed idea, rather than the specific embodiment. In the infringement context, courts look to the claims to define the scope of the patent, and in this context, invention takes on a broader meaning than the embodiment, for the reason noted earlier. Chiang argues that courts determine patent scope by choosing the level of abstraction with which to analyze infringement, and that they do so "*implicitly* and on an ad hoc basis." He suggests that patent law should follow copyright law and acknowledge the levels-of-abstraction problem, its necessity in the context of differentiating unprotected ideas and protected inventions, and the policy discretion involved in the process. I largely agree with his analysis. However, I would push toward a more explicit exclusion of ideas from patent and frame the analysis in a slightly different manner, described in more detail in the following paragraphs.

As noted, invention describes the act of implementing and the implementation. In contrast with ideas, an invention is a discrete thing that can be identified, delineated, and isolated. *Invention is the working embodiment described by a specification.* I agree with Judge Markey and the associated line of cases and commentary.

For patent rights to be *effective as means*, the rights cannot be limited in scope to the disclosed embodiment but instead must be extended to cover a family of related embodiments. The function of claims is to delineate the family of related embodiments.

---

[145] Stevens concurrence (He goes on: "The Court essentially asserts its conclusion that petitioners' application claims an abstract idea").

[146] Chiang (2011).

- Important tangent: *Effectiveness as means* depends, in turn, on what is the relevant economic objective or end. Despite plenty of rhetoric and wrangling, the basic question of whether patent law aims (a) to facilitate markets and correct for supply-side risks associated with high exclusion costs and the cost structure of supply—to facilitate average cost recovery and no more—or (b) to put an additional weight on the incentives to invest scale remains unsettled. The fact that patents provide the power to exclude independent invention seems to push toward the latter objective,[147] but the issue is still open and contentious.[148]

Each embodiment is actually the product of many different ideas at various levels of abstraction, most of which are not novel. Thus, claims should be understood to identify the shared *idea* among the family of embodiments covered by the patent that constitutes the patentee's contribution *to the public domain*. This is where my framing differs from Chiang's. He suggests that the claimed idea is within the scope of the patent and thus owned. I argue that the idea remains in the public domain, but it serves as an indicator for the family of patented embodiments.[149] The public remains free to use the idea, for example, to communicate knowledge or to generate further ideas (e.g., research, workarounds, or improvements). The patent only precludes making, using, and selling embodiments in the family.[150]

Interpreting, construing, and applying patent claims is fundamentally the same exercise that courts perform in copyright cases when they engage in levels-of-abstraction analysis or otherwise attempt to separate ideas from expression. As Chiang argues, claims construction involves evaluating and choosing an appropriate level of abstraction for the idea shared among protected embodiments and consequently the scope of patent protection.[151]

---

[147] According to Cotropia & Lemley (2009), most patent litigation does not involve copying.

[148] See, e.g., Maurer & Scotchmer (2002); Vermont (2006); Lemley (2007). Even if the economic objective is to spur investment in inventive activities above and beyond what average cost recovery would support, it remains unclear that including independent invention within the scope of the patent (rather than recognizing an independent invention defense) is the most efficient way to accomplish that objective. It may very well be the case that other mechanisms for expanding patent scope would be more efficient.

[149] Similarly, Jeanne Fromer describes patent claims as "listing [the] necessary and sufficient characteristics" that delineate "the set of protected embodiments." Fromer 721 (2009). Fromer provides a detailed examination of claiming in copyright and patent law and the scope issues associated with different types of claiming rules. Beyond the fundamental scope issue, she also discusses various costs and benefits of different claiming rules. *Id.* at 722.

[150] *Id.* at 721.

[151] Courts routinely engage is this type of analysis when construing elements of a patent claim and determining the scope of protection afforded by patent. For example, as Burk and Lemley observe:

> In determining the meaning of terms within a particular element, judges practicing patent claim interpretation are engaged in an exercise that to some degree resembles the famous "levels of abstraction test" articulated by Judge Learned Hand for analysis of infringement under copyright law's "idea/expression"

Determining what embodiments populate the set depends on abstraction analysis. The set of embodiments that share an idea may be infinite and growing over time; not all of its members may exist or be enabled at the time of patent filing. The same issue arises in the context of the doctrine of equivalents when courts determine whether embodiments that are not literally within the scope of the claims nonetheless are within the scope of patent protection.

Patent scope is and must be determined through abstractions analysis. Acknowledging the importance of abstraction leaves the door open for tailoring patent scope to the context and type of invention.[152] In some contexts, a low level of abstraction might be chosen to grant "thin" protection, effectively limiting the patent scope to a narrow range of embodiments, perhaps only those embodiments that are currently enabled. In other contexts, a somewhat higher level of abstraction might be chosen to confer "thick" protection, extending protection to embodiments that do not currently exist (or are not currently enabled) but are on the foreseeable horizon. Patent scope can be extended even further, for example, to embodiments that are not foreseeable. I do not make a strong claim about what the scope of patent protection ought to be in general, much less in specific contexts, because such a policy determination depends on the economic and other social objectives, and, as noted, it is not entirely clear that we know what the economic objective is for patent law.

- To illustrate how the underlying economic objective matters, consider the doctrine of equivalents (DOE). The DOE extends protection beyond the literal claims and struggles in particular with after-arising technologies, technologies that did not exist at the time of invention. Often, the after-arising technology serves as a substitute for one of the elements or limitations in a claim, thus taking the new embodiment outside the literal claims. The difficult policy question is whether the DOE should extend patent scope to cover some or all such future embodiments.
- This reflects the basic yet undecided scope issue. If patent law aims only to align incentives to invest in patentable subject matter with incentives that exist in the market but for misappropriation risks, then patent scope should not generally

---

doctrine. They can read a term abstractly, so that a "fastener" becomes anything that attaches two other things together, or they can read the same term more concretely, defining a fastener to be a particular type of connector such as a nail or a U-bolt. Or they may choose a level in between.

Burk & Lemley 31 (2005). Burk and Lemley suggest that "there are no hard and fast standards in the law by which to make the 'right' decision as to . . . the level of abstraction" and that "the indeterminacy is so acute that courts generally don't acknowledge that they are even engaging in [the] inquiry." *Id.* They suggest, much like Hand and many others, that the indeterminacy may be inherent in the "process of mapping words to things." *Id.* at 31, 49. Or it may be inherent in the process of legal line drawing more generally. Tribe & Dorf 1065–71 (1990). In patent law, courts obfuscate the fact that they are making such choices through the overt formalism of claims construction. Chiang calls for a more honest and deliberate approach. Chiang (2011).

[152] BURK & LEMLEY (2009).

be extended to include (all) after-arising technologies. The risk of such technologies is present in markets generally; it is not special in this context. But if the economic objective of patent law is to put an additional weight on the scale in favor of such investments, that is, to provide additional incentives, then extending patent scope in this manner may be an effective way to do so. I do not make a strong claim in either direction because the analysis depends on the type of after-arising technology, whether the technology is the type that can be expected to reduce the fixed costs for entry into the market for patented invention, and the rate of fixed-cost-reducing innovation.

Patent claims describe an idea at too high a level of abstraction when the family of embodiments that would be covered extends beyond patentee's actual contribution and includes embodiments that are insufficiently related to the disclosed embodiment. This may occur when claimed embodiments either already exist in the public domain (prior art) or are not yet enabled (capable of being implemented).

The Supreme Court's analysis in *Bilski* can be understood within this framework. The Court concluded that claims 1 and 4 were not patentable because they were written at too high a level of abstraction and would convey patent scope well beyond the family of embodiments Bilski actually invented. The claims described a family of embodiments that included many preexisting embodiments and many not-yet-invented embodiments; the court described this effect as preempting the field.

The seminal "abstract ideas" case, *O'Reilly v. Morse*, involved nearly identical analysis.[153] Morse owned a patent on the telegraph, and the Supreme Court declared invalid his eighth claim, which read:

Eighth. I do not propose to limit myself to the specific machinery or parts of machinery described in the foregoing specification and claims, the essence of my invention being the use of the motive power of the electric or galvanic current, which I call electro-magnetism, however developed for marking or printing intelligible characters, signs, or letters, at any distances, being a new application of that power of which I claim to be the first inventor or discoverer.

---

[153] Benson does as well. In Benson, the Court held unpatentable a method for converting numerals expressed as binary-coded decimal numerals into pure binary numerals. The Court emphasized the variance of "known and unknown uses," noting that "[t]he end use may (1) vary from the operation of a train to verification of drivers' licenses to researching law books for precedents and (2) be performed through any existing machinery or future-devised machinery or without any apparatus." As in Morse and Bilski, the claim stated an idea at too high a level of abstraction because the family of embodiments/implementations that shared that idea would extend well beyond what the patentee actually invented or enabled others to use. See, e.g., Parasidis 395 (2010); Schaafsma 432 (2010); In re Bilski, 545 F. 3d 943, 954 (Fed. Cir. 2008). See also Lemley et al. (2011).

The Court explained:

> It is impossible to misunderstand the extent of this claim. He claims the exclusive right to every improvement where the motive power is the electric or galvanic current, and the result is the marking or printing intelligible characters, signs, or letters at a distance. If this claim can be maintained, it matters not by what process or machinery the result is accomplished. For aught that we now know, some future inventor, in the onward march of science, may discover a mode of writing or printing at a distance by means of the electric or galvanic current, without using any part of the process or combination set forth in the plaintiff's specification. His invention may be less complicated—less liable to get out of order—less expensive in construction, and in its operation. But yet if it is covered by this patent, the inventor could not use it, nor the public have the benefit of it, without the permission of this patentee.
>
> Nor is this all; while he shuts the door against inventions of other persons, the patentee would be able to avail himself of new discoveries in the properties and powers of electro-magnetism which scientific men might bring to light. For he says he does not confine his claim to the machinery or parts of machinery which he specifies, but claims for himself a monopoly in its use, however developed, for the purpose of printing at a distance. New discoveries in physical science may enable him to combine it with new agents and new elements, and by that means attain the object in a manner superior to the present process and altogether different from it. And if he can secure the exclusive use by his present patent, he may vary it with every new discovery and development of the science, and need place no description of the new manner, process, or machinery upon the records of the patent office. . . . In fine, he claims an exclusive right to use a manner and process which he has not described and indeed had not invented, and therefore could not describe when he obtained his patent. The court is of opinion that the claim is too broad, and not warranted by law.[154]

Many patent scholars and judges have wondered whether the Supreme Court espoused a categorical limitation on patentable subject matter or simply a limitation on claim scope. Apart from the categorical exclusion of abstract ideas from patentable subject matter, patent law recognizes that a patent must enable others to make or practice the invention, which means making an embodiment within the family of claimed embodiments. Moreover, a number of patent doctrines do plenty of work (a) delineating what is and what is not patentable and (b) effectively shaping patent scope. For example, patent law requires novelty, utility, nonobviousness, and an enabling disclosure in a written

---

[154] 56 U.S. 62 (1854). The Court went on to discuss other examples.

description; each of these doctrines serve (a) and (b) and other functions as well. In the line of cases from *Morse* to *Bilski*, the Supreme Court is espousing both a categorical limitation on patentable subject matter and a limitation on claim scope. The two go hand in hand, as described below.

The analytical framework I set forth ends up in a similar place as Chiang.[155] Judges are put in the difficult position of choosing the appropriate level of abstraction to determine the scope of the patent and range of embodiments subject to the patent owner's exclusive rights. Like Chiang, I believe the scope of the claims is and should be influenced by the nature of the actual invention and the characteristics that make it novel, useful, and non-obvious. This steers away from overly formalistic claim interpretation and toward a more deliberate engagement with the underlying scope question and the context.

Theoretically, one potential advantage of my approach is that it is compatible with the notion that ideas are not patentable and only the implementation or embodiments can be patented. The Supreme Court should stop referring to *abstract* ideas and using $E = mc^2$ to illustrate and justify exclusion.[156] Focusing on this extreme and easily made case obscures the underlying issue, as does an overly formalistic approach to claims construction, where judges and the public are led to believe that claim construction inquiry is merely a linguistic exercise, a search for the "true meaning" of claim language.[157] It would be more honest, transparent, and consistent with the First Amendment and copyright treatment of ideas to make clear that ideas are not patentable. Shifting the frame in this fashion leads to a better understanding of what courts and the Patent and Trademark Office are actually doing when evaluating claims, and it also leads to a better understanding of the common task in patent and copyright and reliance on levels-of-abstraction analysis in performing that task.

I recognize that the framework I offer does not provide a clear, bright-line rule or test, and that is what many patent scholars, practitioners, and judges are looking for. In *Bilski*, the Supreme Court rejected the Court of Appeals for the Federal Circuit's exclusive reliance on the "machine or transformation" test.[158] I believe what the Court struggled to say

---

[155] It also resonates well with arguments made by four prominent patent law scholars. Lemley, Risch, Sichelman, & Wagner (2011).

[156] Lab. Corp. of Am. Holdings v. Metabolite Labs., Inc., 548 U.S. 124, 126 (2006), quoting Diamond v. Diehr, 450 U.S. 175, 185 (1981). "The principle means that Einstein could not have 'patent[ed] his celebrated law that $E = mc^2$; nor could Newton have patented the law of gravity.'" *Id.*, quoting Diamond v. Chakrabarty, 447 U.S. 303, 309 (1980).

[157] Chiang (2011).

[158] The Federal Circuit had held that "a "claimed process is surely patent-eligible under §101 if: (1) it is tied to a particular machine or apparatus, or (2) it transforms a particular article into a different state or thing." In re Bilski, 545 F. 3d 943, 954–955 (Fed. Cir. 2008). In some important respects, that test follows the analysis I have suggested, because it differentiated abstract ideas from patentable method inventions based on whether or not the method was implemented on a machine or produced a physical transformation. Thus, one might conclude the Court went in a different direction than I would support. It depends on how one interprets the decision.

is that bright-line rules are inappropriate for deciding cases at the boundary between unpatentable ideas and patentable inventions. Despite its reaffirmation of the oft-expressed and easily stated bright-line rule (abstract ideas are not patentable, which should be *ideas are not patentable*), practical reality requires a standard; it requires levels-of-abstraction analysis in context, much like copyright, albeit with a different set of doctrinal tools.

Finally, in addition to the levels-of-abstraction framework, some other related tools from copyright might be useful in patent law. For example, Mark Lemley asked me to consider patents concerning ideas that have only two different embodiments, say a product and process, each of which is claimed. Such a hypothetical may arise in the case of a patent claiming both an isolated and purified chemical compound and the sole feasible method for its isolation and purification. In such a case, it might be appropriate to import the merger doctrine from copyright law, given the possible social value of the chemical compound and the inability of competitors to design around the patented method. As noted, the merger doctrine limits copyright protection of expression when the idea being expressed is capable of being expressed in an extremely limited number of ways. One could imagine a similar merger doctrine being developed in patent law. I do not take a position on whether this would be attractive policy or whether such a patent doctrine should lead to no patent protection or thin protection. Answering this question depends on how one answers prior questions about the economic objectives or ends of patent law.

* * *

Ideas illustrate the semi-commons structure of intellectual property systems. Ideas are managed as commons by virtue of their exclusion from patent and copyright and inclusion in the public domain. Patent and copyright laws grant limited private rights over outputs from particular uses of ideas. Both patent and copyright laws struggle to filter ideas—to determine whether something is patentable or copyrightable subject matter—and to manage the scope of rights granted to avoid de facto protection of ideas. The next section explores the semi-commons structure of patent and copyright laws more generally.

D. Intellectual Property Laws as Semi-commons Arrangements

The intellectual property laws construct semi-commons arrangements, complex mixtures of interdependent private rights and commons.[159] Semi-commons exist at different scales.

The Court did not turn away from the "machine or transformation" test altogether. The underlying principle (that implementation differentiates unpatentable ideas from patentable inventions) remains valid, and the test remains relevant. Courts should continue to look for machine implementation or physical transformation as an important "clue." See Bilski; Schultz and Samuelson (2011); PTO Guidelines; Lemley et al. (2011).

[159] Heverly (2003); Madison, Frischmann, & Strandburg (2010); Frischmann and Lemley (2007); Frischmann (2007b); Yu 6–8 (2005); Loren (2007); Vetter (2007). On the idea of semi-commons, see Smith (2000).

At a macro level, the cultural environment constitutes mixed infrastructure that should be managed as a commons. As discussed, commons management aims to limit both government and market shaping of the cultural environment and our lives, plans, beliefs, and preferences. Commons management is a strong default position for the cultural environment because users—autonomous individuals as well as social groups and communities—get to shape the environment and choose what to say and do and how to plan their lives, experiences, and interactions with each other and the environment.

Yet, as in the context of the natural environment, a pure open-access or commons regime can lead to tragedy, in this context associated with undersupply of certain types of intellectual resources. Consequently, intellectual property systems enclose and regulate a select (albeit very broad) set of intellectual resources. Thus, an identifiable semi-commons emerges at the macro level, with commons being the default form of management and intellectual property enclosure being exceptional, albeit of broad scope and significant importance. The unenclosed and enclosed are highly interdependent; much of which exists in either space/environment/category depends substantially on complex interactions and various inputs/contributions from the other space/environment/category. Given tremendous difficulties in establishing and maintaining boundaries, and the dynamic and complex nature of cultural-intellectual resource systems, the intellectual property laws also mediate the relationships between the enclosed and unenclosed. As demonstrated with respect to ideas, the First Amendment, copyright, and patent interact with each other and the public domain. The discussion of ideas demonstrates the semi-commons structure and associated interdependence between private and public at the macro level; at the same time, it reveals the semi-commons structure at the meso (or intermediate) level of the copyright and patent systems. Though both legal systems construct private rights and enclose a set of intellectual resources, neither constitutes pure private rights or enclosure. Rather, both copyright and patent laws themselves are semi-commons arrangements that mix both private rights and commons. Both legal systems are designed to sustain incentives and spillovers.

Copyright law creates a semi-commons arrangement—a complex mix of private rights and commons.[160] The rights granted by copyright law—specifically, the §106 rights to reproduce, display, perform, distribute, and make derivative works—provide incentives to create and disseminate works by facilitating transactions and lowering the costs of excluding competitors from using the expression. The supply-side incentives affected by copyright extend beyond the initial investment in creation to investments in content development and dissemination. What must be encouraged is not only works' creation but also their publication, dissemination, and productive use. Like traditional property rights, copyright facilitates transactions over certain uses of creative expression, and thereby enables rights holders to appropriate some of the surplus generated by their investments in

---

[160] The next four paragraphs derive from Frischmann & Lemley (2007), with some modification.

creation, development, and dissemination. In this fashion, the private rights component of copyright law improves investment incentives through the operation of the market mechanism; in a sense, it uses the market to achieve a broader set of economic and social ends.

The commons component of copyright law promotes spillovers; or, to put it another way, the commons component of copyright law avoids market or government allocation of resources for certain ranges of uses and for certain elements of a copyrighted work.[161] Through a variety of leaks and limitations on the private rights granted, copyright law sustains common access to and use of resources needed to participate in a wide variety of intellectually productive activities. Many of these activities generate socially valuable spillovers: benefits realized by consumers, users, and third parties that are external to a creator's decision to produce the work and to any transactions involving the work. For example, due to its limited duration, copyright has generated temporal externalities. A work that enters the public domain is free for public use, and any value derived from this use is external to both the creator's decision to produce the work and any transactions involving the work. Similarly, due to copyright's limited scope, copyright generates externalities that accrue to other creators, even competitors, as these entities can freely use various unprotected elements of a work, such as an idea, theme, or functional feature. Copyright's limited scope may also generate externalities in complementary technology markets: for example, companies can design and build products such as DVD players and iPods that facilitate the enjoyment of copyrighted works. Finally, copyright produces externalities when consumers productively use or reuse works. Creating and consuming creative expression of different types develops human capital, educates, and socializes in a manner that benefits not only creators and consumers but also nonparticipants.

Patent law, like copyright, is a semi-commons that promotes both ownership of rights and spillovers, but the particular ways in which patent law and copyright law permit "leakage" differ significantly. Patent law protections have a much shorter duration than copyright, permitting inventions to enter the public domain more quickly. Patent law also excludes some inventions from protection because requirements for obtaining protection are stricter. Once inventors do obtain protection, however, the right they obtain is much stronger and less leaky than that afforded by copyright law.

Patent law promotes spillovers in several ways. Patents generate externalities by facilitating learning and disclosure.[162] Indeed, patent law, unlike copyright law, requires the patent owner to teach the public how to make and use the invention, and this is often identified as a central function of the patent system, though in practice it is considerably

---

[161] Frischmann 659 (2007b).

[162] Patents may be justified as a publicly preferable means of providing exclusion when compared with alternatives such as trade secrecy. Patents lead to public disclosure of inventions and, at least some, surrounding information and ideas that would otherwise remain secret; such a justification for patents presumes a semi-commons governance regime and not pure exclusion because to be publicly meaningful, disclosure must actually enable productive uses, activities, and opportunities that would not otherwise be publicly available.

less important than the system's incentive effects. Patents lead to temporal externalities—spillovers the occur when the patent expires. Temporal spillovers are quite significant. For example, the overwhelming majority of the social benefit associated with the telephone (and, for that matter, the paper clip) occurred after the basic patents on those technologies expired.

These legal systems sustain commons by excluding resources and designating them unprotectable, but also by sustaining public access to privately owned resources for certain types of uses.[163] In a sense, the legal systems also construct semi-commons at the micro level of the protected expression or invention.[164] At this micro level, copyright law appears to be more sensitive to and accommodating of social demand for commons management of infrastructural expression than patent law is with respect to infrastructural invention. "Copyright encourages and sustains participation in intellectually productive activities that both generate and use expressive works to communicate, entertain, teach, and engage us in many different ways. Many of these activities—e.g., education, community development, democratic discourse, political participation—generate socially valuable . . . spillovers."[165] For example, fair use is a particularly important copyright law doctrine that aims to preserve public capabilities to use copyright protected expression in various ways.[166] As Lemley and I explain:

> Many paradigmatic uses deemed fair involve use of a work to engage in activities that yield diffuse, small-scale spillovers to a community. Using a work for educational purposes, for example, not only benefits the users themselves, but also, in a small way, benefits others in the users' community with whom users have interdependent relations—reading and learning builds socially valuable human capital. Critiquing a work similarly benefits not only the user but also, in a small way, others in the users' community—not only because those others may read the critique itself, but also because engaging in critical commentary is a form of creative and cultural activity that builds socially valuable human capital. We recognize that observing and measuring these spillover benefits is probably an impossible task. That is our point, in fact. As a society, on the whole, we recognize the value of active, widespread participation in these types of activities, and we know that creative expression is essential to participation. Thus, we encourage common access to and use of expression for these types of activities.[167]

---

[163] Litman (1990); LANDES & POSNER (2003); Gordon (1982).

[164] We might connect the idea that the infrastructure theory has a fractal nature in the sense that infrastructural characteristics manifest at different scales with the semi-commons structures (management institutions) that manifest at different scales.

[165] Frischmann 672 (2007b).

[166] Frischmann & Lemley 286–290 (2007).

[167] *Id.* at 289.

Other features of copyright law, such as constraints on the exclusive scope of rights (for example, private display and performance is permissible) or judicial willingness to provide "thinner" protection for certain types of works, also provide breathing space. The levels-of-abstraction framework described above permits judges to adjust the scope of copyright based on the context and nature of the work, and judges routinely filter infrastructural elements of a work in addition to ideas (for example, stock literary elements).[168] Patent law is not sensitive to social demand for commons management of infrastructural invention.[169] The primary commons components of patent law are its mechanisms for exclusion and conferral to the public domain (for example, disclosure, strict qualification criteria, and duration). There is no fair use or functionally equivalent doctrine. Courts implicitly engage in levels-of-abstraction analysis when construing claims and determining infringement, and that provides an opportunity to adjust patent scope, but the analysis is not sensitive to social demand or the infrastructural characteristics of the invention.[170] I do not take a position on whether or not patent law should be more sensitive to such concerns. Other scholars have advanced arguments for a patent fair use doctrine, a more robust experimental use defense, and adjusting remedies when patents on infrastructural inventions are infringed.[171]

Appendix: Basic Research

This appendix provides an abbreviated discussion of basic research as an example of intellectual infrastructure. Before proceeding, it is important to acknowledge that basic research is itself a broad, malleable, and contested concept. There are competing definitions of basic research. In *Science: The Endless Frontier*, Vannevar Bush supplied what is now the classic definition of basic research: research "performed without thought of practical ends."[172] This and various other definitions focus on what motivates or guides researchers, what researchers expect to accomplish or hope to achieve. Some scholars

---

[168] There are various other examples of intellectual infrastructure excluded from intellectual property protection. See *id.* at 286 (historical facts); Lee (2008) (discussing various examples).

[169] Lee (2008). Lee provides an excellent account of how trademark, copyright, and patent law accommodate social demand for access to infrastructural works.

[170] One exception may be pioneering inventions, which may obtain broader scope because of their significance. Sun Studs, Inc. v. ATA Equip. Leasing, Inc., 872 F. 2d 978, 987 (Fed. Cir. 1989); Thomas 58–59 (1995); Lemley 1003 (1997).

[171] O'Rourke (2000) (fair use); Strandburg (2011) (same); Mueller 9–10 (2001) (experimental use); Caruso (2003) (same); Lee (2008) (exploring the concept of intellectual infrastructure, and proposing that "courts should consider the infrastructural use of a patented invention when determining infringement remedies and, in certain circumstances, allow such use to continue by a downstream user contingent upon providing compensation to the patentee.").

[172] BUSH (1954).

refer to basic research as "curiosity-driven."[173] Others implicitly adopt the linear model discussed above and focus on the nonimmediacy of *commercial* applications.[174]

I would put aside what motivates the researchers (curiosity, financial returns, prestige, etc.) and whether the research is commercial or not. Simply put, many different motivations may be in play, and commerciality is not relevant to the definition of basic research (i.e., there are plenty of examples of applied noncommercial research and of basic commercial research).

Given the dual nature of research as a mixed process/product (activity/resource), I approach the definitional question by examining research from both an *ex post* and *ex ante* perspective: From an *ex post* perspective, a research output is characterized by its use, and from an *ex ante* perspective, a research project or investment is characterized in terms of its potential outcomes and uses. Thus, for each potential research activity or investment, there is a probability distribution describing the likelihood that the research will serve as an input for a range of uses. *Ex ante*, public or private investors can estimate this distribution given publicly available and privately held information (hereinafter termed the "use estimate"). The distinction between basic and applied research can be understood by looking to the *variance* of the use estimate. A larger (smaller) variance in the distribution corresponds to basic (applied) research, representing a wider (narrower) range of potential uses and hence greater (less) uncertainty as to a specific use. Therefore, on this view, the distinction between basic and applied research is not dependent on the uses themselves, that is, whether the research is commercial or not. Instead, the distinction rests on the *range of potential uses* and the corresponding *uncertainty with regard to specific uses.*[175]

Over time, moving from basic to applied research might proceed in steps, analogous to Bayesian learning, such that successful research steps affect the use estimates of subsequent research. Often, taking consecutive steps entails producing research and using it as an input to produce dependent or "second-generation" research. The linear model of the innovative process assumes a gradual narrowing of the use estimate as though deviation from the mean does not occur and learning from spillovers is a fiction. In reality, though, progress is nonlinear, meaning that distributions rise, flatten, and shift location dynamically from step to step.

Basic research seems to encompass a wide range of activities and practices among different communities (government, industry, academia, and various other actors and institutions) as well as the research results, the inputs, outputs, and so on. We might

---

[173] Strandburg (2011).

[174] Landes & Posner 305–06 (2003) ("Basic research is distinguished from applied research mainly by lacking *immediate* commercial applications.").

[175] Frischmann 365–66 (2000) (arguing that the difference between basic and applied research is the variance of anticipated applications or uses).

conceptualize basic research as a complex system within the cultural environment. For the sake of brevity, I will not fully explore the contours of the system or the interactions among the various resources and participant communities. Instead, having acknowledged these definitional complications, I proceed to apply the infrastructure theory to basic research.

What makes basic research valuable to society? Again, like a road system, communications networks, and oceans, basic research is socially valuable primarily because of what it facilitates downstream—how it can be used to produce further knowledge and research. It satisfies all three criteria in the general definition of infrastructure and should be classified as public infrastructure: It is nonrival; it creates benefits or value primarily because of the downstream uses, which generally involve the production of additional public goods (e.g., more research, information, knowledge, and learning); and, by my definition, there is wide variation in downstream uses. Again, in my view, what distinguishes basic research from applied research is the variance in expected (or, in some cases, desired or predicted) uses of the research.[176]

It is difficult to estimate the social value of basic research, primarily because of the wide variety of downstream uses that generate public goods and uncertainty with respect to future directions that the cumulative productive processes may go. Basic research, like many infrastructural resources, builds public capabilities to be productive in various ways that are difficult to fully trace. Nonetheless, as with many traditional infrastructures, it is well recognized that basic research contributes significantly to economic growth and social welfare.[177]

As with other infrastructure, recognizing that basic research behaves economically as infrastructure suggests that the social costs of restricting access to the resource can be significant and yet evade observation or consideration within conventional economic transactions. Many others have noted that granting exclusive property rights (e.g., patents) over basic research[178] stifles downstream research, which can impose substantial social costs.[179] This does not mean that no progress will be made. Some avenues of follow-on research may proceed, for example, by initial researchers or others to whom licenses are granted. The point is that basic research may "be encumbered with excessive licensing

---

[176] There are obviously differences between desired, expected, and predicted, but since basic research is rather amorphous and continuous and has a dual product/process nature, I am reluctant to draw any sharp lines.

[177] See, e.g., LANDES & POSNER 305–08 (2003); Rai (1999); Reichman & Uhlir (2003).

[178] While a significant amount of basic research is not patentable, it appears that "more and more fruits of basic research [can] be patented," LANDES & POSNER 308 (2003). In some areas, at least, both the existence and the prospect of patents have had a significant effect on the research process. See *id.* at 305–08.

[179] See *id.*; Scotchmer 32 (1991); Merges & Nelson 869–80 (1990). As Robert Merges and Richard Nelson explain, some private firms recognize the value of open access to basic research and have undertaken efforts to place research results in the public domain. *Id.*

fees and transaction costs,"[180] and the paths taken may be unduly constrained from a social perspective.

Moreover, granting property rights over basic research links resource management with commercialization and introduces the market mechanism's inherent bias for outputs that generate observable or reasonably foreseeable and appropriable returns.[181] Thus, in making decisions regarding access, owners would face the same set of problems that the hypothetical owner of a lake in chapter 11 would face—for example, excessive transaction costs and uncertainty regarding the prospect of appropriable returns.[182] While downstream uses of basic research are not rivalrous in the technical sense (i.e., there is no risk of congestion), users may compete with each other to develop and commercialize the research and may demand exclusive licenses.[183] In granting such licenses, owners may favor uses reasonably expected to generate appropriable returns at the expense of uses more likely to generate positive externalities.[184] This may retard progress in a manner that has substantial social opportunity costs in the sense that socially valuable research paths lie fallow and unexplored.[185]

Consider the case of basic research that has uncertain or low commercial value, which, according to Arti Rai, deserves particular attention:

[I]n the context of research that is demonstrably of low commercial value, there is evidence that upstream proprietary rights have impeded downstream research.

---

[180] Merges (2004).

[181] Not only does this bias affect management of existing research results; it also has dynamic effects on the research process because the prospect of obtaining a patent may skew researchers' incentives and basic scientific norms. See Frischmann (2009a); Lee (2009); Rai 109–13 (1999); Frischmann (2005c); see also SCOTCHMER 127–31 (2004). Scotchmer explains: "[I]t is not easy to compensate the developers of basic technologies. Commercial value generally resides in products that are developed later. If the founders earn some profit, it is only because they can demand licensing fees from later developers. But this requires that later products infringe their patents. Basic scientific knowledge . . . is generally not patentable, in recognition of the fact that the benefits would be hard to appropriate."
  Id. at 129. One reason that basic research should be supported by public sponsors rather than private investors "is that the benefits of basic research are hard to appropriate by private parties." *Id.* at 131–32. To the extent that the public goods applications are sufficiently commercializable (applied and commercial), there is an argument that markets should work quite well in manifesting demand for the infrastructure and that the major impediments to maximizing social welfare originate on the supply side. See *id.* at 127–59.

[182] See chapter 11.

[183] Notably, some of the downstream markets involve further investment in public goods as the innovative process continues.

[184] Cf. Rai (2005) ("[I]n university contexts, where the immediately foreseeable payoffs—commercial or academic—from research is often not high, researchers are unlikely to be willing or able to incur high transaction costs in order to gain access to upstream research.").

[185] In an earlier article, I argued that this constitutes a special type of market failure, which I called "innovative process market failure," because the failure to pursue potential avenues of research involves hidden costs associated with the cumulative, nonlinear nature of the innovative process. Frischmann 374 (2000).

Consider the case of research into a malaria vaccine. The disease burden associated with malaria is very significant, on the order of over one million deaths a year. The social value of a malaria vaccine would therefore be quite high. Nonetheless, because the primary market for such a vaccine would be in the developing world, such research is of low commercial value. . . .

. . .

. . . In the area of agricultural biotechnology, there is perhaps even more compelling evidence that research projects of low commercial value have been significantly delayed, or have not gone forward at all, because of upstream patent rights. Specifically, restricted access to patented technologies has been identified as a significant barrier to development of subsistence crops relevant to the developing world.[186]

More generally, the social costs associated with the market mechanism's inherent bias for outputs that generate observable and appropriable returns may be significant. These costs evade observation because basic research is often an input into and output from cumulative processes involving multiple inputs, multiple outputs, multiple actors, and multiple research avenues heading in different directions. These cumulative processes involve nonlinear progression, feedback loops, (cascading) spillovers, and numerous other complications that frustrate modelers and defy simplification.[187] All of these characteristics contribute to information and transaction cost problems that make relying on property-based, market-driven management of basic research results almost outrageous, much like the seemingly ridiculous hypothetical (in chapter 11) of granting ownership of Lake Michigan to an individual property owner.

Edmund Kitch's "prospect theory" of patents simply does not work well for basic research.[188] His theory is premised on two notions: (1) that the property owner will minimize social waste associated with duplicative efforts; and (2) that the property owner

---

[186] Rai (2005). Rai provides a number of specific examples where upstream patents have impeded downstream progress of research with low commercial value. See *id.* Rai also considers whether collective action may alleviate the problem. See *id.*

[187] Consideration of these characteristics is beyond the scope of this chapter. There is, however, substantial literature in this area. See, e.g., SCOTCHMER (2004); Scotchmer (1991).

[188] See Kitch 265, 276–78 (1977) (likening a patent to a mining claim, where society benefits from efficient exploitation of a patent and its prospects). Kitch argued that IP rights facilitate efficient coordination of research such that duplicative waste is minimized. There are a number of scenarios where this argument holds true, some of which depend on the bargaining positions of primary and secondary researchers, and some of which depend on the innovation types involved. See, e.g., Green & Scotchmer 20, 31 (1995) (discussing bargaining positions of primary and secondary innovators in IP licensing context). Perhaps the most straightforward example of the bargaining position scenario is where valuable information is asymmetrically held by the primary researcher that can be selectively doled out to willing licensees. The latter scenario may occur, for example, in the derivative market for applied incremental research for which duplication is likely, i.e., the range of improvements is narrow.

will best commercialize and license an invention.[189] Neither premise, however, holds up with respect to basic research. Wasteful duplication seems much less likely to be a problem in the context of basic research because of the multitude of directions and research paths that grow out of basic research. One must adopt a rather strong version of the linear model of innovation to support the premise that competitive research efforts within and building from basic research will lead to wasteful duplication.[190] This view assumes that research efforts follow the same course of research, lead to identical results, and are thus economically wasteful. But such an assumption is valid only for relatively applied research projects; two independent research projects having the same extremely peaked use estimate will likely result in duplication because achieving the expected mean use is highly likely. But the likelihood of wasteful duplication diminishes as the variance increases.

- Assume that firms A and B each begin with a shared pool of common knowledge and identical sets of resources (capital, labor, expertise, know-how, etc.). Furthermore, each begins an independent research project X at time t_1 with identical use estimates $P_1(X)$ but without any sharing of information after t_1. The outcome of each firm's project at t_2 yields X_A and X_B. The likelihood that the outcomes are the same depends on the variance of the estimate. When the outcomes are secret and not identical, each firms' new use estimate for continued research is different, creating both different opportunities for progress in the broad sense and different incentives for continued investment. The communication of outcomes from period 1 leads to a separate use estimate.[191]

---

[189] Kitch 276–78 (1977). See Frischmann 372–73, 374–76 (2000); Merges 359, 381 (1992); SCOTCHMER 155 (2004). Scotchmer concludes:

> Thus the licensing platform created by a pioneer patent can undermine competition . . . in the "innovation market" . . . and competition among users of the patented knowledge. It might be better not to give such patents. One alternative is public funding, and another is to let a later innovator who needs the pioneer innovation redevelop it. This leads to cost redundancy, but unless the tool is very expensive, such redundancy may be a lesser evil than retarding the development of later products through restrictive joint ventures or raising their price by facilitating collusion.

> *Id.*

[190] In a discussion of patent races, Scotchmer associates inefficient duplication with the assumption that "R&D costs have a large fixed component [where] if two firms invest, the cost is needlessly duplicated." Scotchmer 273, 275 (1998). She distinguishes the fixed R&D cost process, which leads to duplicative results, from a variable R&D cost process, which leads to duplicative but accelerated results. The latter may be regarded as efficient (i.e., nonwasteful) duplication.

[191] Frischmann (2000).

Various researchers participating in basic research may hasten progress or lead to advances in different directions.[192] If the linear model is dropped, there is little reason to believe that coordination of basic research is akin to mining for ore.

Managing basic research as a commons may have considerable appeal as a means to leverage nonrivalry, maintain the social option value of basic research, and encourage widespread productive use. But how do we overcome the production problem? How do we overcome supply-side problems for basic research?

Basic research is both publicly and privately provided, and there is a continuum of public, private, and hybrid institutions that address supply-side concerns, including grants, procurement, subsidies, regulation, property rights, intellectual property rights, contracts, tax incentives, technology, and social norms. Notably, intellectual property is much less of a factor than public funding. According to William Landes and Richard Posner:

> An enormous amount of basic research is produced every year in the United States and other advanced countries without benefit of patentability. . . . In 1999 half of all basic research in the United States was funded by the federal government, and of the balance 29 percent was financed by universities and other nonprofit research establishments out of their own funds.[193]

By 2010, the portion of basic research funded by the federal government had grown to 60 percent, with academic institutions continuing to act as the second largest source of funding.[194] Universities, many of them publicly-sustained, conduct 55 percent of basic research, with business and industry accounting for less that 20 percent.[195]

Public financing reduces the need to rely on private investment and eliminates supply-side concerns over protecting incentives to invest in the research. In theory, it would appear that the optimal management decision would be to release publicly funded basic research results into the public domain to encourage free, widespread, and potentially competitive use downstream. In a sense, public investment in a basic research commons is precisely the sort of indirect intervention that does not aim for optimality (or optimal

---

[192] As Merges and Nelson argue, "rivalry facilitates technical advance and unified control damps it." See Merges & Nelson (1990). As Richard Nelson put it, "From a social point of view, effective pursuit of technological advance seems to call for the exploration of a wide variety of alternatives and the selective screening of these [alternatives once] their characteristics have been better revealed a process that seems wasteful with hindsight." Nelson 455 (1982).

[193] LANDES & POSNER 306 (2003).

[194] The Science Coalition, Sparking Economic Growth 3 (2010), available at http://www.sciencecoalition.org/successstories/resources/pdf/Sparking%20Economic%20Growth%20Full%20Report%20FINAL%204-5-10.pdf (arguing for increased public investment in basic research, along with increasing university-based research, and pointing out the positive economic benefits and job creation that such investment would engender).

[195] *Id.*

investment in public goods production)[196] but instead aims to support a wide range of "follow-on" activities, by enhancing basic public capabilities,[197] improving the knowledge base on which the public can build, and maintaining flexibility in the opportunities available.

In reality, as one would expect, there are serious obstacles to effectively implementing this solution. To begin with, it depends on government to raise sufficient funds and allocate them efficiently. Of course, government financing of infrastructure always raises these issues, but basic research funding raises some distinct issues. First, in comparison with most traditional infrastructure, basic research is much less tangible and visible to citizens, who may be asked to pay higher taxes to fund it. Second, the demand-measurement problem highlighted by Samuelson may be especially relevant if we substitute tax-paying communities for consumers; communities have strong incentives to conceal their preferences in the hope of free riding on the investments of other communities. Thus, it is not surprising that very little basic research funding comes from local or state governments.[198] Even at the national level, we might expect systematic underinvestment in basic research because of free-riding concerns. The United States is the leading supporter of R&D activities in the world, accounting for 33 percent of worldwide R&D expenditures.[199] Public support for government funding of basic research remains strong, with 84 percent of Americans expressing support for such funding in 2008 (at the height of a long and painful recession).[200]

Another major obstacle is effective management of basic research. In fact, based in part on the perception that the federal government had a very poor record of managing federally funded research results,[201] Congress enacted a series of legislative reforms, such as the Bayh-Dole Act,[202] that aimed to facilitate the transfer of publicly funded technology to the private sector.[203] Most notably, the Bayh-Dole Act permitted and encouraged

---

[196] The demand-measurement problems truly would make such an effort impossible.

[197] Education is the other obvious example.

[198] General R&D funding from nonfederal sources "is small in comparison to federal and business sources"; in 2008 the combined funding from state and local governments, along with academic institutional funds, and nonprofits was a mere 7 percent. National Science Foundation, Science and Engineering Indicators 2010 at 4–14 (2010), available at http://www.nsf.gov/statistics/seind10/pdf/c04.pdf.

[199] National Science Foundation, Science and Engineering Indicators 2010 at 4–33 (2010), available at http://www.nsf.gov/statistics/seind10/pdf/c04.pdf. Japan is the second-largest performer at 13 percent, with China in third at 9 percent of global R&D expenditure. Id.

[200] Id. at 7–29.

[201] See Eisenberg (1996) (explaining and critiquing this perception).

[202] See Bayh-Dole University and Small Business Patent Procedures Act, Pub. L. No. 96-517, 94 Stat. 3019 (codified as amended at 35 U.S.C. §§ 200–211) (2000); see also Stevenson-Wydler Technology Innovation Act of 1980, Pub. L. No. 96-480, 94 Stat. 2311 (codified as amended at 15 U.S.C. §§ 3701–3714 (2000)).

[203] On these legislative reforms, see Eisenberg 1704–09 (1996); Eisenberg (1994); Frischmann 406 (2000); Rai 92–94, 109–15 (1999).

federally funded researchers to obtain patent rights over their inventions. The premise was that patents would facilitate postpatent research, development, and commercialization. That is, in the absence of patents, government-funded research results would languish underutilized because (1) the researchers and their host institutions lacked the incentives and/or capacity to further develop and commercialize the research or to transfer the research results to industry, and (2) even if transfer was feasible, industry lacked sufficient incentives to invest in development and commercialization without the exclusivity made available by patents in the form of exclusive licenses. Granting researchers patent rights, it followed, would enable them to better manage their inventions, and would encourage cooperation between university researchers and industry.[204] Relying on intellectual property to stimulate technology transfer reflected a fundamental shift within the university research community.

The shift has had a profound effect on basic research efforts in certain fields. For example, as noted by Walter Powell, there has been a "sea change in the focus of basic research" in life sciences because of commercialization by universities of basic scientific research results.[205] Moreover, the effort to bring academia and industry closer together may have had significant effects on universities and their science and technology research systems.[206] It is very difficult to gauge this type of institutional change, but there are some indications that the Bayh-Dole Act has had impacts on the management of university science and technology research systems. The *Economist* magazine, which in 2002 heralded the Bayh-Dole Act as "[p]ossibly the most inspired piece of legislation to be enacted in America over the past half-century,"[207] more recently concluded:

Many scientists, economists and lawyers believe the act distorts the mission of universities, diverting them from the pursuit of basic knowledge, which is freely

---

[204] See Eisenberg 1664–66 (1996).

[205] Powell (2001); see also Eisenberg 223 (2001) (suggesting that delays and high transaction costs stifle transfers of biotechnology research tools).

[206] Many have documented the significant increase in commercial activities of universities, including patenting and licensing, for example. There are many different explanations, however. See generally SLAUGHTER & LESLIE (1997) (studying multiple policy instruments and their commercialization impact). In fact, a number of scholars "have argued that much of the increase in commercially oriented university activities, such as patenting and licensing, that has occurred since 1980 was driven by contemporary shifts in intellectual property laws and regimes for funding academic research." Shane (2004) (citing Henderson, Jaffe, & Trajtenberg 119 (1998); Mowery & Ziedonis 399 (2002); Mowery et al. 99 (2001); see also Mowery 16 (2005). Mowery shows that the trend of increased patenting behavior by universities occurred prior to 1980 and the passage of Bayh-Dole. He suggests that, while the relationship between universities and industry may have evolved (been transformed) in the past few decades, transformation should not be attributed to the Bayh-Dole Act itself. *Id.* On university science and technology research systems as infrastructure, see Frischmann 2143 (2009) (applying infrastructure theory to university science and technology research systems and explaining how patents enable a demand pull on the allocation of university research system resources).

[207] *Opinion, Innovation's Golden Goose*, at 3.

disseminated, to a focused search for results that have practical and industrial purposes. Whether that is a bad thing is a matter of debate. What is not in dispute is that it makes American academic institutions behave more like businesses than neutral arbiters of truth.[208]

Despite various expressions of concern about these types of impacts, the empirical evidence is rather light, in part because institutional change may be slow, subtle, and difficult to measure empirically.

There is a rich literature on the impact of the Bayh-Dole Act and related policies, and my objective here is not to engage in that debate. Instead, let me suggest that for basic research, coupling government funding with a clear dedication to the public domain remains a potentially attractive method for sustaining a commons that relies on neither the government nor the market mechanism to manage access. Yet it may not be enough to "release basic research results into the public domain." It is not as if the public domain is the atmosphere that subsequent users can simply inhale and use. Dissemination and effective transfer of basic research to a community of users often requires additional steps beyond mere "release" to the public domain. What those steps may be depends on the context; in some cases, publication of research results in peer-reviewed journals is critical; in other cases, collaboration among researchers in academia and industry may be critical; in some cases, an open-access repository might suffice.

---

[208] *Baying for Blood* 109 (2005) ("For example, a study published in 2003 by Jerry and Marie Thursby, of Emory University and the Georgia Institute of Technology respectively, showed that more than a quarter of the licenses issued by universities and research institutes include clauses allowing the business partner in the arrangement to delete information from research papers. Almost half allow them to insist on publication being delayed."); Reichman & Uhlir 341 (2003) ("Under Bayh-Dole, universities have moved away from policies that favor pure research, both for its own sake and as a tool for advancing higher education. As the costs of education skyrocket, and government funding fails to keep up in many areas, universities have aggressively sought to exploit commercial applications of research results, with an eye toward maximizing returns on investment."). See generally Kesan (2009) (collecting sources).

Modern Debates

13

THE INTERNET AND THE NETWORK NEUTRALITY DEBATE

IN JUST A few decades, the Internet has grown to become an integral part of our society, economy, and daily lives. In addition to the amazing growth in electronic commerce and innovations unimaginable only two decades ago, the Internet has radically increased entrepreneurship, political discourse, the production and consumption of media, social network formation, and community building, among many other things. The Internet has transformed and continues to transform various information- and communications-dependent systems—our economic, cultural, political, and other social systems. Though such a strong claim of transformation may seem hyperbolic, one need only stop and think for a few moments about how the Internet, like other major infrastructures, affects different aspects of our lives. Consider how the Internet provides and shapes opportunities of individuals, firms, households, and other organizations to interact with each other and participate in various social systems. The scale and scope of possible and actual social interactions alone is staggering. Federal Communications Chairman Julius Genachowski stated the following during a speech he made on December 1, 2010:

> Millions of us depend on the Internet every day: at home, at work, in school—and everywhere in between. The high-speed networks we call broadband are transforming health care, education, and energy usage for the better. It's hard to imagine life today without the Internet—any more than we can imagine life without running water or electricity.

The Internet has been an unprecedented platform for speech and democratic engagement, and a place where the American spirit of innovation has flourished. We've seen new media tools like Twitter and YouTube used by democratic movements around the world. . . . Internet companies have begun as small start-ups, some of them famously in dorm rooms and garages with little more than a computer and access to the open Internet. Many have become large businesses, providing high-paying, high-tech jobs in communities across our country. It's the American dream at work.[1]

It is easy to take such routine benefits for granted, as is commonplace for infrastructure. In a sense, this reveals just how much the Internet has seeped into our lives and subtly affected our perceptions of the world and expectations for what we can do. But we should not take these social benefits and opportunities for granted. The infrastructure, its management, and the various infrastructure-dependent systems are not fixed, predetermined, or a given to be ignored. It is important to understand and appreciate how the Internet generates social value, how Internet infrastructure supports widespread user participation in an incredibly diverse range of productive activities, and how managing the Internet infrastructure as a commons sustains a spillover-rich environment.

* * * *

There are many policy debates in the Internet context involving infrastructure. For example, debates about the domain name system, spectrum allocation, standards and protocols, broadband build-out, and peer production and distribution systems involve concerns about managing/governing infrastructural resources. Nonetheless, this chapter focuses on the particularly contentious "network neutrality" debate.[2] At the heart of this debate is whether the Internet infrastructure will continue to be managed as a commons. Ultimately, the outcome of this debate may very well determine whether the Internet continues to operate as a mixed infrastructure that supports widespread user production of commercial, public, and social goods, or whether it evolves into a commercial infrastructure optimized for the production and delivery of commercial outputs.

The network neutrality debate has been going on for over a decade and will likely persist for another. Some may believe that the debate is winding down because the Federal Communication Commission has promulgated "Open Internet" rules, and others may claim that the debate has been and, if it persists, will continue to be a sideshow because there are many other, more important developments afoot. I do not share these sentiments. The FCC's rule is likely only the first step on a long path, for at least three reasons:

---

[1] Genachowski 1–2 (2010).

[2] This chapter builds on and borrows from a series of published articles, including Frischmann & van Schewick (2007); Frischmann & Lemley (2007); Frischmann (2005a). In particular, it owes a lot to the article with Barbara van Schewick, our extensive discussions on this topic, and her recent book. VAN SCHEWICK (2010).

first, it will be challenged in the courts for years; second, it will be implemented at the agency level and will evolve case by case in regulatory proceedings and, consequently, litigation in courts for years; third, it is substantively incomplete, as I discuss below.[3]

A. Internet Infrastructure and Commons Management through End-to-End Design

The Internet consists of many infrastructure resources. Scholars have delineated two macro-level infrastructure resources. The *physical infrastructure* consists of a wide variety of physical networks interconnected with each other, while the *logical infrastructure* consists of the standards and protocols that facilitate seamless transmission of data across different types of physical networks.[4] Both the physical and the logical infrastructure act as essential inputs into end-user production of an incredibly wide variety of outputs, typically described in terms of applications and content. In contrast with the upstream-downstream/input-output terminology used elsewhere in this book to describe the functional relationships between infrastructure and infrastructure-dependent activities and the goods or services that flow from such activities, Internet scholars use layered models of the Internet to distinguish complementary resources as layers based on the functions each layer performs.[5] The number of layers in particular models varies.[6]

For our purposes, the five-layered model illustrated in table 13.1 is sufficient. The physical and logical infrastructures are the foundational layers on which the Internet environment has been built. I refer to the physical and logical infrastructure together as Internet infrastructure and to the applications, content, and social relationships as downstream outputs. In past work, I did not include the social layer,[7] but I do so here to reinforce the point that social goods, including social networks and social capital, are an incredibly important and socially valuable output from Internet use.

---

[3] Regarding the claim that it is a sideshow, I cannot offer a counterargument without getting into the details of other important developments and a comparative analysis. Such a move is unnecessary. While I disagree with the claim, it is perhaps more appropriate to simply emphasize that whatever the candidates for more important developments might be (e.g., interconnection, peering arrangements, spectrum allocation, the domain name system), they are highly likely to implicate the same set of underlying demand-side issues.

[4] Benkler (2000b).

[5] Farrell & Weiser 90–91 (2004); Werbach 57–64 (2002); Sicker & Mindel (2002).

[6] The basic Open Systems Interconnection Model separates Internet infrastructure into the following seven layers: physical; data; network; transport; session; presentation; application. The application layer is the layer with which the user interacts. OSI Model, OSI Model, http://www.osimodel.org/ (last visited Mar. 10, 2011).

[7] I discussed social goods but not a social layer. Frischmann (2005a). On a social layer, see ZITTRAIN 67 (2008) (describing a "'social layer,' where new behaviors and interactions among people are enabled by the technologies underneath"); Madison (2006) (social software); Crawford 699 n. 12 (2005) (social protocol layer).

TABLE 13.1   Five-Layer Model of the Internet

Layer	Description	Examples
Social	Relations and social ties among users	Social networks, affiliations, groups
Content	Information/data conveyed to end-users	E-mail communication, music, web page
Applications	Programs and functions used by end-users	E-mail program, media player, web browser
Logical Infrastructure	Standards and protocols that facilitate transmission of data across physical networks	TCP/IP, domain name system
Physical Infrastructure	Physical hardware that comprises interconnected networks	Telecommunications, cable and satellite networks, routers and servers, backbone networks

The current Internet infrastructure evolved with the so-called "end-to-end" design principle as its central tenet.[8] To preserve its "robustness and evolvability" and to allow applications to be easily layered on top of it, the broad version of this design principle recommends that the lower layers of the network be as general as possible, while all application-specific functionality should be concentrated in higher layers at end hosts.[9] End-to-end design is implemented in the logical infrastructure through the Internet Protocol (IP), which provides a general technology- and application-independent interface to the lower layers of the network.[10]

As a consequence of this design, the lower layers of the network were blind as to the identity of the use (often referred to as "application-blind"); this prevented infrastructure providers from distinguishing between and affecting execution of the applications and content of network communications.[11] In other words, it precludes discrimination based on the identity of the use.

---

[8] There are two versions of the end-to-end arguments. VAN SCHEWICK 96–105 (2010). When I refer to "end-to-end," I am referring to the broad version.

[9] VAN SCHEWICK 96–105 (2010); Isenberg 24–31 (1998).

[10] VAN SCHEWICK 116–23 (2010) (describing how the Internet Protocol implements the two versions of end-to-end arguments). *Internet Protocol: DARPA Internet Program Protocol Specification*, IETF RFC 791 (September 1981), http://www.ietf.org/rfc/rfc0791.txt? number=791 (formally describing IP). Notably, the logical infrastructure—protocols, standards, and so on—are managed as commons.

[11] VAN SCHEWICK 101–3 (2010); Lemley & Lessig 931 (2001).

User identity also was largely obscured. Data packets routed through the various networks that comprise the physical infrastructure utilize IP addresses and do not directly reveal user identity.[12] Of course, access networks know the identities of their own customers,[13] but they did not know the identity of everyone else with whom their customers interact online. Networks could discriminate on the basis of IP address itself—for example, by blocking traffic originating from a particular IP address, perhaps because an end node (destination) is under persistent attack by another end node (source) sending spam or malicious viruses.[14] Such blocking is end-to-end compliant when practiced at the "edges" (end hosts), for example, when end-users choose to block unwanted content using their browser or block spam using their e-mail program or when an e-mail service provider blocks spam at the mail server. In many situations, access networks are vertically integrated and also act as edge providers (end-systems), for example where access networks host content, run server-based applications, and provide related services for their customers. A mail server is an end-point, whether owned and managed by an access network such as Comcast or by a customer of the access network. As noted, blocking traffic at the mail server is a routine method for handling spam and other forms of unwanted content that is end-to-end compliant.[15] On the other hand, if an access network blocked or otherwise discriminated in the treatment of traffic not destined for its mail servers or comparable end-points—for example, by blocking peer-to-peer traffic destined for a customer's home computer—then the access network would violate end-to-end principles.

---

[12] "Every end-user's computer that is connected to the Internet is assigned a unique Internet Protocol number ('IP address'), such as 123.456.78.90, that identifies its location (i.e., a particular computer-to-network connection) and serves as the routing address for e-mail, pictures, requests to view a web page, and [any] other data sent across the Internet from other end-users. This IP address routing system is essential to the basic functionality of the Internet, in a similar fashion as mailing addresses and telephone numbers are essential to the functionality of the postal service and telecommunications system." Register.com v. Verio, 356 F.3d 393 (2d Cir. 2004). See *Glossary of Internet Terminology*, INTERNET CORPORATION FOR ASSIGNED NAMES AND NUMBERS, http://www.icann.org/en/general/glossary.htm (last modified Aug. 13, 2010) ("Internet Protocol Address is the numerical address by which a location in the Internet is identified. Computers on the Internet use IP addresses to route traffic and establish connections among themselves . . .").

[13] Access networks are the subset of infrastructure providers that connect end-users. Some infrastructure providers, such as backbone networks, may interconnect networks but not connect end-users.

[14] Still, user identity was obscure; it was very difficult, if not impossible, to block effectively based on the identity of the user because it is not easy to tie addresses to specific users. For example, in residential networks, IP addresses often are assigned dynamically and shared over time as people log off and on; several users may share an IP address through a network address translator; a server may host a wide variety of different users; and so on.

[15] Comcast filters inbound and outbound spam at the server level and blacklists IP addresses that send excessive amounts of spam. See *What Is Comcast Doing about Spam*, COMCAST, http://customer.comcast.com/Pages/FAQViewer.aspx?seoid=What-is-Comcast-doing-about-spam (last visited Feb. 26, 2011). Comcast does not apply its spam filter to other e-mail applications, such as Gmail. This is acceptable because discrimination effectively occurs at the application layer rather than the infrastructure layers. There may be reasons to be concerned about this practice, but this chapter will not address nondiscrimination rules at the higher layers.

End-to-end design sustains an infrastructure commons by insulating end-users from market-driven restrictions on access and use of the infrastructure.[16] If infrastructure providers follow end-to-end principles strictly, they cannot distinguish between end-uses, base access decisions or pricing on how packets may be used, or optimize the infrastructure for a particular class of end-uses. For the most part, infrastructure providers are ignorant of the identity of the end-users and end-uses.[17] At the same time, end-users and end-uses are ignorant of the various networks that transport data packets (with the exception of access networks).[18] In a sense, shared ignorance is built into the infrastructure through widespread compliance with the end-to-end design principle.[19]

Functionally, the end-to-end principle acts as a limitation on the property rights of network owners, in much the same way that common carriage operates as a limitation on the rights of common carriers, fair use operates as a limitation on the rights of copyright owners, and environmental regulations operate as a limit on the rights of various property owners. But the end-to-end principle is not law, and because circumstances have changed, network owners may decide to abandon it.[20]

There is considerable pressure for change. First, there is pressure to replace the existing "dumb," open architecture with an "intelligent," restrictive architecture capable of differentiating and discriminating among end-uses and end-users. Second, there is pressure for network owners to internalize externalities more fully and appropriate the value of the Internet. This pressure comes from many sources, including the Internet's evolution from narrowband to broadband,[21] the rapid increase in users,[22] demand for latency-sensitive and jitter-sensitive applications such as massively multiplayer online role-playing games (MMORGs) and IP telephony,[23] demand for security measures and spam-regulation

---

[16] LESSIG 46 (2001b); Frischmann 1007–22 (2005a); Frischmann & Lemley 294–96 (2007).

[17] Ohm 1450–51 (2009) (referring to this as a structural constraint right in privacy, because providers did not have the capacity or technology to determine identity).

[18] Frischmann 27 (2001).

[19] Id.

[20] Some have, at least in some contexts. *Comcast Network Management Practices Order*, 23 FCC Rcd 13028, at ¶ 9 (2008), http://hraunfoss.fcc.gov/edocs_public/attachmatch/FCC-08-183A1.pdf. As with many voluntary commons arrangements, defection by community members may be an attractive private strategy, especially if detection is difficult and punishment or enforcement mechanisms are weak.

[21] *Broadband Access Grows 29 Percent, While Narrowband Declines, According to Nielsen//NetRatings*, NIELSEN// NETRATINGS (Jan. 15, 2003); Kerner (2008); Smith 6 (2010) (showing that broadband use overtook narrowband use at the end of 2004, and in May 2010, broadband had been adopted by 66 percent of American adults (increasingly), and narrowband had been adopted by 5 percent of adults (decreasingly)).

[22] Between 2000 and 2010, the total number of global Internet users grew by 444.8 percent. *Top 20 Countries with the Highest Number of Internet Users*, INTERNET WORLD STATS (last modified Aug. 21, 2010).

[23] Regarding MMORGs, World of Warcraft, for example, has over 12 million subscribers as of Oct. 7, 2010. Press release, Blizzard Entertainment, World of Warcraft Subscriber Base Reaches 12 Million Worldwide (Oct. 17, 2010), http://us.blizzard.com/en-us/company/press/pressreleases.html?101007. World of Warcraft has a 58 percent share in the MMORG market as of 2009. Crossley (2009). Regarding IP telephony, Skype has shown immense

measures implemented at the "core" of the Internet (rather than at the ends), and demand for increased returns on infrastructure investments.[24]

In response to these pressures, technology has become available that enables network owners to "look into" the packets traveling across their networks to determine the application or web page they belong to and affect the transport of packets based on this information.[25] This technology violates the broad end-to-end principle, but again, because end-to-end is just a design principle, there is nothing that forces technology to comply with it.[26] Many other methods for getting around end-to-end design and identifying users or uses have emerged. For example, access providers routinely monitor traffic, relying on pattern recognition and other techniques to identify uses—for example, to identify packets used in e-mail, IP telephony, or peer-to-peer applications.[27] In addition, the Federal Communications Commission (FCC) removed most of the regulations that governed the behavior of providers of broadband networks in the past by classifying the provision of broadband Internet access services over cable or DSL as an "information service."[28]

These developments have given rise to the "network neutrality" debate.[29] The central issues are whether and if so how government regulation should disable the ability of network providers to discriminate among uses or users of the Internet.

---

growth since its inception. By August 10, 2010, the service had 560 million registered users, though only 124 million of them used it on a monthly basis. Waters 21 (2010).

[24] Blumenthal & Clark 71 (2001). ZITTRAIN (2008).

[25] Anderson (2007); Cherry 61 (2005); CISCO SYSTEMS, INC., *Network-Based Application Recognition*, http://www.cisco.com/en/US/products/ps6616/products_ios_protocol_group_home.html (last visited Mar. 4, 2011).

[26] VAN SCHEWICK (2010).

[27] These methods include Packet Sniffers/Analyzers (see R. Kayne, *What Is a Packet Sniffer*, WISEGEEK, http://www.wisegeek.com/what-is-a-packet-sniffer.htm (last modified Feb. 24, 2011)) and Deep Packet Capture (see Solera Networks, *Network Forensics*, http://www.soleranetworks.com/network-forensics/our-network-forensics-technology/capture (last visited Feb. 26, 2011)).

[28] Appropriate Framework for Broadband Access to the Internet over Wireline Facilities, Report and Order and Notice of Proposed Rulemaking, 20 FCC Rcd. 14853 (2005) (hereinafter Wireline Broadband Access Order). Before, the FCC's decision to classify the provision of broadband Internet access services over cable modems as an "information service" had been upheld by the Supreme Court (see Nat'l Cable & Telecomm. Ass'n v. Brand X Internet Servs., 545 U.S. 967 (2005), aff'g Inquiry Concerning High-Speed Access to the Internet Over Cable and Other Facilities, Internet Over Cable Declaratory Ruling, Appropriate Regulatory Treatment for Broadband Access to the Internet Over Cable Facilities, Declaratory Ruling and Notice of Proposed Rulemaking, 17 FCC Rcd. 4798 (2002) (hereinafter Cable Modem Declaratory Ruling and NPRM)).

[29] Though the debate has roots in an earlier debate about whether to impose open-access requirements on owners of physical networks, our focus is on the network neutrality debate, as reflected in the recent FCC Report and Order. FCC Report and Order, *Preserving the Open Internet; Broadband Industry Practices*, GN Docket No. 09-191, WC Docket No. 07-52, FCC 10-201, http://hraunfoss.fcc.gov/edocs_public/attachmatch/FCC-10-201A1.pdf (released Dec. 23, 2010).

B. The Network Neutrality Debate

In this section, I first explain why network neutrality is not exactly about neutrality. Because bias of one form or another is inevitable, the real issue is (or ought to be) which type of bias to tolerate. Second, I explain how the debate often is framed in narrow economic terms, and how this framing myopically ignores the most important issues and distorts the debate. Third, I explain how framing the debate in terms of innovation is also too narrow. Innovation is extremely important and a critical source of much social value; however, it is but one of many user activities that generates public and social goods. In short, the current framing of the debate risks missing the forest for the trees. The next section explains how a demand-side approach helps to reframe the debate.

I. NETWORK "NEUTRALITY"

In an influential pair of articles, Tim Wu framed the network neutrality debate by asking whether and how the Internet should be made neutral.[30] Wu and Lawrence Lessig submitted an ex parte letter to the FCC explaining their view that the Commission should embrace network neutrality.[31]

How does the end-to-end design principle relate to network neutrality? Although often conflated, network neutrality is not equivalent to retaining the end-to-end architecture of the Internet.[32] On one hand, the blindness of the network is only one consequence of applying end-to-end principles; end-to-end design is much broader than network neutrality. On the other hand, network neutrality does not necessarily require end-to-end compatible protocols, such as the Internet Protocol. There are alternative means for implementing a nondiscrimination rule.

Implementing a commons via end-to-end network design might appear "neutral" to applications, while shifting to an "intelligent" network design capable of allocating access to the infrastructure based on the identity of the uses (users) appears "non-neutral." Yet end-to-end design is not really neutral. Like commons management in general, it effectively precludes prioritization based on the demands of users or uses. Such prioritization is referred to as differentiated quality of service (QoS)[33] because such an allocation regime would provide quality-of-service guarantees to particular users and uses. End-to-end design effectively disfavors those users or uses that demand such QoS guarantees.

---

[30] Wu (2003); Wu (2004). Wu is credited with coining the term "network neutrality."

[31] Wu & Lessig 3 n. 3 (2003).

[32] Van Schewick 72–73 (2010).

[33] The Internet currently provides best effort data delivery, a simple form of QoS. *Id.* at 7–8. There are different types of QoS, some of which are "more consistent" with end-to-end than others. Lessig 47 (2001b).

One might wonder why an application user might demand guaranteed QoS. The answer is that the Internet infrastructure is congestible and the consequential costs of congestion vary among users and uses. *If and only if there is congestion*, some applications feel the effects more than others, and thus the costs of congestion may be greater for some users than others. Put another way, *user demand for QoS* depends completely on the existence of congestion; users have no need for QoS on an uncongested network.[34] Thus, the shape of user demand will depend on the degree, distribution, and persistence of congestion and the demand for various user activities. In sharp contrast, *provider demand for QoS* does not depend on congestion, because the possibility of extracting greater surplus from consumers via price discrimination makes QoS attractive, even when there is no congestion.

User demand for QoS is a common phenomenon on congestible infrastructure, and it is not unique to or necessarily more severe on the Internet. To take a non-Internet example, consider how congestion might impact drivers on the highway differently—compare the person going to the hospital or an important time-sensitive business meeting with the person going to a friend's house or out to eat. Delays associated with congestion impact these drivers differently. Yet, as discussed in chapter 9, guaranteed QoS/priority is not for sale on most roads.[35] On the Internet, certain applications feel the effects of congestion more intensely than others, and, knowing this, certain application-providers and users might prefer to purchase guaranteed prioritization through QoS. For example, latency- or jitter-sensitive applications, such as World of Warcraft and Skype, might suffer in quality because congestion causes delays in the routing of packets, variations in such delays, or packet loss, and these congestion-related effects can lead customers to value their experience less. (By contrast, a user checking e-mail, surfing the Internet, or using AOL Instant Messenger is less inconvenienced by congestion.) Latency- or jitter-sensitive applications would fare better during congestion on an infrastructure that prioritized access and use according to the identity of the application. Thus, despite the appeal to neutrality, critics of network neutrality are quick to point out (correctly) that

---

[34] One exception is that some users may want to purchase priority for strategic reasons, for example, to crowd out others and/or obtain a competitive advantage.

[35] Of course, in many commercial contexts, priority arrangements are available. Consider, for example, shelf space at the supermarket. Some economists place great weight on the efficiencies of such arrangements in those contexts and attack restrictions on the freedom to do the same in the Internet infrastructure context. But it is important to be clear that those contexts do not involve basic infrastructure at all. Shelf space at the grocery store is rivalrous, and it solely involves the distribution of private goods to consumers (rather than the user-generated public or social goods). Accordingly, for shelf space, the three economic principles discussed in chapter 3 apply, and it seems reasonable to expect that priority arrangements, like many other vertical arrangements among private market actors, would be efficient; the main concern is whether there are significant anti-competitive effects. There is much more at stake in the Internet context. As the next section explains, it would be a major mistake to conflate the Internet infrastructure context with commercial contexts such as shelf space at the grocery store.

nondiscrimination rules are not neutral because they effectively discriminate against users and uses that would benefit under a regime that permits discrimination.

Yet such applications would fare as well on an uncongested infrastructure that did not provide prioritization. The critics assume a congested infrastructure and are most concerned with efficiently allocating scarce infrastructure capacity to its highest valued use, measured, not surprisingly, by users' willingness to pay. The appropriateness of the assumption and the magnitude of congestion and related effects remain quite contentious.[36]

End-to-end design favors one set of applications; shifting to differentiated QoS favors another set. This point escapes critics of network neutrality and remains unappreciated in the debate. But it is worth emphasis: Just as the current end-to-end design favors certain applications at the expense of time-sensitive applications (assuming, for purposes of argument, a congested infrastructure), shifting to a fine-grained QoS regime also would exhibit a systematic bias for particular applications—specifically, for commercial applications that generate observable and appropriable returns. The bias would not be technologically determined, as in the case of end-to-end design; rather, it would be determined by the conventional operation of the market mechanism. Given the ability to discriminate among end-users and end-uses on a packet-by-packet basis and the inability to perfectly price discriminate, infrastructure suppliers rationally may prioritize access and use of the infrastructure via imperfect price or quality discrimination and/or optimize infrastructure design in favor of output markets that generate the highest levels of appropriable returns (producer surplus), at the expense of output markets that generate a larger aggregate surplus (direct consumer surplus, producer surplus, and external surplus).

The bottom line is that one way or another, some bias in the system is inevitable. When confronted with this argument, critics shift gears and suggest that no such bias would occur because all users would obtain access and use. Such a move depends on an assumption either that discrimination will increase output dramatically or that congestion no longer matters. Neither assumption makes sense. I explain these points in further detail below. To overemphasize neutrality or non-neutrality merely distracts from the more important issue, which is how best to manage the infrastructure, given predictable biases.

2. THE ROLE OF ANTITRUST AND REGULATORY ECONOMICS

Network neutrality involves complex interdisciplinary issues, and economics plays a critical role in framing the debate. The central issue is whether government regulation should

---

[36] The congestion-related effects are *not* a consequence of interaction effects or incompatibilities among uses. See chapter 7. (Perhaps the easiest way to recall how such effects arise is to imagine the fighting buffaloes and goats hypo.)

disable the ability of network providers to discriminate among uses or users. This issue triggers familiar economic considerations, discussed extensively in earlier chapters.

Unfortunately, here as in other infrastructure contexts, the case for regulation imposing nondiscrimination rules tends to be evaluated exclusively in terms of antitrust and regulatory economics.[37] As discussed in chapter 5, the antitrust and regulatory economics traditions largely disfavor government intervention into private infrastructure markets for a variety of reasons, most of which permeate the network neutrality debate. Recall that antitrust and regulatory economics adopt the premises that intervention is needed only when markets are not competitive and that even when markets are not competitive, intervention is justified only in very narrow circumstances where demonstrable harm to consumers in the relevant markets can be shown and not outweighed by efficiency gains.

The focus on competition and demonstrable harm to consumers is completely misguided. It distorts the debate dramatically and distracts participants from the more important, fundamental question, which is what type of Internet environment our society demands. Before I attempt to reframe the debate around this question, I highlight three related ways in which the debate is distorted: (1) the supply-chain view of the Internet, (2) the false supplier/consumer dichotomy, and (3) the competition red herring.

a. The Supply-Chain View of the Internet

First, the antitrust and regulatory economics framework views the Internet as a mere supply chain: network access → applications and content → consumers. More "sophisticated" versions of the supply chain view incorporate so-called "two-sided" markets, where economists put networks in between application/content providers and consumers (essentially, applications and content → network access → consumers) and consider how networks will be able to efficiently mediate transactions between each side of the market.[38] But either of these frameworks leaves the partial-equilibrium blinders on and

---

[37] Barbara van Schewick suggested to me that I go too far in this section because proponents of network neutrality regulation have incorporated arguments from outside of antitrust and regulatory economics and fought against the distortions I note in the text. While I support these efforts and have participated in some of them, for example by submitting a comment in the FCC's Open Internet proceeding, I am not convinced that the network neutrality debate has fully internalized the arguments or broken out of the antitrust and regulatory economics framework. I would love to be persuaded otherwise. I do appreciate that in its Report and Order, the FCC expressed similar concerns and an awareness of the broader set of issues that are not well accounted for by the antitrust and regulatory economics framework. Regardless, the point of this section remains relevant and important because the antitrust and regulatory economics framework still has considerable influence.

[38] Weisman & Kulick 87 (2010) (considering auctions, credit cards, dating bars, newspapers, video game consoles, and the Yellow Pages as examples; defining a two-sided market as any market that brings together two distinct user groups that both benefit from the presence of the other); Yoo 96–97 (2010) ("[B]roadcast television . . . brings together two groups: viewers and advertisers."); Ratliff & Rubinfeld 659–60 n. 34 (2010) ("The sale of

reduces an incredibly complex, open system to an inappropriately simple closed system for purposes of analysis, evaluation, and policy making.[39]

The simple supply-chain view assumes complete markets and ignores incomplete and missing markets despite their prevalence in the actual Internet environment. As discussed below, the incomplete and missing markets often involve user-generated public and social goods. The slightly more sophisticated, two-sided market view may incorporate some incomplete markets, but only where the relevant externalities are within the closed system of markets being considered—that is, when the external effect are effects on one side or the other of the mediated market. This is convenient because it allows modelers to examine whether the intermediary will set prices efficiently, but it still assumes away externalities associated with the production, sharing, use, and reuse of public and social goods that are felt outside the closed system. It also fails to appreciate the complexity associated with the fact that the Internet involves many, interdependent many-sided markets and nonmarkets.

Let me make the point using a series of simple illustrations in which CM = complete market; IM = incomplete market; MM = missing market; and NI = network intermediary. (Alternatively, we could illustrate the point by using private, public, social, and network goods rather than markets and network intermediaries.) First, consider the Internet reduced to a two-sided market/closed system:[40]

(1) $CM_1 \longleftrightarrow NI \longleftrightarrow CM_2$

(2) $IM_1 \longleftrightarrow NI \longleftrightarrow IM_2$

In (2), incompleteness in the markets constitutes externalities flowing from one side to the other (from IM_1 to IM_2, or vice versa) and capable of being internalized if the intermediary sets differential prices to account for the externalities.

Second, consider a series of slight transformations that move incrementally toward reality but drastically away from the closed-system view in (1) and (2). Consider what happens when we make the following transformations.

(3) $IM_1, CM_1 \longleftrightarrow NI \longleftrightarrow CM_2, IM_2, MM_1$

In (3), the missing market constitutes externalities that flow outside the system (or off-network) and thus do not flow to any of the other markets within the system.

---

advertising to businesses and the display of advertisements to consumers take place in a *two-sided market* at the hub of which sits the content publisher ... ").

[39] On the problems with these blinders, see Lipsey & Lancaster (1956); Lunney (2008).

[40] I describe this as a supply chain and thus multiple markets with the intermediary being a participant in the various markets, for example, as a service provider. The two-sided market literature sometimes focuses narrowly on a single market with two or more sides.

(4) $MM_1, IM_1, CM_1 \longleftrightarrow NI \longleftrightarrow CM_2, IM_2, MM_2$

(5) $MM_1, MM_2, IM_1, IM_2, CM_1, CM_2 \longleftrightarrow NI \longleftrightarrow CM_3, CM_4, IM_3, IM_4,$
MM_3, MM_4

(6) $MM_1, IM_1, CM_1 \longleftrightarrow NI_1 \longleftrightarrow CM_3, NI_2 \longleftrightarrow CM_2, IM_2, MM_2$

In (6), a second network intermediary connects various user populations.

(7) And so on.

Although we are still not close to reality, it should be clear how the models in (1) and (2) distort dramatically by omission.

Keep in mind that the externalities need not flow to the other side of the two-sided or multisided market; the externalities may flow off the network altogether; the network intermediary is incapable of accounting for, much less efficiently pricing, various types of externalities. The NI certainly has incentives to set prices *as if* the Internet fit model (1) or (2), and it is precisely these distorted (and distorting) incentives that jeopardize the Internet that exists in reality.

b. The False Supplier/Consumer Dichotomy

Second, the framework leads to misconceptions of the actors involved. Specifically, in accordance with the supply-chain view of the Internet, the focus is how network neutrality would affect (a) network providers, (b) application and content providers, and (c) consumers.[41] This framing conflates too much, by creating a false distinction between application and content providers and other end-users and understating the role of consumers as producers. Users produce a wide range of private, public, and social goods, including various applications and content. Google is an end-user, like you, me, or anyone else. We are different in some ways—for example, in the amount of traffic or revenue we generate—but not necessarily in a way that matters (or should matter) to the network neutrality debate. I, you, or anyone else could be the next Google or perhaps the Google of our own "space" on the Internet. Who knows where the next killer app, idea, or YouTube video will come from?

The key point is that viewing the Internet as a means for distributing content, applications, and services to consumers biases the debate in a way that misses the forest for the trees. (As the next section discusses, it reduces the Internet to a commercial infrastructure, although the Internet is a mixed infrastructure.) The social value produced by users as well as the basic capabilities/opportunities for users to be productive are

---

[41] Many commentators recognize the flaws in this point of view. See, e.g., Mehra (2011); BENKLER (2006b). In its Report and Order, the FCC seems to as well. FCC R&O paragraphs 2, 20.

marginalized if not outright ignored. The Internet is much more than a low-cost delivery system for application or content providers or a two-sided market with networks acting as intermediaries between providers and consumers. While the supply-chain view of the relationships among different actors and the corresponding categorization of actors yield a familiar conceptual map, tractable models, and (perhaps) measurable data points, such comforts do not excuse the distortions.

c. The Competition Red Herring

Finally, the debate has been fixated on competition or the lack thereof.[42] As Jonathan Nuechterlein explains:

> most advocacy for net neutrality regulation argues that there is inadequate competition in the market for broadband Internet access and that the government should step in to prevent abuses of the resulting market power. If each American consumer had a choice of ten broadband Internet access providers, *there would be no credible basis for such intervention, because competition would ensure each provider's responsiveness to consumer choice.*[43]

I suspect that many (though not all) proponents of network neutrality would probably concede that regulation would not be necessary if Internet access markets were competitive. The debate has revolved around whether network owners have market power and whether discrimination among data packets causes anticompetitive effects or demonstrable harm to consumers.[44] Proponents of network neutrality regulation claim that network owners have the market power, capability, and incentives to engage in harmful discrimination; opponents claim that the relevant markets are competitive and that any discrimination practiced by network owners is presumably beneficial. To be fair, participants on both sides of the debate appeal to other considerations.[45] For example, an important strand of the debate focuses on innovation, which I discuss below. Another important strand of the debate focuses on the question of what form of public regulation might be appropriate. Does antitrust provide a sufficient check on discrimination, or should the FCC create additional sector-specific regulations?[46] If more regulations are

---

[42] Barbara Van Schewick criticized me for saying this once at a conference. As I mentioned, she told me that the debate has moved on. For her rejection of the idea that competition would make network neutrality regulation unnecessary, see VAN SCHEWICK 255–64 (2010).

[43] Nuechterlein 19, 34 (2009) (emphasis added).

[44] The FCC rejected the idea that only anticompetitive discrimination should be prohibited, FCC R&O paragraphs 77–78, and instead prohibited unreasonable discrimination. I discuss this briefly below.

[45] A survey of the voluminous literature or comments filed in the FCC Proceeding reveals an extremely wide range of arguments.

[46] See, e.g., Nuechterlein (2009).

needed, what form should the regulations take (e.g., a rule versus a standard)? Nonetheless, these strands are heavily influenced by the more basic competition policy framework and its premises. For example, the one "intervention" accepted by both sides of the debate—transparency—suffers from this myopia and its attendant problems. Transparency is perceived as an adequate solution because it would enable consumers to be effective market participants, capable of disciplining access providers by making a fuss about harmful discrimination and switching providers.[47] There are at least three problems with this "solution." First, it presumes that consumers have the time, inclination, and capability to process and react to the information made available. Second, it presumes competition. Third, and perhaps most important, it presumes complete markets in which consumer demand effectively manifests societal demand. Simply put, transparency is important, but transparency alone would not be enough to preserve the social benefits of an open Internet.[48]

Framed as a "lack of competition" problem, the debate ignores demand-side issues by assuming that private demand reflected in markets fully reflects social demand (as the quote above from Nuechterlein suggests). As a result, it fails to appreciate that the social value of the Internet greatly exceeds its market value and that relying on unfettered market allocation of infrastructure access and use runs the risk of demand-side market failures of the sort described in chapters 4 and 5.

Competition alone does not alleviate the demand-side concerns discussed at length in chapter 5.[49] Competition does not ensure an efficient allocation of resources. It does not assure us an Internet environment that maximizes social welfare. Competition does not address these interests for the same reasons that antitrust law is orthogonal to environmental law—antitrust law does not address market failures associated with externalities, whether environmental pollution (negative externalities) or the production, sharing, and productive reuse of public and social goods (positive externalities). Indeed, it is well established in economics that competitive markets overproduce pollution and underproduce public and social goods. Moreover, conventional economic solutions to the underproduction of public goods, such as directing subsidies to public goods producers, do not work well in this context because of the incredible variety of producers and of public goods, and governments' predictable failure in choosing how to direct subsidies in

---

[47] There are other reasons transparency is desirable. FCC R&O paragraphs 53–60.

[48] The FCC also concluded that transparency alone is not sufficient. See *id.* paragraph 61.

[49] First, it does not alleviate concerns about undersupply and underuse of infrastructure, and undersupply of infrastructure-dependent public and social goods. Second, it does not alleviate concerns about dynamic shifts in the nature of infrastructure resources—that infrastructure development may be skewed in socially undesirable directions. This could happen, for example, if private infrastructure owners prematurely optimize infrastructure for uses that they expect will maximize their *private* returns and, in doing so, choose a path that forecloses production of various public or social goods that would yield greater net *social* returns.

this context. Further, the conventional economic solutions do not work well for social goods that are jointly produced in a more distributed fashion.[50]

Even if we assume robust competition,[51] the case for network neutrality remains strong.[52] As the next section discusses in more detail, the Internet infrastructure is a mixed infrastructure that when managed as a commons supports a spillover-rich environment. A tremendous amount of the social value derives from activities by and among users associated with producing, sharing, and reusing ideas and other intellectual and social goods. Spillover effects associated with speech, information flows, social interactions, and other related activities are rampant and arguably should define the relevant policy space.

This does not mean that market power and anticompetitive effects do not matter or do not provide justification for network neutrality regulation, nor does it mean that recognizing the existence and importance of spillovers associated with user-generated public and social goods provides easy, determinate answers. The network neutrality debate is and must be complicated; it should not be reduced to a competition policy framework. It needs to grapple with the demand-side issues, including the social value associated with spillovers from a wide variety of user-generated public and social goods, and the role of commons management in sustaining the social option value of the Internet.

3. INNOVATION

For many, the network neutrality debate is fundamentally about innovation policy.[53] There are very good reasons to focus on innovation. First, innovation itself is crucial because it fuels technological advancement, economic growth, human development, and social progress. Second, the Internet infrastructure has undoubtedly facilitated an incredible amount of innovation, contributed significantly to economic growth, and distributed the capability to innovate widely among Internet users.

---

[50] See chapters 3, 5. On social production, see BENKLER (2006b).

[51] Admittedly, this is a heroic assumption. Still, I will not address the debate over the existence and robustness of competition. For a discussion, see VAN SCHEWICK 251–64 (2010).

[52] I thus strongly disagree with Nuechterlein 42 (2009):

> Proposals for net neutrality rules could have merit only if (i) the broadband Internet access market is inadequately competitive and will remain so indefinitely; (ii) such market concentration will give incumbent broadband providers both the incentive and the ability to discriminate against specific applications providers; (iii) such discrimination would harm *consumers* and not just particular *providers*; and (iv) any such consumer harm would exceed the costs of regulatory intervention. In short, the net neutrality debate, properly conceived, is fundamentally about core antitrust concepts: about market power, market failures, market definition, and the costs and benefits of government intervention in a rapidly evolving, high-technology market.

[53] For an excellent discussion of the relationship between innovation and network neutrality, see VAN SCHEWICK 270–73, 289–92 (2010).

Proponents of network neutrality emphasize, among other things, how an open Internet has supported an incredibly productive innovation system; opponents emphasize, among other things, how government regulation threatens to limit innovation by networks and foreclose opportunities to develop new technologies and services that might thrive in an environment that permitted prioritization and optimization of networks for specialized uses. As Wu has noted, both sides "idoliz[e] innovation."[54] He characterizes the debate in terms of a battle over competing views of what best promotes innovation: an open system that sustains decentralized innovation and prevents centralized control (whether by governments or private infrastructure owners), or an unregulated system free of government interference and subject only to market forces.[55]

Lessig, a major proponent of sustaining the end-to-end design, focuses extensively on the notion of an *innovation commons* and the idea that experimenting and tinkering with—and creating without inhibition—new applications and content are critical productive activities facilitated by the end-to-end architecture of the Internet.[56] In an earlier article, I suggested that Lessig should not focus exclusively on innovation because the term generally referred to commercial innovation;[57] he replied that our disagreement was semantic and made clear that he viewed innovation much more broadly than commercial innovation.[58] I appreciate the broader perspective on innovation and agree that many noncommercial entities innovate and that there are many examples of socially valuable noncommercial innovations. Still, I think that a focus on innovation is not enough.

Innovation is an integral part of the debate, but it ought not be the linchpin on which the end-to-end architecture of the Internet hangs. Innovation—commercial and otherwise—is a vitally important activity furthered by end-to-end architecture. The open Internet greatly enhances users' innovative capability, the capability to experiment, tinker, and put new ideas into practice without the approval of networks acting as gatekeepers.[59] Many users exercise that capability and thereby generate substantial social value. According to Christiaan Hogendorn, "[t]he most dramatic source of spillovers on the Internet is innovation."[60] As one of the critical drivers of economic growth, innovation is an important economic activity to encourage.

Yet innovation entails some degree of novelty, and many of the most valuable Internet applications are not (or are no longer) new, improved, or very innovative—for example, e-mail or instant messaging.[61] While end-to-end architecture undoubtedly promotes

---

[54] Wu 80–84 (2004).

[55] *Id.* at 80–84; Wu 152–54 (2003); Wu & Lessig 5–7 (2003).

[56] LESSIG (2001b); Lessig (2005).

[57] Frischmann (2005a).

[58] Lessig (2005).

[59] Lessig (2004b). See also KELTY (2008) (making similar points with respect to open-source software).

[60] Hogendorn 14 (2010).

[61] Of course, there may be plenty of room for further innovation in these communications technologies.

innovation, bringing us valuable new applications and opportunities,[62] it also promotes the continued use of socially valuable, but perhaps less innovative, applications. To put it another way, we should acknowledge the limits of innovation as a concept because the capability to innovate is but one of the important Internet-enabled user capabilities sustained by a nondiscriminatory infrastructure.

C. Reframing the Debate

This section first discusses the nature of the Internet as mixed infrastructure and the significant role of users in generating social value. It then considers whether commons management is an attractive public strategy.

I. THE INTERNET AS MIXED INFRASTRUCTURE

The Internet satisfies all three demand-side criteria for infrastructure. The Internet infrastructure is a partially (non)rival resource; it is consumed both nonrivalrously and rivalrously, depending on available capacity. The physical infrastructure and certain components of the logical infrastructure, such as domain name space, are partially (non)rival in the sense that they are congestible but not necessarily congested; the risk of congestion depends on the amount of capacity, number of users, and other contextual factors.[63] As the next section discusses, congestion can be managed in a nondiscriminatory manner that sustains the commons and leverages nonrivalry.

The benefits of the Internet are generated at the ends. Like a road system, a telecommunications network, an ocean, and basic research, the Internet is socially valuable primarily because of the wide variety of productive activities it facilitates. End-users generate value and realize benefits through their activities, which involve running applications on their computers; generating, consuming, and using content; and creating and engaging in various social, economic, or other relations with other users. End-users create demand for Internet infrastructure through their demand for applications, content, and relations. Keep in mind that *activities on the Internet* always involve *interactions* among *end-users*; that the interactions may be commercial, educational, social, political, and so on; and that end-users may be individuals, corporations, government actors, or other entities.

Currently the Internet is a mixed commercial, public, and social infrastructure. The Internet is perhaps the clearest example of an infrastructure resource that enables the production of a wide variety of private, public, and social goods. The supply-chain view

---

[62] VAN SCHEWICK (2010).

[63] Moreover, just like other networked infrastructure systems (e.g., transportation), there are many subsystems and components that can be congested at different times. See chapter 9.

of the Internet captures the commercial nature of the Internet: Applications and content providers use the Internet as a means of engaging in a host of commercial transactions with passive consumers. Many Internet-enabled commercial transactions involve the distribution of applications and/or content for personal consumption under (technical and legal) conditions that strictly limit sharing or reuse; thus, although the applications/content are public goods in the technical sense, the transaction effectively concerns passive consumption of a private good.[64] The Internet also acts as an input for information dissemination and exchange for commercial advertising and marketing and facilitates business transactions and information gathering for product development, consumer demand assessment, and operations management.[65] Many Internet-enabled commercial transactions involve the exchange of private goods offline. In these cases, the Internet may reduce the transaction costs or increase the scale of an already existing offline market. Without doubt, the value of the Internet as commercial infrastructure is immense. Here are a few rough estimates:

- According to John Quelch, in the United States the Internet directly and indirectly has led to 3.05 million jobs. The direct monetary value (including advertising services, retail transactions, and payments to Internet service providers [ISPs]) is estimated at $175 billion. Around 190 million Americans spend an average of sixty-eight hours per month online, which means that, by a conservative estimate, the time value of the Internet is around $680 billion per month.[66]
- According to the US Census Bureau, total US commerce in 2008 (the latest year reported on) was about $22 trillion; about $3.7 trillion was in the form of e-commerce, mostly over the Internet, and about 92 percent of e-commerce was business-to-business.[67]
- Globally, the OECD estimates that of the top 250 ICT firms in terms of revenue, Internet firms accounted for $18.3 billion in revenue in 2000, growing to $56 billion in revenue in 2006, with employment growing from 47,539 to 93,380 over that time period.[68]

---

[64] Frischmann 1015 n. 383 (2005a).

[65] Litan & Rivlin 4–5, 19–38 (2001). These processes are often tailored to channeling end-users toward purchasing and consuming commercial products. Balkin 14 (2004).

[66] Quelch (2009).

[67] Bradner (2011), citing U.S. Census Bureau, Measuring the Electronic Economy, 2008 E-Commerce multisector "E-Stats" Report (released May 27, 2010).

[68] *Id.* at 51 (citations removed). According to the Boston Consulting Group, in 2009 the Internet contributed £100, or 7.2 percent of GDP, to the UK economy. Kalapesi et al. 5, 33 (2010). This contribution included online consumption (including cost of access), investment (in telecom companies, hardware/software by corporations), government spending on information and communications technology, and net exports.

Yet the value of the Internet as public and social infrastructure dwarfs its value as commercial infrastructure. I recognize that it is extremely difficult to substantiate such a claim with empirical data that purports to measure value. As many previous chapters explained, it is precisely this difficulty that leads us to take the social value for granted. The public and social aspects of the Internet infrastructure are dramatically undervalued in the current debate. Bringing these aspects of the Internet into focus strengthens the case for managing the Internet infrastructure as a commons.

Consider what makes the Internet valuable to *society*. The Internet's value to society is tied to the range of capabilities it provides for individuals, firms, households, and other organizations to interact with each other and to participate in various activities and social systems. It is very difficult to estimate the full social value of the Internet, in large part because of the wide variety of user activities and interactions that generate public and social goods. Despite this difficulty, we know that the Internet is transforming our society.[69] The transformation is similar to transformations experienced in the past with other infrastructure, but things are changing in a more rapid, widespread, and dramatic fashion.

The Internet is integral to the lives, affairs, and relationships of individuals, companies, universities, organizations, and governments worldwide. It is having significant effects on fundamental social processes and resource systems that generate value for society. Commerce, community, culture, education, government, health, politics, and science are all information- and communications-intensive systems that the Internet is transforming. The transformation is taking place at the ends, where people are empowered to participate and are engaged in socially valuable, productive activities. As Jack Balkin observed, the "digital revolution makes possible widespread cultural participation and interaction that previously could not have existed on the same scale."[70]

The Internet opens the door widely for users[71] to become involved in many different productive activities. Users actively engage in innovation and creation; create new markets and disrupt old ones; create and inhabit new virtual worlds; engage in commercial and noncommercial exchange; speak about anything and everything; maintain family connections and friendships; debate, comment, and engage in political and nonpolitical discourse; organize clubs and protests; meet new people; search, research, learn, and educate; and build and sustain communities. (This paragraph alone could be expanded to a book-length discussion.)

---

[69] National Broadband Plan–Executive Summary, http://www.broadband.gov/plan/executive-summary/; President's Info. Tech. Advisory Comm. 11–20 (1999).

[70] Balkin (2004).

[71] Lest one forget, "users" refers to individuals, corporations, government actors, or other entities using the Internet infrastructure to interact, whether Microsoft or the reader.

These are the types of productive activities that generate substantial social value—value that evades observation or consideration within conventional economic transactions. When engaged in these activities, end-users are not passively consuming content delivered to them or producing content solely for controlled distribution on a pay-to-consume basis. Instead, end-users are interacting with each other to build, develop, produce, and distribute public and social goods. Public participation in such activities not only benefits the participants directly (as indicated by their decision to participate), but also results in external benefits that accrue to society as a whole, *both online and offline.* These benefits are not fully captured, or necessarily even appreciated, by the participants.

Active participation in these activities by some portion of society benefits even those who do not participate. In other words, the social benefits of Internet-based innovation, creativity, cultural production, education, political discourse, and so on are not confined to the Internet; they often spill over. For example, when bloggers engage in a heated discussion about the merits of proposed legislation or the Iraq war, citizens who never use the Internet may benefit because others have deliberated. With respect to weblogs, in particular, political scientists, journalists, economists, and lawyers, among others, have begun to appreciate and more carefully study the dynamic relationships between this new medium of communication and traditional, offline modes of communication and social interaction (whether economic, political, social, or otherwise).

Consider the fact that a significant portion of the content traveling on the Internet is noncommercial, speech-oriented information—whether personal e-mails and web pages, blog or Twitter postings, instant messaging, or government documentation—and the economic fact that such information is a pure public good generally available for both consumption and productive use by recipients.[72] The productive use and reuse of such information creates benefits for the user, the downstream recipients, and even (as discussed above) people offline. These benefits are positive externalities that are not fully appropriated or even appreciated by the initial output producer. The magnitude of the external effects may be quite small on average. Diffusion of small-scale positive externalities, however, can lead to a significant social surplus when the externality-producing activity is widespread, as it is on the Internet.[73] The "killer app phenomenon" is also

---

[72] As is generally the case with speech-related activities, there may be external costs to consider as well (for example, hate speech); the same is true of innovation (for example, malicious software applications).

[73] Widespread, interactive participation in the creation, molding, distribution, and preservation of culture, in its many different forms and contexts, is an ideal worth pursuing from an economic perspective because of the aggregate social welfare gains that accrue to society when its members are actively and productively engaged. This seems to reflect, in economic terms, the basic idea underlying Jack Balkin's democratic culture theory. Balkin (2004); Balkin (2009) This view also complements the arguments, persuasively made by Yochai Benkler, concerning the social value of diversity in both the types and sources of content. Benkler (2001a).

prevalent on the Internet. The history of the Internet is riddled with examples of killer apps emerging from the "backwaters."[74] I discuss a few below.

To illustrate both the small-scale and killer app phenomena, consider YouTube, a video-sharing platform made possible by the Internet. Most videos on YouTube are intended for a small audience, but many probably reach a slightly larger audience. For example, suppose I post a video of my kids singing and dancing. I might send a link to family and friends, expecting the video to be viewed by twenty-five people. Perhaps one hundred people actually visit, watch, and enjoy. This would generate small-scale spill-overs to seventy-five extra people. While YouTube may capture some of the benefits through advertising revenue, the benefits are irrelevant to my own decision to post the video. The benefits are incidental and seem like small potatoes, but they add up consider-ably when millions of people participate in this activity.[75] As you may know, every once in a while (actually, each week), user-generated and posted videos attract millions of viewers and becomes a cultural phenomenon.[76] For example, in May 2007, Howard Davies-Carr posted a video of his two boys, Harry and Charlie, titled *Charlie Bit My Finger—Again!* Apparently, the video "was intended for just one person: the boys' godfa-ther, who lives in the United States."[77] Unexpectedly, the video went "viral" and has now been viewed over 385 million times. That video generated enormous spillovers, social value above and beyond what the poster possibly could have anticipated or is capable of appropriating.[78] Neither the government nor the market would have selected the video ex ante and funded the producer. The bottom line is that an open video-sharing platform

---

[74] ZITTRAIN (2008). Everything from e-mail (Hotmail), web browsers (Firefox), search engines (Google), online auction sites (eBay), matchmaking sites (Match.com), and Instant Messenger (AOL IM) constitute "killer apps" and significantly influence how our society interacts and collaborates online. Dasgupta (2002).

[75] YouTube, like many other sites, also permits users to post comments and interact with each other, and this also may enhance existing social relationships or even create new social relationships. The new relationships may not always be beneficial or the social ties may be incredibly weak; still, the opportunity to socialize is made available and easy, and users actively participate. Related to this is the growth of comment fields in blogs and on news sites, allowing an easy way for the average user to create content, even if it is one sentence.

[76] There are plenty of examples. YouTube Charts, http://www.youtube.com/charts/videos_views?t=a. You can browse videos according to various criteria, such as (a) the most viewed, most discussed, or most favorite on a (b) daily, weekly, monthly, or all-time basis, and (c) by category. It would be interesting to study how these rankings change over time, and to know, for example, whether the ratio of user-generated to commercially produced content has changed.

[77] Chittenden (2009).

[78] YouTube captures some additional advertising revenue but that does not undermine the point about substan-tial spillovers. The advertising revenue cannot possibly fully internalize the externalities. Nor does the fact that the poster also gains financially undermine the point about substantial spillovers. Apparently, "Howard Davies-Carr . . . managed to parlay [the] video of one of his sons biting the other's finger into a lucrative advertising partnership with YouTube. . . .With that kind of attention, spoofs and the ad revenue followed. Davies-Carr won't say exactly how much his family has earned from the video, but the added income made it more possible to afford a new house, he says." Ransom (2010). Both YouTube and the poster capture some of the surplus, but a substantial amount is not appropriated by either.

provides users with a basic capability and keeps social options open; when users choose to exercise the capability, they presumably do so because it sufficiently satisfies their own self-interest, and at the same time they incidentally generate spillovers because they have shared a public good.[79]

These types of spillover-producing activities are *not* limited in any way to YouTube. In fact, there are countless examples of public-good-sharing platforms enabled by the Internet that generate social value in this fashion. Some are proprietary platforms managed by a particular firm; many are not. Some are organized around a particular type of media; others are organized around a particular topic; others are organized around a particular community; others are simply unorganized. Like YouTube, many platforms facilitate more than just sharing. For example, SlashDot.org, Reddit.com, and Digg.com allow users to contribute links to articles, pictures, and a variety of other content, and once the material is submitted, other users vote the contributions up or down, and can comment on each contribution independently of the linked website. User-generated rating systems are a common feature for many commercial and noncommercial websites (including Amazon, Newegg, Barnes & Noble, and CNN, to name just a few).[80]

In fact, there are many infrastructural platforms for producing and sharing public goods. Wikipedia, for example, provides an incredible example of an infrastructural plat- form for creating and sharing cultural content. It is a free online encyclopedia that rivals proprietary encyclopedias such as Encyclopedia Britannica in quality[81] and vastly exceeds its rivals in public accessibility. The Wiki platform is a collaborative authorship tool that facilitates an "open, peer-production model."[82] According to its own "About Wikipedia" entry, "Wikipedia is written collaboratively by largely anonymous Internet volunteers who write without pay. Anyone with Internet access can write and make changes to Wikipedia articles (except in certain cases where editing is restricted to prevent dis- ruption or vandalism). Users can contribute anonymously, under a pseudonym, or with their real identity, if they choose."[83] On a daily basis, 91,000 active users contribute to

---

[79] YouTube is more or less open in the sense that it does not discriminate among users and provides an open platform. But it is worth noting that, unlike some other platforms (e.g., Wikipedia), YouTube limits the ways in which users that view videos can share and reuse the videos.

[80] BENKLER 76–80 (2006b) (describing peer production of relevance and accreditation services at Slashdot).

[81] Giles 900 (2005) (claiming "the difference in accuracy was not particularly great: the average science entry in Wikipedia contained around four inaccuracies; Britannica, about three."). But see ENCYCLOPEDIA BRITANNICA (2006) (claiming Britannica is more accurate than Wikipedia); Poe (2006), (claiming it is a widely accepted view that Britannica is comparable to Britannica, regardless of the debate).

[82] BENKLER 71 (2006b).

[83] Wikipedia: About, WIKIPEDIA, http://en.wikipedia.org/wiki/Wikipedia:About (last visited Feb. 26, 2011). "Wikipedia's greatest strengths, weaknesses, and differences all arise because it is open to anyone, it has a large contributor base, and its articles are written by consensus, according to editorial guidelines and policies." *Id.* Wikipedia is managed as a commons, but it does have a "Protection Policy" that allows administrators to "pro- tect" a page, for example by restricting editing privileges for a limited or indefinite period. There are different

the website.[84] Those users have created more than 17 million articles that attract 78 million visitors per month. Use of the site has increased over the past years. Between February 2007 and May 2010, Wikipedia use increased by seventeen percentage points (among all adults in the United States), while the number of total Internet users has only increased by eight percentage points.[85] Users receive no monetary compensation; their contributions are voluntary. It is quite clear that the actions of the active users generate substantial spillovers.

For many, this is puzzling. Why would people spend so much time and effort editing encyclopedia entries for free? How does such a large-scale open and collaborative enterprise remain stable? As Jonathan Zittrain suggested, Wikipedia is "the canonical bee that flies despite scientists' skepticism that the aerodynamics add up."[86] I do not intend to solve this puzzle; there is likely a complex mixture of motivations that lead active users to be active. Recall the discussion in chapter 12 of various motivations for people to be creative, to express themselves, or to otherwise invest their own resources in being intellectually productive. It is a mistake to assume that active users are engaging in pure altruism, though it surely is one motivating factor.[87] I suspect many active users simply enjoy the activity, and the costs of participating in a meaningful way are dramatically reduced by the platform and supporting social norms and organizational structures.

Consider also Twitter, a real-time messaging service that allows users to post 140-character messages ("tweets") to the world. In September 2010, Twitter had 175 million registered users, and there were 95 million tweets posted each day. According to Pew Research Center's Internet & American Life Project, "Eight percent of the American adults who use the [I]nternet are Twitter users."[88] Twitter users post content on a variety of topics, including updates on their "personal life, activities or interests" (72 percent); "work life, activities or interests" (62 percent); links to news stories (55 percent); "humorous or philosophical observations about life in general" (54 percent); and photos (40 percent), videos (28 percent), and location information (24 percent), among other things. The platform effectively combines aspects of text messaging and blogging with community-building features, and it also interoperates with other social media, including Facebook. While it may be tempting to dismiss the value of tweets as short bursts of nothingness, the messages are valuable communications and may generate spillovers on a small scale as people broadcast their musings, observations, and feelings to the world.

---

levels of protection that correspond to different types of disruption or vandalism. See Wikipedia: Protection policy, http://en.wikipedia.org/wiki/Wikipedia:Protection_policy (last visited Feb. 26, 2011). There are dispute resolution procedures as well. See Hoffman & Mehra (2010).

[84] Wikipedia: About, WIKIPEDIA, http://en.wikipedia.org/wiki/Wikipedia:About (last visited Feb. 26, 2011).

[85] Zickuhr & Rainie (2011).

[86] ZITTRAIN 148 (2008).

[87] Cf. Hoffman & Mehra (2010) (implying that altruism is the relevant motivation).

[88] Smith & Rainie (2010).

Tweets have also contributed in significant ways to political and cultural discourse. As the Open Internet Coalition noted in its submission to the FCC:

> When opposition protests broke out in Iran following the presidential election, the Iranian government attempted to block cell phones and text messaging and deny access to many social networking sites to prevent the spread of speech and discontent. Quickly, however, Twitter became the medium of choice with protesters tweeting minute-by-minute updates, allowing the world to know what was happening in Tehran and giving the protesters a voice when their government did not want them to be heard. Tweets became so vital to the coverage in Iran that Twitter delayed scheduled site maintenance in order for the political organizing in Iran to continue with minimal disruption. Iranians used all forms of new media to organize themselves and their message: Facebook was used to organize rallies, YouTube was used to distribute to videos of protests, and Google Maps was used to track where government tanks were located.[89]

Similarly, more recent uprisings in Egypt can be, at least in part, attributed to online social networking facilitated by Twitter and Facebook. These resources provided an incredible ability to disseminate information quickly and widely; protesters used the communications technologies to rally supporters, organize protests, and take down the government.[90] When the government sought to take down the sites, the people took to the streets. Even after the government seized control of the Internet in Egypt, citizens had ways to tweet about what was going on, either by using a proxy server[91] or by calling a phone number and using a "speak-to-tweet" system.[92] The opposite side of the story, which is rarely mentioned, is that the government also had access to the sites and used them to its own advantage: Activists were rounded up by Egyptian forces based on user information gleaned from Twitter and Facebook.[93]

Of the many social networking platforms on the web, Facebook is the world's largest.[94] Facebook has more than 500 million active users, 50 percent of whom visit the site on a daily basis. Facebook users create and share a tremendous amount of independent content.

---

[89] Comments of Open Internet Coalition, In the Matter of Preserving the Open Internet, GN Docket No. 09-191, WC Docket No. 07-52 (Jan. 14, 2010) (citing Stone & Cohen (2009)).

[90] *Egypt Internet Users Report Major Network Interruptions*, TVNZ (New Zealand) (Jan. 28, 2011), http://tvnz.co.nz/technology-news/egypt-internet-users-report-major-network-disruptions-4008917.

[91] *Id.*

[92] *Egypt Protesters Use Voice Tweets*, BBC (Feb. 1, 2011), http://www.bbc.co.uk/news/technology-12332850.

[93] Gallagher (2011).

[94] MySpace and LinkedIn are two popular social networking sites. The Open Directory Project lists 215 social networking communities. See http://www.dmoz.org/Computers/Internet/On_the_Web/Online_Communities/Social_Networking/.

Facebook Statistics touts the following: There are over 900 million objects users interact with, including groups, events, and user pages; the average user creates ninety pieces of content each month; and more than 30 billion pieces of content (links, news, blog posts, photo albums, etc.) are shared each *month*.[95] In addition to the creation and sharing of various public goods, including speech and cultural content of all sorts, Facebook enables social interactions, the development of old and new relationships, and the strengthening of social ties (even ties that are relatively weak). As a result of these social capabilities, it enables collective action and coordination through social networking that would be incredibly difficult, and perhaps impossible in some cases, without the platform. The spillover effects offline are immense. Again, the wedge between private market value (value captured in market transactions) and social value is substantial.

* * *

I conclude this section with a brief discussion of the basic capabilities that the Internet provides to users and how the availability and exercise of such capabilities may be affecting people.[96]

[The Internet] offers a wide range of opportunities for individuals to participate productively in political, intellectual, and cultural activities. Yochai Benkler describes many ways that peer production occurs through the use of various Internet-enabled communications technologies, including simple e-mail or blog software.[97] These general-purpose, content-neutral, and easy-to-use technologies facilitate participation in wide-ranging discussions in various communities. From the perspective of liberal autonomy, the increased range of meaningful opportunities—the increased choice—is normatively attractive in itself. In addition, society may benefit from actual participation in these activities and the products and/or changes to the cultural environment that such participation can yield.[98]

The Internet facilitates many different forms of and forums for communication that are open in terms of content and users. E-mail, chat rooms, blogs, and web pages are some of the open communications technologies that have greatly enhanced the communication capacities of individuals and groups (on a one-to-one, one-to-many, and many-to-many basis). Digital cameras, video recorders, editing utilities, and resources such as Wikipedia and Second Life are a few of the technologies and platforms that significantly

---

[95] Facebook Statistics, FACEBOOK, http://www.facebook.com/press/info.php?statistics (last visited Feb. 26, 2011). In addition, the 200 million people who use Facebook on their mobile phones are twice as active as non–mobile phone users. *Id.* An update: On October 18, 2011, the Facebook Statistics page indicated that the number of active users had grown to 800 million.

[96] The discussion draws from Frischmann (2007a), which reviews BENKLER (2006b).

[97] BENKLER (2006b).

[98] Infrastructures often provide or enhance basic human capabilities, and when people choose to exercise those capabilities to satisfy their own autonomous needs, society often benefits from spillovers. In future work I will explore the relationships between infrastructure, capabilities, and spillovers.

increase the capacities of individuals to produce digital content that can be shared and collaboratively (re)produced online. Not surprisingly, a significant reduction in costs leads to a significant increase in the quantity of speakers, listeners, and content producers, and thus in speech and content. While the quality of speech and content varies considerably, and one might even regard some barriers to entry in communications as socially desirable, on the whole the societal benefits of this incredible expansion in communication capacities seem to substantially outweigh the harms.

Moreover, as many have observed and discussed, these technologies and their complementary cousins—social software—facilitate more than communications between speakers and listeners or the sharing of content; they enable users to develop meaningful associations with others, such that groups, communities, and social networks may thus coalesce. Users actively participate in meaningful social activities that frankly may be oversimplified when discussed solely in terms of either "speech" or "cultural production." At least in some contexts, the formation of social networks around speech-cultural exchange and intellectual pooling may be the more interesting and important phenomenon.

In addition, a qualitative change that is now under way may eclipse the quantitative change in participation. This qualitative change relates to the liberation reflected in an expansion in the choices we experience—our increased autonomy—but it involves liberation in a somewhat different sense. As Benkler explains:

> The qualitative change is represented in the experience of being a potential speaker, as opposed to simply a listener and voter. It relates to the self-perception of individuals in society and the culture of participation they can adopt. The easy possibility of communicating effectively into the public sphere allows individuals to reorient themselves from passive readers and listeners to potential speakers and participants in a conversation. The way we listen to what we hear changes because of this; as does, perhaps most fundamentally, the way we observe and process daily events in our lives. We no longer need to take these as merely private observations, but as potential subjects for public communication.

The key to this qualitative change is that *people* may change for the better with their experiences. Recall our discussion in chapter 12 of the dynamic and interdependent relationships we have with the cultural environment, how we make and shape it, and how it makes and shapes us. Active, productive users may become more aware, conscious of their (potential) roles as listeners, voters, and speakers, but also as consumers and producers, as political, cultural, and social beings, and as members of communities. They may learn to be productive—or learn to want to be productive, if such desire is not simply latent. This very awareness that one can play different roles and that the environment is not fixed or fully determined by others is encouraging. It encourages participation and the development of facilitative social practices, and perhaps, over time, the adoption of a participatory culture.

Coupled with the empowerment and encouragement for individuals is social empowerment. This enables users to develop and sustain old, existing, and new social relationships on a scale and scope impossible without the Internet. The ability to interconnect with such a vast number of people through a host of different networking technologies and organizational tools enables coordination, group formation, and collective action—capabilities not nearly as easily exercised in pre-Internet days.

The Internet infrastructure serves as a foundational infrastructure in a manner analogous to the natural and cultural environment. As the examples discussed show, the Internet infrastructure supports many mixed infrastructure in the higher layers. There are many Internet applications that provide basic communications and socialization capabilities—ranging from e-mail, chat rooms, instant messaging, and the World Wide Web to peer-to-peer technologies, Twitter, massive multiplayer online role-playing games, and social networking platforms (to name just a few). Many of the applications are appropriately celebrated as innovations with significant economic value, but these applications generate substantial social value above and beyond the private value reflected and captured in market transactions. There are network effects, various types of spillovers among users, and substantial spillovers offline. Though important, it is not enough to celebrate these applications as innovations. In a sense, it is the nature of the innovation that seems to matter most. What is innovative about these applications is their mixed infrastructural nature and the expansion of human capabilities to generate and act on ideas, to communicate, to socialize, to participate, and to be productive and engaged rather than passive.[99]

This section could go on endlessly in many different directions describing the wide variety of user-generated public and social goods. The preceding paragraphs contain a laundry list of areas to explore in future research, including (1) the various systems that the Internet is transforming, (2) different types of higher-layer infrastructure (e.g., infrastructural applications, platforms, and organizational systems), (3) different modes of production,[100] and (4) the opportunities and basic capabilities that the Internet provides to users. Each direction leads to similar observations—the Internet generates substantial

---

[99] Not everyone chooses to exercise the capabilities made available; many Internet users are passive users. This observation does not undermine the point. A recent FCC study indicated that 52 percent of Internet users have submitted a review for a product, 45 percent have uploaded their own content, 23 percent have posted to their own blog or to a group blog, 22 percent have taken a class online, and 14 percent have played a complicated online video game such as a massive multiplayer online role-playing game. Horrigan 16 (2010).

[100] Many of the examples discussed show how the Internet supports infrastructure in the higher layers that enable different modes of production such as commons-based peer production, an important form of nonhierarchical, distributed production by users; collaborative production across organizations (e.g., firms and/or universities); hybrid production that mixes market and nonmarket or proprietary and commons-based production. Participants in these different emerging modes of production capture some of the benefits but often also generate significant spillovers. BENKLER (2006b); Frischmann 1113 (2007a).

social value not captured or reflected fully in markets. The Internet is a spillover-rich environment because of the basic user capabilities it provides and the incredibly wide variety of user activities that generate and share public and social goods.

Finally, I acknowledge that I am very optimistic about how the capabilities that the Internet provides, how people choose to exercise those capabilities, the nature of and outputs from the various activities users engage in, and the various ways in which the Internet is transforming us and our environment. Many people do not share my optimism. There is undoubtedly plenty of bad behavior, harmful speech, and malicious computer viruses, among other things. While this is ultimately an empirical question, I am optimistic for two reasons: First, based on my own experience and an anecdotal survey of various Internet activities, I believe the benefits far outweigh the harms; second, I believe that much, though by no means all, of the harmful conduct can be addressed in a manner compliant with commons management principles, as I discuss below.

2. COMMONS MANAGEMENT

The demand-side case for managing the Internet infrastructure as a commons remains quite strong. To begin with, it is worth recognizing that the universal adoption of end-to-end design protocols reflects a strong private commitment to commons management. Private networks voluntarily chose end-to-end design, interoperability, and interconnection with other networks. It has always been legally and technologically permissible for a private network owner to opt out by ceasing to offer Internet access or transport services and instead maintaining a private network. Networks could have chosen to reject the Transmission Control Protocol/Internet Protocol (TCP/IP).[101] Most successful networks did not.

Recall the discussion in chapter 5 of the business case for commons management as private strategy. I noted five reasons why firms choose to adopt a commons management strategy, such as adoption of and commitment to end-to-end design: (1) consumers generally dislike discrimination; (2) an open, uniform platform may be easier and cheaper to manage than a closed, discriminatory one; (3) a commons management strategy may facilitate joint production or cooperation with competitors more generally, for example, to interconnect and create a more robust meta-network; (4) a commons management strategy may support or encourage value-creating activities by users; and (5) a commons

---

[101] *Transmission Control Protocol: DARPA Internet Program Protocol Specification*, IETF RFC 793 (Sept. 1981), http://www.ietf.org/rfc/rfc0793.txt?number=793 (formally describing TCP); *Internet Protocol: DARPA Internet Program Protocol Specification*, IETF RFC 791 (Sept. 1981), http://www.ietf.org/rfc/rfc0791.txt?number=791 (formally describing IP).

management strategy maintains flexibility in the face of genuine uncertainty.[102] All of these reasons applied, and likely still apply, to private decisions about how to manage the physical networks that jointly comprise the Internet infrastructure.

An astounding number of different networks, both privately and publicly owned, recognized the value of commons management. The collective strategy (commitment, or even social arrangement) sustained the option value of individual networks and the meta-network and avoided premature optimization for any particular use or subset of uses. Persistent uncertainty about the future turned out to be a boon, as anything was possible and no one had the power to control, coordinate, or manage the path of progress.

The network neutrality debate concerns public regulation requiring private networks to comply with commons management, and thus concerns commons management as public strategy. The affirmative case for commons management effectively mirrors the discussion in chapter 5. The Internet infrastructure is a mixed infrastructure, and as such, it faces the two types of demand-driven problems discussed throughout this book: First, it faces concerns about undersupply and underuse of infrastructure to produce infrastructure-dependent public and social goods, which leads to underproduction of those goods. Second, it faces concerns that infrastructure development may be skewed in socially undesirable directions. For example, if private infrastructure owners prematurely optimize infrastructure for uses that they expect will maximize their private returns, and in doing so choose a path that forecloses production of various public or social goods that would yield greater net social returns, the social option value of the Internet is reduced. This latter concern may involve dynamic shifts in the nature of the Internet infrastructure, such as optimizing networks in a manner that shifts from mixed infrastructure toward commercial infrastructure.

Commons management serves the basic functions described in chapter 5. It creates a blunt means for supporting user production of public and social goods. The conventional economic answer to concerns about undersupply of such goods is direct subsidies, but it should be rather obvious why such a solution would be impossible to implement in the Internet context, given the wide variety of activities and the multitude of users. Infrastructure markets subject to commons management have supported such activities and users without the need for government involvement in picking activities or users worthy of subsidy. As chapter 5 explained, commons management effectively creates cross-subsidies among uses/users and eliminates the need to rely on either the market or the government to pick winners by prioritizing or ranking uses (or users). In the Internet context, I would take the cross-subsidy point a bit further. Open infrastructure appears to be what supports the user freedoms and capabilities described in the last section.

---

[102] This includes uncertainty as to how the infrastructure may evolve, what will be technologically feasible, what unforeseen uses may emerge, what people will want, how much people will be willing to pay, what complementary goods and services may arise in the future, and so on.

Micromanagement of user behavior by networks, whether manifested in price discrimination based on who you are or what you are doing or in preferential treatment or ranking of activities, cuts directly against such freedoms and their exercise.

Critically, the same is true at the level of infrastructural applications. Many of the mixed infrastructure applications discussed in the previous section survive as such and thrive through user participation because they exist within an open environment and are managed as commons. From a dynamic perspective, commons management serves the basic function of maintaining flexibility and the generic nature of the resource. It precludes optimization, and in doing so it sustains the infrastructure's social option value.

Many have argued that such regulation is unnecessary because private networks will not defect from the collective strategy of committing to and complying with the end-to-end principle because they recognize—and if they don't, consumers will discipline and force them to recognize—the private value of commons management.[103] I tend to agree that commons management remains an attractive private strategy, mainly because there is considerable uncertainty about future market value—that is, what the future sources of market returns will be. High market uncertainty provides a strong argument for commons management as a private strategy to maintain the option value of the infrastructure. That said, I am much less confident that many private networks agree, that we can count on the disciplining effect of markets, or that networks will not defect whenever feasible.[104] As we discovered in chapter 5, private infrastructure owners have a number of reasons for choosing to reject a commons management strategy, such as opportunities to price discriminate, vertically integrate and optimize for a subset of downstream markets, and control future progress. Similarly, firms may seek to manage user activities more closely—for example, to manage congestion or other types of interactions among users. Finally, firms may be strongly biased in their estimation of the future market value to favor services that they currently offer or expect to offer, sponsor, or otherwise control, and to disfavor those that they do not. Put another way, firms may not recognize that they are operating in a highly uncertain market environment because they are reasonably certain about the potential market value of known or expected services and significantly discount the potential value of uncertain prospects. Nonetheless, it is not necessary to demonstrate that commons management is no longer an attractive private strategy (or that firms no longer believe it to be attractive). There is too much at stake to bet on private strategy coinciding with public strategy.

There is a very high degree of social value uncertainty. It is impossible to predict with any degree of confidence who or what will be the sources of social value in the future.

---

[103] Lee (2008).

[104] Even if firms pledge their commitment to commons management and agree to refrain from discrimination or prioritization, it can be incredibly difficult to detect defections from that commitment. Sashkin 306 (2006); Marsden 12 (2008).

Accordingly, there is no reason to defer to private firms in this context. First, there is no reason to believe that firms are better informed, capable of maximizing social value, or likely to resist the pressure to discriminate, prioritize, or optimize the infrastructure based on foreseeable and appropriable private returns. Second, there is no reason to trust that markets will correct misallocations. Such thinking may be what motivates calls for transparency as a solution, to enable consumers to decide and potentially discipline missteps by networks. But, among other things, this line of thought presumes that private demand fully reflects social demand; it reduces users to passive consumers of commercial infrastructure; and it ignores the social opportunity to leverage the nonrival nature of the infrastructure to enable and encourage user activities that generate public and social goods.

The Internet, like much of the other mixed infrastructure discussed in this book, has been and should continue to be managed as a commons. Doing so has generated immeasurable social benefits. To be clear, I do not claim to be able to quantify these benefits so that they can be put on a scale and compared with the benefits of prioritization; rather, I maintain that the case for shifting away from commons management and toward prioritization simply has not been made. Putting aside rhetorical arguments of the sort discussed in chapter 8, the primary arguments in favor of permitting discrimination and prioritization are related to managing congestion, incentives to invest in infrastructure supply, and managing harmful traffic. While superficially appealing, I do not find these arguments persuasive, as I discuss below. The following section proposes a specific nondiscrimination rule and then addresses these arguments.

C. A Proposed Nondiscrimination Rule and Various Complications

A targeted nondiscrimination rule is an appropriate intervention because it would both preclude differentially allocating and prioritizing access and use of the Internet on the basis of expected private returns and limit infrastructure evolution or optimization on that basis. After briefly introducing the recent FCC Order for preserving the Open Internet, I discuss my proposed nondiscrimination rule, which precludes discriminating based on the identity of the user or use.

On September 23, 2011, the FCC published its Open Internet Order in the Federal Register, to go into effect November 20, 2011. The FCC adopted three basic rules to preserve a free and open Internet:

1.. Transparency. Fixed and mobile broadband providers must disclose the network management practices, performance characteristics, and terms and conditions of their broadband services.
2. No blocking. Fixed broadband providers may not block lawful content, applications, services, or nonharmful devices; mobile broadband providers may not

block lawful websites, or block applications that compete with their voice or video telephony services.

3. No unreasonable discrimination. Fixed broadband providers may not unreasonably discriminate in transmitting lawful network traffic.[105]

The transparency and no blocking rules are important and not very controversial.[106] The rule prohibiting unreasonable discrimination and thus legitimizing reasonable discrimination is more contentious. Some believe the FCC went too far, others not far enough. The FCC expressly rejected the idea that the nondiscrimination rule should only preclude anticompetitive discrimination proven to harm consumers, and thus envisioned a somewhat broader standard. What is (un)reasonable remains to be seen, however. The FCC Order suggested some guidelines, for example, indicating that pay-for-priority is frowned upon, while use-agnostic discrimination may be reasonable. The FCC also emphasized that the rules would be "applied with the complementary principle of reasonable network management."[107] Thus, with respect to discriminatory practices, such as prioritization, there are two separate reasonableness inquiries. While I agree with much of the FCC's reasoning in the Order about the need to sustain an open Internet, I do not believe the FCC went far enough with its nondiscrimination rule. As I discuss below, I would drop "(un)reasonableness" altogether.

For the remainder of this chapter, I do not further examine the details of the FCC rule. That rule is the first step along what promises to be a long path. Although it is intended to provide a stable and predictable regulatory framework, litigation, regulatory implementation, and even intervention by Congress promise to complicate matters and keep the network neutrality debate alive for the foreseeable future. Even if the FCC rule survives legal challenges and legislative overrides, the rule is substantively incomplete. Accordingly, instead of examining the FCC rule, I propose an alternative formulation that corresponds to the basic definition of commons management employed throughout this book.

Congress or the FCC should consider prohibiting broadband Internet providers from discriminating based on the *identity* of the user or use in the handling of packets. "User" may be defined as sender or receiver; "use" may be defined as application or content type; "handling" may be defined as all transport and related services associated with delivery of packets. This simple formulation of a nondiscrimination rule may seem overly strong in that it appears to rule out a significant range of activities that some might

---

[105] Preserving the Open Internet, 76 Fed. Reg. 59,192, 59,192 (Sept. 23, 2011) (to be codified at 47 C.F.R. pts. 0 and 8), available at http://www.gpo.gov/fdsys/pkg/FR-2011-09-23/pdf/2011-24259.pdf.

[106] Implementation involves controversy, but most agree on the basic principles. I focus on the nondiscrimination rule.

[107] *Id.* at 2.

label "reasonable discrimination" or "reasonable network management." Of course, it depends on what those labels apply to.

The proposed rule primarily precludes certain fine-grained forms of price discrimination, quality discrimination, and prioritization. It does not prohibit other forms of price discrimination that are not based on user/use identity, such as typical second-degree price discrimination, and it does not prohibit more efficient methods for managing congestion, such as traditional usage-sensitive pricing or congestion pricing. After discussing how the rule would impact pricing schemes, I explain why disabling application-based prioritization is not as horrible as opponents suggest.

With respect to pricing, the proposed rule precludes many forms of value-based price discrimination. It does not preclude various forms of cost-based differential pricing, including variable load pricing, congestion pricing, and usage-sensitive pricing. The reason is that these and other forms of cost-based differential pricing do not discriminate on the basis of the identity of users or their specific activities (uses). Instead, they discriminate based on quantity of infrastructure use, capacity utilized, and the marginal cost of such use, taking into account contextual details such as timing and available system capacity; none of this includes identity characteristics. Put simply, to implement most forms of cost-based differential pricing, an infrastructure owner need not know *who is doing what*. Rather, the focus is on *when* and *how much*. In sharp contrast, price discrimination relies directly on identity characteristics that aim to best approximate individual users' subjective valuation of infrastructure use—*who and what are essential to the discrimination or prioritization scheme.*

The proposed rule does not preclude all forms of value-based price discrimination; it precludes discriminating on the basis of the identity of the infrastructure user or use. Second-degree price discrimination, for example, may or may not run afoul of this nondiscrimination rule, depending on how the scheme operates. Second-degree price discrimination may present all infrastructure users with the same price schedule for the same basic service with price variations based on the quantity of use / capacity consumed; users decide what to choose from the menu based on their anticipated demand. Third-degree price discrimination, by contrast, tends to categorize consumers based on their identity, specifically based on identity characteristics that serve as effective proxies for consumers' subjective valuations. The categories are not based on cost. *Who is doing what* is central to the scheme. Third-degree price discrimination generally conflicts with the proposed rule. So do finer-grained identity-based price discrimination schemes.

Value-based price discrimination is at the core of the rule because it is estimated appropriable value that drives private allocation, prioritization, and optimization decisions and potentially leads the infrastructure to evolve in a manner that forecloses production of various public and social goods and thereby reduces social welfare. The proposed nondiscrimination rule precludes differentially allocating, pricing, and prioritizing Internet access and use on the basis of appropriable value. As examined extensively in previous chapters, this rule (1) can be a more effective—albeit blunt—means for supporting the production of public and social goods than targeted subsidies, and (2) has important dynamic implications. It maintains flexibility and the generic nature of the Internet. The proposed nondiscrimination rule effectively functions as a social option, which makes economic sense because of persistent and systematic uncertainty about the future sources of both market and social value.[108] It precludes premature optimization by infrastructure owners; preserves the "evolvability" of the Internet[109] by supporting experimentation by users; increases the range of potential value-creating activities; leaves room for unforeseen innovations, markets, and value-creating activities to emerge; and facilitates learning over time.

Disabling identity-based price discrimination is not necessarily costless, although it should not be assumed to be costly either. It *may* involve a trade-off. The two principal potential advantages of price discrimination are (1) increased output and thus reduced deadweight losses when compared with uniform pricing, and (2) increased profits for infrastructure providers that may improve incentives to invest in the supply, maintenance, and improvement of infrastructure. I discussed these issues extensively in previous chapters. Neither of these potential advantages appears to be nearly as significant as claimed by many in the network neutrality debate.

Before proceeding, it is helpful to explain that price discrimination in this context typically would occur in tandem with quality discrimination in the sense that networks would prioritize, shape, or otherwise manage traffic in a discriminatory manner, perhaps according to priced quality-of-service guarantees, but not necessarily in such an explicit fashion. Therefore, I do not discuss identity-based price discrimination schemes divorced from prioritization during congestion (which are pure rent-extraction schemes aimed at capturing a greater portion of the surplus derived from various Internet activities).[110] Few, if any, participants in the network neutrality debate argue in favor of such schemes; opponents of network neutrality regulation almost always argue that prioritization is needed to deal efficiently with congestion.[111]

First, the claim that output would increase if network providers can price discriminate and prioritize traffic is misleading. The case for prioritization depends on an assumption of congestion. In the absence of congestion, there is no need to prioritize traffic, other

---

[108] See ch. 5. GAYNOR (2003); Gaynor & Bradner (2007); VAN SCHEWICK (2010).

[109] See *id.*

[110] For an analysis of these schemes, see VAN SCHEWICK 273–78 (2010).

[111] Comments of Time Warner Cable Inc., In the Matter of Preserving the Open Internet, GN Docket No. 09-191, WC Docket No. 07-52 (Received Jan. 14, 2010), at 66–67; Comments of Cablevision Systems Corp., In the Matter of Preserving the Open Internet, GN Docket No. 09-191, WC Docket No. 07-52 (Received Jan. 14, 2010), at 9–10; Reply Comments of Comcast Corp., In the Matter of Preserving the Open Internet, GN Docket No. 09-191, WC Docket No. 07-52 (Received Apr. 26, 2010), at 35–36.

than plain rent extraction. If the network is congested and infrastructure capacity is scarce, output cannot be increased without making congestion worse or imposing congestion costs on others. If A and B are two use(r)s vying for access and use of a congested resource, prioritization of use(r) A requires deprioritization of use(r) B. The argument for prioritization is really an argument to allocate scarce capacity to uses that would suffer greater consequences from congestion—whether attributed to delay or jitter or packet loss—and thus would realize greater benefits from prioritization. It is not really an argument for increasing output measured by the number of users, uses, or even packets delivered during periods of congestion. Prioritization does not eliminate or minimize congestion. Users A and B *may* adjust their consumption patterns based on how congestion costs are distributed (shared equally or pushed to B because B is less sensitive to timing) and such adjustments *may or may not* lead to increased output over the long run, depending on various factors, but *only if there is sufficient off-peak capacity within an acceptable time frame.* While it is easy to assume the existence and persistence of uncongested periods during which deprioritized users get an opportunity to act, such an assumption is heroically optimistic and plainly unwarranted; as many have pointed out, prioritization creates perverse incentives for network providers to sustain congestion and underinvest in capacity expansion because such a strategy can be more profitable.[112]

Second, the oft-stated claim that increased revenues from price discrimination are necessary to investment incentives is speculative, self-interested, and doubtful. Major providers, such as Comcast, AT&T, and Verizon, have invested considerable sums without any assurance that they would be capable of prioritizing traffic to obtain increased revenues. They would love to capture more of the surplus, but there is no reason to think they are entitled to it, and it is hardly proven that they need it to justify infrastructure investment.[113] As chapter 8 examined extensively, claims that price discrimination is necessary to support incentives to invest are quite easy to state but much more difficult to support theoretically or empirically. Such claims hold only for a special class of cases where (1) the average total cost curve fails to intersect the private demand curve, and (2) price discrimination yields benefits in excess of total costs (i.e., the area under the demand curve exceeds total costs). Even when these conditions are met, there is not necessarily a strong argument in favor of price discrimination. The strength of the argument depends on a number of additional considerations, including (1) a comparative analysis of alternative institutional solutions that might solve the incentive problem in a more efficient manner

---

[112] See, e.g., Economides 8 (2010); Choi & Kim 29–30 (2008).

[113] See, e.g., FCC Order paragraph 40. I addressed this argument elsewhere. Frischmann & van Schewick (2007); Frischmann & Lemley 297 n. 147 (2007) (arguing there are other ways to incentivize capacity upgrades, such as direct subsidization, tax incentives, and government provision of infrastructure). It should be noted that the US government has recently helped broadband providers expand their networks by providing a $7 billion subsidy. Hinsell (2009).

than price discrimination;[114] (2) the magnitude of the net social welfare gains; (3) the option value of waiting and allowing demand to rise, supply costs to fall, and/or economies of scale to kick in; and (4) the social costs of imperfect price discrimination, including the impacts on the productive activities of users and the generation of spillovers.

Thus, even if arguments that price discrimination is necessary to support incentives to invest were supported with empirical evidence (which they are not), this would only prompt a comparative analysis of various institutions for addressing the supply-side problem. There is no reason to believe that prioritization or discrimination based on the identity of the user or use is the most efficient solution. There are plenty of alternatives, including direct subsidization of infrastructure expansion, tax incentives to support infrastructure expansion, funding research aimed at lowering the cost of infrastructure expansion or entry into the infrastructure market, cooperative research and development projects, joint ventures, government provisioning, and so on.

In addition to arguments about alleged benefits of price discrimination—increased output and incentives to invest—opponents of network neutrality suggest that identity-based discrimination or prioritization may be an efficient and thus reasonable way to manage traffic on networks. In particular, two types of traffic management issues arise: (1) managing congestion and (2) managing unlawful, hazardous, or otherwise harmful traffic.

I. MANAGING CONGESTION

End-to-end design works reasonably well because all packets in fact are the same from a delivery cost and congestion cost perspective. Congestion is associated with the buildup of packets in a queue and the delay associated with processing the queue.[115] With regard to queuing, contributions to delay, and thus congestion, one packet is no different than another.

The TCP/IP, an end-to-end control system for managing congestion, operates at the edges of the network.[116] It allows the source and destination (as well as ISPs) to monitor and communicate about queuing delays. When the delay increases, it allows the

---

[114] For example, government subsidy can reduce the average total costs and make the investment profitable without relying on price discrimination. Government subsidies also can be directed at research and development in technologies that may reduce the costs of infrastructure supply and facilitate competitive entry.

[115] For an excellent, accessible explanation, see CRTC Regulatory Policy 2009-657, http://www.cippic.ca/uploads/File/Attachment_B_pt_1_-_Reed_Report.pdf (testimony of Dr. David Reed).

[116] See *id*. See also Speta 245 (2002), which provides an accessible description:

TCP provides the overall "message management" functions that enable computer-to-computer communication. In simplified form, TCP breaks a computer message into the appropriate packet sizes, numbers the packets, creates a check sum so that the receiving computer can check the integrity of the message, provides the information for the reassembly of the message into the proper sequence by the receiving computer, and orders the re-sending of any lost or damaged packet....

end-hosts to reduce the rate at which data is sent until the delay reduces to near zero. There are various technical means for communicating about and responding to congestion; some of these involve managing and prioritizing traffic. But the existence of such means should not lead one to think that packets are different from a delivery-cost or congestion-cost perspective. They are not.

Though packets are the same from a cost perspective, all packets are not the same from a user valuation perspective. Users derive value from the higher-layer uses of delivered packets, and different uses are more or less sensitive to the consequences of congestion. As discussed above, prioritization is primarily about allocating scarcity, typically based on willingness to pay coupled with discriminatory pricing. The economic case for discrimination/prioritization depends on the existence and persistence of congestion. While eliminating congestion completely is not feasible (or even desirable),[117] there are good reasons to direct policy in that direction, or at least toward minimizing congestion, rather than sustaining it to support business models dependent on prioritization. Keep in mind that prioritization as a form of congestion management is offered as a potential justification for dismantling the commons management regime. Simply put, there are more attractive nondiscriminatory means for combating congestion that are compliant with commons management.

Congestion on the Internet should be managed primarily through expanding capacity and implementing usage-sensitive or congestion pricing, rather than accepting prioritization and encouraging persistent congestion. Investment in capacity expansion coupled with pricing sensitive to congestion and/or usage would go a long way toward resolving many of the perceived congestion problems on the Internet.[118] The proposed

---

... IP wraps a header around each packet created through the TCP. This IP header contains the information necessary to route the packets properly from the sending computer to the receiving computer. Thus, the IP header provides the Internet address of the sending computer and the Internet address of the destination computer, as well as the other pieces of information necessary for each network and network gateway to properly handle the packet.

[117] CORNES & SANDLER (1996).

[118] For a detailed discussion, see chapter 7; Frischmann & van Schewick 392–409 (2007). Yoo argues that use restrictions may be a more efficient method for managing congestion than usage-based pricing and that this possibility is a reason to refrain from network neutrality regulation; he suggests that networks should be free to choose among different approaches to managing congestion. Yoo (2006). As discussed in chapter 7, use restrictions may be required where incompatibilities arise among uses, but that is not a problem on the Internet. Rather, the argument for using use restrictions is that network providers may use them as cost-effective proxies in the face of allegedly high transaction costs associated with implementing usage-based pricing. See *id.* The argument is based on faulty assumptions about the costs of metering usage. As Barbara van Schewick and I explain, the costs of metering traffic and implementing usage-based pricing and/or imperfect congestion pricing are not inordinately high; rather, the technology exists and has been available and in practice for years. Frischmann & van Schewick 392–409 (2007). (Since 2007, the technology has no doubt improved and the costs fallen.) We also explain why congestion pricing is imperfect and why this is not surprising or especially troubling. As discussed in chapter 7, even somewhat crude forms of congestion pricing, such as time of day pricing, can have significant efficiency benefits as users internalize some of the external costs associated with the

rule is attractive precisely because it would push providers to focus on capacity expansion and congestion- or usage-sensitive pricing rather than prioritization. Moreover, it would continue to push for innovative solution at the ends. As Lemley and I noted, "Even with a dumb architecture, innovators have figured out how to provide certain degrees of quality of service at the periphery of the network and how to make certain latency-sensitive applications, such as IP telephony, work."[119]

Proponents of prioritization as a necessary or cost-effective tool for managing congestion have failed to make their case, to the extent that they have even tried.[120] There are effective nondiscriminatory means for managing congestion on the Internet, and prioritization is an incredibly shortsighted approach that, at best, aims to mitigate the private costs of congestion for a subset of users. Abandoning commons management and the social values it sustains is much too high a price for society to pay.

2. MANAGING UNLAWFUL, HAZARDOUS, OR OTHERWISE HARMFUL TRAFFIC

Many argue that networks should not only be permitted but should be encouraged to actively police Internet traffic, by monitoring, managing, and regulating unlawful, hazardous, and otherwise harmful traffic.[121] I will not fully address this complex argument here. It involves a number of complications that are beyond the scope of this chapter. My bottom line is that care must be taken when we consider whether to rely on private owners of infrastructure to act as regulators of users' speech and behavior, and innovation at the ends has proven remarkable at addressing problems of all sorts. In many situations, there are nondiscriminatory means for addressing such problems. Finally, as discussed, access networks often operate as end-systems, particularly where access networks run server-based applications and provide related services for customers. Blocking or filtering traffic at the mail server is a routine method for dealing with spam that is end-to-end compliant. This does not conflict with the proposed rule.

---

timing of their activities. *Id.* We explain various advantages of imperfect congestion pricing over use restrictions as proxies. For example, in contrast with use restrictions, congestion pricing does not tax users in off-peak periods. Of course, congestion will not disappear altogether, and congestion pricing (much like quality of service assurances) likely cannot be implemented system-wide because of the many different networks and resources involved.

[119] Frischmann & Lemley 295 n. 143 (2007).

[120] Comments filed in the FCC proceeding and the FCC Order itself provide remarkably thin theoretical or empirical support. See Preserving the Open Internet, 76 Fed. Reg. 59,192, 59, 209-10 (Sept. 23, 2011); Cablevision reply comments, pp. 9–10, nn.21–24; Time Warner Cable reply comments p. 86.

[121] Comments of the Motion Picture Association of America Inc., In the Matter of a National Broadband Plan for Our Future, GN Docket No. 09-51, at 31–32 (stating that the National Broadband Plan should include measures to encourage ISPs to deter unlawful online conduct); Comments of Recording Industry Association of American, In the Matter of Preserving the Open Internet, GN Docket No. 09-191, WC Docket No. 07-52, at 12–13.

The proposed rule could admit narrow exceptions for categorical discrimination against traffic that is demonstrated to be harmful to the network itself. Such an exception is incorporated into the FCC rule as a form of reasonable network management. The FCC Order provides only limited discussion of this issue, however, noting that "spam, botnets, and DDoS attacks" are harmful to networks and also including "unwanted" traffic in the group.[122] More is required. The burden should be on networks seeking shelter in the exception to demonstrate that the traffic in question actually causes harm to network resources or poses a substantial risk of such harm *and* that other end-to-end compliant means are ineffective.[123] It remains unclear the extent to which "spam, botnets, and DDoS attacks" are actually harmful to network resources, *above and beyond congestion*. Usage or congestion-based pricing might reduce the alleged harm considerably by imposing costs on the originators of such traffic, and to the extent that originators are "zombie computers" (i.e., end-user computers that may be infected with a program that sends spam or DDoS attacks without the knowledge of the end-user), congestion pricing would create useful signals to the owners. For each example, viable solutions might be implemented at the ends.

Further, narrow exceptions based on demonstrable harm to users, particularly when users themselves raise a red flag, might be acceptable if shown to be necessary. That said, an exception based on harm to users because of the content itself (e.g., spam) may not be needed. It remains unproven (at least, to my knowledge) that such issues cannot be dealt with effectively at the ends. A slightly different type of harm to users concerns security and the integrity of end-hosts. Zittrain argues that sustaining "generativity" on the Internet may require some security functions to be executed by networks because end-users may not be capable, and the incredibly large number of unsecured end-hosts poses a substantial risk of a "catastrophic security attack."[124] The jury is still out on this issue, and there may be innovative solutions developed and implemented by end-users, including firms or other organizations acting on behalf of and in the interest of individual end-users. Nonetheless, again, narrow exceptions based on security concerns might be warranted. Let me emphasize two points regarding such narrow exceptions: First, the end-to-end design principle does not rule out making the network more secure by bringing certain security functions within the "core," as Barbara van Schewick explains in considerable detail.[125] Second, commons management tolerates such exceptions, as the various examples discussed in this book demonstrate.

---

[122] Preserving the Open Internet, 76 Fed. Reg. 59,192, 59,209 n.102 (Sept. 23, 2011).

[123] To this end, the Order also comes up short, simply stating that "a broadband provider should be prepared to provide a substantive explanation for concluding that the particular traffic is harmful to the network . . ." Preserving the Open Internet, 76 Fed. Reg. at 59,209.

[124] ZITTRAIN 165 (2008).

[125] VAN SCHEWICK 366–68 (2010).

D. Conclusion

My objective in this chapter has not been to make a dispositive case for network neutrality regulation. My objective has been to demonstrate how the infrastructure analysis, with its focus on demand-side issues and the function of commons management, reframes the debate, weights the scale in favor of sustaining end-to-end architecture and an open infrastructure, points toward a particular rule, and encourages a comparative analysis of various solutions to congestion and supply-side problems. I acknowledge that there are competing considerations and interests to balance, and I acknowledge that quantifying the weight on the scale is difficult, if not impossible. Nonetheless, I maintain that the weight is substantial. The social value attributable to a mixed Internet infrastructure is immense even if immeasurable. The basic capabilities the infrastructure provides, the public and social goods produced by users, and the transformations occurring on and off the meta-network are all indicative of such value.

14

APPLICATION TO OTHER MODERN DEBATES

ALTHOUGH THE BOOK seems to culminate with a single modern debate in the previous chapter, this description is a bit misleading because all of the areas discussed in this book are subjects of ongoing debate. For example, as chapter 9 indicated, road infrastructure triggers highly contentious policy issues, including how to manage congestion, reduce environmental costs, and overcome public investment shortfalls. Not only are road infrastructures the subject of modern debate across the country; that debate is actually part of the much larger debate about transportation infrastructure. A more complete discussion must address the various transportation modalities and how they compete and complement each other in various ways. The same can be said about the brief discussion of telecommunication infrastructure in chapter 10. Obviously, modern communications occur on many different interconnected platforms, raising a host of intertwined policy issues. And again, the same thing can be said about environmental infrastructures and intellectual infrastructures.[1] This book necessarily abbreviates the analysis in order to illustrate the basic concepts, highlight the connections between infrastructural resources in different areas, and suggest a general framework for evaluating the case for commons management.

---

[1] As one anonymous reviewer noted, "Any of the illustrative example chapters could be its own book (i.e., you could write a separate book on environmental or intellectual infrastructure). So be careful not to go too far down that path in this book."

Thus, many candidates for further consideration, and comparative analysis, can be found within the categories already discussed.

Let me briefly highlight a few specific candidates.

Google Books is an attractive candidate for a more detailed analysis. Google began to build a massive searchable book collection available on the Internet, akin to a modern Library of Alexandria.[2] Google scanned millions of books from leading research universities around the world, made the collection of digital copies searchable, and provided limited previews or snippets of books subject to copyright protection and full views of public domain books. Google did so without securing permission from authors or publishers who owned the copyrights in millions of books. Class action litigation followed, pitting Google against the Authors Guild of America and five members of the Association of American Publishers. After years of litigation, the parties worked out a very complex settlement agreement. The settlement substantially expanded the scope of the library project, evolving it from Google Print, sometimes called Google Book Search, to Google Books. Among other things, the settlement leveraged the class action process to reach an incredibly broad group of book authors "represented" in the class action and not limited to the actual parties who filed suit against Google, and it required them to opt out of the agreement if they wished to withhold permission from Google. Effectively, the settlement flipped an important default in copyright. Typically, Google would need to seek direct authorization from each copyright owner to make copies and distribute and display them to the public. In other words, copyright owners typically would need to opt in to Google Books, not out. Flipping the default in this context dramatically reduces transaction costs and correspondingly expands the scope of the undertaking.[3] More important, the settlement significantly expanded the range of activities that authors and publishers ostensibly authorized Google to perform. Prior to the settlement, Google arguably acted within the bounds of fair use, in which case permission of copyright owners would not be required. Regardless, the settlement authorized a host of actions— such as commercial distribution and display of digital books to consumers (directly and through institutional subscriptions)—that could not plausibly be justified by fair use.[4] Libraries, authors, academics, competitors, foreign governments, the US Department of Justice, and other entities voiced objections based on a litany of substantive legal

---

[2] On October 9, 2009, Sergey Brin, cofounder and technology president of Google, published an op-ed in the *New York Times* likening the Google Books project to the Library of Alexandria, with the important caveat that Google's library would last forever. Brin (2009).

[3] Many copyright owners are very difficult to identify and track down. Flipping the default (from opt in to opt out) is one way to overcome the so-called orphan works problem. Many people objected to the Google Books settlement because it provided Google with an advantageous position with respect to orphan works. If competitors were able to obtain the same deal as Google—for example, if Congress flipped the default in orphan works legislation—at least some of these concerns would diminish.

[4] See, e.g., Sag (2010).

issues—antitrust, civil procedure, copyright, and privacy. If approved by the court, the Amended Settlement Agreement (ASA) would effectively govern a decent part of the book industry. In March 2011, however, the district court rejected it.[5]

Google Books is a mixed infrastructure with substantial spillover potential associated with dramatically improved public access to millions of books and the ideas, knowledge, stories, and so on contained in them.[6] Google's ownership and management of the collection presents a host of fascinating legal and policy questions. For our purposes, perhaps the most relevant question would be what, if any, form of commons management might be appropriate. Nondiscriminatory access to the collection may be attractive in principle, but for whom? Competitors?[7] Consumers?[8] How would a commons management regime be implemented? Voluntarily by Google and its partners? Imposed and managed through judicial or regulatory proceedings? The ASA provides some insight about what governance regime Google and its partners would choose. A comparative analysis of public institutional options would be interesting. More generally, this would a good example to examine how public versus private financing and ownership of infrastructure affects the potential commons management institutions.[9]

Peer-to-Peer File-Sharing Software (Protocols) is an interesting example of an intellectual infrastructure. The software effectively reduce the costs of transporting and sharing data over communications networks by enabling users—end-points on the networks—to

---

[5] The Authors' Guild v. Google, 770 F.Supp. 2d 666 (S.D.N.Y. 2011) (J. Chin).

[6] With respect to the first infrastructure criterion, the digital collection itself is nonrival but the various data storage, processing, and distribution facilities (e.g., computer and network hardware) are partially (non)rival.

[7] Suppose a competitor, such as Yahoo or Microsoft, sought access to the collection so that they could provide competing services in downstream markets (search, e-book purchases, etc.). What would access for a competitor look like? According to the ASA, access to the "Research Corpus," the set of all digital copies made in connection with the project, would be limited to "nonconsumptive research" by "qualified users," and commercial exploitation of research results (data from nonconsumptive research) would be limited substantially as well (no direct, for-profit, commercial exploitation; no use in competition with Google Books services). Simply put, under the ASA regime, our competitor would be denied access. But would that lead to a successful antitrust claim, perhaps framed as an essential facilities claim? Under current US law, probably not. Google would argue that it does not possess a monopoly, the costs of entry are not prohibitive, and forcing Google to share with its competitors will not only deter competitive entry in this context but will also deter undertakings of this sort in the future. The viability of an antitrust claim would depend substantially on the supply-side analysis, which would require a considerable factual investigation.

[8] With respect to consumers, a nondiscrimination rule would require Google to provide services to users in a manner that does not discriminate based on the identity of the user or use. There are reasons to suspect that Google would not have adopted a commons management strategy. The private benefits of price discrimination might have been too tempting. The ASA indicates that Google planned to discriminate among institutions through its institutional subscriptions, and it contained other hints in that direction with respect to consumer purchases. But since much of the pricing strategy remained obscure, it is difficult to say.

[9] Recall the comparison of publicly owned roads with privately owned telephone networks. Imagine, for example, that a public institution such as the Library of Congress pursued the undertaking or that Google Books was a public-private partnership. In either case, commons management more likely would be a foundational part of the governance regime.

find and communicate with each other directly, rather than through a centralized server or distribution point. As such, the software provides a basic capability to users and serves as a generic input into a wide variety of user activities. The activities involve the sharing of data, much like speech, and users of the protocols, like participants in a conversation, can share and generate public goods as well as social goods. Of course, the example is complicated in large part by the notoriously illegal uses of peer-to-peer software to share copyright protected works such as music and video. That the protocols and software programs implementing the protocols are infrastructural is not especially difficult to see,[10] but what commons management might mean in this context is not as straightforward. The peer-to-peer software and protocols are generally made available to users on nondiscriminatory terms, and in a sense managed as a commons. But rampant copyright infringement can be likened to the tragedy of the commons or environmental pollution in the sense that misuse and overuse of peer-to-peer software (allegedly) causes substantial negative externalities, namely harm to copyright owners.[11] As a result, an important policy issue is whether copyright law should regulate access to and use of the peer-to-peer software: specifically, whether copyright law ought to extend liability for copyright infringement committed by users of a peer-to-peer file-sharing software program to the developers/owners/sellers of the software or to intermediaries who are involved somewhere in the supply chain between software developer and user. There have been a series of lawsuits, with varying results. In *MGM v. Grokster*, the Supreme Court held that peer-to-peer file-sharing services that intentionally induce their users to infringe copyright can be held liable for the actions of their users, but the Court left open what happens when "intentional inducement" is not proven.[12] Existing copyright doctrines of contributory and vicarious liability sketch out secondary liability rules, but the scope of those rules remains uncertain in the peer-to-peer context for a few reasons (e.g., ambiguity in the rules), but mostly because the Supreme Court has earlier created a safety zone from secondary

---

[10] As I argued in Frischmann 338 (2005b): "Like the Internet, P2P systems can be classified as mixed commercial, public, and social infrastructure. P2P systems are (or have the potential to be) nonrival inputs into the production and distribution of a wide variety of private, public, and [social] goods. One person's consumption (or use) of the P2P system does not deplete the amount available for others users to consume. As far as users are concerned, 'the more the merrier.' While major commercial enterprises use P2P systems to distribute content, P2P systems are not (currently) optimized for the unilateral delivery of commercial content. To the contrary, P2P systems are generically designed to support the multilateral exchange of various kinds of content. In contrast with users of a cable system, P2P users can share ideas, beliefs, tastes, and all sorts of information goods that are not owned or commercial. . . . Moreover, P2P systems are more than mere content delivery mechanisms. P2P users create social networks and form relationships with each other across (sub)cultures and geographic space."

[11] The empirical evidence is mixed. See, e.g., Oberholzer-Gee & Strumpf (2007); Peitz & Waelbroeck (2004); Rob & Waldfogel (2006); Zentner (2006); Waldfogel (2010).

[12] Metro-Goldwyn-Mayer Studios, Inc. v. Grokster, Ltd., 545 U.S. 913 (2005).

liability for technologies "capable of substantial noninfringing uses."[13] This is an important live policy debate to which infrastructure theory may contribute.

Open-source software is an example could be approached from a number of different angles. Open source is a commons management regime whereby software developers and users share code, ideas, knowledge, aspirations, and other intellectual resources, collaborate in producing software programs, and develop social goods, including social capital and networks. One angle would be to begin with the open-source regime itself[14] as an institutional infrastructure, much like legal infrastructures such as property, contract, and copyright laws. The open-source regime has fostered an incredible variety of productive user activities. Another angle would be to focus on the enabling infrastructure resources within the open-source communities. For example, Source Forge is an online hosting and meeting place for thousands of open-source projects; it also is a hub for disseminating open-source software.[15] Another angle, which more directly resembles the approach taken elsewhere in this book, would be to focus on particular infrastructural resources managed as an open-source commons. One prominent example is the Linux operating system.[16]

The Linux operating system, an alternative to Windows and the Macintosh OS, was produced and is still maintained by a volunteer collaborative of individual programmers.[17] The Linux collaborative is linked loosely by communications technologies, by members' voluntary allegiance to the project, and by the terms of an open-source license document. Unlike proprietary computer programs, which are distributed to users in object code or executable format only, open-source programs such as Linux are made available in source code form, so that members of the community may modify their copies and, under the terms of the governing license, publish their modifications for use by others. Members of the community may also volunteer their modifications for inclusion in the standard Linux code base. Thus, each member of the Linux community may use material in the Linux commons and may contribute material back to the Linux commons. Each individual member of the community contributes code to the accumulated archive of the Linux kernel, which is the core of the operating system built on Linux.

---

[13] Sony Corp. of Am. v. Universal City Studios, Inc., 464 U.S. 417 (1984). There is debate about the scope of the safety zone and infrastructure theory maps onto it rather well. For more details, see Frischmann (2005b). In fact, in his concurring opinion in Metro-Goldwyn-Mayer Studios, Inc. v. Grokster, Justice Breyer defends Sony's "strongly technology protecting" rule on terms that resonate with infrastructure theory.

[14] Perhaps one could focus even more narrowly on specific licenses, such as the GNU General Public License.

[15] See www.sourceforge.net.

[16] The following paragraph is excerpted from Madison, Frischmann, & Strandburg (2010).

[17] Some of these programmers contribute to the Linux project at the behest of their corporate employers and thus are not volunteers in the strict sense. They are volunteers with respect to the Linux project, however. Their relationship to the Linux community is governed by the same rules as apply to those who participate for other reasons. See, for an exploration of the governance issues involved in the relationship between open-source software projects and commercial firms, O'Mahony & Bechky 440 (2008).

The rules governing use of open-source material and contributions to the open-source commons are partly formal and partly informal. Formally, the software is governed by copyright law and its use is managed by the terms of the General Public License. Informally, the integrity of Linux as an identifiable and stable program depends on a thin hierarchy of informal authority, which extends from Linus Torvalds at the top to the body of individual developers at the bottom.[18] The result is a complete, complex, and successful industrial product that is built and maintained not by a traditional, hierarchical, industrial firm, but by a loose-knit community.

Linux would be an interesting example to explore for a variety of reasons. It seems to show how infrastructure provisioning in a collaborative open environment can work and how maintaining flexibility for users leads to a flourishing, productive community. It also would be quite interesting to examine from an institutional perspective, to see how the commons management regime functions.[19]

* * *

These are just a few examples. There are many others, including the electromagnetic spectrum,[20] the "smart grid," the Internet's domain name system, and university science and technology research systems.[21] Hopefully, at this point you have candidates of your own in mind.

---

[18] KELTY (2008).

[19] On studying commons institutions of this sort, see Madison, Frischmann, & Strandburg (2010). See also various works by Ostrom.

[20] See, e.g., Werbach (2011); Hazlett (2005); Faulhaber (2005); Werbach (2004); Goodman (2004); Faulhaber & Farber (2003); Benkler (2002).

[21] On university science and technology research systems as infrastructure, see Frischmann (2009); Frischmann (2005c).

Conclusion

Shared infrastructures shape our lives, our relationships with each other, the opportunities we enjoy, and the environment we share. Infrastructure commons are ubiquitous and essential to our social and economic systems. Yet we take them for granted, and frankly, we are paying the price for our lack of vision and understanding. Our shared infrastructures—the lifeblood of our economy and modern society—are crumbling. The ASCE Report Card for America's Infrastructure is only one of many indicators.[1] Our shortsighted, piecemeal approach to infrastructure policy must change. We need a more systematic, long-term vision that better accounts for how infrastructure commons contribute to social welfare.

Infrastructure policy is heavily influenced by economics. Accordingly, this book primarily works within economics, drawing together various microeconomic concepts and aiming to expand our economic understanding of infrastructures.

Our current approach to economic analysis of infrastructure oversimplifies the functional economic and social role of infrastructural resources and focuses predominantly on supply-side issues. For example, analysts often classify infrastructure as a public good, acknowledge that it is well understood that markets may fail to efficiently supply such goods, and then proceed to analyze the form of institutional intervention by the government to correct the failure, typically assuming that the degree of intervention should be minimal. Alternatively, analysts often classify the infrastructure market as a natural monopoly and then once more proceed to focus on supply-side issues. If the market

---

[1] See ASCE (2009), discussed in the introduction.

cannot be classified as a natural monopoly, then the case for government intervention dissipates and a strong presumption in favor of deregulation and reliance on competitive markets emerges.

The supply-side analysis is important, but it is misleadingly incomplete. It is not enough to identify the public good nature of infrastructure. That is a fine place to start, but a more nuanced analysis—of what type of public good it is, how it is and can be used, what systemic effects it might have, and so on—is needed.

When reduced to a public good provisioning problem, the functional role of infra-structure is lost; (inter)dependent economic and social systems are reduced to mere markets; and various incomplete or missing infrastructure-dependent markets (or non-markets) are assumed away.[2] Demand for infrastructure is, as in any other market, assumed to be reflected fully and accurately in what people are willing and able to pay for infra-structure. With these assumptions in place, the basic issues that remain are familiar sup-ply-side issues: for example, securing cost recovery and incentives to invest in the face of decreasing-cost phenomena and misappropriation risks. The supply-side issues are impor-tant but tell only half of the story.

This book focuses on the other half—the demand-side issues. Private demand mani-fested in markets by users' willingness to pay for infrastructure does not fully capture societal demand. Private demand ignores the positive spillovers additional infrastructure can generate. The wedge between private and societal demand can lead to undersupply

---

[2] Economists strongly prefer to work with formal mathematical models and quantitative data, for good reasons, but this preference introduces considerable limitations. Among other things, this preference leads many econo-mists to isolate a particular market or two to analyze, holding others constant and assuming them to be complete and competitive. This approach is highly distorting in the infrastructure context because infrastruc-ture resources are often foundations for complex systems of many interdependent markets (complete and incomplete) and nonmarket systems. Economists may cordon off various nonmarket systems and correspond-ing social values because such phenomena are deemed to be outside the bounds of economics. (Recall the dis-cussion in chapter 3 about such boundaries.) But to focus on markets and their interactions and ignore nonmarkets and relevant social values distorts the analysis of infrastructure, whether or not we label the analysis "economic" because it is within the conventional bounds of the discipline. Of course, many economists are well aware of these boundaries and the corresponding limits of their expertise and policy prescriptions. Nonetheless, these limits often are not apparent or well understood by policy makers and other consumers of economic analyses, and even when the limits are understood, there are various reasons why they may be disregarded—for example, ideology or political pressures. J. Scott Holladay, an environmental economist, explained to me:

> When conducting an economic valuation of an ecosystem, we are well aware of our limitations. In a valu-ation study, we identify environmental services and amenities that are valuable but cannot be valued via existing economic methods, and we may assign a non-numerical value to make clear that we are not assigning a value of zero, but when the valuation study is used by policy makers, those non-numerical values may effectively be converted to a zero value and the identified environmental services and ameni-ties truncated from the analysis. Is that a fault of the economist or the policy maker?

To be clear, I am not assigning fault to anyone. Rather, my aim is to examine the consequences of reductionism and shed light on the importance of what is often ignored (or truncated).

and underuse of infrastructure to generate public and social goods (and thus undersupply of such goods). Ignoring that wedge can also lead to investing in infrastructures for uses that generate private returns at the expense of infrastructures (and uses) that would generate greater social returns. Recognizing that this wedge exists requires consideration of critical and underexplored questions: What is societal demand for infrastructure? Why does society want, need, value, or have reason to value infrastructure resources? Why is nondiscriminatory access to such resources so important?

In the context of specific infrastructure, what is the social value of the national highway system? a language? Lake Michigan? the Internet? These infrastructural resources are incredibly difficult to value effectively. Where does one begin? Consider the following lines of traditional economic inquiry: How much does it cost? What would it cost to replace? How much revenue does it generate? How much are people willing to pay for it? How much does it contribute to GDP or economic growth? We are far from being able to answer any of these questions, in part because the "it" is a complex, multifaceted resource which varies considerably across geographic, temporal, and cultural dimensions and for which tracing actual or replacement costs, revenues, willingness to pay for various types of users, and contributions to GDP or growth is incredibly difficult.

Answers to these questions would provide useful data, but it is critical to recognize that *even with such data* the valuation exercise would remain woefully incomplete. Each line of inquiry has its own built-in limitations. Cost is obviously not value. Revenue generated and willingness to pay are good indicators of value only where markets are assumed to be complete and interdependencies and missing markets (externalities) are assumed away. GDP and economic growth focus on some components of social welfare but are myopic and do not capture all components (for example, nonmarket contributions). What is particularly troubling about relying on such valuation measures is that it distorts by omission, leaves difficult value questions unaddressed, and perversely provides a false sense of security that market demand efficiently reflects societal demand. The impact on public policy is dramatic and deeply troubling.

To approach valuation questions intelligently, develop a better understanding of societal demand, and improve policy making, we need to move beyond the impoverished view of infrastructure, accept that the public good classification is only the tip of the iceberg, and grapple with the functional relationships between infrastructure and interdependent systems as well as the reality of various incomplete or missing infrastructure-dependent markets. I acknowledge that this complicates the inquiry tremendously and may make it even more difficult to devise formal mathematical models and to develop quantitative measures that purport to reflect value. I do not find this objectionable, however, because the conventional models and measures obscure as much as they reveal.

Economists—as well as regulators and politicians—recognize that there is a tremendous societal demand for public infrastructures and that infrastructures play a critical role in economic and social development, but exactly why there is demand, how it manifests, how it should be measured, and how it contributes to economic growth and social welfare are not well understood. As a result, infrastructure investment, management, and governance are ad hoc and based on incompletely theorized foundations.

This book develops a more critical, demand-focused theoretic approach. It links *infrastructure*, a particular set of resources defined functionally in terms of the manner in which the resources create value, with *commons*, a resource management principle by which a resource is available to all within a community on nondiscriminatory terms. As noted throughout the book, the link implies a need to carefully evaluate the merits of managing infrastructure as commons in context and with an awareness of the wide variety of interests at stake. Trade-offs among competing values are inevitable and will vary across different types of infrastructures.

The competing values are not always commensurable and easy to trade off against each other. While much of the book's discussion is framed in economics, the book persistently emphasizes the relevance and importance of values not well accounted for by conventional economics. Many of these values are (only roughly) captured in the public and social goods categories or the notion of spillovers, and many reviewers of the book have asked me to expand more on how to integrate noneconomic values. In some of the chapters, I have done so, but I leave a more comprehensive discussion for separate work.

Throughout the book, I have tried to make clear that much like the supply-side analysis, my own analysis has at times been partial, in the sense that I focus on the demand side and do not fully engage the supply side. Part III addressed the most prominent objections to commons management and examined a host of supply-side issues. In many situations, commons management is compatible with market pricing, cost recovery, congestion management, and incentives to invest. Further, Parts IV and V showed how different commons management institutions "fit" different resources, contexts, and provisioning systems. Still, bringing the supply- and demand-side analyses together in a more comprehensive fashion is a task for future work.

Despite my limited attention to supply-side issues, I have advocated the default position of commons management for public, social, and mixed infrastructures. That is, I argue that we should commit to sharing such infrastructure resources in an open, nondiscriminatory manner when it is feasible to do so; that deviations from this baseline objective require justification; and that the burden is on those arguing for the freedom to discriminate. Arguably, this move entails a dramatic shift—perhaps a paradigm shift—away from the conventional position favoring market provisioning and markets "free" from government intervention. Elsewhere, I have criticized this conventional default position.[3] Here, I will just say that multiple market failures are endemic to public, social, and mixed infrastructures, and I see no convincing a priori justification for the opposing

---

[3] Frischmann (2001).

baseline, supporting a freedom to discriminate. In the end, reforming our approach to infrastructure policy requires much more than a public commitment to managing public, social, and mixed infrastructures as a commons, but this would be a significant step forward.

Adopting a capacious view of infrastructure allows us to "see" the wide range of infrastructural resources that we too often take for granted. A demand-side approach assists in making this view more clear and helps explain why it is obscured by our current supply-side focus. Though different in important ways, roads, telecommunications networks, the atmosphere, and ideas are actually similar in very important ways as well. It is critical to appreciate the foundational, enabling role of these and many other shared infrastructures and to see how the same infrastructure policy issues arise across various systems and policy arenas.

Acknowledgments

In writing this book, I have relied *heavily* on the generosity and ideas of others. I am deeply grateful to the many, many people who have helped me. I have been working on the ideas in this book for over a decade. Looking back, it is difficult to acknowledge all of the different people, sources, and ideas that contributed to the book. It builds from over a dozen of my prior publications, dozens of workshops and conferences, and hundreds of conversations.

Some of the core ideas in this book originate in articles I wrote while a law student at Georgetown. Julie Cohen, Avery Katz, and Steven Salop helped me to discover and develop those ideas in the context of innovation and Internet policy arenas. Edith Brown Weiss, Hope Babcock, and Richard Lazarus helped me to see connections between those ideas and the environmental policy arena.

The book builds directly from many published articles and public presentations. I directly build on and borrow from the following articles:

Constructing Commons in the Cultural Environment, CORNELL LAW REVIEW (2010) (with Michael Madison, University of Pittsburgh, and Katherine Strandburg, NYU)

Cultural Environmentalism and The Wealth of Networks, 74 UNIVERSITY OF CHICAGO LAW REVIEW 1083 (2007) (reviewing YOCHAI BENKLER, THE WEALTH OF NETWORKS: HOW SOCIAL PRODUCTION TRANSFORMS MARKETS AND FREEDOM (2006))

An Economic Theory of Infrastructure and Commons Management, 89 MINNESOTA LAW REVIEW 917 (2005)

Environmental Infrastructure, 35 ECOLOGY LAW QUARTERLY 151 (2008)

Evaluating the Demsetzian Trend in Copyright Law, 3 REVIEW OF LAW AND ECONOMICS (2007)

Innovation and Institutions: Rethinking the Economics of U.S. Science and Technology Policy, 24 VERMONT LAW REVIEW 347 (2000)

Network Neutrality and the Economics of an Information Superhighway, 47 JURIMETRICS 383 (2007) (with Barbara van Schewick, Stanford)

Privatization and Commercialization of the Internet Infrastructure: Rethinking Market Intervention into Government and Government Intervention into the Market, 2 COLUMBIA SCIENCE AND TECHNOLOGY LAW REVIEW 1 (2001)

The Pull of Patents, 77 FORDHAM LAW REVIEW 2143 (2009)

Revitalizing Essential Facilities, 75 ANTITRUST LAW JOURNAL 1 (2008) (with Spencer Weber Waller, Loyola University Chicago)

Speech, Spillovers, and the First Amendment, 2008 UNIVERSITY OF CHICAGO LEGAL FORUM (2008)

Spillovers Theory and Its Conceptual Boundaries, 51 WILLIAM & MARY LAW REVIEW 801 (2009)

Spillovers, 107 COLUMBIA LAW REVIEW 257 (2007) (with Mark A. Lemley, Stanford)

I have cut many of the citations from these articles and thus I refer the interested reader to those articles for more depth and additional references.

I am deeply indebted to Mark Lemley, Michael Madison, Barbara Van Schewick, Katherine Strandburg, and Spencer Waller. Our coauthored articles help form the foundation for this book. Working with them greatly improved it and taught me a lot.

Over the past decade, hundreds of people have commented on the articles noted above, spoken with me about the ideas and how to refine or improve them, and contributed meaningfully to this project in other ways. I am particularly grateful to Marvin Ammori, Yochai Benkler, Gaia Bernstein, David Bollier, John Breen, Dan Burk, Adam Candeub, Michael Carrier, Mike Carroll, Barbara Cherry, Julie Cohen, Susan Crawford, Harold Demsetz, Deven Desai, Peter DiCola, David Driesen, Gerald Faulhaber, Shubha Ghosh, Wendy Gordon, Scott Hemphill, Cynthia Ho, Christiaan Hogendorn, J. Scott Holladay, David Isenberg, Brian Kahin, Alfred Kahn, Ariel Katz, Doug Kysar, Peter Lee, Mark Lemley, Lawrence Lessig, Gary Libecap, Doug Lichtman, Michael Madison, Greg Mandel, Mark McKenna, Robert Merges, Michael Meurer, Dan Moylan, Frank Pasquale, Marc Poirier, Giovanni Ramello, J. B. Ruhl, Matthew Sag, Steve Salop, Pam Samuelson, Mark Schultz, Howard Shelanski, James Speta, Christopher Sprigman, Alexander Tsesis, Rebecca Tushnet, Barbara Van Schewick, Spencer Waller, Phil Weiser, Kevin Werbach, Rick Whitt, Joshua Wright, Tim Wu, Christopher Yoo, and Jonathan Zittrain.

For reading and commenting on the entire manuscript, I am deeply indebted to Michael Burstein, Michael Carrier, Christiaan Hogendorn, and Greg Mandel. In addition,

Deven Desai, David Driesen, Shubha Ghosh, Wendy Gordon, Scott Hemphill, J. Scott Holladay, Peter Lee, Matthew Sag, Stewart Sterk, and Spencer Waller read multiple chapters. Their thoughtful comments improved the manuscript greatly.

Many people who I have never met have contributed substantially to this book. I stand on countless shoulders. I have tried earnestly to provide the reader with citations to the relevant literatures, but frankly, given the breadth of disciplines that I have explored in researching and developing these ideas, the bibliography is inevitably incomplete. The bibliography lists hundreds of selected sources; frankly it could list thousands. Still, I hope it serves as a useful reference for entry into these fields.

I thank my dean, Matthew Diller, and my colleagues at the Cardozo Law School for their support. I also thank the Loyola University Chicago School of Law, where I taught for eight years, and my colleagues from Loyola for their support. I particularly thank Spencer Waller for countless hours talking about infrastructure, commons, economics, and many other things.

I have had excellent research assistants at Cardozo and Loyola. They include Cary Adickman, Robyn Axberg, Michael Casey, Atanu Das, Ann Fenton, Yangsu Kim, Ethan King, Kristopher Knabe, Eric Null, Aaron Pereira, and Joe Sanders.

I am grateful to everyone at Oxford University Press for turning my manuscript into a book. Special thanks to Matt Gallaway, Maria Pucci, Christi Stanforth, and Kiran Kumar for all of their hard work. I am also grateful to Mike O'Malley for encouraging me to write this book.

Finally, I thank my family. Their support is what makes everything possible.

Bibliography

Aghion, Philippe, & Peter Howitt (1998), *On the Macroeconomic Effects of Major Technological Change, in* GENERAL PURPOSE TECHNOLOGIES AND ECONOMIC GROWTH (Elhanan Helpman ed.).

ALBERT, STEVEN, & KEITH BRADLEY (1997), MANAGING KNOWLEDGE: EXPERTS, AGENCIES AND ORGANIZATIONS.

ALSTON, LEE J., THRÁINN EGGERTSSON, & DOUGLASS CECIL NORTH (1996), EMPIRICAL STUDIES IN INSTITUTIONAL CHANGE.

ALTMAN, CHARLES F. (1989), THE AMERICAN FILM MUSICAL.

AMABILE, TERESA M. (1996), CREATIVITY IN CONTEXT.

American Society of Civil Engineers (2009), Report Card for American Infrastructure, *available at* http://www.infrastructurereportcard.org/sites/default/files/RC2009_full_report.pdf.

Ammori, Marvin (forthcoming 2012), *First Amendment Architecture*, 2012(1) WISCONSIN L. REV.

Anderson, Nate (2007), *Deep Packet Inspection Meets Net Neutrality, CALEA*, Ars Technica, July 25, *available at* http://arstechnica.com/hardware/news/2007/07/Deep-packet-inspection-meets-net-neutrality.ars.

ANDERTON, ALAIN (2000), ECONOMICS (3d ed.).

Annals of Congress (1817–18).

Appropriate Framework for Broadband Access to the Internet over Wireline Facilities, Report and Order and Notice of Proposed Rulemaking (2005), 20 FCC Rcd. 14853.

Armstrong, Mark, & John Vickers (2001), *Competitive Price Discrimination*, 32 RAND J. OF ECON. 579.

ARNOLD, ROGER A. (2008), ECONOMICS.

ARNOTT, RICHARD (2001), THE ECONOMIC THEORY OF URBAN TRAFFIC CONGESTION: A MICROSCOPIC RESEARCH AGENDA.

Arrow, Kenneth (1962), *Economic Welfare and the Allocation of Resources for Inventions, in* THE RATE AND DIRECTION OF INVENTIVE ACTIVITY (R. R. Nelson ed.).

Arrow, Kenneth J. (1970), *The Organization of Economic Activity: Issues Pertinent to the Choice of Market Versus Nonmarket Allocation, in* PUBLIC EXPENDITURE AND POLICY ANALYSIS (Robert H. Haveman & Julius Margolis eds.).

Arrow, Kenneth J. (1999), *Observations on Social Capital, in* SOCIAL CAPITAL: A MULTIFACETED PERSPECTIVE WASHINGTON: WORLD BANK 3 (P. Dasgupta & I. Serageldin eds.).

Aschauer, David Alan (2000), *Public Capital and Economic Growth: Issues of Quantity, Finance, and Efficiency*, 48(2) J. ECONOMIC DEVELOPMENT AND CULTURAL CHANGE 391.

AT&T (n.d.), A Brief History: The Bell System, *available at* http://www.corp.att.com/history/history3.html.

Averch, Harvey, & Leland L. Johnson (1962), *Behavior of the Firm under Regulatory Constraint*, 52 AM. ECON. REV. 1052.

Aviram, Amitai (2003), *A Network Effects Analysis of Private Ordering*, Berkeley Olin Program in Law & Economics, Working Paper Series 11079.

Baker, Edwin (2007), *The Independent Significance of the Press Clause under Existing Law*, 35 HOFSTRA L. REV. 955.

Baker, Edwin C. (1997), *Giving the Audience What It Wants*, 58 OHIO ST. L. J 311, 350–51.

Balkin, Jack (2004), *Digital Speech and Democratic Culture: A Theory of Freedom of Expression for the Information Society*, 79 N.Y.U. L. Rev. 1.

Balkin, Jack (2009), *The Future of Free Expression in a Digital Age*, 36 PEPPERDINE L. REV. 707.

Balvanera, Patricia, & Ravi Prabhu (2004), UN Millennium Project Task Force on Environmental Sustainability, Ecosystem Services: The Basis for Global Survival and Development, *available at* http://www.unmillenniumproject.org/documents/TF6_IP2_Ecosystem.pdf.

BARNES, PETER (2006), CAPITALISM 3.0: A GUIDE TO RECLAIMING THE COMMONS.

Barnett, Jonathan M. (2004), *Private Protection of Patentable Goods*, 25 CARDOZO L. REV. 1251.

Barnett, Jonathan (2011), *The Host's Dilemma: Strategic Forfeiture in Platform Markets for Informational Goods*, 124 HARVARD L. REV. 1861.

BARON, ROBERT A., & SCOTT A. SHANE (2008), ENTREPRENEURSHIP: A PROCESS PERSPECTIVE.

Barringer, Felicity (2011), *Need a Ride? There Are Apps for That*, N.Y. TIMES, Jan. 20, *available at* http://green.blogs.nytimes.com/2011/01/20/need-a-ride-theres-an-app-for-that.

Barron, Anne (2008), *Copyright Infringement, "Free Riding" and the Lifeworld*, London Sch. of Econ. & Pol. Sch., Law, Society and Economy Working Paper No. 17, *available at* http://ssrn.com/abstract=1272564.

BARSBY, A. W. (1997), PRIVATE ROADS: THE LEGAL FRAMEWORK (2d ed.).

Bassanini, Andrea, & Stefano Scarpetta (2001), *The Driving Forces of Economic Growth: Panel Data Evidence for the OECD Countries*, 33 OECD ECONOMIC STUDIES 9.

Bauer, Steven, & Peyman Faratin (2005), Analyzing Provider and User Incentives Under Congestion Pricing on the Internet, *available at* http://projects.csail.mit.edu/csw/2005/proceedings/bauer_csw05.pdf.

Baumol, W. J. (1990), *Entrepreneurship: Productive, Unproductive and Destructive*, 98(5) JOURNAL OF POLITICAL ECONOMY 893–921.

BAUMOL, WILLIAM J., & ALAN S. BLINDER (2009), ECONOMICS: PRINCIPLES AND POLICY.

Baumol, William J., & David F. Bradford (1970), *Optimal Departures from Marginal Cost Pricing*, 60 AM. ECON. REV. 265.

BAUMOL, WILLIAM J., ROBERT LITAN, & CARL J. SCHRAMM (2007), GOOD CAPITALISM, BAD CAPITALISM, AND THE ECONOMICS OF GROWTH AND PROSPERITY.

Bayhing for Blood or Doling Out Cash? (2005), ECONOMIST, Dec. 24, at 109.

Becker, Mark J. (1998), *Legislative History of the Communications Act of 1934, in* TELECOMMUNICATIONS: LAW, REGULATION, AND POLICY 3, 5 (Walter Sapronov & William H. Read eds.).

Beito, David T. (1993), *From Privies to Boulevards: The Private Supply of Infrastructure in the United States during the Nineteenth Century, in* DEVELOPMENT BY CONSENT: THE VOLUNTARY SUPPLY OF PUBLIC GOODS AND SERVICES (Jerry Jenkins & David E. Sisk eds.), *available at* http://www.as.ua.edu/history/html/faculty/beitofromprivies.pdf.

Bell, Abraham, & Gideon Parchomovsky (2003), *Of Property and Antiproperty*, 102 MICH. L. REV. 1.

BENJAMIN, STUART MINOR, DOUGLAS LICHTMAN, & HOWARD A. SHELANSKI (2001), TELECOMMUNICATIONS LAW AND POLICY.

BENJAMIN, STUART MINOR, DOUGLAS LICHTMAN, HOWARD A. SHELANSKI, & PHILLIP J. WEISER (2006), TELECOMMUNICATIONS LAW AND POLICY, 2nd ed.

Benkler, Yochai (1998a), *Overcoming Agoraphobia: Building the Commons of the Digitally Networked Environment*, 11 HARV. J. L. & TECH. 287.

Benkler, Yochai (1998b), The Commons as a Neglected Factor of Information Policy, Remarks at the Telecommunications Policy Research Conference (September), at http://www.benkler.org/commons.pdf.

Benkler, Yochai (1999), *Free as the Air to Common Use: First Amendment Constraints on Enclosure of the Public Domain*, 74 N.Y.U. L. REV. 354.

Benkler, Yochai (2000a), *An Unhurried View of Private Ordering in Information Transactions*, 53(6) VANDERBILT L. REV. 2063–80.

Benkler, Yochai (2000b), *From Consumers to Users: Shifting the Deeper Structures of Regulation Towards Sustainable Commons and User Access*, 52 FED. COMM. L. J. 561.

Benkler, Yochai (2001a), *Property, Commons, and the First Amendment: Towards a Core Common Infrastructure*, White Paper for the First Amendment Program, Brennan Center for Justice at NYU Law School, *available at* http://www.benkler.org/WhitePaper.pdf.

Benkler, Yochai (2001b), *Siren Songs and Amish Children: Autonomy, Information, and Law*, 76 N.Y.U. L. REV. 23.

Benkler, Yochai (2002), *Some Economics of Wireless Communications*, 16 HARV. J. L. & TECH. 25.

Benkler, Yochai (2003a), *The Political Economy of Commons*, 4(3) UPGRADE.

Benkler, Yochai (2003b), *Lecture, Freedom in the Commons: Towards a Political Economy of Information*, 52 DUKE L. J. 1245.

Benkler, Yochai (2004), *Sharing Nicely*, 114 YALE L. J. 273.

Benkler, Yochai (2006a), *Coase's Penguin, or, Linux and the Nature of the Firm*, 112 YALE L. J. 369.

BENKLER, YOCHAI (2006b), THE WEALTH OF NETWORKS: HOW SOCIAL PRODUCTION TRANSFORMS MARKETS AND FREEDOM.

Benkler, Yochai (2011), *Between Spanish Huertas and the Open Road: A Tale of Two Commons?*, circulated for the Convening Cultural Commons conference at NYU, September 23–24.

Berkman Center for Internet & Society (2009), Next Generation Connectivity: A Review of Broadband Internet Transitions and Policy from Around the World, *available at* http://www.fcc.gov/stage/pdf/Berkman_Center_Broadband_Study_13Oct09.pdf.

Berry, S. Keith (1992), *Ramsey Pricing in the Presence of Risk*, 13(2) MANAGERIAL & DECISION ECON. 111.

Bishop, Richard C. (2003), *Where to from Here?*, in A PRIMER ON NONMARKET VALUATION (Patricia A. Champ et al. eds.).

Bluemel, Erik B. (2005a), *Accommodating Native American Cultural Activities on Federal Public Lands*, 41 IDAHO L. REV. 475.

Bluemel, Erik B. (2005b), *Prioritizing Multiple Uses on Public Lands after* Bear Lodge, 32 B.C. ENVTL. AFF. L. REV. 365.

Blumenfeld, Jeffrey, & Christy C. Kunin (1998), *Local Competition and Universal Service: New Solutions, Old Myths*, in TELECOMMUNICATIONS: LAW, REGULATION, AND POLICY (Walter Sapronov & William H. Read eds.).

Blumenthal, Marjory S., & David D. Clark (2001), *Rethinking the Design of the Internet: The End-to-End Arguments vs. the Brave New World*, 1 ACM TRANSACTIONS ON INTERNET TECH. 70.

Bollier, David (2001), Public Assets, Private Profits: Reclaiming the American Commons in an Age of Market Enclosure, *available at* http://www.bollier.org/pdf/PA_Report.pdf.

BOLTER, WALTER G., JAMES W. MCCONNAUGHEY, & FRED J. KELSEY (1990), TELECOMMUNICATIONS POLICY FOR THE 1990S AND BEYOND.

Bontis, Nick (2005), *National Intellectual Capital Index: The Benchmarking of Arab Countries*, in INTELLECTUAL CAPITAL FOR COMMUNITIES (Ahmed Bounfour & Leif Edvinsson eds.).

Bos, Dieter (2003), *Regulation: Theory and Concepts*, in INTERNATIONAL HANDBOOK ON PRIVATIZATION 477 (David Parker & David S. Saal eds.).

Bourdieu, Pierre (1986), *The Forms of Capital*, in HANDBOOK OF THEORY AND RESEARCH FOR THE SOCIOLOGY OF EDUCATION 249 (J. Richardson ed.).

BOWES, MICHAEL D., & JOHN V. KRUTILLA (1989), MULTIPLE-USE MANAGEMENT: THE ECONOMICS OF PUBLIC FORESTLANDS.

BOYLE, JAMES (1996), SHAMANS, SOFTWARE, AND SPLEENS: LAW AND THE CONSTRUCTION OF THE INFORMATION SOCIETY.

Boyle, James (1997), *A Politics of Intellectual Property: Environmentalism for the Net?*, 47 DUKE L. J. 87.

Boyle, James (2003), *The Second Enclosure Movement and the Construction of the Public Domain*, 66 L. & CONTEMP. PROBS. 33.

BOYLE, JAMES (2010), THE PUBLIC DOMAIN: ENCLOSING THE COMMONS OF THE MIND.

Bradner, Scott (2011), *Eyes in Their Ankles: The Congressional View of Network Neutrality*, Network World, Mar. 14, *available at* http://www.networkworld.com/columnists/2011/031411bradner. html

Branscomb, Lewis M., & James H. Keller (1996), *Introduction*, in CONVERGING INFRASTRUCTURES: INTELLIGENT TRANSPORTATION AND THE NATIONAL INFORMATION INFRASTRUCTURE (Lewis M. Branscomb & James H. Keller eds.).

Breen, John M. (2006), Modesty and Moralism: John Paul II, the Structures of Sin, and the Limits of Law—A Reply to Skeel & Stuntz (unpublished manuscript).

Brenner, Daniel (1998), LAW AND REGULATION OF COMMON CARRIERS IN THE COMMU-NICATIONS INDUSTRY (2d ed.).

Brin, Sergey (2009), *A Library to Last Forever*, N.Y. TIMES, Oct. 9.

Broadband Access Grows 29 Percent, While Narrowband Declines, according to Nielsen// NetRatings, Nielsen//Netratings, Jan. 15, 2003, *available at* http://www.nielsen-online.com/ pr/pr_030115.pdf.

BROCK, GERALD W. (1981), THE TELECOMMUNICATIONS INDUSTRY: THE DYNAMICS OF MARKET STRUCTURE.

BROWN, RICHARD E. (2010), BUSINESS ESSENTIALS FOR UTILITY ENGINEERS.

BROWN, STEPHEN J., & DAVID S. SIBLEY (1986), THE THEORY OF PUBLIC UTILITY PRICING.

Brown, Thomas C., & George L. Peterson (2003), *Multiple Good Valuation, in* A PRIMER ON NONMARKET VALUATION (Patricia A. Champ et al. eds.).

BROWN WEISS, EDITH (1989), IN FAIRNESS TO FUTURE GENERATIONS: INTERNATIONAL LAW, COMMON PATRIMONY, AND INTERGENERATIONAL EQUITY.

Brown Weiss, Edith (1990), *What Obligation Does Our Generation Owe to the Next? An Approach to Global Environmental Responsibility: Our Rights and Obligations to Future Generations for the Environment*, 84 AM. J. INT'L. L. 198.

Brown Weiss, Edith (1995), *Intergenerational Equity: Toward an International Legal Framework, in* GLOBAL ACCORD: ENVIRONMENTAL CHALLENGES AND INTERNATIONAL RESPONSES 333 (Nazli Choucri ed.).

Buchanan, James M. (1952), *The Pricing of Highway Services*, 5 NAT'L TAX J. 106.

Buchanan, James M., & William Craig Stubblebine (1962), *Externality*, 29 ECONOMICA 371.

BULL, ALBERTO (2004), TRAFFIC CONGESTION: THE PROBLEM AND HOW TO DEAL WITH IT.

Bureau of Transportation Statistics (2010), National Transportation Statistics, *available at* http://www.bts.gov/publications/national_transportation_statistics/.

Burger, Joanna et al. (2001), *Introduction, in* PROTECTING THE COMMONS: A FRAMEWORK FOR RESOURCE MANAGEMENT IN THE AMERICAS (Joanna Burger et al. eds.).

Burk, Dan L. (2000), *Patenting Speech*, 79 TEX. L. REV. 99.

Burk, Dan L., & Mark A. Lemley (2003), *Policy Levers in Patent Law*, 89 VA. L. REV. 1575.

Burk, Dan L., & Mark A. Lemley (2005), *Quantum Patent Mechanics*, 9 LEWIS & CLARK L. REV. 29.

BURK, DAN L., & MARK A. LEMLEY (2009), THE PATENT CRISIS AND HOW THE COURTS CAN SOLVE IT.

BURKHEAD, JESSE, & JERRY MINER (2007), PUBLIC EXPENDITURE.

BUSH, VANNEVAR (1954), SCIENCE, THE ENDLESS FRONTIER.

Button, Kenneth (1996), *Ownership, Investment and Pricing of Transport and Communications Infrastructure, in* INFRASTRUCTURE AND THE COMPLEXITY OF ECONOMIC DEVELOPMENT (David F. Batten & Charlie Karlsson eds.).

BUTTON, KENNETH JOHN (1993), TRANSPORT ECONOMICS (2d ed.).

BUTTON, KENNETH JOHN (2010), TRANSPORT ECONOMICS (3rd ed.).

Cain, Louis P. (1998), *A Canal and Its City: A Selective Business History of Chicago*, 11 DEPAUL BUS. L. J. 125, 142–43.

Canoy, Marcel, et al. (2004), *Access to Telecommunications Networks, in* THE ECONOMICS OF ANTITRUST AND REGULATION IN TELECOMMUNICATIONS 161 (Pierre A. Buigues & Patrick Rey eds.).

CARRIER, MICHAEL A. (2009), INNOVATION FOR THE 21ST CENTURY: HARNESSING THE POWER OF INTELLECTUAL PROPERTY AND ANTITRUST LAW.

CARLTON, DENNIS W., & JEFFREY M. PERLOFF (1990), MODERN INDUSTRIAL ORGANIZATION.

Caruso, Andrew J. (2003), *The Experimental Use Exception: An Experimentalist's View*, 14 ALB. L. J. SCI. & TECH. 215.

Cherry, Barbara (2003), *Utilizing "Essentiality of Access" Analyses to Mitigate Risky, Costly and Untimely Government Interventions in Converging Telecommunications Technologies and Markets*, 11 COMMLAW CONSPECTUS 251.

Cherry, Barbara (2006), *Misusing Network Neutrality to Eliminate Common Carriage Threatens Free Speech and the Postal System*, 33 N. KY. L. REV. 483.

Cherry, Steven (2005), *The VoIP Backlash*, 42 IEEE SPECTRUM 61.

Chiang, Tun-Jen (2011), *The Levels of Abstraction Problem in Patent Law*, 105 Nw. U. L. REV. (forthcoming).

Chittenden, Maurice (2009), *Harry and Charlie Davies-Carr: Web Gets Taste for Biting Baby*, TIMES (London), Nov. 1, *available at* http://technology.timesonline.co.uk/tol/news/tech_and_web/the_web/article6898146.ece.

Choi, Jay Pil, & Byung-Cheol Kim (2008), *Net Neutrality and Investment Incentives*, NET Institute, Working Paper No. 08-03, September, *available at* http://papers.ssrn.com/sol3/papers.cfm?abstract_id=1285639.

CHRISTENSEN, CLAYTON M. (1997), THE INNOVATOR'S DILEMMA.

Cisco Systems, Inc., Network-Based Application Recognition, *available at* http://www.cisco.com/en/US/products/ps6616/products_ios_protocol_group_home.html (last visited Mar. 4, 2011).

Cisco Systems, Inc., Network-Based Application Recognition and Distributed Network-Based Application Recognition, *available at* http://www.cisco.com/en/US/products/ps6350/products_configuration_guide_chapter09186a0080455985.html (last visited Sept. 30, 2006).

Coase, Ronald H. (1946), *The Marginal Cost Controversy*, 13 ECONOMICA 169.

Coase, Ronald H. (1947), *The Marginal Cost Controversy: Some Further Comments*, 14 ECONOMICA 150.

Coase, Ronald H. (1960), *The Problem of Social Cost*, 3 J. L. & ECON. 1.

COASE, R. H. (1988), THE FIRM, THE MARKET, AND THE LAW.

Cohen, Amy B. (1987), *Masking Copyright Decisionmaking: The Meaninglessness of Substantial Similarity*, 20 U.C. DAVIS L. REV. 719.

Cohen, Julie E. (1998), *Lochner in Cyberspace: The New Economic Orthodoxy of "Rights Management,"* 97(2) MICHIGAN L. REV. 462.

Cohen, Julie E. (2000), *Copyright and the Perfect Curve*, 53 VANDERBILT L. REV. 1799.

Cohen, Julie E. (2001), *Examined Lives: Informational Privacy and the Subject as Object*, 52 STANFORD L. REV. 1373.

Cohen, Julie E. (2005), *The Place of the User in Copyright Law*, 74 FORDHAM L. REV. 347.

Cohen, Julie E. (2007), *Creativity and Culture in Copyright Theory*, 40 U.C. DAVIS L. REV. 1151.

Cohen, Wesley, Richard Nelson, & John Walsh (2000), *Protecting Their Intellectual Assets: Appropriability Conditions and Why U.S. Manufacturing Firms Patent (or Not)*, NBER Working Paper 7552, February, *available at* http://www.nber.org/papers/w7552.

COLANDER, DAVID (1996), BEYOND MICROFOUNDATIONS: POST-WALRASIAN MACROECONOMICS.

Coleman, James S. (1988), *Social Capital in the Creation of Human Capital*, 94 AMERICAN J. OF SOCIOLOGY S95.

Colvile, R. N. et al. (2002), *The Transport Sector as a Source of Air Pollution*, *in* AIR POLLUTION SCIENCE FOR THE 21ST CENTURY (J. Austin et al. eds.).

Comments of Cablevision Systems Corp., In the Matter of Preserving the Open Internet, GN Docket No. 09-191, WC Docket No. 07-52 (Received Jan. 14, 2010).

Comments of the Motion Picture Association of America Inc., In the Matter of a National Broadband Plan for Our Future, GN Docket No. 09-51 (October 30, 2009).

Comments of Open Internet Coalition, In the Matter of Preserving the Open Internet, GN Docket No. 09-191, WC Docket No. 07-52 (Jan. 14, 2010).

Comments of Recording Industry Association of American, In the Matter of Preserving the Open Internet, GN Docket No. 09-191, WC Docket No. 07-52 (Jan. 14, 2010).

Comments of Time Warner Cable Inc., In the Matter of Preserving the Open Internet, GN Docket No. 09-191, WC Docket No. 07-52 (Received Jan. 14, 2010).

Confessore, Nicholas (2008), *$8 Traffic Fee for Manhattan Gets Nowhere*, N.Y. TIMES, Apr. 8, *available at* http://www.nytimes.com/2008/04/08/nyregion/08congest.html.

Congressional Budget Office (1998), The Economic Effects of Federal Spending on Infrastructure and Other Investments, *available at* http://www.cbo.gov/ftpdocs/6xx/doc601/fedspend.pdf.

Congressional Budget Office (2003), The Long-Term Budget Outlook, *available at* http://www.cbo.gov/ftpdocs/49xx/doc4916/Report.pdf.

Congressional Budget Office (2009), *Using Pricing to Reduce Traffic Congestion*, Study, March.

Congressional Budget Office Testimony (2003), Statement of Douglas Holtz-Eakin, Congestion Pricing on Highways, May 6, *available at* http://www.cbo.gov/doc.cfm?index=4197&type=0.

Cooper, Mark (2005), Making the Network Connection: Using Network Theory to Explain the Link between Open Digital Platforms and Innovation, *available at* http://cyberlaw.stanford.edu/blogs/cooper/archives/network%20theory.pdf (last visited Jan. 20, 2005).

CORNES, RICHARD, & TODD SANDLER (1996), THE THEORY OF EXTERNALITIES, PUBLIC GOODS, AND CLUB GOODS (2d ed.).

Costanza, Robert, et al. (1997), *The Value of the World's Ecosystem Services and Natural Capital*, 387 NATURE 15.

Cotropia, Christopher A., & Mark A. Lemley (2009), *Copying in Patent Law*, 87 N.C. L. REV. 1421.

Cowan, Simon (2006), *Network Regulation*, 22(2) OXFORD REV. OF ECONOMIC POLICY.

Cowan, Simon (2007), *The Welfare Effects of Third-Degree Price Discrimination with Nonlinear Demand Functions*, 38 RAND J. OF ECON. 419.

Crawford, Susan P. (2005), *Shortness of Vision: Regulatory Ambition in the Digital Age*, 74 FORDHAM L. REV. 695.

Crawford, Susan P. (2009), *Transporting Communications*, 89 B.U.L. REV. 871.

Crossley, Robert (2009), *World of Warcraft Dominates MMO Market*, EDGE MAGAZINE, Mar. 24, *available at* http://www.next-gen.biz/news/world-warcraft-dominates-mmo-market.

CRTC Regulatory Policy 2009-657, *available at* http://www.cippic.ca/uploads/File/Attachment_B_pt_1_-_Reed_Report.pdf (testimony of Dr. David Reed).

Crump, David (2001), *Game Theory, Legislation, and the Multiple Meanings of Equality*, 38 HARVARD J. LEGIS. 331.

Daily, Gretchen C., et al. (1997), *Ecosystem Services: Benefits Supplied to Human Societies by Natural Ecosystems*, ISSUES ECOLOGY, Spring, *available at* http://www.epa.gov/watertrain/pdf/issue2.pdf.

Daily, Gretchen C., et al. (2000), *Value of Nature and the Nature of Value*, 289 SCIENCE 395.

Dal Bo, Ernesto (2006), *Regulatory Capture: A Review*, 22(2) OXFORD REV. OF ECONOMIC POLICY 203–25.

Daly, Herman E. (1992), *From Empty-World Economics to Full-World Economics: Recognizing an Historical Turning Point in Economic Development, in* POPULATION, TECHNOLOGY AND LIFESTYLE (Robert Goodland et al. eds.).

Daly, Herman E. (2005), *Economics in a Full World*, 293 SCIENTIFIC AMERICAN 3.

Dasgupta, Partha (2002), *Killer Apps*, Arizona State University, May 1, *available at* http://cactus. eas.asu.edu/partha/Columns/2002/07–01-killer-app.htm.

David, Paul A., & Dominique Foray (1996), *Information Distribution and the Growth of Economically Valuable Knowledge: A Rationale for Technological Infrastructure Policies, in* TECHNOLOGICAL INFRASTRUCTURE POLICY: AN INTERNATIONAL PERSPECTIVE (M. Teubal et al. eds.)

DeGraba, P. (1990), *Input Market Price Discrimination and the Choice of Technology*, 80 AMERICAN ECON. REV. 1246–53.

DEMARTINO, GEORGE (2000), GLOBAL ECONOMY, GLOBAL JUSTICE.

Demsetz, Harold (1967), *Toward a Theory of Property Rights*, 57 AM. ECON. REV. PAPERS & PROC. 347.

Demsetz, Harold (1970), *The Private Production of Public Goods*, 13 J. L. & ECON. 293.

DEPARTMENT OF TRANSPORTATION (2008), REPORT TO CONGRESS.

Deshpande, Manasi, and Douglas W. Elmendorf (2008), *An Economic Strategy for Investing in America's Infrastructure*, BROOKINGS INSTITUTION, July.

DODD, EDWIN MERRICK (1954), AMERICAN BUSINESS CORPORATIONS UNTIL 1860: WITH SPECIAL REFERENCE TO MASSACHUSETTS.

DOERN, G. BRUCE, & MONICA GATTINGER (2003), POWER SWITCH: ENERGY REGULATORY GOVERNANCE IN THE TWENTY-FIRST CENTURY.

Doll, Susan, & Greg Faller (1986), *Blade Runner and Genre: Film Noir and Science Fiction*, 14(2) LIT. FILM Q. 89.

Dreyfuss, Rochelle Cooper (2010), *Does IP Need IP? Accommodating Intellectual Production Outside the Intellectual Property Paradigm*, 31 CARDOZO L. REV. 1437.

DRIESEN, DAVID M. (2003), THE ECONOMIC DYNAMICS OF ENVIRONMENTAL LAW.

Driesen, David M. (2010), *Toward Sustainable Technology, in* ECONOMIC THOUGHT AND U.S. CLIMATE CHANGE POLICY 257 (David M. Driesen ed.).

Duffy, John F. (2004), *The Marginal Cost Controversy in Intellectual Property*, 71 U. CHICAGO L. REV. 37, *available at* http://ssrn.com/abstract=1090648.

Duffy, John F. (2005), *Comment: Intellectual Property Isolationism and the Average Cost Thesis*, 83 TEX. L. REV. 1077.

Eagle, Josh (2006), *Regional Ocean Governance: The Perils of Multiple-Use Management and the Promise of Agency Diversity*, 16 DUKE ENVTL. L. & POL'Y F. 143.

Eastman, Wayne (1997), *Telling Alternative Stories: Heterodox Versions of the Prisoner's Dilemma, the Coase Theorem, and Supply-Demand Equilibrium*, 29 CONN. L. REV 727.

Economides, Nicholas (1996a), *The Economics of Networks*, 14 INT. J. INDUS. ORG. 673.

Economides, Nicholas (1996b), *Network Externalities, Complementarities, and Invitations to Enter*, 12 EUROPEAN J. OF POL. ECON. 211.

Economides, Nicholas (2003), *Competition Policy in Network Industries: An Introduction, in* THE NEW ECONOMY: JUST HOW NEW IS IT (Dennis Jansen ed.).

Economides, Nicholas (2008), *Antitrust Issues in Network Industries, in* THE REFORM OF EC COMPETITION LAW (Ioannis Kokkoris and Ioannis Lianos eds.).

Economides, Nicholas (2010), *Why Imposing New Tolls on Third-Party Content and Applications Threatens Innovation and Will Not Improve Broadband Providers' Investments*, GN Docket

No. 09-191, WC Docket. No. 07-52 (filed with the FCC as "Appendix A" on behalf of Google, Jan. 14).

Edwards, Mathew A. (2006), *Price and Prejudice: The Case against Consumer Equality in the Information Age*, 10 LEWIS & CLARK L. REV. 559.

Egypt Internet Users Report Major Network Interruptions (2011), TVNZ (New Zealand), Jan. 28, *available at* http://tvnz.co.nz/technology-news/egypt-internet-users-report-major-network-disruptions-4008917.

Egypt Protesters Use Voice Tweets (2011), BBC, Feb. 1, *available at* http://www.bbc.co.uk/news/technology-12332850.

Eisenberg, Rebecca S. (1994), *Technology Transfer and the Genome Project: Problems with Patenting Research Tools*, 5 RISK 163, 163–67.

Eisenberg, Rebecca S. (1996), *Public Research and Private Development: Patents and Technology Transfer in Government-Sponsored Research*, 82 VA. L. REV. 1663, 1702–04.

Eisenberg, Rebecca S. (2001), *Bargaining over the Transfer of Proprietary Research Tools: Is This Market Failing or Emerging?*, *in* EXPANDING THE BOUNDARIES OF INTELLECTUAL PROPERTY: INNOVATION POLICY FOR THE KNOWLEDGE SOCIETY (R. C. Dreyfuss et al. eds.) 223–50.

ELLICKSON, ROBERT C. (1991), ORDER WITHOUT LAW: HOW NEIGHBORS SETTLE DISPUTES.

Encyclopedia Britannica (2006), *Fatally Flawed: Refuting the Recent Study on Encyclopedic Accuracy by the Journal Nature*, ENCYCLOPEDIA BRITANNICA (March).

EPSTEIN, RICHARD A. (1998), PRINCIPLES FOR A FREE SOCIETY: RECONCILING INDIVIDUAL LIBERTY WITH THE COMMON GOOD.

Epstein, Larry G. (1999), *A Definition of Uncertainty Aversion*, 66(3) REVIEW OF ECONOMIC STUDIES 579.

Facebook Statistics, Facebook, *available at* http://www.facebook.com/press/info.php?statistics (last visited Feb. 26, 2011).

Faherty, Keith F. (1999), *Mechanical Fasteners and Connectors, in* WOOD ENGINEERING AND CONSTRUCTION HANDBOOK (Keith Faherty & Thomas Williamson eds.).

Farber, Daniel A. (1991), *Free Speech without Romance: Public Choice and the First Amendment*, 105 HARV. L. REV. 554.

Farber, Daniel A. (2006), *Another View of the Quagmire: Unconstitutional Conditions and Contract Theory*, 33 FLA. ST. U. L. REV. 913.

Farber, Daniel A., & Phillip P. Frickley (1987), *The Jurisprudence of Public Choice*, 65. TEX. L. REV. 873.

Farrell, Joseph, & Philip Weiser (2003), *Modularity, Vertical Integration, and Open Access Policies: Towards Convergence of Antitrust and Regulation in the Internet Age*, 17 HARVARD J. L. & TECH. 85.

Faulhaber, Gerald (2005), *The Question of Spectrum: Technology, Management, and Regime Change*, 4 J. TELECOMM. & HIGH TECH L. 123.

Faulhaber, Gerald R., & David Farber (2003), *Spectrum Management: Property Rights, Markets, and the Commons, in* RETHINKING RIGHTS AND REGULATIONS: INSTITUTIONAL RESPONSES TO NEW COMMUNICATION TECHNOLOGIES 193.

FCC Report and Order (2010), Preserving the Open Internet; Broadband Industry Practices (released Dec. 23), GN Docket No. 09-191, WC Docket No. 07-52, FCC 10-201, *available at* http://hraunfoss.fcc.gov/edocs_public/attachmatch/FCC-10-201A1.pdf.

Federal Communications Commission (2005), Appropriate Framework for Broadband Access to the Internet over Wireline Facilities, Report and Order and Notice of Proposed Rulemaking, 20 F.C.C.R. 14853.

Federal Communications Commission (2010), National Broadband Plan: Connecting America, available at http://www.broadband.gov/plan/.

Federal Highway Administration (2006), Congestion Pricing: A Primer (2006), *available at* http://ops.fhwa.dot.gov/publications/congestionpricing/congestionpricing.pdf.

Federal Highway Administration (2008), Report to Congress, 14–10.

Federal Interagency Ecosystem Management Task Force, Memorandum of Understanding to Foster the Ecosystem Approach between the Council on Envtl. Quality et al. (Dec. 15, 1995), *available at* http://www.fhwa.dot.gov/legsregs/directives/policy/memoofun.htm.

FIELD, JOHN (2008), SOCIAL CAPITAL (2d ed.).

Fink, Carsten (2009), *Promoting Checks and Balances, in* INTELLECTUAL PROPERTY AND SUSTAINABLE DEVELOPMENT 363 (Ricardo Melendez-Ortiz & Pedro Roffe eds.).

FISHER, WILLIAM W., III (2004), PROMISES TO KEEP: TECHNOLOGY, LAW, AND THE FUTURE OF ENTERTAINMENT.

FISHER, WILLIAM W., III, & TALHA SYED (forthcoming), DRUGS, LAW, AND THE HEALTH CRISIS IN THE DEVELOPING WORLD.

Flores, Nicholas E. (2003), *Conceptual Framework for Nonmarket Valuation, in* A PRIMER ON NONMARKET VALUATION (Patricia A. Champ et al. eds.).

Freeman, A. Myrick III (2003a), *Economic Valuation: What and Why, in* A PRIMER ON NONMARKET VALUATION (Patricia A. Champ et al. eds.).

FREEMAN, A. MYRICK III (2003b), THE MEASUREMENT OF ENVIRONMENTAL AND RESOURCE VALUES: THEORY AND METHODS (2d ed.).

FREY, BRUNO (2008), HAPPINESS: A REVOLUTION IN ECONOMICS.

FRIEDMAN, MILTON (1962), CAPITALISM AND FREEDOM.

Frischmann, Brett M. (2000), *Innovation and Institutions: Rethinking the Economics of U.S. Science and Technology Policy*, 24 VERMONT L. REV. 347.

Frischmann, Brett M. (2001), *Privatization and Commercialization of the Internet Infrastructure: Rethinking Market Intervention into Government and Government Intervention into the Market*, 2 COLUM. SCIENCE & TECH. L. REV., *available at* http://www.stlr.org/cite.cgi?volume=2&article=1.

Frischmann, Brett M. (2005a), *An Economic Theory of Infrastructure and Commons Management*, 89 MINN. L. REV. 917.

Frischmann, Brett M. (2005b), *Peer-to-Peer Technology as Infrastructure: An Economic Argument For Retaining Sony's Safe Harbor For Technologies Capable of Substantial Noninfringing Uses*, 52 J. OF THE COPYRIGHT SOC. 329.

Frischmann, Brett M. (2005c), *Commercializing University Research Systems in Economic Perspective: A View from the Demand Side, in* 16 ADVANCES IN THE STUDY OF ENTREPRENEURSHIP, INNOVATION AND ECONOMIC GROWTH, UNIVERSITY ENTREPRENEURSHIP AND TECHNOLOGY TRANSFER: PROCESS, DESIGN, AND INTELLECTUAL PROPERTY 155 (Gary D. Libecap ed.).

Frischmann, Brett M. (2005d), *Some Thoughts on Shortsightedness and Intergenerational Equity*, 36 LOYOLA UNIVERSITY CHICAGO L. J. 457.

Frischmann, Brett M. (2007a), *Cultural Environmentalism and the Wealth of Networks*, 74 U. CHICAGO L. REV. 1083.

Frischmann, Brett M. (2007b), *Evaluating the Demsetzian Trend in Copyright Law*, 3(3) REV. OF L. & ECON., *available at* http://www.bepress.com/rle/vol3/iss3/art2.

Frischmann, Brett M. (2007c), *Infrastructure Commons in Economic Perspective*, 12(6) FIRST MONDAY, June, *available at* http://firstmonday.org/issues/issue12_6/frischmann/index.html.

Frischmann, Brett M. (2008a), *Environmental Infrastructure*, 35 ECOLOGY L. Q.

Frischmann, Brett M. (2008b), *Speech, Spillovers, and the First Amendment*, 2008 U. CHICAGO LEGAL FORUM 301.

Frischmann, Brett M. (2009a), *The Pull of Patents*, 77 FORDHAM L. REV. 2143.

Frischmann, Brett M. (2009b), *Spillovers Theory and Its Conceptual Boundaries*, 51 WILLIAM & MARY L. REV. 801.

Frischmann, Brett M., & Mark A. Lemley (2007), *Spillovers*, 107 COLUM. L. REV. 257.

Frischmann, Brett, & Mark McKenna (2011), *Intergenerational Progress*, 2011 WISCONSIN L. REV. 123.

Frischmann, Brett M., & Barbara van Schewick (2007), *Network Neutrality and the Economics of an Information Superhighway*, 47 JURIMETRICS 383.

Frischmann, Brett, & Spencer Waller (2008), *Revitalizing Essential Facilities*, ANTITRUST L. J.

Fromer, Jeanne (2009), *Claiming Intellectual Property*, 76 U. CHI. L. REV. 719.

FTC (2003), To Promote Innovation: The Proper Balance of Competition and Patent Law and Policy, October.

Fudenberg, D., & J. M. Villas-Boas (2006), *Behavior-Based Price Discrimination and Customer Recognition, in* ECONOMICS AND INFORMATION SYSTEMS 377 (Terrence Hendershott ed.).

GAL, MICHAL S. (2003), COMPETITION POLICY FOR SMALL MARKET ECONOMIES.

Gallagher, Ian (2011), *Egyptian Police Use Facebook and Twitter to Track Down Protesters' Names before "Rounding Them Up,"* DAILY MAIL (London), Feb. 6, *available at* http://www.dailymail.co.uk/news/article-1354096/Egypt-protests-Police-use-Facebook-Twitter-track-protesters.html.

GAYNOR, MARK (2003), NETWORK SERVICES INVESTMENT GUIDE: MAXIMIZING ROI IN UNCERTAIN TIMES.

Gaynor, Mark, & Scott Bradner (2007), *Statistical Framework to Value Network Neutrality*, 17 MEDIA L. & POL'Y 24.

Genachowski, Julius (2010), Chairman, Federal Commc'n Comm'n, Remarks on Preserving Internet Freedom and Openness (Dec. 1), transcript, *available at* http://hraunfoss.fcc.gov/edocs_public/attachmatch/DOC-303136A1.pdf).

Ghosh, Shubha (2004), *Patents and the Regulatory State: Rethinking the Patent Bargain Metaphor after Eldred*, 19 BERKELEY TECH. L. J. 1315.

Ghosh, Shubha (2008), *Decoding and Recoding Natural Monopoly, Regulation, and Intellectual Property*, 2008 U. ILL. L. REV. 1125.

Ghosh, A., & Meagher, K. (2004), *Political Economy of Infrastructure Investment: A Spatial Approach.* In NORTH AMERICAN ECONOMETRIC SOCIETY SUMMER MEETINGS AT BROWN UNIVERSITY, PROVIDENCE, USA.

Gifford, Daniel J., & Robert T. Kudrle (2010), *The Law and Economics of Price Discrimination in Modern Economies: Time for Reconciliation?*, 43 U. C. DAVIS L. REV.

Giles, Jim (2005), *Internet Encyclopaedias Go Head to Head*, NATURE, Dec. 15.

Gillis, Justin, & John Collins Rudolf (2010), *Oil Plume Is Not Breaking Down Fast Enough, Study Says*, N.Y. TIMES, Aug. 19, 2010, *available at* http://www.nytimes.com/2010/08/20/science/earth/20plume.html.

Godin, Benoît (2006), *The Linear Model of Innovation: The Historical Construction of an Analytical Framework*, 31(6) SCIENCE, TECHNOLOGY, & HUMAN VALUES 639.

GOMEZ, JOSE A. (2003), REGULATING INFRASTRUCTURE.

Gönenç, Rauf, Maria Maher, & Giuseppe Nicoletti (2001), *The Implementation and the Effects of Regulatory Reform: Past Experience and Current Issues*, 2001(32) OECD ECONOMIC STUDIES I.

Goodman, Ellen P. (2004), *Spectrum Rights in the Telecosm to Come*, 41 SAN DIEGO L. REV. 269.

Gordon, Wendy J. (1982), *Fair Use as Market Failure: A Structural and Economic Analysis of the Betamax Case and Its Predecessors*, 82 COLUMBIA LAW REVIEW 1600.

Gordon, Wendy J. (1993), *A Property Right in Self-Expression: Equality and Individualism in the Natural Law of Intellectual Property*, 102 YALE L. J. 1533.

Green, Jerry, & Suzanne Scotchmer (1995), *On the Division of Profits between Sequential Innovators*, 26 RAND J. ECON. 20.

H.R. Rep. No. 190, 67th Cong., 1st sess. 1 (1921).

Hahn, Robert, & Scott Wallsten (2006), *The Economics of Network Neutrality*, ECONOMISTS' VOICE.

Hamelink, P. (1998), *Environmental Policy and Fiscal Instruments in The Netherlands, in* AIR POLLUTION IN THE 21ST CENTURY: PRIORITY ISSUES AND POLICY 969 (T. Schneider ed.).

Hamilton, Walter H. (1930), *Affection with Public Interest*, 39 YALE L. J. 1089.

Hanifan, L. J. (1916), *The Rural School Community Center*, 67 ANNALS OF THE AM. ACADEMY OF POL. & SOC. SCIENCE 130.

Hardin, Garrett (1968), *The Tragedy of the Commons*, 162 SCIENCE 1243.

HARDIN, RUSSELL (1997), ONE FOR ALL.

Harrington, William et al. (1998), *Overcoming Public Aversion to Congestion Pricing*, Discussion Paper 98–27, RESOURCES FOR THE FUTURE, *available at* http://rff.org/RFF/Documents/RFF-DP-98–27.pdf.

Hausman, J. (1999), *The Effect of Sunk Costs in Telecommunication Regulation, in* THE NEW INVESTMENT THEORY OF REAL OPTIONS AND ITS IMPLICATIONS FOR TELECOMMUNICATIONS ECONOMICS (J. Alleman and E. Noam eds.).

Hausman, J., Ariel Pakes, & Gregory L. Rosston (1997), *Valuation and the Effect of Regulation on New Services in Telecommunications*, 1997 BROOKINGS PAPERS ON ECONOMIC ACTIVITY: MICROECONOMICS 1.

Haynes, Paul (2009), *Before Going Any Further with Social Capital*, Ingenio Working Paper Series No. 2009/02.

Hazlett, Thomas W. (2005), *Spectrum Tragedies*, 22 YALE J. ON REG. 242.

Heal, Geoffrey et al. (2001), *Protecting Natural Capital through Ecosystem Service Districts*, 20 STANFORD ENVTL. L. J. 333.

Heimbuch, Jaymi (2010), *Going Bee-less*, TREEHUGGER, April 19, 2010, *available at* http://www.treehugger.com/files/2010/04/going-bee-less-trials-of-self-pollinating-almond-trees-begin-in-california.php.

HEINZERLING, LISA, & FRANK ACKERMAN (2005), PRICELESS: ON KNOWING THE PRICE OF EVERYTHING AND THE VALUE OF NOTHING.

Helpman, Elhanan (1998), *Introduction, in* GENERAL PURPOSE TECHNOLOGIES AND ECONOMIC GROWTH (Elhanan Helpman ed.).

Hemphill, C. Scott (2008), *Network Neutrality and the False Promise of Zero-Price Regulation*, 25 YALE J. ON REGULATION 135.

Hemphill, Scott, & Jeannie Suk (2009), *The Law, Culture, and Economics of Fashion*, 61 STAN. L. REV. 1147.

Henderson, Rebecca, Adam B. Jaffe, & Manuel Trajtenberg (1998), *Universities as a Source of Commercial Technology: A Detailed Analysis of University Patenting, 1965–1988*, 80 REV. ECON. & STAT. 119.

HENRICH, JOSEPH, ET AL. (2003), ECONOMIC MAN IN CROSS-CULTURAL PERSPECTIVE: BEHAVIORAL EXPERIMENTS, IN 15 SMALL-SCALE SOCIETIES.

Hess, Charlotte, & Elinor Ostrom (2003), *Ideas, Artifacts, and Facilities: Information as a Common-Pool Resource*, 66 L. & CONTEMP. PROBLEMS 111.

Heverly, Robert (2003), *The Information Semicommons*, 18 BERKELEY TECH. L. J. 1127.

HILL, CHARLES W. L., & GARETH R. JONES (2008), STRATEGIC MANAGEMENT: AN INTEGRATED APPROACH.

Hinsell, Saul (2009), *The Broadband Gap: Why Do They Have More Fiber?*, N.Y. TIMES, Mar. 12.

Hoffman, David A., & Salil K. Mehra (2010), *Wikitruth through Wikiorder*, 59 EMORY L. J. 151.

Hogendorn, Christiaan (2010), *Spillovers and Network Neutrality*, OPEN INTERNET COALITION, *available at* http://www.openinternetcoalition.com/files/final_Hogendorn_0108.pdf.

Holmlund, Cecilia M., & Monica Hammer (1999), *Ecosystem Services Generated by Fish Population*, 29 ECOLOGICAL ECON. 253.

Horrigan, John B. (2010), *Broadband Adoption and Use in America*, FCC Omnibus Broadband Initiative, Feb. 2010, *available at* http://hraunfoss.fcc.gov/edocs_public/attachmatch/DOC-296442A1.pdf.

Hotelling, Harold (1938), *The General Welfare in Relation to Problems of Taxation and of Railway and Utility Rates*, 6 ECONOMETRICA 242.

Huddleston, Rep. (1921), Remarks, 61 Cong. Rec. 1988.

Hulten, Charles R. (1996), *Infrastructure Capital and Economic Growth: How Well You Use It May Be More Important Than How Much You Have*, NBER Working Paper No. 5847.

HUME, DAVID (1986), A TREATISE ON HUMAN NATURE (L.A. Shelby-Bigge ed.).

Inderst, Roman, & Greg Shaffer (2009), *Market Power, Price Discrimination, and Allocative Efficiency in Intermediate-Goods Markets*, 40 RAND J. OF ECON. 658.

INTERNATIONAL FINANCE PROJECT (1999), PROJECT FINANCE IN DEVELOPING COUNTRIES.

Internet Protocol: DARPA Internet Program Protocol Specification, IETF RFC 791, Sept. 1981, *available at* http://www.ietf.org/rfc/rfc0791.txt?number=791.

Isenberg, David (1998), *Dawn of the Stupid Network*, ACM NETWORKER, FEB./MAR. 1998, *available at* http://www.isen.com/papers/Dawnstupid.html.

Jaensirisak, S., et al. (2005), *Explaining Variations in Public Acceptability of Road Pricing Schemes*, 39(2) J. TRANSPORT ECON. & POL. 127.

Jefferson, Thomas (1813), Letter to Isaac McPherson, Monticello, Aug. 13.

JONES, CHARLES (1998), INTRODUCTION TO ECONOMIC GROWTH.

Jones, William (1980), The Common Carrier Concept as Applied to Telecom: A Historical Perspective, filed with the FCC as a part of the Competitive Carriers Rulemaking, CC Docket No. 79-252 (1980), and as a part of IBM's reply comments in Computer & Communications Industry Assoc. v. FCC, No. 80-1478 (filed 1982).

Justman, Moshe, & Morris Teubal (1996), *Technological Infrastructure Policy (TIP): Creating Capabilities and Building Markets, in* TECHNOLOGICAL INFRASTRUCTURE POLICY: AN INTERNATIONAL PERSPECTIVE 51–52.

Kahan, Dan M., & Donald Braman (2006), *Cultural Cognition and Public Policy*, 24 YALE L. & POL'Y REV. 147.

KAHN, ALFRED E. (1998), THE ECONOMICS OF REGULATION: PRINCIPLES AND INSTITUTIONS.

KAHN, ALFRED E. (2001), WHOM THE GODS WOULD DESTROY, OR HOW NOT TO DEREGULATE.

Kalapesi, Carl et al. (2010), *The Connected Kingdom: How the Internet Is Transforming the U.K. Economy*, BOSTON CONSULTING GROUP, October, *available at* http://www.bcg.com/documents/file62983.pdf.

Katz, M. (1987), *The Welfare Effects of Third-Degree Price Discrimination in Intermediate Goods Markets*, 77 AMERICAN ECON. REV. 154–67.

Katz, Michael L., & Carl Shapiro (1985), *Network Externalities, Competition, and Compatibility*, 75 AM. ECON. REV. 424.

Katz, Michael L., & Carl Shapiro (1994), *Systems Competition and Network Effects*, 8(2) J. OF ECON. PERSPECTIVES 93.

Kayne, R. (2011), *What Is a Packet Sniffer*, WISEGEEK, *available at* http://www.wisegeek.com/what-is-a-packet-sniffer.htm (last modified Feb. 24, 2011).

Kearney, Joseph D., & Thomas W. Merrill (1998), *The Great Transformation of Regulated Industries Law*, 98 COLUM. L. REV. 1323.

KELLOGG, MICHAEL K., JOHN THORNE, & PETER W. HUBER (1992), FEDERAL TELECOMMUNICATIONS LAW.

Kelly, Daniel (2011), *Strategic Spillovers*, 111 COLUMBIA L. REV.

KELTY, CHRISTOPHER M. (2008), TWO BITS: THE CULTURAL SIGNIFICANCE OF FREE SOFTWARE.

Kerner, Sean Michael (2008), *Narrowband on the Decline in the U.S.*, InternetNews, Nov. 17, *available at* http://www.internetnews.com/stats/article.php/3785496/Narrowband-on-the-Decline-in-the-US.htm.

Kesan, Jay P. (2009), *Transferring Innovation*, 77 FORDHAM L. REV. 2169.

KIDDER, FRANK EUGENE (1899), BUILDING CONSTRUCTION AND SUPERINTENDENCE.

Kieff, F. Scott (2001), *Property Rights and Property Rules for Commercializing Inventions*, 85 MINN. L. REV. 697.

Kitch, Edmund W. (1977), *The Nature and Function of the Patent System*, 20 J. L. & ECON. 265, 276–78.

Klein, Daniel B., & Gordon J. Fielding (1992), *Private Toll Roads: Learning from the 19th Century*, 46 TRANSPORTATION Q. 3.

Klein, Daniel, & John Majewski (2008), *Turnpikes and Toll Roads in Nineteenth-Century America*, E.H.NET ENCYCLOPEDIA (Robert Whaples ed.), *available at* http://eh.net/encyclopedia/article/Klein.Majewski.Turnpikes.

Kline, S. (1991a), *Models of Innovation and Their Policy Consequences, in* JAPANESE/AMERICAN TECHNOLOGICAL INNOVATION (David Kingery ed.).

Kline, S. (1991b), *Styles of Innovation and Their Cultural Basis*, CHEMTECH, August.

Kline, S. J., & Nathan Rosenberg (1986), *An Overview of Innovation, in* THE POSITIVE SUM STRATEGY (Ralph Landau & Nathan Rosenberg eds.).

Knight, F. H. (1921), RISK, UNCERTAINTY, AND PROFIT.

Knudsen, Christian (2003), *The Essential Tension in the Social Sciences: Between the "Unification" and "Fragmentation" Traps, in* THE EVOLUTION OF SCIENTIFIC KNOWLEDGE (Hans Siggaard Jensen et al. eds.).

Komanoff, Charles (1994), *Pollution Taxes for Roadway Transportation*, 12 PACE ENVTL. L. REV. 121.

Komesar, Neil K. (1994), Imperfect Alternatives: Choosing Institutions in Law, Economics, and Public Policy.

KOMESAR, NEIL K. (2001), Law's Limits: The Rule of Law and the Supply and Demand of Rights.

KRACKHARDT, DAVID (1994), ENDOGENOUS PREFERENCES: A STRUCTURAL APPROACH.

Krattenmaker, Thomas G., & Steven C. Salop (1986), *Anticompetitive Exclusion: Raising Rivals' Costs to Achieve Power over Price*, 96 YALE L. J. 234.

Kremen, Claire et al. (2007), *Pollination and Other Ecosystem Services Produced by Mobile Organisms: A Conceptual Framework for the Effects of Land-Use Change*, 10 ECOLOGY LETTERS 299.

KUHN, THOMAS (1962), THE STRUCTURE OF SCIENTIFIC REVOLUTIONS.

Kysar, Douglas A. (2004), *Climate Change, Cultural Transformation, and Comprehensive Rationality*, 31 B.C. ENVTL. AFF. L. REV. 589.

Laffont, J. J., & J. Tirole (1991), *The Politics of Government Decision Making: A Theory of Regulatory Capture*, 106(4) QUARTERLY J. OF ECON. 1089–1127.

LANDES, WILLIAM M., & RICHARD POSNER (2003), THE ECONOMIC STRUCTURE OF INTELLECTUAL PROPERTY LAW.

LANDES, WILLIAM M., & RICHARD A. POSNER (2004), THE POLITICAL ECONOMY OF INTELLECTUAL PROPERTY LAW.

LANDSBURG, STEVEN E. (2008), PRICE THEORY AND APPLICATIONS.

Lazarus, Richard J. (2005), *Human Nature, the Laws of Nature, and the Nature of Environmental Law*, 24 VA. ENVTL. L. J. 231.

Le, Net (2004), *Sunk Costs, Free-Riding Justifications, and Compulsory Licensing of Interfaces*, 1(2) REV. OF ECON. RESEARCH ON COPYRIGHT ISSUES 29.

Le Grand, Julian (1991), *The Theory of Government Failure*, 21(4) BRITISH J. OF POLITICAL SCIENCE 423–42.

Leape, Jonathan (2006), *The London Congestion Charge*, 20(4) JOURNAL OF ECONOMIC PERSPECTIVES 157–76.

Lee, Peter (2008), *The Evolution of Intellectual Infrastructure*, 83 WASH. L. REV. 39.

Lee, Peter (2009), *Interface: The Push and Pull of Patents*, 77 FORDHAM L. REV. 2225.

Lee, Robin S., & Tim Wu (2009), *Subsidizing Creativity through Network Design: Zero Pricing and Net Neutrality*, 23(3) J. OF ECON. PERSPECTIVES 61.

Lemley, Mark A. (1997), *The Economics of Improvement in Intellectual Property Law*, 75 TEX. L. REV. 989.

Lemley, Mark A. (2005), *Property, Intellectual Property, and Free Riding*, 83 TEX. L. REV. 1031.

Lemley, Mark A. (2007), *Should Patent Infringement Require Proof of Copying?*, 105 MICH. L. REV. 1525.

Lemley, Mark (forthcoming 2012), *The Myth of the Lone Inventor*, 110 MICHIGAN L. REV.

Lemley, Mark A., & Lawrence Lessig (2001), *The End of End-to-End: Preserving the Architecture of the Internet in the Broadband Era*, 48 UCLA L. REV. 925.

Lemley, Mark A., & David McGowan (1998), *Legal Implications of Network Economic Effects*, 86 CALIF. L. REV. 479.

Lemley, Mark, Michael Risch, Ted Sichelman, & R. Polk Wagner (2011), *Life after* Bilski, 63 STANFORD L. REV. 1315.

Lenhart, Amanda, et al. (2004), Pew Internet & American Life Project, Content Creation Online.

LERNER, A. P. (1944), THE ECONOMICS OF CONTROL.

Lessig, Lawrence (2001a), *Copyright's First Amendment*, 48 U.C.L.A. L. REV. 1057.

LESSIG, LAWRENCE (2001b), THE FUTURE OF IDEAS: THE FATE OF THE COMMONS IN A CONNECTED WORLD.

Lessig, Lawrence (2004a), *Coase's First Question*, 27(3) REGULATION 38.

LESSIG, LAWRENCE (2004b), FREE CULTURE: HOW BIG MEDIA USES TECHNOLOGY AND THE LAW TO LOCK DOWN CULTURE AND CONTROL CREATIVITY.

Lessig, Lawrence (2005), *Re-Marking the Progress in Frischmann*, 89 MINN. L. REV. 1031.

Levin, Richard, Alvin Klevorick, Richard Nelson, & Sidney Winter (1987), *Appropriating the Returns from Industrial Research and Development*, 3 BROOKINGS PAPERS ON ECONOMIC ACTIVITY 783.

Levine, Mark (2009), SHARE MY RIDE, N.Y. Times, Mar. 5, *available at* http://www.nytimes.com/2009/03/08/magazine/08Zipcar-t.html.

Levinson, David (2005), *The Evolution of Transport Networks, in* HANDBOOK OF TRANSPORT STRATEGY, POLICY AND INSTITUTIONS VOL. 6 (Kenneth Button & David Hensher eds.).

LEVY, SIDNEY M. (1996), BUILD, OPERATE, TRANSFER: PAVING THE WAY FOR TOMORROW'S INFRASTRUCTURE.

Lichtman, Douglas (2000), *Property Rights in Emerging Platform Technologies*, 29 J. LEGAL STUD. 615, 617.

Liivak, Oskar (2010), *Rethinking the Concept of Exclusion in Patent Law*, 98 GEO. L. J. 1643.

Lincoln, Abraham (1838), The Perpetuation of Our Political Institutions: Address before the Young Men's Lyceum of Springfield, Ill. (Jan. 27), *in* ABRAHAM LINCOLN: HIS SPEECHES AND WRITINGS 76 (Roy P. Basler ed., 1946).

Lindsey, Robin (2006), *Do Economists Reach a Conclusion on Road Pricing? The Intellectual History of an Idea*, 3(2) ECON. J. WATCH.

Lindsey, Robin, & Erik T. Verhoef (2000), *Traffic Congestion and Congestion Pricing*, Tinbergen Institute Discussion Paper No. 101/3, *available at* http://dspace.ubvu.vu.nl/bitstream/1871/9420/1/00101.pdf.

Lipsey, R. G., & Kelvin Lancaster (1956), *The General Theory of the Second Best*, 24 REV. ECON. STUD. 11.

LITAN, ROBERT E., & ALICE M. RIVLIN (2001), BEYOND THE DOT.COMS: THE ECONOMIC PROMISE OF THE INTERNET.

Litman, Jessica (1990), *The* Public Domain, 39(4) EMORY L. J. 965.

Liu, K. C. (2008), *Rationalising the Regime of Compulsory Patent Licensing by the Essential Facilities Doctrine*, 7 INT'L REV. OF INTELL. PROP. & COMPETITION L. 757.

LOCKE, JOHN (1975), AN ESSAY CONCERNING HUMAN UNDERSTANDING, BOOK II, CH. I, NO. 1 (Peter H. Nidditch ed.).

Loren, Lydia Pallas (2007), *Building a Reliable Semicommons of Creative Works: Enforcement of Creative Commons Licenses and Limited Abandonment of Copyright*, 14 GEO. MASON L. REV. 271.

Losey, John, & Mace Vaughn (2006), *The Economic Value of Ecological Services Provided by Insects*, 56(4) BIOSCIENCE 311.

Luban, David (1995), *The Social Responsibilities of Lawyers: A Green Perspective*, 63 GEORGE WASHINGTON L. REV. 955.

Lunney, Glynn S., Jr. (2002), *Fair Use and Market Failure: Sony Revisited*, 82 B.U.L. REV. 975.

Lunney, Glynn S., Jr. (2008), *Copyright's Price Discrimination Panacea*, 21 HARV. J. L. & TECH. 387.

Lynch, Sheila (1996), *The Federal Advisory Committee Act: An Obstacle to Ecosystem Management by Federal Agencies?*, 71 WASH. L. REV. 431.

MacKie-Mason, Jeffrey K., & Hal R. Varian (1995), *Pricing Congestible Network Resources*, 13(7) IEEE J. ON SELECTED AREAS IN COMMUNICATIONS 1141.

Madison, Mike J. (2005), *Law as Design: Objects, Concepts, and Digital Things*, 56 CASE W. RES. L. REV. 381.

Madison, Mike J. (2006), *Social Software, Groups, and Governance*, 2006 MICH. ST. L. REV. 153.

Madison, Mike J., Brett M. Frischmann, & Katherine Strandburg (2010), *Constructed Commons in the Cultural Environment*, 95 CORNELL L. REV. 657.

Mandel, Greg (2008), *When to Open Infrastructure Access*, 35 ECOLOGY L.Q. 205.

Mansfield, Edwin, et al. (1981), *Imitation Costs and Patents: An Empirical Study*, 91 ECON. J. 907.

Mansfield, Edwin (1986), *Patents and Innovation: An Empirical Study*, 32(2) MGMT. SCIENCE 173.

Mansfield, Edwin (1988), *Intellectual Property Rights, Technological Change, and Economic Growth, in* INTELLECTUAL PROPERTY RIGHTS AND CAPITAL FORMATION IN THE NEXT DECADE 3, 8 (Charles Walker & Mark Bloomfield eds.).

Markey, Howard T. (1983), *Why Not the Statute?*, 65 J. PAT. OFF. SOC'Y 331.

Marsden, Christopher T. (2008), *Net Neutrality: The European Debate*, 12(2) J. INTERNET L. 1.

Maurer, Stephen M., & Suzanne Scotchmer (2002), *The Independent Invention Defense in Intellectual Property*, 69 ECONOMICA 535.

May, Anthony et al. (2004), *Optimal Locations and Charges for Cordon Schemes, in* ROAD PRICING: THEORY AND EVIDENCE (Georgina Santos ed.).

McAdams, Richard H. (1997), *The Origin, Development, and Regulation of Norms*, 96 MICH. L. REV. 338.

McCollum, Daniel W. (2003), *Nonmarket Valuation in Action, in* A PRIMER ON NONMARKET VALUATION (Patricia A. Champ et al. eds.).

McElligott, Sean (2009), *Addressing Supply Side Barriers to Introduction of New Vaccines to the Developing* WORLD, 35 AM. J. L. & MED. 415.

McLEOD, KEMBREW, & PETER DiCOLA (2010), CREATIVE LICENSE: THE LAW AND CULTURE OF DIGITAL SAMPLING.

McNERNEY, REBECCA A. (1996), THE CHANGING STRUCTURE OF THE ELECTRIC POWER INDUSTRY.

Meade, James E. (1944), *Price and Output Policy of State Enterprise*, 54(215/216) ECON. J. 321.

MEADE, JAMES E. (1973), THE THEORY OF ECONOMIC EXTERNALITIES: THE CONTROL OF ENVIRONMENTAL POLLUTION AND SIMILAR SOCIAL COSTS.

Mehra, Salil K. (2011), *Paradise Is a Walled Garden? Trust, Antitrust and Consumer Dynamism*, 18 GEO. MASON L. REV. 889.

Merges, Robert P. (1992), *Rent Control in the Patent District: Observations on the Grady-Alexander Thesis*, 78 VA. L. REV. 359, 381.

Merges, Robert P. (2004), *A New Dynamism in the Public Domain*, 71 U. CHI. L. REV. 183 (2004).

Merges, Robert P., & Richard R. Nelson (1990), *On the Complex Economics of Patent Scope*, 90 COLUM. L. REV. 839.

Merges, Robert P., & Richard R. Nelson (1994), *On Limiting or Encouraging Rivalry in Technical Progress: The Effect of Patent Scope Decisions*, 25 J. ECON. BEHAV. & ORG. 1.

Meurer, Michael J. (2001), *Copyright Law and Price Discrimination*, 23 CARDOZO L. REV. 55.

MILL, JOHN STUART (1869), ON LIBERTY.

Millennium Ecosystem Assessment (2005), Ecosystems and Human Well-Being: Synthesis, *available at* http://www.millenniumassessment.org/documents/document.356.aspx.pdf.

Miller, Zane L. (2007), *Urban Life and Urban Landscape, in* READING LONDON at xvii (Erik Bond ed.).

Mimura, Carol (2010), *Nuanced Management of IP Rights: Shaping Industry-University Relationships to Promote Social Impact, in* WORKING WITHIN THE BOUNDARIES OF INTELLECTUAL PROPERTY (Rochelle Dreyfuss, Harry First, & Diane Zimmerman eds.).

MORRIS, WILLIAM, & MARY MORRIS (1988), MORRIS DICTIONARY OF WORD AND PHRASE ORIGINS (2d ed.).

Morton, Pete (1999), *The Economic Benefits of Wilderness: Theory and Practice*, 76 DENV. U. L. REV. 465.

Mowery, David (2005), *The Bayh-Dole Act and High-Technology Entrepreneurship in U.S. Universities: Chicken, Egg, or Something Else?, in* 16 ADVANCES IN THE STUDY OF ENTREPRENEURSHIP INNOVATION AND ECONOMIC GROWTH, UNIVERSITY ENTREPRENEURSHIP AND TECHNOLOGY TRANSFER: PROCESS, DESIGN, AND INTELLECTUAL PROPERTY 39 (Gary D. Libecap ed.).

Mowery, David, & Arvids A. Ziedonis (2002), *Academic Patent Quality and Quantity before and after the Bayh-Dole Act in the United States*, 31 RES. POL'Y 399.

Mowery, David C., et al. (2001), *The Growth of Patenting and Licensing by U.S. Universities: An Assessment of the Effects of the Bayh-Dole Act of 1980*, 30 RES. POL'Y 99.

Mueller, Janice M. (2001), *No "Dilettante Affair": Rethinking the Experimental Use Exception to Patent Infringement for Biomedical Research Tools*, 76 WASH. L. REV. 1.

Musgrave, Richard (2009), *Merit Goods, in* THE NEW PALGRAVE: A DICTIONARY OF ECONOMICS 452 (3d ed.).

MUSGRAVE, RICHARD, & PEGGY MUSGRAVE (1984), PUBLIC FINANCE IN THEORY AND PRACTICE (4th ed.).

Nachbar, Thomas B. (2008), *The Public Network*, 17 COMMLAW CONSPECTUS 67.

NAGLE, JOHN COPELAND, & J. B. RUHL (2006), THE LAW OF BIODIVERSITY AND ECOSYSTEM MANAGEMENT (2nd ed.).

Nash, Jonathan Remy (2007), *Trading Species: A New Direction for Habitat Trading Programs*, 32 COLUM. J. ENVTL. L. 1.

Nash, Jonathan Remy (2008), *Economic Efficiency versus Public Choice: The Case of Property Rights in Road Traffic Management*, 49 B.C.L. REV. 673.

Nash, Jonathan Remy, & Richard L. Revesz (2001), *Markets and Geography: Designing Marketable Permit Schemes to Control Local and Regional Pollutants*, 28 ECOLOGY L. Q. 569.

NATIONAL ACADEMIES PRESS (2006), STATE AND FEDERAL STANDARDS FOR MOBILE-SOURCE EMISSIONS (2006).

NATIONAL RESEARCH COUNCIL (1987), INFRASTRUCTURE FOR THE 21ST CENTURY: FRAMEWORK FOR A RESEARCH AGENDA.

NATIONAL RESEARCH COUNCIL (2005), VALUING ECOSYSTEM SERVICES: TOWARD BETTER ENVIRONMENTAL DECISION-MAKING.

Nat'l Cable & Telecomm. Ass'n v. Brand X Internet Servs., 125 S. Ct. 2688 (2005), aff'g Inquiry Concerning High-Speed Access to the Internet Over Cable and Other Facilities, Internet Over Cable Declaratory Ruling, Appropriate Regulatory Treatment for Broadband Access to the Internet Over Cable Facilities, Declaratory Ruling and Notice of Proposed Rulemaking, 17 F.C.C.R. 4798 (2002).

National Surface Transportation Policy and Revenue Study Commission (NSTPRSC) (2007), Transportation for Tomorrow: Report of the National Surface Transportation Policy and Revenue Study Commission 3–20 (December).

Nelson, Richard (1982), *Government Stimulus of Technological Progress: Lessons from American History, in* GOVERNMENT AND TECHNICAL PROGRESS 451 (Richard Nelson ed.).

Nelson, Richard R. (1987a), *Roles of Government in a Mixed Economy*, 6 J. POL'Y ANALYSIS & MGMT. 541.

Nelson, Richard (1987b), *Understanding Technical Change as an Evolutionary Process, in* LECTURES IN ECONOMICS.

Netanel, Neil W. (2005), *Copyright and "Market Power" in the Marketplace of Ideas, in* ANTITRUST, PATENTS AND COPYRIGHT 149 (Howard Shelanski & Francois Leveque eds.).

NETANEL, NEIL W. (2008), COPYRIGHT'S PARADOX.

Network Forensics, Solera Networks, *available at* http://www.soleranetworks.com/network-forensics/our-network-forensics-technology/capture (last visited Feb. 26, 2011).

Neuman, Janet (2007), *Thinking Inside the Box: Looking for Ecosystem Services within a Forested Watershed*, 22 J. LAND USE & ENVTL. L. 173.

Nimmer, Melville B. (1970), *Does Copyright Abridge the First Amendment Guarantees of Free Speech and Press?*, 17 UCLA L. REV. 1180.

Noam, Eli M. (1994), *Beyond Liberalization II: The Impending Doom of Common Carriage*, 18 TELECOMM. POL'Y 435. Sec. III.3.

NOAM, ELI M. (2001), INTERCONNECTING THE NETWORK OF NETWORKS.

NORTH, D. (1990), INSTITUTIONS, INSTITUTIONAL CHANGE AND ECONOMIC PERFORMANCE.

NORTH, DOUGLASS C. (2005), UNDERSTANDING THE PROCESS OF ECONOMIC CHANGE.

Nuechterlein, Jonathan E. (2009), *Antitrust Oversight of an Antitrust Dispute*, 7 J. TELECOMM. & HIGH TECH. L. 19.

NUECHTERLEIN, JONATHAN E., & PHILIP J. WEISER (2005), DIGITAL CROSSROADS: AMERICAN TELECOMMUNICATIONS POLICY IN THE INTERNET AGE.

Oakland, W. H. (1987), *Theory of Public Goods, in* 2 HANDBOOK OF PUBLIC ECONOMICS 485 (Alan J. Auerbach & Martin Feldstein eds.).

Oberholzer-Gee, Felix, & Koleman Strumpf (2007), The Effect of File Sharing on Record Sales: An Empirical Analysis, 115 JOURNAL OF POLITICAL ECONOMY 1–42.

OCHOA, ORLANDO A. (1996), GROWTH, TRADE, AND ENDOGENOUS TECHNOLOGY.

Odlyzko, Andrew (2004a), *The Evolution of Price Discrimination in Transportation and Its Implications for the Internet*, 3 REV. OF NETWORK ECON. 323.

Odlyzko, Andrew (2004b), *Privacy, Economics, and Price Discrimination on the Internet, in* ECONOMICS OF INFORMATION SECURITY 187 (L. Jean Camp & Stephen Lewis eds.).

OECD (1962), THE MEASUREMENT OF SCIENTIFIC AND TECHNICAL ACTIVITIES: PROPOSED STANDARD PRACTICE FOR SURVEYS OF RESEARCH AND DEVELOPMENT.

OECD (2000), KNOWLEDGE MANAGEMENT IN THE LEARNING SOCIETY.

OECD (2006), INFRASTRUCTURE TO 2030: TELECOM, LAND TRANSPORT, WATER AND ELECTRICITY.

OECD (2008), ENVIRONMENTAL POLICY, TECHNOLOGICAL INNOVATION AND PATENTS.

OECD (2010), GLOBALISATION, TRANSPORT AND THE ENVIRONMENT.

Ohm, Paul (2009), *The Rise and Fall of Internet Surveillance*, 2009 U. ILL. L. REV. 1417.

OLSON, MANCUR (1965), THE LOGIC OF COLLECTIVE ACTION.

O'Mahony, Siobhán, and Beth A. Bechky (2008), *Boundary Organizations: Enabling Collaboration among Unexpected Allies*, 53 ADMINISTRATIVE SCIENCE QUARTERLY 422.

Opderbeck, David (2009), *Deconstructing Jefferson's Candle: Towards a Critical Realist Approach to Cultural Environmentalism and Information Policy*, 49 JURIMETRICS 203.

Opinion, Innovation's Golden Goose (2002), 2002 ECONOMIST TECH. Q.3.

O'Rourke, Maureen A. (2000), *Toward a Doctrine of Fair Use in Patent Law*, 100 COLUM. L. REV. 1177.

Ortiz-Moctezuma et al. (2010), *Development of Transportation Infrastructure in the Context of Economic Growth, in* DYNAMIC SYSTEMS, ECONOMIC GROWTH, AND THE ENVIRONMENT.

OSTROM, ELINOR (1990), GOVERNING THE COMMONS: THE EVOLUTION OF INSTITUTIONS FOR COLLECTIVE ACTION.

OSTROM, ELINOR (2005), UNDERSTANDING INSTITUTIONAL DIVERSITY.

Ostrom, Elinor (2007), *A Diagnostic Approach for Going beyond Panaceas*, 104 PROC. NAT'L ACAD. SCI. USA 15181.

Ostrom, Elinor (1998), *Reflections on the Commons, in* MANAGING THE COMMONS 95 (John Baden & Douglas S. Noonan eds.).

Padmore, Tim, & Hervey Gibson (1998), *Modeling Regional Innovation and Competitiveness, in* LOCAL AND REGIONAL SYSTEMS OF INNOVATION 45 (John De la Mothe & Gilles Paquet eds.).

PAPANDREOU, ANDREAS A. (1994), EXTERNALITY AND INSTITUTIONS.

Parasidis, Efthimios (2010), *A Uniform Framework for Patent Eligibility*, 85 TUL. L. REV. 323.

Patterson, L. Ray (1987), *Free Speech, Copyright, and Fair Use*, 40 VAND. L. REV. 1.

Pearce, David (1998), *Auditing the Earth*, ENVIRONMENT, March, at 23.

PEAT, F. D. (2002), FROM CERTAINTY TO UNCERTAINTY: THE STORY OF SCIENCE AND IDEAS IN THE TWENTIETH CENTURY.

PEGRUM, D. F. (1944), *Incremental Cost Pricing: A Comment*, 20 J. OF LAND AND PUBLIC UTILITY ECON. 60–63.

Peitz, Martin, & Patrick Waelbroeck (2004), *The Effect of Internet Piracy on CD Sales: Cross-Section Evidence*, CESIFO Working Paper No. 1122, January.

Peltzman, Sam (1976), *Toward a More General Theory of Regulation*, 19(2) J. OF L. AND ECON. 211–40.

PELTZMAN, SAM (1998), POLITICAL PARTICIPATION AND GOVERNMENT REGULATION?

Pickert, Kate (2009), *Postcard from Hughson*, TIME, Mar. 12, *available at* http://www.time.com/time/magazine/article/0,9171,1884835,00.html.

PIGOU, ARTHUR CECIL (1920), THE ECONOMICS OF WELFARE.

PINK, DANIEL H. (2010), DRIVE.

Plowden, Stephen (2005), *Memorandum, in* ROAD PRICING: THE NEXT STEPS (House of Commons: Transport Committee).

Poe, Marshall (2006), *The Hive*, ATLANTIC ONLINE, September, *available at* http://www.theatlantic.com/magazine/archive/2006/09/the-hive/5118/

Poirier, Marc R. (2006), *Modified Private Property: New Jersey's Public Trust Doctrine, Private Development and Exclusion, and Shared Public Uses of Natural Resources*, 15 SE. ENVTL. L. J. 71.

Poirier, Marc R. (2008), *Natural Resources, Congestion, and the Feminist Future: Aspects of Frischmann's Theory of Infrastructure Resources*, 35 ECOLOGY L.Q. 179.

Pollack, Malla (2002), *The Multiple Unconstitutionality of Business Method Patents: Common Sense, Congressional Consideration, and Constitutional History*, 28 RUTGERS COMPUTER & TECH. L. J. 61.

Poole, Robert W. Jr. (1996), *Private Toll Roads, in* PRIVATIZING TRANSPORTATION SYSTEMS 165 (Simon Hakim et al. eds.)

Portes, Alejandro (1998), *Social Capital: Its Origins and Applications in Modern Sociology*, 24 ANNUAL REVIEW OF SOCIOLOGY 1–24.

Posner, Richard A. (1986), *Free Speech in an Economic Perspective*, 20 SUFFOLK U. L. REV. 1.

Powell, Walter W. (2001), *Networks of Learning in Biotechnology: Opportunities and Constraints Associated with Relational Contracting in a Knowledge-Intensive Field, in* EXPANDING THE BOUNDARIES OF INTELLECTUAL PROPERTY: INNOVATION POLICY FOR THE KNOWLEDGE SOCIETY 251, 263–65 (Rochelle Cooper Dreyfuss et al. eds.).

Power, Alison G. (2010), *Ecosystem Services and Agriculture: Tradeoffs and Synergies*, PHILOS. TRANS. R. SOC. LOND. B. BIOL. SCI.

Preserving the Open Internet, 76 Fed. Reg. 59,192, 59,192 (Sept. 23, 2011) (to be codified at 47 C.F.R. pts. 0 and 8), *available at* http://www.gpo.gov/fdsys/pkg/FR-2011-09-23/pdf/2011-24259.pdf.

President's Info. Tech. Advisory Comm. (1999), *Information Technology Research: Investing in Our Future, available at* http://www.ccic.gov/ac/report/pitac_report.pdf.

PUTNAM, ROBERT (2000), BOWLING ALONE: THE COLLAPSE AND REVIVAL OF AMERICAN COMMUNITY.

PUTNAM, ROBERT D. (1993), Making Democracy Work: Civic Traditions in Modern Italy.

Quelch, John (2009), *Quantifying the Economic Impact of the Internet*, WORKING KNOWLEDGE–HARV. BUS. SCH., Aug. 17, *available at* http://hbswk.hbs.edu/item/6268.html.

Rai, Arti Kaur (1999), *Regulating Scientific Research: Intellectual Property Rights and the Norms of Science*, 94 Nw. U. L. REV. 77.

Rai, Arti Kaur (2005), *Proprietary Rights and Collective Action: The Case of Biotechnology Research with Low Commercial Value, in* INTERNATIONAL PUBLIC GOODS AND TECHNOLOGY TRANSFER IN A GLOBALIZED INTELLECTUAL PROPERTY REGIME (Jerome Reichman and Keith Maskus, eds.).

Rainie, Lee (2010), *Internet, Broadband, and Cell Phone Statistics*, PEW INTERNET, Jan. 5, *available at* http://www.pewinternet.org/⊠/media//Files/Reports/2010/PIP_December09_update.pdf.

Ramsey, Frank P. (1927), *A Contribution to the Theory of Taxation*, 37(145) ECON. J. 47.

Ransom, Diana (2010), *Earning Cash with YouTube Videos*, WALL ST. J., June 18, *available at* http://online.wsj.com/article/SB10001424052748704122904575314851538643196. html?mod=WSJ_SmallBusiness_LEADNewsCollection.

Ratliff, James D., & Daniel L. Rubinfeld (2010), *Online Advertising: Defining Relevant Markets*, 6 J. COMPETITION L. & ECON. 653.

Reed, David P. et al. (1998), *Commentaries on "Active Networking and End-to-End Arguments,"* 12(3) IEEE NETWORK 66.

REGIONAL STUDIES ASSOCIATION (1989), BUILT ENVIRONMENT: VOLUME 15.

Reichman, J. H., & Paul F. Uhlir (2003), *A Contractually Reconstructed Research Commons for Scientific Data in a Highly Protectionist Intellectual Property Environment*, 66 L. & CONTEMP. PROBLEMS 315.

Reply Comments of Comcast Corp., In the Matter of Preserving the Open Internet, GN Docket No. 09-191, WC Docket No. 07-52 (Received Apr. 26, 2010).

Revesz, Richard L. (1999), *Environmental Regulation, Cost-Benefit Analysis, and the Discounting of Human Lives*, 99 COLUM. L. REV. 941.

Revesz, Richard L., & Robert N. Stavins (2007), *Environmental Law, in* HANDBOOK OF LAW AND ECONOMICS, VOL. 1 (A. Mitchell Polinsky & Steven Shavell eds.), *available at* http:// www.hks.harvard.edu/fs/rstavins/Papers/Environmental_Law_and_Policy_Handbook_ Chapter_by_Revesz_&_Stavins.pdf.

Rey, Patrick, & Jean Tirole (2007), *A Primer on Foreclosure*, reprinted in III HANDBOOK OF INDUSTRIAL ORGANIZATION (Mark Armstrong & Rob Porter eds.) 2145–2220.

Rich, Giles S. (1942), *The Relation between Patent Practices and the Anti-Monopoly Laws—Part II, 24 J. Pat. Off. Soc'y 159 (1942)*, reprinted in 14 FED. CIR. B. J. 21 (2004).

Rob, Rafael, & Joel Waldfogel (2006), *Piracy on the High C's: Music Downloading, Sales Displacement, and Social Welfare in a Sample of College Students*, 49(1) J. OF L. & ECON. 29.

Robinson, Glen O. (1991), *Regulatory and Institutional Change, in* AFTER THE BREAK-UP: ASSESSING THE POST-AT&T DIVESTITURE ERA (Barry G. Cole ed.).

ROBINSON, GLEN O. (2008), COMMUNICATIONS REGULATION.

Robinson, Glen O., & Dennis L. Weisman (2008), *Designing Competition Policy for Telecommunications*, 7 REV. OF NETWORK ECON. 509.

ROBINSON, JOAN (1933), THE ECONOMICS OF IMPERFECT COMPETITION.

Romer, Paul (1986), *Increasing Returns and Long Run Growth*, 94(5) J. OF POLITICAL ECON. 1002.

Romer, Paul M. (1996), *Why, Indeed, in America? Theory, History, and the Origins of Modern Economic Growth*, 86 AMERICAN ECON. REV., PAPERS AND PROCEEDINGS.

Rose, Carol (1986), *The Comedy of the Commons: Custom, Commerce, and Inherently Public Property*, 53 U. CHICAGO L. REV. 711.

Rose, Carol (2003), *Romans, Roads, and Romantic Creators: Traditions of Public Property in the Information Age*, 66 L. & CONTEMP. PROBS. 89.

ROSENBERG, NATHAN (1994), EXPLORING THE BLACK BOX: TECHNOLOGY, ECONOMICS, AND HISTORY.

ROSSI, JIM (2005), REGULATORY BARGAINING & PUBLIC LAW.

Rudolf, John Collins (2010), *Coral Die-Off Took Scientist by Surprise*, N.Y. TIMES, Nov. 6, available at http://green.blogs.nytimes.com/2010/11/06/coral-cataclysm-took-scientist-by-surprise.

Ruggles, Nancy (1949), *Recent Developments in the Theory of Marginal Cost Pricing*, 17 REV. ECON. STUD. 107.

RUHL, J. B., STEVEN E. KRAFT, & C. L. LANT (2007), THE LAW AND POLICY OF ECOSYSTEM SERVICES.

Ruhl, J. B., & James Salzman (2007), *The Law and Policy Beginnings of Ecosystem Services*, 22 J. LAND USE & ENVTL. L. 157.

Sag, Matthew (2010), *The Google Book Settlement and the Fair Use Counterfactual*, 55 N.Y.L. SCH. L. REV. 790.

Saltzer, Jerome H. et al. (1981), *End-to-End Arguments in System Design*, 1981 SECOND INTERNATIONAL CONFERENCE ON DISTRIBUTED COMPUTING SYSTEMS 509.

Saltzer, Jerome H. et al. (1984), *End-to-End Arguments in System Design*, 2 ACM TRANSACTIONS ON COMPUTER SYS. 277.

Salzman, James (1997), *Valuing Ecosystem Services*, 24 ECOLOGY L. Q. 887.

Salzman, James (2006), *A Field of Green? The Past and Future of Ecosystem Services*, 21 J. LAND USE & ENVTL. L. 133.

Salzman, James, & J. B. Ruhl (2000), *Currencies and the Commodification of Environmental Law*, 53 STAN. L. REV. 607.

Salzman, James, Barton H. Thompson Jr., & Gretchen C. Daily (2001), *Protecting Ecosystem Services: Science, Economics, and Law*, 20 STAN. ENVTL. L. J. 309.

Samuelson, Pamela (2006), *Enriching Discourse on Public Domains*, 55 DUKE L. J. 783.

Samuelson, Paul A. (1954), *A Pure Theory of Public Expenditure*, 36 REV. ECON. & STAT. 387.

Samuelson, Paul A. (1958), *Aspects of Public Expenditure Theories*, 40 REV. ECON. & STAT. 332.

Sashkin, Davina (2006), *Failure of Imagination: Why Inaction on Net Neutrality Regulation Will Result in a de Facto Legal Regime Promoting Discriminatory and Consumer Harm*, 15 COMMLAW CONSPECTUS 261.

Sawkar, Anu R. (2008), *Are Storylines Patentable? Testing the Boundaries of Patentable Subject Matter*, 76 FORDHAM L. REV. 3001.

Sax, Joseph L. (1970), *The Public Trust Doctrine in Natural Resources Law: Effective Judicial Intervention*, 68 MICH. L. REV. 471.

Schaafsma, Paul E. (2010), The Case for Financial Product Patents: What the Supreme Court got Right and Wrong in Bilski v. Kappos, and a Suggestion for Reasonable Line on Business Method Patents, 92 J. Pat. & Trademark Off. Soc'y 398.

Schatz, Thomas G. (1977), *New Directions in Film Genre Studies (A Response to Charles F. Altman)*, in 2 FILM HISTORICAL-THEORETICAL SPECULATIONS 44.

SCHATZ, THOMAS G. (1981), HOLLYWOOD GENRES.

SCHERER, F. M. (1984), Innovation and Growth: Schumpeterian Perspectives.

SCHERER, F. M., AND D. ROSS (1990), INDUSTRIAL MARKET STRUCTURE AND ECONOMIC PERFORMANCE.

Schmalensee, Richard (1981), *Output and Welfare Implications of Monopolistic Third-Degree Price Discrimination*, 71(1) AM. ECON. REV. 242.

SCHMIDT, GORDON W. (2003), DYNAMICS OF ENDOGENOUS ECONOMIC GROWTH: A CASE STUDY FOR THE ROMER MODEL.

Schultz, Jason, & Pamela Samuelson (2011), *"Clues" for Determining Whether Business and Service Innovations Are Unpatentable Abstract Ideas*, 15 LEWIS & CLARK L. REV. (forthcoming 2011).

Scotchmer, Suzanne (1991), *Standing on the Shoulders of Giants: Cumulative Research and the Patent Law*, 5(1) J. OF ECON. PERSPECTIVES.

Scotchmer, Suzanne (1996), *Protecting Early Innovators: Should Second-Generation Products Be Patentable?*, 27 RAND J. ECON. 322.

Scotchmer, Suzanne (1998), *Incentives to Innovate*, PALGRAVE ENCYCLOPEDIA OF LAW & ECONOMICS 273, 275.

SCOTCHMER, SUZANNE (2004), INNOVATION AND INCENTIVES.

Segal, David (2010), *Should BP's Money Go Where the Oil Didn't?*, N.Y. TIMES, Oct. 23, *available at* http://www.nytimes.com/2010/10/24/business/24claim.html.

Sen, Amartya (1993), *Capability and Well-Being*, *in* THE QUALITY OF LIFE (M. Nussbaum and A. Sen eds.) 30–53.

SEN, AMARTYA. (2009), THE IDEA OF JUSTICE.

Sen. Rep. No. 75, 67th Cong., 1st Sess. 1 (1921).Shane, Scott (2004), Encouraging University Entrepreneurship? The Effect of the Bayh-Dole Act on University Patenting in the United States, 19 J. BUS. VENTURING 127, 129.

SHAPIRO, CARL, AND HAL R. VARIAN (1998), INFORMATION RULES: A STRATEGIC GUIDE TO THE NETWORK ECONOMY.

Sicker, Douglas C., & Joshua L. Mindel (2002), *Refinements of a Layered Model for Telecommunications Policy*, 1 J. ON TELECOMM. & HIGH TECH. L. 69.

SIDAK, J. GREGORY, & DANIEL F. SPULBER (1998), DEREGULATORY TAKINGS AND THE REGULATORY CONTRACT.

Simarmata, Djamester A. (1998), *Regulatory Reform and International Market Openness*, *in* REGULATORY REFORM IN THE GLOBAL ECONOMY.

SLAUGHTER, SHEILA, & Larry L. LESLIE (1997), ACADEMIC CAPITALISM: POLITICS, POLICIES, AND THE ENTREPRENEURIAL UNIVERSITY.

SMALL, KENNETH A., ET AL. (1989), ROAD WORK: A NEW HIGHWAY PRICING AND INVESTMENT POLICY.

Smith, Aaron (2010), *Home Broadband 2010*, PEW INTERNET, Aug. 11, 2010, *available at* http://www.pewinternet.org/~/media//Files/Reports/2010/Home%20broadband%202010.pdf.

Smith, Aaron, & Lee Rainie (2010), *8% of Online Americans Use Twitter*, PEW INTERNET, Dec. 9, *available at* http://pewinternet.org/Reports/2010/Twitter-update-2010.aspx.

Smith, Henry E. (2000), *Semicommon Property Rights and Scattering in the Open Fields*, 29 J. LEGAL STUD. 131.

Solow, R. M. (2000), *Notes on Social Capital and Economic Performance*, *in* SOCIAL CAPITAL: A MULTIFACETED PERSPECTIVE 6 (P. Dasgupta & I. Serageldin eds.).

SORENSEN, PAUL ET AL. (2008), MOVING LOS ANGELES: SHORT-TERM POLICY OPTIONS FOR IMPROVING TRANSPORTATION.

Speta, James B. (2002), *A Common Carrier Approach to Internet Interconnections*, 54 FCLJ 225.

Spulber, Daniel F. (1986), *Second Best Pricing and Cooperation*, 17(2) RAND J. OF ECON. 239.

Srinivas, Krishna Ravi (2010), *Open Source Drug Discovery*, *in* INCENTIVES FOR GLOBAL PUBLIC HEALTH: PATENT LAW AND ACCESS TO ESSENTIAL MEDICINES (Thomas Pogge et al. eds.).

Staff of House Comm. on Science (1998), 105th Cong., 1st sess., Unlocking Our Future: Toward a New National Science Policy 8 (Comm. Print 1998), *available at* http://www.access.gpo.gov/congress/house/science /Cp105-b/science105b.pdf.

Steinmueller, W. Edward (1996), *Technological Infrastructure in Information Technology Industries*, *in* TECHNOLOGICAL INFRASTRUCTURE POLICY: AN INTERNATIONAL PERSPECTIVE (M. Teubal, D. Foray, M. Justman, & E. Zuscovitch eds.).

Steins, Nathalie A., & Victoria M. Edwards (1999), *Platforms for Collective Action in Multiple-Use Common-Pool Resources*, 16 AGRIC. & HUMAN VALUES 241.

STERLING, CHRISTOPHER H., ET AL. (2008), SHAPING AMERICAN TELECOMMUNICATIONS.

STIGLER, G. J. (1966), THE THEORY OF PRICE.

Stigler, G. (1971), *The theory of economic regulation*, 2 BELL J. ECON. MAN. SCI. 3–21.

Stole, Lars A. (2007), *Price Discrimination and Competition*, *in* 3 HANDBOOK OF INDUSTRIAL ORGANIZATION 2221.

Stone, Brad, & Noam Cohen (2009), *Social Networks Spread Defiance Online*, N.Y. TIMES, June 16, at 11.

Strahilevitz, Lior Jacob (2000), *How Changes in Property Regimes Influence Social Norms: Commodifying California's Carpool Lanes*, 75 IND. L. J. 1231.

Strandburg, Katherine J. (2011), *Patent Fair Use 2.0*, U.C. IRVINE L. REV. (forthcoming 2011).

Sutton, Paul C., & Robert Costanza (2002), *Global Estimates of Market and Nonmarket Values Derived from Nighttime Satellite Imagery, Land Cover, and Ecosystem Services Valuation*, 41 ECOLOGICAL ECON. 509.

Tassey, Gregory (1995), *Infratechnologies and Economic Growth*, *in* TECHNOLOGICAL INFRA-STRUCTURE POLICY: AN INTERNATIONAL PERSPECTIVE 59 (Morris Teubal et al. eds.).

TAYLOR, CHARLES (1995), PHILOSOPHICAL ARGUMENTS.

TAYLOR, JOHN G., & AKILA WEERAPANA (2009), ECONOMICS.

TAYLOR, PAUL W. (1986), RESPECT for Nature: A Theory of Environmental Ethics.

TEUBAL, MORRIS ET AL. (1995), TECHNOLOGICAL INFRASTRUCTURE POLICY: AN INTERNATIONAL PERSPECTIVE.

Texas Transportation Institute (2010), Urban Mobility Report, *available at* http://tti.tamu.edu/documents/mobility_report_2010.pdf.

Thierer, Adam (2005), *The Real Net Neutrality Debate: Price Flexibility versus Price Regulation*, TECH. LIBERATION FRONT, Oct. 27, *available at* http://techliberation.com/2005/10/27/the-real-net-neutrality-debate-pricing-flexibility-versus-pricing-regulation/.

Thomas, John R. (1995), *The Question Concerning Patent Law and Pioneer Inventions*, 10 HIGH TECH. L. J. 35.

THOMSON, J. M. (1974), Modern Transport Economics.

THUMANN, ALBERT, & D. PAUL MEHTA (2008), HANDBOOK OF ENERGY ENGINEERING.

Tiebout, Charles M. (1956), *A Pure Theory of Local Expenditures*, 64(5) J. OF POL. ECON. 416.

TIROLE, JEAN (1988), THE THEORY OF INDUSTRIAL ORGANIZATION.

Top 20 Countries with the Highest Number of Internet Users, Internet World Stats, *available at* http://www.internetworldstats.com/top20.htm (last modified Aug. 21, 2010).

Transmission Control Protocol: DARPA Internet Program Protocol Specification, IETF RFC 793 (Sept. 1981), *available at* http://www.ietf.org/rfc/rfc0793.txt?number=793.

Tribe, Laurence H., & Michael C. Dorf (1990), *Levels of Generality in the Definition of Rights*, 57 CHI. L. REV. 1057.

TUCKER, IRVIN B. (2008), MICROECONOMICS FOR TODAY.

Turner, R. Kerry, et al. (2003), *Valuing Nature: Lessons Learned and Future Research Directions*, 46 ECOLOGICAL ECON. 493.

Turow, Joseph (2005), *Have They Got a Deal for You: It's Suspiciously Cozy in the Cybermarket*, Washington Post, June 19.

Turow, Joseph, Lauren Feldman, & Kimberly Meltzer (2005), OPEN TO EXPLOITATION: AMERICAN SHOPPERS ONLINE AND OFFLINE, A Report from the Annenberg Public Policy Center of the University of Pennsylvania.

Tushnet, Rebecca (2009), *Economies of Desire: Fair Use and Marketplace Assumptions*, 51 WM. & MARY L. REV. 513.

U.S. Department of Transportation (DOT), Transportation Statistics Annual Report, Condition of U.S. Highway Bridges: 1990–2007 (2008), *available at* http://www.bts.gov/publications/transportation_statistics_annual_report/2008/pdf/entire.pdf.

S Environmental Protection Agency (US EPA), Carpool Incentive Programs (2001), *available at* http://www.commutesolutions.com/letsride/Resources/commuterchoice/carpool.pdf.

S EPA, Ecological Research Program Multi-Year Plan FY 2008–2014 app. A (Feb. 2008) (Draft Review).

US EPA, Office of Water (1995), *Controlling Nonpoint Source Runoff Pollution from Roads, Highways and Bridges*, Aug. (EPA-841-F-95-008a).

US EPA, Transportation and Air Quality, *available at* http://www.epa.gov/oms.

VAIDHYANATHAN, SIVA (2001), COPYRIGHTS AND COPYWRONGS: THE RISE OF INTELLECTUAL PROPERTY AND HOW IT THREATENS CREATIVITY.

Van Schewick, Barbara (2008), *Architecture and Innovation: The Role of the End-to-End Arguments in the Original Internet*, PhD Dissertation, Technical University Berlin 2005, MIT Press, Boston.

VAN SCHEWICK, BARBARA (2010), INTERNET ARCHITECTURE AND INNOVATION.

Varian, H. R. (1985), *Price Discrimination and Social Welfare*, 75 AMERICAN ECONOMIC REVIEW 870–75.

Varian, Hal R. (1996), *Differential Pricing and Efficiency*, 1(2) FIRST MONDAY.

Vermont, Samson (2006), *Independent Invention as a Defense to Patent Infringement*, 105 MICH. L. REV. 475, 484.

Vetter, Greg R. (2007), *Open Source Licensing and Scattering Opportunism in Software Standards*, 47 B.C. L. REV. 225.

VISCUSI, W. KIP, JOSEPH E. HARRINGTON, & JOHN M. VERNON (2005), ECONOMICS OF REGULATION AND ANTITRUST (4th ed.).

VON HIPPEL, ERIC (2005), DEMOCRATIZING INNOVATION.

Waldfogel, Joel (2010), *File Sharing and Sales Displacement in the iTunes Era*, INFORMATION ECONOMICS & POLICY.

WALKER, GILBERT (1942), ROAD AND RAIL.

Waters, Richard (2010), *Investors Wary of Hype for Skype*, FINANCIALTIMES (London), Aug. 10, *available at* ProQuest, Document ID 2107145931.

Weinberg, Jonathan (1999), *The Internet and "Telecommunications Services," Universal Service Mechanisms, Access Charges, and Other Flotsam of the Regulatory System*, 16 YALE J. ON REG. 211.

Weiser, Phillip J. (2003), *The Internet, Innovation, and Intellectual Property Policy*, 103 COLUM. L. REV. 534, 564–68.

Weisman, Dennis L., & Robert B. Kulick (2010), *Price Discrimination, Two-Sided Markets, and Net Neutrality Regulation*, 13 TUL. J. TECH. & INTELL. PROP. 81.

Werbach, Kevin (2002), *A Layered Model for Internet Privacy*, 1 J. ON TELECOMM. & HIGH TECH. L. 37.

Werbach, Kevin (2004), *Supercommons: Toward a Unified Theory of Wireless Communication*, 82 TEXAS L. REV. 863.

Werbach, Kevin (2007), *Only Connect*, BERKELEY TECH. L. J., 1234.

Werbach, Kevin (2011), *The Wasteland: Anticommons, White Spaces, and the Fallacy of Spectrum*, 53 ARIZONA L. REV.

Whitt, Richard S. (2004), *A Horizontal Leap Forward: Formulating a New Communications Public Policy Framework Based on the Network Layers Model*, 56 FED. COMM. L. J. 587.

Whitt, Richard S. (2009), *Adaptive Policymaking: Evolving and Applying Emergent Solutions for U.S. Communications Policy*, 61 FED. COMM. L. J. 483.

Wigod, Aaron M. (2002), Comment, *The AOL-Time Warner Merger: An Analysis of the Broadband Internet Access Market*, 6 J. SMALL & EMERGING BUS. L. 349.

WILKIN, PETER (2001), THE POLITICAL ECONOMY OF GLOBAL COMMUNICATION.

Williamson, Oliver E. (1971), *The Vertical Integration of Production: Market Failure Considerations*, 61(2) AM. ECON. REV.

Wilson, Kevin G. (2000), Deregulating telecommunications: U.S. and Canadian telecommunications, 1840–1997.

Wilson, Robert (2002), *Architecture of Power Markets*, 70 ECONOMETRICA 1299.

Wireline Competition Bureau, Notice of Proposed Rule-Making, *Received* Oct. 22, 2009, *available at* http://fjallfoss.fcc.gov/ecfs/comment_search/input?z=hoocw (under Proceeding Number, input "09–191" and under Name of Filer, input "Wireline Competition Bureau" and input "10/22/2009" under "Date Received").

Wu, Tim (2003), *Network Neutrality, Broadband Discrimination*, 2 J. TELECOMM. & HIGH TECH. L. 141.

Wu, Tim (2004), *The Broadband Debate: A User's Guide*, 3 J. TELECOMM. & HIGH TECH. L. 69.

WU, TIM (2011), THE MASTER SWITCH.

Wu, Tim, & Lawrence Lessig (2003), Letter to Marlene H. Dortch, Secretary, FCC, CS Docket No. 02-52 (Aug. 22), *available at* http://faculty.virginia.edu/timwu/wu_lessig_fcc.pdf.

Yen, Alfred C. (2003), *Eldred, the First Amendment, and Aggressive Copyright Claims*, 40 HOUSTON L. REV. 673.

Yoo, Christopher S. (2003), *Rethinking the Commitment to Free, Local Television*, 52 EMORY L. J. 1579.

Yoo, Christopher S. (2004), *Would Mandating Broadband Network Neutrality Help or Hurt Competition? A Comment on the End-to-End Debate*, 3 J. TELECOMM. & HIGH TECH. L. 32.

Yoo, Christopher S. (2006), *Network Neutrality and the Economics of Congestion*, 95 GEO. L. J. 1947.

Yoo, Christopher S. (2007), *Copyright and Public Good Economics: A Misunderstood Relation*, 155 U. PA. L. REV. 635.

Yoo, Christopher S. (2008), *Network Neutrality, Consumers, and Innovation*, 2008 U. CHI. LEGAL F. 179.

Yoo, Christopher S. (2010), *Innovations in the Internet's Architecture That Challenges the Status Quo*, 8 J. TELECOMM. & HIGH TECH. L. 79.

Yoshida, Yoshihiro (2000), *Third-Degree Price Discrimination in Input Markets: Output and Welfare*, 90(1) AM. ECON. REV. 240.

Yu, Peter K. (2005), *Intellectual Property and the Information Ecosystem*, 2005 MICH. ST. L. REV. 1.

Yujie, Liu (2011), *Beijing's New Traffic Rules Surprise Some Drivers*, CHINA DAILY, Jan. 5, *available at* http://www.chinadaily.com.cn/bizchina/2011–01/05/content_11798638.htm.

Zentner, Alejandro (2006), *Measuring the Effect of File Sharing on Music Purchases*, 49 J. OF LAW AND ECON. 63–90.

Zhao, Yidi (2011), *Beijing Residents Rush to Register Cars on New Quota*, BLOOMBERG NEWS, Jan. 3, *available at* http://www.bloomberg.com/news/2011–01-02/beijing-residents-rush-to-register-new-cars-to-meet-china-s-quota-system.html.

Zickuhr, Kathryn, & Lee Rainie (2011), *Report: Wikipedia Past and Present*, PEW INTERNET, Jan. 13, *available at* http://www.pewinternet.org/Reports/2011/Wikipedia/Report.aspx.

ZITTRAIN, JONATHAN (2008), THE FUTURE OF THE INTERNET AND HOW TO STOP IT.

Index

Figures, notes, and tables are indicated by *f*, *n*, and *t* following the page number.

Abstraction-Filtration-Comparison approach, 290
Abstractions analysis, 288–91, 295–98, 300–301, 305
Algorithms, 290, 293, 294
Amazon.com, 95
Amended Settlement Agreement (ASA), 360, 360n7–8
American Public Transportation Authority, 207n65
American Recovery and Reinvestment Act, 223n64
American Society of Civil Engineers (ASCE), ix–xi, x*t*, 210, 365
Annenberg Public Policy Center, 95
"Anonymous crowding," 141
Antitrust law
    common carrier regulation and, 103, 104
    essential facilities doctrine and, 101–2, 107
    government intervention and, 105–6, 107
    network neutrality debate and, 326–30
    telecommunications and, 217, 219–21
Arnott, Richard, 151–52n27
ARPANET, 82
Arrow, Kenneth, 37, 47n70, 77
ASA (Amended Settlement Agreement), 360, 360n7–8

ASCE. *See* American Society of Civil Engineers
Aschauer, David, 21
Association of American Publishers, 359
Atmospheric commons, 206n60
AT&T, 84, 219, 220–21, 352
AT&T v. Iowa Utilities Board (1999), 185
Authors Guild of America, 359
Autonomy, 257n10
Average cost pricing, 13, 170, 175–79, 175n29, 180*f*, 181
Averch, Harvey, 172
Aviram, Amitai, 87n27, 88n34

"Baby Bells," 220
Backhaul services, 212–13
Backward compatibility, 280, 283
Baker, Ed, 53n78
Baldwin, Carliss, 98
Balkin, Jack, 336, 337n73
Barnes, Peter, 246
Barron, Anne, 42
Bayesian learning, 306
Bayh-Dole Act, 312–14, 313n206, 314n208
Bekar, Clifford, 23
Belch, Toby, 289
Beliefs influenced by ideas, 51–52, 51–52n76, 257
Bell System, 214, 216, 219, 220

Benkler, Yochai, 93, 258, 260, 262, 268–69, 342–43

Berkman Center for Internet & Society, 222n61

Biases in infrastructure management, 79, 82–83, 84, 99

Bilski v. Kappos (2010), 255, 292–95, 298, 300–301

Bit Torrent, 154

Blogs and bloggers, 52, 337

Bloomberg, Michael, 203n46

Blumenfeld, Jeffrey, 214n12

BOOT (build-own-operate-transfer) models, 190n2

Botnets, 356

Boudin, Michael, 290n117

Bourdieu, Pierre, 47

Bowling Alone (Putnam), 46n61

Boyle, James, 256n8, 273

BP oil spill, 239–40n42

Bradner, Scott, 98

Brandeis, Louis, 281

Breen, John, 257–58

Breyer, Stephen, 185–86

Bridges, x, 191, 210

Brin, Sergey, 359n2

Broadband Internet access, 222n61, 223–24, 317, 323, 330, 348–49

Brown Weiss, Edith, 245, 246

Buchanan, James M., 143

Build-own-operate-transfer (BOOT) models, 190n2

Burk, Dan L., 296–97n151

Bush, Vannevar, 305

Button, Kenneth, 192, 193, 194n15

California, emissions standards in, 208

Capacity consumption, 149, 150–51

Capacity cushioning, 150, 198

Capacity expansion of infrastructure, 142–44, 155, 156, 198, 199

Capital goods, 24, 33–37, 34t, 63

Carlaw, Kenneth, 23

CBO (Congressional Budget Office), 197–98, 202

Census Bureau, 335

Chain-Linked Model, 272

Chappe, Claude, 211

Charlie Bit My Finger — Again! (YouTube video), 338

Cherry, Barbara, 103, 104, 104n32

Chiang, Tun-Jen, 291–92, 295, 296, 300

Chicago, Lake Michigan and, 239, 239n39

Chicago, prosperity of, 6–7n10

Chile, road system in, 199n29

China, road energy consumption in, 207n61

Clark, Kim, 98

Clay, Henry, 195n17

Clean Air Act, 208

Clean Automotive Technology research, 207

CLECs (competitive local exchange carriers), 185, 185n39

Climate change, 190, 206, 232, 241

Clubs
club goods, 32
discriminatory, 144n18
membership in, 146, 149
theory of, 144–45, 145n19, 149n26

Coase, Ronald, 37, 38–39, 129, 130–32, 131n37, 134, 205

Cohen, Julie, 257n10, 270, 270n54

Coleman, James, 46, 48n72

Collective action, 139, 229, 342, 344

Comcast, 154, 321, 321n15, 352

Comedy of the commons, 228, 231, 247

Commerce
e-commerce, 335
road systems and, 6–7, 7n11, 193–94

Commercial infrastructure
commons management and, 100, 105–7
demand-side issues with, 72–73, 76
government intervention and, 100, 105–7
as infrastructure resources, 67–68, 67t, 68n7
price discrimination and, 181
uncertainty and, 113

Common carrier regulations
AT&T and, 220
commons management and, 94
competition and, 103–4, 105
under English common law, 6n8
nondiscrimination and, 157
price discrimination and, 119
supply-side incentives and, 160
telecommunications and, 217, 218–19

Common nail example, 276–78, 276n80, 283–84

Commons and commons management, xv, 60, 91–114. *See also* Comedy of the commons; Tragedy of the commons
atmospheric, 206n60

"commons destroys incentives" claims, 159, 160–65, 174
  congestion and, 92
  end-to-end design and, 319–23
  government intervention in, 94, 99–114
    commercial infrastructure and, 100, 105–7
    public, social, and mixed infrastructure and, 100, 108–14
  infrastructure link to, 368
  infrastructure pricing and, 117–35. *See also* Infrastructure pricing
  intellectual infrastructure and, 259–60, 284–301
  Internet and, 334, 345–48
  management, defining of, 3, 7–9, 8–9*n*16, 91
  nondiscrimination and, 7–8, 92, 93–94, 100–105
  price discrimination and, 117, 118–25
  price regulation and, 117, 125–29
  private business strategy and, 93–99
  "public commons," 8
  roads and, 190, 194–209
  semi-commons, 230, 231, 248, 255, 274, 301–5
  spillovers and, 6, 9, 94
  supply-side issues and, 159–60, 175–86, 368
  telecommunications and, 217–22
Communications Act of 1934, 218, 220
Communications infrastructure. *See* Telecommunications
Community identity, 239, 239*nn*39–40
Competition and competitors
  common carrier regulations and, 103–4, 105
  destructive, 170–71
  essential facilities doctrine and, 102
  marginal costs and, 15
  monopolies and, 106, 107, 175, 182–86
  network neutrality debate and, 327, 330–32
  nondiscriminatory access for, 100–101, 106–7
  open access for, 101–2, 106–7
Competitive local exchange carriers (CLECs), 185, 185*n*39
Complementary efficiencies, 97
Computer Associates v. Altai (1992), 290
Congestion, 115, 136–58. *See also* Congestion pricing
  approaches to, 31–32, 141–49, 141*f*
    capacity expansion and, 142–44, 155, 156, 198, 199

congestion pricing, 118, 146–49, 155–56, 175, 198
    commons management and, 92
    environmental infrastructure and, 235, 240
    heterogeneity and, 149–55
      capacity consumption, 149, 150–51
      cross-crowding, 149, 151–52, 156–57
      use restrictions, 144–46, 149, 152–57, 198
    on Internet, 138, 142, 145, 156, 325–26, 334, 351–55, 354–55*n*118
    management of, 155–58
    in networks, 88*n*34
    partially (non)rivalrous infrastructure and, 136–41, 155
    roads and, 137–38, 143–44, 190, 192, 196–204, 325
    use restrictions and, 144–46, 149, 152–55, 156–57, 198
Congestion pricing
  approaches to, 118, 146–49, 155–56, 175, 198
  for roads, 190, 198, 199–204, 201*n*37
  for telecommunications, 217
Congressional Budget Office (CBO), 197–98, 202
Consumers
  false supplier/consumer dichotomy and, 327, 329–30
  free-rider dilemmas and, 265
  marginal costs and, 166*n*15
  network neutrality debate and, 329–30
  nondiscriminatory and, 100–102, 103
  price discrimination and, 93, 95–96, 98
Consumption goods, 24, 33–37, 34*t*
Cooperation as commons management strategy, 93, 96
Copyright
  free-riding dilemmas and, 267
  Google Books and, 359
  ideas and, 255, 281, 282
  Linux operating system and, 363
  markets and, 109
  peer-to-peer software and, 361
  as semi-commons, 302–3, 304–5
Copyright Act, 285
Cordon charges, 202
Cornes, Richard, 29, 30*n*15, 32, 139*n*5, 140
Costanza, Robert, 233*n*23
Cost pricing. *See* Average cost pricing
Covad, 185*n*39

Cowan, Simon, 124n14
Criminal justice systems, 44
Cross-crowding, 149, 151–52, 156–57
Cultural environments, 254, 256–60
Customers. *See* Consumers

Davies-Carr, Howard, 338, 338n78
DDoS attacks, 356
Deadweight losses
    average cost pricing and, 176
    essential facilities doctrine and, 107
    government intervention and, 106
    intellectual property and, 268
    investment incentives and, 169, 174
    marginal costs and, 77, 106, 129–30, 167
    monopoly pricing and, 126–27, 174–75
    patent law and, 264
    price discrimination and, 17, 17n17, 120, 121,
        123–24, 172, 351
    pricing schemes and, 16
    social costs of, 78
    subsidies and, 132
    supply-side incentives and, 167–68
Decreasing-cost phenomena, 12–15
Degradation of resources, 137, 137n2, 235, 235n31,
        240, 245, 247
Demand-side issues
    commercial infrastructure and, 72–73, 76
    commons management and, 59–60
    demand-manifestation problems, 66, 72–78,
        74–75f, 78f, 85, 105, 108
    environmental infrastructure
        and, 230, 247, 248
    government intervention and, 132
    infrastructural status and, 81–82
    infrastructure resources and, xi, xii–xiii, 19,
        59–60, 368–69
    market failure and, 40, 61, 90, 91
    merit goods and, 45–46
    network effects and, 87–90, 87n27
    nonrival goods and, 36–37
    optimality condition and, 54, 57
    private demand and, 74–75, 74–75f, 111, 121,
        180, 181, 366–67
    public infrastructure and, 56, 69, 72, 74,
        76–77
    roads and, 191–92
    social infrastructure and, 42, 69, 71, 72, 74,
        76–77

societal demand and, 59–60n1, 63–66, 74–75,
        74–75f, 111, 121, 180, 366–67
    supply problems and, 72–78
    telecommunications and, 217, 222
Demsetz, Harold, 6n9, 37, 39n38, 41–42n48, 70
Department of Transportation (DOT), 198, 210
Depletion of resources, 235
Depreciation of resources. *See* Degradation
        of resources
Deregulation, 182, 213
Deshpande, Manasi, 21
Development economics, 10, 19
Diamond v. Diehr (1981), 293, 294
Differential pricing. *See* Price discrimination
Digg.com, 339
Doctrine of equivalents (DOE), 288n113, 297
DOT (Department of Transportation), 198, 210
Drug discovery example, 278–79
DSL broadband, 323
Duffy, John F., 106, 131, 176

E-commerce, 335
Economics. *See specific types, e.g.,* Infrastructure
        economics
Economides, Nicholas, 87, 89
Economies of scale, 171, 192, 194, 353
Economist (magazine) on Bayh-Dole Act, 313–14
Ecosystems and ecosystem services, 230, 236–37,
        243, 244, 249–52
Education, 45, 49, 110
Egypt, social networking in, 341
Eldred v. Ashcroft (2003), 285–86
Electric power industries, 183–84
Elmendorf, Douglas W., 21
Encyclopedia Britannica, 339
Endogenous growth theory, 22
End-to-end design of Internet, 319–23, 320t, 324,
        326, 333, 353, 356
Energy Department, 109n40
Environmental infrastructure, xvi–xvii, 4,
        225–52
    capacity management and, 157
    congestion and, 235, 240
    delineation of, 230, 234–46
        direct nonmarket uses, 240, 241–43, 250
        indirect nonmarket uses, 240, 243, 250
        market uses, 240–41, 250
        nonhuman and unborn users and, 244–46
    management of, 230, 246–48

multiple-use management and ecosystem
  services and, 230, 249–52
as nonmarket goods, 44
as nonrivalrous good, 63n2
tragedy of the commons and, 9
valuing of, 230, 231–34
Environmental Protection Agency (EPA),
  207, 208
Environmental science, 232, 232n14
Essential facilities doctrine
  commons management and, 94, 105
  competitors and, 106–7
  compulsory licensing schemes and, 279n86
  monopolies and, 107n37
  nondiscrimination rules and, 101–2, 107
  supply-side incentives and, 160
  telecommunications and, 219
Estache, Antonio, 19
Externalities. *See also* Negative externalities;
  Spillovers; Third-party effects
  congestion and, 139, 140
  environmental infrastructure and, 240
  microeconomics and, 24, 29, 37–42,
    39n40, 43
  public infrastructure and, 49, 55, 69, 90
  social infrastructure and, 43, 48–49,
    70–71, 90
  speech and, 50, 51–53, 76
  supply-side issues and, 39
  tragedy of the commons and, 139
E-ZPass system, 202

Facebook, 340, 342n95
Facilities, sharing of, 185–86
"Factors of production," 34
Fair use doctrine, 304–5, 359
Farber, Daniel A., 284
Farrell, Joseph, 97
Federal Communications Commission (FCC)
  on anticompetitive discrimination, 330n44
  antitrust suits and, 220
  AT&T and, 84
  broadband regulation and, 222, 323
  broadcast licenses and, 145
  cellular telephone service and, 212
  Comcast and, 154
  on Internet users, 344n99
  interstate regulation by, 213
  network neutrality and, 324

Open Internet and, 318–19, 327n37, 348–50,
    356, 356n123
  on transparency, 331n48
Federal Highway Administration
  (FHWA), 198, 203
Feedback loops, 272, 309
FHWA (Federal Highway
  Administration), 198, 203
Field, John, 47
Firms. *See* Private infrastructure providers
First Amendment, xi, 255, 260, 282, 284–86
Fixed costs, 13, 166, 177–78, 222–23, 266, 266n43
Flat-rate pricing, 147, 150
Freeman, A. Myrick, III, 240
Free markets. *See* Markets and market
  mechanisms
Free-rider dilemmas
  capacity expansion and, 143
  commons and, 160–63, 160n1
  consumers and, 265
  excludability of resources and, 26
  externalities and, 39
  facilities sharing and, 183
  information resources and, 9
  intellectual infrastructure and, 261,
    262–63, 266
  optimality conditions and, 56
  private property rights and, 9n19
  public goods and, 49
  rivalrousness of consumption and, 28, 29–30
Fromer, Jeanne, 296n149
Future generations, 230, 244–46, 248, 256

Gaynor, Mark, 98, 99
GDP (gross domestic product), 367
Genachowski, Julius, 317–18
General Public License, 363
General-purpose technologies (GPTs), 22–23,
    276, 276n79
Genericness of infrastructure, 64, 65, 79, 86, 152
Ghosh, Arghya, 19–20, 21
Ghosh, Shubha, 170–71, 172
Gifford, Daniel, 17
Global warming. *See* Climate change
Gmail, 321n15
Godin, Benoît, 271–72
Gold plating (economic), 172
Google, 329
Google Books, 359–60, 359n3, 360nn7–9

Google Book Search, 359
Google Maps, 256*n*5, 341
Google Print, 359
Gordon, Wendy, 259*n*20
Gottschalk v. Benson (1972), 293, 298*n*153
Government intervention and regulations
  basic research and, 311–13, 314
  commercial infrastructure and, 72, 105–14
  commons and, 94, 99–114
  demand-side issues and, 132
  environmental infrastructure and, 230
  excludability of resources and, 26
  externalities and, 38
  infrastructure provision by, 14
  market failure, 6, 18
  natural monopolies and, 171–72, 366
  network neutrality debate and, 326–27
  role of, 4, 6, 18
  social goods and, 71, 77–78
  supply-side issues and, 160, 165, 168, 175
  in telecommunications, 223–24
GPTs. *See* General-purpose
  technologies
Greenhouse gas emissions, 190, 206–7
Gross domestic product (GDP), 367
Growth theory, 22, 269*n*50

Hand, Learned, 288–89, 296–97*n*151
Hanifan, L. J., 46
Hardin, Garrett, 7, 139, 144
Hardin, Russell, 48*n*72
Harrington, Joseph, 13, 170, 170*n*20
Harvesting processes, 33, 33*n*24
Hazardous materials, 205
Health care, 45, 110
Hedging concept, 294, 295
Hemphill, Scott, 123*n*13
High Occupancy Vehicle
  (HOV) lanes, 199–200, 199*n*30
Highways. *See* Roads
Hogendorn, Christiaan, 333
Holladay, J. Scott, 366*n*2
Holmes, Oliver Wendell, 285
Hotelling, Harold, 129–33, 134, 167
HOT lanes, 200
HOV (High Occupancy
  Vehicle) lanes, 199–200, 199*n*30
Huddleston, George, 220
Hulten, Charles, 21

IBM, 279
Ideas
  abstract, 292–95, 298, 300
  First Amendment, copyright, and patent
    jurisprudence and, 284–301
  "ideas out, expression in" rule, 291
  invention and patent scope and, 255, 295–301
  use and consumption of, 51–52
ILECs (incumbent local exchange carriers),
  184–85, 185*n*39
Illinois Boat Registration and Safety Act,
  248*n*77
Incentives. *See* Investment incentives; Supply-
  side issues and incentives
Incidental beneficiaries, 49*n*73
Incumbent local exchange carriers (ILECs),
  184–85, 185*n*39
Inderset, Roman, 133*n*41
"Information services," 323, 323*n*28
"Infra-infrastructure," 231, 231*n*10
Infrastructural capital, 33–34*n*24
Infrastructure economics, xiv, 10–23. *See also*
  Infrastructure pricing
  decreasing-cost phenomena and, 12–15
  macroeconomics perspective on, 11, 19–23
  market provisioning and pricing and, 15–17
  microeconomics perspective on, 10–19
  supply-side issues, 12–15, 18–19, 365–66
Infrastructure pricing, 115, 117–35. *See also*
  Infrastructure economics
  price discrimination, 117, 118–25
  price regulation and, 117, 125–29
  subsidies and marginal costs and, 117, 129–35
Infrastructure Report Card (2009), 210
Infrastructure resources, xiv, 59–60, 61–90.
    See also specific infrastructure types (e.g.,
    Environmental infrastructure)
  commercial, 67–68, 67*t*, 68*n*7
  delineation of, 4, 61–66, 62*t*, 65*f*
  demand for, 63, 63*t*
  demand-manifestation and supply problems,
    72–78, 74–75*f*, 78*f*, 85
  demand-side analysis and network effects,
    87–90, 87*n*27
  dynamic nature of, 79–86
    infrastructural status and, 79–82, 80*f*
    prioritization, optimization, and design,
      79, 82–86
  Lessig's figure and, 86–87, 86*f*

public and social, 67*t*, 68–72
pure, 67, 68
Innovations
    infrastructural resources and, 22
    linear model of, 271–72, 306, 310
    network neutrality debate and, 324, 332–34
    spillover from, 38
    uncertainty and, 85
    value-creating user activities and, 97
Input-output relationships, 270–71
Institutionalism, 21
In-system behaviors, 11–12
Intel, 279
Intellectual infrastructure, xvi–xvii, 4, 225–26,
        253–314. *See also* Intellectual property
    basic research as, 305–14
    commons management of, 259–60, 284–301
    cultural environment as, 254, 256–60
    delineation of, 255, 275–81
    economic characteristics of, 254–55, 261–75
        activities, products and processes, 268–75
        (non)excludability, 254, 254*n*1, 261–64
        nonrivalry, 254, 254*n*1, 261, 264–68, 274
        supply-side problems, 261–68
    ideas as, 281–301
        abstract, 292–95, 298, 300
        First Amendment, copyright, and patent
            jurisprudence, 284–301
        invention and patent scope, 255,
            295–301
    as semi-commons, 255, 274, 301–5
Intellectual property. *See also* Copyright; Patents
        and patent law
    economic theory of, 42
    externalities and, 39, 41
    free riding and, 161, 263, 267*n*44, 288
    government intervention and, 108–9
    investment incentives and, 267–68, 267*n*44
    as semi-commons, 302
Interaction effects, 151
Interconnections
    network effects and, 87*n*27
    regulations on, 127, 127*n*22
    in telecommunications, 216, 221
Interexchange networks, 212
Internet, xvii, 317–57. *See also* Network
        neutrality debate
    broadband, 222*n*61, 223–24, 317, 323, 330,
        348–49

congestion on, 138, 142, 145, 156, 325–26, 334,
        351–55, 354–55*n*118
demand for, 81–82
end-to-end design and, 319–23, 320*t*, 324, 326,
        333, 353, 356
infrastructure of, 8*n*16, 82*n*18
network neutrality debate, 318–19, 323–34,
        346, 357
    antitrust and regulatory economics in,
        326–30
    commons management and, 334, 345–48
    competition and, 327, 330–32
    false supplier/consumer dichotomy and,
        327, 329–30
    innovation and, 324, 332–34
    mixed infrastructure and, 318, 334–45,
        346–47
    neutrality concept, 324–26
    reframing of, 334–48
    supply-chain view and, 327–29, 330, 334–35
    nondiscrimination rule for, 348–56
    harmful traffic and, 355–56
Internet & American Life Project, 340
Internet Protocol (IP), 320–21, 321*n*12,
        321*n*14, 324
Internet service providers (ISPs), 335
Interstate Highway System, 191
Inventions, 255, 291–92, 291*n*123, 295–301, 303
Investment incentives
    average cost pricing and, 175–79
    "commons destroys incentives" claims, 159,
        160–65, 174
    intellectual property and, 267–68, 267*n*44
    intellectual resources and, 261–62, 265–66
    patent law and, 296, 296*n*148, 297–98
    price discrimination and, 175, 179–82, 351,
        352–53
    unbundling and, 184–85
IP. *See* Internet Protocol
IP telephony, 332
Iran, Twitter in, 341
Irreducibly social goods, 43, 46, 47–48, 48*n*72
ISPs (Internet service providers), 335

Japan, broadband Internet in, 223
Jefferson, Thomas, 281–82
Jitter-sensitive applications, 322, 325
Johnson, Leland L., 172
Justice Department, 359

Kahn, Alfred, 15, 18, 41*n*45, 163–64, 179
Kieff, Scott, 276*n*80
"Killer application" phenomena, 76, 337–38, 338*n*74
Kingsbury Commitment, 219–20
Kitch, Edmund, 309–10
Kline, S. J., 272
Knowledge, tacit, 261
Kudrle, Robert, 17
Kunin, Christy C., 214*n*12

Lake Michigan, 239, 239*n*39, 309
Landes, William, 311
Languages, 69
Latency-sensitive applications, 322, 325
Lee, Peter, 81
Lemley, Mark, 42, 68*n*7, 87–89, 296–97*n*151, 301, 304, 355
Lessig, Lawrence, 86–87, 324, 333
Lessig's figure, 86–87, 86*f*
Levels of abstraction. *See* Abstractions analysis
Library of Alexandria, 359, 359*n*2
Licenses, 73, 73*n*11, 145, 279*n*86, 307–8
Light-duty vehicles, 208
Lindsey, Robin, 200–201
Linux operating system, 362–63, 362*n*17
Lipsey, Richard, 23
Local exchange networks, 212, 222–23
London, cordon pricing in, 202
Losey, John, 250–51
Lotus Development Corp. v. Borland International, Inc. (1995), 290*n*117
"Lumpy" fixed costs, 13, 166
Lunney, Glynn S., Jr., 265*n*42

Ma Bell. *See* Bell System
"Machine or transformation" test, 300–301*n*158
Macroeconomics, 11, 19–23
Magnetic Resonance Imaging (MRI), 272–73
Malaria vaccines, 309
Malvolio, 289
Management, defining of, xiii–xiv, 3–9
    commons management, 3, 7–9, 8–9*n*16
    infrastructure resources and, 3–7
Marginal Cost Controversy, 129–35, 143
The Marginal Cost Controversy (Coase), 130
Marginal costs
    congestion and, 139, 150
    consumers and, 166*n*15

controversy over, 129–35, 143
deadweight losses and, 77, 106, 129–30, 167
infrastructure pricing and, 117, 129–35
market provisioning and, 15
optimality condition and, 53
partially (non)rival resources and, 31, 62, 137–38
price discrimination and, 120
rivalrousness of consumption and, 26, 27
for roads, 192
subsidies and, 117, 129–35
supply-side incentives and, 166–67, 168–69
Market failures
    bias and, 84
    demand-side, 40, 61, 90, 91
    externalities and, 38, 40
    government intervention and, 6, 18
    public and social infrastructure and, 71–72, 74, 108
Marketplace of ideas metaphor, 285
Market provisioning. *See also* Markets and market mechanisms
    excludability of resources and, 26
    infrastructure economics and, 14–17
    of intellectual resources, 265, 268
    marginal costs and, 168
    price discrimination and, 175
    in telecommunications, 216
Markets and market mechanisms. *See also* Market provisioning
    incomplete markets, 70, 328, 366
    missing markets, 37, 38, 41, 70, 328, 366
    rival goods and, 34, 35–36
    rivalrousness of consumption and, 27, 28
    two-sided, 327–29, 328*n*40, 330
Markey, Howard, 291–92, 295
Mathematical formulas, 294, 295
McGowan, David, 87–89
MCI, 219
MCI v. AT&T (2008), 107
Meagher, Kieron, 19–20, 21
Merger doctrine, 290, 290*n*119, 301
Merges, Robert, 307*n*179, 311*n*192
Merit goods, 43, 45–46, 45*n*59, 48, 70, 110
Meta-environments, 258, 275
Meta-networks, 96, 216, 221, 345–46, 357
Metering of resources, 147, 156
MGM v. Grokster (2005), 361
Microeconomics, xiv, 24–57

consumption goods and capital goods and, 24, 33–37, 34*t*
  nonrivalrous goods and, 36–37
  rival capital goods, 35–36
  rival consumption goods, 34–35
externalities and, 24, 29, 37–42, 39*n*40, 43
infrastructure economics and, 10–19
optimality conditions and, 53–57, 53*n*80
public and private goods and, 24–33
  (non)excludability and, 24–26, 25*t*, 29, 33
  (non)rivalrousness of consumption and, 24–33, 25*t*, 31*t*
    partially (non)rival goods and, 30–33, 30*n*15, 31*t*
    takeaways on, 32–33
social goods and, 24, 42–49, 43*n*53
  externalities and, 48–49
speech and, 24, 50–53, 50*n*75
Microprocessor chip example, 279–80, 283
Microwave transmission technology, 215–16
Mid-Texas Communications Systems, 219
Mill, John Stuart, 52*n*76
Millennium Ecosystem Assessment (UN), 235
Mixed infrastructure
  commercial infrastructure and, 78
  commons and, 100, 108–14
  cultural environment as, 258–59, 302
  environmental infrastructure as, 230, 237
  Google Books as, 360
  government intervention and, 108–14
  Internet as, 82, 318, 332, 334–45, 346–47
  language as, 69
  nondiscriminatory management of, 94
  price discrimination and, 181
  roads as, 194, 196
  social infrastructures as, 71
  telecommunications as, 211, 217
MMORGs (multiplayer online role-playing games), 332
Mobility, personal, 189
"Modular industry structures," 97
Monopolies. *See also* Monopolistic pricing; Natural monopolies
  applications markets and, 97
  competition and, 106, 107, 175, 182–86
  essential facilities doctrine and, 101
  government regulation of, 18
Monopolistic pricing
  deadweight losses and, 174–75

essential facilities doctrine and, 107
investment incentives and, 125, 174
nondiscrimination and, 106, 129, 129*n*32, 169, 176
price regulation and, 126–27
Morton, Pete, 236–37
Mowery, David, 313*n*206
MRI (Magnetic Resonance Imaging), 272–73
Multiplayer online role-playing games (MMORGs), 332
Multiple-use management (MUM), 230, 249–52
Musgrave, Richard, 45, 45*n*59, 110
Music sampling, 273

Nachbar, Thomas, 103–4, 104*nn*28–29, 104*n*32
Nails. *See* Common nail example
National Institutes of Health, 109*n*40
National Research Council (NRC), 4*n*1, 64, 208, 251–52
National Science Foundation, 109*n*40
National Surface Transportation Policy and Revenue Study Commission, 210
National Vehicle and Fuel Emissions Laboratory, 207
Natural monopolies
  demand-manifestation problems and, 72–73
  facilities sharing and, 186
  government intervention and, 131, 171–72, 366
  market characteristics and, 166, 170–74
  regulatory economics and, 12, 13–14
  roads and, 189, 192
  subadditivity and, 13*n*10
  supply-side issues and, 166, 170–74
  telecommunications and, 213, 215, 216, 219–21
Negative externalities
  congestion and, 138
  environmental resources and, 9, 241
  pollution as, 108
  roads and, 190, 196, 206, 209
  use restrictions and, 157
Nelson, Richard, 307*n*179, 311*n*192
Nesting analyses of infrastructure, 256, 256*n*5
Network effects
  congestion vs., 140–41
  demand-side analysis of, 87–90
  interconnections and, 87*n*27
  roads and, 192
  telecommunications and, 214, 216, 217
  value-creating user activities and, 97

Network neutrality debate. *See also* Internet
  antitrust and regulatory economics in, 326–30
  commons management and, 346
  competition and, 330–32
  false supplier/consumer dichotomy and, 329–30
  identity-based discrimination and, 353
  innovation and, 332–34
  neutrality concept, 324–26
  price regulation and, 128n26
  supply-chain view of, 327–29
Network standardization, 104
Neuman, Janet, 249
Neutrality, network. *See* Network neutrality debate
New growth theory, 22
News reporting, 109, 110
New York City, congestion pricing in, 202–3, 203n46
New York Times on Google Books, 359n2
Nondiscrimination rules
  common-carrier regulations and, 94, 103–4, 119, 157
  commons and, 7–8, 92, 93–94, 100–105
  congestion and, 158
  dynamic vs. static efficiency and, 163–64
  essential facilities doctrine and, 107
  facilities sharing and, 182–83
  government intervention and, 100–105, 106
  Internet and, 348–56
  investment incentives and, 175
  merger approvals and, 107n37
  monopolistic pricing and, 129n32, 169, 176
  need for, 4–5, 6
  network neutrality and, 324
  partially (non)rival infrastructure and, 137
  price discrimination and, 118–19, 122–23, 125, 168
  price regulation and, 125–29, 159
  in public, social, and mixed infrastructure, 108, 110, 113
  road systems and, 7
  spillovers and, 7
  supply-side incentives and, 159–60, 165
  telecommunications and, 217
Nonexcludability
  of goods, 24–26, 25t, 29, 33
  intellectual infrastructure and, 254, 254n1, 261–64

Nonhuman users, 230, 240, 244–46, 248, 249
Nonlinear pricing, 175
Nonmarket goods, 43–45, 46, 48, 70, 238–39
Nonmarket uses of environmental infrastructure, 240, 241–43, 250
Nonmarket valuation techniques, 44
Nonrivalry and nonrivalrous goods. *See also* Partially (non)rivalrous goods
  commons as, 93
  consumption and, 24–25, 25t, 26–30, 31t, 32–33, 36–37
  environmental resources and, 234–35
  infrastructure resources and, 62–63
  intellectual infrastructure and, 254, 254n1, 261, 264–68, 274
  Lessig's figure and, 86
  speech and, 53
North, D., 43n51
NRC. *See* National Research Council
NSFNET, 82
Nuechterlein, Jonathan, 330, 332n52
Nussbaum, Martha, 246

Odlyzko, Andrew, 96
OECD, 10n1, 20, 335
"One Policy, One System, Universal Service" slogan, 214
"On the shoulders of giants" effect, 254, 260, 268–70, 269n51, 274
Open Internet Coalition, 341
Open Internet rules, 318–19, 327n37, 348–50, 356, 356n123
Openness and open access. *See also* Transparency
  commons management and, 8, 91–92
  for competitors, 101–2, 106–7
  government intervention and, 94
  infrastructure resources and, 94–95
  open-access repositories, 314
  price regulation and, 127, 127n22
  telecommunications and, 217, 221–22
Open-source software, 362–63
Open Systems Interconnection Model, 319n6
Optimality conditions, 53–57, 53n80
Optimization of infrastructure, 79, 82–86, 108, 195–96n18
Options theory, 112
Orange County (California), road-pricing scheme in, 201–2

O'Reilly v. Morse (1854), 298–99, 300
Orphan works problem, 359*n*3
Ostrom, Elinor, 256*n*5

PANYNJ (Port Authority of New York and
    New Jersey), 202
Parker v. Flook (1978), 293–94
Partially (non)rivalrous goods. *See also*
    Nonrivalry and nonrivalrous goods
  commons as, 93
  congestion and, 136–41, 155
  environmental infrastructure as, 235–37, 247
  infrastructure resources and, 62–63
  Internet as, 334
  public and private goods as, 30–32, 30*n*15,
      31*t*, 33
Patent Act of 1952, 292
Patent and Trademark Office, 300
Patents and patent law
  basic research and, 307*n*178, 308*n*181
  Bayh-Dole Act and, 313
  commercial infrastructure and, 73
  copyright law and, 255, 301
  free-riding dilemmas and, 267
  ideas and, 282
  as intellectual property regime, 109
  inventions and, 291–92, 291*n*123, 295–301, 303
  patent pools, 96
  prospect theory of, 309–10
  scope of, 255, 295–301
  as semi-commons, 302, 303–4, 305
  supply-side issues of, 263–64
Path dependencies
  capacity expansion and, 143
  congestion pricing and, 147
  defined, 85*n*24
  environmental infrastructure and, 228
  optimization of infrastructure and, 85, 94
  use restrictions and, 152
  value-creating user activities and, 97
Peak load problems, 123, 142, 175, 197
Peak shaving, 144*n*17
Pearce, David, 233*n*23
Peer-to-peer file-sharing (P2P), 360–62, 361*n*10
Pegrum, D.F., 131
Personal mobility, 189
Pew Research Center, 340
"Picking winners" among infrastructure users
  commons management and, xv

First Amendment and, 285
  government intervention and, 111, 112
  ideas and, 52
  infrastructure management and, 9, 94
  public goods and, 109
Pigou, A. C., 38–39, 56
Plagiarism, 288
Poirier, Marc, 63*n*2, 245*n*63, 246, 246*n*72
Pollution, 108, 190, 192, 196, 206–9, 208*n*71
Port Authority of New York and New Jersey
    (PANYNJ), 202
Portes, Alejandro, 48*n*72
Positive externalities. *See* Spillovers
Posner, Richard, 284, 311
Powder River Basin, 79
Powell, Walter, 313
Power, Alison, 238, 238*n*37, 252
Price cap regulations, 126
Price discrimination. *See also* Price regulations
  common carrier regulation and, 103
  commons management and, 117, 118–25
  consumer opinion on, 93, 95–96, 98
  deadweight losses and, 167–68, 172, 351
  infrastructure investment and, 169
  infrastructure pricing and, 117, 118–25
  Internet and, 350–53
  investment incentives and, 175, 179–82, 352–53
  monopolies and, 106
  nondiscrimination and, 118–19
  path dependency and, 85
  perfect, 16–17, 17*n*17
  public goods and, 265*n*42
  roads and, 195
  Robinson-Patman Act and, 107*n*36
Price regulations. *See also* Price discrimination
  commons and, 117, 125–29
  in electric power industries, 184
  infrastructure pricing and, 117, 125–29
  natural monopolies and, 172
  sharing regimes and, 164
Prioritization of infrastructure access
  government intervention and, 112
  infrastructure resources and, 79, 82–86
  Internet and, 351–52, 353, 354–55
  price discrimination and, 121
  roads and, 195–96
  use restrictions and, 153, 156
Prisoners' dilemma problems, 9*n*19, 96
Private goods, 24–33, 335

Private infrastructure providers, 15, 78, 82–85

Property rights
    basic research and, 307–8
    end-to-end principle and, 322
    excludability of resources and, 26, 33
    externalities and, 39, 39n38
    free riding and, 161n4
    infrastructure resources and, xii
    rivalrousness of consumption and, 27, 29
    tragedy of the commons and, 139, 228–29

Property trusts, 246

Prospect theory of patents, 309–10

Provisioning services (ecosystem services), 243

P2P (peer-to-peer file-sharing), 360–62, 361n10

"Public bads," 230, 238n36. See also Negative
    externalities

Public choice theory, 221

"Public commons," 8

Public domain
    basic research and, 311, 314
    ideas and, 162, 286
    manufacturing processes in, 73
    patents and, 296, 298, 303, 305
    private ownership and, 260

Public goods. See also Public infrastructure
    basic research and, 307
    environmental infrastructure and, 238
    impure, 30, 30n15, 32, 62
    microeconomics and, 24–33
    optimality condition and, 53–57
    production of, 66
    public infrastructure resources and, 68–69,
        366
    public welfare economics and, 12
    pure, 62
    speech and, 50–51, 50n75
    underproduction of, 331

Public infrastructure. See also Public goods
    commons and, 100, 108–14
    demand-side issues with, 74, 76–77
    externalities and, 49, 55, 69, 90
    government intervention and, 108–14
    as infrastructure resources, 67t, 68–72
    nondiscriminatory management of, 94
    price discrimination and, 181

Public transit, 207, 207n65

Public welfare economics, 12–13

Pure infrastructure, 67, 68

Putnam, Robert, 46n61, 47

Quality of service (QoS), 324–26, 324n33

Quelch, John, 335

Rai, Arti, 308–9, 309n186

Railroad systems, infrastructural status of, 79–80

Ramsey, Frank, 16

Ramsey pricing, 16, 122–23, 123n12, 127, 131

R&D activities. See Research and researchers

Rate-of-return regulations, 126

Rationing of resources, 145–46, 152–53, 155–56,
    190, 199

Real options theory, 85, 98

Real-time System Management Information
    Program, 204n50

Recreational activities, 232n18, 237–38n35,
    241–43, 248, 248n77

Reddit.com, 339

Regional Bell Operating Companies, 220

Regulating services (ecosystem services), 243

"Regulatory capture," 213, 213n6

Regulatory economics, 12, 13–14, 40–41, 326–30

Report Card for America's Infrastructure
    (ASCE), x–xi, xt, 143n14, 365

Research and researchers
    government support for, 109, 109n40
    as infrastructure, 77, 78f
    linear model of, 271–72, 306, 311
    spillovers and, 272–73

Revealed preference methods, 233, 233n20

Revesz, Richard, 227, 234

Rich, Giles, 292

Ride sharing, 199–200, 199n30

Rival goods, 86

Roads, xvi, 4, 187, 189–210
    commerce and, 6–7, 7n11, 193–94
    commons management and, 190, 194–209
        congestion and, 137–38, 143–44, 190, 192,
            196–204, 325
        environmental pollution and, 190, 192,
            206–9, 208n71
        interaction effects and, 204–5
    economic characteristics of, 191–94
    infrastructural status of, 79–80
    in-system behavior and, 11
    Interstate Highway System, 191
    modern debate on, 358
    nondiscrimination and, 7
    overview, 190–91
    public investment and, 209–10, 209n76

supply-side issues and, 191–92, 195, 209

Robinson, Glen, 163, 164, 184

Robinson-Patman Act, 107*n*36

Romer, Paul, 30, 269*n*50

Rose, Carol, 6–7, 193

Rosenberg, Nathan, 271–72

Rubbernecking, 197

Ruhl, J. B., 243, 243*n*56, 250

Rule of law, 44

SAFETEA-LU, 204*n*50

Safety risks on roads, 196, 204–5

Salzman, James, 233–34

Samuelson, Paul, 53–54, 55, 56, 264*n*38, 265, 277*n*82, 312

San Diego, road-pricing scheme in, 201

Sandler, Todd, 29, 30*n*15, 32, 139*n*5, 140

Science: The Endless Frontier (Bush), 305

Science (periodical) on commons, 7

Scotchmer, Suzanne, 269*n*51, 310*nn*189–90

Second Life (virtual game), 342–43

Self-help mechanisms, 262–63

Semi-commons, 230, 231, 248, 255, 274, 301–5

Sen, Amartya, 246

Shaffer, Greg, 133*n*41

Shakespeare, William, 289

Shelf space at supermarkets, 325*n*35

Sidgwick, Henry, 56

Singapore, road-pricing system in, 201, 202

Skype, 325

SlashDot.org, 339

Social capital, 43, 46–47, 47*nn*70–71, 48

Social goods. *See also* Social infrastructure

   demand-side issues with, 74, 76–77

   environmental infrastructure as, 238

   externalities and, 43, 48–49, 70–71, 90

   irreducibly, 43, 46, 47–48, 48*n*72

   microeconomics and, 24, 42–49, 43*n*53

   nondiscriminatory management of, 94

   production of, 66

Social infrastructure. *See also* Social goods

   commons and, 100, 108–14

   government intervention and, 108–14

   as infrastructure resources, 67*t*, 68–72

   price discrimination and, 181

   public infrastructure resources and, 68–69

Social options, 94, 230

Social surpluses, 76, 194

Software, 88–89, 290, 360–63

Solow, Robert, 22, 47*n*70

Solow residual, 22

Source Forge, 362

South Dakota, railroads in, 79

Southern Pacific Communications, 219

South Korea, broadband Internet in, 223

Spam (e-mail), 321, 321*n*15, 355–56

Speech

   economic concepts of, 24, 50–53, 50*n*75

   externalities and, 50, 51–53, 76

   First Amendment and, xi

   Internet and, 337, 343

   nondiscrimination and, 104

   optimality conditions and, 56

   political, 284–85

Spillovers (positive externalities)

   cascading, 271

   commons and, 6, 9, 94

   congestion pricing and, 156

   copyright law and, 303, 304

   cross-subsidies and, 111

   cultural environment and, 260

   deadweight losses and, 77, 121

   demand-manifestation problems and, 85

   environmental infrastructure and, 242, 248

   Google Books and, 360

   infrastructure and, 5–6, 6*n*8

   innovation and, 38

   in-system behavior and, 11–12

   Internet and, 332, 333, 337, 338–40, 344–45

   marginal cost pricing and, 134

   market failures and, 61

   network effects and, 87–88, 89–90

   nondiscrimination and, 7

   patents and, 303–4

   price discrimination and, 17, 123*n*13, 125, 181, 182

   public and social infrastructure and, 69, 108

   research and, 272–73

   roads and, 193, 194

   social demand curve and, 74–75

   social surplus and, 76

   user-generated, 10

Stated preference methods, 233, 233*n*20

Stavins, Robert, 227, 234

Steinmueller, W. Edward, 5

Stevens, John Paul, 294–95

Stockholm, cordon pricing in, 202

Subadditivity of cost functions, 13*n*10

Subsidies
average cost curve and, 179
commons management and, 346
congestion and, 144
infrastructure pricing and, 117, 129–35
intellectual property and, 109, 275
marginal costs and, 117, 129–35
price discrimination and, 120, 181
public goods and, 70, 77, 111, 331–32
social goods and, 71, 77, 110–11
telecommunications and, 214–15, 216, 223
Supply-side issues and incentives, 115, 159–86
basic research and, 311
"commons destroys incentives" claims, 159,
160–65, 174
dynamic vs. static efficiency and, 160,
163–65, 163n8, 166, 167
free riding and, 160–63, 160n1
government regulation and, 160,
165, 168, 175
commons management conflicting with,
159–60, 175–86, 368
average cost pricing, 175–79, 175n29
monopolies and competitive markets
and, 175, 182–86
price discrimination and, 175, 179–82
copyright and, 302
demand-manifestation problems
and, 72–78
economic characteristics of, 166–75
cost structure and, 166–69, 174
natural monopoly and, 166, 170–74
excludability of resources and, 26
externalities and, 39
infrastructural status and, 81
infrastructure economics and, 12–15, 18–19,
365–66
intellectual infrastructure and, 261–68
network neutrality debate and, 327–29, 330,
334–35
patent law and, 296
public and social infrastructure
and, 71–72
rivalrousness of consumption and, 28
roads and, 191–92, 195, 209
telecommunications and, 213–14, 222
"Supra-market" returns, 176, 179
Surpluses, social, 76, 194
Sweden, broadband Internet in, 223

Tacit knowledge, 261
Taxation
on basic research, 312
on fuel, 207, 210
marginal cost pricing and, 130–31, 132, 134
roads and, 196
Taylor, Charles, 47–48, 48n72
TCP/IP. See Transmission Control Protocol/
Internet Protocol
Technologies. See also specific types
after-arising, 297–98
complementary, 303
excludability of resources and, 26
infrastructural resources and, 22–23
infrastructural status of, 80–81
microwave transmission, 215–16
transfer of, 312–13
Telecommunications, xvi, 4, 187–88, 211–24
commons management and, 217–22
antitrust and, 217, 219–21
common carrier regulations and, 217,
218–19
open access regulation and, 217, 221–22
demand for, 81
economic characteristics of, 213–17
incumbent local exchange carriers and, 184–85
modern debate on, 358
overview, 212–13
private investment and, 222–24
supply-side issues and, 213–14, 222
Telecommunications Act of 1996, 184, 221, 222
Telephone services, 14, 212–13, 332. See also
Telecommunications
Third-party effects, 12, 37, 41–42n48, 53, 56. See
also Externalities
Thursby, Jerry and Marie, 314n208
Tillamook State Forest, 249
Time-of-day pricing, 147, 151, 201
Time-of-week pricing, 201
Tolls, 195n17, 196, 200, 201–2, 203
Torvalds, Linus, 363
Total factor productivity, 22
Trade secrets, 73n11, 303n162
Tragedy of the commons
carrying capacity and, 142
congestion and, 138–39, 146
environmental resources and, 9, 228–30,
231, 247
free riding and, 160

peer-to-peer software and, 361
private property rights and, 9*n*19
roads and, 196
"The Tragedy of the Commons" (Hardin), 7
Transaction costs, 77, 108
Transmission Control Protocol/Internet
    Protocol (TCP/IP), 345, 353–54,
    353–54*n*116
Transparency, 331, 331*n*48, 348–49. *See also*
    Openness and open access
Transportation infrastructure. *See* Roads
Transportation Statistics Bureau, 208
Trusts, property, 246
Tushnet, Rebecca, 276
Twelfth Night (Shakespeare), 289
Twitter, 318, 340–41

Unborn users. *See* Future generations
Unbundling of telecommunications,
    184–86, 185*n*39, 221
Uncertainty in commons management, 93, 98,
    99, 112–13
Underprovision of infrastructure, 15, 108, 109
United States
    basic research in, 311, 312
    bridges in, 210
    broadband in, 223
    economic growth in, 22
    greenhouse gas emissions in, 207
    infrastructure in, 21, 143, 143*n*14
    Internet in, 335
    personal mobility in, 189
    road system in, 189–91, 192, 194–95*n*17,
        198, 199
    social capital in, 46*n*61
    telecommunications in, 184–85, 212–13
    universal service in, 216
Universal service, 214–15, 216, 221, 223
University activities, 313–14, 313*n*206
Urban Mobility Report (2010), 198*n*24

User restrictions
    congestion and, 144–46, 149, 152–57, 198
    on roads, 205
Utilitarian economics, 273–74*n*75

Vail, Theodore, 214
Value-creating user activities, 93, 96–97
Value-of-service pricing, 215
Van Schewick, Barbara, 146, 154, 327*n*37,
    330*n*42, 354*n*118, 356
Variable load pricing, 122–23, 124
Vaughn, Mace, 250–51
Verizon, 352
Vernon, John, 13, 170, 170*n*20
Viscusi, W. Kip, 13, 170, 170*n*20

Waste
    research duplication and, 309–10
    of resources, 143–44, 199
WDR (World Development Report), 21
Weblogs. *See* Blogs and bloggers
Weiser, Philip, 97
Weisman, Dennis, 163, 164, 184
Welfare economics, public, 12–13
Western Electric, 219, 220
Wikipedia, 339–40, 339–40*n*83, 342–43
Wildland ecosystems, 236–37
World Bank, 48
World Development Report (WDR), 21
World of Warcraft, 325
World Wide Web. *See* Internet
Wu, Tim, 84, 324, 333
Wyoming, railroads in, 79

Yoo, Chris, 154, 354*n*118
YouTube, 318, 338–39, 338*n*75, 338*n*78, 339*n*79

Zipcars, 280*n*90
Zittrain, Jonathan, 84, 340, 356
"Zombie computers," 356

Lightning Source UK Ltd.
Milton Keynes UK
UKOW04f1204250914

239170UK00001B/42/P